PILGRIM PEOPLE

BOOKS BY ANITA LIBMAN LEBESON

PILGRIM PEOPLE
JEWISH PIONEERS IN AMERICA

PILGRIM PEOPLE

Updated Edition

by Anita Libman Lebeson

MINERVA PRESS
New York

Library of Congress Cataloging in Publication
Data
Lebeson, Anita Libman, date
  Pilgrim people.

  Bibliography: p.
  Includes index.
  1. Jews in the United States—History. I. Title
E184.J5L566 1975   973'.004'924   75-2199
ISBN 0-308-10156-1

Minerva Press Edition, 1975 (A Funk & Wagnalls Imprint)

Manufactured in the United States of America

ISBN 0-308-10156-1
1 2 3 4 5 6 7 8 9 10

"The Pilgrim" by Edwin Markham, reprinted
by permission of Mrs. Virgil Markham.

FOR

David R. Lebeson

⇶   It was as if he tried by his fine gift of courage to prove
that his people had in them great depths of sacrifice and
deep wells of patriotism, a quiet willingness to offer their
lives for their country—and never to count the cost.

Pilgrim People, p. 366 ⇷

CONTENTS

PREFACE

THE TIME has come to write a full-length history of Jews in America. It is a tale worth telling. For the history of Jews in the Western hemisphere need not be forgotten lore. Its romance, excitement, adventure are ripe for a chronicler. Its montages are challenging. Its implications are significant. It is part and parcel of American History.

The Jewish immigrant who crossed the Atlantic—from the days of the expulsion from Spain to the days of the expulsion from Germany—brought a great heritage, was heir to a noble culture. Stripped of all material possessions, he arrived here with the skills he had acquired in his native land. No government sponsored Jewish early colonization. No rich landholding companies enticed the Jewish immigrant with promises of fertile lands and generous subsidies. From the start, Jewish immigrants were on their own. They challenged the wilderness. They fought for the ramparts. They died on every battlefield. Jewish entrepreneurs bought land, traded with the Indians, helped to develop the hinterland, built ships and sailed them, helped tie the distant parts of the world together.

The historian who writes the narrative of so challenging and vital a people as the Jews must bring to his task more than an Olympian detachment. He needs to probe deep into the hearts and minds of the immigrants. He needs to study both the cultural setting and the cultural heritage, to distinguish between what Jews brought to their new homes and what they borrowed from their neighbors.

The story of Jews in America holds up a mirror—a mirror large enough to show not only the Jew, but also his cultural environment. It discovers not only the role of the Jews in the drama of American history, but also their relation to the other participants in the cast.

History has been described as a record of man's struggle against nature, against his fellow man and against himself. The history of Jews in America follows this pattern. Perhaps the bitterest struggle of all has been the one the Jew has been fighting with himself—looking deep into his soul, weighing and measuring his worth, questioning, searching for surcease from strife and finding only more strife.

His heritage belongs to all. The most cherished possession which

the Pilgrim Fathers brought with them was Hebraic culture. To take
away the Old Testament influence from the annals of early American
history is to rob it of its spice and flavor. The very texture and life-
blood of the early covenants by which the founders of this nation
lived, the strength of their philosophies, the meat of their sermons,
the sinews of their early educational systems were founded on Jewish
thought.

If all this were not reason enough for writing the chronicle of Jews
in America, there is still another trend to be noted—a new trend in the
field of American historiography. There have been many fine new
additions to the growing library of works on American history in
recent years. Many of these works, written by great scholars of sound
reputation and high purpose, omit completely all references to
Jewish participation in the building of America. It is as if the hand
that writes on the wall gets writer's cramps when it comes to the
Jewish contribution. In volume after volume, the name of the Jew
is conspicuous by its absence. One can not say this is by design. These
are men of integrity and scholarship. Yet by some feat the record of
the Jew has been expunged. His past performances are consigned to
the limbo of things forgotten. His heroes are without honor—
unsung, unremembered.

The Jew is a character who might never have been—the ghost
in Hamlet, the faint voice heard off stage, the figure without substance forever destined to live in a land of shadow, to wander lost,
unnoticed, in a forgotten world.

The Quakers and Shakers, the Oneida Community, the followers
of the frailest prophets and the most evanescent ideologies may be
found in these books. The achievements of the Jew are lost in a
vacuum. It may be that the fault lies with the Jews themselves. Perhaps their scholars, so busy pursuing other gods, have forgotten
Jerusalem and its influence. Perhaps the facts are scattered and are
hard to assemble.

It is time that this story was told.

In the preparation of this work which began in 1943 and continued
until 1949, many libraries were visited and many scholars were consulted. With unstinting generosity scholars gave of their time and of
their knowledge. Permission was freely granted to quote from published works and to abstract unpublished manuscripts.

Pilgrim People was written at the Newberry Library. To Dr.
Stanley Pargellis, librarian of the Newberry Library, the writer is
especially indebted. His ready ear and wise counsel were freely
available. His interest in the manuscript was unfailing from its begin-

ning until the end. One of the trustees of the Newberry Library, Dr. William B. Greenlee, freely granted me access to his valuable manuscript collection and to his published and unpublished papers. Dr. Ruth Lapham Butler, custodian of the Ayer Collection, was helpful in interpreting the data pertaining to Columbus and to cartography. Dr. Pierce Butler translated the earliest extant Brazil Prayer—Dios Con Ysrael. Many staff members of the Newberry Library were most helpful on many occasions. To Mrs. Gertrude L. Woodward of the Rare Book Room, to Mrs. Mabel J. Erler and to Mrs. Bess C. Finn I am indebted for help freely given over the years. Mrs. Barbara Boston McNeil assisted with the preparation of the bibliography.

Dr. Judah Rosenthal, librarian of the College of Jewish Studies of Chicago, translated a letter of Aaron Lopez written in 1770 and assisted me in verifying Hebrew dates. Dr. Nathan Goldberg kindly sent me a number of Yivo publications of which he is the author and called my attention to numerous pertinent works published by that organization. Mrs. Elizabeth Libman assisted me in translating these works from the Yiddish. Mr. David Luna was indefatigable in translating old Portuguese and Spanish documents. Miss Eleanor Senn while at the Bibliothèque Nationale translated many French documents. She also prepared the index for Pilgrim People. Dr. Jeanette Fellheimer of Yale University ably assisted me in abstracting the twenty-six volumes of the Occident.

Dr. Lewis Hanke, head of the Hispanic Foundation of the Library of Congress facilitated the use of materials in his department and made numerous valuable suggestions. Mr. Peter Petcoff of the Division of Maps of the Library of Congress assisted me in identifying numerous maps and in the preparation of the cartographical data. Mr. Isaac Goldberg, formerly of the Semitic Department of the Library of Congress and now of the Hebrew Union College Library, was generous with time and suggestions. Professor Alexander Marx, librarian of the Jewish Theological Seminary of America assembled for ready use many documents, papers and books of early Americana Judaica. Rabbi Louis Finkelstein, president of the Jewish Theological Seminary of America, and Rabbi Moshe Davis, dean of its Teachers' College, showed a warm interest in the work and were helpful in the clarification of problems arising from the interpretation of the role of the Jew in American life. Judge Ulysses S. Schwartz of the Superior Court of Cook County, Illinois, generously gave me access to some of his papers and discussed with me many important aspects of the American Jewish scene.

Dr. A. S. W. Rosenbach, former president of the American Jewish

Historical Society, very kindly granted me permission to photostat many documents belonging to the Society, as well as those belonging to the Rosenbach Collections. It is difficult to express my sense of indebtedness to Mr. Isidore S. Meyer, librarian of the American Jewish Historical Society. For with endless patience he assembled unpublished manuscripts, diaries and notebooks and was unsparing of his time and effort in facilitating their use. His help was immeasurable; his interest constant. He carefully read the entire manuscript and made numerous suggestions for its improvement. Rabbi David de Sola Pool of the Shearith Israel Congregation of New York, friend and mentor of many years, gave counsel and encouragement when it was sorely needed, allowed me to consult his unpublished manuscripts, pointed out ways in which the manuscript could be condensed, assisted me in translating Sephardic terms, interpreted the role of early Jewish settlers in America. He read the manuscript carefully and made many valuable suggestions for its improvement. Dr. Joshua Bloch, chief of the Jewish Division of the New York Public Library, as he had done in the years when *Jewish Pioneers in America* was being written, gave generously of his time and experience in helping plan the research for *Pilgrim People*. It was he who pointed out the wealth of social history to be found in the pages of the *Asmonean*. In many conferences he helped clarify and interpret the role of the Jew in the building of America. He was quick to encourage and help, ready with counsel and criticism. It is a privilege to acknowledge my indebtedness to him. To Mr. Robert H. Glauber who skilfully cut out thousands of words, my warm thanks are due. Mr. Stuart Brent read the manuscript and was helpful to its author in many ways. Mrs. Marguerite H. Munson edited *Pilgrim People* for publication, adding much to its readability, bridging over many gaps in the narrative, making innumerable suggestions for its improvement.

As first written *Pilgrim People* comprised some eight hundred thousand words. It would have required about four volumes to contain the history of Jews in America. To abridge the manuscript it was necessary to rewrite it many times. Inevitably much that was important had to be sacrificed. To my husband, who in his capacity of first reader followed the narrative through all of its mutations, I am indebted for astute criticism, constructive suggestions and never-failing help. To him especially I am most grateful.

Winnetka, Illinois   ANITA LIBMAN LEBESON
March 22, 1950.

PILGRIM PEOPLE

CHAPTER I

The Dream of Sanctuary

LONG, LONG ago, so runs the legend, there was a place where valiant Jews lived in abundance and prosperity. A mighty river flowed around this land. Within its boundaries beautiful houses embellished with towers were built for dwelling places. There were no servants in this land. For each man and woman tended his own garden. Cattle grazed peacefully in deep green fields. The land was a cornucopia pouring forth its abundance for all. Life was happy. Faith was sturdy. There was neither grief nor evil. And no child died during the lifetime of his parents.

The Ten Lost Tribes of Israel were at home here.

Here in the *Diary of Eldad the Danite* was escape and adventure. Little wonder that it became a popular classic pored over by those who could read and retold by the illiterate. The year was 880. The time was dark and feudalism had a firm grip on the populace. Life was rugged. Diversions were few. Wars were interminable. Ten years before, by the Treaty of Mersen (870), Charlemagne's Empire had been cut up into three kingdoms and the seeds for many centuries of strife were firmly planted on European soil. Mohammedans were girding for battle. Already northern Africa and Spain and Sicily were penetrated. The Slavs and Hungarians were flexing their biceps. The men of the North were looking out for lands to conquer.

Why the Cinderella people should have seized upon this fairy tale is no mystery. They greeted the adventures of Eldad "with wild rapture." The fame of this utopia spread among Christians and Jews— for even the mysterious hero of Christendom, Prester John, was to be found in its pages. Nearly three hundred years passed before a Jew-

1

ish traveler decided to track down this fabled land where even the rivers suspended movement on the Sabbath day and where Jews dwelt in peace and security, unmolested and unharmed. But he was not the only one. There were others.

Who were these travelers who were like needles in the haystacks of Europe and Asia? Intrepid of spirit they must have been. For they braved unknown danger when present troubles would have sufficed. They courted disaster and death. Something drove them on. Was it curiosity, boredom, the search for utopia? Each single traveler was in his way the advance emissary for others. Did he then go out to seek a possible haven for his oppressed coreligionists? Were new markets and more liberal laws the magnets? Perhaps all these factors were at work.

Here was a scattered people, uprooted from the land it loved, stumbling, with many a backward glance to Zion, over the highways of the world. A small folk, not really wanted anywhere. Tolerated here—rejected elsewhere. Concerned about its own dark fate and brooding about its vanished brethren—the Ten Lost Tribes of Israel. Was it not true that "the Jews have not for their mansion any peculiar Countrey"? Their possessions were light and portable. They had no fields to till, no forests to call their own. They were perforce a pilgrim people.

Jews then were mobile. Did Charlemagne wish to communicate with the fabulous Harun-al-Rashid, a Jew named Isaac was of the diplomatic party. The Caliph of Cordova sent a deputation to Germany toward the close of the tenth century. One of the members of the Caliph's party, Ibrahim ibn Yakub, reported this journey. From the days of the Midrash there were revolutionaries among the Jews, bold fellows who claimed the earth was round! Inspired by this daring concept, they felt they could always return to the point of origin. Abraham ibn Ezra, Estori Parchi, Petachia of Ratisbon were travelers of note. But the prince of medieval mobility was Benjamin of Tudela who found that "obscure and unknown places are full of the glory of Jews."[1]

Geography was then and for a long time had been a mixture of myth and fable. Any information which was even remotely factual, such as Benjamin's, was an improvement on existing knowledge. To travel at all was remarkable. To come back with fact instead of fable was a boon to commerce, to the exchange of ideas between distant parts of the world, to the spread of culture patterns.

In spite of the overwhelming dangers and the terrors, Jewish mobility is amazing. There were always men shuttling back and forth from known dangers to unknown. The romance of Jewish travelers is still to be written. Some of them wait to be identified. Their peregrinations are still to be traced. Pursuing some hidden quest of their own, these restless, roving spirits penetrated into many unknown corners of the earth. We meet them in many lands, in every generation. They were the naïve and the gullible. The men who believed in miracles and in fairy tales. They pursued utopias. They followed hunches. They believed in divination and necromancy, in abracadabra and astrology. So they walked the lanes and dusty roads and sailed the ships and caravels and jounced on camels and on donkeys. And their trails were as cords binding distant places to each other.

On their travels they learned many things. They verified much that they had read in the Midrash and the Talmud. For was it not written that the earth was like a ball thrown from hand to hand? Did not the thirteenth-century mystic, Moses de Leon, steeped in the wisdom of Persia, student of Vedanta philosophy, write in the Zohar that when it is day on one side of the earth night blots out the other? He may have read the narrative of Rabbi Petachia of Ratisbon who started out from Prague in 1175 and returned fifteen years later full of the wonders of the lands he had seen, from Assyria to Zion. Estori haFarhi, onetime resident of Spain and France settled down to years of hard work in Palestine. For seven years he studied the land and its relics, the history and the legends of Palestine. The fruits of his research were written down under the title *A Knop and a Flower*. It was to become a priceless legacy to scholars of later generations.

Such a bold spirit was Fernão Mendes Pinto, who has but recently been identified as a Jew. His book of travels, *Peregrinação*, is a classic which the Portuguese are proud to claim as their own. Pinto has been acclaimed as a great literary figure and branded a magnificent liar. In twenty-one years of "peregrinations," he saw many hitherto unknown places. He was one of the first Europeans to visit Japan. It was he who introduced those islanders to the musket. Captured thirteen times, sold into slavery seventeen times, he managed to survive his vicissitudes, because of an innate, incurable optimism, an indomitable opportunism and a belief in himself and his destiny.[2]

The account of his travels, written with verve and charm, still endures. He is a symbol of a mobile, restless, adventurous folk, a true pilgrim in spirit.

He who writes history performs an act of faith. The historian selects a fact here, a person there—seeking to recreate a vanished scene, to capture a mood, to clothe a skeleton in flesh and blood. He breathes upon the dead bones of the past—and lo! they come to life. The history of the Jews is unlike that of any other people. It is distilled anguish. It is crystallized grief. It is the dirge of a people cut away from the land they love, yet always faithful to it. It is the story of an exiled band of pilgrims with Zion etched on its heart. The survival of the Jews is a major miracle of history. A people condemned to death and annihilation, to fire and torture—drowned in all the rivers of Europe, besieged in all its cities, yet always a remnant managing to survive—the Eternal Remnant of Israel. What does a man do when condemned to death? He spins fantasy in his dying hours. He reads the Bible as the clock ticks away the last few moments of his life.

So the Jews. They took refuge in daydreams. They drew maps charting known continents. They dreamed of uncharted utopias, of islands where they could find a haven. They studied the stars, finding consolation in otherworldliness, in the contemplation of untainted planets and undefiled constellations. They became the astronomers and geographers, the astrologers and cartographers of their day.

Superstition presided over the birth of geography. For geography, like all early sciences, belonged partly in the realm of fairy tale. Legendary accounts of mythical lands rivaled in fantasy the stories of the strange monsters who peopled the terrifying stretches of surrounding unexplored oceans. Legends told by uninhibited travelers helped shackle exploration and discovery. Fishermen and voyagers are notorious tellers of tall tales. Pliny and Solinus, Mandeville and Comas let their imaginations roam unchecked. Benjamin of Tudela could spin a yarn with the best of them. Fantasy was added to fact to make the contrast between the known world and the unknown as great as possible. Even the illiterate could feast on pictures. So maps were embellished with curious addenda. The famous Hereford Map included the Terrestrial Paradise. There were griffins and there was even the Land of the Seven Sleepers! Whimsey and chimera, phantom and fiction lurked in *mappa mundi*.

But the arteries of commerce and the stark courage of bold men gradually ate away the gingerbread house of geographical knowledge. The astronomer too left the astrologer's cocoon. He devised instruments which helped the mariner. The Arab who had contributed much to the science of mathematics had shown the way. The Arabian *kamal* was perfected into the astrolabe.

Jews were the middlemen of science. Language, which is the medium of exchange of scholarship, was no barrier to the Jew who lived now under the Crescent and now under the Cross. Whatever one culture knew was brought by these itinerants to other groups among whom perforce they resided. From the days of Ptolemy, the Jew carried this knowledge from place to place, serving as the catalytic agent, spurring the use of new tools and skills—skills that depended on mental powers rather than on physical possessions. One of the earliest of scientists in this field was an Arab, Massahala, who became converted to Judaism. The work of Levi ben Gerson, also known as Leo Hebraeus, was invaluable. His acquaintance with Arabic science facilitated his scholarly labors.

Just as the sick man is always preoccupied with his health, so is the unwanted one always concerned about the elsewhere. The present dwelling-place bristling with harsh reality is but a threshold away from the land that is yet to be discovered, where the climate is pleasant, crops abundant and there is room for all. What is Jewish history but the shifting of geographic centers?

So it was that Jewish astronomers taught by Arabs and fellow Jews prepared the Toledo Tables in 1070. Two Jewish astronomers completed the Alphonsine Tables for the ruler of Castile. In 1310 Isaac Israeli readapted them. Six years later, another Toledo Jew, Joseph ibn Wakkar, continued the work. Toward the end of the fourteenth century Immanuel ben Jacob made numerous valuable additions to this field. Soon many other famous names were added to the roster. But Jewish scholars did not carry on their work in a vacuum. There was constant collaboration, translation and adaptation in the realm of scholarship. Not only did they travel from one land to another—they leaped the hurdle from civilization to civilization, from Orient to Occident. They learned from the Arabs. They taught the Christians.

So seeking shelter, they dispensed knowledge.

On his journey from fact to reality, the historian walks with care. Not for him the fanfare, the unmerited accolade, the tower built of grains of sand. Slowly and meticulously he hews to the line, following accepted methods, known procedures. In launching inquiry on the role of the Jews in the era of exploration and discovery, the overwhelming evidence has been selected from Christian scholars. The supplemental data come from Jewish sources. For the purpose is to establish facts, not to glorify them. So the contribution of men like Professor Edgar Prestage of the University of London, Charles de La Roncière of the Bibliothèque Nationale, the eminent scholar, Armando Cortesão, the erudite William B. Greenlee of the New-berry Library, now takes precedence.

The world of the Jews on the eve of the Age of Discovery was "one world." They turned up in the most unexpected places. At harbor towns where fleets of ships came and went on all sorts of missions. On the high seas. In Africa, in India and in many islands that were the jumping-off-places for the vast unknown. Not all this roaming was due to the spirit of adventure. Much of it was due to necessity. Some of it was due to the lack of security. Some due to expulsions. Migration has always been twofold. Rejection alternates with acceptance, hope with failure.

With the Jews the sequence was logical and inexorable. They studied the stars. They made maps which helped navigators. They helped develop astronomical measuring devices to aid in locating the position of ships on the high seas. They were invited to go on journeys to facilitate map-reading, the taking of bearings, the measur-ing of distances from the Equator and the making of mathematical calculations. They were taken along as linguists and interpreters who might help make arrangements with the natives of newly discovered lands. And last of all there was an inexhaustible supply of convicts, *degradados*, relapsed Jews and suspect Marranos who were available to man the ships when the voyage was hazardous and regular seamen were wary and reluctant about signing up for tilts with monsters and griffins, for storms and cataclysms, for cannibals and jungles.

The maritime proficiency of the Jews, their skill in the making of maps and instruments so needed in the developing field of navigation made these specialists greatly sought after. Where Jews were needed, protection replaced prejudice and expediency became the guide to tolerance. Scholars basked in the sun of royal favor. When Pierre le Cérémonieux of Aragon wanted a silver astrolabe, he turned to Jews of Perpignan. The royal clock of Barcelona was checked by their instruments. Mossé Jacob, David Boujoru, Natan ou Acan del Barri—three simple Jews of Perpignan lost their anonymity, all because they mastered special skills.

From Avignon to the Balearic Islands to Majorca such specialists were found. But it was Majorca which became "the center of an exclusively Jewish science." To this island gravitated scholars whose concern was with the wider world. The Rabbi of Majorca was also a student and a specialist in the making of astrolabes. Rabbi Ysaac Nifoci and his coreligionist Bellshons were the official suppliers of astrolabes to Prince John of Aragon, as well as the translators of important astronomical works. Map-making became the grand art of Majorca—and at the apex of their profession were two Jews who achieved *"un éclat incomparable."* They were Abraham and Jehuda Cresques.

La Roncière places the beginning of the cycle of important maps which issued from Majorca as the middle of the fourteenth century. For the Ordinance of 1354 provided that each warship should be furnished with two maps. Abraham Cresques was without a peer there. He was the great virtuoso of the drawing boards. He had the talent. He now found a ready market for his wares.

Portolan charts based on scientific observation of seamen were painstakingly drawn. Growing out of coastal sketches roughly drawn by navigators, they became more detailed as more information was made available. These charts differed from maps, for they were designed as aids to navigation. Largely they date back to the thirteenth century. The three succeeding centuries witnessed the flowering of this art. The invention of the compass and other instruments extended the keys to navigation to captains of sailing ships. Life was expanding to include wider horizons. History was being made under the Portuguese, in the cloistered study of the ascetic Prince Henry, in the academy which he established at Sagres, where Jewish talents flowered. It was in this little world, and more particularly on the island of Majorca, that the science of the geographer, the map-maker, the astronomer was highly prized.

Let us review briefly the skeletal facts of Portuguese history at this era.

At about the time that William was casting covetous glances at the white cliffs of Dover, in 1065, King Ferdinand died and the monarchy, as in a proper fairy tale, was divided among his three sons. The wars and invasions that followed are not of immediate concern here. Nor are the marriages and amours of the royalty and gentry of moment. We need not pause to distinguish the illegitimate from the legitimate offspring of these alliances. The history of Portugal is a tangled web of wars, intrigues, invasions, conquests. The Moors alternately won victories and were vanquished (1055-64). Sancho I carried on the war against the Moors. In 1189, he equipped a fleet of forty vessels. Sancho II established an arsenal. King Diniz expanded the navy. The snowball was rolling downhill. "From the beginning, the sons of Israel had aided the development of the navy," says Leite. "To each ship or galley ordered built by the crown they gave as a tenure an anchor and a cable."[3] The psychological implications are interesting! So when John I came to the throne in 1385, his accession marked the beginning of an age of expansion. Of his six children, Duarte succeeded him, and Prince Henry the Navigator became most famous. The time was ripe. The age of discovery had found its leaders.

The status of Jews in Portugal was similar, on the whole, to their position in Spain. Much depended on royal favor. The emergence of nationalism, the growing influence of the Church, the constant need for new sources of money to finance the navies, the military campaigns of Portugal, all reflected on the position of Jewry. The Church was always a factor. King Diniz (1279-1325) held his ground against the demands of the Church. His successor was more yielding. King John I protected the Jews. He tried to stem the tide of antisemitism which was rampant in Spain. John II accepted some Jewish refugees as permanent residents from his neighboring country—in exchange for a handsome fee: six hundred families for sixty thousand gold crusados. Skilled laborers who were desperately needed paid a low fee. Others, subject to a poll tax, were granted temporary residence rights. They were then to be provided with ships for the next stage of their exodus. What befell them when, their money mulcted, they could no longer pay their way, was slavery and exile. The history of the Island of St. Thomas picks up the sorry tale.

The growing antisemitism in Spain and Portugal was in part contemporaneous with emerging nationalism. It was also testimony to the growing power of the Church. The tribunal of the Inquisition was in existence in Aragon from the thirteenth century. Castile took over the tribunal in order to treat with dispatch the matters pertaining to New Christians. The new developments of the Inquisition were spawned in the fertile brain of Torquemada. In 1488 it was going full blast. Two years later it moved to Majorca. What happened in 1492 belongs to history—American history.

One of the most prized maps in the history of geography was the Catalan Atlas of 1375 of *"Cresques lo Juheu."*

Abraham Cresques was attached to the royal household of John, the prince of Aragon. His official title was impressive: "Astrologer, Master of World Atlasses and Compasses." Prince John was his enthusiastic admirer and patron. It is a matter of record that when the prince saw one of Abraham Cresques' maps, beautifully drawn and embellished, he exclaimed, "This is the most beautiful map that ever I have seen!"[4]

In his professional work Abraham Cresques was happy. Over his drawing table either at the palace library or in his home, he was sure of an admiring audience. His maps were prized. A *mappa mundi* of his making was the gift par excellence. There is serenity and deftness in his work, proof of true virtuosity. He died in 1387, four years before the major persecutions of Jews which compelled his widow and his son to change their religion. To his death he bore the title *"Cresques lo Juheu."* Five hundred and fifty years after completion of his Catalan Atlas, the head of the Bibliothèque Nationale was to describe it as *"la quintessence des connaissances géographiques du moyen âge . . ."* Nordenskiöld says, "The Atlas Catalan forms the most comprehensive work of the fourteenth century. It is particularly rich in historico-geographical mythical legends in the interior of countries."

The maps of Jewish cartographers spurred dreams of empire. Jews helped equip the navy through the fleet tax. But they did more. Jews took part as soldiers in the Battle of Ceuta and died for the glory of Portugal and for the privilege of extending its boundaries. It was on this expedition that Prince Henry the Navigator tasted battle and the heady wine of conquest. His enormous curiosity and his thirst for knowledge grew into a lifelong, insatiable craving. He began to ask questions, interrogated men of every rank. He called in Jewish and other travelers and pumped them for information about the south coast of Guinea and the interior of Africa.

Prince Henry the Navigator was not squeamish. He overlooked no document. He snubbed no scholar who could contribute to his knowledge. His familiarity with the great portolanos of the Jews of this era is thorough. The Catalan Atlas was much prized at Sagres. It was the prize portolano of all, from the opening of the period of scientific cosmography in 1300 until the curtain was rung down after the discoveries of Columbus and Vasco da Gama and Cabral. Many great scholars were attracted to Henry's Academy of Sagres. Their contributions to geographic knowledge were invaluable. Here were forged many keys which opened the doors to the unknown.

The undisputed head of this group of scientists was Jehuda

Cresques, whom Hamy calls "*l'illustre fondateur de l'École de Sagres.*" Jehuda Cresques was a skilled navigator, instrument and mapmaker, who taught the Portuguese navigators all that he knew of these sciences. He had been educated by his father. Lovingly, painstakingly, Abraham had taught his son all that he knew. At first Jehuda was a pupil, then a collaborator of his father's. Jehuda Cresques was converted through force. His baptismal name was Jacobus Ribes.

Of the circumstances which preceded Jehuda Cresques' move to Sagres, there are several accounts, all of them in fairly close accord with each other. Prestage tells us that in the Villa do Infante of Prince Henry, at Cape St. Vincent, many ships put in for repairs and refitting. From the navigators aboard, Henry always sought information about their latest discoveries. Each new discovery was duly recorded on the maps which Henry tried to keep up to date. "This last task was performed by Master Jacome, an expert cartographer and maker of nautical instruments, whom he persuaded to come from Majorca and enter his service in exchange for a high salary."[5] But it is to La Roncière that we are indebted for the best and most valuable information on our Master Jacome or Jehuda. For he describes in well-documented detail, first the work of Abraham Cresques, the father, and then of Jehuda Cresques, his gifted son. For Jehuda Cresques was in his own right a scholar of great stature. Not content with inheriting his father's reputation, he added to it. He was attached to the royal household, like his father before him. His maps also were deemed worthy of being used as royal gifts. He was versatile in many ways. At one time King John I of Aragon sent a number of gifts made by Jehuda Cresques—an astrolabe, a map of the world, an hourglass and an almanac for the ensuing three years—to the Count of Foix, in exchange for two pedigreed greyhounds!

About the contribution of Master Jaime or Jacome there is unanimity from the time of his contemporaries to the latest authorities writing in this field. Thus Kimble writing in 1938 states that Jacome was the "most famous of all men" to be drawn to Sagres. To the school he brought a new point of view, that of scientific inquiry, the stressing of fact over fantasy, the importance of actual voyages over armchair speculations—the laboratory method in place of the romantic approach to the world in which he lived.

So great was the influence of Jehuda Cresques and his father that La Roncière designates as "*Les Cresques et Leur École*" that section of his work devoted to the dawn of the age of exploration and discovery. They did, in fact, found a school, establish a scientific dynasty, tear apart the opaque draperies of ignorance, prepare the way for the great adventure.

His place as court cartographer was secure. In addition to his other duties, Jehuda Cresques was also a teacher. It is with several of his pupils that we now concern ourselves.

For there were others. Famous colleagues of the Cresques whose beautiful maps delight the connoisseur to this day. There was Gabriel de Vallsecha whose name added glory to the Majorcan school. There was Mecia de Viladestes. In the Bibliothèque Nationale of Paris there is a map dated 1413 which is signed by Viladestes. He has been identified as a Marrano. This portolano was at one time in the library of the Convent of Val de Cristo. In this map there is traced the navigation in African waters of Jacome Ferrer of Majorca. The Viladestes map is largely based on the Catalan map of Abraham Cresques. Mecia de Viladestes was listed as a convert in 1401 and in that year was issued a permit to leave Sicily.

"The ex-Jew, Mecia de Viladestes, furnished more accurate documents than his coreligionist, Abraham Cresques," says La Roncière. He knew the location of many an oasis. He knew trans-Saharan routes unknown to his fellow scientists. He described and drew costumes and shields. Like his colleagues he also knew and noted where Jews lived.

The torch is passed from hand to hand. The Cresques', Mecia de Viladestes and then another illustrious name—that of Gabriel de Vallsecha. Here was a cartographer whose map became famous because it was used by Americus Vespucius.

A number of maps by Gabriel de Vallsecha were presented by D. Pedro to his brother. One of these maps, drawn between 1434 and 1439, "is our authority for the earliest known Portuguese voyage to any part of the Azores." Vespucci boasted the ownership of a "geographical skin" by Gabriel Vallsecha.

High in the ranks of the scholars and sages was Abraham Zacuto, who had improved the astrolabe which Vasco de Gama used. From Camoëns, most celebrated author of Portugal, who wrote *The Lusiad* in the sixteenth century, to F. Cantera Burgos of the University of Madrid, who wrote *El Judio Salmantino Abraham Zacut* in the twentieth century, Zacuto has been recognized and honored. The tributes have come largely from Christian sources. Zacuto was an author of note. His *Sefer Yohasin* covered the period in Jewish history from the Great Assembly to the end of the Talmudic period. But it is more than a *Book of Genealogies*, for it contains a sketch of universal history, which begins, logically, with Creation and ends with the close of the fifteenth century.

Zacuto was born around 1450. He died in 1510. During the crowded years between much happened. This scholarly Jew was born in Salamanca, was expelled from Spain, emigrated to Lisbon where he became astronomer to King Manuel and wrote numerous works, among them a history of the Jews and the *Almanach Perpetuum*. In 1493 he received an honorarium as Royal Mathematician.

King Manuel also relied on Zacuto's knowledge in matters nautical. The scholar had explained his theory of storms to the king, the use of his tables, the times most suited to navigation, the manner of determining the position of a vessel by observing the sun at high noon and the North Star at night. The King then sent pilots to Zacuto for instruction. He taught them the use of the astrolabe, by the application of his tables. He gave them numerous charts to facilitate their work.

Vasco da Gama, before he left Lisbon, met Zacuto in private conference. Unattended, the two men conferred in a monastery and Zacuto carefully briefed Vasco da Gama on his forthcoming expedition. What took place where these two men met we can only guess. But could the shadows on the wall have been cast by other shades, like that of Abraham ibn Ezra, whose studies had laid the foundation for the facile scholarship and the ready understanding of Zacuto? One of the crypto-Jewish navigators, Pedro Nunes, who accompanied Cabral on his expedition to Brazil, wrote from the newly discovered land to King Manuel in 1500 that their discoveries were not due to chance but to the thorough briefing which they had received. He said, "When our mariners started they were supplied with best information, and provided with instruments and rules of astrology and geometry."[6]

The *Almanach Perpetuum* was written in Hebrew. It was translated into Latin by Zacuto's disciple and pupil, Joseph Diego Mendes Vizinho (or Vecinho). It was published in Leiria in 1496. The printer like the author and translator was a Portuguese Jew, Samuel de Ortas, who with his son Abraham owned a printing press in Leiria until 1496.

There are extant sixteen copies of the *Almanach Perpetuum*, according to Fontoura da Costa. One of them is in the library of the Jewish Theological Seminary of America. From the sheaf of notes on the greatness of Zacuto's *Almanach Perpetuum* only a few may be cited. Prestage notes that this work was used by Columbus. Its timing was perfect. For it was written between 1473 and 1478 and thus formed the backbone of scientific navigation for Columbus, Vasco da Gama and Cabral.

In his definitive work, *A Marinharia dos Descobrimentos,* Fontoura da Costa writes that there are many other scholars of Jewish origin who aided Portuguese navigators in their discoveries. An important instrument of marine observation was perfected by Pedro Nunes. Other scholars are belatedly recognized. But in the astronomical chain forged in the development of *ciência nautica* at least three links out of a total of seven were contributed by Zacuto. Yet, withal, these honors garnered in his lifetime were as unavailing as were posthumous tributes. For his hard work, his scholarly reputation, his importance in furthering the skills of navigators and explorers—none of these things could purchase his personal happiness. He clung to his Judaism with tenacity. He gathered strength from his ancestors rather than from his contemporaries.

Thus when I was in Spain and in other Christian countries after my books on astronomy were published, I was known as Rabbi Abraham Zacutus, the Salamancan. I was justified in taking pride because of this.[7]

Honors might pile up, recognition might not be wanting, scholarly acclaim grudgingly or freely given might be had—but against the rising tide of nationalism, against the floods of antisemitism, Zacuto was helpless. In 1496 Abraham Zacuto and his son Samuel again joined the others, the lesser pilgrims, and went journeying from Portugal in search of sanctuary. For the expulsion of the Jews fell like the sharp blade of a guillotine upon the Jews of Portugal as it had fallen on the Jews of Spain in 1492. He went to Africa, to Turkey. His wanderings ended when life itself ended.

Zacuto had a son. But he also had a disciple. A man who was his spiritual heir, his co-worker, his collaborator, his translator. He was Joseph Vizinho, sometimes known as *"Maître Joseph le Juif."* He was the last of the great Jewish cartographers whose inspiration had derived from Majorca. For gradually the Majorcan school had succumbed to the pressure, the proscriptive measures, the persecution which was its reward for the great services it had rendered. It had fallen into a state of dissolution—and the glory had departed from Majorca.

The school of navigation which Prince Henry the Navigator had so carefully assembled and so assiduously headed was destined to survive. John II of Portugal went on with Henry's hobby. Here was a threshold personality, a man who straddled the Middle Ages and looked wide-eyed into the new age of science whose sun was just rising. Prestage describes John II as "a very solicitous inquirer into the secrets of the world, that is, well versed in cosmography." Prince Henry had had his Jacome of Majorca. John II had "appointed a committee of experts, including the Jews, Joseph Vizinho and Abraham Zacuto." Vizinho became an integral part of John II's scientific circle.

Vizinho was a contemporary and an associate of Isaac Aboab, "*último gaón de Castilla*," a man of attainment and of great personal prestige. He worked as well with his Christian colleagues as with his Jewish confreres. He was no closet cosmographer. For he was sent by his royal patron on a scientific mission to Guinea to measure the altitude of the sun. He worked on scientific committees, called *Juntas*. He translated, taught, traveled, studied, perfected measuring devices, tested them on field trips. A man of parts!

CHAPTER II

New World—Old Problems

➨➨➨ I, David, have seen the distressing sight and the disturbing
spectacle; how . . . the intelligent Jews are diminishing;
how the learned are disappearing from among us. . . .
—*From a document proposing the
creation of a Jewish College in
Mantua, March 22, 1564.*   ᴸᴸᴸ

COLUMBUS DESERVES the spotlight in a history of Jews in the
Western Hemisphere because of still persistent questions. First, was
he a Jew? No matter how our subject may squirm or shield his eyes
from the glare of floodlights or pretend that he wants his antecedents
to remain unknown, he must face his twentieth-century critics.
Second, did his discoveries change the lot, revolutionize the desti-
nies, affect the future of our protagonists, the Pilgrim People? Third,
what connection did he have with the Jews of his age? Did they contribute materially to his undertaking? Were they an integral part of
his enterprise? Let us consider the "known" facts.

Here is a thumbnail sketch of Columbus for those whose curiosity
is dormant and whose credulity is quiescent. The question marks
deal only with uncertain dates. His birth—Genoese. His early training—at sea. He lived for some years in Lisbon, where he married
and where a son was born. He proposed to reach India by sailing
west. He was spurned by Portuguese officials. Eventually he met with
success in Spain. He set sail on his historic voyage on August 3, 1492.
His pilot was Juan de la Cosa. The Pinzón brothers, Vicente and
Martín, each commanded a vessel, with himself in charge of the first.
He met with great successes and great reverses and died in Valla-
dolid believing that he had found a westward passage to Asia.

Just a simple tale with great reverberations! But is it quite as
simple as it seems?

15

Columbia Encyclopedia says that the discover of America (1451-1506) was "almost certainly" born in Genoa. It is a challenging statement. What, if anything, is "almost" certainty? Why did the chronicler, Columbus, fail to record his birthplace? The fault originates with the discoverer. Columbus perpetrated a deliberate hoax on historians. He chose to do so. All his life he scattered ambiguities in his writings with a lavish hand. If they have now sprung up to bedevil the historical fraternity and to obscure the facts of his life, he has only himself to blame. Said Vignaud, who devoted a lifetime to the study of the Columbian question, "Columbus never said one word of truth about what personally concerned him."[1]

In one of his letters is found the following Delphic note:

I am not the first Admiral of my family, let them give me what name they please; for when all is done, David, that most prudent King, was first a shepherd and afterwards chosen King of Jerusalem, and I am a servant of that same Lord who raised him to such a dignity.[2]

His son Ferdinand insisted that his father's "progenitors were of the blood royal of Jerusalem."

The ghost of Columbus walks through the pages of his writings wearing strange disguise. Why this transformation? Why should a vain, proud, demanding, self-assertive, pompous person who craves titles, has delusions of grandeur, insists on proper respect and public deference, why should such a man be less than himself? Why the coy anonymity alternating with the regal manner?

First, because Columbus wished to have his antecedents blotted out. Second, if he was a Jew, he did not dare to be known as one, although his writings are sprinkled with Old Testament allusions, although his major contacts before and after his great discovery were Jewish, although he complained of his treatment at the hands of Christians and berated them for their cruelty when writing to Jews or crypto-Jews. "If one wishes to cover up his traces, he must above all, not betray his origin,"[3] wrote Houben in 1935.

To those writers who flatly argue for Columbus as a Genoese, there has always been one hard nut to crack—the discoverer did not at any time use Italian. Not only that, but his New World nomenclature is Iberian and fails to introduce the nostalgic note, the autobiographical emphasis which would come from giving to even one remote spot in the newly found lands the subtle tribute of naming it for a place in his "native" Italy. Such Olympian indifference is not seemly. What can his reason be? Cecil Jane, a meticulous scholar, disposes of that consideration with ease. The man was an illiterate most of his life, he asserts. Hence Columbus left no Italian writing for posterity. However, he seems to have learned how to write late in life and then, proud of his newly acquired skill, he annotated his books in pompous, fulsome, newly acquired prose. He probably dictated his earlier works, hence the grandiose diction, the tangled, confusing style—in which Lombroso was to find centuries later evidence of mental instability. Jane feels that the Columbian marginal notes should be considered of a piece with his other writings, especially his *Libro de las Profecias*, which is charged with Biblical prophecy, which dwells on divine promise to rebuild Jerusalem and which hints broadly that he—Columbus—was the divinely chosen instrument to accomplish these ends. So this great "illiterate" annotated his Pliny in Castilian. And so when he wrote to Pope Alexander VI instead of using Italian, which was to be expected, he again wrote in Castilian.

Professor Morison gives a nod of approval. He finds no document, no inference, no hint of Semitic origin in his protagonist. "The usual line of Jew-Columbus argument is to distort his signature into something of cabalistic significance." He insists that Columbus applied Biblical language "to his own life and adventures; it is ridiculous to read into this passage a secret admission of Jewish blood, or an ambition to provide a new home for a persecuted race."[4]

Because of this dense Columbian fog, books on the subject are still being written and sober scholars calling each other harsh names. Thus Charles E. Nowell writing on *The Columbus Question* in 1939 says, "There is a lunatic fringe of writers determined to establish far-fetched theories regarding the Columbus enterprize."[5] Salvador de Madariaga's *Christopher Columbus*, published in 1940, categorically states that our protagonist was a Genoese of Sephardic stock. Madariaga is not on any more solid ground than Morison. Despite the exhaustive research, the marshaling of facts carefully cited, the giant question mark overshadows the text.

It is refreshing to turn to facts, to dates, to movements traceable on maps. Let us go back a little and pick up a few threads, starting to weave our tapestry anew. There is solid, incontrovertible ground. We have dates, names, places, letters. We know that whatever his antecedents, whatever the biographical uncertainties, fate threw Columbus into Jewish circles. They befriended him and rebuffed him. They were his admirers and his detractors. They played a role in his personal reverses at the courts of Portugal and Spain and but for their intercession with Ferdinand and Isabella, Columbus might have been deprived of their sponsorship.

It was in 1476 that Columbus' campaign in Portugal and his applications for royal support collapsed. For while King John was not averse to lending an ear to Columbus, his scientific advisors voted thumbs down every time on Columbus' proposals. The man impressed them as a dreamer and his plans as impractical. The three experts who were consulted at this time—D. Diogo Ortiz, Bishop of Ceuta, Dr. Rodrigo of Pedras Negras, the King's personal physician who wielded much influence at court, and Joseph Vizinho, the Jewish scholar and scientist, a favorite pupil, disciple and translator of Abraham Zacuto—felt that little of benefit could result from the projected expedition. But had not the cupidity of Columbus been so great, the King might well have vetoed his advisors and given Columbus the requested help. The terms proposed by Columbus were so unreasonable that the King decided to turn him down.

In the latter part of his stay in Portugal Columbus traveled to Guinea in West Africa and made numerous scientific observations. These he used later for purposes of comparison. This expedition to the Gold Coast proved very useful to him. He was more than a casual witness in 1485 to a meeting between King John II and Joseph Vizinho, when the latter returned from his field trip to Guinea and reported his observations to the King. Certainly if King John II wished to undertake a costly and hazardous westward voyage, he had men in his court who were accomplished navigators, tried and true, into whose hands such a venture might be safely placed. "The age was one in which skilled navigators abounded, and Columbus can but have been aware that, in practical knowledge of maritime matters, he had many equals and perhaps many superiors even among those who sailed with him."[6]

In 1485 Columbus, frustrated in Portugal, accompanied by his five-year-old son, Diego, went to Spain. There too he made little headway. Three years later he wrote an exploratory letter to King John II, to find out whether he would again be welcome in Portugal. The King answered cordially. In December of 1488 Columbus returned to Lisbon in time to be a spectator at the triumphal return of Bartholomeu Dias after rounding the Cape of Good Hope. It was a bitter pill for Columbus to swallow after the long years of waiting and pleading, of urging and conspiring. Angrily he shook the dust of Portugal from his boots. His hopes next turned to a nobleman of

Andalusia, Luis de Cerda, whose grandmother had been a Jewess. De Cerda's hospitality was famous. There Columbus rested for a while, trying to blot out the memory of his failures and the importunings of his creditors. He improved his time by persuading his host to provide him with a letter of introduction to the King and Queen of Spain. He was then ready to take on Ferdinand and Isabella.

Columbus now resolutely built his plans on Spain. For here he would be made or broken. This was almost his last stand. Next to Palos, the monastery of La Rabida was towering high on a bluff. Here Columbus and his young son found hospitality and patronage. Armed with letters of introduction, Columbus called on Ferdinand and Isabella. He found not only the court, but the entire kingdom in a state of turmoil. For there were serious rifts in the ranks of the powerful. Gradually they penetrated to every level of society. Old Christians, New Christians and Jews contended for power. The *converso*, or New Christian, was the despised middleman, caught between the aversion of those whose ranks he had joined and the aloofness and contempt of those whose ranks he had deserted.

Yet Columbus, wily diplomat that he was, knew that he must walk the tightrope, that he must seek friends in all three camps, that he must alienate and estrange no one. Whatever his antecedents, his letters show that he knew just the right note to strike with representatives of each of the three groups. He was by turns pious and orthodox in his dealings with Christians. He was factual and straightforward when writing to Jews, peppering his writing with Old Testament allusions, quoting liberally from the Prophets. He complained of Christians when writing to *conversos*, striking just the proper shade of ambiguity. Verily, all things to all men.

Columbus and Isabella had established some rapport in 1486. This was now to be continued. The renewed negotiations had secured the friendly interest of two Jews, Don Abraham Senior of Castile and Don Selemoh of Aragon.

If Madariaga is to be taken literally—and whatever reservations one may have on his theory about Columbus being of Jewish stock, his text shows exhaustive research and discerning well-documented scholarship on the history of Spain—the Jewish influence in Spain was incalculable. No Spanish ruler got along without them. Until 1492, Jews were financiers, royal advisers, key military officials. Under the title of *alfaquim*, a man might be a royal scribe, a diplomat, a courtier, a physician to the royal family. "Surrounded by court intrigue and always uncertain of the ambitions of their truculent vassals, the Castilian Kings leaned heavily on their Jewish counselors whose fidelity was not marred by conflicting loyalties."[7]

But as the months dragged out, Columbus' temper was worn thin. He nursed his grievances. He determined to leave Spain forever and next to try his fortunes in France. But friends dissuaded him and once more they interceded with Isabella. The Queen agreed to see him and even sent him money to buy a new suit of clothes and a mule. She was in a mellow mood. Granada had surrendered, ushering in the year 1492 with triumph and fanfare. Let Columbus be brought before her! But being a woman she once more changed her mind about this persevering petitioner. Again he packed his few belongings and planned his final exit from Spain. It was at this point that fate, a few Jews and Luis de Santangel took a hand in his affairs.

Luis de Santangel, *escribano de ración*, was one of the most influential men at court. He was a member of one of the wealthiest, most powerful Jewish families of Aragon, a family of social prestige, dignity and status. The Santangels, like many other families, subjected progressively to social pressure, official discrimination and outright persecution, joined the steady procession of converts to Christianity, those reluctant pilgrims who stumbled a little as they walked—for their glances were ever turned backward to the faith they had forsaken.

Santangel endorsed wholeheartedly the cause of Columbus. It may have been compassion that moved him. For pity is akin to personal grief. He could not bear to see this shabby petitioner leave Spain with empty hands. So Luis de Santangel hurried to Isabella. With ready eloquence he argued the cause of Columbus. Perhaps it was also his own cause and the deep, ineradicable love for his own people that moved him to action and to passionate pleading. For he might have dreamed of the new lands somewhere beyond the vast horizon as a place of refuge for the Jews—"a sort of Zionist movement." And so what one of his great biographers, John Boyd Thacher, calls "The Triumph of Columbus" was in reality the triumph of the *converso*, Luis de Santangel, visionary and champion of the perennial lost cause of history—the cause of the Jews.[8]

Santangel argued well. But, the Queen demurred, there was quite a sum of money involved. She might have to pawn her jewels. This, Santangel earnestly assured her, would not be necessary. He would himself furnish a part of the money. Santangel was a man of his word. He advanced at least half of the necessary amount. Besides, he well knew that some of the Queen's jewels were already pledged to finance the recently completed military campaign. "Moveover, Santangel's reasoning was irresistible. So little risk for so vast a gain!" Thus Morison.

Santangel was not alone in his partisan role. Columbus had other Jewish friends at court. High on the list of his influential friends, Columbus rated Gabriel Sanchez, the treasurer of the kingdom. There is no need to review his biography. It is like that of other Jews who traded baptism for survival. It was a poor bargain. Permanent security always eluded them. Gabriel Sanchez was a patriot who zealously served the King, who shares the honor of having befriended Columbus. As a *converso*, he was *persona grata*. But his immunity was too dearly bought. His father was burned in effigy in 1493. His brothers and sisters were burned at the stake for being adherents of Judaism.

Columbus had still another powerful friend to uphold him. Not a *converso*, but a steadfast Jew he was. His name—Don Isaac Abravanel. The family had lived both in Spain and in Portugal. Don Isaac was on cordial terms with Alfonso V of Portugal. When he fled to Castile, he soon became indispensable to Ferdinand and Isabella. He shares with Santangel and other Jews the honor of having helped in financing the expedition of Columbus. So much has been written on Don Isaac Abravanel that his name is widely known, his accomplishments greatly celebrated. It would be easy at this point to leave the main road and to travel a part of the way with this scholar, sage and prolific writer. His enthusiasm for scholarship, his breadth of interest, are truly amazing. Yet everything he considered was within one frame of reference—its bearing on Jews. To be a mystic and yet practical, to know the uses of solitude and still to be able to practice the art of diplomacy, to cherish contemplation and wisdom and yet to be able to plunge into varied activities—that seems scarcely to describe Don Isaac Abravanel.

"Jews had an important part given them in the American drama," says that great authority on Columbus, John Boyd Thacher. "Few names among the *dramatis personae* were more illustrious than those of Luis de Santangel and Gabriel Sanchez. When the craze against the Jews was at its height in Spain; when persecution sorely tormented them, when their property was confiscated and their lives in peril, many apostatized and pretended to accept the Christian faith. . . . Few of these conversions were real."[9]

It was against such men that the Spanish Edict of Expulsion of March of 1492 was directed. While Columbus waited happily for the outfitting of his ships, for the completion of innumerable details, for the beginning of his great adventure, the Jews of Spain stunned by calamity were mechanically performing their rites of mourning. For them to leave the land they loved and had served so well was like looking into the face of death.

"So that, after having banished all the Jews from all your Kingdoms and realms . . . you ordered me to go with a sufficient fleet to the said regions of India."[10] In these words Columbus recorded the twin events which were inexplicably bound up with each other: *expulsion and exploration.*

The expulsion was well timed. Isaac Abravanel and Abraham Senior had pleaded before Ferdinand and Isabella for an extension of time. They got two days of grace. On the ninth day of Ab, the day of mourning for the destruction of Jerusalem, the exodus began.

"The last sound Columbus heard as he was preparing to sail from the Old World was the wailing of the Jews," writes Thacher. With that melancholy dirge mingling with the untroubled sound of plashing waves of the Atlantic, Columbus faced westward.

We turn now to the final act of the drama in Spain. It is not a scene to linger on. Its sight and sound are reminiscent of the nightmare years recently witnessed. Death wears a universal face—its pace and manner are unaffected by time and place. It is the same story found on the pages of all newspapers since 1933.

We have a contemporary eyewitness account of the expulsion from Spain filed with the same meticulous care that our best reporters use today. And despite the fact that the reporter was also an active participant in the drama, himself experiencing the anguish and the poignant sorrow of becoming a *displaced person*, no note of self-pity creeps into his news story. It is superb reporting.[11]

I was at court when the royal decree was announced. I wearied myself to distraction in imploring compassion. . . . But as the adder closes its ear with dust against the voice of the charmer, so the King hardened his heart against the entreaties of his suppliants. . . .

The King was abetted by the Queen who

urged him to continue what he had begun. We exhausted all our power for the repeal of the King's sentence; but there was neither wisdom nor help remaining. . . . Our nation bewailed their condition with great lamentations; for there had not been such a banishment since Judah had been driven from his land. They exhorted and encouraged each other to keep firm to the law: *Let us surmount every trouble for the honour of*

*our nation and our religion. . . . If they leave us with life, we will live;
if they deprive us of it, we will die; but never let us violate our holy law.*

In measured prose worthy of a place beside the Gettysburg Address, our report concludes:

Let us abandon our settlements, and seek for homes elsewhere. . . . In one day, on foot and unarmed, 300,000 collected from every province, young and old, aged and infirm, women and children, all ready to go anywhere. Among the number was I, and with God for our leader, we set out.

The despatch is filed for eternity by Don Isaac Abravanel.

Columbus commanded the flagship. It was the largest, most imposing of the three vessels, even boasting a covered deck. Vicente and Martín Pinzón headed the two caravels—the *Pinta* and the *Niña*.[12]

The details of that epoch-making voyage are well known. But two questions concern us now. What scientific equipment used on this voyage was made by Jews. Were there any Jews aboard?

The first of these questions has already been answered in these pages. Did not Jewish cartographers again and again make their inestimable contribution? Did not Jewish scholars enlarge the knowledge of the Admiral of the Ocean Seas?

Had not his association with the Jewish scientists and mathematicians taught him much? Joseph Vizinho had reported his observations on his famous field trip to Guinea in the presence of the discoverer who had later verified these observations. Of Zacuto's *Almanach Perpetuum* with its tables of declination, which was the most important work in any sailor's library, much has been written here. But even before it was printed in 1496, manuscript copies of the *Ephemerides* of Zacuto were long available to mariners. For it had been written between the years 1473-78, while Zacuto was professor at the university of Salamanca. There were at least three copies in Hebrew still extant in 1912, at Lyons, Valencia and Munich. And while we are assigning "credits," let us not forget Levi ben Gerson, whose cross-staff, which he called *baculus Jacob*, Martin Behaim reintroduced to the Portuguese on the eve of the discoveries.[13]

A forgotten contemporary of Levi ben Gerson who died in Perpignan in 1370, was an instrument maker known as Tsevi Herz, a Jew who is associated with the city of Prague. His valuable astrolabe is noted for engraved Hebrew inscriptions. Tsevi Herz made a notable scientific contribution to the art of navigation.

The mariners who sailed with Columbus were no strangers to the astrolabes, the maps, the weather charts of Jewish scientists. But Jews were more than closet contributors to the Columbian undertaking. There were Jews who made that voyage with Columbus.

Eighty-seven out of ninety crew members have been identified by name and occupation. Only a few can be recognized as Jews. For how could they survive and sail if they were so known? The names of some of the sailors have a familiar sound, similar to names of known Jews and *conversos*. Kayserling lists the following *conversos*:

Luis de Torres—linguist, who was to serve as translator, for he knew Hebrew and Arabic.

Alonso de la Calle—a former resident of Jew's Lane for which he was named.

Rodrigo Sanchez—who was related to Gabriel Sanchez, treasurer of Spain.

Maestre Bernal—ship's surgeon who had worn the shirt of a *sambenito* in 1490.

Dr. Marco—a surgeon.

According to Morison, who gives the crew list of each vessel, Rodrigo Sanchez, listed as comptroller, was on the *Santa Maria*. Luis de Torres, interpreter, was a fellow passenger. Also on the flagship were Maestre Juan Sanchez, surgeon and Bartolomé de Torres, able seaman. These last two are not identified as to origin. On the *Pinta*, under Captain Martín Pinzón there was a Maestre Diego, listed as an apothecary, and an able seaman who had two sets of names: Juan Rodriguez Bermejo, alias Rodrigo de Triana. The latter is considered a Jew by some authorities. Kayserling scoffs at it and rejects Rodrigo de Triana in toto. However the belief as to his origin persists.

Henry Harrisse in his *Christophe Colomb* says of the men who accompanied Columbus that there were many Jews among them. He credits a Jew with the first glimpse of the new world. Ravenstein also stresses the fact that *degradados* were numerous in the ships' personnel. That among these men with a "record" there might have been relapsed Jews is not unlikely.

The *Pinta* was the best sailor of the three ships. So it came to pass that "a sailor called Rodrigo de Triana saw this land first." On his flagship, Columbus too was straining his eyes. He thought he saw a light. "He also told Rodrigo Sanchez de Segovia, whom the King and Queen sent with the fleet as Inspector, who saw nothing." Thacher notes in connection with the flickering light which Columbus noticed that Indians often went about at night with torches. Columbus in an account given to Antonio de Torres some time later spoke of the danger of fire. "However this may be," writes Thacher, "Columbus claimed and obtained the reward . . . for having first discovered land." The able seaman who first saw land was furious. After his services were completed he left for Africa where he renounced Christianity and returned to his former faith.

It was truly landfall and no mirage. . . . The calendar said it was Friday, October 12, 1492.

The voyage which had begun at the conclusion of a day of mourning for the destruction of Jerusalem, the ninth day of Ab, was ended on Hoshana Rabbah, the twenty-first day of Tishri. It was Succoth, the Festival of Booths, in the year 5253, the "day of willow-sprigs." On that day the pious sing *Hosanna* as they reverently carry the Torah scrolls and on that day the blessings for the ensuing year are determined on high.

The expulsion on a day of mourning! The discovery of a New World on a day of rejoicing! A new world was opened up!

"The Admiral called the two captains and the others who landed," so reads the *Journal*, "and Rodrigo Descoredo, Notary of all the Fleet, and Rodrigo Sanchez of Segovia and told them to bear him witness and testify that he . . was taking possession of the said isle." San Salvador, Guanahani or Watlings Island, call it what you will, was now proudly claimed by the Admiral of the Ocean Seas for their Majesties, Ferdinand and Isabella.

Next envoys were selected, linguists who could be expected to converse with the natives and report to Columbus what mysteries the unknown island shielded. One hundred and twenty-eight years before the Pilgrim Fathers gazed with thanksgiving and with awe upon the New World, a representative of the Pilgrim People was first chosen to explore with a shipmate this virgin land. The two men who were dispatched to make these historic observations were Luis de Torres, interpreter, and Rodrigo de Jerez, able seaman, both crew members of the flagship.

It was Luis de Torres, "who had been a Jew," in the words of Columbus, who was to head the diplomatic mission to the Emperor or Grand Khan. For this undertaking, Columbus had "prepared with pathetic punctilio." The "ambassador," Luis de Torres, carried with him a Latin passport, a Latin letter from Ferdinand and Isabella, and a gift. Luis was given six days in which to accomplish his mission. Rodrigo de Jerez was chosen as his companion because he had once visited Guinea and had met its Negro King and was supposedly well versed in matters of protocol. They had two native guides. They were to look for spices as well as for other information. Beads were given them to be used in exchange for food.

Again we turn to the *Journal* of Columbus for our narrative of the adventures of Luis de Torres and his companions.

Yesterday in the night, says the Admiral, the two men whom he had sent inland to see the country came back and told him how they had gone twelve leagues as far as a village of fifty houses, where he says there were a thousand inhabitants, as a great many live in one house . . . the Indians received them with great solemnity.

A detailed report was brought back by Luis de Torres of the people, of their customs, of the vegetation, of the animals they encountered and of all the strange sights they saw. Not the least of the wonders was the smoking of herbs—tobacco—which reminded the "ambassador" of the paper tapers which boys light "on the day of the Passover of the Holy Ghost." But, alas, for all the languages which Luis de Torres spoke, he could not converse with the inhabitants of the New World. It was most humiliating for a scholar, a linguist and a gentleman to conduct his historic interviews in sign language.[14]

Although linguistic skills failed him, his powers of observation did not. He was the first European to visit the natives of the New World, the first to describe their life before it was corrupted by contact with the white man, the first to discover the use of tobacco. He was the first Jew to settle in Cuba. He was granted a royal pension by Ferdinand and Isabella. The rest of his life was lived out in the New World.

In this fashion the discovery of the New World was begun, "the greatest event which has happened since the creation of the world," wrote one historian in 1552.

The discovery of Columbus sounded the starting gun for a transatlantic race. There were many important voyages to come. The Portuguese standard was now being ferried to many a distant outpost. And often and often, Jews were aboard. . . . The era of maritime activity begun by Prince Henry the Navigator gathered momentum through the years. The voyages of Eannes, of Gonçalves, of Velho were but steppingstones. We cannot at this point entertain the theory which has been advanced by some scholars that the Portuguese may have discovered America forty years before Columbus.

The controversial subject is amply covered by Prestage, by Morison, by Cortesão, and others.[15] The Portuguese were busy. They shared their information with as few as possible. They invited strangers to their land and exploited them. Their ambitions were limitless and were soon in conflict with those of Spain. Pope Alexander VI, being an Aragonese, had pro-Spanish leanings and his four papal bulls left only the crumbs for the Portuguese. Protests from Lusitania were loud and vehement. Something would have to be done to protect the rights of the Portuguese.

The Jews of Portugal followed these proceedings with keen interest. For the numbers of Jews who had lived in Lusitania for centuries had had their ranks recently swelled by exiles from Spain. The largest group of refugees had crossed over into Portugal in 1492. They were received with anxiety by their coreligionists. But King John made a paying business of his "hospitality." There were some hundred thousand emigrés, estimates Cecil Roth. Each of these was now taxed eight crusados in return for a limited permit to remain in the country. The King undertook to furnish ships at the expiration of the transit permits.

But again royal promises proved worthless. Ships were late, inadequate, unseaworthy, manned by sadists. The unfortunate passengers were dumped on the neighboring coast of Africa. Those who could not be accommodated on the ships were sold into slavery. Little children were torn from their parents. Some were taken to S. Thomé, an island off the coast of Africa. Others were clutched to their mother's breasts, as these frantic, driven women jumped headlong into the ocean.

King John died and went to his reward in 1495. His kinsman who succeeded John II was King Manuel, "the Fortunate." He reversed some of the anti-Jewish policies of his predecessor. The Jews who had not yet left Portugal were allowed to remain. But these "halcyon" days of legalized residency were soon terminated. For the twenty-six-year-old ruler was about to make an alliance with the daughter of Ferdinand and Isabella. The coy young bride refused to accede to the marriage until the Jews in Portugal joined their exiled brethren and took to the highways of the world. On the fifth day of December in 1496, Jews and Mohammedans were given ten months to leave the country.

But Manuel being an ambitious man did not really want to let the Jewish people go. He planned to herd them into the Christian fold by fair means or foul. Now hell broke loose. On Passover of 1497 Jewish children were ordered to be forcibly baptized. Snatched from the arms of their frenzied parents, they were dragged away to make their obeisance to the Prince of Peace. Some parents chose to die with their children. Others went mad. Now all the foul means at the disposal of the majority were invoked against the helpless minority. Some Jews were walled alive into dungeons. Others, leaden-footed, more dead than alive, presented themselves to the authorities to be "restored" to society by baptismal waters. The stubborn remnant who still held out were declared to be slaves. By these measures virtually all the Jews of Portugal became New Christians. In this crucible of death and murder and bestiality, the most tenacious brand of crypto-Judaism was born. From the ranks of these people came the very earliest settlers, the first pioneers of the New World.

Against a background of matrimonial alliance, pogroms and conversion by persecution, Manuel began to lay plans for his next undertaking—the ambitious plan involving an expedition to India. To head this expedition Manuel the Fortunate selected Vasco da Gama, a member of his household and a first-rate navigator. The best available information was to be given the explorer. Bishop Diogo Ortiz furnished the books and maps that were so necessary, "while Abraham Zacuto provided astronomical instruments." Zacuto had developed a theory concerning the prediction of storms. He was once more levied upon for instruction, advice and information.

But far more interesting from our point of view than the assistance given Da Gama by Abraham Zacuto, was the composition of the crews. For they were largely *degradados,* convicts or banished men without a future. While these *degradados* were anonymous we do find some reference to indicate the presence among them of New Christians who certainly had little to lose by setting off on such hazardous journeys.

Among the men who listened to Zacuto may be found the names of the following *degradados*: Damião Rodrigues, João Machado, João Nunes, Pero Dias, Pero Esteves.

Another who figures prominently in contemporary accounts was the *"renegado"* Gaspar da Gama. For when Vasco da Gama sponsored his baptism, Gaspar chose the name of his Christian godfather as his own. Gaspar da Gama was a sailor with a past. He was about forty years old when he was impressed by Vasco da Gama. He was blond, tall, attractive, with a prepossessing personality. He recalled visiting many distant lands and had joined numerous expeditions.

In the *Journal of Vasco da Gama* there is an interesting description of Gaspar's first appearance on board ship. He spoke "Venetian" well, was richly dressed in linen and carried a sword in his belt. He greeted the officers effusively, protesting vigorously that he was a Christian who had become a Moor under duress but at heart had never wavered in his support of Christianity. Viewed with suspicion by those who met him, called a renegade Moor, or a renegade Jew, he was accused of being able to shed his faith with the ease of a reptile. Correa called him a Castilian whose real name was Alonso Perez. But he did not fool anybody. He was known to his associates as "the Jewish pilot."

King Manuel knew him as a Jew and so referred to him in one of his letters. He was ubiquitous. Travel was in his blood and change of address was a commonplace experience. He was Cabral's interpreter as well as Vespucci's. In a letter of Vespucci dated June 4, 1501, Manuel praises Gaspar's knowledge of languages and mentions his extensive travels in Asia. So indispensable did he now become that he was invited to go along on several important expeditions. He won more royal favor. King Manuel appointed him a cavalier of his household. He was granted a pension. He could make friends and influence his comrades. Lest we seem too hard on the mercurial Gaspar da Gama, let us note that enforced baptisms were common on these voyages. The *degradados* who composed the crews refer to this religious rite as a frequent occurrence.

But the importance of Gaspar da Gama does not end with his association with King Manuel and Vasco da Gama. Two men whose names belong on the roll of honor as great discoverers of this age, utilized his skills and his information. They are Pedro Álvarez Cabral and Americus Vespucius. In 1500, Gaspar da Gama was in the company of Cabral as mariner and interpreter on the way to the East. Vespucci found him both trustworthy and useful on two of his voyages.

There was a historic scene at Cape Verde when Cabral met the ships which were commanded by Vespucci. Vespucci described Gaspar da Gama as "the best-informed man among Cabral's followers." His description of Gaspar as a fount of information and experience is an eloquent tribute to this Jewish adventurer. Cabral headed a fleet of thirteen ships and twelve hundred men who had been assembled to man the ships.

Gaspar Judeo was one of the two official interpreters of the fleet. The other was Gonçalo Madeira, of whose antecedents nothing is known. But there were linguists in the fleet, men who knew Arabic and other languages. One sailor who knew Arabic well was Ayres Correia. Who these linguists were, it is of course impossible to state with certainty. But all historians are agreed on one point—that many *conversos* were members of Cabral's personnel. One of the mystery-men was Master John, or João.[16] "Mestre João was well equipped with astrolabe, quadrant, and ephemerides."[17]

Who was this Master John? He was a Galician astronomer, an astrologer, a physician and surgeon. His title, "Master," implies that he had also been an instructor. It was largely as an astronomer that Master John employed his time. He studied the constellations of the Southern Hemisphere. He sent a sketch of the Southern Cross in his letter to the King. "It is probable that he, like so many men of his profession at that period, was a converted Jew,"[18] says Dr. Greenlee. He served both as a physician and scientific navigator on Cabral's voyage.

Cabral's landfall was made during Easter week, in April, 1500. When the armada first approached land, it was both a welcome and an imposing sight. A towering, circular mountain, like a sentinel rose before them, while below it smaller ranges nestled close. And far, far below that, was an expanse of flat shore with tall green trees. They anchored at the mouth of a big river and Nicholas Coelho, accompanied by Master John, was sent in a boat to interview the curious natives who appeared with bows and arrows in their hands. Coelho signaled to them to put down their weapons. They complied. The sea was choppy and the time unfavorable for prolonged salutations and exchanges of compliments. But Coelho gave the natives three caps and received an elaborate feather headdress in return. Then they left. Cabral then ran up the coast toward the north in search of a good harbor. When they finally found a suitable anchorage, it was a bay large enough to accommodate a fleet. Again Nicholas Coelho was called in. This time Bartholomeu Dias and a *degradado*, Afonso Ribeiro, were sent with him.

This event—the discovery of Brazil—has been covered at length by countless historians. One of the pithiest descriptions is that of Professor Renard who says simply: "In 1500 Álvarez Cabral was driven by a storm to the coasts of Brazil, which the government peopled with exiled Jews and convicts."

This summary account will do for our purposes.

In the South Atlantic, washed by the tides of countless centuries, there is an island named for a Jew. "Isolated in the vast solitude of the Atlantic there looms up out of the surging ocean the island of Fernando Noronha facing in every direction of the globe." Travelers nearing the green coast of Brazil have seen it. The name is on every map. The man to whom that island was presented and for whom it was named is just emerging from the thick ooze of oblivion. His life can be reconstructed from thousands of footnotes. He is a bit like Adam, for he too is made out of dust, the dust of many libraries. Now like a castaway he is about to be rediscovered. The Pilgrim People acclaim him as a hero of great stature, an explorer and a discoverer of their very own.

Out of the opaque layers of the past, he emerges. Belated accolades salute him. His full name seems to have been Fernão Pereira Pestana de Loronha. He was also known as Fernando Loronha, Fernando Noronha, Fernando della Rogna. Both his name and his religion underwent numerous enforced mutations.

Fernando de Loronha was called by the King *"cavaleiro de nosa casa."* He was given the freedom of the city of Lisbon. As a *cavaleiro* he had access not only to the best homes in Lisbon and Portugal but also to the King's palace. In person and in manner, he must have been highly acceptable. He achieved a position of unquestioned leadership not only in court circles, but in the society of New Christians. *Conversos* were prominent in the economic and cultural life of Portugal. Both Jews and converts looked up to Loronha. For he was a strong character, adventurous, bold-spirited. Yet in spite of his personal aplomb and the assurance of his movements, despite his great wealth and social triumphs, there were pathetic evidences of his having remained at heart a loyal, unconverted, secret Jew. We have fragmentary clues as to that. There was the ship he once purchased and renamed the *Judea*. There was the harbor discovered and named Cananéa, a harbor which was 32° South on the map, just as the place in Palestine for which it was named was 32° North. There were the Jewish settlers whom he took along with him on his very first voyage, and the little settlements, the very first in South America, which he founded for these *conversos*. Were these acts of allegiance or atonement? Who can say?

The South American discovery teased and intrigued the imagination of the royal house. The insatiable craving for wealth could now be assuaged. What more natural than to call upon a familiar figure at court, an enterprising entrepreneur like Fernando de Loronha and to man the expedition with New Christians clamoring to leave Portugal by any means? Fernando de Loronha had a number of barcos at his disposal. At least five we can identify by name: the *Nazarre*, the *Tryndade*, the *Santa Caterina*, the *Bretôa*, and the *Judea* were among them.

There was the land. Here were the ships and personnel. They all added up to a new expedition, the purpose of which was primarily to enrich the King. A contract was drawn up. This contract may have been a clear-cut business venture, but to the Jews of this era, it was a passport to a golden opportunity. From where they sat in Portugal, the new land was peopled by friendly natives, mysterious and undefined in resources, distant from the ministrations of the Holy Office—a veritable paradise to the persecuted, the driven and the hunted Jews of Iberia.

Loronha paid handsomely for his concession. Diffie estimates that the privilege of risking his neck and his ships for King and country was worth something in the neighborhood of fifty thousand dollars per annum to Loronha. However, if spices and dyes could be brought back to Portugal, the venture would be cheap at any price.

There were others who were ready to explore all the commercial possibilities in Brazil. There were Florentine merchants in Lisbon eager to join in the new ventures. One of these men was Bartolomeo Marchioni. Another was Amerigo Vespucci. But above and beyond reasons of adventure or profit, there were men to whom a new home meant a new lease of life. It was for these dispossessed people that Fernando de Loronha became the spokesman. So Fernando de Loronha presided at a meeting of the *conversos* who first undertook the exploration and commercial development of Brazil. Some historians, wishing to detract from the importance of this conference, say that Jews also called on Italian bankers and merchants and other nationals to work with them and that Loronha's chairmanship of this meeting of *conversos* means very little. The banding together of New Christians was of utmost importance however. Their subsequent activities and carefully worked-out plans clearly indicate the extent to which they put their hearts into this venture. There were other meetings of Jews who were interested in the development of Brazil. They wanted to become colonists. Thus Calmon writes that under Loronha Jewish colonization in Pernambuco and Bahia was of foremost importance. Of the earliest settlers, Jews were in the majority.

One of the men who figured often in the Loronha business ventures was Amerigo Vespucci. The reason that Vespucci and other Italians were ready partners with *conversos* in this and subsequent undertakings seems to be, according to Dr. Greenlee, that Italians had no aversion to working with Jews. The profit motive overshadowed other psychological hurdles. At any rate, they got along very well.

The first expedition whetted their appetites. The second venture to the land of parrots and other fascinating inhabitants lasted three months. During that time forty-four days of foul weather were endured. But what was a simple "act of God" like a tempest or a rough sea to those who had known the rigors of man-made monsoons?

Furthermore, a group of newly converted Jews, or New Christians, viewed the far-off land as an opportunity not only for trade but also as a likely refuge from persecution in Portugal. Since King Manuel sought to economize in every way at this time to obtain funds for the India fleets, the second voyage to Brazil may be considered largely as a private venture. It was financed chiefly by Marchioni and the New Christians headed by a prominent shipowner in Lisbon, Fernão de Loronha, who probably went as the commander. It seems evident that the Florentine, Amerigo Vespucci, also was among the notables present on this voyage.[19]

There were three caravels that set sail in May of 1501 in the second armada. They sailed west until they passed the rockbound shores of the island that was later to bear the name of our Jewish protagonist. Then they came to the mainland of Brazil. The first actual landing was made at São Roque. Then the caravels rounding the eastern coast of Brazil, continued in a southerly direction along the coast. The southernmost point of shore which these sea-weary navigators touched must have looked like the promised land to them. For they linked it with the land of Canaan in their minds. And Cananéa is there to remind us of that identification. Vespucci and Loronha were again a team. But now they separated. Loronha went north, back to the island he had first sighted. Now he landed there. Thence by way of the Azores, he returned to Lisbon. A syndicate of New Christians was formed and articles were drawn up for exploiting the new land.

The story of the first lease of the land of the parrots is covered in detail in *Historia da Colonização Portuguesa do Brasil.* Here Loronha is referred to both as concessionaire and associate of the New Christian settlers.

The concession which King Manuel issued to Loronha was specific as to its aims and vague as to geography. What the King had in mind could be summarized as profits and empire. What Loronha had in mind was settlements and trade. In the new land there was at least one very much desired product. That was brazilwood or dyewood. In the *Terra Nova* there grew a large tree. From the logs of this tree, a red dye which was very popular in Europe could be extracted.

The island which Loronha first discovered was confirmed to him and to his heirs. There were two important documents involving Loronha. One was his contract with the King to explore, settle, and develop the commerce of Brazil. The other involved the gift of the island which he discovered and which was renamed in his honor. Later, in a charter issued by King João III in 1522, this grant was continued and confirmed.

After the initial period of exploration of the coastline and of searching for the marketable brazilwood, the caravels explored some of the bays with a view to settlement. To Bahia de Todos os Santos— the Bay of All Saints—goes the honor of being the first port in Brazil. At Cape Frio, *conversos* established a fort, the first colonists' settlement in Brazil. Bearing the products of the new land in the holds of their ships, some of the men now returned to Lisbon. Others, more daring and less bound by ties in Portugal, stayed on in the new settlement. But even those who went back to Lisbon were irrevocably joined to the new land. Barcos, caravels and ships shuttled back and forth between Portugal and Brazil. Dyewood, slaves, tropical birds, skins of animals, monkeys and other pets were among the exports. Loronha's *Bretôa* was the best known of these enterprising vessels. Loronha continued to head the exodus of New Christians to the New World.

It would be well if having presented Loronha as a man of energy, of vision, of compassion for his fellow *conversos*, it could also be stated that his own sympathies had been enlarged, that he frowned upon the prevailing custom of slavery. But there was no compunction in him, no record of fleeting regret, no holding back from adding human cargo to the other products that he exported from Brazil. This holds true of other Jewish settlers as well. They had no more conscience in the matter than their Christian contemporaries. Jewish pioneers were of no greater moral stature than other early settlers. They were among those present at the founding. That is all.

CHAPTER III

The End of the Settlements

➤➤➤ Referring to the new Jews and Christians, I shall tell this to your Excellency: In Constantinople, while eating with the ambassador of the Most Christian Emperor, the ambassador of Chios, and many gentlemen and Christians, I remembered a discussion which was promoted critically blaming the emperor and Your Highness for causing the Jews to go to Turkey; they said that the Turks, before the coming of the Jews, were of inferior intelligence and deficient in weapons, and now because of the Jews there was plenty of everything and they had developed their industries and mechanical handicrafts, and so the discussion continued unfavorable to Your Highness.
—LUCIO D'AZEVEDO, *Historia dos Christãos Novos Portugueses.* ⇇⇇

WE NOW enter on the creative era of Jewish history in America—the period of pioneering and settlement. Gilberto Freyre believes that the Sephardic Jews were largely an effete aristocracy, an anemic bourgeoisie. According to him, their activities for centuries had been for the most part concerned with scholarship and commerce—occupations which developed brain rather than brawn. Now we witness a miracle, the refutation of such charges in the laboratory of Brazil.

For the Jews proved to be hardy pioneers in the dense wilderness of the new land.

It is simple to state that the first settlements in Brazil were made by New Christians, that its earliest settlers were *conversos.* We locate Bahia and Cape Frio on the map. "Here," we read of Cape Frio, "the fort was erected and the New Christians established a little settlement, the first in Brazil." It is simple to reconstruct the details of the earliest commercial ventures, for we know what cargo the barcos and

35

caravels carried. It is all a matter of record. We also know about some of their larger undertakings.

As for the Jew, there is evidence to the effect that he was one of the most active agents in the winning of a market for the sugar-producers of Brazil, a function that, during the first century of colonization, he fulfilled to the great advantage of this part of the Americas. He would appear to have been the most efficient of those technicians responsible for setting up the first sugar-mills. The history of patriarchal society in Brazil is, for this reason, inseparable from the history of the Jew in America.[1]

In these words, the foremost sociologist of Brazil acknowledges the Jewish contribution to the history of the largest country of America.

But it is very frustrating at the same time. There is so much the historian wants to know which is hidden from him. What manner of folk were they? Had the generations of persecution and of pushing around hardened them? What were their moods? How did they react to the stark realities of life in the opulent wilderness of Brazil? How long before their families followed them? What were the folkways of these people who sought so eagerly to discard the enforced and unwanted rites of their new religion? Had they forgotten how to be Jews? Had their Judaism undergone mutations due to its subterranean existence, like a plant forcibly deprived of the sun? We know that many of them retained the flame of their ancient faith. But in what form? The transition period was one of spiritual uncertainty, of deep psychic unrest, of tension, of inner turmoil. Could the busy lives, the manifold activities, the restlessness have been symptomatic?

For centuries Jews of Iberia had lived as neighbors of the Moors and Christians. Now they met the head-on impact of the natives of Brazil, of their strange ways, of their suspicion and aversion, of their childlike trust and hospitality. Some there must have been who recoiled from the Indians. Others who came to terms with them, loved them, used them, and by means of toys and trinkets exploited them. We know that there were bold men among the Europeans who found it possible to take the leap which led them to become permanent settlers in the camps of the Indians. Like the hero of the fairy tale who owned seven-league boots, they were able to span the bridge between two diverse cultures and to fit themselves into the folkways and mores of a more primitive society than their ancestors had known for countless generations.

One such man was João Ramalho, the Daniel Boone of the South American wilderness.

There are some authorities who state categorically that this Robinson Crusoe character, João Ramalho, was a Jew. There are others who vehemently and heatedly deny the fact, protesting that it is sheer nonsense and sheer impudence to assume that the first European hero of the Brazilian jungle was a member of the Jewish fraternity.

João Ramalho was the oldest Brazilian settler of European stock. He lived in São Vicente and he married an Indian princess. He helped the Portuguese establish themselves in Brazil. Thus Nowell.

He was perhaps the most famous of the earliest European settlers of Brazil. His claim to fame rests on his begetting of many *mestizo* children. Thus Freyre. João Ramalho was a Marrano, shipwrecked off the coast of Brazil, writes A. M. Friedenberg. He married the daughter of Chief Tybiriçá. He became the head of a famous mameluke family, Diffie informs his readers. He was suspect by the Holy Office, adds Gurgel. He is called "the notorious João Ramalho" by Dr. Greenlee, who recounts briefly his adventures and experiences in *The First Half Century of Brazilian History*.

The possibility exists that João Ramalho was a member of one of the expeditions headed by Loronha and that he may have even been one of the earliest settlers of Cananéa. For forty years João Ramalho walked untrodden paths through the jungles of Brazil. During that time he established such warm, friendly relations with the natives that again and again his intercession in behalf of Europeans saved many a hopeless situation. He acquired the stature of a national hero. Legend and romance cluster about his deeds. It is likely that Ramalho may have been a *degradado*, one of those convicts or escaped sailors of whom we read so often in the early records of New World settlement. Nowell says:

Ramalho therefore must be given the benefit of the doubt; it is possible that this human derelict was the first permanent European inhabitant of continental America.[2]

Through the rhythm of migration, like that of a pendulum swinging back and forth over the Atlantic, now over Europe and now over the New World, through repeated voyages, close contact was established between East and West. Each migrant who made the transition from the known world to the unknown was tied by a thousand bonds to the culture he had left behind him. A man may be running away, yet he paints his future in terms of what he knows, subtracting only the grosser evils of his known existence from the envisioned tomorrow. The past is never really left behind. Like the house of a turtle it is the boundary of a man's existence. The new environment may present new problems. But the techniques for solving them he learned in Europe. The tools and skills he once knew are applied to solve the mathematics of his new world. Thus we have a unified picture.

In its earliest stages, Brazilian cultural development exhibited two divergent phenomena—great mobility and immediate stability. In other words, some men were restless wanderers, piercing thick jungles, looking for gold, for rare spices, for rare birds and furs. Others, from the very beginning, dug in. They built substantial homes for themselves. They planted and reaped and were glad of a permanent address at last. In all this, South American history parallels that of North America.

Following the shore line, the bays and safe harbors, the first settlements were built. Then the great rivers became the arteries to the interior. There was alternate digging in and scattering out, concentric waves forming one beyond the other. And although there were both Jews and non-Jews among the earliest settlers, it is strange how from all sides, testimony of the importance of Jewish influence on the form and spirit of early Brazilian colonization keeps pouring in.

Portugal now settled down as a colonizing power. The Jewish merchants did not permit their interest in Brazil to lapse. Contracts and grants were renewed whenever possible. Settlements were extended. Forts and towns were added.

In 1530 under the leadership of Martin Afonso de Souza colonization took another spurt forward. Twelve captaincies were established, each under its own *donatario*. And deeper and deeper went the penetration of the vast land of the pampas.

It was the promised land to these migrants. So they determined to make a go of it. Each season brought new settlers, better organization, greater stability. Side by side with these constructive forces, violence, gambling, drunkenness—all the dissolute habits of frontier community life—could be observed. Yet in spite of the readily accepted carnival of sin and debauchery, it was still a crime to be a Jew. A man could be challenged for his faith, here as in Portugal. The Holy Office and its Inquisitors were zealous sleuths. So friars would meet the incoming boats and board them "to inquire into the religious health" of the immigrants. A quarantine on ideas and conscience was attempted. Even in the New World the Jews had to go underground. For with the founding of the Jesuit order, dispatch and efficiency had been added to religious zeal. There was much to be done. "Checking the intrusion of Protestantism, investigating the conditions among the newly converted Jews, establishing the Inquisition . . . and carrying on a serious dispute with the Papacy"[3] called for organization and planning.

Then in 1580 Portugal and Spain were united under the Spanish King Philip II. This union lasted until 1640, with the center of influence being moved to Madrid.

Brazil was at first largely dominated by the one-crop culture, the sugar cane industry. But as the planters familiarized themselves with the prodigality and bounty of Brazilian soil, other products were gradually added. Toward the end of the sixteenth century, some two-hundred sugar mills were owned by the Jews of Brazil. They were busy places. The sugar mills required many hands. Spirited bidding for additional slaves kept adding a steady stream of Negroes to the plantations. Expansion, prosperity, greater demand for sugar in European cities—all of these things were the barometers which determined the per capita price of each Negro. Christian planters and Jewish planters were rivals for a cheap labor supply. In the early settlements of Brazil, notably in and around Bahia, the first modern city of Brazil, there were many skilled artisans, many small merchants, and farmers.

Some Jewish settlers lived in the environs of Bahia. Others were heads of plantations in the surrounding country. There were congregations in Bahia and in Olinda, near Recife. When in 1621 another outburst of activity by the Inquisition occurred, many *conversos* fled to neighboring countries for refuge. In 1619, eight boatloads of refugees from the Inquisition landed at Rio de la Plata.

This pattern of Jewish infiltration was true not only of Brazil but of other South American colonies. In his *Alien Strands in the Racial Fabric of Chile*, Professor Isaac Joslin Cox has found many corroborative data. He notes that people of "doubtful" ancestry could buy their citizenship in Chile. So Nicolas Pérez, who described himself as of Jewish, Greek and Turkish ancestry, paid an all-time-high price for the privilege of citizenship—four thousand pesos. Proximity to Brazil made Chile a haven for surgeons, physicians and scholars, as well as for carpenters, mechanics and bakers. In 1541 one hundred and fifty "Spaniards" came to Chile and taking native wives begot many children. Some of these "Spaniards" are supposed to have come originally from Germany. They called themselves *Flores*, suggesting, as Professor Cox points out, that the original name might have been Blumenthal. "Many of the Spanish names . . . form an interesting study in family origins. This is particularly true with respect to the Jews whose record in the Iberian Peninsula, despite change of names and intermarriage, suggests considerable Semitic admixture in Chilean blood." Protection could be bought. It was a lucrative business for Chileans, particularly when the scent got warm and the thud of sandaled feet of Inquisitors came near. "Two Portuguese of foreign birth in Santiago were forced to pay nearly fifty thousand pesos to escape deportation."

If it wasn't the Inquisition, it could be brigands, corsairs, pirates, or other notables. So in 1579 Sir Francis Drake captured the ship of Nemo da Silva, a *converso*, which was busily engaged in coastwise trade off Brazil. For fifteen months the reluctant Da Silva was exploited for his knowledge of Caribbean and South American waters. Then he was abandoned in Mexico. Here the Inquisition caught up with him, found him guilty of Judaism and condemned him to perpetual exile.

Yet in spite of such constant hazards Jewish entrepreneurs continued their varied activities. They took all sorts of risks. Life was short and precarious. But they made the best of it. They established factories, built forts, brought the manufactured products of Europe to the homes of the new settlers. *Conversos* maintained unbroken contact with their unbaptized relatives. They knew what was available for export, what was in demand in Europe. They were the middlemen, the link people, who welded the East to the West. They were also the planters, the millowners, the manufacturers. The early history of Brazil was in large part the history of Jewish exploration, settlement and pioneering.

Not only did commerce flourish. Ideas and scholarship and poetry thrived. Freyre in an article titled *"Os Começos da Literatura Israelita na America"* calls our attention to the importance of *"literatura israelita"* in the early history of Brazil.

The creative force which was unleashed in the New World inexorably overcame every obstacle. It was a far cry from the drawing table of Abraham Cresques, the astronomical studies of Zacuto and Vizinho, to the peregrinations of Gaspar Judeo, to the reports of Master John, to the discoveries of Fernando de Loronha. But the torch of Jewish scholarship and invention was carefully tended. The flame flickered and did not die.

Now another European nation enters the arena. It was the second century of Brazilian history.

Even before the West India Company was organized, Holland had great plans for her future expansion. Humane Dutchmen dreamed

of founding transatlantic colonies, untainted by slavery. The rivalry
between Spain and Holland was of long standing. The Dutch were
going to be different colonizers, they thought. And so they were—
somewhat. There was the same hunger for silver and gold. There
were spices and dyes beyond the Atlantic. There were colonists who
were ready to pack up at a moment's notice—clamoring for land,
pledging their muscle and energy to its cultivation and development.

All the noble intentions of the Dutch with regard to slavery did
not stand up. The slave trade was highly profitable. Cheap labor was
needed. The institution remained. Brisk trade followed compromise
with conscience. It is not surprising that the time came when the
States General at the Hague approved the monopoly of the West
India Company on the following three items: the slave trade, muni-
tions, and the export of dyewood. Humanitarians could rant and
plead for antislavery. But each slave earned the Company a profit of
240 per cent. In the face of such lucrative returns, all scruples went
skidding.

Nor need the Jewish participants of the West India Company present themselves for accolades. For they were in there, pitching for
profits like the Christians. And whether there are 7 names of Jews
out of a total 167 shareholders, as there were in 1656, or whether
there were 72 Jewish shareholders out of a total of 111, as there
were in 1674—the facts are incontrovertible. They were all in it
together! So Recife became known as "the port of the Jews" and
its main street as *Rua dos Judios*. Tokens of Semitic penetration!

A steady stream of crypto-Jews had been pouring into Amsterdam. Many Portuguese Jews were among them. The West India
Company of Holland now took a better look at Brazil. It was a perfect setup. A vast tract of land was here, poorly fortified, potentially
profitable, like a ripe plum in a forbidden orchard. . . . to the Rio de
la Plata, where eight boatloads of Jewish refugees landed, to other
sheltered bays and harbors, there came these perennial pilgrims
seeking shelter and refuge. They came and settled on the land.

As their influence increased and as Dutch penetration grew more
marked, the spirits of the Jewish settlers of Brazil underwent a
marked elevation. It was a happy day in 1624 when the first important foothold was secured in Brazil by the Dutch. How greatly did
the Jews who had gone underground yearn for the reaffirmation of
their ancient faith. How welcome was the news of Dutch successes
to their Jewish relatives in Holland. In large numbers they now left
Holland for Brazil, persuaded of the auspicious omen of Dutch military success. But just eleven months later, the Dutch were driven out

by the Portuguese and the Inquisition again sprouted its flowers of evil. Once again Judaism went underground.

This was but the first of a series of seesaw campaigns in which the prize fell now to the Dutch, now to the Portuguese. In 1630 the Dutch managed another foothold in Brazil. They captured Olinda and the outer harbor of Recife. It was the initial part of a campaign which eventually included most of Pernambuco. Within two years a sufficient stretch of land was acquired to be named New Holland.

Meanwhile Portugal was biding her time. The reckoning was made whenever her armies drove out the Dutch. In 1625, five Jews had been condemned for their Dutch sympathies. A decade later it was rumored that the entire campaign was the brain child of three Amsterdam Jews: Alvarez Franco, Manuel Fernandez Drago and Moses Cohen (Antonio Vaz Henriques), who not only conceived the military plans but went along to take a part in the battles.

The Dutch conquest of Pernambuco gave a great boost to the census of the Jews. *Conversos* lost no time in acknowledging their true faith. Dutch domination again meant large numbers of Jewish immigrants. In 1642, two sensitive young scholars, Isaac Aboab and Moses Raphael de Aguilar led two hundred Jewish settlers to Brazil. Even Menasseh ben Israel at one time considered emigrating to the Western Hemisphere. He had, like a great actor about to forsake the stage, issued a public statement of farewell to his European friends and relatives. But other interests detained him. He did not cross the Atlantic. In one year alone six hundred Jews, many of them originally from Germany, Hungary and Poland, who had tarried in Holland awaiting news of any haven in which they might be received, were unloaded at Recife. These Ashkenazic Jews had served galling apprenticeships as menials to the Sephardim in Holland. They were active, ambitious, eager to make good. Many were great scholars who lacked recognition because they lacked wealth. It did not take them long to establish a foothold in Brazil. They were linguists. That helped. They were poor. That helped. They had been pushed around enough and they were tired of it. That helped too. No matter how the former Sephardic residents rebelled against these energetic, impoverished immigrants, they were determined to make good. They would not be denied. They came in tatters. Few of them had more than one shabby suit of clothing. How they managed in the face of their galling poverty, confronted by the phalanx of opposition of the earlier settlers to make a go of things, no one can say. They became brokers in a hundred transactions. They became peddlers. They became laborers. They became intermediaries. "The Christian merchants found themselves," as Azevedo says, "reduced to the role of spectators of the Israelite business."[4]

Definitely the "Golden Age" for Jews in Brazil was during the years 1637 to 1644 under Count John Maurice, writes Friedenberg in reviewing *Watjen's Colonial Empire in Brazil*. Count John Maurice had liberalized the laws pertaining to Jews. If a magnet were needed for a crypto-Jew, what better one could there be than to be allowed freedom of worship?

So wholehearted were Jews in enjoying their new privileges that in 1638 Count Maurice succumbed to complaints of Christians. He said he was "compelled" to prevent Jews from being too open in their practice of Judaism. For Calvinists and other zealots were not happy at such brazen display of devotion to an ancient faith. Perhaps the transformation of ragged immigrants into prosperous brokers had its share of influence on Christians, for it seemed to be adding insult to injury to have these ragamuffins become gentlemen of means so fast.

Jews of Brazil were planters, merchants, tobacco-growers and merchants, soldiers, sugar-refiners, brokers, storekeepers, peddlers. But this list does not begin to cover the occupational diversity found among them. There were professional men too. We know there were Jewish doctors and poets and scholars. There was a *converso*, Balthazer d'Affonseca, who was an outstanding engineer. He was commissioned by John Maurice in 1640 to build a bridge connecting Recife with Mauricia. The original estimate, based on the use of stone, was for a total cost of two hundred forty thousand guilders. But the bridge was finished in wood at about half of the proposed cost. Balthazer d'Affonseca, his son and his grandchildren were among those who were freed of the oppressive disguise of crypto-Judaism by the coming of the Dutch. There was also a prospector or mining engineer who went about poking in the hills and thought he had found a gold mine. But it was probably fool's gold and Bento Enriquez was sadly deflated. There was a Jewish lawyer appropriately named Cardoso whose permit to practice law stirred up a hornet's nest of protest. It took the intervention of several influential Jews of Amsterdam to uphold lawyer Cardoso's right to continue the practice of law. This is but one more example of the fellowship between the Jews of Holland and those of Brazil.

The tenacious insistence on their rights by Jews brought benefits to others in Brazil. "Heathens, Jews and Roman Catholics" were all lumped into a kind of unholy alliance and while being given many privileges, were considered as stray sheep whom the Protestants sought most earnestly to convert. Clergymen eagerly, indefatigably attempted to make converts. They watched closely for stray evidences of blasphemy, for contentiousness, for criticism of the established faith. Sermons were sometimes protested as being unfriendly to Christianity and when in 1639 a rabbi attacked corruption in government, it soon came to the attention of the officials. This sermon did not contribute to the popularity of the Jews. Jews were eventually forbidden public worship in Brazil.

"The Brazilian Jews did not take the order to close the synagogues too seriously,"[5] says Bloom, for these worthies even built themselves another synagogue without bothering to get official permission. Complaints on this and many other scores continued to mount. From the restrictions which were now applied we may infer much indirect evidence to shed light on social relations between Christians and Jews. Jews were now expressly forbidden to build new synagogues. They could not marry Christians. Extramarital relations with Christian mistresses were henceforth tabu. It is likely that the last two prohibitions were equally popular with Jewish officials and respectable burghers. But this period of group friction may be characterized as a honeymoon compared to the days of strife ahead.

Events in Europe were changing. Quick echoes could be detected by the listening ear in the New World. A climax was nearing. The signs were as clear as an approaching summer thunderstorm. Lines were sharply drawn—religious and national lines. The hour of Portuguese challenge to the Dutch was approaching. New Holland was on thin ice. Catholics were on one side, Dutch and Jews on the other.

Now the sugar crop was poor for three successive years, 1642-43-44. Jewish sugar planters and refiners had their backs to the wall. Bankruptcy stared them in the face. Jorge Homen Pinto who owned nine sugar mills and required 370 slaves to run them owed more than seven hundred thousand guilders to the West India Company. For they had sold him slaves on credit and so had become deeply involved in his sugar empire. Many lesser Jewish planters and refiners were also in the red and the West India Company made numerous "adjustments," settlements, compromises. Other debt-ridden settlers, not only the Portuguese, began to toy with the idea of a change in government. For in what better way could they get rid of their debts? The Jews were willing to struggle in their economic morass, preferring Dutch rule to Portuguese at any cost. When sundry officials and planters put out feelers to the Portuguese, the grapevine in Marrano circles in Portugal saw to it that the Jews of Brazil were warned.

Nieuhoff, a contemporary chronicler, tells us that on "the 30th of May 1645, a letter without a name was delivered to the great council by one Abraham Markado, a Jew, subscribed only 'Plus ultra.' "[6] The paper was written in Portuguese and warned the Dutch that a large army was being readied for a surprise attack. The Portuguese Ambassador to the Hague, while professing great friendship for the Dutch, was secretly helping the plotters in Brazil, fomenting rebellion.

The Jews decided to call for help.

Abraham de Azevedo was the representative of the Jews of Dutch Brazil. He was sent to Holland from Recife to ask for help against Portugal. And so intrigue in Brazil was accelerated while in Europe the West India Company and the Dutch Government were lulled to sleep.

Negotiations dragged out in diplomatic double-talk while acts covert and overt in the New World brought war ever closer. It is hard to summarize those grim days. The spirit revolts from such stark tragedy. The siege of Recife is the old bitter story of any beleaguered city, like Richmond or Madrid. Jews began leaving Recife in evergrowing numbers from 1645 on. All hope was now lost. For the Jews the day of reckoning was approaching. Catastrophe mounted.

In 1646 a ship from Brazil was wrecked. Of its 148 passengers, "mostly Jews," only 28 were saved. On June 1, 1646, an ultimatum was sent the beleaguered city by the Portuguese. Jews determined to die fighting. The city held on grimly. Bread ran out. Soldiers threatened to desert. So what little food was left was allocated to them. When two Dutch ships arrived bringing food, late that month, it brought some shred of hope as well.

There were heroes and martyrs galore in those days among the defenders of Recife. Woe to a Jew if the Portuguese got their hands on him! "Why are Jewish prisoners of war martyred unto death in so beastly a manner. Are they worse people than we?"[7] asked one humane negotiator. Nevertheless Jewish prisoners were separated from other prisoners of war. Again and again the States General tried to secure equal treatment for all prisoners. In vain did they protest of the "horrible procedures" against Jews. A few were liberated on conversion. Many were turned over to the amenities of the Inquisition without mercy, thus anticipating the Nazis of our shameful era. From 1646 on, things became worse in Recife and many Jews became guerillas and commandos in those days of bitter privation, of war and of danger, of fighting unto death. On January 27, 1654, the Portuguese commander entered Recife. New Holland was lost to the Dutch.

An era had closed. The curtain was lowered on more than one hundred fifty years of colonizing, of exploration, of vision, of privation, of hardship, of courage, of dreams of security and of plans for a new life under the Western skies.

Now once again the old familiar order was restored to Brazil. And again the black-robed friars were free to conduct their inquiries as to "the religious health" of the inhabitants: *Who are you? Who were your ancestors? What manner of men were they? What of their faith? And yours?*

The victorious Portuguese commander who regained the land from the Dutch, Francisco Barreto, had proclaimed an amnesty. Jews were not to be molested. They were given ninety days to wind up the affairs of more than one hundred and fifty years. They were allowed to "sell" their possessions, their mills and factories and stores. It was a buyer's market. The fruit of their labors was harvested by those who remained. They departed the land. "The synagogues were destroyed, the stones of the Jewish burial ground overturned, and the Jewish settlement ended."

But they could not be obliterated. They left many traces of themselves forever impressed on the history of the land they had helped to discover. They had contributed to the racial strain of the Portuguese and the Brazilian peoples. They had bequeathed "the Sephardic tradition of intellectuality" as well as "a fondness for learned trappings, legalism, juridical mysticism," says Freyre[8] Truly in small ways and in great the Jews left their ineradicable mark upon the history, the course of events, the traditions, manners and customs of Brazil. The individuals departed. Their way of life remained.

Some of the "miraculously expelled" Jews went from Brazil back to Holland. Others scattered to many places in Central and North America. Still others returned to their crypts and hiding places, donning once more the cloaks of "secrecy and mystery."

CHAPTER IV

Of Grain and Gold

JEWS WENT to England now on one errand, now another. In 1410,
King Henry IV called upon the papal physician, Dr. Elias Sabot, to
come from Italy to England. Dr. Elias came and brought a *minyan*
of ten men with him. At least the good doctor made sure that he
could say his prayers.

The most dynamic and certainly the most influential Jewish resident of England at this time was Dr. Rodrigo Lopez.

In the Folger Shakespeare Library, in a document titled *In
Judaeorum,* we read:

> Doctor Lopus, the Queenes Physician, is
> descended of Jewes: but himself A
> Christian, & Portugall.
> He none of the learnedest, or expertest
> Physicians in yᵉ Court: but one, that
> maketh as great account of himself, as
> the best: & by a kind of Jewish practis,
> hath growen to much Wealth, & sum
> reputation: as well with yᵉ Queen herself,
> as with sum of yᵉ greatest Lordes,
> & Ladyes.[1]

He was on the staff of St. Bartholomew's Hospital in 1561. In
1586 Queen Elizabeth made him a physician of her household. His

influence grew. His interests extended far beyond the dispensing of pills and poultices. He was involved in court intrigue. He was not above using his influence to intervene in behalf of a friend. He even managed to secure royal favors for Sir Francis Drake. Nor did he neglect his own interests. He had his friends and a number of grateful patients. They availed him little. He died on the gallows.

We now trace briefly the trail of the Jews which leads us through green mansions and over deep rivers and over steppingstones of islands—eventually to North America. Here are a few dates which mark the movements of the Pilgrim People:

> Brazil—1500
> Lima—1533
> Concepción—1600
> Barbados—1628
> Surinam—1639
> Curaçao—1650
> Cayenne—1650
> Martinique—1654
> New Amsterdam—1654

Jews were careful to seek out, insofar as it was in their power to do so, colonies of those nations that were less hostile to them. This accounts for the fact that they preferred Dutch and English colonies and stayed away from those under the French flag. In the French possessions of Martinique or St. Christopher, there were relatively few Jews to be found. Their occupations were restricted under the French and the official attitude may be described as one of disdain toward Jewish settlers. Pomeroon, Surinam and Jamaica became through necessity the places to which Jewish immigration was directed.

How shall we tell the story? Chronologically? Geographically? Biographically? On the twentieth of April in 1655, two Jews petitioned for the right to settle in the Barbados as Jews. They were a physician, Dr. Abraham de Mercado and his son, David Raphael de Mercado. Their petition was granted by Oliver Cromwell. Dr. Abraham de Mercado had been an elder of the congregation at Recife in Brazil. Menasseh ben Israel, the great Amsterdam rabbi, had dedicated a book to him in 1641. So we have it. One case defies time, geography and classification. This instance may be multiplied many times over.

Soon this scholarly physician was joined by other Amsterdam

Jews. Bethencourt lists among these new Barbados settlers eminent Sephardim from Portugal, Spain, Holland and England. There were women too. In 1676 Rachel Torres, resident of the Barbados, applied to the community of Amsterdam for assistance in procuring for herself a dowry. This bit of information is important for a number of reasons. First, it shows how the custom of providing for the marriage of Jewish women was maintained. Second, it proves the keen sense of responsibility which the mother community in Amsterdam felt for the indigent virgins whom they had exported. They sent dowries overseas. They also assisted their bachelors to seek other homes. One of the notables who had achieved fame as a poet and member of the Academia de los Floridos, Daniel Levi de Barrios, sent his son to Barbados. One young woman was an orphan whom the Dutch community had apparently dispatched to the Barbados in accordance with the time-honored practice of keeping the indigent on the move. Before long there were enough of these dowerless virgins, deserving orphans, and sons of poets, together with other gentry, to found two synagogues on the island and start numerous families.

In an early journal describing the growth of the British West Indies, there is found an interesting reference to Barbados. The entry, made in March of 1654, deplores the number of foreigners who have made their way there.

The chief church is mostly Presbyterian; the Independents have their conventicles . . . the Jews have their sinagogs . . . and what is bad as all the rest, places of trust, both military and civil, are put into such men's hands.[2]

Still David Raphael de Mercado managed to become the largest taxpayer in Barbados. Such a man might be criticized, but he carried considerable weight.

It must be noted that just as the philanthropic activities of Amsterdam were expedited by sending the poor abroad, these indigent immigrants, grateful for their new lease on life, on achieving a measure of wealth, never forgot their parent community. More than one such settler sent money back to Amsterdam to be used for others. The pattern is so universal as to allow for generalization. First come the individuals driven for economic, religious and personal reasons to find a solution to their problems in the New World. Second, families are established. Third, synagogues are created. Fourth, a communal life comes into being. Fifth, there is maintained a chain of contact with the places and the people left behind, with the uncles and the aunts, the friends and the business associates, and the elders of the parent community.

Where there is open hostility the pattern presents variants. Peru may be cited as an example of another form of settlement. Here there was little or no acceptance of Jews. There was constant group tension and group conflict. The Jews went underground. For Peru lost very little time in establishing the official machinery for the running down of heretics.

Yet there are times when the very opposite is true. When the Jewish settler instead of being ferreted out was invited to come in by the front door. This policy was practiced by the Dutch in Surinam. One such document, discovered by Oppenheim, speaks volumes:

> It seems the States of Holland are making a plantation betwixt Surinam and Cartagena in the West Indyes, wherein they go very wysly and pollitickly to work aiming chiefly at a trade there with the Spanyard; for which purpose they hav sent hether to invyt many families of Jews and granted them many priviledges and immunitys, which they hav printed and sent hether. I intend your Honour a coppy thereof enclosed if I can get it translated in tym. Spainish is become now the Jews mother-tongue not only in thes parts but throhout al the Turks dominions; in which respect they wil be very useful to the Duch in theyr plantation; and many opportunityes may present for them to converse with the Spanyard by reason of their civility. If our planters at Surinam took the sam course it would be much to their advantage. About 25 famillyes of Jews go hence for the Holland plantation; som of them told me they nothing dout but to introduce a trade very speedily with the Spanyard there who ar in most extream want of all European commoditys.[3]

This letter was written in 1658. We know that Jews were in Surinam as early as 1639. By 1643 they had progressed to the point of having a rabbi. A vast green meadowland eventually came to be called Joden Savanne, "Jewish Savannah." There was a second influx of Jews which arrived from England with Lord Willoughby. A third group of migrants was led by David Nassi, who was also known as Joseph Nuñez de Fonseca. They came from Cayenne after the French took it over. This last group of pilgrims were largely refugees from Brazil who took to the many highways of this hemisphere when the Portuguese came back in full force. Since these emigrés were seasoned farmers and plantation owners, hardened by life under the most rugged conditions, they made excellent settlers.

When Surinam was conquered by the English, there were Jews there. Before long, members of the Jewish community of Surinam were in great financial straits because of the application of the Navigation Act of 1651, and because of the war which was then being waged by England upon Holland.

There was a Jewish colony on the Pomeroon between the years 1658 and 1666. Oppenheim considers it as second in importance after Brazil, from the point of view of Jewish history. It was an agricultural community in which the settlers farmed the soil and tilled the fields. In the history of this early Western Guiana colony there are several incidents which throw light on the pioneering Jews of this section of the country.

On November 1, 1657, two ships were equipped to transport colonists to Western Guiana. A provision was made that the Jewish colonists should be allowed to take along their own food. On Monday, November 12, 1657, "a committee of the Jewish nation" helped to draw up a number of articles for the colonization of the "Continental Wild Coast." This document fixed the payment for Negroes, estimated the exemption in taxes to householders building their own homes in the new country, and provided for the establishment of a military group to protect the colonists. Of particular interest to us is the following:

For the special exemptions heretofore proposed by the Jews they request a binding resolution, in such form that the said exemptions may be made subject to the laws of this country. Commissioners grant this.[4]

Oppenheim feels that the profitable experience of the Dutch in its liberal treatment of Jewish colonists was enough to persuade the English to consider the presence of Jews in their midst as an economic asset and to cause them to compete in concessions with the Dutch. Many of the provisions of the Dutch grants of privileges to the Jews seem to have been copied verbatim by the English. Not only the need for Jewish settlers was responsible for this growing liberality. We note an awareness on the part of the Jews themselves of the fact that they are playing an important, dynamic, indispensable role as pioneers. Jews felt that the time had now come when they could assert their demands, when they could trade sugar mills and ships for the right to live as Jews and as equals with their Christian neighbors. There are records of Jewish petitions to the government citing many precedents. These petitions demand rights and privileges which are enjoyed elsewhere. The Jews openly state that their coreligionists await clarification of their status before settling in large numbers in the wilderness.

In 1665 a government grant assured the safety of Jewish refugees in Surinam. The accession of Charles II officially changed the name of Surinam to Willoughby Land, in compliment to Lord Willoughby who was one of its proprietors. The Jews of Surinam were important in the land because sugar was important. Their presence there insured at least a trickle of the precious substance to England. So we have the strange spectacle of privileges being bought by sugar loaf. Another factor that led to the acceptance of the Jews was the desperate need for able-bodied settlers. Tropical diseases played havoc with the population. The grant of 1665 was to serve as a guarantee of their rights to the Jews already in Surinam, and as bait for the expected new Jewish settlers.

The grant of 1665 was an extraordinarily sweeping one to have been made, and, so far as we know, is the first of its kind granted by the English to Jews anywhere. Its terms read almost, in view of the situation at the time and its liberality, as if it were forced from the authorities who feared for the life of their colony.[5]

Another synagogue of Surinam was established in 1685. At the ceremonies which launched this undertaking, Rabbi David Prado assisted. He remained in the colony until his death twenty-eight years later. A noteworthy settler at this time was Samuel Nassy, who distinguished himself as a soldier in the defense of Surinam against the French. He too was a former student of the *Yeshiva* of Amsterdam. The names of the settlers who left Amsterdam for Surinam read like a roll of honor. We have met their relatives again and again, as scholars, as defenders of their convictions, as martyrs of the Inquisition. The commander of the Pomeroon had his work cut out, adjusting differences, settling disputes, quieting turbulent elements.

Jamaica in the West Indies had its crypto-Jews prior to 1655, when they were known as members of the Portuguese Nation. Some of the Brazilian refugees of 1654 came to this large island. The English had fortunately conquered Jamaica in 1655. Impressed by the excellent record made by Jews as colonizers under the Dutch, the British were in a hospitable frame of mind. Jews, moreover, were of considerable assistance to the British in the capture of Jamaica. A pilot, Campoas Sabbata, and Simon de Caceres gave them sufficient help to be rescued from anonymity.

Jewish settlers showed a peculiar aptitude for agricultural pursuits. Their sugar plantations had achieved renown from the earliest days in Brazil. Now in Jamaica they became known as coffee-growers.

They also exported dyewood, ginger, indigo, cocoa. Between 1663 and 1683 many petitions by Jews are on record asking that the oath of citizenship be so worded as to permit a Jew to become endenizened. By 1670 the Jews had so demonstrated their value as colonists that Jewish immigration was actually sought and encouraged, and thirteen years later they won a partial victory—the right of residence. But it was not always smooth sailing. Competition with Christian planters became more acute. Their resentment grew with rivalry. Hurricanes and an earthquake wrought economic havoc. When times are hard, group tensions increase.

When Jamaica was invaded in 1692, following a shattering earthquake, it is said that the Jews behaved so stalwartly that the entire community was aroused to admiration. So great was the impression created by their fortitude that King William appealed to the Legislature in Jamaica in their behalf, when English merchants in that island tried to take away from the Jews their hard-won privileges. In that same year a group of Jewish petitioners addressed themselves as follows:

That whereas your peticŏners having inhabited for Severall years in your majesties Island of Jamaica and by that most terrible Earthquake which happened there on ye 7th of June Last have Lost all they had in the World humbly begg your majesties favour to be made free Denizons.[6]

There were then listed in the records of Jamaica and Barbados twenty-two heads of households, among whom was at least one woman. They asserted that unless proscriptive measures against them be abated that "it will be the Utter Ruine of so many poor Families that live in that Island and by whose meanes (altho' in such low Circumstances) the Trade there is very much promoted and augmented."[7]

But the Jamaica Assembly was controlled by Christian competitors. No relief was given the Jews. Instead a special tax was imposed upon their community. It worked great hardship. Twelve Jews were required to collect this tax from their brethren. It was not until 1740 that the fight was finally won. In that year foreigners were granted permission to become naturalized. Jews were quick to take advantage of the law passed by Parliament. The tide had turned.

So Jewish pilgrims found permanent homes for themselves. Thick impenetrable jungles, swift rivers, mountains, swamplands, great expanses of water—all these hazards were met and conquered. Hostility, aversion, persecution—these too were surmounted. Internal dissension was swiftly suppressed. Discipline was stern, swift, harsh. Authority was unquestioned, implicitly obeyed. The Jewish community was a strong entity and presented a solid phalanx to a hostile world.

There was marked occupational diversity among Jews. Farmers and trappers we have met. Manufacturers of dyes and sugar we also know. Shipowners are numerous. Planters and slaveowners were everywhere. How shall we classify a "gold-finding Jew"? For we find such a reference in 1664. Or two Jewish brothers who formed a syndicate to mine copper in Jamaica in 1664? Or vanilla and pimento growers? We find in a letter addressed to the Dutch West India Company in 1684 the following statement:

The Jew Salomon de la Roche having died some 8 or 9 months ago, the trade in vanilla has come to an end, since no one here knows how to prepare it so as to develop the proper aroma and keep it from spoiling.[8]

Another Jew, Moses Isaac de Vries, became indispensable as an interpreter.

I have frequently felt the want of a good sworn interpreter of the Indian languages, such as there is in Surinam, and this want has often been to our loss. I have frequently been assisted by the Jew Moses Isackse deVries, but he being now dead there is not a good faithful one to be got, and I am afraid to trust to the negroes or creoles, who say or conceal whatever they wish.[9]

In addition to his linguistic talents he also became a noted sugar operator. A coreligionist of de Vries was Isak Israel Lorenzo, known better by his nickname, "Isaac the Jew." He was proficient in the Carib language and was employed by the government in Surinam. Yet a Spanish document of 1743 complains of the way the Jews swarm between the banks of the Amazon and the Orinoco.

The subject is inexhaustible. So we close with two interesting episodes. One involves Gabriel Milan, the Jewish Governor of St. Thomas. The other concerns a contract between King Charles II of England on the one hand and Sir William Davidson and Abraham Israel de Piso and Abraham Cohen on the other.

Gabriel Milan was born in Germany in 1631. He was an adventurer from his youth. For he went from his birthplace to France where he enlisted in the French Army under Mazarin. After France came Amsterdam. The soldier became a merchant. He prospered. He next undertook some successful commissions for members of the

Danish court. For Denmark, encouraged by the example of Holland and prodded by the financial success of Dutch Jews, had determined to follow a liberal policy toward Jews. In 1622, King Christian IV of Denmark invited the Jews to settle in his kingdom. His letter addressed to the Jewish community of Amsterdam offered them religious freedom and other privileges. But in Denmark, as in other countries, the nod of approval of one monarch was succeeded by the frown of the next.

In 1670 Gabriel Milan visited Copenhagen where he married the daughter of the King's Jewish physician, a member of the famous De Castro family. His fortunes fluctuated and days of opulence were followed by periods when he claimed he had not a crust of bread. His poverty and the yearning, like Sancho Panza, to be made governor of an island induced this man who had boasted in Amsterdam of his loyalty to Judaism, to turn Christian in Copenhagen. He received his wish with his baptism.

In 1684, Milan was appointed Governor of St. Thomas. The Directors of the Danish West India Company excused their appointment on the grounds that he knew many languages, had excellent training in commerce, "had good common sense and needed the position."

But he was a prime rascal and power went to his head. He was an inefficient administrator, arrogant, cruel.

There were sixteen in his household. A grown son, Felix, and four younger children and enough servants to make up sixteen, besides Milan and his second wife. He fired his lieutenant and put his son Felix in his place, fell out with the captain of the ship, "began to play fast and loose with his council" and started scheming with planters, setting them against each other. He imprisoned his predecessor and his wife, put on airs, assumed the title of excellency, served twelve-course dinners, became sick, lost his youngest son, revived his quarrel with Captain Meyer, whom he accused of mistreating "an unfortunate Jew" and whom he called an antisemite. The Captain finally skipped without the Governor's permission. Milan's misdemeanors multiplied. His arrogance and scheming grew. He was taken back to Denmark where, stripped of all of his titles and honor and property, he was executed in 1689 and his property confiscated.

Jews had their rascals as well as their great men.

In the fourteenth year of his reign, Charles II made a contract with a Baronet and two Jews.

The document is titled:

> His Ma[ts] Contract wth S[r]
> W[m]Davidson M[r] Ab:
> Israel & Abraham Cohen
> for ye Mines Royall of Gold
> in Jamaica. & the Denizacõ
> of the 2 Last of them[10]

The King had been informed by Davidson, Cohen and Israel that there was a gold mine in Jamaica. They were willing "to bee at the charge & hazard in ye discovery and working thereof." The King too was "willing." The agreement was drawn up.

Permission was granted for the working partners to erect any necessary buildings. Sir William, Abraham Cohen and Abraham Israel were to receive "One full third part (the whole in 3 parts to bee divided)" of the yield of the mine. The operating partners were to receive thirty acres of land in Jamaica. There follow a number of other important conditions. Then the important paragraph which endenizens the two Jewish partners. The manuscript reads:

And whereas the said Abr: Israel & Abr: Cohen being Aliens borne in parts beyond the seas cannot trade and traffique as y[e] naturall borne Subjects of this his Ma[ts] Realme, w[th]out his Ma[ts] Licence and indulgence to them in that behalf His Ma[tie] therefore doeth think fit, & is graciously pleased for y[e] better carrying on of the said Worke and their encouragement therein to make them free Denizens of this his Kingdome of England.[11]

There were Jews who valued their rights as citizens above gold.

CHAPTER V

Hebrews Encounter Hebraism
in America

→>> That all the Hebrews shall be admitted for Burgezes . . .
Grannting to anny Persons of anny Nation anny Previl-
ledges, the Hebrews shall enjoy them alsoe.
> —*Priveleges Granted to the People*
> *of the Hebrew Nation That Are to*
> *Goe to the Wilde Cust* <<<

THE EARLY settlers on the doorstep of America were not aware
of the huge continent that loomed before them. Only its outer edge
had been explored. They were caught between the vast ocean they
had crossed and the vast continent they faced. So each little trading
post and fort was like a nut, a tight solid little nut in which dwelt
tight-minded little people. Like-mindedness became important. The
color of a man's skin and the cut of his garments identified him as a
friend. For who could trust the naked savage, his skin red and his
purpose sinister? And was not the dense and trackless forest which
surrounded the clearing, thick with danger, overrun with enemies?

Under such conditions it is natural for men to feel secure with
those who resemble them. It is understandable that they bristle like
frightened animals when confronted by someone who is cut from a
different cloth. Surrounded by a new environment, unexplored and
mysterious, the old becomes invested with nostalgia, with the warm
affectionate cloak of memory. It was true in the Old Dominion. It
was true in New Netherlands and in Georgia. It was a pattern, a mold
cut to fit any transplanted band of Europeans struggling for a foothold, trying to wrest a living from an unfamiliar scene, attempting
to create a new society without violating too much cherished and
time-honored customs, without abandoning folkways that were
familiar and mores that carried authority and stability.

In the brief history of the Dutch penetration of the Hudson and

Delaware River Valleys all these factors were discernible. The main trading posts of New Amsterdam and Fort Orange, the strings of patroonships along the Hudson River were bits of Holland transplanted. In the harsh and strident personality of the Director-General, ostentatious and unstable, with his silver-encrusted wooden leg and his showy clothes, there were faint reminiscences of parental authority, of childhood and security. The people were few and the land was vast. The New Amsterdam population under the Dutch did not exceed some sixteen hundred people. All of the New Netherlands numbered some ten thousand souls.

So the river valleys bloomed with settlers. The parent company yearned only over profits. The authoritarian government of the colony and the Reformed Church were in control. The Indians were valued as agents of the fur trade, with only an occasional missionary sent out to invite them to partake of Christianity. There was little emphasis on the intangibles which the English colonists valued— charters of liberties and assemblies to legislate their laws.

This was the setting and this the atmosphere into which a band of Jewish pilgrims, "healthy but poor," attempted to inject themselves with consequences not devoid of drama.

Between 1621 when Elias Legardo came to Virginia and 1654 when the *Peartree* brought Jacob Barsimson to New Amsterdam, there were scattered Jewish settlers along the Atlantic seaboard leaving their faint imprints on their times. Barsimson's arrival was duly recorded as follows:

Jacob Barsimson, Jew, Debtor.
    For freight and board on his coming hitherward
A°. 1654, 8 July, per ship *Peartree* ....36 (guilder)[1]

He was followed within a few weeks by twenty-three coreligionists, "big and little." They were under a cloud from the start for there was not enough money between them to pay for their passage. They were battered victims of circumstance. For their departure from Brazil had been of necessity hurried. Their expectation of funds from Holland was legitimate. But they arrived before their remittances. A judgment was asked by the ship's master and obtained. All household goods on the bark were to be sold.

Those must have been desperate days. For by the sixteenth of September the judgment was executed and was still insufficient to settle their debts. At first David Israel and Moses Ambrosius were jailed for the balance due. Then Asser Levy was arrested. But after they had been confined several weeks in jail, the crew of the *St. Charles* relented and the three debtors were released. Then Jewish debtors and Christian creditors settled down to a truce awaiting their money from Holland. It was the old dramatic plot in reverse, with Master Jacques de la Motte playing Shylock.

It was an inauspicious beginning. They were alien. They were not wanted. They were poor. Peter Stuyvesant was moved to action. He sharpened his quill and engaged in a long-drawn-out correspondence with his superiors in Holland. He found Jews "repugnant." He foresaw that their indigence would make them "a charge in the coming winter." Besides they were known to be "a deceitful race" and should therefore "be not allowed further to infect and trouble this new colony."[2]

The Directors of the Dutch West India Company did not see eye to eye with the disgruntled Stuyvesant. They took pains to point out that the Jews had incurred great losses in the war in Brazil, that they were large shareholders of the Company, that they were therefore to be allowed to remain, to trade and to travel about. While letters were exchanged, other Jews came to the colony. This time from Holland. Now Domine Megapolensis added his complaints to those of Governor Stuyvesant. "The godless rascals" wanted to build a synagogue. Still more Jews were coming from Holland. The colony swarmed with "many atheists and various other servants of Baal among the English . . . it would create a still greater confusion if the obstinate and immovable Jews came to settle here."[3]

Hard-koppig Piet tried his best. But he lost the argument. The Directors wrote Stuyvesant a conciliatory letter saying that they foresaw the same difficulties as did the Governor of New Amsterdam from the continued residence of Jews there, yet they could not overlook "the large amount of capital which they still have invested in the shares of this company." It was a potent argument. Now Stuyvesant complained that the doors were in very truth opened not only to Jews but to Papists and others as well. To make matters worse, the Jews insisted on "the free and public exercise of their abominable religion." Where were they all heading? The colony was overrun with aliens and nonconformists—Waldensians, Huguenots, Baptists, Presbyterians, Quakers. "You may therefore shut your eyes," the Directors wrote to the complaining Governor, "at least not force people's consciences, but allow every one to have his own belief, as long as he behaves quietly and legally."[4]

But the Jews somehow could not be ignored. Their names appear on petitions, in court records, in business transactions, in applications for special privileges. They are cited for violations of laws, for reversing the Sabbath. They are a constant "problem." They needed land for the quick and the dead.

July, 1655

Abraham deLucena, Salvador Dandrada and Jacob Cohen, Jews, in the name of the others, petition the Honorable Director General this day to be permitted to purchase a burying place for their nation, which being reported to the meeting and voted on, it was agreed to give them the answer that inasmuch as they did not wish to bury their dead (of which as yet there was no need) in the common burying ground, there would be granted them when the need and occasion therefor arose, some place elsewhere of the free land belonging to the Company.
Dated as above.[5]

There were other ways in which Jews showed their unyielding nonconformity. The records bristle with pleas and petitions, with official rejection and occasional reluctant consent to their requests. Less than a year after their initial appearance in New Netherlands, Jewish traders petitioned the authorities to be allowed to trade in New Sweden on the Delaware River. This was refused. But since Jews already had a trading expedition in that region, undertaken without official consent, they were allowed to send two agents to the South River to wind up their affairs.

It was more than trading privileges that these Jewish settlers wanted. They battered with all their might and main against discrimination. They wanted more than negative acceptance. They demanded the right to perform their civic duties like other settlers. When the Indians were on the warpath and the community was threatened, several Jews voluntarily contributed one hundred guilders to the defense fund. Jacob Barsimson and Asser Levy being poor were near the bottom of the list of donors. Each gave six guilders. Driven by pride and poverty, these two now determined to take up the fight for the right to bear arms in the common cause. The record is eloquent:

8 November [1655]

Jacob Barsimson and Asser Levy request to be permitted to keep guard with other burghers, or be free from the tax which others of their nation pay, as they must earn their living by manual labor. [After a vote, the answer was given:] Director General and Council persist in the resolution passed, yet as the petitioners are of opinion that the result of this will be injurious to them, consent is hereby given to them to depart whenever and whither it pleases them. Dated as above.[6]

They refused to depart. It pleased them to remain. They were accepted as guards. The next rung up the ladder was the claim to burghership. On April 11 of the year 1657, we read:

Asser Levy, a Jew, appears in Court; requests to be admitted a Burgher; claims that such ought not be refused him as he keeps watch and ward (*tocht en wacht*) like other Burghers; showing a Burgher certificate from the City of Amsterdam that the Jew is Burgher there. Which being deliberated on, it is decreed, as before, that it cannot be allowed, and he shall apply to the Director General and Council.[7]

Now the entire Jewish community formed a solid phalanx behind Asser Levy. It took ten days for the authorities to yield to their persuasion. On April 21, 1657, Jews were admitted to citizenship. It was a milestone and a victory. It is a date to remember in the annals of Jewish history in America.

New Netherlands was a bridge between the stern, disciplined, rockbound life in New England and the easy cavalier society of the Old Dominion to the south. But both were English and the Dutch wedge between must have stuck in the throats of the English. Something had to be done. Besides the Dutch prospered. The fur traders exchanged rum and arms for peltry. There was constant friction along the outposts. "Even the Pilgrims far away at Plymouth . . . grumbled about the trading cruises of the Dutch."[8] Quickly, painlessly the British fleet sailed into New Amsterdam and New Amsterdam in 1664 became New York.

For the Jews the transition was not hard to make. They had nothing to fear from the English. They lived in New York and fought and worried and met the onslaught of time and aggression and hostility as they had done in New Amsterdam. Lived and died. And on their tombstones they summed up the brief arithmetic of their lives. There they recorded what they believed about this life and about the hereafter. All that was permanent and imperishable in brief biographies they chiseled out of granite. One such person is a symbol of many a forgotten generation of a time long vanished. He was so lost as to be, but for his name, anonymous.

Of the subject of this sketch, Benjamin Bueno de Mesquita, nothing other is known than that according to his tombstone he was buried in the year 1683.[9]

Yet friends and family he must have had. For the survivors saluted the going out of his life in this way:

> Beneath this stone is buried
> He who was Benjamin Bueno de Mesquita
> Died—and from this world was taken
> On the fourth of Heshvan. His blessed soul
> Here from the living separated.
> Wait for thy God! who will revive
> The dead of His people in mercy
> To enjoy without end Eternity.
> 1683.[10]

This ancient document in stone is a token of the faith of the survivors and a summary of their philosophy of life and death and eternity,—marking the last rite of passage of a seventeenth-century Jew in America.

Both at home and abroad there were Jews and crypto-Jews living on British soil. Chemists and physicians, "gold-finding" engineers and shipowners, merchants and brokers, scholars and craftsmen, were among these settlers. With her defeat of Holland, England had her appetite whetted for more conquest. France was to be next. In this grand strategy Jews were not a factor. So they came and went on the seaboard and on the islands belonging to England. Their fortunes were erratic, as were the laws of the various colonies. In the "Coppie of the Liberties of the Massachusetts Colonie in New England" there was no welcome for the Jew. It held the door open for those "professing the true Christian Religion." The Maryland Toleration Act stipulated that "no person in this province professing to believe in Jesus Christ shall be in any way troubled, molested, or discountenanced for his or her religion." The Mennonites of Pennsylvania excluded "Usurious Jews, English stiff-necked Quakers; Puritans; foolhardy believers in the Milennium."[11] In the face of such barriers the mere presence of Jews in the colonies seems remarkable. Only their long experience with the rebuff direct and indirect, with official austerity and unofficial frowns, with open reluctance and devious dodges all designed to keep them out, to keep them moving, to exterminate or transform them—only these attitudes had somehow inured the Jews. Perhaps they had no time for introspection. It took all the talents they had just to survive. Let us meet a few of these early settlers.

In 1621, Elias Legardo, its first known Jew, came to Virginia on the *Abigail*. Soon other settlers with Jewish names appear on the records of the Old Dominion. In 1624 a woman named Rebecca Isaacke was a resident of Virginia. A "Portuguese" whose brother was a London merchant was there also. Familiar names like de Torres, Rodriguez, Abraham, are found in the records. But the specific identification is sometimes lacking.

There is no guessing about a pioneer in near-by Maryland, one Jacob Lumbrozo, called "ye Jew doctor." He came to Maryland in 1656 and immediately began his medical practice. He must have been a man of parts. His coming was an event of note. A court record of Maryland dates an event as occurring "soone after ye arryvall of ye Jew." He was busy both as a "chirurgeon" and as a litigant. In one year he sued nine debtors. Among them was one patient, David Fereira, whom he sued for seven months' medical care. But other lawsuits often involved business transactions, such as the sale of four hundred pounds of tobacco "and caske." Lumbrozo must have been an irascible fellow. For in 1658 he was tried for blasphemy and saved only by a proclamation of general amnesty in honor of Richard Cromwell. His trial did not curb his many activities. They multiply as he grows in consequence. He sends for a wife. He is endenizened in 1663 and applies for a tract of land. His estate is called "Lumbrosie's discovery." He imports a servant and becomes a country squire. His tobacco is shipped to London and he has numerous business correspondents in Virginia. Finally "calling to mind the transitoryness of all Sublunary things," he makes his last will and testament leaving the bulk of his estate to his wife and four thousand pounds of tobacco to his sister Rivka in Holland. A son is born posthumously to Elizabeth and she promptly marries again. That is a thumbnail sketch of just one Jewish pioneer.

Before 1700 there are scattered along the seaboard individuals or householders or heads of families whose names are unmistakably Jewish. But there is no organized group life, no indisputable religious or communal officiation. Nevertheless New England is deeply involved in the Hebraic tradition. Puritanism is responsive to the teachings of the Old Testament. The Prophets, major and minor, are familiar names. There are Isaacs and Deborahs growing up in many a Christian home. Hebrew is a language cherished and esteemed. Not in vain had the Pilgrim Fathers sojourned in Holland, living as neighbors of the Jews there. For had they not known the same hardships, the same exclusion from Dutch craft guilds, the same grinding discipline of poverty?

But Puritan Massachusetts is cold, its code is rigid. It is human and natural to seek as friendly an environment as possible. So the Jews looked next to Roger Williams and to his colony of Rhode Island. Besides dissenters have a magnetic attraction for other nonconformists. Himself driven out by the unyielding Puritans of Massachusetts, Roger Williams determined that religious freedom would be the bedrock of his own colony. Scoffers might thrust their rapiers of criticism, but he held fast to his democratic convictions. As an exile, he welcomed to his colony other nonconformists. Says a Jewish historian of their early experiences in Newport: "A happy chapter of the Jew in the New World began."[12]

In 1643 Roger Williams went to England to get a charter for his new colony. While there he wrote his famous pamphlet "The Bloudy Tenent of Persecution," containing among other subjects a plea for the rights of Jews. This publication had no small influence on the course of events in England which led to the resettlement of Jews. Such a policy went hard against the grain of men like Cotton Mather to whom Newport was but "the common receptacle of the convicts of Jerusalem and the outcasts of the land."[13] Cotton Mather, ambivalent, morbid, intractable, son of Increase Mather, presents the opposite point of view from Roger Williams, combining within himself that strange dichotomy so characteristic of many Americans who came after him, of bristling hostility toward Jews and a passionate desire to embrace them in the bosom of Christianity. This pattern of alternate rejection and blandishment appears often in American history as the story of its Jewish minority unfolds. It is the old story of the sanctioned and unsanctioned groups—with sanction originating with the majority.

The exact date of the arrival of Jews in Newport is uncertain. The scholar whose research work in this area was most exhaustive, Oppenheim, states that there were Jews in Newport in the spring of 1658. Owing to their activity as Masons we can find further verification in the history of that organization.

In the Spring of 1658, Mordecai Campannall, Moses Peckeko (Pacheco), Levi, and others, in all fifteen families, arrived at Newport from Holland. They brought with them the three first degrees of Masonry, and worked them in the house of Campannall; and continued to do so, they and their successors, to the year 1742.[14]

The history of the Masonic order accepts this place and time as marking the inception of the order in North America. They organized a religious community, *Kahal Kadosh*, and selected Mordecai Campanal as its head. The first services were conducted in his home. There one day they recorded a twin event—attending religious services and climaxing the occasion with the induction of Abraham Moses into the mysteries of Masonry. By February of 1677 the augmented Jewish community purchased, from Nathaniel Dickens, its first cemetery.

There were enough Jews living in Newport to have a street called "Jew's Street." There were enough in number to warrant the Surveyor General to bring suit against them for violation of a clause in the Navigation Acts. A Major William Dyre "hath caused the estates of Severall Jews . . . to be seized to bring to a Tryall as Aliens."[15] However justice held its own in Rhode Island. The defendants were acquitted and the Major was ordered to pay court costs. But the Jews of Newport wanted more than such a decision. So they petitioned the General Assembly for clarification of their status. They got it:

Voted, in answer to the petition of Simon Medus, David Brown and associates, being Jews, presented to this Assembly, bearing date June 24th, 1684, we declare that they may expect as good protection here, as any stranger, being not of our nation, residing amongst us in this his Majesty's Colony ought to have, being obedient to his Majesty's laws.[16]

That seemed fair enough. More Jewish settlers arrived. In 1694 the Jewish community was increased by a number of families who came from the West Indies. More were on the way.

Boston's first tax list shows that "Ye Jew" Rowland Gideon was assessed eighteen shillings. He was engaged in selling tobacco and in the year his name first appears, 1674, it also turns up on the Court records when he and his partner Barruch sued a man for 100 pounds. In invoking justice, Rowland, or Rohiel, pleaded that the same law be applied to "the Stranger and Sowjournner—as for the Israellites." Within five years of his debut on Boston's tax list, Rowland Gideon secured his papers of denization conferring right of residence in all English colonies. With his wife Bathsheba he became a plantation owner on the island of Nevis. He moved to London and by 1698 was given the freedom of the City of London—the first Jew in history to have that distinction. At the opening of the eighteenth century Rowland Gideon was treasurer of the Bevis Marks Synagogue of London.

As the years marched toward the eighteenth century the Jews of New York made the transition toward a cohesive communal life. In 1674 Governor Andros when taking command of the colony was ordered to permit "all persons of what Religion so ever" to live there in peace. But that was only negative tolerance. For the 1683 Charter of Liberties and Privileges excluded Jews by limiting its benefits to professing Christians. To clarify their position the Jews petitioned in 1685 for the right to conduct their services openly. Their plea was rejected on the grounds that public worship was for those who professed faith in Christ. So they continued using their homes as synagogues. Since 1682 they had been meeting in a little house on Mill Street where services were conducted. The cottage was recognized as a synagogue by the community, for in that year Domine Selyns wrote, "The Jews, Quakers, and Labadists have their separate meetings." A former resident of Newport, Saul Brown, a prosperous and enterprising merchant, officiated at religious services. At his death in 1682 there was already a functioning religious community. His successor was Abraham Haim deLucena who at first divided his time between his clerical and business duties. Soon he found that he must make a choice. He gave up his activities as a merchant and devoted all his time to his growing congregation. The congregation was coming of age. A map published in 1695 locates the synagogue on Beaver Street. By October of 1700, a piece of land is described as adjoining the synagogue. It is clear that the rejection of their petition for the right of public worship did not legislate the Jewish community out of existence.

Step by step, the Jews of New York were achieving personal and communal recognition. It was not easy. Constant vigilance, constant effort were involved. In 1685, one Jewish resident complained that his trading privileges were restricted. Governor Dongan insisted that Jews could not engage in retail trade according to law as that right was reserved only for citizens. They were required to limit themselves to wholesale trade. Those who lived "up the Hudson" could not engage in foreign trade, which meant that their residence was limited to the New York City area if they would be exporters and importers, as so many Jews were. More and more the distinction was drawn between the endenizened and those who were not naturalized. Jews next sought the privileges of freemen. Among those who were naturalized from 1687 on, there were merchants and shopkeepers. But there was a greater occupational diversity than one would expect. Among the Jewish freemen there were three chandlers, a butcher, baker, distiller, tobacconist, tailor, brazier, cordwainer, vendue master, saddler, goldsmith, watch-maker and a peruke-maker. There was an enlisted soldier who was dunned for the price of a gun. There were a few bankers. In 1700, Lord Bellamont of New York wrote to the Lords of Trade: "Were it not for one Dutch merchant and two or three

Jews that have let me have money, I should have been undone."

In spite of all their difficulties, Jews had prospered. When we consider the poverty-stricken band of pilgrims who arrived in 1654,—remembering that three members of their community were thrown into debtors' jail—it comes as a distinct surprise to find one of the three, in 1664, being called to a meeting of wealthiest citizens. In just one decade Asser Levy had made that transition! The occasion was packed with drama. The English fleet was threatening New Amsterdam. Money had to be raised to defend the city. Asser Levy advanced one hundred florins. It was a lost cause. In October of the same year, Asser Levy took the oath of allegiance to England and was levied upon to the extent of two florins a week for the support of the victorious English soldiers. The change in sovereigns did not check Levy's growing importance. His business transactions covered a wide variety of enterprises. He bought land. He built a slaughterhouse. He owned a thriving tavern near the Wall Street section. He was trusted by Christians as well as Jews. Often he was called in as referee to settle arguments. He was named by men of other religious denominations as well as his own as executor of their estates. Johannes de Peyster and Jacob Leisler, a leader of the Rebellion, were among those who used his good offices as an intermediary. His influence and reputation carried weight far beyond the boundaries of his immediate community. His request to reduce a fine imposed on Jacob Lucena was effective in another colony. He was liberal with his money. It is characteristic of the man to find that when the Lutherans wanted to build a church in 1671, it was Asser Levy who advanced them money.

But above all, above wealth and prestige and growing authority and recognition, was his jealousy of his rights. For Asser Levey would brook no insult, condone no slight, accept no injustice. He had a clearly conceived idea of the dignity and importance of the individual, of status, of all the factors involved in maintaining personal prestige. It included all the appurtenances of the solid citizen: the ownership of a sword and of pistols, of thirteen tablecloths and twenty-four napkins, and household silver and goblets, and many pictures and two looking glasses and a Sabbath lamp, as well as "a parcel of old books, also a negro boy valued at 20 pounds." Dearer to him than mere ownership of these solid things were matters involving his personal honor and the maintenance of his rights. He was engaged in countless lawsuits which concerned not only broken contracts and unfulfilled promises but far less tangible grievances.

Asser Levy was a strong man.

The record bulges to overflowing. It is for the historian an embarrassment of riches. In the accounts of Crown revenues received in the port of New York from 1703 to 1709 from Jewish merchants, we learn the names of the chief figures engaged in international trade. We know what type of goods was brought in at the port of New York and the kind of goods shipped out. These data are of general interest. One of the striking facts noticed in a study of these lists is that even in the earliest years of the eighteenth century there were women engaged in commerce. On the twenty-fifth of May, 1705, Sarah Meyer imported seventy-five gallons of rum on the *Frederick*. Whether the good lady kept a tavern or had a powerful thirst the record does not state. On March 22, 1707, Hester Brown brought in twenty-five gallons of rum "In Ye Sloop Flying Horse."

Often the same names occur again and again. Among the most enterprising of merchants was Abraham de Lucena. Other names that appear on these customs lists are also familiar. They are Joseph Bueno, Issac Gabay, Lewis Gomez, Isaac Marques, Moses Levy and Joseph Nunez.

These are but a few of the active merchants who paid duty listed as "Customs inward." The "Customs outward" brought in smaller revenues and were largely imposed on rum and furs.

The frequency with which rum appears on these records shows us all too clearly that Jews like Christians had their share of traffic in the infamous triangle: rum—molasses—slaves. Jews, however, did not import many slaves, although some were slaveowners.

Addison has said of the Jews that they were "the instruments by which the most distant nations converse with one another and by which mankind are knit together in general correspondence." When we study the places to which Jews transmitted their orders and from which they received goods, we find all of them to be cities in which they had relatives, in which there were groups or communities of coreligionists whom they knew, who were no strangers to the men in New York, in Rhode Island or in Boston.

This sense of group solidarity expressed itself in other ways than in commerce. There were touching anecdotes showing the close dependence of Jews on each other, proving that the bonds of kinship were not severed by migration.

When the Congregation Honen Dalim on the Island of St. Eustatia in the West Indies was destroyed by a tropical storm, it was to the

Congregation Shearith Israel in New York that the members appealed for funds for the restoration of their house of worship.

The building of religious edifices had a peculiar attraction for Jews. It made a nonsectarian appeal. Again and again in those early days when Christian groups were raising funds, Jewish donors proved liberal. And whether the appeal went out to build a steeple of the Lutheran Trinity Church of Philadelphia or to replace damaged Torah scrolls in the West Indies, Jewish donors were ready to contribute.

Records have come down to us showing how often men assumed the debts of near or distant relatives. There are papers which prove that kinship was often stretched beyond the point of reason or logic. When there was no relationship, then association in a synagogue, casual acquaintance or even the mere claim of one Jew upon a fellow Jew would seem enough. That is why it is so difficult to contain these men in a paragraph. A man may be a calloused importer of rum, an untroubled owner of slaves, a keen businessman. Yet he may also be warm, kind, generous, openhanded to the poor. The more these names on customs records come alive, the more resistant are they to arbitrary classification.

Here was Moses Levy who was born about 1665. His youth was spent in London. He was a merchant, and the owner of many ships engaged in trade with Africa, probably some slave trade. After accumulating a substantial fortune in London, he went to America. Early in the eighteenth century he landed in New York City. His activities were manifold. He took an active interest in the Congregation Shearith Israel and in communal affairs. "Meanwhile his vessels continued to make their way in foreign waters and occasionally pick up a prize, which was then considered an act of distinction." But what price status, wealth, recognition? His entire life was summarized in thirty-five words on a bit of granite:

> O Frail Adam,
> What the Earth Surely Produces
> Death by His Power Reduces.
> Thy Heavenly Part Man Being Fled,
> Alas, The Other Parts Are Dead.
> Mr. Moses Levy depar^d this Life June the 14th 1728 [17]

Just as Jews were a factor in international trade, so were they among those who tended to break down intercolonial isolation. They were not hampered by insular concepts. Having been a mobile folk for many centuries, they continued their migrations between the colonies unimpeded. The important historic era, the years from 1700 to 1775 when a sense of nationalism was emerging, needed to be served by men who could cross over from New York to Pennsylvania without too great an effort. The Jews of Newport were not strangers to their coreligionists in Georgia. In having converse with each other they also aided the cause of national unity. They were prodigious visitors and interested correspondents. Little escaped them. They were avid for news of each other.

The Sheftall papers yield an amusing fragment. Young Sheftall Sheftall who is away from home, writing to his father, Mordecai Sheftall, on the eve of Passover—making, no doubt, a wry face as he contemplates a week's revolution in his usual diet—says: "This is Aref Pasoch my small gutts is warring with the Big Ones." The knowledge of the restrictions imposed on Jews by their dietary laws—*Kashruth*—is shared by their Christian acquaintances. A Christian friend, John Wereat, writes to Mordecai Sheftall: "If you go to Mount Hope carry your Knife with you that you may not return hungry."[18] This refers to the specially sharpened knife used by Jews for mitigating the slaughter of animals.

There is a wholesome relationship expressed here. A recognition of differences in usage and in religion. There is acceptance of these differences without squeamishness or fuss. It is the evolving American formula. It makes for friendship with one's neighbors of whatever faith.

Jews were psychologically adaptable. They were not overawed by distance. Their ships traversed the high seas. Their inland voyages followed the trails and the rivers. Their young sons were dispatched to woo brides in distant places. They helped each other build synagogues. They exchanged information and commodities. They shipped their poor and their orphans and widows from place to place trying to distribute the burden of philanthropy more equitably. Their young boys were sent to the larger cities to be educated. They undertook protracted social visits. They assisted the newest immigrants in getting started in frontier outposts.

Often young Christian boys were entrusted to Jews for training and education. There are many such instances of interfaith trust and reliance. Among the papers of Aaron Lopez of Newport there is a postscript to a letter written by Ray Sands to Aaron Lopez on March 30, 1769, which serves as an excellent example of mutual good will and co-operation.

P.S.

Sir

    hear is a young Lad Amongs Us has a grate inclination
to be brought up in the Marchants way and his farther
Moved to me ^{to} apply to you to know whether it
Madents Sute you to take him he is a Lad of about
fifteen years of Age his father is Aman of Intrust
And will Due any thing to Surport him in the
branch of his inclination And if there shood be a
Vacancy with you and the Lad Shood Sute ( ) wood
be glad you wood take him
Please to Let Me know your
Mind About ye Matter   R. Sands[19]

There was one other way in which Jews could serve as unifying
links in the great community. The "hawkers and walkers," the peddlers
and itinerant merchants, the trappers and fur traders were important
dispensers of news as well as of pots and pans and calico. To the
dwellers in isolated frontier shacks, human contact with the outer
world was invaluable. The channels of communication were meager.
The mail was either nonexistent or slow or carried by an occasional
traveler. The tradesmen who came and went between the seaboard
towns and the frontier outposts brought those precious contacts with
the world which the frontier folk had left behind. The warm welcome
awaiting the peddler was repaid in many ways. The accent in which
the news was dispensed—Spanish, German, Portuguese—could be
overlooked. Such a courier was needed. To a man schooled in rejection that in itself was a rich and satisfying experience. Many friendships were begun and flourished from these casual contacts. These
frontier meetings are not to be overlooked in studying the growth
of a national spirit. For they conferred both upon the itinerant immigrant merchant and on the settler who may have once been an indentured servant, a sense of shared interest, a sense of belonging, a
sense of independent existence, a sense of security which neither had
known in his old days. It was a network within whose boundaries
patriots grew up and the spirit of independence was nurtured.

The *New York Evening-Post* on December 17, 1744, carried a
notice which is an example of one of the many services these
"hawkers and walkers" performed:

        The Albany Post, Abraham Alstine,
        intends to set out To-morrow, any
        Gentlemen that has Letters may
        send them to his House on the
        Broad-Way near the Fort.

It did not matter too much that some of these men spoke languages other than English or spoke broken English. They delivered the mail. They brought news of the seaboard. They sold scarce commodities. The welcome mat was out for them.

In view of their turbulent past, it is remarkable that Jews of colonial times insisted on being recognized as Jews. When Judah Hays's name appears on a petition in New York in 1729, he calls himself "an Israelite & merchant." Both he and David Hays were given the freedom of the city of New York in 1735. When Jews are sworn, it is on the Old Testament.

To this practice of referring to Jews as such we owe some of our knowledge of their earliest history. The Boston tax list of 1674 lists three names: Rowland Gideon "Ye Jew," Raphael Abandana, "Samuel the Jew." Connecticut in 1659 fined a man called simply "David, the Jew," twenty shillings for an unspecified offense. In Massachusetts Solomon Franco, the Jew, is given a stipend of six shillings a week "till he cann gett his passage into Holland." Official generosity is coupled with an ultimatum—that he get out of the colony within ten weeks.

It is, however, when we consider the organization and development of Jewish communal life in those early days, that patterns of social organization emerge. Then the relationship of the *in-group* to the *out-group* lends itself to summary. For we see the social imbalance, the tentative compromise, the growing accommodation, the mutual adjustments, the competition and conflict, as well as the rapprochement and sympathy—all woven into the composite fabric of life in America.

Such were the men and events in the momentous days at the close of one century and the beginning of another in America.

In far off Ukraine as the giant clock that strikes the passing of the centuries was marking this event, Israel ben Eliezer—the Baal Shem—was born in 1700. No greater contrast is possible. The Jews in America were firmly planting their feet in reality. On this side of the Atlantic great strides were made in commerce, in education, in the building of religious communities, in the making of a new nation. On the other side, in direst poverty, in an atmosphere of hairsplitting legalism, the Jews of Eastern Europe lived a life of retreat from reality. Their finest minds had devoted their greatest talents to interpreting passages of law and lore while difficulties hemmed them in and privation was their daily portion. The simple and illiterate folk had no spokesman, for none cherished them or planned for them.

The Baal Shem became the voice of the masses. He taught them that to seek good in life, to cultivate happiness, to enjoy the pleasures of the senses, was to serve God truly and well. So was born the Hassidic sect with its mysticism, its legend and its folklore.

Between Judaism in America and Judaism in Eastern Europe there was a gulf as wide as the miles of land and ocean that separated them on the map. And when they met, as meet they did in America two hundred years later, there were few here who understood these followers of the Baal Shem and fewer still to hold out a fraternal hand to them.

We turn now to some of those communities, in Rhode Island, in New York, in Pennsylvania, in Georgia, in New Orleans. We note their fragmentary beginnings, their dynamic growth, their evolution, their hardening into fixed molds, their continuance or their decline and fall.

CHAPTER VI

Seaboard Synagogues
and Lonely Outposts

>>> The Christian Religion was never intended, nor ought, to
leave the Rights of Mankind *in a worse condition than it
found them.*
—SOLOMON ABRABANEL, London, 1736 <<<

AS THE eighteenth century approached, many changes were evident
in American Jewish life. The emphasis shifts now from the individual,
the bold adventurer and rugged pioneer, to group life in America.
Groups and communities acquire color and substance. Man is gregarious and social by nature. The culture he builds is the end product of
group effort and association. The age of great men, of Fernão de
Loronha and João Ramalho and Asser Levy, gives way to the rise
of communities, the building of synagogues, the undertaking of
schools and fraternal associations. When there are many people to
choose from, a man will divide the world into those who are like
him, the *in-group*, and those who are unlike, the *out-group*. This is the
core of the concept of the "Chosen People." A man accepts and
approves of his "looking-glass self," says Cooley. Individuals are
animated by "the consciousness of kind" says Giddings. These are
basic concepts which must be kept in mind when the new, emerging
communal patterns of Jewish life in America are studied. Otherwise
Jewish history becomes a phenomenon in a vacuum.

In 1699 on the threshold of the new century, the Jews of America
found in John Locke a spokesman for their rights and liberties. For
the *Fundamental Constitutions* written by this great man for the
colony of Carolina specifically recognized the rights of Jews and other
dissenters.

If we allow the Jews to have private houses and dwellings amongst us,
why should we not allow them to have synagogues?[1]

74

So under the aegis of this kindly philosopher who said that courtesy, friendship and soft usage are better than force, Jewish history in South Carolina had its beginnings.

That the "Grand Model" of government did not work out, need not concern us. That it was a clumsy, unwieldy, cumbersome document does not matter. That Carolina early was divided into a "respectable" colony for landed proprietors to the South and a home for the poor and for the runaway to the North, is also irrelevant. The fact remains that under the constitution prepared by Locke, there was sanctuary. Jews readily availed themselves of the privileges granted them. It was enough.

The seaboard from New England south to the Carolinas and Georgia was dotted with new settlements. Hammer blows made new rhythms as men transformed forests into clearings. The rich, fertile earth was plowed and men harvested the crops which they had wrested from the land. Down the rivers they sailed their heavy-laden boats. Over the tortuous mountain passes others doggedly plodded. The land was a magic carpet unrolled for the pioneers. All things were possible. Anything might happen. The land was new and hopes were young and all eyes were fixed on the morrow. There was room for all. Each was bounded only by himself. His horizons were unlimited. He had shed the skin of his past. The future was a garment of his own making.

But the land was a subtle mistress. Gradually character and personality and way of life were shaped to conform with rugged, stony hills, with broad and hospitable and sunny acres. By the opening of the eighteenth century there was a discernible flavor of regionalism throughout the land. The Puritan way of life had taken root in New England. The plantation system was established in Virginia and in South Carolina. And between these two systems there had evolved the middle colonies which constituted a bridge, economically, geographically, psychologically, between them. In all of these places, the Jews found a niche for themselves. Sometimes it was but a narrow corner where Jews dwelt on sufferance. At other times it was on broad acres which a man could proudly call his own.

Hebrew and Hebraism had always been prevalent in the Puritan mind. The Old Testament was well thumbed. The Prophets were more than mere names. They were household words. They were the names given to dearly loved children. Hebrew was a language early included in the Harvard curriculum. Many of the Puritan sermons were Hebraic in ideology and content. It is not surprising that in 1634 a code of laws was titled "Draft of the Model of Moses, his Judicials." Nor that in 1658 Plymouth colony adopted the Jewish code as a model. One need only leaf through Dr. Rosenbach's exhaustive bibliography of early Judaica-Americana to find the breadth of interest in Hebrew and Hebraism shown by some of the founders of our nation. They were veritably "the new Israel." One scholar, Hans Kohn, sees their entire cultural milieu as an expression of self-identification with the ancient Hebrews. The sociologist and cultural anthropologist can also point out many similarities. The attitudinal self-consciousness of the Puritan, his system of social controls, his uneasy conscience were Hebraic. It was not only in nomenclature. It was in the way that the Puritans were oriented toward all of life. It was in their theocratic society, in their moral rigidity, in their messianism.

In 1640 the *Bay Psalm Book*, with a preface by Richard Mather, was the first book published by English settlers in America. It was translated directly from the Hebrew, using Hebrew type for the first time in North America.[2]

Sermons and private undertakings to convert Jews were a commonplace.[3] The Reverend Increase Mather of Boston preached a series of sermons titled "The Mystery of Israel's Salvation Explained and Applyed." Cotton Mather wrote a book "to engage the Jewish Nation, unto the religion of their Patriarchs." He was forever alert to the possibility of converting Jews to his way of thinking. One of his books contains an appendix on the "Conversion of a Jew." The subject was almost a fixation with him. Such entries as the following show with what earnest devotion Cotton Mather threw himself into his self-appointed task:

July 4-5, 1713. Vigil-prayer. For the conversion of the poor Jew, who is this Day returned once more unto New England, and who has now for 19 years together been the Subject of our Cares and Hopes, and Prayers.

August 29, 1713. Prayer. For the conversion of the Jew for whom I have been so long and so much concerned![4]

Samuel Sewall's diary and the private notebooks of many of his contemporaries contained numerous references to this all-engrossing subject.[5]

The hunting down of religious quarry was a sport to every one's liking. The occasional convert was warmly welcomed. But they never quite accepted him. Always a faint aroma of suspicion clung to the baptismal robes. Perhaps the following letter will show how "conversion" did not transform a Jew nor insure him acceptance and fellowship. James Logan writes to Henry Goldney as follows:

Philad^a 7-3-1723

In some of my letters to Captain Annis I took notice that Isaac Miranda, an apostate Jew or fashionable Christian Proselyte, was gone over to transact some affairs in which our Gov^{er} is concerned, and particularly in relation to ye mine beyond Susquehanna. I have since rec'd a very pressing application from some inhabitants of the Lands on this side of the River over against that mine, who have not yet obtained Titles to their settlements, are apprehensive that he has some design or Instruction to procure a right and turn them out of their possessions & Improvem^{ts}, which would be very unjust. I can only say at present, that the man ought in general to be guarded against for all his notions in relation to you, if I mistake not, will be found Insidious.[6]

J.L. [James Logan]

Never free of suspicion. . . .

These were the beginnings of Jewish history in the colonies. Let us look at them now in the eighteenth century, tracing their growth, examining their structure, meeting the children of the earliest settlers and the newcomers. For the times were dynamic. There was change on every side. The country was growing, stretching its boundaries. Jews changed with the times, moved on to new places. They settled in New Biloxi as well as in New York.

In many ways the synagogue was the vital center of Jewish communal life.[7] To the synagogue went the children to attend the school which was maintained by the congregation and usually presided over by the cantor. Here the elected trustees determined procedure, dues, decorum, salaries, fines and penalties. Strict discipline was maintained not only over the behavior of the congregants, but also over their kitchens, their meat supply, their utensils used for cooking, over the home religious observances.

Every synagogue had its constitution and by-laws. These were revised from time to time. Usually a special book was used for recording both the written instrument of government and the names of the members who agreed to abide by the rules so drawn up. Shearith Israel had such a code of laws in 1706 and again in 1728.[8] These records mirror our protagonists. Its discipline was ironclad. Its authority was unquestioned. Within its orbit the dread weapon of excommunication could be wielded. So the mores were rigidly

CONSTITUTION

Of the Congregation of

Shearith Israel,

As reported by a Committee on the nineteenth day of May, one thousand eight hundred and five.

FOR the better enabling the rulers of this Congregation to govern the same agreeably to the immutable principles of justice, and for the purpose of promoting harmony, peace and unity among the members thereof, as a religious society, a full and respectable meeting of the Congregation was held on the twenty-eighth day of April last, which meeting was opened by Mr. Aaron Levy, acting Parnas, when Mr. Isaac Moses was chosen Chairman, and I. M. Gomez Secretary......Mr. A. Levy then stated to the meeting the object for which they were convened, whereupon it was moved and seconded, that a Committee of five be appointed to draft and report a suitable CONSTI-TUTION and BYE-LAWS.....The following gentlemen were thereupon nominated and chosen, viz. Messrs. Ephraim Hart, I Hart, sen. J. B. Kursheedt, M. Myers and M. L. Moses, who by virtue of the powers vested in them do recommend the following Constitution, as embracing proper fundamental principles, upon which all laws are to be hereafter predicated, so far as the same shall be consistent with the Act of Incorporation.

CONSTITUTION, &c.

ARTICLE I.

Name.

THE Congregation of Israelites in this City shall hereafter and forever be known as a body corpo-rate by the name, stile and title of THE CONGREGATION OF SHEARITH ISRAEL in the CITY of NEW-YORK.

ARTICLE II.

To be govern-ed by six Trus-tees.

SEC. 1. THE spiritual as well as temporal concerns of this Congregation, shall be confided to fix Trustees, to be elected in the manner and form prescribed in and by the act of incorporation, whose duty it shall always be to elect a Parnas or Parnasim from amongst their board, he or one of them pre-siding in the board, and possessing all the powers out of it, that may be granted by the laws to be estab-lished.

Trustees to e-lect Parnas.

Officers.

SEC. 2. The officers of this Congregation shall always be a Hazan, Shochet and Shamas, and such other officer or officers as may hereafter be deemed necessary and elected by the Congregation.

ARTICLE III.

Prayers &c. to be read in He-brew.

English.

THE fixed PRAYERS, the PARASA, and HAPHTORAS shall forever be read in the original Hebrew lan-guage, but the board of trustees may on public thanksgivings, or other special occasions direct the Ha-zan or any other suitable person to deliver an address, sermon, or moral lecture in English.

ARTICLE IV.

Parnas may cause offenders to be punished.

THE Parnas or Parnasim may at all times cause any offender or offenders against this Constitution, or any of the laws of the Congregation to be punished in such manner as may hereafter be provided.

ARTICLE V.

Certain prop-erty ever to re-main unsold.

What may be leased, and for how long.

Electors to be notified.

Two thirds to be a majority.

THE Synagogue and Burying places, shall ever be the joint property of all Israelites who are or may hereafter become electors of this Congregation, and the same shall never be sold, mortgaged or shut up, by any person or persons under their authority, nor shall any of the leases of that part of the property of this Congregation adjoining the BET-HAIM, now on lease be renewed for a longer term than twenty-one years—and if the board of trustees shall deem it necessary, or conducive to the interest of the Congregation, to dispose of any other real estate, they shall cause the electors residing within the juris-diction of the corporation of this city, to be duly notified to assemble at the usual place of meeting or such other place as they may appoint, when two thirds of the members present agreeing shall be consid-ered a majority.

upheld. Powerful sanctions were delegated to the Parnas and the Elders. Lapses from grace were costly, for they led to social isolation. Readmission to communal life had to be earned. Thus membership was a privilege to be cherished.

When in 1729 the original Sephardic membership had been sufficiently augmented by Ashkenazim, non-Iberian Jews, it was decided that the time had come to build a synagogue. Now the record is well documented. Here is a "Coppey of Sundry Accounts—relating to the building of the new Sinagogue." They authorize the payment of four shillings to "Mr. penant for drawing the writings with the Carpenters." The same gentleman earns six shillings for drawing up a contract with the "masson." Negroes were used as unskilled labor. Their owners were compensated—"pd ye Wido fonseca for negro hire . . . £ 1/5/10 1/2." Skilled workers were paid in commodities or money. They used tea, loaf sugar, "a barl. Strong Beer." It was an enterprise involving Jews and non-Jews. From G. Stuyvesant they bought bricks. From John Roosevelt white lead "and sundries."

The erection of the synagogue on Mill Street, the first in North America, was an oblation of magnitude to the Jews of New York and to their friends in distant places. The *Haham*, chief Rabbi, of Curaçao collected 264 pieces of eight. Special contributions came from Jamaica, from Barbados, from London, from other American colonies. As for the Jews of New York, it was their beloved project! Money was pledged, contributed, pledged again. They paid for single stones, for parts of windows, for equipment, for decorations. One devout member contributed, "for work done for ye ten Commandmts," at the rate of a shilling per commandment. One member contributed building lime which was to be paid for if the treasury permitted "and in case of failure of any money being left, Mr. Moses Gomez will have done Kodez" (a worthy deed). A woman in Barbados, Mrs. Lunah Burgos, sent forty pounds to build a wall around the cemetery. Another woman gave ten pounds to buy a Torah.

Finally the little brick structure on Mill Street was completed. We can only guess at the emotions of pride and thanksgiving which were lavished on it. How they must have cherished this symbol of freedom of worship, this opportunity of walking in dignity and pride, dressed in their best as becomes the Sabbath, of stepping over their own holy threshold, of openly acknowledging their faith. What prayers of gratitude must have welled up on the Passover day in 1730 when Moses Lopez de Fonseca rose before the congregation to intone the prayer of dedication.

The congregational records now extant go back to the year 1727, the earlier documents having been lost. At first the minutes were kept in Portuguese. Then both English and Portuguese were used. Finally the record is entirely in English.

The maintenance of a congregational school was one of the earliest concerns of Shearith Israel. One year after the completion of the Mill Street synagogue, on the last day of Passover, 1731, a "Yeshibat" was dedicated. Five years later when David M. Machado was engaged as "reader" of the congregation he was also obliged

to keep a publick School in due form for teaching the *hebrew Language*, either the whole morning or afternoon as he shall think most proper, and any poor that shall be thought unable to pay for their children's Learning they shall be taught gratis.[9]

By 1747, the school was keeping regular hours. School was in session from nine to twelve daily and from two to five on Thursday afternoon. The instructor was to be paid a load of wood per annum and eight shillings each quarter for each scholar enrolled. "Also, that the parness or one of the adjuntos shall visit the said School weekly." In 1755 the educational curriculum was further expanded. The Reader's salary was increased

on Condition that he opens a School at his own house every day in the week (Fryday afternoon Holy Days and Fast days Excepted) & teach such poor children Gratis that shall have an order from the Parnas Presidente, the Hebrew, Spanish, English, Writting & Arithmetick.[10]

School was in session the year around. The hours varied. In the summer, the children were kept at their studies from nine to twelve and two to five. In the winter, from ten to twelve and two to four. Once a month the trustees of the synagogue agreed to visit the school "to examine the children and judge if the scholars under the Hazans care advance in their learning."

It is likely that Jewish children of the well-to-do had private tutors as did the wealthier Christian families. There was no secret made of the poverty of some of the children who were taught free upon presenting a statement of their inability to pay tuition. It was an early and not too happy application of "the means test" so glibly described in current social work textbooks. Certainly no effort was made to minimize the importance of wealth or to mitigate the rigors of poverty. What the effect was on the little children who had this arbitrary economic pattern superimposed upon them, we do not know. It was a long cry from democracy in education.

But if educational methods were cavalier, they were mild compared to the summary administration of sweet charity. The happiest disposition of a case was one which facilitated and expedited the client's removal to some other spot on the map. Every indigent person was encouraged to migrate. It is a ready solution that has endured to our own days of *The Grapes of Wrath*, to keep the poor moving in search of work, of security and of a more permanent address.

The congregational minutes of Shearith Israel are a study of group life in early America.[8] They should serve to illustrate the methods of social control. They are a blueprint of a synagogue in action as an instrument of government, of education, of philanthropy, as a vehicle for religious experience. Within the orbit of the congregation a man's life could be lived out. From the synagogue was but a short distance to the Beth Hayim—the ultimate resting place where only those in good standing might be interred. It was a small, homogeneous group with strong ties and an enduring ethnocentrism. Decorum had to be preserved for the sake of the larger community as well as for the successful functioning of the inner group. The folkways and mores were maintained and perpetuated. A façade of strength and unity was upheld. An integrated relationship with the greater community was established.

Discipline was stern and the elders alert for signs of infractions of the rules. The backslider, the nonconformist, the Sabbath-breaker was swiftly punished. He had to conform to continue as a Jew. The trustees of the congregation were eternally vigilant. They took their responsibilities seriously.

But here and there, very slowly, a breach was made. The young people found ways of eluding constant surveillance. It was easy to forget dietary laws when traveling with Christians. A young dandy going out into society might "forget" the Sabbath and shave. There were instances of fraternizing which led to intermarriage. There were many bridges which spanned the gaps between Jew and Christian. Gradually the synagogue yielded a little. Some of the rigidity and inflexibility went out of the elders. The customs of the country, its language, were encroaching upon early insularity. The revolutionary spirit was abroad in the land. It penetrated into the synagogue.

One of the signs of change was Isaac Pinto's translation of the Sephardic Ritual into English. It was printed by John Holt in 1766. Pinto meticulously acknowledged the sacredness of Hebrew and firmly voiced his belief "that it will again be reestablished in Israel."

But he pleads the necessity for an English prayer book because Hebrew is "being imperfectly understood by many, by some, not at all." Here then was a realistic attempt at compromise. They were moving toward secularization. Yet on some matters they refused to yield. In 1763, a rule was adopted which forbade any officers of the congregation from attempting to make converts. Marriages were not to be performed between Jews and proselytes.

As we come closer to the fateful years which marked a crisis in American history, another and far more action-packed period of activity begins for American Jews. But of these activities and of the war years, more later.

Other communities sprang up in many places. Along the Atlantic coastline, down to the gulf there are Jewish travelers and settlers.

The earliest mention of a Jewish resident of the colony of Connecticut is dated 1659. In that year "David the Jew" was fined twenty shillings for "tradeing provision from children" in the absence of the heads of their households. Two years later, Jews living in Hartford were ordered to leave at the end of seven months. Jacob Lucena ran afoul of the law in Connecticut in 1670 and was jailed until his fine of twenty pounds was paid. This was reduced to half the amount when Lucena petitioned the authorities, "considering he is a Jew, to shew him what favors they may." The intervention of Asser Levy reduced the fine by another five pounds. "Davie, a Jew" and "Jacob, a Jew" were among householders in 1669-1670 who had "quantities of grain." Jacob owned a number of horses which he transported to New York. The description of his horses is detailed—such as, "browne mare with a slitt in the off eare"—but unfortunately no description is found of their owner.

In the eighteenth century there are more detailed records for the colony. The Pinto brothers were patriots of New Haven in 1775. Solomon Pinto was an officer of the Seventh Regiment of the Connecticut Line serving until 1783. He became one of the founders of the Society of the Cincinnati in his State. Two of the Pinto brothers were wounded in combat. Another patriot soldier was David Judah.

It was to Connecticut that Gershom Seixas, the ardent patriot, fled with the Scrolls of the Law from his congregation in New York. There he remained from 1776 to 1780, being joined by a number of his congregation.

Delaware figured in the records of New Amsterdam from 1654. In the following year Isaac Israel and Benjamin Cardosa were traders there. Pressure brought to bear on the home office of the Dutch West India Company soon extended trading privileges to their coreligionists. But the records are meager. For it was in the neighboring colonies that Jews in colonial America lived their lives and made their contribution.

Jewish history in Massachusetts was far from the unrolling of a red carpet. From 1649 on, when Solomon Franco was allowed a pittance of six shillings a week to tide him over for ten weeks—on condition that he leave at that time—there was no welcome mat for Jews in that colony. It was one thing to pay lip service to their ancestors, the Prophets. Quite another to accept their descendants, the immigrants! Solomon, "ye Malata Jew," ran afoul of the law in 1668. His offense —traveling on Sunday. Rowland Gideon fared better. He was one of the first Jews of the colony to become endenizened. There came a gradual amelioration of the position of the Jews in Massachusetts. For by 1720, one of their number, Isaac Lopez, was elected a constable in Boston.

At least two of their number, the Frazons, descendants of Brazilian Jews, were known to the Reverend Samuel Sewall, "to whom I am beholden for a sight of the Spanish Bible." Another Jew was the owner of a snuff mill! With a partner he acquired a tract of land in 1733 and set a part of it aside for a cemetery. As for the Jews' connection with Harvard—thereby hangs a tale.[11]

The early education of Jewish children was largely a parochial affair. The synagogue considered the education of young children an integral part of its function. A traveler who visited Newport in 1760 was favorably impressed by the beautiful synagogue then in the process of building. "It will be extremely elegant within when completed," he wrote, "but the outside is totally spoilt by a school which the Jews would have annexed to it for the education of their children." Some of the well-to-do merchants and successful brokers and physicians had private tutors for their children, others sent them abroad. Not all colleges accepted Jewish students. But disqualifications collapsed as Jews became benefactors of colleges. This was the case with Brown University of Rhode Island. In one year, three Jews, Israel Joseph, Michael Lazarus and Moses Lindo, were among those who subscribed to the school's support. That prejudice was like a balloon that could be pricked by donations may be seen from the following resolution voted by the trustees of Brown and communicated to Mr. Lindo by the President and Chancellor:

(1770) The sum of twenty pounds having been reported from Mr. Moses Lindo, a Jewish merchant of Charleston, it was thereupon "Voted, That the children of Jews may be admitted into this Institution, and entirely enjoy the freedom of their own religion without any restraint or imposition whatever."[12]

To appraise properly the relationship of Jews to higher learning at this time, two facts must be borne in mind. Colleges were very small in population. In 1680 at Harvard there were a scant twenty students. They were completely sectarian. Theological subjects taught by clergymen loomed large on every curriculum. The classics and Greek, Latin and Hebrew were means to an end—the training of clergymen and of professional men. As early as 1653, Michael Wigglesworth, Harvard's Instructor in Hebrew, was petitioned by his reluctant students that they "might ceas learning Hebrew."[13]

The time came when Harvard was again looking about for a teacher of Hebrew. It coincided with the occasion when an Italian Jew named Judah Monis was looking for a job.

Judah Monis was born in 1683, in Italy. Of his early years we know little. But by 1716 he was a freeman of New York. He was listed then as a merchant. Four years later he turns up in Boston. Here he seems to have met a number of crusading preachers, especially Increase Mather and a Mr. Leverett. He received an honorary Master of Arts degree from near-by Harvard in 1720. He was then still an unconverted Jew. But his Christian friends labored with him for two years. The vacancy at Harvard, the blandishments of his new friends—it all added up to a public baptismal ceremony. On March 27, 1722, Judah Monis, ex-Jew, delivered an oration entitled "Truth" and publicly avowed himself a Christian. All of his life Monis was to deliver speeches protesting the sincerity of his conversion and the "Confession of his Faith." All of his life his sincerity and dedication to truth were to be questioned. Hannah Adams, first American woman historian, flatly avers that Harvard required the change in religious status from Monis as a condition to his securing the teaching position.[14] Always his new-found friends referred to him as "the converted Jew" or the "Christianized Jew." He was never one of them. Miss Adams, whose own connection with Harvard was very close, and who probably knew some of the older colleagues of Monis, states that all of his life he observed Saturday as his Sabbath.

In his spare time Monis worked on a Hebrew grammar. It was completed in 1726. He waited for several years until its publication. Hebrew type had first to be imported from England. When it was finally published in 1735 it was the first complete Hebrew book published in America. There had been prior to this date some occasional use of Hebrew chiefly in religious works published under the aegis of Harvard. An occasional Hebrew autograph, an inscription in a book, a phrase in a diary or sermon was testimony of a man's erudition. The subject was very unpopular at Harvard. Monis' classes were small. His unhappiness mounted. On occasion when his financial crises made his life particularly difficult, he received an added subsidy from Harvard. The last time was in 1760.

Being a Christian did not help him much. Still when he wrote his will in 1764 he reaffirmed his new faith. But even on his tombstone, his friends saluted him as *Rabbi* Monis. For more than forty years he walked a solitary path flanked by his past which he rejected and his present which he never fully realized.

This is an attitude of psychological dualism which needs clarification from Christians. For the Monis episode is not isolated. It persists to our own day.

Other colleges too taught Hebrew. The president of King's College wrote that "as soon as a Lad has learned to speak and read English well, it is much the best to begin a learned education with Hebrew . . . the mother of all Language and Eloquence." King's College had its Jewish friends. A fund-raising campaign in 1762 utilized the talents of Moses Franks, son of Jacob Franks and brother of Phila Franks who had married Oliver de Lancey, one of the governors of the college. Moses Franks was a member of the influential firm of Nesbitt, Colebrook and Franks, which had advanced money to the British Government during the French and Indian War. The class of 1774 had a Jewish graduate, Israel Abrahams. After the Revolution when King's College became Columbia, Rabbi Gershom Mendes Seixas of Shearith Israel was appointed one of the regents of the college.

Yale had several graduates who were listed as of Jewish extraction. The first three known Jews to receive their degrees from Yale were the Pinto brothers—Abraham, Solomon and William. They were the children of Jacob and Thankful Pinto. They were born in New Haven. Ezra Stiles knew them and referred to them in his *Diary*. They were Revolutionary patriots and served in the Army throughout the War.

At the University of Pennsylvania Jews were found from its earliest days. Between 1760-68 there were six Jewish students in its Academy and College. Among the most noted of its Jewish graduates was Moses

Levy whose father was one of the signers of the Non-Importation Resolutions. He enrolled in 1769 and was one of the three students who graduated in the class of 1772. He became a member of the Legislature, holding other public offices until 1822 when he was chosen presiding judge of the Philadelphia District Court. In 1802, his own college elected him a trustee, a position he held for twenty-four years, until his death. In 1804, he is mentioned in Jefferson-Gallatin correspondence as a worthy candidate for Attorney-General of the United States.

Another alumnus of the University of Pennsylvania was Zalegman Phillips of the class of 1795, whose father had fought in the Revolutionary War. In Lancaster, Pennsylvania, Franklin College was established in 1787 and appropriately named for its founder. In its first year, there were four Jewish students: Jacob and William Franks, and two of the children of Michael and Miriam Gratz, Hyman and Richea Gratz, who inaugurated student life there. Richea Gratz was one of the first American women to receive college training.

If these numbers seem small, it is because the total numbers involved are very small. When a score of students constituted the total enrollment of a college, when only three students graduated in one year, their numbers loom large in terms of percentage. So we must emphasize the fact that before 1783 there were only two medical schools in the country—Columbia and the University of Pennsylvania. By the time the War was over there were not half a hundred doctors graduated from both institutions. Of course the practice of medicine was not restricted to graduates of American colleges. Always there were men like Dr. Lumbrozo of Maryland and Dr. Nunez of Georgia who were among the newcomers to this land and who brought their medical knowledge with them. There was in Virginia in the early eighteenth century a Dr. Siccary of Virginia who was described as a Portuguese Jew. In the records of Virginia, Dr. Isaac Levy who practiced medicine in the Illinois Country between 1779 and 1786 is mentioned. To Lancaster, in 1747, came Dr. Isaac Cohen who thus announced his arrival:

Dr. Isaac Cohen from Hamburg in Germany, who studied seven years in the City of Copenhagen, informs the public that he has lately arrived in Lancaster, where he intends to practice physic and the art of healing, at the house of John Hatz, inn keeper. . . . N. B. Poor persons cured gratis if they can show a certificate from a clergyman that they are really poor. He expects letters addressed to him to be postpaid and those who live at a distance and desire his aid will please send a horse for him.[15]

During the Revolutionary War, Dr. Philip Moses Russell of Pennsylvania served as a surgeon. In Georgia, Dr. Moses Sheftall, son of a noted patriot, served both in the Legislature and as a surgeon in the Chatham Regiment. He helped found the Georgia Medical Society in 1804. Near-by South Carolina had three Jewish physicians in the years immediately preceding and during the Revolution—Dr. Nathan Levy, Dr. Levi Myers, and Dr. Sarzedas.

New York had more Jews practicing medicine than any other colony. Two are mentioned in the minutes of Shearith Israel in 1742. One of them was a Bohemian Jew, a "Chirurgeon" named Dr. Woolin. In the following decade three other doctors are mentioned in the congregational records. On the eve of the Revolution, Dr. Isaac Abrahams graduated as a physician in New York. A graduate of the Royal College of Surgery, Dr. Joel Hart, also practiced in New York. He was one of the founders of the Medical Society of the County of New York and became one of the trustees of the New York College of Physicians and Surgeons.

Finally there was a young boy, a medical student, Walter Jonas Judah, who lived but a brief twenty years. He was born in New York in 1778. While a medical student at Columbia's Medical School he volunteered to help in the care of patients stricken by the yellow fever epidemic which was raging throughout the city. He contracted yellow fever while caring for the sick. His tombstone in the Bowery Cemetery of Congregation Shearith Israel bears this simple tribute:

Worn down by his exertions to alleviate the sufferings of his fellow citizens in that dreadful contagion that visited the city of New York in 1798.[16]

Just as Shearith Israel Congregation was related to Bevis Marks in London, so did it bear a close kinship to the Jewish community at Newport, Rhode Island, the Congregation Yeshuat Israel. Newport is proud of its dead Jews. The synagogue has recently been dedicated as a national shrine. Their cemetery inspired Longfellow to write "The Jewish Cemetery at Newport," saluting these pre-Revolutionary pioneers.

The early Jewish residents of Newport were simple folk. Among them were lowly soap-boilers and brass workers, as well as more prosperous merchants and traders. Their commercial ventures extended to New York, as well as the West Indies. But they made little impression upon the commerce of the seventeenth century. They accepted gratefully the assurance of the General Assembly, made in

1684, that they would be treated in the same way as other foreigners of that province. After 1750 the Newport Jewish community quickened to life. Members of the influential and energetic pioneer families —the Lopez, Rivera, Polock, and Hart families—looked upon Newport and saw that it was good. What a paradise it must have seemed to these emigrés, refugees and exiles, who had found a temporary home in the West Indies!

They were an asset to any community. They owed much to Newport, but Newport also owed something to them. They were good citizens, energetic and indefatigable entrepreneurs and industrial pioneers. As early as 1705, Jews had introduced soap-making to Rhode Island. Jacob Rivera introduced the sperm oil industry in America. By 1760, there were seventeen factories engaged in the making of candles, and preparation of sperm oil. They brought many other industries as well.

But always their first project was the communal launching of a synagogue. When the Lisbon earthquake of 1755 shook loose a few more Jews into Newport, the time was ripe. Soon Rabbi Isaac Touro and a cantor arrived. They acquired a suitable "Lot of Land" and succeeded in raising "a small Fund." But unfortunately they found "our Abilities not equal to our wishes." Naturally they turned to their brethren in New York. Their appeal struck a warm response.

On August 1, 1759, the cornerstone for their synagogue was laid. To Aaron Lopez went that honor. The architect chosen was a disciple of the famous Sir Christopher Wren, Peter Harrison, who had attained a considerable reputation as the builder of the Redwood Library. Harrison's plans show a striking similarity to the synagogues of Amsterdam and London, with which he may have been familiar. Slowly, painstakingly, the Jews of Newport nursed the enterprise, collecting pence and pounds in their own midst and from other congregations until the nearly two hundred thousand bricks were paid for. It was a heavy obligation for Newport Jewry. They had even to borrow a Torah scroll from Shearith Israel to begin functioning as a synagogue.

So "the Time of Consecrating the holy Fabrick" neared. On a Friday afternoon in December of 1763, on the first day of Hanukah, 1,928 years to the day after the festival was initiated by Judas Maccabeus, the Jews of Newport reverently and in silence heard the three knocks on the closed doors, then the voice of the Rabbi calling, "Open for me the gates of righteousness." The doors were flung open and the procession filed in chanting the Twenty-Ninth Psalm.

The mood was not always one of exaltation.

There were other things on their minds at this time. The Navigation Act stipulated that only the endenized could carry on trade in the colonies. Some of the Jewish residents of Newport had been naturalized in New York. But Rhode Island flouted the tradition of its great founder. The new applicants were rejected:

The petition of Messrs. Aaron Lopez, and Isaac Elizar, persons professing the Jewish Religion, praying that they may be naturalized . . . it appears that the free and quiet enjoyment of the Christian religion . . . were the principal views with which the colony was settled . . . no person who does not profess the Christian religion can be admitted free of this colony.[17]

To make the reversal of history complete, Massachusetts accepted Aaron Lopez' application and he was naturalized there.

Here was a man who was one of the outstanding tycoons of his era. Certainly he was the most successful example of the pre-Revolutionary Jewish merchant. He was a native of Portugal who came to Newport in 1752, at the age of twenty-one. With his father-in-law, Jacob Rodriguez Rivera, who was known as "the honest man," Lopez saw the commercial possibilties of Newport harbor. He became the proud owner of a fleet of thirty sailing vessels. A record of his seafaring and commercial activities would serve as a cross section of American colonial economic history. His letters, papers, inventories, deeds, which are in the possession of the American Jewish Historical Society could literally fill volumes. The men who addressed themselves to him on personal matters and matters of business knew that he was a person of probity. One of his correspondents addressed him as "the exalted leader, dear and upright." Another refusing to submit a bill for three weeks' work implied that he would leave the matter of payment to Lopez' generosity. Moses Seixas wrote to Lopez that "I was fully sensible that the natural benevolency of your disposition wou'ld stimulate you to administer some ease to my truly agitated mind." As his debtor, Seixas did not wish to incur "a suspicion of disingenuity." Ezra Stiles, President of Yale University, when he learned of the death of his friend wrote: "He was a Merchant of the first Eminence; for Honor & Extent of Commerce probably surpassed by no Mercht in America." Of his personal characteristics Stiles wrote that Lopez was noted for "a Sweetness of Behav. a calm Urbanity an agreeable & unaffected Politeness of Manners . . . the most uni-

versally beloved of an extensive Acquaintance of any man I ever
knew."

More than forty Jewish families came to Newport because of him.
Other rich men joined the Tory cause. Not Lopez. His espousal of
the patriot cause almost ruined him. He eluded the British when they
captured Newport and moved to nearby Leicester in Massachusetts.
His magnificent home was later endowed and converted into the
Leicester Academy by Lopez.

In 1755, there came to Newport a scholarly Christian preacher
whose interest in the Old Testament, in Hebrew, and in Jews forms the
basis of the most vital source material we have on the Jews of Newport.
That man was Ezra Stiles, graduate of Yale and later its noteworthy
president, and the work, his *Literary Diary*. Frequent are the entries
descriptive of Jews he met, of absorbing theological discussions, of the
habits, customs and ways of life, of this, to him, strange group of
people. Had these settlers of Newport materialized out of the pages of
the Old Testament, he could not have regarded them with greater
interest.

He may have studied Hebrew in his youth. Or he may have been
self-taught. His son-in-law writes: "Some light, indeed, he derived
from the Jews at Newport, particularly from their Huzzans, or
teachers." He took long walks with these men, improved his knowledge at every opportunity and gradually "he began to spell and read
the Psalter." Even before he began his *Diary*, he often referred to his
contact with Jews.

The fact is that Stiles was an extravert. He had a decided flair for
social relationships. He cultivated Jewish friends. He encouraged
them. He knew and conversed with six rabbis. At least one of them
he described as an Ashkenazi, Rabbi Moses Bar David. As was his
custom, Ezra Stiles called on this visitor and following the established
protocol, the visiting Rabbi returned the call the same day. Stiles
showed Rabbi Moses his copy of the *Zohar*. The Rabbi indicated his
complete rapport with its mysticism. How these two managed to
convey to each other their innermost thoughts is not recorded. For
the Rabbi came from Poland and presumably knew only Hebrew and
Yiddish. Yet he managed to cover, in addition to the *Zohar*, "the
Messiah, angels, and general Subjects that would be of mutual concern
to mystics."

It is quite possible that Rabbi Isaac Touro acted as interpreter
on these occasions. Touro came to Newport in 1759 from Amster-

dam by way of the West Indies. He is a strange man whose beginnings are vague and whose end is a mystery. There is a tombstone in Newport Cemetery marking the place where he is *not*
buried. For the first rabbi of Newport died and was buried in
Jamaica. He came to Newport as a young man after having studied
at the rabbinical seminary of Amsterdam. He met Reyna Hays,
sister of Moses Michael Hays of Boston, and married her in 1773.
Their two sons were Judah and Abraham Touro. The Revolutionary War sent the Touros wandering out of Newport, to New York
and then to Kingston. It is likely that Touro was Tory in sympathy
for his efforts at keeping the New York congregation going when
its patriotic Rabbi Seixas, had chosen to throw in his lot with the
Revolution, and his later leaving the country for a British possession may well be an indication of Touro's real sentiments. However, while he lived in Newport his relations with Ezra Stiles were
most warm.

One day there came to Newport, a dusty, travel-worn pilgrim.
He was Haym Isaac Carigal, native of Hebron in Palestine. He
had been a rabbi since twenty and had preached in Europe and
in England and in Curaçao. Aaron Lopez, who knew Ezra Stiles
well, brought the visiting Rabbi, Haym Isaac Carigal, to call on the
noted diarist. "The Rabbi is aet. 39, a large Man, neat and well
dressed in the Turkish Habit." They talked of everything apparently, from cabbages to kings. They touched on the Gemara,
the two Talmuds and many other subjects. "We conversed much
and freely," Stiles records on another occasion, "he is learned and
truly modest, far more so than I ever saw a Jew."

On March 8, 1773, "it being the Eve of Purim," Dr. Stiles
went to synagogue. "There I saw Rabbi Carigal. . . . He was dressed
in a red Garment with the usual Phylacteries and habiliments, the
white silk Surplice; he wore a high brown furr Cap, had a long
Beard. He had the appearance of an ingenious & sensible Man."
A month later, April 8: "This day is Passover with the Jews. I
went to the synagogue. The Chocam Rabbi was there. . . . He behaved modestly and reverently. Some part of the Singing in the
Synagogue this day was exceeding fine & melodious."

It is interesting that Rabbi Carigal attended Dr. Stiles' church
also.

The time came when Rabbi Carigal once more prepared to
set off on his travels. They promised to write to each other. The
Rabbi assured him, says Dr. Stiles, that

he would always write to me from any part of the World wherever he should be. He again took leave of me very affectionately praying God to bless me. I told him I parted from him with great Reluctance, and should ever retain an affection for him—that it was probable we might never see each other in the Land of the Living and wished we might after Death meet together in the Garden of Eden and there rejoyce with Abraham, Isaac and Jacob, and with the soul of the Messiah till the Resurrection. He wished me reciprocally and my Family every Blessing and desired me to write him by every opportunity—said he loved me from the Heart, had my name in his Book, and should send it to Jerusalem, where I should be soon known as I was here.

So their meetings ended and their letters began.

Not all the Jews of Newport were rich, influential, urbane, well educated. Some were poor and shabby. Others were in perpetual difficulties. Some, like Moses M. Hays and Myer Polock, met with temporary reverses: "By various Losses at Sea and other inevitable misfortunes they are rendered insolvent Debtors." Some Jews found time for the amenities, for membership in their Masonic Lodge, in the Philosophical Society, in the Redwood Library. Others labored in the stench of an abattoir. They sent "Casher Fatt, Tongues and Cheeses" to Surinam, Barbados and Jamaica. One shipment sent by David Lopez on board the brigantine *Hannah* contained forty kegs of beef and "two geeze pickled." Another communal enterprise was the baking and exporting of Matzoth for Passover. It was written of one Newport Jew that

> Beneficent as Abraham, he constantly relieved
> The woes of poor and needy, afflicted and bereaved.

This may very well have been the height of the social ladder of the Jews of Newport.

Pennsylvania is because of its location the "Keystone" or pivotal seaboard colony. It is the rendezvous of the North and South. Great rivers and their tributaries thread the land. Both ocean and lakes are accessible. Mountain ridges in the west are carved by deep gorges. There are valleys, plateaus, rivers, forests. The land is fertile and beautiful. Waterways are the first highways of travel. At strategic places men pitch their tents, build forts, establish settlements. Through the surrounding forests stalks the stealthy Indian. Each day is packed with danger. Life is a pitched battle, with the odds evenly distributed. The immigrants are recruited from many places. Among the Schwenkenfelders, Labadists, New

Born, New Mooners, Separatists, Zion's Brueder, Ronsdorfer, Inspired, Quietists, Gichtellians, Depellians, Mountain Men, River Brethren, Brinser Brethren, Society of the Woman of the Wilderness—Jews of Pennsylvania also made a niche for themselves.

William Penn had been generously endowed with land. Settlers were badly wanted. To secure these immigrants, he offered to sell land for as low as ten dollars a hundred acres. He placated the Indians by his fairness, so they did not constitute a hostile fringe to the new settlements. He further allowed complete religious freedom and instituted a democratically chosen assembly. His policy, almost naïvely honest, brought rich rewards. Pennsylvania prospered.

In 1703, a directory of Philadelphia lists Jonas Aaron as a Jewish resident of that city. Across the river, Benjamin Levy is in residence. Soon they are joined by others, men of affairs, merchants, entrepreneurs, traders. Between 1700 and 1750 the population of the Quaker colony grew from twenty thousand to two hundred thousand. Philadelphia outdistanced New York, attaining cultural leadership and becoming the cradle of our nation. And over all this there brooded first the spirit of its benign founder and then the genius of its great son, Benjamin Franklin. Was it not pertinent that Benjamin wrote two of his parables, the "Parable against Persecution" and the "Parable on Brotherly Love," in language that in mood and rhythm approximated the Bible?

It was culturally a dynamic scene. When strange folkways dwell cheek by jowl, there is a form of social contagion by means of which one group is "infected" with the ideas of its neighbors. It is a reciprocal process. There is a curious influence ascribed to Jews of Pennsylvania. Julius Friedrich Sachse, in his discussion of *The German Sectarians of Pennsylvania*, tell us that Jewish Indiantraders, whose headquarters were near Schaefferstown from 1720 on, made themselves strongly felt among the Pennsylvania Germans. In their wanderings from community to community in search of peltry, they soon became acquainted with isolated religious groups, each one intent on fanning the flames of its own fanaticism. These German settlers, "whose reason was almost dethroned with religious excitement and vagaries," on coming in contact with Jewish traders were deeply influenced by their beliefs. We must remember that each religious community was then in the experimental and formative stage, a period when enthusiasm is rife and the adherents ready to grasp at any belief which has survived the initial experiment. Jewish religious practices seem to have been widely imitated. Circumcision was practiced. Dietary laws were strictly observed. Even to this day the descendants of these early Judaized Germans do not mix milk with meat dishes. Several German families not content with a partial following of the Mosaic code "returned to the old dispensation, and with these accessions quite a Jewish community was formed in Lancaster county."

They built a log house of worship on an old Indian trail, "the first synagogue in the American desert." This building was known as the Schul. Here, according to Sachse, the shofar was blown long before its sound was heard elsewhere in the colony. They employed a Hazan, whose home adjoined the synagogue. The advent of the new moon was piously observed by these Jewish Christians. Near by they buried their dead. To what extent these practices actually made Jews of these theologically confused Christians, we are not in a position to say. It is still an unsolved problem, even to the chronicler of this group, Mr. Sachse.

But one fact remains undisputed, that the Jewish traders of the wilderness were so thoroughly grounded in Jewish theology and practice as to inspire both the respect and imitation of some of the German Pietists with whom they came in contact. Jews of Pennsylvania also had their own mystic, a Philadelphia-born ascetic who called himself Jacob Philadelphia and was steeped in the occult, in the Cabala, in metaphysics as well as in mathematics. Many legends cluster about him. He lectured in England and on the continent of Europe, regarding himself as a scientist. But to the populace he always remained a votary of the occult and the miraculous.

Geographically, Jewish groups in colonial Pennsylvania were established chiefly in Easton, Lancaster, Reading and Philadelphia. Of the eleven families in Easton, for example, Meyer Hart and Rachel, his wife, were one. When that town was surveyed, it was found that the eleven heads of families were classified as follows: Clerk of Court, Lawyer, Carpenter, Smith, Ferryman, two Tavern Keepers, a Baker, Butcher, Mason, and Shopkeeper. These eleven families, in all about forty souls, were clustered about a little frontier stockade, in a place where the war-whoop of the Indian was a familiar and much dreaded sound. From the first, Meyer Hart identified himself wholeheartedly with his little community. He prospered. By 1763, his county tax was larger than that of any other taxpayers in Easton. He then owned three houses, several

Negroes, and his store. He had advanced to the position of inn-keeper. In the following year, 1764, he was naturalized. When he came to Easton, Meyer Hart's name was at the bottom of the tax list. Five years later, when the somewhat enlarged community built a school, Meyer Hart's name led the list of contributors. The cause of free public education in Easton was advanced by the shopkeeper's donation of twenty pounds of wrought nails, which were at a premium in the wilderness.

The coming of two other Jews was not an unmixed blessing for Meyer. A lawsuit inaugurated by Hart, the prosperous landowner, against Barnet Levy, his indigent tenant, gives us a glimpse of strife among the Hebrews: "A petition of Meyer Hart of Easton, complaining of the sheriff of the county of Northampton not exe-cuting process directed to him by the justices to remove a tenant from his possession." Whether or not Barnet Levy was dispossessed, we do not know.

Meyer Hart's importance grew. His son Michael, "the stuttering Jew," enlisted in Captain Hagenbuck's Company, in August of 1776, and was made a corporal. The father's prestige advanced so that in the following year he was put in charge of British prisoners. In 1778, Meyer Hart was David Hart's agent for victualing British prisoners. Their participation in Revolutionary activities belongs in another chapter.

Lancaster, Pennsylvania, was the home of one of the most am-bitious Jewish colonial entrepreneurs. Joseph Simon was an Indian trader, merchant and landowner on a vast scale. He came to Lan-caster several years after the town was laid out. He is definitely known to have lived there in 1740. The only member of his race to have preceded him, was the lawyer, Isaac Miranda, who died in Lancaster in 1733. Miranda, however, was known as the "fashion-able Christian."

To estimate fully the activities of Joseph Simon, one must keep in mind the quick tempo of events in colonial America about the middle of the eighteenth century. There was a charged excitement in the air. No longer was the tidewater the sole theater of action. Stirring scenes were being enacted in the hinterland.

A new generation of leaders was emerging, schooled for the greater adventures still to come. The West was a new training ground. It offered acres, fertile and verdant. And immigrants wanted land. Not for them were the quit-rents of the seaboard. They cast longing eyes on the rich bottomlands of the Ohio and Mississippi Valley.

While the diplomats of Europe were sharpening their pens and their wits for the coming conflict, the pioneer stolidly made his way through the trackless forest, pitching his tent wherever he saw promise of crops and food and more permanent shelter. Through the forests stalked the Indian, sullen, resentful, nursing a smoldering hatred for the white invader which waited an excuse to flare into war. Catholic France was beginning to look to its defenses. Canada and the Mississippi Valley were to be held for the glory of the King and the Church.

Indian trails led over mountain gaps and passes, through gorges, and along river banks. Rivers, worming their way through the forests and valleys, resounded with new cries. Wooden wagon wheels creaked their tortuous way to this Mecca of pioneers. Canoes, bateaux, flatboats swayed their precarious way down the rivers which led to the lands of promise. All roads led to the West.

In 1744, in the "Journal of Treaty with Six Nations" drawn up at Lancaster, mention is made of Jews and Jewesses recently arrived from New York. Three years later, Richard Locke in writing of the religious population at Lancaster said, "Here are ten families of Jews." The population of Lancaster Jewry was augmented by Isaac Nunez Henriques, a member of a prominent family of Georgia Jews. Between them, Simon and Henriques acquired the deed, as trustees, to the Jewish cemetery at Lancaster, in 1747. Of a regularly organized congregation there seems to be no trace. Lancaster Jews supported the Philadelphia congregation, and met for worship at the home of Joseph Simon, where a kind of private synagogue was maintained.

Joseph Simon was the backbone of this group. He and another coreligionist, Joseph Solomon, were the first two Jews to be naturalized in Lancaster. This was in 1749. They were sworn on the Old Testament. Simon was a man of boundless energy, who led a life of constant excitement. He had an interest in every sort of enterprise, and an incurable bent for partnerships. Among his business associates were Barnard and Michael Gratz, David Franks, Levy Andrew Levy, Solomon Etting, Robert Callender, William Trent, George Croghan, Alexander Lowry and others. It seems to have been his practice to induct his sons-in-law into the business. Levy Andrew Levy, Michael Gratz, Levy Phillips and Solomon Etting married daughters of Joseph Simon. He began as a shopkeeper. Then followed an active development of the Indian trade, and he "soon became one of the most prominent Indian traders and merchants,

and one of the largest land-holders in Pennsylvania . . . his enterprizes extending not only over Pennsylvania, but to Ohio, and
Illinois, and to the Mississippi River."

Joseph Simon had additional headquarters at Fort Pitt, to which
the Shawnee were encouraged to bring furs. A firm of rival competitors, Baynton, Wharton and Morgan, eager to divert the lucrative pelt trade to themselves, established a rival post on the Scioto
River. On October 4, 1766, the Fort Pitt traders registered a protest
with Sir William Johnson, Indian Superintendent, against the establishment of this rival post. Joseph Simon was one of those who was
opposed to the rival Scioto settlement. The Lancaster group of merchants were part of the new and the wonderful times. They were at
the threshold of the Western frontier.

The bateaux floating down the Ohio and its tributaries carried
cargoes of coarse clothing, foodstuffs, rum, wine, tea, coffee, sugar,
spices, blankets, ammunition, soap, shoes, and countless other articles
invaluable to the sparsely populated settlements. Among the "Indian
goods," trinkets, bits of jewelry, cheap laces, earrings, and armbands
were included.

Pack trains followed the Indian trails to the interior. When in
1755, General Braddock arrived at the Big Crossing settlement, his
troops met the pack trains of Joseph Simon. Eight years later a pack
train belonging to twenty-two traders was attacked by Indians at
Bloody Run. Most of the cargo, valued at eighty thousand pounds, was
lost. Some of the pack-carriers were killed. In 1768, William Trent
presented a claim to the Indians for indemnity in behalf of the traders.
They secured title to a vast tract of land. Of the twenty-two men
whose claims were thus recognized by the Indian chiefs, David
Franks, Joseph Simon and Levy Andrew Levy were Jews. The
Indiana Land Company was formed. The land owned was augmented
by another grant to Joseph Simon and associates in 1773. Jews
whose names occur in the second land grant are: Joseph Simon,
Levy Andrew Levy, Moses Franks, Barnard and Michael Gratz,
Moses Franks, Jr., Jacob Franks and David Franks. But there was a
fly in the ointment. For Virginia refused to recognize the validity
of these deeds. All the potential landowners became involved in
long-drawn-out lawsuits.

Philadelphia was then a bustling, thriving city. It boasted substantial homes and substantial living. There were a number of

wharves and counting houses near the waterfront. Ships from distant places were like so many paintings hung in its harbor. Merchant ships and privateers docked side by side. Sonorous church chimes rang in many an important arrival, and greeted the farmers who brought their produce on market day. Along the river front farmers, businessmen, sailors, immigrants, Negroes, sober-clad Quakers and exotic privateers rubbed elbows. Life was good. Food was abundant. Eating became a fine art. It was practiced at home and at the taverns and coffee houses. Here Lucullus as well as George Fox had his following.

In this opulent, cosmopolitan, thriving city, Jews found their niche. By 1740 they owned a burial ground, always a sign of numbers. Here against its wall eleven years later a target for sharpshooting was set up. In the *Pennsylvania Gazette* of September, 1751, a notice was inserted asking "sportsmen to forbear (for the future) firing" against the cemetery wall, as the practice was found to be damaging to the tombstones. What it did to the spirits of Philadelphia Jewry is not stated. From 1740 on they met for regular worship. Here there were German as well as Sephardic Jews, and although the former were in a minority they made a definite place for themselves both in the business circles of their city and in its social life. Members of the Gratz and Franks families were people whose presence would enrich any community.

To the counting house of David Franks there had come one day a somewhat travel-worn young man whose name was Barnard Gratz. He was then about twenty-one years old. This youthful pilgrim had been born in Langendorf, which is in Upper Silesia. He and his brother Michael, two years his junior, had received a classical education in the little village of their birth, and on top of that had acquired a distinct "London finish" during a residence in England. This "London finish" meant adequate knowledge of how to dress, speak and deport oneself with genuine propriety. To such lengths was this gentility carried that one of his London cousins warned Michael that there was time enough for such fine manners after his life's ambition was realized. Michael wanted to be a "nabob."

They wrote Hebrew and Yiddish with ease, and had an adequate, though phonetic, knowledge of English. The geography of the day they knew reasonably well. Their mathematics was adequate for their business requirements. Their books were kept with systematic exactness. They could flourish a quill with the best of them, at times with copperplate precision, at other times lapsing into a more comfortable, fairly legible script. Both brothers made friends easily, had a boundless energy, a zest for life, a love of adventure, a flair for business, and a loyal devotion to family.

There is a portrait of Barnard Gratz (after he had become a successful merchant) by Thomas Sully, which portrays him as a shrewd, keen-eyed, stocky, short-necked man, with a high receding forehead, and a concentrated, earnest expression. His younger brother is a somewhat different type. He looks like a round-faced benevolent Pickwick, with a double chin, rotund body, small pudgy hands. The same high forehead is there, the same keen, penetrating eyes. It is the elder of the two brothers who first applied to David Franks for a position. He began working for Franks in 1754. An auspicious beginning it was. Barnard's employer was good-natured, sociable, and hospitable. He had married a non-Jew, was lax in his Jewish observances, was chiefly concerned in becoming a recognized member of the colonial gentry. His counting house was an excellent training school for an ambitious young man. Soon Barnard was eager to start out in business for himself. So he wrote to London urging that his brother Michael come over to take his place with David Franks, warning him, however, that the position called for "industry, and good nature, and no pride." Michael had no difficulty in filling his brother's shoes. He had begun on an adventurous career long before joining his brother. The struggle between England and France was not then confined to North America. Attention was centered on India as well. So Michael had set out for India during the years 1757 and 1758. The family had its finger on the pulse of two economic battlefronts. Barnard was in America, and Michael in India. Now Michael was ready in 1759, after making his will, to come to America.

Distant places always had a lure for Michael Gratz. Shortly after he took up his residence in North America, between the years 1759-63, his ledgers listed transactions with Georgia, Halifax, Guadaloupe, St. Christopher and London. At the same time, his brother Barnard was sending cargoes down waterways to the West, and becoming more and more of a factor in piercing the American wilderness, and in supplying the men who were so arduously engaged in pushing the American frontier to the Mississippi and beyond.

In 1761 we find Barnard Gratz sending an agent to Quebec. It took sixty days to make the voyage and the ship docked "a mear wreck." Barnard is informed that "your fourteen pair of leather breeches got all wet on board the sloop, likewise much rat-eaten. . . . I am likewise a sufferer," laments his agent, "as my chest and whatever articles I had in the cabin were under water." It is interesting that the writer finds that "shoes are a most unsalable article. . . . Neat dancing pumps would have sold well. Pumps and moccasins are wore in this place, Summer and Winter, by all except soldiers." Another market to the north was Newport. The Gratz brothers lost no time in making connections with the leaders of the Rhode Island Jewish community. So we find Jacob Rodriguez Rivera writing to Michael about personal as well as business matters. He includes greetings from the Lopez family as well as his own. The letter is written in informal manner, and argues a friendly familiarity between both groups.

Despite the fact that the two brothers signed the Non-Importation Resolutions, they managed to send heavy pack trains into the interior. In 1768 their agent, William Murray, established a flourishing outpost for the brothers Gratz in the Illinois country. A year later he reports goodly profits at Kaskaskia and calls for more goods. Late in the same year, Joseph Simon of Lancaster outfits a pack train for Ephraim Blaine. The Gratz brothers maintain representatives in London. They have business interests that range from Canada, down to the Mississippi and its tributaries, as well as along the Potomac. George Croghan and Joseph Simon transact business at Fort Pitt. In 1774 when William Murray gets word that some forty Indians have been killed by white people on the Ohio, he expresses concern for Joseph Simon who has not been heard from: "His scalp will be in danger on his return to Illinois." In 1775, Thomas Wharton writes to his brother complaining that Simon, Levy and others of the Lancaster group in the Indiana Company are too much disposed to a compromise with Virginia.

The extent of the Gratz operations in North America and the West Indies is too large to be discussed at length here. A whole volume is devoted to a partial summary of their activities.

Some hazardous journeys were delegated by the brothers to others. But many a dangerous voyage to distant places was undertaken by the two brothers themselves. Michael usually made his will on the eve of an expedition. Just before setting out for St. Eustatia and Curaçao in 1765, Michael drew up a new will revoking "all former Wills and Powers." He informed his brother of his safe arrival at St. Kitts in a very short note, it "Being just Sh'b't." The Sabbath was observed even in the outposts!

One of the best ways we have of looking closely at our protagonists is through their elaborately posed portraits and through their casual, unstudied letters. The former are posed as to mien and apparel, often inscrutable as to expression. It is as if by closing their lips and placing a well-bred mask on their faces they meant to defy future generations to pierce the façade, to guess at the drama and conflict and secret life within.

Portraits of colonial Jews and their dames show them to have adopted wholeheartedly the dress of the period. With the possible exception of the visiting rabbis or travelers, the eighteenth-century Jew tried to dress like his neighbors. Their contacts with the European markets and their connections with the London, Lisbon and West Indian sources of supply meant that in the matter of finery their ladies need not stint. Men too affected the waistcoats, knee-breeches, powdered wigs, buckled shoes and ruffled shirts of the period. Let anyone examine the orders of Washington to his London agent to be convinced that a military career and interest in dress were not incompatible.

It is much easier to generalize about externals than to interpret the inner life of these people. One wonders what mental processes were concealed behind the smiles and smirks of the elaborately dressed women. What were their thoughts, emotions, the details of their daily life? So far very little of this kind of material is available. The richest single source of information is in the papers of the Gratz family. An occasional letter by Miriam Simon Gratz to her husband or her brother-in-law lifts the curtain, and takes us into the warm intimate family circle of a Jewish pioneer.

Miriam's early letters to her husband are written in a stilted, dignified, somewhat formal vein. During his frequent absences from home, she familiarized herself with the details of the Gratz business. Michael was well posted on all that went on.

"My dear Michael," she writes in 1774, "I received your agreeable form by Mr. Lyon, which gave me infinite pleasure to hear that you are well." Then like a true daughter of the prudent Joseph Simon, she tells him that she will have to postpone her trip to Lancaster because of unfinished business in Philadelphia. A lucid business report follows. She signs herself "Your ever loving and affectionate wife until death." Then the feminine postscript: "Do come home as soon as you can." The wealth of her affection for her family is evidenced again and again.

In addition to strong family ties, there was a feeling of kinship between Jewish communities on the Western Continent. In a surprisingly short time after his arrival at a new place, a Jewish newcomer would establish contact with coreligionists in distant places. We have seen how communities called upon each other for help in building synagogues, and with what readiness they sent the poor off to other congregations. We have noticed too the commercial interdependence of Newport, New York, Philadelphia, Charleston.

Whatever the cause, the effect of such an economic network between commercial centers, was a very salutary one. When we recall the difficulties of travel and the resultant isolation of groups for months on end, the loose structure of the colonies becomes apparent. It is true the "essential forms of colonial culture were English in their origin." But it is equally true that "the eminent advocates for the Scotch, Irish, Dutch, Swiss, Welsh, Swedes, and Jews" who "have entered pleas against this ruling" have excellent reasons for claiming some peculiar contribution to the prevailing English culture.

The contribution of the Jew was that he triumphed over the untraveled wilderness. His pack trains carried much-wanted goods through the trackless forests: needles, and calico, and medicine, and sugar, and spices and tea. Many a Swiss Family Robinson or Dutch or English, as the case may be, marooned in the backwoods, welcomed gladly the solitary trader, or the pack train, bearing luxuries and necessities and news.

Maryland, founded by Catholics, was primarily designed by the Calverts as a place of refuge for members of their sect. Its Toleration Act was notoriously hostile to non-Christians. This Act was more honored in the breach than in the observance. For although it provided that those who denied the divinity of Jesus be put to death, it was never carried out. Following the passage of the Naturalization Law of 1740, a number of Jews availed themselves of that privilege.

In the early eighteenth century a Colonel Levy was condemned to death in Virginia for his share in an insurrection in 1711. But the record of Michael Franks and Jacob Myer was happier. They were with George Washington in his Ohio campaign. A landowning family, the Israel family, was known in Virginia from 1757. They are immortalized by "Israel's Gap," a Virginia mountain pass. A Hezekiah Levy was a member of a Masonic Lodge to which George Washington belonged.

The Carolinas and Georgia from their earliest days had Jewish inhabitants. Here too as elsewhere, the Jew adopted the customs, habits and point of view of his environment. Religiously he may differ, psychologically he is at one with his surroundings. The artisan, craftsman, mechanic or petty farmer was attracted to the north of Carolina. The more ambitious immigrant who wished to simulate the life of the aristocracy at home, who hungered for vast estates and a new feudalism, went south. From the beginning there were more slaves and indentured servants in the south than in the north. After an indentured servant had served his term, he frequently settled down near his former master on a small land holding. This group was augmented by runaway servants who settled in North Carolina in the vicinity of Albemarle. They too lived on small farms. Social distinctions were much more pronounced here. Employers did not fraternize with their former servants. Class lines were sharply drawn. The freed serving man formed the nucleus of the despised poor white class of the South. The history of Jews in North Carolina dates from 1665, when some people came from Barbados to find refuge there.

Governor Archdale's interpreter in South Carolina in 1695 was a Jew. Two years later there was passed an act "for the making aliens free of this part of the province and for granting liberty of conscience to all Protestants." Of the sixty-four nonconformists who availed themselves of its privileges, there were four Jewish merchants. In each case the applicant was described as "an alien of ye Jewish Nation." Simon Valentine, one of this group, is known to have been a resident of Charleston in 1696, and from that year on is mentioned often in the records. He was the earliest known Jewish landholder in South Carolina. He was endenizened prior to 1709. Soon there were a number of others who acquired large tracts of land in addition to carrying on mercantile activities and sharing in the events of early colonial history.

Even in the very early days of the colony, Jews from diverse places were found there or had business connections with relatives in the Carolinas. Thus in 1710, a resident of New York, one Abraham Isack, about to set out to sea, makes his will in South Carolina. Jacob Franks of New York had a correspondence with his nephew, Moses Solomons, who with David Franks was a member of the St. Andrew's Society of Charleston. Jews and Huguenots actually voted for members of the Assembly in 1703. This temerity was not unrebuked. Great alarm was expressed and protest lodged in London against so pernicious a practice. Nothing came of it however. There is no later evidence here of any similar interference with the Jew's exercise of voting priviliges.

The Jews of Charleston were a cosmopolitan group. To that community men of many lands were attracted. In 1749 the Congregation Beth Elohim was organized. Moses Cohen who had come from London was elected Rabbi. The religious community was modeled on the one in Bevis Marks of London. The Reader of the Congregation was Isaac Da Costa. He was a native of London, visited Newport, met Ezra Stiles and so found his way into the immortal *Diary*. In addition to his duties in the newly organized synagogue, Da Costa was a merchant, an administrator of an estate and with his partner was widely interested in shipping under the firm name of Da Costa and Farr. He was decidedly a "joiner." He was a member of King Solomon's Lodge, No. 1, the oldest in the colony, and was a steward of the Palmetto Society. When the British came, he refused to "take protection" and so was banished from the colony. His possessions were confiscated. He made his way with his son to Philadelphia and having survived countless dangers died "by the wound of a splinter in his hand." Joseph Tobias, Parnas of Beth Elohim, was endenizened in Charleston in 1739. His grandson Jacob was a member of Captain Drayton's Militia in 1775. The congregation had its school. It had its cemetery on Coming Street. The Hebrew Benevolent Society was established in 1784. The Hebrew Orphan Society founded in 1801 was the first organization of its kind to place orphans in foster homes. Simple tradesmen they may have been. Yet their record is impressive.

The Jewish merchants of those early days dealt in the usual imported staples which included both luxuries and necessaries. They advertised "Good Old Barbados Rum," as well as wine, sugar and lime juice. They bought rice and indigo. They dealt in land and horses. Even Negroes figure in their advertisements.

Besides merchants, there were men who brought technical skills to the new colonies. Such a person was Moses Lindo who was an expert dyer and was known as an excellent judge of cochineal and indigo. He came to South Carolina "to purchase Indico of the Growth and Manufacture of this Province, and to remit the same to his Constituents in London." He was held in public esteem, a petition being circulated to make him a public inspector. For ten years Moses Lindo was Surveyor and Inspector-General of Indigo for South Carolina. Lindo's hobby was the study of herbs and plants to be used as dyes and medicines. In the *Philosophical Transactions* of 1763 he reports a new dye. He also reports in a letter to the *Gazette* "the CURE of that grievous and common disease among the negroes called YAWS."

In 1773 there came to South Carolina a young English Jew named Francis Salvador. He was a member of a well-known, much respected, wealthy Jewish family of Portuguese and Dutch antecedents. Their Hebrew family name was Jessurun Rodrigues, which in the course of their wanderings underwent many mutations. Eventually the family took root in England, just when we do not know. Their denization papers, however, are dated in 1719. In 1745 a grant was made permitting the family to use its ancient coat of arms. The Salvadors reached financial eminence. Members of their family ranked among the merchant princes of the day. Joseph Salvador was the first Jewish director in the East India Company, as well as the president of the Portuguese congregation of London. This family was noted for its generosity and for frequent loans they made to the British Crown.

In addition to amassing wealth, they acquired large tracts of land in South Carolina and other colonies. When, owing to the failure of the Dutch East India Company and the earthquake at Lisbon, the family fortunes shrank, Francis decided to emigrate to South Carolina.

He left his wife and four children in England and came here to prepare a home for them. To the family holdings more land was added, until he owned close to seven thousand acres of land. He bought slaves and settled down to the routine of a gentleman planter. His excellent English education, his extensive travels, together with great personal charm, endeared him to his associates.

With his friend Richard Rapley, who lived with him at Cornacre or Coronoca, he identified himself with the Revolutionary element of his colony and was soon recognized as a leader not only of his community but also of the Provincial Congress which met at Charleston and in which he served as a deputy. He took part in those stirring sessions when statehood was first considered and finally achieved by his colony. Together with C. C. Pinckney, famous Revolutionary statesman, he was present on the historic day when the Provincial Congress became the General Assembly of the State of South Carolina. Francis Salvador had thrown himself into Revolutionary politics with all the ardor and zeal by which Jews are so often identified when a cause bears promise of universal freedom and overthrowal of despotism.

The leading patriots of South Carolina accepted him as one of them. Associated with Salvador on committees in the Provincial Congress were C. C. Pinckney, Patrick Calhoun, John L. Gervais, Edward Rutledge, LeRoy Hammond and others. According to one authority, Salvador received a splendid liberal education including all the accomplishments suitable to his wealth and place in society. "His manners, were those of a polished gentleman; and as such he was intimately known and esteemed, by the first revolutionary characters in South Carolina. He also possessed their confidence in a great degree; as his literary correspondence with them, sufficiently proves."[18] Again and again his name is found on prominent legislative committees. Often it is he who presents the report for his associates. That he is known to be "of the Jewish nation" is no detriment to him. His advice carries weight in the legislative halls. His help is very welcome when hostilities begin. The Cherokee Indians, whom the patriots made repeated attempts to conciliate, were won over by the British and encouraged to attack the frontier. When they heard that the British fleet was arrived and was stationed in Charleston harbor, the Indians, on July 1, 1776, overran the frontier and the holocaust began. Some of the refugees took shelter at the home of Salvador. As soon as he learned the news, Salvador, like Paul Revere, "forthwith mounted his horse, and galloped to Major Andrew Williamson's residence, twenty-eight miles from thence." The people of the border were practically without arms or ammunition. They were completely at the mercy of the Indians. Major Williamson tried to gather men to repulse the Cherokee invasion, but "so great was the panic, that although he dispatched expresses on all sides, only forty men were collected in two days. With these, accompanied by Mr. Salvador, he marched on the 3rd of July, to the late Captain Smith's house."

It was in this campaign that Francis Salvador lost his life. The Indians had planned a surprise attack on the patriots. Major Williamson's horse was shot down under him

and Mr. Francis Salvador, who was riding alongside of the Major, was shot through the body and left leg: and falling among the bushes, he was unfortunately discovered by the Indians immediately, and scalped. . . . He retained his senses to the last; and when Major Williamson came up and spoke to him, he anxiously asked whether the enemy was beaten? And upon being told that they were, he replied, he rejoiced at it: when shaking the Major by the hand, he bade him farewell—and died.[19]

So ends the life story of the first Jew to give up his life for the cause of American Independence.

Although German or Ashkenazic Jews were in the minority in Charleston, they were by no means less important to its communal life. Philip Hart, who had emigrated from Hamburg, became one of the officials of the congregation of Charleston—in itself no small achievement. He had the energy typical of his group. A philanthropically inclined merchant he was, whose name is found as a contributor to a number of charitable institutions. He fought in the Revolution in Lushington's militia company. His charitable and communal activities were continued until his death in 1796.

The Sephardic community of London, like many another metropolitan group, was perplexed by the poor they had always with them. But poverty and debt were not confined to the Jewish section of the population. James Oglethorpe, like Charles Dickens in another generation, sympathized with the wretched inmates of the debtors' prisons. He enlisted the co-operation of a number of other philanthropists and a movement for a new colony was launched. The colony of Georgia was established in 1732. In the following year came its first contingent of settlers.

Among the earliest of settlers in Georgia were some Jews who brought with them a Scroll of the Law and a circumcision box. Before long they had received a gift of a Hanukkah Menorah and some Hebrew books. They were ready to conquer the wilderness! The manner of their arrival was in itself quite a story.

In order to collect funds to finance the transportation of settlers, a number of committees were named to collect money. One of these groups consisted of three Jews—Salvador, Baron Suasso and Da Costa, who was the first Jewish director of the Bank of England. They gathered not only money but Jewish colonists as well. For some one among them had hit on the idea that Jewish money should finance Jewish immigrants. They got some twelve families of German Jews together, chartered a ship, and sent them off to Georgia. When the trustees got wind of this scheme, their anger was great. That their pet colony should be thus overrun was unthinkable. They demanded the surrender of both money and "commissions." In vain. The committee did not give up its "commissions" until their purpose was accomplished.

To make matters still worse for the harassed directors, some forty Portuguese Jews of independent means decided to emigrate to Georgia at about the same time. Of this number a few were refugees from the Portuguese Inquisition. Whether the indigent German Jews and the more affluent Portuguese came on the same ship is a matter of doubt. But there is no doubt as to their joint status in Georgia. They were considered members of the same "category"—a fact probably unpalatable to the Sephardim who disliked snobbery but practiced it with a high hand.

Oglethorpe heard loud outcries from the trustees. He was asked not to encourage the Jews. He was appealed to, to prevent their settling in Georgia. Nevertheless in the face of opposition in England and in Georgia, Oglethorpe accepted these unwelcome pilgrims. He wrote to the trustees in praise of their thrift, industry, and dependability. He particularly mentioned the medical exertions of Dr. Nunez in caring for the sick of the colony. The trustees in reply asked Oglethorpe to pay Dr. Nunez for his services, but under no circumstances to hand out any land to him or to his coreligionists. But Oglethorpe had a happy faculty of ignoring such instructions as he did not care to accept. A congregation was formed in 1734 and the Jews were at home in Georgia.

Jews were allowed to buy land. That this land was sold rather than distributed seems obvious, for the German Jews received none. The deeds are all made out to the wealthy Portuguese contingent, and in many cases they were allotted more than one farm. In one case, David Cohen Del Monte received thirty farms. This is three times as much as was allowed to any Christian in the colony. Evidently each man was permitted to buy as much land as he wished.

Georgia was intended by its founders to be a silk-raising and wine-producing colony. The Portuguese Jews, both the original settlers and those who came later, were experts in these industries. One of these Sephardic settlers, Abraham De Lyon was so successful as a vintner that his vineyard became a showplace. "Nothing has given me so much Pleasure since my Arrival as what I found here," writes William Stephens, agent of the trustees, in 1737, after a visit to De Lyon's farm.

In a tract published in Charleston in 1741 dealing with Georgia, the inhabitants among other grievances include one of interest to us: "*Abraham De Leon, a Jew*, who had been for many years a Vineron in *Portugal* and a Free-holder in *Savannah*, cultivated several kinds of Grapes . . . to great Perfection." Oglethorpe withheld from him a subsidy, granted him by the trustees for the purpose of further developing this industry. His work as a vintner was considered of such importance by his neighbors that they wanted it subsidized.

The hardships of building homes in a new land should have sufficed. Man-made strife complicated matters. Stubbornly the Portuguese Jews refused absolutely to have anything to do with German Jews. The lines were rigidly drawn.

Four things kept the Sephardic and Ashkenazic elements apart: status, money, land and place of birth. Were it not for the journal of a Protestant minister who came to Georgia with his congregation in 1734, this little German Jewish group would have been completely forgotten. As it is, when the German Jews heard of the arrival of seventy-eight Salzburgers and their minister, they felt that upon them rested the obligation of making these *"landsleute"* feel at home. They could not do enough for the Christian newcomers.

Times grew bad in Georgia. Gradually early settlers began to leave the colony. By 1741, this exodus had become so general that the Journal of the Trustees states, "On the West side of Savannah lies the Township lots of the Jews, all gone to other Colonies except three or four." Of these some went to South Carolina, others to New York, still others to Pennsylvania. But by 1750, most of these wanderers found their way back to Georgia. In the following year, the trustees sent a converted Jew, Joseph Ottolenghi, to superintend the silk industry in the colony. He was born in Italy and emigrated to London where he joined the Episcopal Church.

After their return to Georgia, Jews adjusted more readily. Among the members of the Masonic fraternity, a branch of which was organized by Oglethorpe, there were at least four Jews. One of these, Moses Nunez, also held the post of Searcher for the Port of Savannah and Indian Interpreter.

Now it was the vast river valley that became the setting for a drama of conflict, of plot and counterplot. This rivalry grew more acute as the economic importance of the Mississippi Valley became evident. The English undersold the French. The French became of necessity more successful in winning the confidence and friendly co-operation of the Indians. Canadians built forts in an attempt to cut off the English. British economic advance continued from the Hudson Bay to the Mississippi. King William's War and Queen Anne's War, although they germinated in Europe, easily took root in American soil. Soon any hostility in Europe was like a stone flung into water, the rings grew wider and wider and eventually touched the North American Continent. The keener the economic rivalry between France and England in Europe, in India, on the Guinea Coast, the more marked that rivalry in the Mississippi Valley. English land speculators and fur traders recognized no boundary to the west. The land was fertile, well watered, accessible, well stocked with game.

Food was abundant. The peltry trade was brisk and remunerative. Far-visioned men saw the valleys peopled with new settlers, and were eager to buy land for resale. The Ohio Land Company, consisting of prominent Virginians and Englishmen, was organized in 1749. Céleron de Bienville, who knew the ways of the forests, and a large group of French Canadians were chosen to defend the French interests in the Ohio.

The plans of the French were definite. They would accept no English settlements west of the Alleghenies.

It was at this time that George Washington appeared on the scene. Lieutenant Governor Robert Dinwiddie of Virginia sent this twenty-two-year-old surveyor to the French commandant to demand the immediate withdrawal of the French. In the delegation accompanying George Washington were two Jews, Michael Franks and Jacob Myer. The French answered by erecting Fort Duquesne on the Ohio. Washington tried to dislodge the French in vain. General Braddock was sent from England. He too met with defeat. The Seven Years' War was on.

In the meanwhile David Franks was given the commission of supplying the Virginia expedition. On June 27, 1758, David Franks writes to Washington: "I wish you a Successful Campaign." The war was to prove basic training for the conflict few men expected.

On every hand there is documentary evidence that Jews were in the thick of things, that the dust of the road and the smell of gunfire was in their nostrils. In the account of the "Startling Experience of a Jewish Trader" we read of "a trading Jew," named Chapman.

An entry in the *Diary of the Siege of Detroit* by Major Roberts, dated May 22, 1763, reads:

They had taken Chapman and his merchandize, as also a Cannoe with five Englishmen coming from Sandusky yesterday, among whom were Mr. Smallman and two Jews.[20]

On the sixteenth of May, 1760, Captain William Trent, Joseph Simon, David Franks and Levy Andrew Levy entered into a partnership in the western fur trade. In the course of their business association Joseph Simon, David Franks and later Michael Gratz acquired from Captain Trent a seven thousand and five hundred-acre tract of land in Cumberland County, Pennsylvania. This group (Franks, Trent, Simon and Company) was, according to the U.S. Supreme Court, "the heaviest loser by Indian raids during the Pontiac war." Land was then cheaper than money. According to a letter to Michael Gratz,

Peter R. Livingston, because of the money famine in New York, is compelled to draw money against unsold goods in Philadelphia. This condition is widely prevalent. Attacks by Indians, always a menace to the westbound pack trains, became more serious in 1763 and flamed into formidable proportions under the leadership of the avenging Pontiac, to whom the white man was an execrable enemy.

Early in 1763, David Franks informed Michael Gratz of the uprising:

The Indians have begun a war near the Forts; killed and taken several people and traders, and Levy (?) is a prisoner.

Sporadic Indian outbreaks were frequent. Jewish traders, like others, accepted these dangers. The extent to which the success of a Western venture depended on the humor of the Redskins may be seen from the following letter of Michael to his elder brother, who is in London, in 1769:

The Seneca Indians are much discontented on account of the purchase money that was given at the last treaty to the nether Indians, and their share not yet received *by* them, which makes them very insolent and daring, though it is thought they want nothing but presents and rob, if they can, *in the* meantime. So I am *in* no ways sorry that we did not send any more, as I am much afraid of what we have there already, if an Indian war should happen.

He goes on to describe the activities of the "Black Boys" who deal in Indian contraband, such as firearms. These "Black Boys" are white backwoodsmen who painted like Indians and took great liberties with the traders, usually cheating both Indians and white men. On another occasion, their Illinois agent writes with grave concern about a rumor that reached him that some forty Indians had been killed by whites on the Ohio. "If this intelligence is true it would be much against us and greatly endanger my scalp."

Levy Andrew Levy was often in the midst of Indian business, warfare and intrigue. John Campbell relies greatly on information furnished by Levy. "I have heard nothing from Pittsburgh," he writes, "but what Mr. Levy acquainted you of. I am in great hopes that the unfortunate affair will be made up for the present at least. . . . Mr. Levy will write you if we want any Indian goods." In a letter to Levy, in 1774, Campbell tells him of a threatened Indian attack:

Almost all the settlements on the West side of the Monongahela River are deserted and a great number of people on this side of the mountains are moved off. . . . Send off immediately to Philadelphia for the 400 weight, powder, for the garrison and for a union flag of five yards to hoist for the Fort. . . . The spirit of the people is inflamed so that they can scarcely be restrained from falling on the Indians before the fate of the traders at the Shawnee towns is known,—if they are killed or captivated. . . . I expect there will be near two thousand men in Indian country soon.

The two Gratz brothers were becoming more and more concerned by the state of Indian affairs on the Ohio. Barnard writes to his brother:

Yours of the 24th of May (1774) is duly received, with the packet of news of Indian affairs on the Ohio, which was the first account here. I showed it to Sir William Johnson, who blames Cresap much. I am very sorry such a thing happened as I am afraid our traders may suffer, though I hope they will get in safe.

To the Gratz brothers the Western front becomes more important after 1765. Up to that year they had been engaged in a lively importing business. Michael Gratz went as far as to purchase his first ship *The Rising Sun* from his Newport correspondents. He visited Curaçao and St. Christopher in 1765 and in spite of being shipwrecked, reached Philadelphia in time to sign the Non-Importation Agreements. The embargo on British goods was carefully observed. The East learned in a crude way to make necessary articles at home. Patriots spurned imported finery. Homespun goods were worn with pride by a people becoming nationally conscious.

Now the Gratz brothers, like most of their coreligionists, resolutely turn their backs on England, and concentrate all of their activities on affairs west of the Alleghenies. They become more closely allied with Joseph Simon and his associates. Their affairs are developed to ever greater importance. They become landowners on a grand scale. Their correspondence with prominent men is vast. It concerns everything from sale of land to politics.

In 1772 the Gratz brothers write to Croghan congratulating him "on the good news of the Chartered Government." During the following year, Barnard makes a trip north where he tries unsuccessfully to dispose of some of their joint land holding. He writes of this to Croghan and then goes on:

But on my arrival at Philadelphia, Governor Franklin was here. I waited on him and told him the reason of my not having sold any of the land.

When Sir William Johnson dies, Miriam Simon Gratz writes the news to her husband. "By the first opportunity, you'll let Mr. Croghan know about Sir William's death." On the eve of the Revolution a group of nine men address themselves to Samuel Wharton to ask him for the original Indian deed on their land grant, in order that it may be recorded in Virginia. They style themselves "a number of Sufferers by the Indian War in 1763." Among the "sufferers" are William Trent, Joseph Simon and George Croghan. In April of 1776, Joseph Simon and Levy A. Levy receive a letter from Thomas Wharton assuring them that he is looking after their interests.

The Gratzes also become interested in the Illinois country.

It took the British two years to take over the Illinois country. For the Indians there made a determined stand against the British. In 1765 both sides were ready for peace. The man chosen for the task was a wily diplomat, a successful Indian trader, a grandiloquent Irishman. It was George Croghan.

On the twenty-third of March, 1765, Croghan had bought from Joseph Simon and Levy A. Levy a consignment of goods for the Illinois country. The total amounted to more than two thousand pounds. It consisted of clothing, blankets and much Indian goods, such as hair trinkets, hair plates, silver armbands, "Ear Bobbs, and Bells."

Joseph Simon made frequent consignments to the Illinois country, as did David Franks, who was a member of Franks, Trent, Simon and Company. It was about this time that Simon's ventures in Indian trade became so extensive as to merit an introduction to Sir William Johnson.

In 1767 the Reverend Thomas Barton of Lancaster wrote to Sir William Johnson as follows:

WORTHY SIR:-
. . . Give me leave, Sir, to introduce to your knowledge Mr. Joseph Simon, a worthy, honest Jew and Principal merchant of this place, who has always been employed as a victualler to the troops that have been quartered here and has given general satisfaction.

When the Gratz brothers entered the Illinois market, they chose as their agent a canny Scotch-Irishman with a rich and sparkling sense of humor. William Murray's letters form the comic relief in this somewhat complicated and involved Illinois venture. "A plague!" he writes, being down with a malarial chill. "Why did you not send some good spirits, sugar, tea, Port wine, if possible, and some little *et ceteras* for my own use? . . . I must go to bed and sweat. God bless you." Michael's answer to this was that not want of feeling, but scarcity of goods "on account of Non-Importation" prevented him from sending the supplies demanded by Murray.

During the years 1770-73 the firms of Joseph Simon and his associates, and the firm of David Franks and Company which included the Gratzes, Murray, Rumsey, Ross, and David Franks, gradually increased their operations. Murray remained in the Illinois country until after the outbreak of the Revolutionary War.

William Murray continues the acquisition of land for himself and his associates. In 1774-75, he secures the Wabash Grant. This was but one of a number of land schemes and companies in which directly and indirectly Jewish merchants were concerned. George Croghan was the organizer of the Grand Ohio Company, on which many prominent men had their eye. Benjamin Franklin wrote to his son that "the Ohio Affair seems now near conclusion," but cautioned him to say nothing as yet, "for many things happen between the cup and the lip." Wharton was sponsor of the Vandalia Grant in the Ohio region. This was followed by the Wabash Grant. Simon and Campbell became interested in the Ohio Company of Virginia and a little scheme fathered by the Gratz, the "Indiana." These are but a few of the land ventures and projects which were for the most part extinguished when the colonists mobilized their strength to overthrow their common enemy, England.

Jean Baptiste Le Moyne, Sieur de Bienville founded New Orleans in 1718.[21] In the following year two Jews, Jacob and Romain David, a shoemaker and a tailor, settled in a near-by plantation. Three other Jewish immigrants joined the colony in the same year; one of the three was a soldier, Louis Solomons.

Other traces of Jewish residence in Louisiana exist. They are slim and fragmentary. In the *Louisiana Historical Quarterly*, two Jews, Mendes and Solis, are mentioned as factors in the developing of the cane sugar industry.

There is, however, one hitherto unknown aspect of Louisiana Judaica which after more than two centuries has just come to light.[21] This story hinges on a document in the Ayer Collection of the Newberry Library, pointing to Elias Stultheus, called *"le Juif."*[22]

It is one of those episodes in history which involves drama, adventure, romance, intrigue, excitement, plot and counterplot. The setting is graphically portrayed here. The story of "the real Manon" belongs in it. Curiously enough, Baron de Villiers' account goes back to Dr.

Michel Nostradamus, a Marrano of St. Remy, astrologer and physician. It was to his Jewish ancestry that Nostradamus attributed
his gift of prophecy and to that prophecy that Villiers dated the fore-
knowledge of French empire in Louisiana. He predicted that France
would extend her domain to far-off countries. To Villiers the *"pays
lointain"* of Nostradamus might well have meant Louisiana.

New Orleans from the first days looked like "a very miserable
village." But from its clustering legends, from its romances, licit and
illicit, dozens of operas, novels and *romans* have been written, not the
least of them dealing with "the sinner Manon [who] is too much the
symbol of a courtesan to own a birth certificate." But there is sufficient evidence to suspect that this woman was a stowaway in the hold
of the *Dauphine*, as many others probably were on other ships. Of
Manon we need but add that her real name was Anique Benjamin.

All early historians, all documents, "dusty archives" and later works
are unanimous in their agreement on one subject—that there were
Jews in the Louisiana country from the earliest years of the eighteenth
century. Terrage, Penicaut, La Harpe, Margry, René Le Conte,
Cochut, Thiers, Deiler, all agree on the presence of Jews in varying
numbers in the lower Mississippi basin. Many works mention *"le Juif"*
Elias Stultheus who came to play a very important role in one chapter
of early Louisiana history. He was the chief director of the vast Law
concessions.

John Law, central figure in a grand scheme known as the Mississippi
Bubble, whose agent Elias Stultheus was, is the forerunner of such
men as Ivar Kruger and Samuel Insull. By a "curious process of complex annexation and assimilation, John Law had succeeded in erecting
the most stupendous financial fabric that has ever been presented to
the world."

To manage his vast colonizing and financial enterprise in the Mississippi Valley he chose a Jewish agent, *"particulier de Law, le Juif
Elias Stultheus."* Law furnished authority by remote control. Stultheus was the director on the scene.

Villiers writes:

From 1717 up to 1722 not only vagabonds, deserters and smugglers
were sent to Louisiana as an administrative measure. The government of
the Regency deported likewise a certain number of people of standing.
The names of these exiles cannot be found in the general correspondence
and many items concerning them seem to have been destroyed inten-
tionally.[23]

Could some of these exiles, who were not the sweepings of French cities but "people of standing" and *whose records were deliberately destroyed*, could some of them have been Jews? Such historical sabotage had been used against the Jews before. Among the *Documents* in Margry, we read that there came on seven ships from France *"plus de quatre mille personnes, tant Francois qu'Allemands et Juifs."* The fact that the director-general in charge of the new colonization was a Jew, that Jews came here and became literally lost people, all of this requires further study. It is akin to "the policy of mystery and secrecy" of Portugal.

Of the hazards, and the conditions under which the crossing was made, conditions well described as "murderous," we have an excellent account. It also shows the active role Elias Stultheus had in the settlements of New France which took the settlers as far as the Arkansas.

In Louisiana nothing was prepared to receive the colonists. All of them were lacking provisions, medicine and clothing. Instead of leading them immediately toward the interior of the country, they were made to wait on the sandy coast of the Mississippi delta. One party of Germans died at Nouveau-Biloxi, where they had been living close together. They died of misery or of undulant fever, the scourge of this country, but their stay in this country had been a short one.

Under the direction of a special agent of Law, the Jew Elias Stultheus, the survivors left and went to the concession of Arkansas at the end of spring. Their number was diminished to such a degree that the plan of settling some of them at the Détour aux Anglais had to be abandoned. Immediately they began to cultivate land which was still very swampy and quite unsuited for Europeans to work in the open.[24]

It is extremely difficult for the historian, from the passenger lists available, to identify those who were Jews. Let us cite two examples here. Only those who like Stultheus were called *"le Juif"* may be spoken of with certainty. Among the passengers on the death-carrying ships were families named Heidel and Zweig, translated later to Labranche.

Usually such settlers were lumped under the general designation *"Les Allemands."* Says Deiler:

As Penicaut informed us that in 1719 the ship *"Les Deux Freres"* brought a number of German people, "with all sorts of merchandise and effects which belonged to them," and as these evidently were people of some means, who wanted to become independent settlers, we may assume that they were the founders of *"le premier ancien village allemand,"* one and a half miles inland from the Mississippi River.[25]

"Law's Germans" were sent up the Mississippi River to New Orleans. Then up the Arkansas River. Their land "extends about forty miles up the Mississippi on both banks."

How many of the settlers were Jews, we do not know. There is a Bavarian immigrant, for example, named Simon Kuhn. One of his daughters married a Labranche (Zweig). There were many others of this group that are open to question.

Deiler, who has done persistent and thorough research in this field, traced the channels of one transplanted name:

Remarkable was the fate of the name "Hofmann." The forms Ofman, Aufman, Eaufman, Haufman, Ophman, Oghman, Ocman, Hochman, Haukman, Hacmin, Aupemane, Augman, Olphman, and Ocmane were not the only changes that occurred. The family came from Baden and thus "de Bade" was often added to the name. In course of time the people forgot the meaning of "de Bade," and a new name was formed, "Badeau," with a feminine form, "Badeauine."[26]

Even Elias Stultheus may have had another name, as well as another spelling, for we learn that Law's agent on the Arkansas was called Levens. We have no way of knowing whether another Jewish agent whose name may have derived from Levin or Levinson assisted Elias in his many affairs.

La Compagnie des Indes had a very brief but stormy existence. The year 1720 saw the financial empire which Law had managed to evolve, totter and collapse. On the shores of the Mississippi delta, in the harbors of New Orleans and New Biloxi, men with heartbreak written on their weather-beaten faces watched in vain for the help they hoped for but which did not come.

When the news of the collapse of Law's vast financial structure finally reached the stranded settlers, they were at their wits' end. Both the Compagnie in France and the bewildered settlers in New France had no plan of action. Their hopes had been so high, the actual situation so grim and unpromising. They had barely cleared the ground, barely had time to erect rude shelter. Crops had not yet been planted. They had been led to believe that the Compagnie would stand in the role of paterfamilias. Now they were deprived of leadership, of sustenance, of authority. John Law was a bankrupt and a fugitive. His agent made a valiant effort to carry on.

It seems incomprehensible that the directors of the company in Louisiana, under these circumstances, should have waited from the 4th of June to beyond the middle of November of the same year to decide to take Law's concessions over; and even after they had decided to manage the concessions in the future for their own account, the resolution was not carried out, as Law's agent on the Arkansas, Levens, refused to transfer the business to the company or to continue it in the company's name. Furthermore, as this man, in spite of his refusal to carry out orders, was left undisturbed in his position, it happened that the German *engagés* in the meantime received help neither from one side nor from the other to bridge them over to the harvesting time of their first crop, but were forced to ask help of their only friends, the Arkansas and the Sothui Indians. Finally, when help from this last source failed, and small-pox broke out among the Indians and the Germans, they were forced to give up all and abandon the concession.[27]

So ended one brief chapter in Louisiana's history and of the *"particulier de Law, le Juif Elias Stultheus."*

Some Jews remained in Louisiana. When in 1724, Governor Bienville issued his notorious *Code Noir*, Article One of the Black Code "decrees the expulsion of the Jews from the colony." Article Three bans them from the province forever.

CHAPTER VII

Jews Are in Everything
and Out of Everything

➤➤➤   For the hire of Beds, furniture, etc. to accomodate my
family during the time the president occupied mine . . .
$12.00.

> —*From bill submitted by Colonel
> Isaac Franks to George Washing-
> ton*   ⫷⫷⫷

JEWS DID not fare badly under the English law, if we distinguish
between "civil rights, including the power to protect from wrong both
person and property, and political rights, the power to take part in the
legislation and government of a country." Protection of person and
property seems to have been universally conceded the Jewish resident. The exercise of voting power and a share in the government
were not universally his. Each colony determined the political status
of the nonconformist or alien. During the colonial period and until
State constitutions were drawn up, the legal status of the Jew was
uncertain. In practice the Jew seems to have been accorded a measure
of equality as to civil rights and debarred in some colonies from the
enjoyment of political rights. Numerous examples have been given of
Jews who became endenizened.

In Maryland the Jewish residents were without any civil rights
according to law, but in practice they were tacitly allowed a number of
undefined privileges. Their position in that colony was so uncertain
that Jews avoided Maryland. In 1776, the profession of Christianity
was definitely invoked as a prerequisite for office-holding there. This
disability remained on the statute books until 1825, when a determined
effort on the part of energetic Jewish opponents led by an eloquent
Irishman secured the amendment of this law. North Carolina in its
constitution of 1776 allowed freedom of worship but disqualified
Jewish office-holders. In New York, in the contested election of

119

1737, it was voted "that none of the Jewish profession could be admitted as evidence in the controversy now pending." New Jersey granted religious freedom to all but Papists. But few Jews are found in that colony. Between 1702 and 1776 no Jews were naturalized there. The New Jersey constitution of 1776 granted full civil rights to "protestant" inhabitants. New York in its constitution of 1777 placed Jews on a status of complete equality with other residents.

The years before the American Revolution unroll. So much is happening. So many new characters emerge on the historical scene. The times are gravid here and in Europe. These are the years of great productivity for the Baal Shem Tob, founder of Hassidism, for Moses Haim Luzzato, great Jewish philosopher, for Elijah, Gaon of Vilna, for Moses Mendelssohn, founder of the Haskalah (Enlightenment) movement in Europe. How much awareness there is in America of the intellectual questions that agitate European Jewry, it is impossible to state. Contact was maintained on both sides of the Atlantic. Lopez of Newport had a correspondent in Poland.

The time had not yet come for American Jewry to make its first tentative movements in the direction of evaluating itself in relation to the intangibles of life, to the world of ideas, to concepts of other-worldliness. It was a period of action, not of contemplation, in America. Later Mendelssohnian rationalism was to penetrate American Jewish consciousness, challenging orthodoxy and tradition. Later too there were to come the religious reforms, the severance of age-old ties, the pragmatic compromises, the yielding to social pressure, the accommodation to new social conditions. The gulf between a Jew in Vilna and a Jew in Virginia was wider than the ocean and taller than the mountains between them.

It was a time of great contrasts. In 1752, a young doctor of Vilna returned to his native city after sitting at the feet of the great Luzzato, and was sent in the same year to the Hague to represent the Vilna Jewish community at a conference. In 1752, in Williamsburg, Virginia, the American public had its first opportunity to meet Shylock. *The Merchant of Venice* was produced there on the fifteenth of September. It was the first of many importations. The American theatergoer came to know "the usual disagreeable type of stage-Jew." There were unpleasant doctors, Christians masquerading as sinister characters by pretending to be Jews. There were Jewish barbers and purveyors. There was the cowardly rascal, Shadrach Boaz, whose popularity was so instantaneous that he became a magnet for plagiarists who copied him often and with distorted variations. Crooks and forgers and cheats were served up as types of Jewry.

At the same time American Jews were risking their lives and fortunes in all the frontier outposts. They were mobilizing their ships and arms and their young men for the coming struggle. They were building Christian church steeples with their contributions and helping many a sectarian college weather its financial crisis. The facts were there. The performance of American Jews was known. Yet there is a pronounced ambivalence on the part of Christians in their relationship with Jews. Men were willing to apprentice their young sons to Jewish brokers and at the same time were laughing uproariously at portrayals of repulsive Jewish characters who were as unlike the Jews they knew as creatures from Mars would be.

Here is their paradox.

Jews were both *in* everything and *out* of everything. They mingled with Christians yet preserved their insularity. They lent a ready ear to new ideas. They considered the synagogue an impregnable citadel. They made many compromises. They were unyielding.

There are striking exceptions to this practice of either voluntary or enforced insularity. Jews often had Christian business partners. Occasionally the highest confidence was expressed by a Christian in entrusting a Jew with a difficult mission. In 1774, the General Provost wrote to Barnard Gratz that he was sending his little daughter to Barnard and asking that he take charge of her and attend to her education.

Conversion and intermarriage were two factors which constantly made inroads into the ranks of colonial Hebrews. From the earliest period Puritan divines thundered sermons at the wilfully deaf children of Israel. Tremendous energy was expended by these would-be saviors of the Jews. Eternal salvation was constantly dangled before them, like hay before a stubborn mule. Considering the efforts involved, the rewards were few and unsatisfactory. There was always that corroding doubt left as to the sincerity of the convert. So often material and social rewards were more coveted than eternal salvation. It was a sad state of affairs. Converts like Isaac Miranda, "the fashionable Christian," never quite succeeded in completely divesting themselves of their former religion. Miranda was often dubbed "the apostate Jew." This suspicion clung even unto the third and fourth generation. The biographies of Yale graduates include such entries as "Isaac Isaacs . . . of

Jewish extraction." He was one of the pillars of the Episcopal Church
in Norwalk, Connecticut.

From the days of the Mathers, Cotton and Increase, to the more
liberal Ezra Stiles, conversion of the Jews was an all-engrossing subject. This effort was continued into the nineteenth and twentieth centuries. The files of the *Occident*, a nineteenth-century Jewish periodical, from its first volume of 1843 throughout the existence of the
journal, frequently discussed the work of societies for "Evangelizing
Jews." The stronger the efforts at conversion, the greater was the
resistance of the Jew.

The citadels of orthodoxy were assailed in America. The rationalists,
"enthusiasts," ethical reformers were having their field day. The *Age
of Reason* was at hand. The time was ripe for Thomas Paine to write:

Had it been the object or the intention of Jesus Christ to establish a new
religion, he would undoubtedly have written a system himself. . . . He
was a Jew by birth and by profession.[1]

But it took a long time for these ideas to light up the Jewish question
or to mitigate prejudice.

Neither their religion nor their insistence on civil rights prevented
Jews from owning slaves. They were known to have imported slaves
in 1661. In 1720 a Jew exchanged merchandise for slaves he had
brought in his own ship from Guinea.

When, in 1741, it was discovered that New York Negroes had con-
spired against the white population, and had planned to burn the city,
a large number of Negroes were arrested and transported or condemned to death. Some of these slaves belonged to Jewish owners.
Cuffee, belonging to Lewis Gomez, had planned to burn his master's
house. Machado's house was burned by his Negroes. A few were
acquitted, among them servants belonging to Judah Hays and Samuel
Myers Cohen.

A list of Jewish businessmen, brokers, land operators, vendue
masters, auctioneers, shipowners, bankers, insurance agents, book-
sellers, chemists, doctors, gentlemen, butchers, bakers, farmers,
vintners would be a cross section of every walk of colonial life. Even
a random perusal of the tremendous store of available material would
convince the casual reader that Jews were an important segment of the
population.

Whether they met at the Masonic Lodge, or at the dancing assembly,
whether they bought and sold from each other, Jews and Christians

encountered each other in many ways. When the President of
Harvard delivered a sermon before the Massachusetts Legislature,
averring that, "The civil polity of Israel is doubtless an excellent general model, allowing for some peculiarities," he was admitting Jews to
membership in a common culture.

Jewish settlers in America were men and women hardened by
adversity. From their earliest days on the western shores of the
Atlantic, they had shared the dangers and the rugged life with other
immigrants. But in addition they had fought hard to overcome the
disabilities imposed on them as Jews, disabilities they had known in
Europe and refused to accept in the New World.

So when American grievances burst their bonds and the Revolution,
once the handwriting on the wall, became a reality, Jews were ready.
They were not strangers to the rugged life, to the battle for human
rights. It was their war, their land, their cause. They were willing to
die for abstract beliefs and ideals—and they did.

There was no sweet accord among all Americans on the need for
armed conflict. The American people did not rise up as one man.
Some there were who failed to rise at all. Some made of their conduct
a perfunctory and meaningless gesture, straddling every issue, sitting
out every bloody engagement, concerned only with saving their skins
and their property. "One third Whig; another Tory; and the rest
mongrel," John Adams is quoted as saying. In England as in the
colonies, men were divided on this critical issue. There was Burke,
the great conciliator. There was David Hume who defended the
American cause. There was an English Jew who pleaded for peace.
This man was Abraham Wagg, born in England in 1719, who emigrated to America, and in a clumsy way attempted to reconcile the
land of his birth with his adopted home, convinced that there was a
fundamental unity of interest binding all English-speaking peoples.
In New York, where he lived in 1770, Wagg earned his living as a
"wholesale grocer and chocolate manufacturer." He married Rachel
Gomez, a daughter of one of the blue-blooded Sephardim, an alliance
which could not but lend prestige to any member of the Jewish community of New York. The outbreak of the Revolution found Abraham
Wagg unmistakably loyal to the Crown. A series of misfortunes, including a personal injury which lamed him, the death of a child and
serious financial reverses determined his removal to England, where
he lived from 1779 until his death in 1803.

Among the papers which Abraham Wagg left behind him is a memorial found in the Public Record Office, entitled: "The Sentiments of a Friend to Great Britain and America." It is written in New York, in August of 1778. The memorialist begins with an apology, for the subject of his petition "is seemingly a paradox," and the hope that their "Excellencies will excuse the presumption and rudeness of a common person to pretend for to dictate to such superior characters."

The letter urges upon Parliament the adoption of the terms proposed by Congress on the seventeenth of June, 1778, which call for the immediate withdrawal of the British fleet and army, a definite acknowledgment of the independence of the United States.

He summarizes his plea by urging "that Great Britain shall acknowledge the thirteen united states of North America Free and independent."

Right along there were many signposts pointing toward the coming Revolution. In 1754 Benjamin Franklin had already "discovered the essence of the conflict." In the same year, Isaac Myers of New York called a meeting at the Rising Sun Inn and organized a company of bateau men which he headed as captain. There were other Jews who joined in a military expedition across the Allegheny Mountains. In 1755 when the Braddock campaign ended in failure and the colonies were alerted to the growing dangers in the French and Indian campaigns, Benjamin Cohen was chosen as a member of the Provincial Council of Pennsylvania and Attorney-General of the colony. The rumblings and mutterings of Indians bent on blocking the British were fast turning into military campaigns. Many Jews were among the Indian traders who suffered grievously in these engagements. The Amherst Papers are a depository of much illuminating information on the role of Jews in the skirmishes and battles of this period. Men named Jacob Wolf and Jacob Wexler served in the ranks. Lieutenant Joseph Levy was on the scene of the Cherokee uprising in South Carolina in 1761. A Captain Elias Meyer was a member of the Royal American Regiment whose activities, judging from the Amherst Papers, during the years 1761-63, were manifold. His recommendation for promotion stated that he was an engineer who had previously served thirteen years as a lieutenant.

As important to the cause of the colonies as Indian traders and soldiers were the shipowners. Such men as Samuel Jacobs, owner of the *Schooner Betsey*, have been lately discovered and belatedly receive posthumous accolades. His vessel loaded with a cargo of fish was about to set sail for Oporto and return with goods from Portugal. But the *Schooner Betsey* was seized at Quebec and pressed into British service and used finally to evacuate the beleaguered British troops. A claim for damages submitted to Amherst by the owner of the *Schooner Betsey* was later allowed him.

The Non-Importation Agreement of 1765 had nine Jewish signers: Benjamin Levy, Hyman Levy, Samson Levy, Joseph Jacobs, David Franks, Mathias Bush, Michael and Barnard Gratz and Moses Mordecai. In 1770 the issue before every businessman was whether to import or not.

How did Jewish Tories fare?

One Jew of Rhode Island, because he had imported tea, and violated the Non-Importation Agreement, "was stripped of all he was worth and driven out of the island. His brother shared in his misfortunes but did not survive them." Another Newport Jew "was inhumanly fired upon and bayoneted, wounded in fifteen parts of his body, and beat with their muskets in a most shocking manner . . . and died of his wounds a few hours after, universally regretted by every true lover of his King and Country." This man who fell a martyr to the Tory cause was Isaac Hart, merchant of renown, and patron of fine arts. Moses Hart of Rhode Island figures in the British archives as having presented a claim of two thousand pounds for loss of property incurred as a supporter of the King. A Philadelphia Tory, named Mordecai Levy, was compelled to make a public retraction of his belief in July, 1775. "I now take this opportunity of declaring that my conduct proceeded from the most contracted notions of the British Constitution and the rights of human nature," he admitted.

David Franks, Philadelphia Tory, was well known. A number of contracts were let to him for providing food for troops and prisoners. He is called "agent . . . for victualling troops of the King of Great Britain" in the *Journal* of the Continental Congress. In 1778 Congress allows Franks to go to New York on condition that he will promise not to give out any information to the enemy. A month later an indiscreet letter of his addressed to Moses Franks is intercepted and David Franks is "conveyed to the new gaol in this city." He does not like "the new gaol," so he manages to effect his discharge. From then on he is a marked man under constant surveillance. In 1780 Franks is given just fourteen days to get into the enemy lines. But he objects because the pass is only for himself, his daughter and her maid. He feels he cannot travel without a manservant for himself and two servants for his daughter. After another exchange of letters, Franks is given twenty-four hours to leave Philadelphia. That is the last we hear of him there until after the war. His Tory sympathies cost him much of his wealth and his social position. Like other propertied men among both Jews and Christians, Franks was typical of the group whose wealth, prestige and commercial interests dictated their allegiance to the King and made them unwilling to identify themselves with the proletarian mob shouting slogans for liberty.

As early as 1775 the importance of privateering had been recognized. The Continental Congress legalized the capture of enemy vessels and encouraged patriots to wage war on the high seas. American shipowners had so ardently thrown themselves into their assignment that by 1778, they had seized or destroyed 733 ships, carrying cargoes worth over ten million dollars. The importance of this phase of the American struggle for liberty should not be underestimated. The mistress of the seas was being challenged in her own stronghold. Among the Jews who were owners or part-owners of ships manned with guns were M. M. Hays of Boston; Isaac Moses and Benjamin Seixas of Philadelphia; Abraham Sasportas of Philadelphia. Moses Levy of Philadelphia in partnership with Robert Morris (famous financier of the Revolution and a non-Jew) owned the *Havannah* and the *Black Prince*. Isaac Moses and Matthew Clarkson owned the *Cornelia*, the *Marbois* and the *Mayflower*. Isaac Moses & Co. owned the *Chance* and the *Fox*. For the fifty-four guns carried on the ships owned by him and his associates, Mr. Moses asked Congress that gunpowder be furnished. Congressional encouragement endorsed privateers and privateering.

Of the ships and sloops and brigantines owned by Aaron Lopez a whole volume could be written. They plied the coastwise route. They sailed to Portugal and England and France and the West Indies. The letters of Lopez to his captains—Reply, Wiswall, Hathaway and others—are written with the authority of a tycoon accustomed to issuing orders. He dealt in many commodities—tobacco, corn, turpentine, white beans, beeswax, lumber and slaves. "In my Instructions to Captn Hathaway (to whom be pleased to deliver the Inclosed) I directed him to make all possible dispatch at Carolina as I had immediate use for the Slaves he was to bring."

Levi Solomons testified to being present on the man-of-war *Gaspee*, where he saw Colonel Ethan Allen "with a pair of irons on his legs

and a sentry standing before him with a pistol in his hand." Another
Jew, in 1776, had his sloop taken from him and succeeded in recap-
turing it. In 1776 Aaron Lopez delivered gunpowder and a whale
boat to the colony of Rhode Island for which he was allowed twenty-
two pounds. Other shipowners, like the Gratz brothers, who had
privateering interests have already been mentioned. Carter Braxton,
one of the signers of the Declaration of Independence, wrote to
Michael Gratz: "I have at length been able to adjust finally the account
of the unfortunate privateer in which you had a share."

Throughout the war, Jewish shipowners continued their patriotic
enterprises. So many letters have been preserved that the historian
works in an embarrassment of riches. Here is one such letter written
by Haym Salomon which in the midst of war is concerned with
finance as well as trivia—teacups, kerchiefs and sheeting:

Philadelphia 23rd July 1781

Mr Carl (   )
  Gottenburg—
    Sir:
       By recommendation of Mr Pollard, I take the Liberty to
enclose Eight First Bills on Paris drawn by Francis Hopkinson on the
Commissioner of the United States of America at Paris Amounting to
198 Dollars equal to 990 Livres Tournois for which you will please to
Ship & first Vessell Bound to this place and to my address the following
Articles Viz: One Box with a few Dozen Tea Cups and Saucers only a
few Peices of the Best Quality of Flag Silk Henkercheifs—and the
Amount of the remainder in Russia Sheeting.
Yours.
Haym Salomon[2]

Of military participation in the war, there was no lack. Wolf
lists a number of officers and men whose record was one of distinction and heroism. There were instances of all the men in a family
shouldering arms for freedom's sake. There were David Hays and his
son Jacob, both of whom "fought in various battles for independence."
His house and store were burned down by Tories. There were the
three Pinto brothers, students at Yale. Two of them were wounded
in battle. Sometimes whole communities were scattered by the exigencies of war. Jews, like their Christian neighbors, were swept by
the tides of war now here, now there.

The record of individual soldiers is sometimes pathetically brief.
For death quickly overtook them. So the military career of Ensign
Mordecai Davis may be summarized briefly: Enlisted January 5,

1776, died August 12, 1776. These Revolutionary War patriots were realistic men. They drew their wills on the eve of battle:

Most Humbly bequeath my soul to God my maker and my body to the Earth from whence it came. As to my Worldly Estate my will and Desire is 'that all my Just Debts be accurately Paid and after that I bequeath Five hundred Pounds curr^{cy}. to the Jewish Synagogue of Chas. to be Remembered there every Chipoor. Five hundred Pounds to Rabbi Moshé to say Kadish a Twelve month, My House and wearing Apperle to my Friend Lazarus Levy Fifty Pounds to Abraham Jones Shames and all the rest of my Estate that shall remain after the above Legacies and my Debts are Paid, I give and bequeath all the rest to my hearty Friends Benjn Phillips and Ephraim Abrahams or the last Surviving Party and If the Almighty Spares my life that I return * * *[3]

So wrote Jacob I. Cohen, a member of the Charlestown Regiment of Militia, called "The Free Citizens." He volunteered for military service early in the war, serving under Moultrie and Lincoln. Madison's papers contain many references to this courageous patriot.

Jews were not unaware of the important role which they assumed in the common struggle. If they were heroes, they did not underestimate their heroism. If to fight for freedom was a distinction, then they merited their share of the glory. They bled and died for the freedom which they proposed never again to surrender.

"It is well known among all the Citizens of the 13 united states," thus reads a letter to the Federal Convention, written by Jonas Phillips, one of the signers of the Non-Importation Resolutions, "that the Jews have been true and faithful whigs, & during the late Contest with England they have been foremost in aiding and assisting the states with their lifes and fortunes, they have supported the cause, have bravely fought and bled for liberty which they can not Enjoy." He refers to the proposal to require acceptance of both Old and New Testaments as part of the newly considered constitution.

The patriot cause had its Jewish advocates everywhere. In New England there were many Jewish supporters of the Revolutionary cause. Of the Jews of Newport, the Reverend Frederick Denison says: "The Jews were friends of the colonies in the Revolutionary struggle. They gave liberally of their means to sustain the Patriot cause. In some cases they served in the Continental armies." Aaron Lopez lost heavily in the British raid on Newport. Not only quantities of goods, but a number of his ships were sacrificed. In 1780 James Wilson and William Lewis wrote to Congress in behalf of Aaron Lopez: "The Character of Mr. Lopez, as a Friend to the Liberties and Independence of the United States, is clear & unimpeached. . . . He is a Merchant of extensive Business, is active, enterprizing and public Spirited."

The residents of Newport, of whom quite a number were Jews, suffered greatly when their city was captured. Some eight thousand British and Hessians occupied their city. The enemy destroyed 480 houses, burned many ships, cut down trees and orchards, pillaged the beautiful library, then one of the best in America, and took away many of the town records. A number of the Newport residents fled to other places, taking refuge where they could. Some went to Leicester, Massachusetts. Others made their way to Boston and near-by places. So it is that many Jewish families were scattered and their rich and colorful communal life was not resumed after the War.

The Congregation Shearith Israel of New York witnessed strife and dissension brought on by difference of opinion on the issues at stake. There were Tories among the members to whom the rebels were "rabble." They felt that their loyalty and allegiance was due to the King. Old families, from a sense of indebtedness to the Crown, refused to compromise their reputations by siding with the patriots. Lines were sharply drawn. Bitter feeling was expressed on both sides. Jonas Phillips made some converts for the patriot cause among his fellow worshipers at the synagogue. But the real synagogue champion of the Revolution was its Rabbi, Gershom Mendes Seixas. When news came that the British were approaching New York, he decided to close the synagogue rather than keep it open under British protection. There were many men in the congregation who had been so outspoken against the Crown that they felt they would be better off in another climate. So the synagogue was closed and the Rabbi, a native of New York and a zealous patriot, saw to it that every ceremonial object— the scrolls and prayerbooks and candlesticks—was taken away.

When Tory Jews under the leadership of a Broad Street furrier, opened the synagogue, the place looked like Mother Hubbard's cupboard. Here in this bare building a few dreary services were chanted during the British occupation. But this happened on very rare and special occasions. The little synagogue presented a dismal sight stripped of its familiar brass candlesticks, its tablets, and its scrolls. The departing patriots had taken the warmth and the color with them.

Some of the Shearith Israel refugees went to Connecticut. Among them was Rabbi Seixas, bearing the purloined scroll and other synagogue objects. There he lived until 1780, when he removed to Philadelphia, following many of his congregation. Here he contributed his energies to the founding of another synagogue, Mickvé Israel. At the close of the War, the triumphant Reverend Seixas restored himself and the ceremonial articles of which he was the voluntary custodian, to the reunited congregation of New York. These historic objects are now to be seen in the present Shearith Israel synagogue. The minutes of his congregation have a most significant interruption. There are no records between September 27, 1775, and December 8, 1783.

The patriots and the Loyalists of the Congregation Shearith Israel may have settled many an argument in verbal skirmishes. But at the same time a number of Jewish soldiers were dying under fire on the outskirts of the city. One Jewish officer, Colonel Bush, describes the Battle of Long Island which began in a watermelon patch. The British "made great havoc among our men," he writes. The casualties on both sides were very heavy, he notes. There is more news of other Jewish patriots, some serving in naval engagements, others in the farthest outposts.

There were so many patriots among the Jews of New York that it is impossible to describe them all. Perhaps one of them whose proudest boast was that he was a native New Yorker will serve as an example. He was Colonel Isaac Franks. Isaac Franks was born in New York in 1759. He was still in his teens when he joined Colonel Lasher's Regiment in 1776. This regiment was annexed to the Continental Army under the command of General Washington. He took part in the Battle of Long Island and in the retreat to New York. Young Isaac Franks was captured by the British. After being held a prisoner for almost three months, he escaped "in a small leaky skiff with one single paddle to the Jersey shore." During the next four years he was in the Quartermaster's Division. In 1781, he was commissioned ensign in the Seventh Massachusetts Regiment. At the end of a year, "being severely afflicted with the gravel," he was compelled to resign. The years immediately succeeding the War find him in reduced circumstances. Later his fortunes improved. He was the recipient of a Revolutionary pension the last four years of his life and held several civil posts. With Dr. Benjamin Rush he bought vast tracts of Indiana land.

His home in Germantown was known to be comfortable, for President Washington leased it during the winter of 1793, when a yellow fever epidemic was raging. The bill for occupancy, presented to the President, is amusing. In addition to the rent which was sixty-six dollars for two months, Washington paid for a missing flatiron, one fork and four platters. He also was charged for "the damage done to a large double Japand waiter made use of in the service of the president." The sum of two dollars and fifty cents was expended by Franks "for Cleaning my house and putting it in the same condition the President rec'd it in." The fact remains that the Franks home was once the nation's Capitol.

His service to the State of Pennsylvania was recognized in 1794 when Franks was made a Lieutenant Colonel in the Pennsylvania Militia. He often recalled his military record with pride, not failing to add that he was "a native born Citizen and a uniform Republican."

Among other New York Jews who were in the Army may be mentioned Jonas Phillips, David Hays, who was with a New York contingent at Braddock's Field and an officer, Asser Levy, who was probably a grandson of the fighting butcher of New Amsterdam days. In his plan for the defense of New York, which Major General Lee submitted to General Washington (March, 1776), he stated that the East River could be protected from the British as follows: "A battery for this purpose is planned and in some forwardness at the Jews Burying Ground." On a tablet which marks this spot is the legend: "During the War of the Revolution it was fortified by the Patriots as one of the defenses of the City." Here under patriot guns slept the Jewish fathers of New Amsterdam who had consecrated this cemetery in 1656.

Gershom Mendes Seixas may be said to be typical of the generation of native American Jews who served the cause of the patriots with unswerving ardor. His maternal grandfather, Moses Levy, lived for some years in London and became the owner of numerous merchant vessels. When in about 1701 he migrated to New York, he became active in the affairs of Shearith Israel, serving as its Parnas for a number of years. His daughter Rachel married Isaac Mendes Seixas, a native of Lisbon who migrated to America, became a merchant and was one of the signers of the Non-Importation Resolutions. Gershom Mendes Seixas was one of their six children. He was born in New York in 1745. When a boy of five, he appeared before his elders in the congregation to read the prayers. From that moment on, his life's course was planned. At the age of twenty-one he was elected rabbi of Shearith Israel, a post which he held for half a century. He must have been a silver-tongued orator. Rabbi Seixas was in the pulpit when word reached him that the British were approaching New York. The sermon he preached on that occasion was so eloquent that even the Tories wept.

Rachel and Isaac Seixas could well be proud of their children. They were all ardent patriots. Gershom's brother, Benjamin, was an officer of the New York Militia. Abraham Seixas was a colonel of the

Georgia Brigade of the Continental Army and served throughout the entire war. His sister Grace was a brilliant woman, reputed to be a sparkling conversationalist who was well versed in politics, finance and national affairs.

When Rabbi Seixas full of Revolutionary ardor and religious zeal went to Philadelphia in 1780, he plunged into a campaign to establish another synagogue. His restless energy soon communicated itself to others. Land was bought in 1782. In the stirring days of 1782-83, the Jews of Philadelphia joyfully celebrated two events: peace and the dedication of their synagogue. As "liege subjects to the Sovereignty of the United States of America," they invited the State officials to the ceremonies of the dedication of Mickvé Israel. Patriots like the brothers Gratz, Haym Salomon and others could point with pride to this simultaneous service to their God and to their country. It was indeed a year of well-earned jubilee to Philadelphia Jewry.

Rabbi Seixas returned to New York in March of 1783. His zeal was undiminished, his restless energies needed still greater scope. One of his first reforms was to substitute the use of English for Spanish wherever it supplemented the Hebrew language. He became one of the original incorporators of Columbia College and one of its trustees, being the only non-Episcopalian to serve in that capacity. His relations with the Episcopal clergy were of the warmest. Often members of the Episcopal clergy were invited by Rabbi Seixas to sit near him at services at Shearith Israel. He became a student of American Jewish history, furnishing Hannah Adams with much valuable information for her *History of the Jews*. Rabbi Seixas utilized his historical information when in 1800 he delivered a lecture at St. Paul's on the history of the Jews of New York.

The Jews of Lancaster who had close family ties and business interests with the Philadelphia patriots were also characterized by their adherence to the Revolutionary Movement. Joseph Simon's name appears again in the *Journal* of the Continental Congress. Blankets for the military hospital, rifles and drums for the Army, provisions for prisoners, or women and children, are only a few items for which this enterprising Lancastrian served as purveyor.

With others of their fellow citizens, Joseph Simon, Barnard Gratz, Levy Andrew Levy, Levy Marks and Meyer Solomon, pledged themselves at Lancaster in 1777, to maintain one or more messengers "to ride between Lancaster and General Washington's army with & for intelligence." Another of their number, Joseph Cohen, was in

service in the Revolutionary Army. Michael Hart was on the muster
roll of a military company in 1776. Myer Hart took charge of the
British prisoners' camp in his vicinity.

Philadelphia became a place of refuge for many patriotic Jews. On
the eve of the Revolution, Philadelphia Jewry was ably headed by
Barnard Gratz. He was then the Parnas, or presiding elder, of the
congregation, which since 1747 had been meeting in a small house
in Sterling Alley. His brother Michael, as well as numerous kinsmen
and their former employer, David Franks, were all members of this
little synagogue.

David Franks was a Tory at heart and in deed. He belonged to the
minority among his coreligionists. Yet in 1765 his name was inscribed
with other patriots on the famous Non-Importation Resolutions. But
his financial interests were closely bound up with the British. He had
been an active agent for them in getting supplies for their troops in the
French and Indian Wars. His Tory sentiments led to his arrest in
1778. Only the influence of his brother Moses could extricate him
from his troubles. He was one of a group of exchanged prisoners who
was ordered out of the country on his release. He went to England.

Prior to his brush with the law, David Franks had founded the *New
Jersey Journal* in 1778. The paper ran about four years. The rhythm
of a printing press becomes a habit hard to shake. After the War he
returned to this country and published the first *New York City Directory*. His subsequent movements are not easy to trace. He returned
to Philadelphia for a while to supervise his vast land holdings which
stretched from Pennsylvania and Virginia to Indiana and the Illinois
country. Frankstown, Pennsylvania, is named for him. His will, pro-
bated in England, describes him as a gentleman of Isleworth, County
of Middlesex.

Like many a fairy-tale father, David Franks had three daughters.
The youngest of these, Rebecca, left behind her legends and anecdotes
attesting to her personal popularity with the British and to her Tory
sentiments. Rebecca was gay, flirtatious, brilliant, lighthearted, witty,
beautiful and popular. She is a contrast to the home-loving, retiring,
patient, simplehearted patriot, Miriam Gratz; to the devoted and
sacrificing Mrs. Minis, or the dutiful and valiant Mrs. Sheftall. Not for
her the gray days, the heavy heart so many other women knew.

Rebecca Franks knew many officers in the British and American
ranks. She was admired and respected by all of them. It remained for
Charles Lee, the vain, showy, treacherous, loose-mouthed, ill-bred,
slovenly general who was a thorn in Washington's side until he was

court-martialed and suspended, to write her a vulgar letter containing coarse, ribald, gross jests and boorish innuendoes. That her answer put the boorish general in his place, proves Rebecca equal to any emergency. His letter of apology attempts to explain his impropriety: "My acquaintance with you is too slender to take any liberties which border on familiarity." Thus he defends his Rabelaisian impudence, calling it but an "effort to make you laugh for a moment in these melancholy times."

A much more pleasant acquaintance was that with the ill-fated Major André. He was to be seen, while a paroled prisoner, at the home of David Franks, where he idled away some of his time, and occupied the rest of it by painting a miniature of the beautiful Rebecca, which he presented to her with his compliments. Another Tory belle whom Rebecca knew well was the beautiful Margaret Shippen, who later married General Arnold. To a member of the Shippen family, Rebecca wrote, after the British Army had evacuated Philadelphia: "Poor Nancy I know how she must have felt."

After her marriage Rebecca and her husband moved to England. They lived in Bath where the assemblies and balls must have satisfied Rebecca as they did the heroines of Jane Austen's books. At any rate she was lost to America and Judaism at the same time.

It is a study in contrasts, of which Rebecca and her Tory friends are examples. For the British took their war comfortably. Their men were well fed and well clothed. Frequently their troops maintained not only themselves but numerous camp followers. "Burgoyne's forces were accompanied by approximately two thousand women," says one historian. Their officers too were dedicated to the complete enjoyment of life. "Howe was a gay man of the world, loving ease, wine, gambling, and the society of ladies. . . . Enamored of indolence, drink, and high living, eager to effect peace by conciliation."

While Howe was in Philadelphia, Washington was in Valley Forge. "The cold was intense, supplies of clothing were not to be had, provisions were scarce, it was impossible to care properly for the sick. Cold, hungry, and half-naked, the men moved about like ragged spectres."[4]

How fortunate for American history that the War was won by the "ragged spectres."

During the time that Rebecca Franks was describing the vacuity of social life in New York, a young Jewish soldier, Solomon Bush, was writing to a friend, in November of 1777, that he hoped to be able to say that "New York is ours before long." Though "the surgeons pronounced my wound Mortal," his chief concern is "to be able to get Satisfaction and revenge the Rongs of my injured Country." And another Jewish patriot, Benjamin Levy, on learning that Robert Morris and his family might have to be evacuated from Philadelphia offered him shelter: "We have one spare bed our house is good and large." He adds: "As these are not times for compliments and ceremony, I need not give you assurances of making you welcome."

There was at least one Jew starving with the rest of them at Valley Forge. He was Dr. Phillip Moses Russell, surgeon's mate in the Second Virginia Regiment. He was born in 1745. In 1775 he enlisted under General Lee, later joining the Virginia Regiment. He was at Valley Forge during 1777-78. His devotion to duty merited a letter of commendation from General Washington. Among others who served in the Virginia contingent was Captain Jacob Cohen, who served under Lafayette and who remained in the service until after the surrender of Cornwallis. The Virginia Line included such names as Isaac Israel, Andrew Moses, Moses Franks, Francis Goldman, Joseph Hart, Benjamin Jacobs, John Isaac, Juda Levi, Ezekiel Moses, Samuel Myers, Levin Philips, George Solomon, David Stern, Lewis Steinberger and Henry Samuel. Some or all of these men might have been Jews. We know nothing about them, other than that their names appeared on the Virginia records.

There was a nineteen-year-old bank clerk named Reuben Etting who was working in Baltimore when the War broke out. He joined the patriot forces and fought with them until his capture by the British in 1780. When his captors learned that he would not eat pork, they put him on a diet of hardtack and pork. Emaciated, weakened by his self-imposed fast, he contracted tuberculosis and died shortly after his release.

Among the Revolutionary War notables was Major Benjamin Nones, a native of Bordeaux, France. He came to the United States in 1777 and lost no time in joining the fight. He was at first a private and served under Count Pulaski. Captain Verdier wrote of him:

Benjamin Nones has served as a volunteer in my company. . . . his behavior under fire in all the bloody actions we fought has been marked by bravery and courage which a military man is expected to show for the liberties of his country, and which acts of said Nones gained in his favor the esteem of General Pulaski as well as that of all the officers who witnessed his daring conduct.

Major Nones, with those under his command at the Battle of Savannah, "shared the hardships of that sanguinary day."[5] He became a major of a company of four hundred men "composed in part of Hebrews." They were attached to Baron De Kalb's command. De Kalb was severely wounded at the Battle of Camden, South Carolina, on August 16, 1780. Three Jewish officers allegedly bore their dying chief from the battlefield. They were Major Benjamin Nones, Captain Jacob De la Motta and Captain Jacob de Leon.

No account of Jewish participation in the Revolutionary War is complete without a sketch of an enigmatic personality, David Salisbury Franks. He was a patriot whose spectacular career and checkered history made him the center of a controversy which took a long time to simmer down. Jefferson said of him, in a letter to James Madison:

He appears to have a good eno' heart, and understanding somewhat better than common, but too little guard over his lips. I have marked him par ticularly in the company of women where he loses all power over himself, and becomes almost [lacking]. . . . This is in some measure the vice of his age but it seems to be increased also by his peculiar constitution.[6]

In another letter: "He is light, indiscreet, active, honest, affectionate."

David Salisbury Franks was born in Philadelphia. His trail leads from Philadelphia to Canada, back to Philadelphia, then a number of times to Europe and back. He first achieves temporary prominence in a Montreal street brawl and lands in jail. From a brief autobiography:[7] "I suffered a short tho rigorous imprisonment on Account of my attachment to the Cause of America." As a matter of fact, it was a difference of opinion as to the heinousness of a crime that had been committed—the crime being the daubing of a bust of the King, and labeling it: "This is the pope of Canada and the Fool of England." A Frenchman who saw this exclaimed that the dauber ought to be hanged. To which Franks retorted, "In England men are not hanged for such small offences." Franks was accused of calling so great a crime just a "small offence." So to teach Franks the importance of lese majesty, they imposed a bail of ten thousand pounds. It was enough to make any offender take notice.

His prison days were brief. His friends secured his freedom in six days.

"When the Northern Army retreated from Canada," he goes on with his narrative, "I joined it as a Volunteer & continued attached to that army with some little intermission until the reduction of General Burgoyne." In 1778 we find him in Philadelphia after that city had been evacuated by the British. The next year he volunteers again, and goes to Charleston, where he serves as aide-de-camp to General Lincoln. "In 1780, I was in Arnold's military Family at West Point until his Desertion to the Enemy."

Now as it happened, it had fallen to the lot of David Salisbury Franks to receive the appointment as aide-de-camp to General Arnold in 1778. He was given the rank of major and entrusted especially to see to the safety of the beautiful Margaret Shippen Arnold, the General's wife. For "while Gen. Arnold was in command of West Point he frequently sent her to different, and sometimes distant parts of the country." Of his superior's plans, Franks was in complete ignorance. "General Arnold was guarded and impenetrable to all around him," his aide-de-camp tells us, in discussing his chief's "detestable scheme." Poor Major Franks! He was destined to spend much of his time in clearing his own reputation and that of his associates of any previous knowledge of Arnold's betrayal. Arnold himself, in a letter written to General Washington from the *Vulture*, seeks to vindicate his intimates of any charges that may be brought against them. "In Justice to the gentlemen of my Family, Colonel Varick and Major Franks," he says, "I think myself bound to declare, that they . . . are totally Ignorant of any transactions of mine that they had reason to believe were Injurious to the Public." Still these men were under a cloud. They were arrested, tried and acquitted. Major Franks was unhappy and dissatisfied. So he wrote to General Washington: "I had here nothing but a Name unspotted I trust, untill Arnold's baseness gave the Tongue of Calumny Grounds sufficient to work upon against any one unhappily connected with him." He laments the fact that "A conscious Innocence of the abominable and groundless charge of Perjury may cheer, yet cannot support me thro' a World, too easily misled by false Reports and Prejudices." So again he invites investigation. Washington allows it. And for the second time, Major Franks is cleared.

In 1781 Robert Morris sent the Major with papers to Jay who was then at Madrid. Then to Franklin at Paris. Here he acquired a taste for diplomatic service abroad. He loved good times and he was, like Franklin, a great favorite with the ladies. We have on record the testimony of a woman who knew him, whose opinion of Franks did not coincide with that of Jefferson. "He was respected and welcomed wherever he went, for his social humor and manly candor," writes Mrs. Gibson. Evidently what seemed candor to the women, was interpreted as indiscretion by the men. Having acquired a taste for diplomatic life, he put himself in the way of any appointment that was likely to take him abroad. The intervention of his friends accomplished his ends. "When Mr. Jefferson was going to Paris, one of the Commissioners, for making a Treaty of Peace, he took me into his family," Major Franks writes. "In the Winter of the year 1784 Congress dispatched me to Europe with a Copy of the Ratification of the definitive Treaty. . . . In 1785 I went to Marseilles," as Vice Consul. Franks evidently was pleased with his French appointment for Jefferson wrote to Monroe, on November 11, 1784.

He is very anxious to be continued in it & is now there in the exercise of his office. If I have been rightly informed his services & sacrifices during the war have had their merit and I should suppose Congress would not supersede him but on good grounds.

Major Frank's narrative continues:

In the fall of 1786, Mr. Barclay was commissioned by our ministers for making a Treaty . . . with the Emperor of Morocco & I was appointed his Secretary. . . . After Mr. Barclay's return to Spain . . . I was sent by him with it from Madrid to Paris & from thence by Mr. Jefferson to London to get Mr. Adam's signature to it. . . .
Thus I have devoted Eleven Years of the best Part of my life to the Service of my Country, in all which time, I am bold to say that I have ever been actuated by a disinterested Zeal for her Honor & Prosperity.

Like Micawber, the Major finds himself in pecuniary difficulties as the years go on. He too is always "hoping for something to turn up"; applying for positions; making "disinterested tenders of his Services"; or asking that his due "Emoluments" be granted him. In 1789 he received four hundred acres of land in payment of his war service. He had the distinction too of being one of the original members of the Pennsylvania division of the Society of the Cincinnati, an organization of officers of the Revolution.

Curiously enough, our definite information about him stops at this point. Like his early years, his last ones still await the further investigation of historians. We meet him again in connection with an unhappy land venture. That marks the end of his career.

In the Southern theater of the War, the British also found concerted and vigorous opposition.

That South Carolina had its full quota of inflammable young rebels eager to uphold the Revolution is a matter of record. From the first they strained their ears for news from the north. On the twenty-fourth of July, 1776, Drayton wrote to Salvador, that early Jewish martyr to the patriot cause: "No news yet from Philadelphia; every ear is turned that way, anxiously listening for the word, independence. I say God speed the passage of it, Amen say you."

The majority of the Jews of South Carolina lived in Charleston, then Charles Town. Every South Carolinian between sixteen and sixty was required to enroll in the militia of his district. So the Jews of Charleston became members of Captain Lushington's Company. They fought in several engagements. David N. Cardozo (later sergeant major) distinguished himself for great valor. Another of their number, Joseph Solomon, lost his life in the Battle of Beaufort. In 1780 the British besieged Charleston. General Lincoln was bottled up in the city and after a two months' siege was compelled to surrender. Lushington's Company figured prominently in the defense of the city.

There are fourteen Jews who took part in the defense of their city as members of the Country Militia. There were eight Jews in the Charles Town Regiment of Militia. Two of the latter, David Sarzedas and Philip Minis, had fought in the Revolutionary Army of Georgia and had then gone to South Carolina. Another soldier, Markes Lazarus, was a sergeant major who had seen three years of active service. Abraham Seixas fought as a lieutenant in the Continental Line in Georgia and as a captain of militia in Charleston. Jacob Cohen, prominently associated with the Congregation Beth Elohim, was imprisoned by the British on the ship *Torbay*. There were also three merchants who fought in the War. They were Emanuel Abrahams, Abraham Cohen and Gershon Cohen. Mordecai Myers of Georgetown furnished supplies to the American Army.

Among the accessions to the Jewish population of Charleston were two men who came over with the Hessians, Samuel Levy and Levy Solomon. They made Charleston their home after the War.

Of another Charleston Jew, Myer Moses, General Sumter said that

his treatment of the American wounded and prisoners were such as to entitle him to the good wishes and gratitude of all those who had the success of the Revolution at heart. After the fall of Charleston, his treatment of the wounded and prisoners who were taken and sent to Charleston was extremely friendly and humane, they being in the greatest possible distress.[8]

As early as 1772, there was a Dr. Nathan Levy practicing medicine in South Carolina. In the distant Illinois country another Dr.

Levy, Isaac, was practicing his profession during the years of the Revolutionary War. A year before the War's end, Dr. Levy sued one of his patients for professional services. Mr. Buteaux, the patient, claimed that he was not completely cured. Dr. Levy countered by accusing his patient of not following orders. Mr. Buteaux had consumed sixty pills in two days to accelerate his recovery. Dr. Levy testified that such a large dosage would have killed the patient. The decision was awarded to the doctor.

From seaboard to crudest outpost, like "the wild region then known as Illinois Country," Jews gave a good account of themselves. In war and in peace, exchanging rifle shots or provisioning troops, dressing wounds or alleviating suffering among noncombatants, they were actively engaged in advancing the common cause.

At the outbreak of the Revolution, the Jewish population of Georgia was much depleted. Some forty families remained there. Yet even in so small a group there were a few who stood out as ardent patriots. Georgia was split into two camps. Each one contrived to meet and draw up resolutions. Among the Tory signers was Moses Nunez. Among the patriots of Georgia were Mordecai Levi and Sheftall Sheftall, Philip Jacob Cohen, Philip Minis and Cushman Pollock. Also there were Lieutenant Abraham Seixas and Lieutenant David Sarzedas.

Among the thousands of Sheftall papers, there is much of general interest to the historian of the Revolutionary War. Many mercantile enterprises are covered. The issue of Continental paper money is frequently discussed. There are papers dealing with the adventures of the Sheftall-owned, armed *Schooner Hetty*. There are many illuminating anecdotes, admonitions, maxims, advice. Mordecai Sheftall was a man of parts. His father Benjamin had belonged to that romantic, exciting chapter of history associated with the founding of Georgia. Mordecai was born in the earliest days of Georgian colonial history, in 1735, one of the first European children born in Georgia. He lost no time in joining the military forces of his colony at the outbreak of hostilities. He performed many services in the field. On one occasion Mordecai wrote to his son, Sheftall Sheftall: "General Jackson . . . has said . . . that he owes his life to the Attention of D^r. Sheftall."

The British listed Mordecai in their Disqualifying Act as "Chairman of the Rebel Parochial Committee." In 1778 Mordecai Sheftall was appointed by Major General Howe as Deputy Commissary of

Issues for South Carolina and Georgia. In the same year, members of the Minis and Cohen families were mobilizing money for the Revolution. Philip Minis advanced six thousand nine hundred dollars to the paymaster of troops then in Georgia. Minis, Cohen and Pollock also loaned to the patriot cause more than six thousand dollars which was later paid by Congress.

When in 1778 the British attacked Savannah, Mordecai Sheftall and his son were among those captured by the enemy. In the *Capture of Mordecai Sheftall*, a journal which he kept, are many fascinating anecdotes. Under date of December 29, 1778, he writes:

This day the British troops . . . landed early in the morning . . . they entered, and took possession of the town . . . on our arrival at the creek . . . we found it high water; and my son, not knowing how to swim, and we, with about one hundred and eighty-six officers and privates, being caught, as it were, in a pen, and the Highlanders keeping up a constant fire on us, it was thought advisable to surrender ourselves prisoners. . . . On our way to the white guard house we met with Colonel Campbell who inquired of the Major who he had got there. On his naming me to him, he desired that I might be well guarded, as I was a very great rebel.

While he was in jail, this "very great rebel" wrote his wife, Frances, a letter which was probably meant to reassure her, and to spare her any unnecessary anxiety. That is the only way to account for his ambiguous remark, "I am fully as well treated as I could expect," and "I must acknowledge that I have met with much Genteel treatment from the officers than I was formerly led to believe we should receive." Another letter expresses great concern for the education of his children. He writes to his wife:

I am happy to here that you are once more become Mistress of your own house . . . home is home, as the old saying is, I must beg you will put the poor children to school that they may not be intierly lost, in this Corrupt Age.

When he was released on parole, he managed to get to Philadelphia where with other patriots he helped organize Mickvé Israel. At the close of the Revolutionary War, Mordecai received a grant of land from the government, as compensation for his patriotic services.

Philip Minis has the distinction of being "the first white male child" born in Georgia. His parents reached Georgia just five months after Oglethorpe. There were some forty settlers in the vessel which brought, among others, the Minis family consisting of Abigail and Abraham Minis and their daughters Esther and Leah.

Members of the Minis family, in addition to advancing money to the patriot cause, had two sons, William and James, in the Georgia Line. Even their women were known as "great whigs." Mrs. Philip Minis brought food to the Sheftalls when they were captured. After the British seized Savannah, Mrs. Minis and her daughter Judith were first ordered to keep to the house and later banished from the town. When the French troops approached Savannah under D'Estang in 1779, he relied upon Philip Minis for information as to the best place to land the troops. Sheftall Levy corroborated Minis' advice and a French document goes on to say that "the two gentlemen Philip Minis and Sheftall Levi will conduct the force of men whenever ordered to do so." Lieutenant Abraham Seixas, who has already been mentioned, was frequently sent on dangerous missions to other military encampments bearing letters and important information for the officers. He was sent from Georgia to Charleston with news for General Lee. In the correspondence between Greene and Marion, Pollock is also mentioned as a messenger.

The patriotism of the Jews of Georgia was challenged in 1778 by a woman whose accusation has long since been lost. It seems that she charged the Georgia Jews with running away to Charleston. There has been preserved a refutation of these charges signed by "a real *American* and a true-hearted Israelite." The facts were that when the merchants who happened to be from home learned that the British had landed, they "proceeded post haste to Georgia, leaving all their concerns unsettled, and are now with their brother citizens in the field, doing that which every honest American should do."

The record of Jewish participation in the military campaigns of the Revolution is packed with incident. From the counting house and the general store, from the brokerage firm and the shipping concern, men and boys in their teens dropped their civilian activities and equipped themselves often at their own expense, to fight for freedom. Isaac Franks was only seventeen when he fought under the command of George Washington. The two sons of David Bush of Pennsylvania were distinguished officers of the patriot Army. One of them was Major George Bush. The other was Lewis Bush. Lewis enlisted in Washington's Army at the outbreak of hostilities. By the ninth of January in 1776 he was commissioned a first lieutenant. His courage under fire and his qualities of leadership soon won him new honors. In June of the same year he was promoted to captain. In March of

1777 he was made a major. His military career ended when he was mortally wounded at the Battle of Brandywine in September of 1777.

Jewish patriots are but vaguely known. In June of 1948 a Boston bookstore, having come into possession of a "superb piece of Washingtoniana" wanted more information about Atkinson and Solomon Bush, who inscribed this rare volume to Washington. Their query read: "And Colonel Solomon Bush? Was he, in 1779, the deputy adjutant general of the Pennsylvania Militia?" He was. In one of his letters to Henry Lazarus, Solomon Bush describes his "deplorable condition." He writes that his "thigh was broke and the surgeons pronounced my wound Mortal." He recovered and lived to be made a pensioner of his grateful country.

But not every battle of the Revolutionary War was fought with guns and mortars. It was an economic struggle as well. While some of their Jewish brethren were in the field, others enlisted in the uphill struggle to secure financial support for the men in uniform. Were not many of the grievances against which the colonists chafed concerned with a revolt against the financial burden imposed on them? Charles A. Beard wrote that if Congress had been adept at raising money, the War would have been of short duration: "In the field of material goods and actions, they met almost insuperable obstacles." It was a staggering burden. "All financial resources had to be raised from the void—and with great discretion."

Providentially it was at this point that a Polish Jewish immigrant pitted his talents against "the void" and wrought a miracle.

Haym Salomon was born in Lissa, Poland, in 1740. Of his early education and background there is little information. We know that he had traveled widely. We know that his departure from his native country coincided with its partition. Like Kosciusko and Pulaski, he migrated to America. Warmly these men espoused the patriot cause. They knew each other here and may have been acquainted in Poland. Haym Salomon was a young man of thirty-two when he opened his Broad Street office as a broker and commission merchant. Before long, Salomon joined the Sons of Liberty. He was soon launched as a patriot. With his friend, Alexander MacDougal, he was almost immediately implicated in anti-British activities. He was arrested in September of 1776. At Provost Prison, crowded with men of many nationalities, Salomon's linguistic abilities stood him in good stead. Soon he was given the post of prison interpreter and, after a short time, released. Promptly he plunged into courtship, wooing and winning Rachel Franks, sister of Colonel Isaac Franks. It was not a bad marriage for a young Polish-Jewish immigrant. He must have been a presentable young man, for it was not easy to crash Sephardic society. Scarcely a year had passed after his marriage to Rachel when the British charged him with being a spy. He was court-martialed and sentenced to die. But his old friends rallied to his cause. With their help he escaped. The Sons of Liberty are credited with his deliverance by some authorities. There is a considerable accretion of legend that has grown up around Haym Salomon. Some of it is still to be sifted.

His own narrative is by far the most trustworthy. He writes that he had been in residence in New York for some time before the British occupation, "and soon after taken up as a Spy and . . . committed to the Provost." His knowledge of languages made him useful. He was turned over to the Hessian Commander. Here he was able to help a number of French and American prisoners to escape, as well as to influence some Hessian officers "as were inclined to resign." These activities "rendered him so obnoxious to the British Head Quarters that as he was already pursued by the Guards . . . he made his happy escape from thence."

Behind him he left a considerable personal fortune as well as "his distressed Wife and a Child of a Month old at New York waiting that they may soon have an Opportunity to come out from thence with empty hands."

Empty-handed he came to Philadelphia in 1778. When he died in that city seven years later, the government was vastly indebted to him. He held government certificates totaling more than three hundred fifty thousand dollars. His estate claimed that Salomon's notebooks showed entries of specie advanced to the superintendent of finance amounting to more than two hundred thousand dollars. There were also a number of promissory notes given him by various people whom he had from time to time assisted.

Little less than genius could have transformed an impoverished refugee into a financier of first rank. That all of this was accomplished in a few years makes it seem all the more a gigantic feat. How did he do it? Some idea of the scope of his business we may get from his own advertisements in the Philadelphia papers.

Thus on November 6, 1782, he styles himself:

Broker to the Office of Finance, to the Consul General of France, and to the Treasurer of the French Army. . . .

Buys & sells on commission Bank Stock, Bills of Exchange on France, Spain, Holland, and other parts of Europe, the West Indies, and inland bill. . . .

He represented the French consul, as well as Chevalier de la Luzern, the French ambassador. He rendered service to the agent of the King of Spain, Don Francisco Rendon, who wrote: "I am entirely indebted to the practical kindness of Mr. Salomon to support my credit with any degree of reputation." Some inkling as to the vast sums of money that must have passed through his hands may be had when we realize that he "was sole negociator of all the war subsidies of France and Holland."

The family records claim such names as Jefferson, Willson, Ross, Duane, Reed, Madison, Mercer, Arthur Lee, Rittenhouse, Pendleton, Randolph, among those who had recourse to his treasury. To Robert Morris, the financial wizard of the Revolution, large amounts were advanced from time to time. In Morris' diary, Salomon's name is mentioned more than seventy times.

In 1782 Madison wrote to Edmund Randolph: "I have for some time been the pensioner on the favor of Haym Salomon, a Jew broker."

A month later, Madison again tells Randolph:

The kindness of our little friend in Front Street, near the coffee-house, is a fund that will preserve me from extremities, but I never resort to it without great mortification, as he obstinately rejects all recompense. The price of money is so usurious that he thinks it ought to be extorted from none but those who aim at profitable speculations. To a necessitous delegate, he gratuitously spares a supply out of his private stock.

In his petition to Continental Congress, Haym Salomon outlined his war experiences modestly. Salomon makes no extravagant claims, asks only for the opportunity to work. He remembers to intercede for a distressed comrade. The qualities of restraint and understatement are apparent and endearing.

But it is through his letters that we learn more of Salomon as a man, as a patriot and as a forthright Jew.

Here are accounts of transactions, foreign and domestic, large and small, important and trivial. His correspondents are diplomats of status, prestige and dignity. They are also little fur trappers exchanging peltries for much-needed goods. There are "unknown" names. But the names of the country's great and cherished are here also. Yet complicated as his affairs must have been, all is in order. Each transaction, big or small, is handled on its merits, calmly, with dispatch. Only occasionally does one come across a reference to the pressure of his affairs when he writes: "Multiplicity of Business hardly Gives me time to think what I am doing."

These letters are in the handwriting of several clerks in the employ of Haym Salomon who were apparently under orders to copy incoming letters and who took dictation from their chief. Most of the clerks signed their initials. One of them, Sam L. Hays, signs his name with a bold flourish, "Am for H. Salomon," and is distinguished by his poor spelling. He writes about a draft which he will try to get "excepted and advice you thereof." He is glad to "here" from his correspondents. Other clerks have their own idiosyncrasies. But through these letters one mind shines through, the mind of a keen man, a man of probity and honor who thinks clearly and settles his affairs with dispatch.

The letters come from many places, cover many subjects. So Philemon Dickinson offers Salomon "a Gentmans Bond" for "2000 Silver Dollars" and several business appointments adding, "I will pay you handsomely if you Succeed." Salomon has an agent in Gothenburg named Carl Soderstrom who writes him on November 5, 1781:

Shall be very Glad of having Your approbation of what have done for You Recommending my Self to Your future orders when You Speculate this way & Assure You upon Some previous notice to procure You every article You Should want to the Lowest prices possible.

Jonas Phillips of Sparks Court, Duke's Place, London, represents Salomon there after the War. James Cummings represents him in Paris during the War years.

He has numerous agents in various parts of this country with whom his relations are most cordial. The extent to which he is trusted by his friends is only matched by his own confidence in their integrity. Only on rare occasions does he become irritated with trifles or with the dilatory tactics of one who seems not to be acting in good faith. He writes a very sharp letter to a correspondent in Richmond: "My patience is almost Exhausted with your Proceedings with regard my handkerchiefs."

He is even approached by an agent who is trying to raise money for the relief of captured British officers. The letters which follow should be of general interest to students of American history. In February of 1782 he is informed that "There is a number of Officers here Belonging to Cornwallis's Army, which are in great want of money and must draw on New York, but find it difficult to Sell their Bills."

It is through fragments of information about general conditions during the war that we grasp many details of life under stress. There is a hunger for news as the ordinary channels of information are blocked. We read in the *Letter Book*:

I shall be Glad of Some of Your News Papers Our Press has been Stopt ever Since Cornwallis made a Descent in the Country (   ) Are Kept at present without News of Any Kind particular foreign.

As the war draws toward its conclusion he writes to one of his friends in Virginia:

Philad⁣ᵉ 12 March 1783

Felix Gilbert Esqʳ
  Buckingham County
   Virginia
. . . Trade is entirely at a Stand, and Peace is yet in Suspence I think we Shall have Peace. I sent you Several Newspapers for youre perusal.

Besides matters of general concern two phases of Haym Salomon's letters are of interest. One is his firm recognition of his rights as a Jew. "Holly Days" are observed, noted, duly celebrated. His Christian correspondents are notified of interruptions in business due to these observances in a matter-of-fact way. There is no hedging or undue explaining. It is not necessary. His constant preoccupation with his relatives in Europe who seem to exist in a chronic state of financial embarrassment is noticeable. So he exports goods to his London agents, the "Purpose being to Relieve Some poor Relations that I have in Europe." The letter is dated April 30, 1783, just twelve days after George Washington had proclaimed the end of the War. A letter written by Haym Salomon the day before mentions his joy at having at last heard from his parents. He closes with the following admonition which is autobiographical as well:

NB. Please to mention to my father the Difficulty that I have laboured under in not having any learning & that I Should not have Known What to have done had it not been for the languages that I learned in my travels Such as French English etc—Therefore would advise him & all my Relations to have their Children well educated particularly in the Christian language. & Should any of my Brothers Children have a good head to learn Hebrew would Contribute towards his being Instructed.

As his health failed, Salomon began to resent the importunings of his numerous relatives. Overwork and anxiety have worn his temper thin. He issues an ultimatum to his impecunious clan: "I desire no relation may be Sent." Two years after he wrote this letter, his labors were over. He died in 1785.

It would be easy to be carried away by the great and the prominent. The historian would then be like a proud householder calling attention to family portraits done by masters while furtively fingering the keys to the closets where the family skeletons are hidden. It is too easy to assume that even the great and elite were always faultless.

If we read the tombstone of Aaron Lopez, we may come away with the feeling that such an impeccable character is indeed "an ornament" to society.

> He was a merchant of eminence
> of polite and amiable manners.
> Hospitality, Liberality and Benevolence
> were his true characteristics
> An ornament and valuable Pillar to
> the Jewish Society of which he was a
> member. His knowledge in commerce
> was unbounded and his integrity irreproachable
> thus he lived and died, much regretted,
> esteemed and loved by all.

Yet we know that at least a part of his income was derived from the labors of "seasoned" slaves. And we ask ourselves whether a Jew who annually recited the Passover service in thanksgiving for emancipation from slavery should not have, with his brethren, made some overt gesture of understanding and compassion. There were half a million slaves in the country at the outbreak of the Revolutionary War. While it is true that there were very few men among the Christians who spoke out against slavery, still one of their number, John Woolman, published a pamphlet in 1746 crying out against the unholy system.

Yet Aaron Lopez died insolvent, maintains his most recent chronicler.[9] His insolvency was a credit to him for he "became impoverished chiefly on account of his adherence to the American cause." He who at one time was sole or part owner of 113 ships, risked and lost his fortune during the course of the War. If the historian could take the liberties of a novelist, there might be a moral here.

There are so many other correctives to the historian's exuberance. Here is an article on David Emanuel, "The First Jew to hold Office

By the SUPREME EXECUTIVE COUNCIL

of the Commonwealth of *Pennsylvania*.

WHEREAS *Solomon Raphael* —— the Bearer hereof, intending to follow the Business of a Pedlar within the Commonwealth of *Pennsylvania*, hath been recommended to Us as a proper Person for that Employment, and requesting a Licence for the same: WE DO hereby licence and allow the said *Solomon Raphael* to employ himself as a Pedlar and Hawker within the said Commonwealth, to travel with one Horse and to which *[illegible]* lend divers goody merchandize until the *twenty first* Day of *March* next; Provided he shall, during the said Term, observe and keep all Laws and Ordinances of the said Commonwealth to the same Employment relating.

GIVEN under the Seal of the Commonwealth, at Philadelphia, the *twenty first* Day of *March* —— in the Year of our LORD One Thousand Seven Hundred and eighty seven.

ATTEST.

This license issued to Solomon Raphael by Benjamin Franklin is the property of the American Jewish Historical Society. Unlike many of his contemporaries, Franklin's contact with Jews was "slight although friendly." His name, however, heads a list of non-Jewish contributors in 1788 when the congregation Mickvé Israel of Philadelphia conducted a fund-raising campaign addressed to their fellow citizens "of every Religious Denomination."

of Governor of One of the United States."[10] It was a career that included military duties in the War. It included selection as a justice of the peace in Georgia in 1774. It encompassed a romantic, hairbreadth escape from death at the hands of the Loyalists. It ended in his baptism and his loss to the Jews. So his importance to Jewish history is negligible. He deserves little notice except possibly as a symbol of a small but steady trickle of Jews who gradually left the fold, who founded Christian families with never a backward glance, who gave their descendants none of that warm loyalty which those who are part Scotch or part Irish always boast.

So the social historian weaves his narrative, seeking to balance the dark with the light, the great with the small, more concerned with the total tapestry than with any single part of the design. The ledger of a merchant prince is important. But so is a peddler's license. Especially one signed with the greatly respected name of Franklin. In Solomon Raphael's license "to follow the Business of a Pedlar," we glimpse not only one man's right "to expose and Vend," but a whole army of "hawkers and walkers" whose fallen arches and calloused feet made them dream of the department stores they would some day found—and did!

What sentiments B. Franklin entertained for S. Raphael at the moment he affixed his signature to his hawker's license, we do not know. But we do know from a letter which Franklin wrote from Paris on May 27, 1777, that he dreamed even then of America as a place of refuge for the oppressed of Europe and their kith and kin. It was addressed to his nephew. It reads in part:

I continue amazingly well & hearty for my Age, and hope to Live to See the End of these Troubles, and our Country establish'd in Freedom, when it will soon become great & glorious, by being the *Asylum of all the Oppress'd in Europe,* & the Resort of the Wealthy who love Liberty from all Parts of this Continent, to establish themselves & Families among us.[11]

The Franklin letter typified the absence of any noticeable antialienism in America at this time. It was part of a prevailing state of good will and interfaith co-operation of which there are many examples. During the Revolution, Sheftall and fellow members of a charitable organization managed to express that state of good will. They founded the Union Society. For some of the time Sheftall was its president. It was a unique attempt to combine Protestants, Catholics and Jews in a social service brotherhood. Some of their meetings were held while they were prisoners of the British, for according to the rules of their fraternity any three members constituted a quorum. Perhaps a common cause, a threat to security, a common enemy as a target for hate, made for group solidarity and unity. It is possible that William James was right in his pleas for "a moral equivalent for war." During the critical days of the Revolution, the factors for unity outweighed the factors that divided men.

Whether the events concern the great or the obscure, there is drama in the times. There are dense forests. There are Indians war-bent or barter-bent. There are crude log huts and stately mansions. There are assemblies and balls and imported costumes and powdered wigs. There are the men in leather breeches and the women in calico. And between the seaboard and the frontier there are differences which are at times irreconcilable. Yet strangely there is also much accord. The American narrative is a story of contradictions, a tale made up of wondrous things. A court document, a newspaper ad-vertisement, a last will and testament, a handbill announcing a public meeting—they are all a part of history. The known great and the unknown little folk are characters in the same passing drama, sub-ject to the same laws of life and death and oblivion. All are enhanced by the miracle of time and all partake of the enchantment of its passing. Is there not a touch of romance in the annals of the Con-tinental Congress which state:

RESOLVED, That it be referred to captain George Morgan, Eneas Mackay, Esq., and captain John Neville, to adjust and determine all matters of difference between Coquataginta, or Captain White-Eyes, and Messrs. Bernard Gratz and Michael Gratz.

Who shall say that the following advertisement announcing the advent of Jacob Philadelphia is less intriguing than any tale of Edgar Allan Poe? The time is January, 1777.

All lovers of Supernatural Physic are hereby informed, that in a few days, the world renowned Magician, PHILADELPHUS PHILADELPHIA whom Cardanus already mentioned in his book *"de natura supernaturali"* wherein he designates him as the "Envied one of Heaven and Hell," will arrive here by the ordinary Post-chaise, although it would have been an easy matter for him to have come through the air.

Who would not wish to be present at a meeting at the Indian Queen Tavern as announced in the *Pennsylvania Gazette*, January 12, 1780?

The Proprietors of Indiana are requested to be punctual in meeting, agreeable to their adjournment, at the Indian Queen Tavern, in Philadelphia, on the First Monday in February, at Four o'Clock P.M. By Order

DAVID FRANKS, President.

Jan. 5, 1780

The initiation ceremony in Boston of Abraham Jacobs into the mysteries of the Masonic order takes on added significance when his membership certificate bears the signature "Paul Revere, Master."

Historians have harvested a few notable men. The skilled hands of Jewish stonecutters chiseled many a salute to departed Jews who are forgotten. Their work remains. Yet they are unknown. Names like Isaac Navarro, simple craftsman. Or the anonymous silversmiths. One of them, Myer Myers, was elected president of the New York Silversmith Society in the year of our nation's birth. There was an eighteenth-century Jewish artist in Charleston, South Carolina, named Joshua Cantir. Later David Lopez of that city was the architect and builder of the present synagogue Kahal Kadosh Beth Elohim, the fourth oldest congregation in the United States, organized the day after Rosh Hashanah in the year 1749.

There are other forgotten men and women, the fleeting names, the vaguely remembered families. Such a man was Abraham Mordecai who settled in Montgomery, Alabama, in 1785. He came from Pennsylvania and chose to make his home among strangers. Such are the occasional names of Jews that we find on tax lists, court summonses, engaged in lawsuits, applying for licenses. Such are the names found on the records of many congregations.

There are the newspaper advertisements and the wedding announcements and the posthumous eulogies which taken all together make a ready harvest for the historian. Sometimes a sentence or two sums up a lifetime:

In Memory of
Walter J. Judah

Student of Physic, who worn down by his Exertions to Alleviate the sufferings of his fellow Citizens in that dreadful Contagion that visited the City of New York in 1798 fell a Victim in the cause of Humanity the 5th of Tishri A.M. 5559 Corresponding with the 15th of September 1798 Aet. 20 Years 5 Months and 11 Days.

Then again it may be a summary of a lawsuit which in just three brief sentences outlines a crisis for all Jews:

The case of Stansberry v. Marks, reported in 2d Dallas, page 213, was tried on Saturday, April 5, 1793. The defendant offered Jonas Phillips, a Jew, as his witness, but he refused to be sworn because it was his Sabbath. The Court therefore fined him £10.

Yet we know that Jews availed themselves of the right to be sworn on the Old Testament. Such notations as the following are frequent:

On the 26th Day of December in the year of our Lord 1792 Before me Richard Peters Judge of the District Court of the United States in & for the Pennsylvania District came David Franks of the City of Philadelphia Gentleman & being duly sworn on the five Books of Moses (he being a Jew) doth depose and say. . . .

A vigorous challenge to an unjust law, a frontal attack on an unfair decision in the courts of any of the states frequently called forth the greatest skills of our protagonists. So in 1797, Solomon Etting and his father-in-law, Barnard Gratz, began a campaign to permit the Jews of Maryland to hold office. "A bill drafted originally for that purpose by William Pinkney, and called the Jew Bill, was championed, session after session at great sacrifice and even at the cost of defeat for office, by Thomas Kennedy of Washington County." Yet in near-by Pennsylvania and in other States, Jews were holding public office.

These rights were dearly won. They called for tact, for persistency, for unyielding determination. But they also mobilized the finest Christian talent to help them. They appealed to the best in Christianity—to justice and fair play. In 1787 Jonas Phillips had addressed the Federal Convention in these words:

I the subscriber being one of the people called Jews of the City of Philadelphia, a people scattered & dispersed among all nations do behold with Concern that among the laws in the Constitution of Pennsylvania, there is a Clause Sect 10 to viz—I do believe in one God the Creatur and governor of the universe the Rewarder of the good & the punisher of the wicked—and I do acknowledge the Scriptures of the old & New testament to be given by divine inspiration—to swear & believe that the new testament was given by divine inspiration is absolutely against his Conscience to take any such oath—By the above law a Jew is deprived of holding any publick office or place of Government which is a Contridictory to the bill of Right Sect 2 viz. . . .

Six years later he was willing to pay the cost of his allegiance to Judaism.

There were the lonely Jews like John Hays of Cahokia who moved to that tiny Illinois village in 1793. There were the anxious Jews, fearful lest a holiday or a Memorial Day be forgotten or the dietary laws should go by the board for want of a kosher meat supply. So David Hays wrote to his brother Michael in 1784: "I send you by Jacob ¼ mutton kil'd yesterday, also your Deed; & wish you a good fast Shabos; also Monday is yorsite for Mother."

It was not always easy to be a Jew, to live on a cultural desert island cut off from the sustaining warmth of contact with one's own, to remember to orient one's religious life according to one calendar and secular life according to another. To long for holidays and celebrations with family and friends—and to celebrate them quietly, lonesomely, within the narrow radius of one's own home. To nibble the "cake of custom" without friends is to rob it of all taste and flavor. Often the crumbs turned to ashes and all zest was gone out of life. . . . Then came the faint sense of nostalgia. Then the longing for family and friends constricted the heart. Then the minor strains of the folk tune *"Schwer zu sein a Yid"* ("It is hard to be a Jew") welled up from the very bowels of a man and the edges of morale were worn frayed and thin.

The commercial activities of Jews were manifold. They ranged from what a man could carry on his back to vast real estate holdings involving hundreds of thousands of acres. Of some of the great financiers mention has been made—Haym Salomon, Joseph Simon, Barnard and Michael Gratz. There were others. Benjamin Levy and Benjamin Jacob, for example, were appointed as signers of bills of credit. Jacob Hart, a Baltimore Jew, loaned money to Lafayette. Hyman Levy's name is found in the *Journal* of the Continental Congress as having supplied the Army with goods. Isaac Moses of New York subscribed three thousand pounds for purchasing provisions for the Army. Turning again to the Gratz papers we find numerous items referring to large sums of money being advanced to needy patriot leaders. So Edmund Randolph draws on Barnard Gratz for eight hundred fifty pounds. James Madison gives Michael Gratz a receipt for four thousand eight hundred thirty-seven "Continental dollars." Michael Gratz and John Gibson give George Rogers Clark more than one thousand four hundred dollars to be used in his Western campaign.

In the *Calendar of Gratz Papers* in the Gratz Collection in St. Louis, there are many blueprints for a history of the westward movement which is contemporaneous with the epic drama on the seaboard. In 1748-52, the Ohio Company of Virginia was organized. In 1754 Benjamin Franklin proposed at the Albany Congress to carve new colonies in the great Mississippi Valley. The Pontiac Conspiracy broke out in 1763. On the seventh of October, 1763, the King forbade further settlements in the West. An associate of the Gratz brothers, George Croghan then went to England "in the interest of the sufferers of the Pontiac War and of Western Colonization and is disgusted. . . ." Croghan returned and began in 1765-66 operations in the Illinois country. On March 23, 1765, "he secures Indian goods . . . from Simon, Levy and Company (Joseph Simon of Lancaster) to outfit his first Illinois expedition." It was a considerable venture involving two thousand pounds worth of goods. Others joined in until there was a sizable movement under way, organized by those who favored the establishment of Western colonies. In 1768 we come across the following entry:

June 8, William Murray at Carlisle writes to Barnard Gratz in Philadelphia, as he is starting West, via Fort Pitt, leaving his Pennsylvania business in the hands of the Gratz Brothers in Philadelphia.

Exactly one month later, on July 8, Michael Gratz writes to William Murray asking him to open up a branch of the Gratz brothers in the Illinois Country. William Murray carries on in spite of many difficulties. April 24, 1769, "William Murray writes the Gratz brothers from Illinois that ague will disappear when the country is settled." Barnard Gratz is preparing to leave for London and is provided with a letter of introduction to London merchants. In the meanwhile Colonel George Croghan is supplied with sundry goods by the Gratz brothers which are to be used in trade with the Indians. In the late summer of 1769,

August 21: Michael Gratz writes to Barnard Gratz in London, on business with William Murray in Illinois, on Baynton, Wharton and Co's "land affairs," on the interests of Joseph Simon, and on the results of political complications, making it difficult to get supplies for the West.

At the close of the year, December 28, 1769, we note that

Michael Gratz writes from Philadelphia to William Murray in Illinois that the failure to send more goods is not due to lack of confidence but to the results of the Non-Importation policy which makes it almost impossible to get them.

On the first and second day of March of the year 1770, Colonel George Croghan turns over a vast tract of New York land, on the

Mohawk River in Albany County—nine thousand and fifty acres—
to Michael Gratz. The sum paid to Croghan was one thousand eight
hundred pounds. And so it goes!

It is when we begin to examine the real estate contracts and deed
polls of the Revolutionary War period and the years immediately
following, that we become vastly impressed with the magnitude of
Jewish business transactions. One of the Pennsylvania tracts of land
bought by Isaac Franks from Enoch Edwards was called "Little
Paris." It was "Situate on Wheeling Creek in Washington County."
It is quaintly bounded by a dogwood tree on one side and a walnut
tree on another. One fifth of any gold or silver ore that might be
found on the land was, however, to revert to Enoch Edwards.

Another Pennsylvania "Indenture" involved a section called "Lo-
cust Bottom." The purchaser was Solomon Marks, the younger. The
seller was Augustine Regnaud. With the land title went "all and
singular ways woods water and watercourses rights priveleges members and appurtenances whatsoever thereunto belonging."

One transaction involved land sold by Isaac Franks to Dr. Benjamin Rush.

One of the most bustling, energetic of men was Aaron Levy. He
was very likely one of the most successful in his field. For the vast
land holdings, the sales and purchases of lands in his name, are
evidence of his many enterprises. He had imagination, too. He stands
out as the first Jew in America to found a town and name it for himself. He was born in Holland in 1742 and came to this country
while in his late teens. From Northumberland, Pennsylvania, which
was his headquarters, he started a network of trading operations. He
traded with the Indians. He furnished supplies to his colony. Later
he moved to Lancaster where he kept a shop and became a partner of
Joseph Simon. He was a patriot. During the War, he advanced "a
large sum of money to the Continental Congress" through Robert
Morris. He helped furnish supplies to the Army. But it was the acquisition of land which was his dearest ambition. He named the town
which he founded Aaronsburgh. In the naming of the streets, he let
his fancy have free reign.

One of the streets was named for his wife Rachel to whom he was
deeply attached. They had no children. His will, made in Philadelphia where he had taken up residence in 1782, gives us some insight
into his friends and associates. He attained some prominence there,
described himself as a "Gentleman" and was one of the founders of
the Congregation Mickvé Israel.

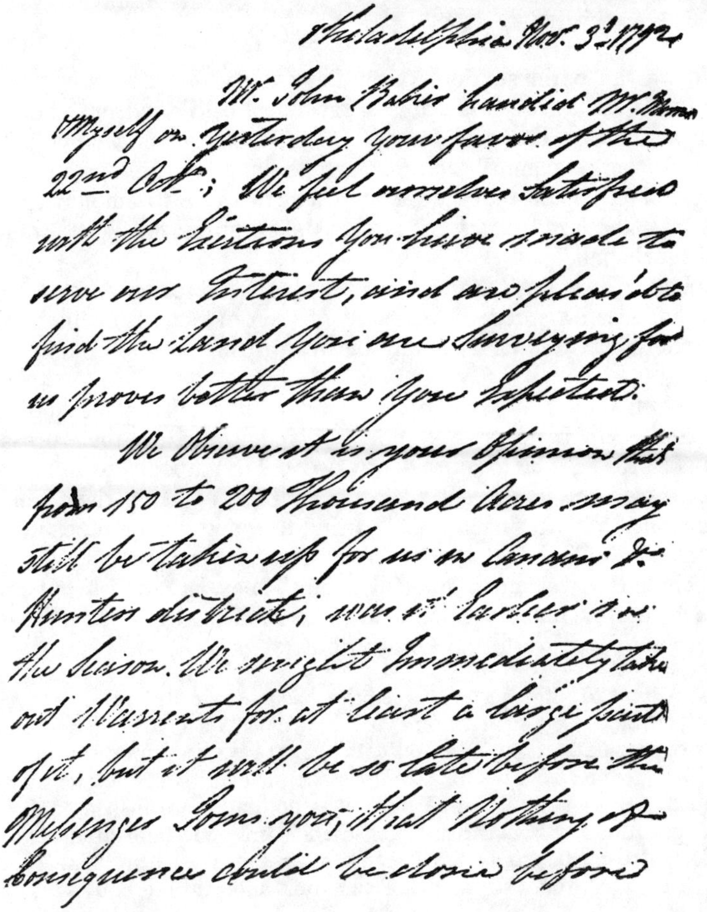
Philadelphia Nov. 3d 1792

Mr. John Baker handed Mr. Morris & Myself on Yesterday your favor of the 22nd Oct.; We feel ourselves Satisfied with the Exertions You have made to serve our Interest, and are pleased to find the Land You are Surveying for us proves better than You Expected.

We Observe it is your Opinion that from 150 to 200 Thousand Acres may still be taken up for us in Canaan & Hunters districts, was it Earlier in the Season. We might Immediately take out Warrents for at least a large part of it, but it will be so late before the Messenger Joins you, that Nothing of Consequence could be done before

This letter is addressed to Aaron Levy in Northumberland County. It is dated Philadelphia, November 3, 1792 and expresses satisfaction with Aaron Levy's "Exertions" as a surveyor. The letter is signed by Walter Stewart for Robert Morris. The concluding paragraphs read:

"We therefore Wish You if Possible to get a part of this Land Survey'd as it Stands, bringing with You all the Requisite drafts & Papers, & when you are on the Spot We will either take out the Warrents Ourselves, or assist You to get some other persons to Enter into the Business.

"It is Unnecessary for us now to Answer the Other parts of Your letter as it can best be done when We meet." Property of the American Jewish Historical Society.

He was an optimist. For Aaron Levy undertook not only to sell such lands as he had in his possession but also to "find out and discover a Tract or Tracts of Land." In one such agreement made between Aaron Levy and Walter Stewart, he undertook to locate several tracts of land of ten thousand acres each, the total to amount to "at least Fifty thousand Acres not already taken up on the West Branch of Susquehanah."

Robert Morris was the third partner of this enterprise. After Aaron Levy had been assured of his share of the land, the remaining two partners divided the land equally between them.

Of commoner clay were other Jewish settlers, the poor and the landless. There is no mystery nor secrecy surrounding their prosaic lives—if prosaic it be to journey down rivers in flatboats, to follow an ox-team trudging its uneven way over prairies, or along river banks; to hew one's way to shelter and security; to found communities in the wilderness.

Their letters written in colorful Yiddish may lack polish but they have an earthy humor which makes them delightful reading. One correspondent writes to the Gratz brothers:

I also want to inform you that I have been sick in bed for two weeks (may you be spared such trouble!). I had caught a cold and it got the better of me. Later I got it in my feet. I cannot walk even now. And our *chacham* [genius] of a doctor says it is rheumatism. But since he knows so much, I don't believe him. I think it is nothing more than a cold, for I first got it in my back, then with stitch in my side, and after that in my feet. It can't be *Zipperlein* because I am not a wealthy man. Thank God, I have recovered so far that I can walk about in the house.[12]

One needs to mark well the close relationship between Christians and Jews in the most critical years of our nation's history. In war and in peace they stood shoulder to shoulder. In the busy teeming cities, in the lonely little outposts, they shared the work and the danger, the planning and the building, the worry and the glory. There is but one generalization that may safely be made about the Jews who witnessed the birth of our nation—that they defy generalization. For there were poor and ragged Jews living on communal charity. There were Jewish capitalists living on vast estates. Their portraits were painted by Gilbert Stuart and other great painters. They imported their clothing and their furniture from abroad. Their children went to the best schools and danced in the most fashionable assemblies. They were slaves of fashion and rigidly conformed to every social code espoused by their Christian neighbors. There were ignorant men among them who knew little English and less Hebrew. There were men of learning. There were professional men and scholars who consorted with their non-Jewish equals. There were Jewish peddlers. But they were not alone, for itinerant "hawkers and walkers" were to be found aplenty in Christian ranks. Jewish society was a pyramid like its Christian counterpart—only smaller.

Among these early pioneers, there were men to love and to admire. There were men to shun and to avoid. There were women who braved every danger, smuggling letters and supplies to prisoners, risking life to nurse and hide wounded soldiers. There were women who flirted and danced through the years of heartbreak and of sacrifice. There were men who kept hammering away at discrimination and prejudice. There were a few who eased their lives by marrying Christian women. They entered the host culture forsaking their own. Haym Salomon could write to the greatest leaders of his day that he was taking time off to observe his holy days. But there were always those who found it easier to evade and to escape their responsibilities as Jews.

Some men filled their letters only with business details. Others were responsive to every political change and mood, placing the events that concerned the nation far above any personal affairs.

The Sheftall family of Georgia may have merited the respect of all who knew it. There were many like them. But not all Jews of that state inspired respect and admiration. If one of them stepped out of bounds or was guilty of a breach of faith or of misconduct, there were the usual careless generalizations, the sloppy statements, the categorical innuendoes. Here is a brief paragraph culled from "Cursory Remarks on Men & Manners in Georgia. By A Citizen, 1784," which points out the great vulnerability of the Jew and "the slender tenure of goodwill" which is vouchsafed him.

The Jews are a race of men well acquainted with the scorns and persecution of all the rest of the world. Surely, then, it was a most forward, not to say unguarded action, in one of these whose religious situation makes him the most vulnerable man on earth to endeavour to disfranchise an Indian of privilege which he himself held by the slender tenure of goodwill; indeed if we believe Mr. Adair, in his History of the Indians, we might go farther and call it a most *injudaic* action, for the writing strongly insists the Creek Indians and the Jews are very nearly allied; he hazards a conjecture that the former are really and truly one of the Tribes of Jacob, who came, by some means or other, to be lost in the wilds of America.[13]

Even so great a friend of the Jews as Ezra Stiles occasionally lapses into careless reporting when he attempts to pin the Tory label on many of his Jewish neighbors. He forgets that when he was himself accused of lack of zeal for the King, he stoutly denied it. On April 7, 1775, just a few days before the Battle of Lexington, he said, "That I have ceased to pray for the King & Royal Family is so far from being true that I constantly pray publickly for the King every Lords day & on every public Occasion."

CHAPTER VIII

Freedom Is Dearly Won

➤➤➤ WE, the Master, Wardens and Brethren of King David's Lodge, in Newport, Rhode Island, joyfully embrace this opportunity, to greet you as a Brother, and to hail you welcome to Rhode Island. . . . Permit us then, illustrious Brother, cordially to salute you, with three times three, and to add our fervent supplications, that the Sovereign Architect of the Universe may always encompass you with his holy protection.

> —*Address of the Master, Wardens and Brethren of King David's Lodge, to George Washington, President of the United States of America* ◄◄◄

FREEDOM DID not fall like an overripe plum into the laps of American Jewry. It was dearly won. It was earned on the battlefield and harvested in every community. It was the fruit of an unceasing struggle requiring eternal vigilance. Perhaps the Jews found part of the answer to religious freedom in numbers. For there is no denying the fact that the diversity of Protestant sects and the presence of Catholics made some workable compromise essential. Separation of Church and State was the answer. The Revolution left its mark on organized religion. In 1775 nine of the thirteen colonies had established churches. Almost at once the Anglican clergy in five states lost their special privileges. Deism and Unitarianism made sizable inroads into the ranks of the more orthodox Christian churches.

When the crisis came, Jefferson, Paine, John Adams, Washington, Franklin, Madison, and many lesser lights were to be reckoned among either the Unitarians or the Deists. It was not Cotton Mather's God to whom the authors of the Declaration of Independence appealed; it was to "Nature's God."[1]

161

In the United States, events as well as abstract ideas shaped the destiny of the Jews. The Declaration of Independence, the Revolutionary Movement and the War itself, had crystallized in the mind of the American Jew his thoughts on the subject of equality. The War opened new political vistas. The Jew became a more articulate member of society. The role of passive, sluggish acceptance of civil disabilities was discarded for a more alert, more aggressive, more belligerent attitude. The Revolutionary Movement in North America, the reforms of the French Revolution and the Napoleonic Era in Europe, were like gusts of fresh air in a stale ill-ventilated chamber. The Jew breathed more freely in France and the United States.

Thomas Jefferson, author of the Declaration of Independence, is without a doubt the foremost figure in the movement for religious toleration in the United States. His own State, Virginia, early became the battleground where nonconformity was pitted against acceptance of an established religion. In 1776 a convention met in Virginia in order to draw up a constitution for the new State. Among the provisions debated was one which provided for religious toleration. Madison opposed the use of the word *toleration*, maintaining that freedom of worship was a *right* inherent to mankind, and not a *privilege* granted by a benevolent government. His interpretation was accepted.

In 1779 Jefferson introduced a bill for establishing religious freedom. This measure was held in abeyance for several years. In the meanwhile the slender finances of the Virginia Episcopal Church, which felt the want of a State subsidy, as well as the widespread acceptance of radical revolutionary doctrines imported from France, caused the people of Virginia to view the religious situation with alarm. Friends of the established church felt that they had fallen upon evil days. Christianity, they urged, should be re-established in Virginia. In 1784 Patrick Henry submitted a bill for subsidizing the Christian religion in his State. Jefferson was then in France. But James Madison proved an able spokesman for the Jeffersonian theories. Nevertheless, the opposition won by a vote of 47 to 32. Patrick Henry's resolution was adopted and he was made chairman of a committee to draft a suitable bill.

This measure became a storm center in the legislative halls. At the instance of Madison, it was submitted to the voters of Virginia. In order that his point of view be thoroughly understood, Madison prepared a *Memorial* and *Remonstrance* against the bill which was widely circulated and signed. Public opinion overwhelmingly supported the author of the *Remonstrance*. Thanks to him, religious freedom was safe in Virginia. Jefferson was satisfied that "within the mantle of its protection, the Jew and the Gentile, the Christian and Mahometan, the Hindoo, and Infidel of every denomination" were safe.

Each State had its own separate problem to solve. There is a noticeable pattern which repeats itself. Max J. Kohler summarizes the situation in New York in these words:

Thus prior to the Revolution the Jews in New York enjoyed in practice full civil rights; their legal status was less satisfactory, however, and various political rights were withheld from them. By the first Constitution of the State of New York, adopted in 1777, they were put on an absolute equality with all other subjects, that State having been the leader in actually granting full religious liberty.[2]

The results of the American struggle for religious freedom were far-reaching. French political reformers, like Mirabeau, warmly endorsed the Jeffersonian attitude. To Jefferson, the French acceptance of his views was a source of great satisfaction.

To what extent ideas of toleration were colored by acquaintance with patriotic Jews, or by a sense of indebtedness which many Revolutionary leaders felt toward individual Jews, is a matter of speculation. Whatever its ideological antecedents, the Virginia act and those patterned on it gave a powerful impetus to Jewish emancipation in Europe, as well as in America. The subject was widely discussed. Hebrew sources record the victory with triumph and invoke the American example repeatedly. They argue that the emancipation of Jews has not brought the much dreaded influx of Jews to the United States and France, whereas it did contribute materially to the economic prosperity of these more enlightened nations.

It was a hard, uphill fight. The issue raised its head in other States and not always with the same gratifying results. A correspondent writes in *The Pennsylvania Evening Post* in 1776, expressing the fear that unless Christianity is specified, "Jews or Turks may become in time our greatest landholders . . . so as to render it not only uncomfortable but unsafe for Christians." Again another contributor who styles himself "A Follower of Christ" writes to the same paper in 1777, complaining that

The Pennsylvanians have made a new constitution . . . by which Jews, Turks, and Heathens may not only be freemen of that land, but are eligible for Assemblymen, Judges, Counsellors and Presidents or Gov-

ernors. . . . Will any Christian power call this state for the future a
Christian state? Will it not be an asylum for all fugitive Jesuits and
outcasts of Europe?[3]

In North Carolina the Episcopal Church was the established
denomination from 1701. After a determined effort, Protestant dissenters secured a modification of this law, excluding both Catholics
and Jews from the enjoyment of similar freedom. By the constitution
of 1776, Jews as well as Catholics were debarred from office-holding.
There was a liberal element which continued to wage an unsuccessful campaign against these religious restrictions. On the whole the
subject was ignored. Catholics were elected to office. But when, in
1808 and 1809, a Jew, Jacob Henry, was twice elected to the Legislature, the whole subject was reopened. A political opponent challenged Henry's right to hold office. Henry defended his position with
eloquence, invoking the Bill of Rights of the Federal Constitution.
He appealed to their sense of fair play, as well as to his constitutional
rights. Two Catholic office-holders helped him. He was seconded by
the enlightened minority of the State. By an adroit interpretation of
the law Jacob Henry was allowed to retain his seat, but the disability
clause remained. It was not until the year 1868 that the new Constitution withdrew the disqualifying clause. The champion advocate
of Jewish rights who hurled editorial bolts at this backward State,
was Isaac Leeser. In the pages of his journal, the *Occident*, and elsewhere, he continued to press the subject.

Another laggard State, even more reluctant to recognize the principle of religious liberty than North Carolina, was New Hampshire.
Until 1876, Jews and Catholics were ineligible to hold certain offices
there.

These new items chronicling both defeat and victories trickled
through to the Jews of Europe. What the channels of communication
were, we can only guess. Letters went back and forth across the
Atlantic. Articles and books and newspapers carried the news.
Travelers came here to visit and returned home to praise, to tell the
wonders of the new age, of the marvels of democracy in practice.
Shabby, poverty-stricken immigrants made good, became prosperous
and sent presents to Europe and money for transportation to America. The pendulum of communication swung back and forth.

Teamwork during the critical war years brought Christians and
Jews together. There is no need to review at length the extent to
which Jews of colonial and Revolutionary times co-operated in many
important ventures with prominent non-Jews. The evidence is over-

whelming. Colonel Franks was associated with Dr. Benjamin Rush in 1784 in the purchase of nineteen tracts of Indiana land. The Gratz brothers numbered among their land-holding associates men who helped make history at this time. The extent to which Philadelphia Jewry was esteemed by their contemporaries may be gathered from a subscription list for the support of the synagogue which in 1788 had such names as those of Benjamin Franklin, Charles Biddell, William Bradford, and David Rittenhouse among the subscribers. In Newport, in Charleston, in Savannah, the story is repeated.

George Washington, in his frequently quoted correspondence with the various Hebrew congregations, shows an open and liberal attitude at all times.

The Jews of Savannah sent to the first President of their country a warm expression of their regard:

Sir:- We have long been anxious of congratulating you on your appointment, by unanimous approbation, to the presidential dignity of this country, and of testifying our unbounded confidence in your integrity and unblemished virtue. Yet however exalted the station you now fill, it is still not equal to the merit of your heroic services through an arduous and dangerous conflict, which has embosomed you in the hearts of her citizens.

Our eccentric situation, added to a diffidence founded on the most profound respect, has thus long prevented our address, yet the delay has realized anticipation, given us an opportunity of presenting our grateful acknowledgments for the benediction of heaven through the magnanimity of federal influence and the equity of your administration.[4]

In answer the President replied:

I rejoice that a spirit of liberality and philanthropy is much more prevalent than it formerly was among 'the enlightened nations of the earth, and that your brethren will benefit thereby in proportion as it shall become still more extensive; happily the people of the United States have in many instances exhibited examples worthy of imitation.

The Newport Jews were no less articulate. They saw the historic significance of their position clearly:

Deprived as we hitherto have been of the inalienable rights of free citizens, we now—with a deep sense of gratitude to the Almighty Disposer of all events—behold a government erected by the majesty of the people—a government which to bigotry gives no sanction, to persecution no assistance, but generously affording to all liberty of conscience and immunities of citizenship, deeming every one of whatever nation, tongue or language, equal parts of the great governmental machine.

To the Newport Jews, Washington replied:

May the children of the stock of Abraham who dwell in this land continue to merit and enjoy the good will of the other inhabitants—while every one shall sit in safety under his own vine and fig tree and there shall be none to make him afraid.

But Washington, too, saw the larger meaning, the deeper significance of these events. For in his reply to Newport, he included this significant sentence:

The citizens of the United States of America have a right to applaud themselves for having given to mankind examples of an enlarged and liberal policy—a policy worthy of imitation. All possess alike liberty of conscience and immunities of citizenship.

Succeeding Presidents and statesmen were engaged from time to time in an exchange of letters with Jews. Some of these papers have a more than casual significance. They contribute materially to our ability to interpret the times, the great leaders and the Jews in relation to both.

John Adams on the occasion of the dedication of the Mill Street synagogue in 1818, wrote to Mordecai M. Noah:

I have had occasion to be acquainted with several gentlemen of your nation, and to transact business with some of them, whom I found to be men of as liberal minds, as much honor, probity, generosity and good breeding, as any I have known in any sect of religion or philosophy.

I wish your nation may be admitted to all privileges of citizens in every country of the world. This country has done much. I wish it may do more; and annul every narrow idea in religion, government, and commerce.

"If I were an atheist and believed in blind eternal fate, I should still believe that fate had ordained the Jews to be the most essential instruments for civilizing the nations,"[5] our second President once wrote in a private letter. Like his distant relative, the author Hannah Adams, he had a lifelong interest in Jewish History.

That Thomas Jefferson, the apostle of liberalism, should have frequently expressed himself on the subject of Jewish emancipation, is to be expected. He had a warm, sympathetic understanding of the position of minority groups subjected to the domination of an aggressive majority. Liberal laws he felt were "the only antidote to this vice. .... But more remains to be done, for although we are free by the law, we are not so in practice; public opinion erects itself into an Inquisition, and exercises its office with as much fanaticism, as fans the flames of an Auto-da-fé."

He writes to a Jewish correspondent of. his deep awareness of the intolerance inherent in most men:

Your sect by its sufferings has furnished a remarkable proof of the universal spirit of religious intolerance inherent in every sect, disclaimed by all while feeble, and practiced by all when in power. Our laws have applied the only antidote to this vice, protecting our religious, as they do our civil rights, by putting all on an equal footing.[6]

On the subject of education, Jefferson expressed himself in forthright terms when he wrote to Isaac Harby that Jewish students should be excused from all compulsory "Theological Reading."

Jefferson practiced what he preached. He seems to have been without any prejudice. In 1804 in letters exchanged between Gallatin and Jefferson, a "Mr. Levy of Philadelphia" is seriously considered for the post of Attorney-General of the United States. Jefferson was a close personal friend of one family of that name. It was this family which, after his death, bought Monticello, the Jefferson home. At one time Commodore Uriah Phillips Levy was the owner both of Monticello and the Monroe estate. It was Commodore Levy who in 1833 presented the nation with a bronze statue of Thomas Jefferson. This statue was the first object of this kind ever owned by the United States Government. It was altogether fitting and proper that a Jew should thus commemorate the services of this great liberal.

James Madison, like his distinguished contemporary, was well disposed toward this little minority group. "The history of the Jews," he once wrote, "must forever be interesting." His correspondence with Jews is varied and colorful. In 1812 President Madison received a letter from a woman in London in which she turned over to him 131 shares of stock to be used "for the Defence of the United States." The letter uses several words in Hebrew script, refers to the fires of the Inquisition, closes with the pious hope for the restoration of "the Kingdom of Jehovah." During his presidency, Madison appointed Dr. Joel Hart as the United States Consul at Leith, Scotland. In a letter to Mordecai M. Noah in 1818, Madison expressed himself as "having ever regarded the freedom of religious opinions and worship as equally belonging to every sect."

Letters between Jews and Christians were not limited to the polite exchange of high-sounding principles. Among the thousands of letters that have been preserved there are simple expressions of friendship like the letter written by Colonel Isaac Franks expressing his grief at the death of Dr. Benjamin Rush. For theirs had been a friendship of thirty-three years. Ever on the alert, they did not hesitate to call to account their Christian acquaintances who were guilty of misusing the word "Jew." "You know I am your friend, and therefore I write to you freely," wrote Solomon Etting to Henry Clay, adding that he felt "both surprized and hurt by the manner in which you introduced the expression 'the Jew' in debate in the Senate of the United States." Henry Clay's answer disclaims any "unfavorable interpretation." Of America's first woman historian, one of her friends said, "If you want to know Miss Adams, you must talk to her about the Jews." For she had "faithfully studied their history, and she venerated the antiquity of their origin. . . . She felt for them as a suffering and persecuted people. . . . It was the long contemplation of this chosen race that induced her . . . to write their history." It was the newly emerging spirit of democracy which marked its leaders as philosemites.

The land we know. Let us consider its settlers. The total population in 1789 was just under 4,000,000, of whom some 700,000 were slaves. Philadelphia, the largest city, numbered 42,000 people. The largest settlements were along the seaboard. According to an estimated figure in the census of 1790, there were in the neighborhood of 109,000 settlers in the valleys of the Ohio and the Cumberland. When in 1800 the Government was moved to newly laid out Washington, planned by Major L'Enfant, a French engineer, the capital was but half finished. But eleven critical years of government by compromise had been achieved. Three new States had been admitted to the Union. Treaties were made with Indians at the instigation of President Washington. Indian traders, of whom many were Jews, were to be licensed henceforth. His labors finished, Washington bade his people a moving farewell and turned his office over to John Adams.

The student of Americana-Judaica will do well to keep in mind the main events and personalities of American history at this formative period of national history. It is our frame of reference. The Jews, always a minority group, can only be studied in relation to the activities and events which affected all Americans. While general statistics at this time were largely speculative, for the Jews they were especially so. We can only deal with the men and women whose names were preserved to us because of their official connection with the founders of the nation, because of their signal service in one way or another. We know that Manuel Noah, father of Major Mordecai Manuel Noah, gave his all in serving his country, having been chosen by Francis Marion to go north as aide-de-camp to Washington. But do we know the little men who fought and starved and died in many bloody campaigns? We know that Major David S. Franks and Colonel Isaac Franks attained prominence. We recall that Benjamin Nones rose from the ranks to head as Major "a Hebrew legion" of four hundred men in De Kalb's command. But what of the four hundred? There are so many unsolved riddles, so many unraveled plots.

Not the least of the mystery plots is the one which concerns our first Secretary of the Treasury, Alexander Hamilton, the financial genius who is credited with building the monetary structure of the new nation. He was a native of the British West Indies, studied at King's College, was a friend of Washington's. Gertrude Atherton, whose generosity is responsible for erecting a monument to Mrs. Rachel Levine, Alexander Hamilton's mother, after exhaustive research in Denmark and St. Croix managed to stir up a hornet's nest of unsolved riddles. Rachel was technically still John Levine's wife when young Alexander was born. However, this too belongs more in the realm of romantic fiction than to that of history.

It is with our third President, Thomas Jefferson, that fact piles upon fact and the structure becomes a veritable monument to be cherished by every student of American Jewish history. A linguist, educator, lawyer, mathematician, scientist, musician, farmer, statesman, diplomat, author, architect, public servant, humanitarian—yet Jefferson was modest withal. In his epitaph he chose to commemorate but three of his achievements:

Here was buried Thomas Jefferson, author of the Declaration of American Independence, of the statute of Virginia for religious freedom, and father of the University of Virginia.

His nature was a bubbling fountain of good will. It was logical that Jews should turn to him, that he should lend a willing ear and a ready hand whenever they approached him. Jews may have been in a minority, but Jefferson did not forget them or their needs. He insisted that the University of Virginia be founded as a nonsectarian institution, that courses in Christian theology be optional with the students. By proclamation he made Thanksgiving Day a day in which Jews could freely partake.

That he had Jews on his mind in establishing these reforms, is made clear again and again by Jefferson in his writings. "I have thought it a cruel addition to the wrongs which that injured sect have suffered," he wrote in the evening of his life from Monticello, "that their youth should be excluded from the instructions in science afforded to all others in our public seminaries, by imposing upon them a course of Theological Reading which their consciences do not permit them to pursue."[7]

Among the Jefferson papers are several letters from Moses Myers and Joseph Marx and a firm called "Cohen & Bros." They cover a number of subjects. Here is a report of the Sanhedrin called together by Napoleon in which his correspondent assures Jefferson:

Should any part of their Deliberations, or Sentiments expressed by any Member of that Body, tend to confirm the liberal and enlightened views, expressed by yourself, of that persecuted Race, when last I had the honor and pleasure of an interview, it will prove to me a source of high gratification.[8]

On another occasion a simple gift which Joseph Marx presents to Jefferson elicits the acknowledgment that "its highest value is placed in the motives of the giver." Another time the subject involved concerns a financial transaction at the office of the United States Bank. Again "Marx & Brown" are compelled to decline an invitation of Thomas Jefferson's, "their attendance being required at Court."

The subject is by no means exhausted. But it is hoped that enough evidence has been cited to show that Jefferson's liberalism was practiced not alone on an abstract philosophic level but carried out in deed, in simple acts of courtesy, tact and consideration. His was democracy in action. That is why he was so attentive to the happenings in Europe. There is a consistent parallel in events in France at this time. On September 27, 1791, the French National Assembly abolished all discriminatory laws. French Jews rejoiced with good cause. Four years later French influence had extended as far as Holland. Wherever the French Army advanced thereafter, there blossomed emancipation for the Jews. It was a happy harvest and an omen of events to come. Napoleon's Proclamation of 1799 had promised Jerusalem to the Jews. In 1806 the Assembly of Jewish Notables had met at his invitation. In 1807 the Sanhedrin was convened. We know how eagerly Americans watched these changes in the tides of

Hebrew fortune. From Jefferson to the merest clerk in some outlying country store, there was rejoicing on the part of some Christians and all Jews of the tolling of freedom's bell.

As the nineteenth century took up the torch from the faltering hands of the eighteenth, an old patriot of the Revolution, a combat-weary veteran, none other than Benjamin Nones, picked up his quill pen and wrote an angry letter to an editor.

To the Printer of the Gazette of the United States.

Sir,

I HOPE, if you take the liberty of inserting calumnies against individuals, for the amusement of your readers, you will have so much regard to justice, as to permit the injured through the same channel that conveyed the slander, to appeal to the public in self defence. . . .

I am accused of being a *Jew*, of being a *Republican*, and of being *Poor*.

I *am* a *Jew*. I glory in belonging to that persuasion. . . .

I am a *Republican*! Thank God I have not been so heedless and so ignorant of what has passed, and is now passing in the political world. I have not been so proud or so prejudiced as to renounce the cause for which I have *fought*, as an American, throughout the whole of the revolutionary war, in the militia of Charleston, and in Polaskey's legion, I fought in almost every action which took place in Carolina, and in the disastrous affair of Savannah, shared the hardships of that sanguinary day, and for three and twenty years I felt no disposition to change my political any more than my religious principles. . . .

I am a Jew, and if for no other reason, for that reason am I a republican. . . .

But I am *poor*; I am so, my family also is large, but soberly and decently brought up. They have not been taught to revile a christian because his religion is not *so old* as theirs. They have not been taught to mock even at the errors of good intention, and conscientious belief. . . .

I know that to purse proud aristocracy poverty is a crime, but it may sometimes be accompanied with honesty even in a Jew: I was bankrupt some years ago; I obtained my certificate and was discharged from my debts. . . .

This is a long defence Mr. Wayne, but you have called it forth, and therefore, I hope you at least will not object to it. The public will now judge who is the proper object of ridicule and contempt, your facetious reporter, or

Your humble servant,

BENJAMIN NONES.[9]

PHILADELPHIA, August 11, 1800.

A year after this letter appeared in print, Myer Polonies, a Polish Jew, died in New York. In his will he left nine hundred dollars, the interest to be used for the founding of a Hebrew School as an integral part of the synagogue activities. Ten years later the Legislature of New York voted a grant to the Polonies Talmud Torah. And when "an aged and virtuous virgin in Israel," Miss Rachel Pinto, died she added to the school treasury by leaving the magnificent sum of six hundred and sixty-one dollars and ninety cents.[10] If Jewish children were to be equipped to write letters to editors, there was only one way to prepare them.

Now an age of mobility dawned. Men and their families took to the roads or hewed new ones. A giant tide of humanity overflowed the mountains, rolling westward. Frontiers were mobile barriers knocked down like hurdles in a race.

Wagon wheels turned toward the setting sun, biting deep into the virgin soil. The "Flying Machine" was a covered wagon that traveled fast—a day and a half between New York and Philadelphia in 1771. Stage coaches ran regular schedules. The Conestoga wagon was used for long overland journeys, down to the days of the California gold rush. Painted bright red and blue with a white cloth cover, its colors were symbolic of the new nation. Bridges upheld by hewed logs came into use. Soon the Pony Express went rumbling over them. Rivers tempted men. The flatboat and barge or keelboat carried passengers into the fragrant river valleys. The pirogue, a large canoe which could transport a family and a number of tons of household goods, was a familiar sight. Packet boats advertised for passengers. The first ferry-boat was put into service between New York and Hoboken in 1804. The steamboat, first conceived by John Fitch in 1785, was by the turn of the century a sturdy and lusty child.

It was the age of the itinerant. There were men on foot and on horseback, unattached men whose love of the road replaced other ties, wife and children and home. There were itinerant preachers, teachers, clergymen, lawyers, doctors, dentists, actors and minstrels. Many a craftsman spent the winter months at his bench and then took to the road with the first thaw. Peddling was once an honorable Yankee calling. It lost caste only when Jews began plodding over the trails and roads in goodly numbers. A man began as a pack peddler. Then he bought a horse and wagon and finally achieved the dignity of a permanent address. As the merchant class gained stability and status, there was a noticeable snubbing of the roving peddler. Competition was keen. The merchant resented the itinerant salesman. "Doubtless some of the peddler's undesirable reputation was due to

propaganda fostered by merchants." Wealthy Jews who achieved
social equality with their Christian neighbors worried on their plushy
estates lest their precarious social standing be jeopardized by a flat-
footed immigrant who carried his wares and his *talith* on his back.
How would a man like Luis Gomez, with an estate in the country in
Marlborough-on-the-Hudson and a creek that flowed into that sluggish
river named "Jew's Creek" in his honor, how would such a man feel
about these his road-weary brethren? For an itinerant schoolmaster
or peddler or cobbler is a romantic character until he is found to be a
Jew. Then he ceases to interest most people.

"The ways are preparing and the roads will be made easy," wrote
Washington. But the rigors of the road were incalculable, especially
for the orthodox Jew who had his diet to worry about. So well known
were these difficulties that it does not surprise us to find a non-Jewish
traveler who left New York for St. Louis in 1845 writing:

After a while I had my dinner,—ah! such a dinner—two glasses of
bonny clabber sweetened with dirty brown sugar. . . . They set before
me . . . a little square chunk of fat salt pork; but I told them I could
no more eat it than if I were a jew [sic].[11]

Eventually troubles and hazards were surmounted and we find
these wanderers everywhere following now one calling, now another.
There are so many interesting characters like "Old Mordecai" who
founded the city of Montgomery, Alabama. He began as a butcher
and in the course of a long life tried his hand at one thing and another, taking time out to serve three years in the patriot Army of the
Revolution. At War's end he found a permanent home in a place
desolately named Buzzard Roost in what is now Georgia and became
a trader among his neighbors, the Cusseta Indians.

There were indentured servants among Jews who found life unbearable and solved their personal problems by running away. Such
a person was young Wolf Samuel who left Amsterdam without money,
promising to pay for his passage one week after his arrival. He was,
with other impecunious immigrants, sold in open market. For seventy-
six dollars which his master paid for young Wolf Samuel, the boy
was pledged to work for thirty-eight months. His letters from Pitsch-
bodem (Peach Bottom), in Pennsylvania, are full of unrelieved unhappiness. In desperation he wrote to the officials of his township, "to
make you known my sad condition." His letters were intercepted.
He took to the road. In the *York Recorder*, May 24, 1820, there

appeared an advertisement offering five-dollars reward for his return. Wolf Samuel made good his escape.

The years sped on as swiftly as a rushing river. There were momentous changes brewing. When Washington took the oath of office a second time, France was in the major throes of her Revolution. "Liberty, equality, fraternity" made welcome music on both sides of the Atlantic. But gradually as terror became the tool and handmaiden of the Goddess of Reason, as war and aggression against neighbors evolved into a martial pattern, as bloodshed replaced philosophic concepts and casualty lists supplanted ideologies—France alienated her friends. Washington proclaimed our neutrality on April 22, 1793. He walked a tightrope between France and Great Britain. To make the situation more acute, the British were inciting the Indians to rebel against the steady march of the white man into his grazing grounds and green valleys beyond the Alleghenies. John Jay negotiated a treaty with England, but her continued violation of all promises and all solemn pledges aroused the American public. They resented the treaty and the treaty-makers. Jay was burned in effigy in Georgia. Hamilton was stoned in New York. Washington was exposed to "censure, abuse, and vilification."

In this atmosphere of internal strife and bitter factionalism, of strained relations with European powers and growing party and political differences at home, another election was held and another President selected. The Federalists chose John Adams. The Republicans, whose standard-bearer was Jefferson, carried the election in 1801, four years later. Across the Atlantic Napoleon Bonaparte was master of France. England and France were girding for war. At this moment, the vast plains of Louisiana became a prize which England coveted and France could not defend. Robert Livingston was our minister in France. Jefferson wanted Louisiana. We acquired it in 1803 and so doubled the area of our land. Almost a century before, Elias Stultheus, "le Juif," and other pioneers had sweated and toiled over it, had felled its timber and tilled its fields and forded its rivers and wallowed in its marshes, and sickened and died there. Now this vast domain was to add fourteen States to the Union and to add untold wealth and resources to our national economy. Within two months of the Louisiana Purchase, Meriwether Lewis and William Clark headed an expedition which led them across the Rocky Mountains and along the Columbia River to the Pacific Ocean. The inexorable march from coast to coast was under way.

Now there took place a chain of events in Europe which dragged this nation into war. In the life-and-death struggle between Napoleon and England a fuse was lighted which precipitated us into armed conflict with England. Between 1793-1802 our maritime trade had become impressive. Ships built in American harbors sailed to every port of the world. By 1810, ninety-one per cent of our foreign trade was carried by American ships. It was now that England's high-handed policy, her ignoring of our sovereignty, her impressment of American sailors, her crass disregard of international law, made war inevitable. But England provoked us not only on the high seas and within sight of our harbors. She supplied the Indians with guns and gunpowder. It was necessary to take to arms to subdue the Redskins. William Henry Harrison defeated the Indians at Tippecanoe. "It was the men of the agricultural frontier who . . . at last brought about the declaration of hostilities against England in 1812."

We turn now to that war and to the Jewish soldiers who fought in it, from Private Jacob Appel to Private Abraham Yuxsheimer, with one brigadier general, a number of lieutenants and captains and a colonel to add to the list.

There were about three thousand Jews in the United States when the War of 1812 broke out. Of this group a number are found in the Army and Navy. Many of these are sons of Revolutionary patriots.

There was Aaron Levy, son of Hayman Levy, and son-in-law of Isaac Moses, ardent Revolutionary patriot. Aaron was paymaster in the Army in 1800. In 1812 he attained the rank of captain. His promotions brought him the rank of major in 1815, and lieutenant colonel in 1816. Another familiar name is that of Haym M. Salomon, son of the patriot and financier, who was an officer in the War. The Phillips family, which included Jonas Phillips, a soldier in the War of the Revolution, listed his son Joseph in the War of 1812, as well as two other members of the family, Naphthali Phillips and Dr. Manuel Phillips, who saw service. The Seixas family numbered three officers—Captains Abraham, Moses B. and Solomon Seixas. David G. Seixas, son of the patriotic Rabbi of Shearith Israel, was also in service at this time. Other Jewish families are represented: Sampson Simson, an ensign, and Samuel Noah, West Point graduate, who fought as a private. Benjamin Gratz, son of Michael Gratz, as well as Joseph and Simon Gratz, were among the Pennsylvania volunteers. Two members of the Nones family are found in the ranks.

There were others, officers and men who carried on the tradition established by their Revolutionary forefathers. Their ranks were augmented by a number of foreign-born Jews who took up residence in the United States after the Revolution. Interesting is the name of a Jewish soldier, Bernard Hart, whose grandson, a non-Jew, was the novelist Francis Bret Harte. Bernard Hart was a division quartermaster during the War.

Southern Jews enrolled in the war against England with characteristic enthusiasm. Among them were Meyer Moses, a militia captain, Jacob De La Motta, a surgeon in the Army; Abraham A. Massias, first a captain, later a major; Hyam Cohen, a lieutenant in the First Regiment; Chapman Levy, a captain of militia.

In the search for a "typical" family, the historian is overwhelmed by an embarrassment of riches. Perhaps the Cohen family of Maryland will do.[12] Israel and Judith Cohen were the parents of a large family. Their sixth child was Mendes Cohen. He was still in his teens when he joined the Twenty-Seventh Regiment of his State under the impression that he would be joining a fighting unit assigned to defend Washington. When he found that he was mistaken he managed to secure a transfer to Captain Nicholson's Fencibles. He was in Fort McHenry with seven other Jews when it was bombarded. Colonel Mendes Cohen's account of the bombardment is one of his family's treasures. When Francis Scott Key wrote "The Star Spangled Banner" there were three Cohens, an Etting, an Israel Davidson, as well as three soldiers named Moses, Myers and Solomon on the scene.

There were some others whose contribution to the War lifted them out of the rank and file. Such a man was Harmon Hendricks, a New York merchant, who subscribed $40,000, one of the largest individual subscriptions, for bonds to finance the War. Levi Charles Harby of South Carolina was an intrepid midshipman in the Navy during the War. He was captured by the British and spent eighteen months in a prison in Dartmoor. Colonel Nathan Myers was in command of a brigade near New York City at the outbreak of the War. Joseph B. Nones, a midshipman in the Navy, was secretary to Henry Clay when the latter, as one of a commission of three, was sent to Ghent to the Peace Conference. Joseph was the son of Major Nones of Revolutionary War fame. He served at one time on the *Guerrière,* a member of Decatur's staff. Nones retired from the service in 1822.

Captain Mordecai Myers showed a decided aptitude for Army life. He was born in Newport, Rhode Island, in 1776, at the outbreak of the Revolution. After receiving his education in New York, he lived for some time in Richmond, Virginia. While in New York, he studied military science for two years. In 1812 Myers secured his commission as Captain in the Thirteenth U.S. Infantry and tackled war in earnest. At Sackets Harbor he distinguished himself by rescuing some one hundred and fifty seasick, shipwrecked sailors. They were found in capsized schooners which had carried hospital stores. The survivors had indulged too freely in medicinal liquors and were "nearly all intoxicated." He succeeded in getting these befuddled warriors to shore, although it required the aid of the crews of two larger boats that had been put in his charge.

Captain Myers saw active service in the Canadian campaign. At the Battle of Chrysler's Farm, near Williamsburg, while leading a charge against the British, he was severely wounded. Invalided for four months, he nevertheless returned to service and carried on until the end of the War.

Mordecai Myers, skilled though he seems to have been in military arts, found the intricacies of the King's English a bit too much for him. A letter of his written in 1813 describes with complete lack of modesty his activities in the War. He addresses his friend Mr. Naph-thali Hart:

DEAR NAPH:
   . . . the time has arrived when the nation requirs all its advocats. Sum must spill there blud and others there *ink*. I expect to be amongst the former and I hop you are amongst the latter.

He muses sadly on the changes wrought by war and the fortunes made and lost by "Mercantil" men. Then in a philosophical vein, he continues:

It is a fine thing to abandon the persute of welth. I never ware hapy in Persute of Riches and now that I have abandoned it I am much more contented. . . . My Dutys are hard and Trying to the Constitution but I continue in good helth as yeate.

Then comes a rather interesting bit of information about the blockade:

I Abserve by the news papers that most of our Southern ports are blockaded, that I expected it is done with a view to call the attention of Government to defencive operations In sted of Affensive ones. But I hop we are competent to both. If we receive the necessary reinforcements and a good Genl we ken conqure the uper Province & be at Montreal by Octobʳ and then proced to the Seage of quebeck at our Lashure.

His optimism is boundless. The letter continues with a recital of his numerous camp duties and his weighty responsibilities. "I have anough to do but am content," he concludes.[13]

While the Jews of America stood side by side with other citizens in the War of 1812, dramatic events were transpiring in Europe, events which turned the Jewish world upside down, injected controversy, threatened their precarious peace of mind. For eighteen days, from June 28 to July 16, 1812, Napoleon was in residence in a palace in Vilna, the Jerusalem of the Diaspora. Some Jews prayed for the defeat of Napoleon, others, like the brothers Goldsmid, helped finance his wars. "The consideration given to the subject of 'Jewish rights' at the Congress of Vienna, held at the close of the Napoleonic Wars, proved of considerable importance in the history of Jewish emancipation," writes one historian. "Jewish communities were officially represented at the Congress, although their spokesmen were not actually heard at any official sessions."[14]

There was the usual diplomatic double-talk. Prince Metternich reassured Mr. Baruch of Frankfort-on-the-Main that "all well-acquired rights of every class of inhabitants are confirmed." But they were not easy. At a dinner party at the home of Prince Hardenberg, held in 1815, the Edict of Emancipation of Jews of 1812 was table talk. One of the guests said, "It cannot possibly be prudent forever to maintain the old discrimination against Jews by Christians, and even to increase the prejudice."[15] But though imprudent, it was the course adopted. Europe acquiesced.

The Jews of Vilna were reading Ben Franklin, surreptitiously. The Jews and enlightened Christians of America were following events in Europe openly, with full realization of the larger issues involved. Momentous years these, on both sides of the Atlantic. In America Hannah Adams was at work on her *History of the Jews*. In Italy, in 1812, Isaac Samuel Reggio was busy translating the Five Books of Moses into Italian. In Germany Meyer Anselm Rothschild on his deathbed in 1812, knew that his five sons were securely established in the capitals of Europe. In Germany the Christian scholar Baron Wilhelm von Humboldt took up the cudgels for the Pilgrim People.

Events in Europe and America were intertwined. Jewish emancipation in America gave the impetus to ghetto-bound Jews of Europe to look up, to nurture the hope of improving their lot, to migrate some day to America.

Social mobility was spurred by many colonization plans, some of them related to programs for conversion of Jews to Christianity. "The American Society for Meliorating the Condition of the Jews" coupled missionary efforts with colonizing ventures. In 1825 this group had more than two hundred branches. The founders were not actuated purely by missionary motives. There was an element of self-reproach involved as well. Christian society, it was held, owed the Jews "reparation for the wrongs they have received at the hands of Christians. All the Christian nations of the world are deep in the guilt of persecuting the Jews; and for this they need national expiation." The plan was to acquire land, erect buildings, and equip the Jewish converts with necessary tools, for they were "to be *principally* employed in agricultural and mechanical operations." That Jews were by nature adapted to life on the soil was to them a matter of certainty. The directors in their second annual report, in 1824, stated:

It is a matter of undisputed Scriptural History, that no nation was ever more attached to agriculture than the Jews in Palestine; and that it was only for the short period in which Solomon sent his ships from Ezion-Zaber to Opher, that they engaged in commerce. And though it were ever so averse from agriculture; yet it must be permitted to assign the true reason . . . because the Jews *in their dispersion* have almost everywhere been denied the privilege of acquiring and cultivating land. Commerce, therefore, was the only road left open to them, particularly the retail trade. . . . The result of a fair experiment will no doubt prove, that in this respect, the character of the Jew, like that of all other men, is the effect of education and of circumstances.

In 1825, the directors leased a four-hundred-acre farm at Sawpit on the East River. European agents were engaged for the purpose of popularizing the colony. All was ready for an invasion of "Hebrew Christians." At the end of a year the directors were reluctantly compelled to abandon their project. Hebrew Christians had failed to materialize. So another utopia died in embryo.

This group was not the first. A ladies' club doing business under the mellifluous title of "The Female Society of Boston and Vicinity for Promoting Christianity among the Jews" had been established in 1816. Its patron saint was Hannah Adams. They continued their operations until 1843. But they met with nothing like the public acclaim and influential sponsorship of the "American Society for Meliorating the Condition of the Jews." For half a century, from 1820 to 1870, this society continued its high-sounding endeavors. They were beating their heads against a stone wall. The collective headache which ensued involved not only the founder of the group, an ex-Jew born Levy and transformed to Frey. It must certainly have affected the sponsors, who numbered among them such notables as John Quincy Adams, Elias Boudinot, General Stephen Van Rensselaer and DeWitt Clinton. The history of this organization is a history of failure in two periods. The first two decades the Society tried to find and transport for colonization in America, European Jewish converts. That failed. The last thirty years the Society concentrated its blandishments on Jews already established in America. That failed also. Yet efforts at conversion were never completely abandoned.

To live as Jews was but to serve an apprenticeship for the promised larger life. Why then respond to missionary overtures? Yet interest in Jews and things Jewish continued to agitate Christian clergymen. When in 1815 phylacteries were discovered in Pittsfield, Massachusetts, the stir created showed that the fairy tale about American Indians being the Ten Lost Tribes of Israel still had its believers.

The concern with colonization had ancient roots. In 1783, a German Jew, addressed a *Memorial* to the President of the United States in which he described the wretched life led by Jews of Germany. He told of the barriers which surrounded them, of the miserable living they earned as petty shopkeepers and tradesmen. America offered escape. Their hopes for the new world were modest: "to establish colonies at our own cost, and to engage in agriculture, commerce, art and sciences. . . . Supposing that two thousand families of us would settle in a desert of America and convert it into a fertile land, will the old inhabitants of the provinces suffer by it?" he asked. This dream of European Jewry for a new start in America saw its slow and gradual fulfillment, but not by an early mass migration. That was to come later. A definite plan to colonize Jews on the upper Mississippi and in the Missouri region was proposed by a land speculator who was probably interested in disposing of his land holdings. He published a pamphlet in London in 1819 in which he advocated the purchase of land in America by wealthy Jews of Europe for the benefit of the poorer ones. Indigent Jews could be sent there to found agricultural communities. That project also failed.

Then a Jewish promoter, Moses Elias Levy, from St. Thomas in the West Indies, dreaming of becoming a landed proprietor, bought vast stretches of land in Florida. One of his tracts of land in Alachua County embraced thirty-six thousand acres, much of it acquired while the land was still a part of Spain. Actual settlement on this land began in 1820. Levy spent eighteen thousand dollars in bringing the first settlers to Florida. In 1823, fifty people were settled on the land. These pioneer Florida "tourists" were brought to Florida at Levy's expense. Twenty-five houses were built; a road of forty-five miles laid; three hundred acres were cleared and placed under cultivation. Levy hoped to found a model agricultural colony there. Levy is to be remembered for suggesting a plan for the abolition of slavery, and for his son who could not cope with the name of Levy and changed it to Yulee.

Levy's colony was open to settlers of all faiths. There was, however, an exclusively Jewish colony established in 1837. In that year,
eleven New York Jews bought land in Ulster County of their State
and founded a colony named Sholam. The colonists were educated
people, who cultivated the arts and music, and brought with them
beautiful paintings and elaborate household furnishings. One of their
first acts was to address a request for help in building a synagogue, to
Shearith Israel in the City of New York. Action on this appeal was
postponed. The colonists struggled along for four years. Their artistic
and musical talents were of no help in founding an agricultural community. In 1842, the colony failed, as did many a similar group.
Idealists, like the followers of Robert Owen and members of the
Brook Farm experiment, seem doomed to failure.[16]

Out of war and out of strife, a new period in American history now
emerges. Peace had come to the land and to Europe in 1815. There
was time now to take sides, to take stock, to take a look around at our
neighbors to the south. For we had come of age. We were young and
strong and dreaming dreams of the future. No boundary was strong
enough to contain us, no frontier rigid enough to hold back the tide
of migrants. It was good to be alive, good to feel one's strength, good
to look ahead to an unlimited future. So Americans viewed with considerable interest, with decided fellow feeling, the events in Latin
America. The American Revolution in the north had been victorious.
The American Revolutions in the south were a long-delayed echo. It
was high time. In 1812, when the United States was poised on the
brink of war, in Caracas, Venezuela, nature took a hand. A violent
earthquake rent that city leaving thousands of dead and dying in its
wake. Was it a sign, asked the Venezuelans, a sign from Heaven,
signifying its displeasure with the men and with the women who had
listened to the dulcet-voiced words of revolutionaries? Reaction set
in. One of the men who had survived that earthquake was the gallant
dreamer, the stouthearted, dauntless soldier, Simón Bolívar.

The liberation of Hispanic America was indeed a struggle against nature
—not only nature . . . but even more against human nature. Beside this
titanic epic the story of the liberation of North America is a pastoral tale
told on a summer day.[17]

All enlightened Americans followed the ensuing years with eager
interest. It is not too much to suppose that Americans named Nunez,
Lopez, Carvalho were more than casual spectators of the battles that
were fought in country after country to the south. For had they not
heard tales from their grandparents, tales of those pioneering days,

when Jews were the very first to come ashore, to clear the wilderness, to erect crude dwellings, to establish plantations and synagogues? Many an American Jewish child of Sephardic stock must have heard the stories told, stories grown mellow and entrancing, wistful and nostalgic, as the years dulled the anguish and the sorrow and blurred the fine edge of memory.

England was now an amputee. Spain was next. During the Napoleonic Wars, the Spanish colonies had tasted freedom of trade. Now Spain was trying to apply the tourniquet. It chafed. Spain's tentacles reached from Cape Horn to three hundred miles north of San Francisco. All of South America, save Brazil and Guiana was hers. One after another, the colonies revolted. Republics blossomed where tyranny once held sway. In Europe the Holy Alliance had waxed strong in its unholy suppression of hard-won freedom. Was America to be next?

Now James Monroe, friend of Thomas Jefferson, was in the White House. His Secretary of State was John Quincy Adams. It was his genius which formulated the plan. It was his Chief who announced it to the world on December 2, 1823. The Monroe Doctrine declared itself on the side of its fellow Americans to the south. It was an umbrella under which all freedom-loving Americans—North and South —could take shelter, and did. We recognized our southern sister republics and served notice on Europe to respect American interests as separate and independent from European concerns. Were we totally disinterested? Hardly. General Andrew Jackson had, at the invitation of Monroe, wrested Florida from Spain's weak grasp. Florida was formally "ceded" to the United States in 1821. Among its settlers who watched the transfer of ownership and speculated on how it would affect them were a London planter named George Levy; a watch-maker also from London, called Lewis Solomon; a grocer from Holland, one Levy M. Rodenburg; a planter from South Carolina, whose name was Isaac Hendricks. It is not unlikely that they were Jews.

Europe, bled by wars, ruined by endless military campaigns, discouraged by the giant snuffers of the Holy Alliance, held little hope for the average man. Labor was often more plentiful than opportunities to work. New and cheaper help was constantly displacing more highly paid and more experienced workers. The introduction of machines in the cotton mills of New England meant that many a skilled craftsman and artisan found himself without work. Farmers who had done years of back-breaking work on their little stony, hilly farms, were hard hit by the resulting depression which affected all of New England. They saw their homes as financial morasses from which it would be well to be freed. This discontent was fertile soil for the Western land agent and land speculator. Green acres beckoned the farmer. Adventure loomed large in the minds of repressed youth. Escape from the soul-destroying quest of work was there for the jobless. Opportunity to give their children a better start in life than they could have in the East urged on the work-worn parents. This was the genesis of that vast migration, which uprooted the maladjusted, the malcontents, the jobless, the adventurous, and sent them westward to seek their fortunes and to make their homes.

Among them there were Jewish pioneers.

No matter what other enterprises Jews of America were engaged in, they were from the very first interested in its land. A handbill signed by Barnard Gratz, dated Albany, May 26, 1773, advertises two parcels of land, one of twenty-five thousand acres and the other of nine thousand. Isaac Franks, alone or together with Benjamin Rush, bought large acreage of Pennsylvania land. A letter from Robert Morris to Aaron Levy expresses the satisfaction Mr. Morris feels at Levy's "Exertions" and refers to his surveying the land for Robert Morris and his associates. An indenture Daniel Levy made with Edward Burd and Robert Kemble in 1794 involved eleven hundred acres. A tract of land "on the waters of Bald Eagle Creek" and named "Farmer's Delight" was endorsed in Hebrew by Aaron Levy in 1796. Other Jews received land in compensation for Revolutionary War services.[18]

Far beyond the reaches of the Ohio, north as far as Canada, Michigan and Wisconsin, west to the Illinois and Ste. Genevieve, later St. Louis, south to New Orleans, plucky Jews made their solitary way. The records are scattered and incomplete. We can only follow these bold pioneers haltingly for their story is still fragmentary. It is an epic narrative, full of romance, adventure and excitement.

Canadian Jews early made their way into Michigan and Wisconsin. Ezekiel Solomon of Montreal settled in Mackinac in 1763. Records indicate that he lived in Michigan until 1816. Ezekiel Solomon was one of the few English survivors of the Indian attack upon Mackinac in 1763. With a few others, all of whom suffered terrible privations, he was taken to Montreal by the Ottawas and ransomed. A man of stark courage, he again forsook the safety of Montreal for the dangers of Mackinac. When the British withdrew from Michigan he went with them to the English settlement of Drummond's Island, where land

To be fold, the following Lands, fituate, lying, and being on the South Side of the *Mohawk's-River*, in the County of *Tryon*, viz.

ONE Tract containing Nine Thoufand Four Hundred and Fifty Acres of very fine Land, adjoining to the well-known Settlement of *Cherry-Valley*, between the *Adaquictinga-Creek*, or Branch of the *Sufquahana-River*, and the main Stream thereof, being Part of the Townfhip of *Belvidere*, through which a Branch of *Schenneveffes-Creek*, and that Branch of *Sufquahana-River*, Commonly called *Cherry-Valley-Creek*, both run, and make confiderable Quantities of low, or interval Lands: And alfo fundry other Tracts of very fine Lands, containing, together, about Twenty Five Thoufand Acres, adjoining *Lake Otfego*, (which is but eight Miles from a large *German* Settlement on the *Mohawk-River* ;) being Part of a Tract of One Hundred Thoufand Acres of Land, granted to GEORGE CROGHAN, Efq; and others. For Terms of Sale apply to the Subfcriber, who will attend at *Kinderhook*, at the Houfe of Mr. JOSEPH SIMONS, from the firft of *June* till the feventh: From the ninth till the fourteenth, at Mr. TITES, in *Johnftown*, County of *Tryon*: From the fifteenth to the twenty-firft, at the WIDOW VERNON's, in *Albany*; From the twenty-fecond to the twenty-ninth, at the Houfe of Mr. ROBERT CLENCH, in *Schenectady*; where Purchafers may treat with him for any Quaintity of faid lands; for which an indifputable Title will be given, by the Subfcriber.

BARNARD GRATZ.

ALBANY May 26, 1773.

Barnard Gratz, whose name appears on this advertisement, was, with his brother Michael, active in many enterprizes. He worked for David Franks on his arrival to America. He was joined by his brother and the two started out in business for themselves. The operations of the Gratz Brothers in North America and the West Indies were extensive. They identified themselves with the Patriot cause and with other merchants signed the Non-Importation Resolutions. Barnard Gratz was the uncle of Rebecca Gratz. Property of the American Jewish Historical Society.

was issued to him. Levy Solomons of Montreal had large business dealings with Mackinac at this time. Another likely member of the same family, William Solomons, was the interpreter to the English officials in Mackinac. His name too occurs as late as 1816.

The far-flung interests of the Franks family reached the outposts of the Northwest before the close of the eighteenth century. Jacob Franks was an English Jew who came to Green Bay in 1794, one of its earliest settlers. In that year he succeeded in acquiring titles to large tracts of land from the Indians. From then on, he had many irons in the fire. He built a dam at Rapides des Pères. He established a blacksmith shop, and engaged a skilled workman to manage it. The first sawmill and gristmill in that part of the country were among his enterprises. He exported huge quantities of deer tallow, and employed the only carpenter and joiner in the territory to work for him, from 1800 on. For his first three years in that trackless country, Jacob Franks was in charge of a trading post, which was established in Green Bay by Ogilvie, Gillespie and Company of Montreal. At the end of that time, he was the owner of a trading post of his own. To this post came Indians and *coureurs de bois*, bartering peltry for sugar, tea, rum. They soon became the fast friends of this energetic Jew. In 1797, when Jacob Franks went to Canada to buy the outfit for his trading post, he brought back with him his sixteen-year-old nephew, John Law, from Quebec. John was the son of an English captain and Jacob Franks' sister. The bond of friendship and kinship was very close between Jacob Franks and John Law. One early traveler speaks of Franks and his nephew as "Jews extensively embarked in the fur trade here." Whether John Law took his part-Jewish extraction seriously, it is impossible to say. At first he worked for his uncle; later he went into business for himself. He was a lieutenant in the British Army in the War of 1812; took part in the defense of Mackinac against the Americans. John Law married a half-breed, daughter of an Englishman and a Chippewa mother. He died at Green Bay in 1846.

We have described the land ventures of many Jewish brokers like the Gratz brothers and their associates. One of these companies involved certain sections of the Ohio region. A group of men including James Wilson, Levi Hollingsworth, Charles Willing, Dorsey Pentecost, and Michael and Barnard Gratz were associated in the joint holding of a tract of land, of three hundred and twenty-one thousand acres, drained by the tributaries of the Ohio River. Joseph Simon was active in the development of communities near Louisville. Other Jews were indomitably pushing their way down the Ohio.

In 1817, Joseph Jonas of Plymouth, England, came to Cincinnati —the first Jew in that region. He had been attracted by reading the descriptions of the beauty of the Ohio Valley, as well as by its economic opportunities. Undeterred by the advice of his friends who urged him to remain in the East, where he could maintain his religious contacts, he went west. He became an object of curiosity there. Many people who had heard of Jews, but never seen them, came to look upon him. Having seen him, they accepted him as one of them. In 1819, three other English Jews joined Jonas who had become established as a watch-maker and silversmith. Soon others followed. And in the fall of that year this little handful of Israelites ushered in the High Holidays with prayers. Their experience was a happy one. One of their number wrote in 1842, that if the Jews "will only conduct themselves as good citizens in a moral and religious point of view" they will be well received by their "Nazarene" neighbors.

A cemetery was acquired in 1821. A congregation, Bene Israel, was organized in 1824. And Jewish communal life was firmly established. They launched a building campaign, and like their older sister-congregations circularized their coreligionists, appealing for contributions from England, from Barbados, from Charleston and Philadelphia. Donations came in, in generous amounts. The synagogue was dedicated in 1836. This Hebrew community was proud of its accomplishment. The members of the group dramatized themselves, conscious of being the makers of history. It is possible that they were fired by the romantic imagination of Joseph Jonas, a man of pronounced literary tastes. The circular letter he wrote to appeal for funds concludes:

It is also worthy of remark that there is not a congregation within 500 miles of this city and we presume it is well known how easy of access we are to New Orleans and we are well informed that had we a Synagogue here, hundreds from that City who now know and see nothing of their religion would frequently attend here during holidays.

This letter was written in July, 1825. At that time accessibility depended upon navigation. The Mississippi and the Ohio were the arteries between the New Orleans Hebrews and their Cincinnati coreligionists.[19]

It is true that the Jews of Louisiana had tried to found a congregation in 1824. They failed. But they managed to exert some pressure as a group. For in 1828 one of the laws of Louisiana provided "that no Israelite child shall be excluded either from the schools, from

the Temple or the burial ground on account of the religion of the
mothers." The first official's name signed to this document is that of
Labranche, a member of the old Zweig family. Intermarriage must
have been the rule. For there are numerous provisions in the articles
governing the Jewish community of Louisiana which refer to intermarriage and the children of such unions:

Any Israelite member being married to a strange woman shall have
the privilege of interring the said wife in the walls of the burial ground.
. . . All children born of an Israelite and not having abjured the religion
of the father shall be entitled to burial. . . . All prayers offered shall be
after the custom of the Portuguese Israelites.[20]

In this way did a little minority group seek to effect a compromise
with the harsh realities of life, realities leading in the direction of
assimilation or accommodation, of extinction or integration.

CHAPTER IX

The Era of Native Sons
and Daughters

→⟫⟫   Wert not thou he from whom my spirit caught
Its proudest aspiration to high thought?
—PENINA MOÏSE in *The Mercury*
December 27, 1828   ⟪⟪←

IN THE formative years of our nation's history there were born in this land men and women whose lives influenced deeply the thoughts of the American Jewish community. Through their personal histories we may trace the ideas and the events that were of moment to their coreligionists here and abroad.

In a time when the young republic was evolving, when boundaries were stretching and new horizons beckoned, when national consciousness quickened the pulses and the two Americas were developing their universe of discourse, the Jews of America recognized the talents of three men and two women. Judah Touro was born in Newport in 1775, Rebecca Gratz in Philadelphia in 1781, Mordecai Manuel Noah in Philadelphia in 1785, Isaac Harby in Charleston in 1788, Penina Moïse in Charleston in 1797.

The first of these was Judah Touro, of whom Max J. Kohler said that he was "one who would probably by common consent, be singled out as the most prominent American Jew of the first half of the nineteenth century."[1] Be that as it may, he typified the highest and most ideal type of Jew in America to some historians, and was merely a rich merchant who acquiesced to slavery with complacency, according to another writer. It was Judah Touro's proud boast that his birth coincided with the outbreak of the American Revolution. He lived to see his country grow bitter, acrimonious, heavily involved in the question of slavery. Touro died four years after the Compromise of 1850, in his beloved Southern city, New Orleans.

Judah Touro was the son of Isaac Touro who had come from

Jamaica to serve as the rabbi of the Newport congregation. It was Rabbi Touro's privilege to inaugurate religious services in that beautiful little Newport synagogue, in which so many men and women had found inspiration. Isaac Touro and his friend, Ezra Stiles, were often to be seen walking the shaded streets of Newport, talking, arguing, discussing everything from the Hebrew alphabet to the Cabala. It was the young Rabbi who welcomed Haym Isaac Carigal to Newport. He married Reyna Hays, the sister of wealthy Moses Michael Hays of Boston.

To Isaac and Reyna Touro three children were born—Abraham and Judah and Rebecca. The Revolution saw the Newport community scattered. The Touros too left the city and moved eventually to Kingston, Jamaica. Here Isaac Touro died, in 1783. The young widow was offered a home by her brother, M. M. Hays, who had already attained marked business and social success in Boston and whose warm hospitality extended far beyond his personal family. She accepted his offer. In four years she died. Their uncle assumed entire charge of the young orphans. They were well educated, given excellent business and social training. For to Hays's home came eminent non-Jews as well as Jews. Harrison Gray Otis, son of James Otis of Revolutionary fame; Thomas H. Perkins, who proposed the first American railroad; the Reverend Samuel J. May, a leader in the abolitionist movement— were among those who frequented the Hays home. It was an interesting household. For young Judah growing up, it held an added attraction, his cousin Catherine Hays. He may have formed "a romantic attachment" for her. He never married and after sixty years of separation, he remembered Catherine in his will. At any rate the astute father of a wealthy daughter and uncle of an impecunious nephew effected a lasting separation. The Boston adventure was over. In his uncle's counting house he had had a thorough apprenticeship in business. He was ready for other pastures.

So Judah Touro, in 1802, made his way to New Orleans. The voyage from Boston, which began in October, 1801, and lasted until February, 1802, was so arduous that Judah resolved never to repeat the experience. He kept that promise.

New Orleans was then a bustling little city of between eight and ten thousand people. Here Touro opened a small store and began dispensing Yankee notions. He prospered. His honesty, integrity, industry, good faith won him many friends. With keen farsightedness he invested his surplus wisely. Wealth came to him. In a quiet, unostentatious way he began to cultivate his hobby, that of large-scale philanthropy. Here was his peculiar genius. He combined a warm sympathy for humanity, with sufficient means to help the needy. And he gave quietly, generously, openhandedly, to Jews and Christians and to several Negro slaves to enable them to buy their freedom.

Touro's benefactions endeared him to many. The fact that his disbursements knew no limitations of sect or creed was an effective step in the direction of interfaith co-operation. Schappes gives as proof of the propaganda value of such donations the fact that Colonel J. W. D. Worthington cited Touro's generosity to Christians in arguing for the abolition of Jewish disabilities in Maryland in 1822. Although even here opinion was not unanimous. For Touro was said by one contemporary to practice "true Christian liberality."

Says Theodore Clapp:

He was born, reared, and had lived, and died in the Hebrew faith. It was the faith of his father, who was a learned and most esteemed rabbi. It was the faith that had been handed down to him by a long line of illustrious ancestors, reaching back to the patriarchal ages of the world. . . . It was the faith of Jesus himself, who was a Jew, and who declared that the religion of the Old Testament contained all that is requisite to guide us to eternal joy.

Another deep and lasting friendship with a non-Jew was between Touro and Rezin Davis Shepherd in whose home Judah lived for forty years. Touro speaks of him in his will as "my dear, old and devoted friend . . . to whom under Divine Providence, I was greatly indebted for the preservation of my life when I was wounded on the last of January, 1815." Touro refers to the time when he served as a volunteer under General Andrew Jackson, on the plains of Chalmette, when New Orleans was being defended against the British. He was severely wounded, and left dying on the field, where his friend, Shepherd, found him. He had already received first aid. Shepherd procured a cart and brought him to a hospital base where he received the medical care that saved his life.

Touro's list of benefactions is long. He gave contributions to his birthplace, New Orleans, to synagogues, to many cities, to his nation. When the Bunker Hill Monument was dedicated it was found that Judah Touro had contributed ten thousand dollars, one of the largest gifts, toward its completion. Yet he was incensed when his donation was made known, preferring to remain in the background in the role of anonymous giver. He contributed to, but kept aloof from, the Ashkenazic congregation which was organized in New Orleans in 1826. When in 1846 a Sephardic congregation was organized, he became an active participant in its affairs. He endowed his own religious congregation, the Dispersed of Judah liberally. He continued the support of the Touro Infirmary, part of the Hebrew Hospital of New Orleans. He left bequests to other Hebrew congregations, to charitable organizations, to schools, to various orphan homes, and almshouses, to hospitals in other cities; to the Newport synagogue, to the "North American Relief Society for Indigent Jews of Jerusalem, Palestine." One of his largest bequests is the sum of fifty thousand dollars to Sir Moses Montefiore, "to ameliorate the condition of our unfortunate Jewish Brethren, in the Holy Land."

Here then is a blueprint for a Jewish philanthropist. What of Judah Touro, the man? He was simple, quiet, modest, frugal, unassuming, warmhearted, sympathetic, generous, kind. Was he "democratic"? It would appear not, for he carefully eschewed contact with the poorer Jews of New Orleans. His upbringing in the wealthy home of his uncle in Boston had apparently confirmed Touro in "consciousness of kind." He could keep his Judaism in abeyance until fellow Sephardim were available in New Orleans. His most serious shortcoming was, according to one authority, his failure to see the abuses of slavery. Some Southerners were aware of it. "The best intellect of America outside the region of practical politics has been on the anti-slavery side." One need only recall the Grimké sisters, daughters of a wealthy South Carolinian plantation and slaveowner who became ardent abolitionists. One need only read, as Touro might have, being of their time, their burning, passionate denunciations of slavery in *The Liberator*. He was not on the side of the oppressed, although he gave generously to the indigent. "Touro's generosity had no religious or geographical boundary, but it stopped short of Negro slaves or Negro freemen. Not one Negro institution, or institution to aid the Negro, and there were such in 1854, was a benefactor of a Touro bequest," writes Schappes. His city operated an infamous slave mart. If his heart was wrung by it, he does not show it. He owned but one slave whom he set free after making sure of his future security. The Negro slaves in the Shepherd household where Touro lived were all freed through his efforts and assisted to a fresh start in life. That was as far as he went. He was a Southerner, a conservative, a Sephardic Jew, a wealthy man. He adjusted to his environment without qualm or scruple. His money, which he could not take with him, he left to found asylums, orphanages, libraries. He was one of the first Zionists of America. For he helped Warder Cresson, a convert to Judaism, establish a Jewish agricultural settlement near Jerusalem in 1850.

He must have been a lonely man. His life, for all its wealth, has but the incidents which an onlooker, not a participant, enjoys. He was always a guest at another's board. Always a spectator, seldom an actor in the drama of a life that began with the Revolution and ended in the year when the New England Emigrant Aid Society was recruiting a band of thirty men and women, Free-Soilers, to go to Kansas in 1854. There was no mistaking then the shape of things to come.

"Who was he that Americans of the olden faith delight to honor?" asks Morais. "Did he surpass his contemporaries in knowledge, or did he make his power felt in Federal government? These questions which naturally suggest themselves, are answered by the simple mention of one word—Philanthropy."[2] With that astute and kindly summary the case for Judah Touro rests.

"My dear Ben," wrote Rebecca Gratz to her soldier brother shortly after the War of 1812 broke out,

We found Jo here on a short visit but he return'd to camp this morning and we feel forlorn without you and him . . . your military zeal is very fine but I hope your wishes will not prevail—an armistice would be more glorious to the country than all the laurels its heroes can gather. . . . John departed south this morning to join his General. . . . We sit and bewail you much more like women than patriots and turn pale at the thought of a battle.[3]

The woman who wrote the letter was young. She was richly endowed with gifts. She was charming, graceful, accomplished, humane, gentle. Her life stretched out to 1869, a goodly span. Rebecca Gratz ranks without question as one of the greatest of American Jewesses. Beauty, intellect and a character of rare sweetness were hers; a keen, penetrating mind, high ideals of service, a strong sense of family ties, devotion to friends, and a deep sense of obligation to all mankind. One can extol her virtues, eulogize her excellencies, dwell on her philanthropic and educational services—and build up a portrait of a female paragon, whose very virtues become the dull background for a life of monotonous and unrelieved good works. Such a portrait would be false. So we must steer clear of hyperbole, and try to give instead a picture of the warm, pulsing tenor of her life. Of her daily thoughts, her reading, her friends, her observations, her mothering of all the orphans of her own family, and of the orphans of her city, of her graceful acceptance of the ups and downs of life, her philosophical adjustments to her own peculiar problems, of her ardent championship of the oppressed of all sects—of her manifold interests we can speak with ease and with certainty.

What were her antecedents?

Her father was Michael Gratz, brother of Barnard, whose name has often appeared in these pages. Her mother was Miriam Simon, daughter of that enterprising landowner and Indian trader, Joseph Simon, whose ceaseless energy helped open up the West before the Revolution. Of Miriam, too, much has been said. She was the most representative Jewish woman of the colonial period—a true mother in Israel. To Michael and Miriam Gratz, twelve children were born. Of the children who grew to maturity, Rebecca was by far the most outstanding. She is best known as the original of Rebecca in *Ivanhoe*. Among her many devoted friends, Rebecca Gratz numbered the Ogden Hoffman family. It was in the office of Judge Ogden Hoffman that Washington Irving studied law and to his daughter Matilda that he became engaged. Miss Hoffman's untimely death did not end the friendship which sprang up between Irving and Miss Gratz. Their mutual esteem and admiration continued through life.

Washington Irving frequently enjoyed the hospitality of the Gratz home and introduced others there. In 1807, he wrote to Rebecca about the proposed visit to Philadelphia of Thomas Sully, the artist: "I think I can render him no favor for which he ought to be more grateful, than in introducing him to the notice of yourself and your connections." In the autumn of 1817, Washington Irving visited Scott, who had long been a warm admirer of the American author. For several delightful hours these two men roamed about the fields near Abbotsford, swapping tales, talking like two kindred spirits and warm old friends. For each of them it was a great meeting. It laid the foundation for a genuine friendship. "To this friendship," says Gratz Van Rensselaer, "we owe the character of Rebecca in 'Ivanhoe.' " For Scott was then mulling over in his mind the story of *Ivanhoe*. During their conversation, Irving mentioned his own personal tragedy, the death of Matilda Hoffman. He dwelt on the close friendship and the many services rendered by Rebecca Gratz to her friend. He described with real enthusiasm Rebecca's charm, beauty, goodness, and sweetness of character. He told of her many philanthropies, of her loyalty to friends, of the universal admiration which she aroused in all who knew her. Scott was interested. "He immediately determined to introduce a Jewish female character and, on the strength of Irving's vivid description, he named his heroine Rebecca." When Scott finished his novel in 1819, he sent a copy to Irving, and wrote him, "How do you like your Rebecca? Does the Rebecca I have pictured compare well with the pattern given?"[4]

Rebecca Gratz read *Ivanhoe* in 1820. She wrote, on the fourth of April, to her sister-in-law: "Have you received Ivanhoe? When you read it tell me what you think of my namesake Rebecca."

And again, on the tenth of May, 1820, she wrote:

I am glad you admire Rebecca, for she is just such a representation of a good girl as I think human nature can reach—Ivanhoe's insensibility to her, you must recollect, may be accounted to his previous attachment —his prejudice was a characteristic of the age he lived in—he fought for Rebecca, tho' he despised her race—the veil that is drawn over his feelings was necessary to the fable, and the beautiful sensibility of hers, so regulated yet so intense, might show the triumph of faith over human affection. I have dwelt on this character as we sometimes do on an exquisite painting until the canvas seems to breathe and we believe it is life.

Rebecca could well sympathize with her namesake whose love for someone not of her faith stood as an unsurmountable barrier between them. She too, it is said, faced the same problem and her case as that of her fictional namesake saw "the triumph of faith over human affection." When Irving returned to America, he called on Rebecca Gratz and undoubtedly acquainted her with Scott's portrait of her which was then in preparation.

This source of the character was known to Miss Gratz. . . . Shrinking as she did from publicity she would seldom acknowledge the fact, and when pressed upon the subject would deftly evade it by a change of topic.[5]

Scott's pen portrait of Rebecca might well have been written about Miss Gratz, of whom there are two excellent likenesses, the one by Sully, the other by Malbone. Sully said

that he had never seen a more striking Hebraic face. The easy pose, suggestive of perfect health, the delicately turned neck and shoulders with the firmly poised head and its profusion of dark, curling hair, large, clear black eyes, the contour of the face, the fine white skin, the expressive mouth and the firmly chiseled nose, with its strength of character, left no doubt as to the race from which she had sprung. Possessed of an elegant bearing, a melodiously sympathetic voice, a simple and frank and gracious womanliness, there was about Rebecca Gratz all that a princess of the blood Royal might have coveted.

Among the manuscript collections of the American Jewish Historical Society there is a letter which Rebecca wrote to Mary Eliza-

This last portion of a letter written by Rebecca Gratz, November 23, 1802, to her friend Mary Elizabeth Fenno of Pearl Street, New York, is the property of the American Jewish Historical Society. It is typical of many letters which Rebecca Gratz wrote during her lifetime. It is warm, affectionate, full of humor. Indeed the joke attributed to Mark Twain about the reports of his death being somewhat exaggerated is here anticipated by almost a century. Rebecca Gratz writes "Miss Pemberton whose death you lament with so much sensibility is much better. . . ."

beth Fenno of Baltimore in 1802. It is a long and revealing letter. Here Rebecca Gratz invites her friend to become a regular correspondent. "My Affection for you will ever make it a pleasant employment to write," says Rebecca. She shows a keen interest in the simple social diversions, in the romances and engagements and reconciliations of her friends. Then she introduces a humorous comment, whose origin has in the past been attributed to Mark Twain: "Miss Pemberton whose death you lamented with so much sensibility is much better."

The letter mentions many names of Christian and Jewish friends. The impression it conveys is that there was a natural social intercourse between the groups and that to Rebecca and her friends such distinction did not occur.

Quite apart from their Jewish significance, the letters of Rebecca Gratz are an important contribution to social history. For the running comment on men, on books, on the arts, on important events, of a keen and observant mind during those significant years 1811-66, cannot but be a marked addition to American history. During those years, three wars were fought, a continent spanned, cities built, slaves emancipated. During those years American literature was enriched and firmly established by the work of such men as Irving, Longfellow, Whittier, Lowell, Emerson, Thoreau. Through her we feel the rhythm of the times—more than half a century of comment on events which included the steamboat, the Erie Canal, the building of railroads; whose scope embraced the important intellectual and political issues, followed the ups and downs of many a prominent career and which closed during the dark days of Reconstruction.

Harriet Martineau, Anthony Trollope, Sir Walter Scott, Carlyle, Mary Wollstonecraft, Shelly, Cooper, Fanny Kemble, Grace Aguilar, Prescott, Sir Bulwer-Lytton, Charles Dickens, are but a few of the men and women whose works are discussed in her letters. Politics frequently concern her. Henry Clay, her close friend, is very often mentioned. More than at any other time, she became a partisan during his Presidential campaigns, following with the keen eagerness of a loyal friend the numerous political ups and downs of this great man.

Religion and religious observances are often mentioned. In her personal life, Rebecca was a consistently devout, observant Jewess. Each day began and ended with prayer. She was self-critical, constantly examining herself searchingly. Little wonder that Isaac Leeser dedicated his catechism to Rebecca.[6] She welcomed social and philanthropic service and filled her life with the performance of numerous duties and obligations. She made a home for her unmarried brothers. She mothered and reared the nine orphaned children of her sister, Rachel Moses. Yet in review we see much of her life as a thread of vicarious experience. She was the typical spinster who submerges her own heartaches in those of her nephews and nieces, who is a spectator not an actor in her own biography. We read her letters and think what a mother she could have been. We think with regret that she was a little wasted. . . .

In her twenty-first year she became the secretary for the "Female Association for the Relief of Women and Children in Reduced Circumstances." She was a founder of the Philadelphia Orphan Society in 1815. The Hebrew Sunday School Society, the first of its kind in America, was founded by her. This was a significant Jewish service which she performed for her religious contemporaries and for all Jewish posterity. She began an educational movement which survives to this day and which forms the basis for Jewish religious education in America. At her suggestion, and through her efforts, the Jewish Foster Home was founded.

Besides her home and public duties, Rebecca Gratz found time to keep in close touch with her scattered family, and her hosts of relatives and friends. She was often called in to nurse the sick and never did she fail to give aid and assistance and comfort to those who called upon her. Her work for her own people went on.

Had our heroine no faults? It must be recorded that like Judah Touro she seemed insensitive to the subject of slavery. A careful reading of her *Letters*, a thorough search in the pages of the twenty-six volumes of the *Occident*, give us few hints of her awareness of the institution of slavery, of the work of the abolitionists, of the Underground Railroad, of other women who enlisted in campaigns of social amelioration. She writes in 1820: "One of the curses of slavery is the entire dependence the poor mistress is reduced to— when she is rich enough to have all her wants supplied by numerous servants." That is hardly a degree of social awareness which we might be led to expect from a person of Rebecca's attainments. She read widely, voraciously. Yet there is no mention of *Uncle Tom's Cabin*—or of its author, Harriet Beecher Stowe. Slavery was on everyone's mind in 1852. It was the burning question in politics. Rebecca's friend, Henry Clay, had but two short years before accomplished the Compromise of 1850. Daniel Webster's superb seventh of March speech had supported the Compromise. In 1852, the Free-

Soil party entered a candidate in the Presidential race. Where was Rebecca then? She was interested in the "Deaf & Dumb Institution." She threw herself into the needs of the "Orphan Asylum Society." "If you have had measles in your Orphan Asylum," she writes to one of her friends, "we have had small pox & varialoid—between thirty & forty were sick at the same time—one died." She noted the smallest illness of those within the radius of her knowledge. It is most difficult to understand. Could some of her letters have been lost or wilfully suppressed by her correspondents? Was it a rare sense of tact, the fear of offending her many friends and relatives in the South? She is so cautious, walks her tightrope with such skill. She writes in December of 1859: "That miserable Harpers Ferry affair will be made use of to keep up excitement. I hope when the executions are over, peace will be restored." A year later, one of her letters reads: "I suppose every good citizen feels it his duty to be at the post where his influence is strongest. I hope that Kentucky is free from secession principles or dangers—and that our beloved Union may survive the dangers that threaten." She attempts so gallantly that her words stir within us an answering echo of sympathy for her dilemma, to reconcile the various factions of her family, to resolve her personal loyalty to the Union with her family loyalty and love for each and every person dear to her. When Howard Gratz visited their home, she writes of his "politics so antagonistic." Philadelphia "is decidedly Unionist," she adds. And when in 1861 the inevitable conflict erupted and gunfire was heard at Fort Sumter on January 9, 1861, Rebecca wrote a letter to Benjamin Gratz dated January 21, 1861, in which she said:

I pray fervently that Kentucky will be firm in the Union—the seceders are bringing ruin on their own heads as well as the deepest distress on the whole country—would that the spirit of conciliation proposed by Mr. Crittenden could obtain a triumph, I believe most of the southern states would gladly reconsider their hasty movements, and leave S Carolina to her evil counsels.

Gradually we note that as her years lengthen, her mood is saddened. She knows that she has somehow missed the high adventure, the personal narrative. She writes to Ann Boswell Gratz for news of "your domestic history—there is too much sameness in mine to afford much on record—my only visits are to the family—or the Institutions I have adopted as part of my avocations." And as the War goes on and the suffering is brought within her orbit, she complains on April 15, 1863, that "the presence of war is unheeded—except indeed in the active works of charity for the sick & wounded brought to our hospitals. My Dear brother, I am too old to do any good, but feel deep interest in all this & pray for better times."

Her last available letter written May 13, 1866, was a letter of condolence on the loss of his son, Hyman Cecil Gratz, addressed to "My beloved Ben." She writes:

My heart claims the privilege of sharing your affliction—of mourning with you the loss of your precious son—long separation from those we love is among the severest trials of this life. . . . Oh My brother my heart mourns for you . . . to miss the daily intercourse of your son—his warm affectionate heart was ever so full of love that he was endeared to all who came under its influence, and my memory of all the overflowing kindness of his life will keep his memory ever green in our hearts.[7]

Soon her own memory would be cherished by her friends everywhere. She was tired. She had traveled a long road since 1781. Her own life was a record of overflowing kindness.

We come now to another protagonist through whose life we share the drama of his generation. Four years after Rebecca's birth in Philadelphia, Mordecai Manuel Noah was born there. He died in New York in 1851.

Mordecai Manuel Noah's antecedents were typically American and Jewish. From 1750 on, members of his family are found in the directories of South Carolina.[8] His father was a citizen of Charleston, was known as an ardent patriot who contributed liberally to the Revolution and who fought under General Marion. His mother was Zipporah Phillips, daughter of a Philadelphia patriot. He grew up in Philadelphia near a tavern which flaunted a painting of the Federal Convention. He used to stand before it marveling "at the assembled patriots, particularly the venerable head and spectacles of Dr. Franklin, always in conspicuous relief."

Across the street from this old tavern was the American Theater. As a boy, Noah joined a troup of amateur actors who frequented this playhouse. "I had an early hankering," says Noah, "for the national drama, a kind of juvenile patriotism, which burst forth, for the first time, in a few sorry doggerels in the form of a prologue to a play." To his lot fell some part of "the honour of cutting the plays, substituting new passages, casting parts, and writing couplets at the exits." This company of Thespians did not last long: "The expenses were too heavy for our pockets; our writings and performances were sufficiently wretched, but as the audience was admitted without cost, they were too polite to express any disapprobation." From his boy-hood on, he was a regular patron of the Chestnut Street Theater.

I seldom missed a night; and always returned to bed, after witnessing a good play, gratified and improved: and thus, probably, escaped the haunts of taverns, and the pursuits of depraved pleasures, which too frequently allure and destroy our young men; hence I was always the firm friend of the drama, and had an undoubted right to oppose my example through life to the horror and hostility expressed by sectarians to plays and playhouses generally.

The Franklin library, as well as the theater, claimed many of his boyhood hours. Later he studied law and entered politics in Charleston, South Carolina. As one of the young "war hawks," he ardently advocated the War of 1812 and as editor of the *Charleston City Gazette* he wrote many an inflammatory article favoring the war movement. In 1811, Noah had been offered the post of United States Consul at Riga in Russia. This offer he declined. Two years later he was appointed Consul at Tunis, with a special mission to Algiers. Here Noah distinguished himself by rescuing several Americans who were held as slaves in the Barbary States, as well as by protesting vigorously against his country's paying an annual tribute to Moroccan pirates. Monroe recalled him, it is alleged because of his religion, but there is no substantiating proof for this charge. Upon his return to New York, Tammany received him with open arms. He continued a staunch Democrat, identifying himself with Jacksonian democracy, became a Surveyor of the Port, and judge of the Court of Sessions, and gradually established a firm claim to "civic esteem."

Nor was this all. Noah was a facile, witty, brilliant journalist. The *Advertiser, Courier and Enquirer, Evening Star* and *Sunday Times* were among the papers founded or edited by him. At this time American literature was in its infancy. It was the generation of Cooper and Irving. Noah, who knew these men, also made his contribution to the literary harvest of his day. His plays, *The Fortress of Sorrento, Paul and Alexis, She Would be a Soldier, Marion; or the Hero of Lake George, Grecian Captive*, and *The Siege of Tripoli*, were successfully produced and well received by the public. But they were merely light interludes in a life crammed full of many absorbing activities.

Noah tells us that his "line . . . has been in the more rugged paths of politics." He claims to have been for the most part "peaceably employed in settling the affairs of the nations, and mildly engaged in the political differences and disagreements which are so fruitful in our great state." These "mild disagreements" led to fist fights, street brawls, and duels, but it was all in a day's work to him. Noah continued his diatribes without regard to personal safety. He supported Andrew Jackson. He adhered to Tammany. He broke with Van Buren and championed Harrison. Partisan to the bone, Noah saw only what he wished to see—his side of the argument.

What manner of man was he? Seen through the eyes of a non-Jewish contemporary who says, "I knew Major Noah well," we get this portrait:

Physically, he was a man of large muscular frame, rotund person, a benignant face, and most portly bearing. Although a native of the United States, the lineaments of his race were impressed upon his features with unmistakable character. . . . He was a Jew, thorough and accomplished. His manners were genial, his heart kind, and his generous sympathies embraced all Israel, even to the end of the earth.

When at the height of his political career, he suddenly defected, and joined his former political enemies, he both baffled and infuriated his friends. He was accosted by a former crony who indignantly asked him, "Are Democracy and Whiggery the same, as you have left the one and gone over to the other?"

Noah replied that they were still "as wide apart as the east is from the west!"

"Then how comes it you went over to the opposite side?" queried his irascible friend.

"My dear sir," answered Noah with an air of wonder at the other's naïveté, "it is the party which has changed, not I! The truth is, I found, to my surprise, that the *principles* had gone over to the other side; and as I could not honorably desert my principles, or suffer them to desert me, I had, in all conscience, to go over too!" Lockwood, to whom we are indebted for this anecdote, comments: "Was ever a party slip so admirably made, or political somersault so deftly done?" And truly in those days of shifting party principles and insecure party affiliations, the principles changed sides as often as their adherents, and a party platform was like the platform of a public conveyance where each side takes its stand as a matter of convenience. It is true that Major Noah was a "visionary, somewhat, and an enthusiast altogether." He often succeeded in arousing his adversaries to a frenzy which at times he richly deserved.

There are many letters extant, addressed to men of national prominence. In 1819 Noah wrote to Van Buren, the future President and frequent correspondent, "not in the way of condolence but rather of congratulations as your removal from office will have done much good to our cause and I am fully persuaded that it can do you no harm as the republican party will ever take pleasure in affording that protection & confidence to men of principle which they loudly claim." At another time Noah wrote to Van Buren to thank him for his "friendly attentions." This letter bears an interesting notation: "He has been app'd Sheriff but I have no recollection of having taken a part in promoting it."

He seems to have had the faculty for baffling, annoying, irritating, inflaming and enraging his associates. His were no halfway measures. In what he wrote and what he said, impulse and enthusiasm often carried him away. His letters illustrate well the extent to which Noah enmeshed himself in the political webs of his day.

On one occasion Van Buren advises Noah to "let the few individuals who entertain different views talk on, but don't notice them in your paper—they will soon be lost in the general mass."

Noah was sensitive and unwilling to be derided by his enemies. "I am not in a situation to be ridiculed by my opponents," he writes to Van Buren. Yet in spite of his ambition to appear favorably in the public eye, he was the storm center of many a political squabble. A correspondent on two successive occasions wrote: "Noah, of the Advocate, appears determined to wage war—His attack on the Speaker is base and contemptible, and will only injure himself." Again: "You will have seen M. M. Noah's course respecting our proceedings here, Is this man mad? . . . No good will end his career."

Rufus King wrote to Van Buren at various times discussing the opposition to Noah's candidacy for office, and suggesting that Van Buren's friendship with Noah was a drawback to the former's political ambitions. "I have seen the Articles, which your imputed Friendship for Noah procures you but they are so insignificant and so general, that they can not be worth your attention."

Often Van Buren was embarrassed by Noah's editorial policy. "Beseech our friend Major Noah to let the Morgan affair alone. I am sick, heart sick at his reckless indiscretion upon that subject. It is passing strange that a man so capable can commit so great a blunder as unnecessarily & unwisely to run in the face of so irresistible a current of public opinion as exists upon this subject in many Western counties." This refers to a Masonic exposé. Noah being a Mason, while Van Buren was not, there was decided difference of opinion between them on this incident.

Noah was much in the public eye. His movements and his political affiliations were critically watched. Whatever he said or did brought down on his head the hyperbolic epithets of his critics. So one of them speaks of "a foolish publication of Noah of some garbled statement." He had a way of inspiring violent contempt or great enthusiasm.

And yet his friend Lockwood could say of him: "His versatility was wonderful—sometimes, perhaps, audacious." Sheriff, judge, major, consul, politician, dramatist (or rather playwright) and journalist, with a style racy, easy, genial and humorous, what a wealth of incidents the life and times of Noah would unfold!

If Mordecai Manuel Noah could be carried away on the subject of politics, what was to be expected of him when he threw his ardor and passion and temperament into a consideration of the Jewish problem? Whatever his virtues may have been—and they were many —moderation was not among them. His mind, agile, alert and fertile, had a habit of exaggeration. He saw things on a grand scale. Pouncing upon a hypothesis he would persuade himself that he was dealing with a solid fact. There were no halfway measures with him. A cause was wholly good or utterly hopeless. You were either his friend or his enemy.

Added to all this was a childlike habit of dramatizing men and situations. This tendency stemmed from his youth, when he saw life as a stage-crazed enthusiast sees it, as a succession of histrionic incidents exploded at dramatic moments before an enthusiastic audience. His exuberance grew with years of pen-pushing in the service of not-too-clean politics. A lively imagination, a Hebraic susceptibility and sympathy for suffering, "a genial, frank, childlike ingenuousness," a keen sense of the dramatic, an ardent desire to be the deliverer of his people, an unrestrained, hyperbolic type of mind—of this stuff was the American Messiah made.

A contemporary of Noah's tells us that on one occasion a benevolently disposed woman, who was asked to support a society for evangelizing Jews, wrote to ask Noah his opinion of the practicability of such a movement. His letter was an erudite exposition of the beliefs and ideals of the Jews, "their ancient hereditary traditions, their venerable history, their hope of a coming Messiah;" and concluded by expressing the probability that the modern Gentiles would "sooner be converted to the Jewish faith, than that the Jews would be converted to theirs."

When objections were raised to Noah's being made sheriff of New York because of his faith, it left him completely undisturbed. "Pity," said one of his critics to Noah, "that Christians are to be hereafter hung by a Jew." "Pretty Christians," answered the new sheriff, "to require hanging at all."

Another incident of his career as sheriff of New York illumines his character. When, in 1822, a yellow fever epidemic menaced the city, Noah released all the prisoners confined in the debtors' jail, on Ludlow Street, a sort of American Marchalsea. He brought down on himself an avalanche of bills and claims for damages from righteous, indignant creditors. These claims Noah and his bond-signers had to pay. In addition to his other troubles, Noah was denounced by several city clergymen, who, in scoring his rule, interpreted the plague as a divine visitation upon New York, a just punishment, for having chosen a Jew as its sheriff.

With unclouded faith he regarded the American Indians as the descendants of the Lost Tribes of Israel. He refused to entertain any doubts on the subject. "He could lecture on the origin of the American Indians," writes Samuel Lockwood, "with a complacent assurance that set the venerable Albert Gallatin, and all the other American ethnologists, aghast." In his sketchy, breezy way Noah had familiarized himself with this subject, as with a number of others, and once his mind was made up, the "facts" were to him indisputably convincing. He saw this as he saw all the aspects of the Jewish question, with the clouded eye of a partisan.

"If the Indians of America are not the descendants of the missing tribes, again I ask, from whom *are* they descended?" With such incontrovertible logic Noah shouted down the opposition.

Out of his partisanship for the Jewish people, the Ararat plan was born.

During his travels through Europe, Noah saw the misery, the hopeless degradation of its Jews. Driven into economic rat-holes by restrictive measures, this oppressed and persecuted people lived only on the memory of its past greatness, nursing the hope of some future Messianic miracle which would deliver them from the morass into which they had sunk.

From time to time champions had arisen, who like Lessing and Dohm saw the majesty of this people, the Pagliacci among nations, who caricatured, reviled, defamed, disparaged, lampooned, could

still rise to moments of sublime grandeur. The preceding generation
had had its Mendelssohn who taught the submerged Jews of that day
to hold up their heads, and who wrested from his Christian contemporaries an unwilling but sincere admiration. Yet even Mendelssohn felt that the Hebrews were thoroughly unprepared for any
colonization project. He said in 1770:

> The greatest difficulty standing in the way of the project seems to me
> to be the character of my nation. It is not sufficiently prepared to under-
> take anything great. The oppression under which we have been living
> for so many centuries has deprived our spirit of all vigor. It is not our
> fault . . . I cannot even assure myself that my widely scattered people
> possess the co-operative force, without which the most carefully laid
> plans must fail.

Then came the French Revolution. It gave the Jews a measure of
freedom. It widened their horizon, renewed their dreams—dreams of
a reborn Israel. Of this world-wide, postrevolutionary spirit, Noah
was the typical expression. Palestine was the ultimate solution, as he
saw it. But before European Jews could be made ready for the up-
building of an agricultural state, they must have two things—an immediate refuge for the persecuted and homeless and downtrodden, as
well as a place where they could be taught to live on and with the soil.

"My faith does not rest wholly in miracles," Noah once said.
"Providence disposes of events, human agency must carry them out."

It was as the savior of his people that Noah preferred to be regarded. The biggest histrionic thrill of his life came to him when, as
"The Judge of Israel," he attempted to restore his people to their
former greatness.

As early as 1820, his plans for his coreligionists were well known.
On September 7, of that year, John Quincy Adams wrote of Noah
in his diary: "He has great projects for colonizing Jews in this
country, and wants to be sent as Chargé d'Affaires to Vienna for
the promotion of them." In the same year, 1820, Noah petitioned the
State Legislature of New York for a grant of land on Grand Island.
The committee reported favorably, saying: "The committee did not
doubt, but that the recent persecution of the Jews in various parts of
Europe, may favor the views of the petitioner, and that the settlement of Grand Island would be a desirable object to this State."

This bill did not pass.

Grand Island was a spot on the "Niagara frontier." It was then a
beautiful wooded island, quiet, isolated, and well stocked with wild

game, a hunter's paradise. Situated on the Niagara River, equally
distant from Lake Erie and the Falls, it comprises 17,381 acres. The
land was fertile and admirably suited for intensive gardening.

In 1825, Grand Island was surveyed and subdivided into farm lots.
The State of New York announced through the press that the land
was open for settlement.

Now Major Noah, in whose mind the idea of colonizing Jews had
long lain dormant, was suddenly galvanized into action. Grand Island was to be set aside for the Jews. It was to be their refuge and
asylum which they sorely needed.

Noah persuaded his friend Samuel Legget to buy about two thousand five hundred acres of land. This was to serve as a nucleus for a
Jewish city which would eventually include the entire island. The
times, he argued, were auspicious. The Erie Canal was nearing completion and would bring Grand Island directly in the path of the new
commerce which was to transform the backwoods into a metropolis.

Through his paper, the *National Advocate,* he disseminated his
colonization idea. When lots on Grand Island were listed for sale, a
number of other capitalists joined in a fever of speculative buying.
Despite much skepticism and opposition Noah's propaganda and
preparations continued. He was fortunate in finding one Jewish
disciple in the person of A. B. Seixas of New York, who constantly
encouraged Noah.

On a hot August day, this Jewish Don Quixote, followed by his
Sancho Panza, Mr. Seixas, packed their belongings and left New
York for Buffalo. Buffalo was then a village of two thousand five
hundred souls, of whom all but one were strangers to Noah. But that
one, Mr. Isaac S. Smith, whom he had known in Tunis, was easily
enlisted in support of Major Noah's plans.

A cornerstone had been ordered which bore the imposing inscription:

ARARAT
A City of Refuge for the Jews
Founded by Mordecai Manuel Noah *in the Month of Tizri*
Sept. 1825 & in *the* 50th *year* of
American Independence

A great rush of settlers was expected to coincide with the dedication of the stone. Many spectators were awaited to witness the attendant ceremonies. It was decided to hold the entire ceremony in the
Episcopal Church of Buffalo. The great day was ushered in with "a

salute fired from the court house." Nor was this all. The versatile Noah on this day not only occupied the center of the stage, but himself reported the occasion in *The Buffalo Patriot*. So his reporting preserved for posterity much of the flavor of the occasion. At ten o'clock, on September 2, 1825, the Masonic and military escort met, and at eleven, the procession began. In full Masonic and military regalia came the paraders, in their midst "The Judge of Israel, in black, wearing the judicial robes of crimson silk, trimmed with ermine and a richly embossed gold medal suspended from the neck."

They entered the church and marched down its aisles while the band blared out the Grand March from *Judas Maccabeus*. After the services were "read emphatically" by the Episcopal minister who had so hospitably welcomed the celebrants, "Mr. Noah rose and pronounced a discourse, or rather delivered a speech," (let it not be forgotten that this quotation is from Noah's pen) announcing the reorganization of the Jewish government.

On this day was given to the world the "Proclamation to the Jews," in which he announced the approaching realization of the prophecy that the Jews

are to be gathered from the four quarters of the globe, and to resume the rank and character among the governments of the earth . . . to be restored to their inheritance, and enjoy the rights of a sovereign, independent people. Therefore, I, Mordecai Manuel Noah, Citizen of the United States of America . . . and by the grace of God, Governor and Judge of Israel, have issued this my Proclamation, announcing to the Jews throughout the world, that an asylum is prepared and hereby offered to them, where they can enjoy that peace, comfort and happiness, which have been denied them through the intolerance and misgovernment of former ages.

This city of refuge was to be called Ararat.

There follows a bombastic summons to the Jews throughout the world. He revives, reviews, enjoins, commands, orders, wills, abolishes, invites, imposes taxes, names commissioners—always in the grand manner. "I command," "I abolish," says this self-elected prophet.

The result?

Favorable publicity in a number of newspapers, considerable discussion and general friendly interest in the plight of the Jews of Europe was evinced by a number of Christians. Typical of such comment was an editorial in the *Albany Gazette*:

Here they can have their Jerusalem without fearing the legions of Titus. . . . Here they can lay their heads on their pillows at night without fear of mobs, of bigotry and persecution.

But as for the Jews, they ridiculed Noah and repudiated his project. Jews are notoriously hypercritical of each other.

Noah, however, with his every-ready wit and newspaper at hand, replied to all the jeers and flings in good humor, and lost none of the prestige of his character and position, either politically or morally. He was known to be eccentric in many things, and this was put down as the climax of his eccentricities.

In attempting to defend himself, Noah published a letter from two German Jews, Doctor Gans and Doctor Zunz, which he had received in 1822. In this letter they described the misery of their lot and spoke of Noah's activities as "animating the abject spirits of the members of an oppressed creed." This document then goes on to discuss the possibility "of *transplanting a vast portion of European Jews to the United States.*" It was an intimation of the mass migration of German Jews which was to come at a later date.

Noah's activities in behalf of the Jews fall into three stages. His first project conceived at the consecration of Shearith Israel synagogue in 1818, was to mobilize the seven million Jews into an active campaign against Turkey's dominion in Europe. That was to be followed by a re-establishment of the Jews in their ancient homeland. *He ranks therefore as the first Zionist in America.*

His second plan dealt with the establishment of Ararat, which was to be an agricultural training school for future Palestinian settlers.

The third phase of his grand strategy for solving the Jewish problems was resettlement in the land of Zion. In analyzing the hopes and ambitions of Jews centering about Palestine, Noah sounded a modern note. He challenged reawakened Jewry of the world to "do something for themselves; they must move onward to the accomplishment of that great event foretold—long promised—long expected."

With keen penetration he assessed the Near East situation—the rivalries, the intrigues, the race to extend spheres of influence. He realized the strategic importance of Palestine and the fact that "the combined force of Russia, Turkey, Persia, and Egypt, seriously threaten the safety of British possessions in the East Indies." Indeed much of Noah's philosophy sounds the prophetic note. "From the Danube, the Dneister, the Ukraine, Wallachia and Moldavia, the best of agriculturists would revive the former fertility of Palestine!" Today the pioneers of Israel have transformed desert spaces into fertile farming communities.

On another occasion in a speech on the "Restoration of the Jews," he makes the following searching observation:

England must possess Egypt, as affording the only secure route to her possessions in India through the Red Sea; then Palestine, thus placed between the Russian possessions and Egypt, reverts to its legitimate proprietors, and for the safety of the surrounding nations, a powerful, wealthy, independent, and enterprising people are placed there, by and with the consent of the Christian powers, and with their aid and agency, the land of Israel passes once more into the possession of the descendants of Abraham. . . . Every attempt to colonize the Jews in other lands has failed; their eye has steadily rested on their own beloved Jerusalem, and they have said, "The time will come, the promise will be fulfilled."[9]

In the same city of Charleston, South Carolina, where Mordecai Manuel Noah had been a journalist, another Jewish newspaperman was born in 1788.[10] His father, Solomon Harby, emigrated from England to Jamaica, then to Charleston. Of other members of his family, Isaac Harby writes:

My maternal grandfather contributed pecuniary aid to South Carolina, and particularly to Charleston, when besieged by the British. My father-in-Law was a brave grenadier in the regular American army, and fought and bled for the liberty he lived to enjoy and to hand down to his children.

Solomon Harby was "among the first to set an example to his Jewish brethren, of giving a liberal education to his children," his son tells us. Isaac was educated in a well-known academy, that of Dr. Best. As a very young man he was an assistant teacher in Charleston College, and began publishing articles in local newspapers. In 1808, Harby shouldered the financial problems of his family, whose sole support he became on the death of his father. He opened a school at Edisto Island, and proceeded to dispense education in the traditional manner. He stated his goals in a simple advertisement:

The subscriber has opened an Academy in Bedon Alley No. —, where will be taught the usual branches of an English Education, viz. Elocution, Arithmetic, Penmanship, Grammar, Geography—also the Latin and Greek Classics, Composition and the first books of Euclid's Elements.

He pledges himself, not only to pay every attention to the routine of his Pupil's improvement, but also to instruct them in the principles of virtue and patriotism. To instil into their minds honour and morality; and so far to effect the wish of the noble Spartan, as to teach Boys those things *when they are young,* which will prove most useful to them, *when they become men.*

ISAAC HARBY.

Two educational departures should, however, be noted. He shared the games of the boys and entered with abandon into all of their sports.

Besides being a schoolmaster, Harby was in his day, a well-known journalist. He was both an occasional contributor, and assistant editor and editor of several Charleston papers. In 1814, he bought the *Investigator* and became the ardent champion of the Republican cause in the South. The name of the paper as well as its policies were changed. Harby espoused the cause of Madison, and made his subscribers like his paper. Other journalistic ventures claimed his pen. He contributed to the *Charleston Mercury,* wrote popular essays, reviews, dramatic criticisms. Like Noah, he wrote plays, and saw them produced. In 1828, Harby decided to move to New York, which was then, as it is now, the Mecca for playwrights and journalists. He had lost his wife to whom he had been devoted. He had nursed her through a long and painful sickness, himself worn down by the strain of watching her unbearable suffering. His health was never regained.

Once in New York, he opened a school, contributed dramatic reviews to the *Evening Post* and other papers. But six months of hard work and privation led to his untimely death. He was barely past forty when he died.

During his short life Harby, like Noah, made a distinct contribution to his people. His great eloquence, his ebullient enthusiasm, his most ardent zeal was devoted to the formation of the "Reformed Society of Israelites," which was, in the last analysis, an attempt to make Judaism take root and feel at home in America.

"Where is he that does not feel a glow of honest exultation, when he hears himself called an American?" asked Isaac Harby. "America truly is the land of promise," he avers in his "Discourse on the Jewish Synagogue." So it was that this impassioned Jewish dissenter sowed the seed for that far-reaching movement which had as its aim the adjusting of Judaism to the American environment.

When he died, his friends and members of his family lamented his untimely loss. Penina Moïse, a lifelong friend, wrote:

Art thou not linked with every record dear,
That memory loves to trace from childhood's sphere?
Wert not thou he from whom my spirit caught
Its proudest aspiration to high thought?[11]

"For the student of Jewish history, Isaac Harby is best known, however, because of his activities in the Charleston Jewish Reform movement, which is so largely identified with his name," says Max J. Kohler. It is obvious that like all zealots, he could kindle enthusiasm by the sheer appeal of his personality. When Penina Moïse paid tribute to Isaac Harby's "mental radiance," she was expressing lyrically what countless others felt.

Something of his spirituality, mysticism, prophetic vision, devotion to Judaism can be felt in his speeches and his writings. His personality was singularly free of inner conflict. He knew his goals and the roads that led to them. He treasured his American heritage. He cherished his Jewish background. Within him these two traditions reached a happy flowering. To reconcile the one with the other involved no inner struggle. It was, for him, a matter of simple logic.

As an American he could boast of his ancestors. As a Jew he could write frankly to Thomas Jefferson of his plans for his coreligionists:

CHARLESTON, 14th January, 1826

SIR,

With patience and industry, we hope, in a few years, to be able to establish a mode of worship, simple and sensible; suited to the liberality of the age, improving to the Israelite, and acceptable to the Deity. The example set by the University, which owes its noblest characteristics to your judgment and philanthropy, offers a bright pattern to any similar institution in our country. May you, honoured sir, live to see your warmest wishes realized in the results.

With sentiments of gratitude and admiration,

I am your ob't. serv't.

ISAAC HARBY

His discourse and essays attracted much favorable attention.

L. C. Moïse, his biographer, writes:

The Library of Southern Literature, in giving a résumé of the life of Isaac Harby, calls him an editor and dramatist, but makes no mention of him as a religious reformer. Historians have signally neglected to give this man his proper place in the Jewish Reform movement, which fact may be accounted for by lack of appreciation on the part of those of his own faith. For in his capacity as religious leader lies the most important and the most abiding work of his useful life.

The movement for Judaism in American dress did not, however, originate with Harby. It had pre-Revolutionary origins. When in 1766 Isaac Pinto translated the Sephardic ritual into English in order to extend the influence of the synagogue to those whose native tongue was English, he was pointing the way to reform. For during the stirring days of social, political, and civil progress which marked the movement of the years, the synagogue had remained stationary. Nevertheless, the same rules which weighed so heavily upon the founders of Shearith Israel, continued in force for another century. Excerpts from the constitution of the Congregation Beth Elohim in Charleston adopted in 1820 differ but little in content from the rules of Shearith Israel adopted one hundred years earlier. Within the synagogue walls the hands of time moved slowly. Conformity, strict and inflexible, was the rule. Social ostracism threatened the offender. Fines, penalties, punishments, excommunication and expiation were so many swords held over the Jewish community. "This constitution of 1820, then," Elzas tells us, "reveals the Synagogue as a severely autocratic institution. It controlled its members, both within the Synagogue and without."[12]

It was inevitable that there should be murmurs of protest in the ranks of those whose lives were spent in an atmosphere which enshrined the past and ignored the immediate present. It seems natural that this protest should become articulate in Charleston where the Jews were largely native, cultured, enlightened and educated, as well as closely identified with the Revolutionary movement.

What did the agitators for reform want? In the light of the practices of present-day Judaism, their demands, first presented in 1824, to the vestry of Beth Elohim, are very modest. They asked that portions of the service be read in English, as well as in Hebrew; that the reading be abridged "and everything superfluous excluded"; that the Rabbi expound a portion of the Bible in English, every week "like all other ministers," so that they may know something of their religion which so few of them really understood.

This petition was tabled without discussion.

In 1824, "The Reformed Society of Israelites" was organized. Its purpose was to make "such alterations in the customs and ceremonies of the Jewish religion as would comport with the present enlightened state of the world." Abridged their purpose was:

First, that the bulk of the services be in English, so that they be understood.

Second, "to discontinue the observance of such ceremonies as partake strongly of bigotry."

Third, to abolish repetitious and superfluous portion of the services.

Fourth, to include an English sermon, in which "the principles of the Jewish faith, and the force and beauty of the moral law, may be expounded to the rising generation."

The Society continued until 1833. But during its brief existence it had paved the way for a more liberal, more enlightened spirit in American Jewry. This movement for synagogal ceremonial reform later gained adherents from the ranks of many of the newcomers. Among them was Isaac Mayer Wise, a Bohemian Jew whose coming to America gave the reformers a powerful leader. In 1848, he issued a call to American Rabbis. Isaac Leeser, in whose *Occident* the call was published, ably seconded Rabbi Wise. The accession of David Einhorn and Samuel Hirsch helped the reform movement, but that story belongs in a later chapter.

Before dismissing the subject, let us beware of oversimplification. Human motives are often far from simple. To what extent the urge for reform was due to the desire to achieve a rhythm of conformity with American trends, we can not say. That was certainly a part of it. Another reason was the loss of some of the young Israelites who, following their hearts, intermarried and eventually through their own indifference or their children's choice, were separated from the Jewish community. But was there not still an additional hidden cause for this separatist movement? Had not Jews in America, Sephardic Jews especially, nurtured their own separatism? Had they not become devotees of "consciousness of kind"? As Jews from Poland and Bohemia and Germany made their way into various American communities, did not American Sephardic Jews shrink a little from the contact? We know how they frowned on "intermarriage," these aristocratic Sephardim. Their ears shrank from hearing the beloved Hebrew pronounced in some strange and shrill accent. Better perhaps to limit Hebrew prayers, to yield to those who preferred to hear English spoken. Assimilation with Christians was easier for some of them than assimilation with the impecunious Jewish foreigner who had but recently fled abject poverty and direst hardship in Europe. Men of status and substance do not fraternize with those who lack them. Did not Erasmus write in his book of manners to beware of men who walked about with their hands folded behind their backs? In this way is the fabric of social ostracism woven.

So we have the setting—Charleston. We have the plot—revolt against tradition. We have the protagonist—Isaac Harby, "whose buoyant brilliancy could e'er dispense vivacity and vigor to the sense." And whether one clings to tradition or adheres to reform, does not really matter. For Isaac Harby's personality is to be cherished as peculiarly American and indelibly loyal to Judaism. His character was the sum of all that made him. His brief lifetime, from Washington's days to the time of John Quincy Adams, was one of high achievement as well as of promise cut short. And if he knew but little of his Jewish contemporaries in Europe—both he and the founder of the Haskalah Enlightenment Movement belonged to the same era—yet he labored with all his zeal, with all his many talents, with his failing strength and his gifted pen, for integration and fruition, for intelligent participation in religious services, for an easier and more liberal Judaism in America.

Penina Moïse was born in Charleston in 1797 and died there in 1880.[13] Her parents were French Jews who emigrated from Alsace to the West Indies and, in 1791, to Charleston.

Penina's mother was a great beauty. Penina, one of nine children, was conscious of her own inferiority. She was nearsighted, yet her one great escape was in reading. This was a forbidden luxury. So she would creep up to the attic of their house with books and note paper and read by the faint light which filtered through the little dusty windows. Even at night when the moon was bright she would go back to her books undeterred by the shapeless shadows, the eerie noises, that made the attic seem haunted. When she was twelve years old, her father died. From the bitter sense of loss, from the poverty into which the family was now plunged, Penina was never to recover emotionally. The traumatic experience was to color the rest of her days. Schooling stopped. She had to find ways of helping to support her family. Still every spare moment was given to reading. The extent of Penina Moïse's self-education was phenomenal. She showed her literary ability at an early age. In 1830, her poems and prose began to appear in print. She was a prolific author. She was a contributor to the *Charleston Courier, Boston Daily Times, Godey's Lady's Book,* the *Occident* and the *Charleston Book,* as well as other publications.

Although her work was sometimes light and humorous, her best efforts were those when as an aroused Jewess she championed her people. Her interest in her coreligionists amounted to a passion. Like Rebecca Gratz, she was active in Sunday School work. She was a pillar of Beth Elohim at Charleston. She wrote a collection of beautiful hymns for the use of her congregation which came to be widely accepted.

Then, too, she was the unofficial poet laureate of her city. Many civic events were celebrated by her. Penina Moïse became well known throughout the South. The intellectuals of her city paid her tribute. Her Friday afternoons were well-known gatherings of the elite of Jewish Charleston.

She was blind for twenty-five years. Yet despite her blindness, she conducted a successful girl's school and continued her writing. Her pupils read aloud to her. Together this blind preceptress and her charges read the works of George Eliot, Charlotte Brontë, Walter Scott and many other classics. She was adored by her pupils and much respected by her community. Here was a pioneer woman in the field of education and literature. She was a typical Southerner reflecting its tradition and ideology in her work and in her writing. With her as with Harby, environment inexplicably shaped her thinking. The folkways and mores of the South were hers in full measure. Her large family shared with her her convictions, her ardent Southern partisanship, her spiritual kinship with her environment. Columbus Moïse of New Orleans, banker and postmaster of his city, was one of the family. Edwin Warren Moïse of Charleston (born in 1811) was an ardent Southern patriot and a judge during the Confederacy. His namesake (born in 1832) in the same city organized his own company of 120 men and equipped them largely at his own expense. Company A of the Seventh Confederate Cavalry had Moïse as its Captain, fought under General Lee during the War Between the States.

The importance of Penina Moïse lies not only in her poems, which were treasured by her generation. Through her writing and in her life she reveals herself and the dilemma of the American Jew. So many were celibate. So many intermarried and were lost. Even where faith was steadfast and loyalty to parental culture was whole-hearted, the individual Jew paid a bitter price for remaining in the fold.

Penina Moïse left beautiful hymns as her legacy to future generations. Through these hymns not only her religious beliefs but her deepest innermost thoughts and yearnings are made evident. There is no mistaking her sentiments when she wrote:

> Halleluja! May our race,
> Heirs of promise and of grace,
> Enter Heav'n beyond Life's goal,
> Blessed Canaan of the soul!

She was a mystic and a believer. When she became the successor to Sally Lopez as Sunday School Superintendent, she could indulge both her love of teaching and her innate piety. She became celebrated even among her Christian friends for her religious fervor. So that when a noted English Bishop died she was invited to contribute a memorial poem. She could turn from threnodies to worldly subjects with ease. In 1838 when the great fire of Charleston leveled the synagogue, she rose to the occasion with a poem. Another time when her congregation was sharply divided on whether to install an organ, Penina found it an excellent opportunity to air her views on music. The synagogue was rebuilt in 1841 and consecrated two years later. Again her fellow Jews turned to her for the hymn of consecration.

Her life was not to be lived out in a loveless vacuum. Her enthusiastic biographer wrote of her unhappy romance: "Romance entered Miss Penina Moïse's life in early womanhood, coming in a form that spoke pleadingly to her heart. But, alas! it had to be denied . . . she could not be tempted even by love to transgress the rules of her religion's exclusiveness and step without its pale." Then he adds that she was all the better for having once loved and been loved in return. This first love of hers overshadowed later "offers" which she rejected: "More than one offered her love, but she remained true to her own heart."

One of her rejected suitors sent her "an aeolian harp," which she kept in one of her windows because of the pleasant vibrations of the strings when the wind swept by them. Her troubles, her poverty and her valetudinarianism kept her much in the public eye. She suffered from gradually deteriorating eyesight, from neuralgia and from insomnia. Yet when a yellow fever epidemic struck her community she enlisted as a nurse and carried on valiantly. She endorsed the principles of the South wholeheartedly. She was "a strong states-rights woman" and advocated secession.

During the War, Penina, her sister and niece "refugeed to a little town" in the interior. Partisan to the core, she was often inspired to write martial poetry in honor of soldiers of the Confederacy. When the War was over, Penina and her family were as destitute as every one else. They opened a school. Penina, who was then blind, gave "oral lessons." She seemed to have a marked sensitivity to light and wore dark blue glasses to protect her sightless eyes. Invariably she wore a white Swiss muslin cap. Then around her face she tied a black silk kerchief "to fight off attacks of the fiend neuralgia."

Her hands were never still. "Her fingers were ever busy—ripping

—generally something black in silk, fold after fold." A somber figure, blind, handicapped by ill health, shrinking from light even though she could not see it, trusting to the magic pain-killing attributes of a black silk kerchief tied about her face, preoccupied with ripping black silk stuff. . . . Were not these symptoms of inner mourning, testimonials to a dark, loveless, wasted life?

If these indications of a serious psychic malaise, of a deeply ingrained anhedonia, were individual characteristics, they would merit scant mention. But the larger implications are deeply significant. They are revelations of the price paid by "marginal" men and women caught by conflicting loyalties, bound to two cultures, torn between what they wanted and what the community expected of them.

Penina Moïse was articulate in words and in manner. So because she revealed herself, she performed a service to the many men and women in America who shared her tragic dilemma. The perpetual finger-moving, ripping and picking at cloth were eloquent signs of a deep-seated protest—a manifesto of subconscious resentment. The stern choice made by Penina confronted a growing number of Jews in America. For they were lost to their people if they intermarried and lost to themselves if they did not. And the alternative of rejection of religious community and siblings, or rejection of self, presents no happy solution.

Here then we have five Jews—Touro, Gratz, Noah, Harby, Moïse. All were born in the last years of the eighteenth century. All had certain characteristics in common. They were all as one in their keen pride in their American heritage. All had the finest educational facilities the times afforded. All were synagogued Jews. All reflected the opinions and prejudices of the wealthy, aristocratic segment of Jewry. With the exception of Rebecca Gratz, they were Sephardic, Southern in sympathy and allegiance. All of them gave their finest talents to their fellow Jews. Touro dispensed great wealth. Penina her poetry. Rebecca good works. Harby tried to bring about through acculturation the welding of Judaism and Americanism. Noah dreamed of a Jewish state and of a return of the oppressed of European Jewries to Zion. It was a great generation that could produce such men and such women. They were good for all Americans to know. They were articulate Jews loving their native land no less because they cherished their ancient heritage.

"The poor man retains the prejudices of his forefathers without their faith, and their ignorance without their virtues." So wrote D. C. Gilson in his introduction to Tocqueville's *Democracy in America*.[14] These were the *elite*. What of the rank and file? They were also the poor, the unlettered, the hard-working, the itinerants—whose horizons were limited, whose contacts outside their own community were few and circumscribed.

In 1793, in the case of Stansberry *vs*. Marks, a Jewish witness refusing to be sworn on Saturday was fined ten pounds. In 1805, the Congregation Shearith Israel accused one Caleb Vandenburg of affixing a seal upon meat which resembled theirs. Caleb attributed the offense to his sense of humor. The authorities could not see it in that light.[15]

The Market Committee to whom was referred the memorial of the President and Trustees of the Congregation of Shearith Israel report that they have examined the Subject and have conferred with Caleb Vandenburg who acknowledges he put the seals on the Meat, but did it in a joke, but the affidavits of two of the Congregation declare that he offered the Meat for sale as Cosher or fit for that Congregation to eat, and as we do not see any good cause why this Board ought not to protect this religious People in their religious Rights when not inconsistent with the Public Rights. We therefore are of opinion that Caleb Vandenburg be Suspended of his License as a Butcher.
New York Sep[r] 2th 1805.

GEORGE JANEWAY
J[a] DRAKE

Eight years later Benjamin S. Judah and Isaac Gomez, Jr., were still concerned with the matter. They carefully explained to the authorities that

it is not lawful for a Jew to eat of the flesh of Any Animal unless killed inspected and sealed by certain persons called Shochets duly authorized by the Trustees of the Synagogue that certain persons unauthorized by their Trustees had taken upon them the Office Shochet and they prayed the interference of the Common Council to prevent such impositions. Whereupon an Ordinance was passed entitled "an Ordinance to prevent impositions in the sale of Jews meat in the public Markets."[16]

In 1816 the Commonwealth of Pennsylvania *vs*. Wolff tested whether "a conscientious Jew could perform worldly labor on Sunday and be exempt from a Sunday statute." This was not upheld. Three years later the courts held in the State of South Carolina *vs*. Carvalho that "disturbing a congregation of Hebrews was an indictable offence at common law, although the offender was a member of the same."

In 1831, in Phillips *vs.* Gratz, it was decided that "excusing a Jewish plaintiff from attending court on Saturday is a matter of discretion, not of right." From 1833 on there were a number of lawsuits testing the validity of Sunday nonobservance.[17]

Gradually as Jewish peddlers began to usurp the field which Yankee hawkers considered their own, the areas of tension between the poor of both groups were considerably increased.[18] If the student of history is to maintain a semblance of objectivity, he must be careful to relate these tensions to the complex factors, social, economic, psychological, religious, which are involved. Material and nonmaterial culture traits are concerned. Differences in dress, food, language, occupations, observances of days of rest, recreational activities—all are areas of potential friction. Not all differences were resolved in courts of law. Some were amicably adjusted. Others created conflict. The host culture had the advantage of numbers. The minority group compensated by assuming that it was a "chosen people."

These areas of conflict tended to diminish as individuals in both groups approached each other in skill, in knowledge, in education, in wealth. Numerous examples are found in the field of medicine. Kagan's exhaustive study titled *Jewish Contribution to Medicine* discusses many medical biographies, records of accomplishment and of success.[19] Here is Dr. Joel Hart, born in Philadelphia, September 14, 1784. He graduated from the Royal College of Surgery in London. On his return to America he became a founder of the New York College of Physicians and Surgeons. Later President Madison appointed him as the United States Consul at Leith, Scotland, a post he held from 1817 to 1832. He then came back to his native land and for another decade practiced medicine here. Here certainly was a career unmarred by difficulties due to racial origin, religious or cultural differences. Nor does the life history of Dr. Manly Emanuel present evidence of any undue hardships. He was born in Davenport, England, February 5, 1795, and was graduated from St. George's Hospital in London in 1816. After receiving his degree, he emigrated to the United States and established his medical practice in Philadelphia. He died July 3, 1880. The tenor of his days was unruffled.

A man endowed from birth with many gifts was Dr. Isaac Hays, nephew of Rebecca Gratz, whom Kagan considers "the most outstanding figure among the early Jewish physicians." He was born in Philadelphia July 5, 1796. In 1820, he received his M.D. degree from the University of Pennsylvania. He was a pioneer American ophthalmologist and became a noted surgeon. He edited many medical books. Dr. Hays became an editor of the *American Journal of the Medical Sciences*. Then he founded and edited *Hays' Journal* which for more than fifty years was considered "the best American medical monthly." As if these accomplishments were not enough, he was one of the founders of the Franklin Institute and of the American Medical Association. He seems to have straddled two sets of mores without friction, conflict, inner tension, anxiety. Only a person who had successfully adjusted to his immediate environment and to the "great society" could have crowded so much constructive activity into one lifetime. Important ophthalmological instruments were perfected by Dr. Hays. In addition, he was an indefatigable worker in several hospitals and dispensaries. For four years he was president of the Academy of Natural Sciences of Philadelphia. His most enduring contribution was the drafting of a code of ethics for the American Medical Association—a code which was adopted by many medical societies throughout the land.

Dr. Daniel L. M. Peixotto was born in Amsterdam in 1800. His family moved to New York when he was seven. He was a physician at nineteen, having graduated from Columbia. After several years in the West Indies, he returned to New York specializing in gynecology. Preventive medicine was an obsession with him and he became a pioneer in the field. When only twenty-five, he helped found the Academy of Medicine. With two other physicians he undertook the editing of the first Medical Journal published in English, *The New York Medical and Physical Journal*. In 1829 he became its only editor. Invited to become president of Willoughby Medical College in Cleveland in 1836, he occupied that post as well as acting as dean of its faculty for a number of years. One of his pet projects was a "Society for Assisting the Widows and Orphans of Medical Men." Before his death in 1843, he found time to enter the political arena. An intimate friend of Andrew Jackson, he actively participated in the political campaign preceding his election. He edited a pro-Jackson paper called the *True American*. Yet he found time to be active in Jewish communal affairs. Rachel Seixas, whom he married, was a member of a well-known New York Jewish family.

So again we have an example of an individual whose social heritage —immigrant, Dutch, Sephardic, American, academic, professional— was an amalgam of many influences, a harmonious distillation of the culture traits of all of them. Can we in all fairness say that the diffusion of the ideas and practices current in one group is of no benefit to the other? That the cross-fertilization of ideas, of attitudes, of philosophies is of insignificant value? Is not the founding of a society for the care of indigent widows and orphans of the medical profession in line with Jewish practice of philanthropy? And did not Daniel Peixotto study to be a doctor in a Christian university? It is when the fusion of two ideologies produces a good and useful citizen, that we know that the process which made him is one which the society that made him should accept with approval.

The Jews, as they identified themselves in dress and customs and way of life with those about them, were more readily accepted by their Christian neighbors. A *Geschichte der Jehudim*, published in Germany in 1821, in discussing the position of Jews in the Southern United States, reads: "In dress and manner the Jews of Charleston do not differ from other citizens. Open-hearted and hospitable, like all Carolinians," they play a creditable part in the social and political life of their State. So impressed were Europeans with the American attitude of liberality toward Jews and with the fact that they were permitted to hold office that they dwelt on the subject again and again in their books, magazines and letters. A pamphlet written in London in approximately 1830, by Dr. Barnard Van Oven, entitled "An Appeal to the British Nation on behalf of the Jews," cites the existence of a number of Jewish office-holders in the United States.

Harriet Martineau, who visited the United States, and was familiar with the superior status of Jews on the Western Continent, wrote in 1834: "The disgrace of the exclusion of the Jews is so deep that, as soon as their lordships in the Upper House become fully conscious of it, they will be in a prodigious hurry to get rid of it."

Their fight for equality, therefore, was a fight that American Jews were waging, not only in their own behalf, but indirectly for their coreligionists in Europe. The astonishing part of it all is that numerically speaking, American Jews were but a small fraction of the total population. Statistics are in this case not particularly reliable. Nevertheless, they are of relative importance. In 1818, Noah estimated the Jewish population of the United States at about 3,000. In 1826, Isaac Harby is authority for placing the number at 6,000. The American Almanac gave the number as 15,000 in 1840. In a *History of the Jews* published in 1848, the numbers leaped to 50,000.

What were the factors involved in this sudden accession in population? Let us look to Europe first. The French Revolution and the Napoleonic reforms removed a number of restrictions, and raised

countless hopes in the hearts of European Jews. The wave of reaction that followed, especially between 1830-48, quickly snuffed
them out. While the spirits of European Jews were downcast by the
reverses they experienced, American Jews were making social and
political headway. The contrast was obvious. Many Europeans of all
sects and races sought at this time to escape from their debt-ridden,
impoverished, reactionary countries. All roads led to America.

Even before 1848, Jews in the United States were not all drawn
from the ranks of Spanish and Portuguese Sephardim. From very
early times there were German and Polish Jews among them.[20]
English Jews, so often identified with the Sephardic element, were in
some instances originally German Jews who like Jacob Franks went
from Germany to England and then to America. Members of the
Salomon, Philips, Gratz, Hart, Levy, Simpson, Moses families were
Ashkenazim—Polish or German Jews. Georgia from its earliest days
included German as well as Portuguese Jews among its pioneers.
Amusing are the details of social snobbery exhibited by the Sephardim
toward the Ashkenazim. The ostracism, the isolation to which German
Jews were relegated by their Spanish coreligionists was no greater in
many cases than the treatment accorded Jews by their stiff-necked
Christian neighbors. Jews did not always practice among themselves the toleration they were so anxious to receive from Christians.

But the German Jews had energy and pluck and perseverance.
They achieved material success. That is invariably followed by social
recognition. A member of the wealthy Bleichroeder family, who
emigrated to America, was readily accepted by the upper strata of
Jewish society from the first. He wrote to his family in 1807: "It is
particularly this cultured class of Jews which has treated me so generously and assisted me with advice and deed." A traveler in the
United States, Israel Joseph Benjamin, who wrote *Drei Jahre in
Amerika,* made a careful study of German Jewish immigration here.
He found that German Jews began to come to America in great numbers in 1836. Bavaria with her severe marriage and economic laws
was instrumental in forcing the largest number of Jews to emigrate.
They were a destitute and poorly educated group. But they were hard-
working, ambitious, pious men. They became peddlers, carrying their
packs to distant dwellings, to farmhouses, to little villages which were
swallowed up in the surrounding wilderness. An early German traveler
says of the Jews: "They generally begin as peddlers, stopping at every
farm house, and the farmer is obliged to buy something to get rid of
them."

The prevalent error that German Jewish migration was turned on like a faucet in the middle of the nineteenth century should be emphatically scotched. Here is a note in 1900, taking cognizance of the centennial of a German Jewish congregation. "The Congregation, Rodeph Shalom of Philadelphia, has just celebrated the one hundredth anniversary of its foundation, the celebration taking place December 21 to 23, 1900," writes Rabbi Henry Berkowitz. We have the deed executed in 1801 for the purchase of a cemetery. We know that the charter of 1802 was replaced in 1812.

Certainly the presence of Ashkenazic Jews in our social fabric is one to be reckoned with. Polish and Central European Jews might be snubbed by their contemporaries—but not by the historian who would do justice to his task.

When the daughter of Gershom Mendes Seixas, his favorite child, married an immigrant, a young German Jew who had come to the United States in 1796, the event must have occasioned no little comment in "elite" Sephardic circles.[21] And well might the gossips wag their tongues! Gershom Mendes Seixas was born in New York in 1745. He became minister of Shearith Israel in 1766 and continued in his post for almost fifty years. We know how he led and rallied to the patriot cause nearly all of New York's Jewry. We know of his helping to organize Mickvé Israel, the new congregation in Philadelphia. He helped found Columbia College and was one of its trustees. It was a career of dignity, of status, of unimpeachable social position. Sarah Abigail Seixas' husband had a totally different background. Israel Baer Kursheedt was born in Germany in 1766. Thoroughly grounded in Hebrew in his native land, he came to the United States at the age of thirty. And such was the charm of his personality that he became the favorite son-in-law of Rabbi Seixas and for a time even the president of Shearith Israel! Yet not for long. After a residence in Richmond, Virginia, during the years 1812-24, he returned to New York and became a trustee of the newly organized congregation of B'nai Jeshurun, founded in 1825, which was formed by a group of seceders from the parent congregation. The rift was occasioned by one group of worthies choosing their own *shochet*. "The secession of B'nai Jeshurun in 1825 . . . and further secessions . . . brought about a state of anarchy in the Jewish community," says Grinstein. Certainly Mr. Kursheedt was no milk-and-water personality. Yet it is to his father-in-law's letters to the educated immigrant from Germany, that we are indebted for a close look at Jewish life in America during the War years.

Dr. David de Sola Pool, who has edited the letters and interpreted them, makes some interesting observations about the penetration of Ashkenazic vocabulary, customs, folkways into the sacrosanct Sephardic circles: such words as *Shule* (Synagogue), *Good Shabess* (Good Sabbath), *kindbett* (childbirth), *rudle* (gossip), *schofel* (rascal). "The free usage of Ashkenazic terms is to be interpreted not as a gracious Sephardic concession . . . but as a reflection of the usage in the New York Jewish community of the time," says Dr. Pool. If the Sephardim learned about *Kugel* (pudding) from the Ashkenazim, the former taught the latter the delights of *Olmendigas* (meatballs). It would appear from these letters that we will have to revise radically our notions of what constituted the "elite."

From these letters we learn of the impact of the War on the people of New York. By 1813, foodstuffs were high in price and scarce, "the poverty in the city is great." The blockade had already been felt in every port city and far inland. By 1814, Rabbi Seixas wrote freely of his sufferings the past two years. The receiving of his allotment of Matzoth and sugar for Passover was no small bit of news. The synagogue, more than seventy-five years old, was crowded and in poor repair. The congregational treasury was in a "reduced state." Trustees quarreled and resigned. Military reverses were met by "fasting, humiliation & prayer" and duly commented upon in sermons by the good Rabbi. Collections for victims of the War were the order of the day. His sermons were geared to current events. It was not difficult to convince his congregants that "War was an Evil of the greatest magnitude, by David's declaration to Gad."

Yet Rabbi Seixas could refer to Spinoza as "the apostate Jew" and impute to him the "free-thinking among the english." He refuses to become involved in controversy which was then agitating Christian circles. George Bethune English had published a work comparing the Old Testament with the New. Christian ministers like William Ellery Channing and Edward Everett considered Christianity challenged in its very stronghold. Mr. English was quite plainly shopping for a new religion, for he eventually became a Mohammedan! But in the interim this seeker after a way of life called on Rabbi Seixas who "heard him quite patiently." Rabbi Seixas reports the occasion to Kursheedt:

Mr. E. came at about 5 Stayed until 8—being engaged for the evening —he certainly is a man of great reading—besides being a classical scholar—& well versed in the hebrew grammar—gained a gold medal at the college—for the best treatise on the origin of points—I forgot to mention that Daddy (David) likes him & came in to be one of the

Company—you may depend there was no lack of conversation—he was here *before* dinner on *Shabbat* and was invited to Tea—he has told somebody, & the by-word has passed through many somebodies, until it reached cousin Becky—who told it to me, that he had gained more knowledge of yr Father, in the short conversation he had with him, than from all the Books which he has read—if so of me, what will he say of our dr [dear] K? after conversing with him! tomorrow he sets off for Phi[a] how long to remain there—uncertain—thence to Richmond.

Around each Jewish settlement there are clustered stories of significance. Some of the events loom large in the biographies of individuals. Others have social implications for "the great community." Sometimes a grateful non-Jewish visitor left a tribute to Jewish hospitality, as did Captain Alexander Graydon who described his impression of the Etting home on the eve of the Revolution:

York, I must say, was somewhat obnoxious to the general charge of unsociableness under which Pennsylvania had always labored; or if I wrong her, I was not the kind of guest that was calculated to profit of her hospitality. Perhaps I approached her under unfavorable auspices, those of a young man debauched by evil communications; or perhaps there was want of congeniality between her manners and mine. Be it as it may, there was but a single house in which I found that sort of reception which invited me to repeat my visit; and that was the house of a Jew. In this I could conceive myself at home, being always received with ease, with cheerfulness and cordiality.

At other times our attention is vigorously attracted to the existence of crude, raw hatred for Jews. The story is found in the *Letters of Rebecca Gratz.*[22]

Under date of September 2, 1832, she writes:

I received a letter—a heart-rending letter, a few days ago from our dear Sally Minis—giving an account of the situation of the family, in consequence of that unfortunate affair of Philips, and at his request stating the particulars, by which he is exonerated from the stigma the newspaper account left on his character—

Before we go on with Rebecca's account of "the unfortunate affair," it may be well to refresh the reader's mind about the background of the Minis family in America. It was founded by Abraham Minis, who was one of the original forty Jews who came here in the earliest days of Georgia's history. As early as 1733, he was a landowner. He lived to be one hundred and one years old His son Philip was the first white child born in Savannah. During the Revolution, Philip was a patriot, enlisting himself and his fortune in the patriot cause. But more than that—his wife and daughter were known as "great whigs." It was they who smuggled food to the imprisoned Sheftalls. Eventually these brave women were confined to their own quarters by the British and then ordered to leave town. Philip Minis, who was involved in a duel, came by his militant nature honestly.

Rebecca's narrative goes on:

He was consulting some of his friends at the races in April about naming a horse, when Mr. Stark passing by said "Name him Shylock" and afterwards called him a "D——d Jew"—Minis challenged him then —he apologized, and the affair slumbered—until some of Starks friends induced him to retract his apology, and another challenge was sent & accepted—a difference about the hour of fighting arose between the seconds. Mr. S——s friend wished them to meet on the same day— Minis's insisted that a sufficient time was not allowed to settle his affairs, and proposed the dawn of the next morning or any hour after that they would prefer—the seconds parted without coming to any agreement and Mr. Stark with his friend went to the ground at 5 o'clock that afternoon, although assured that the other party would not meet them then—they returned and publicly pronounced Minis a coward—the next morning they met accidentally at the city Hotel—Minis reproached Stark for his conduct—he drew a pistol and advanced. Minis did the same, and fired instantly—Stark fell mortally wounded—and Minis immediately expressed his determination to give himself up to the civil authorities—and is now in close confinement—where he must continue until January—as his father is a judge in the inferior Court, and Mr. S's nearest relation is a judge in the Superior Court, and so a new election must take place before he can be tried.

The importance of this incident goes beyond its anecdotal value. It indicates a mood, a temper which the youth of American Jewry, bred as patriots by parents and grandparents who had fought and pioneered, displayed on every occasion. Rebecca Gratz tells us that

Henry Etting too has had a fight at the navy yard in Boston but no serious consequence is likely to result—our Sister had a few sleepless nights to endure on his account, as a Mother's fears have so many objects—but the Capt and other officers have sent testimonials of his good conduct in the affair.

She refers to the son of Solomon Etting and Rachel Gratz Etting. Rachel was the daughter of Bernard Gratz and a cousin of Rebecca's. Henry became a midshipman in 1818, a commodore in 1830 and was retired as a captain in 1861.

Such men cannot be pushed around.

Now we come to an anomaly. We reconstruct the history of an American Jewish family largely from the pages of the *Virginia Magazine of History* and the *North Carolina Historical Review*.[23] Let us meet the Mordecai family. It is an interesting problem in historical methodology. First we construct the genealogy. Then we follow the family saga from before the days of the Revolution to the twentieth century. It is not "typical." For no family is ever typical. Yet it follows a pattern which is not strange to the culture of America, which is a native pattern.

We begin with Moses Mordecai of Bonn, who was born in 1707. He married an Englishwoman, Elizabeth Whitlock, who became a Jewess and "dropped her baptismal name for that of Esther." Moses Mordecai lived first in New York then in Philadelphia. He was one of the signers of the Non-Importation Agreement. He died in 1781. Moses and Elizabeth had a son named Jacob, who was born in 1762, in Philadelphia. He was educated in the best private schools of his native city and completed his schooling in the counting house of David Franks. In 1774 he was a sergeant of a rifle corps. As a member of this corps, he had the privilege of being a member of the escort party when the members of the Continental Congress moved into Philadelphia. Jacob Mordecai married Judith Myers in 1784. They had six children. Moses Mordecai "became a leading member of the North Carolina bar." Samuel Mordecai "became an outstanding merchant of Richmond" and wrote a history of that city. Solomon Mordecai studied medicine in Philadelphia and "became a popular physician" in Mobile, Alabama. George Washington Mordecai "settled in Raleigh and became an eminent lawyer, railroad president and president of the bank of North Carolina." Alfred Mordecai became a major in the U.S. Army and "refused to fight or make arms" against the South during the Civil War. The youngest son, Augustus Mordecai, became a farmer near Richmond.

Judith Mordecai, the mother of these boys, worn out no doubt by the strains of bearing her family, died when her eldest son was eleven years old and her youngest baby but seventeen months old. After two years Jacob married the half-sister of his former wife, Rebecca Myers. They had seven children. Of this second group of children, Emma, the youngest of his seven daughters, was the most interesting. She "devoted her long life (1812-1906) to educational and religious work, in which she played a prominent part." In this way Padgett characterizes the various members of our "sample" study.

Now it seems that the philoprogenitiveness of Jacob Mordecai made great financial demands on him. His business affairs lagged and he was hard put to it to make ends meet. So like many another man before and after him, he turned to teaching. Between 1809-19 he ran a school which "was an unqualified success from a cultural as well as financial standpoint."

That Jacob Mordecai had a winning, warm personality, an attitude of gallantry toward women, considerable personal charm and erudition, is made clear by Rebecca Gratz, who wrote a description of his visit to her home in 1832. It occurred within six years of his death. Rebecca writes on February 16 of that year:

I dare say I mentioned old Mr. Mordecai's visit in the fall—and how much delighted we were with the patriarchal manner and wisdom of his conversation—since his return he has twice written to me, and sent me valuable papers of his own writing which I consider quite a treasure, the last was a character of "David King of Israel."

The Warrenton Female Seminary gained considerably from the personality of the erudite and charming director. All evidence we have points to a highly successful school. It was nonsectarian and the daughters of near-by well-to-do families were successfully educated there. Rachel Mordecai, his eldest daughter, was a pedagogue of great ability. Nor was the second Mrs. Mordecai idle. Despite the seven daughters she bore she found time for the school.

Young Samuel Mordecai attended the Warrenton Academy in North Carolina. At fourteen he went to work for his uncle, Samuel Myers, in Richmond. Then he became a cotton broker in that city. He had other gifts as well as an aptitude for business. When the Richmond synagogue commemorated with "Humiliation and Prayer," the burning of the Richmond Theater on December 26, 1812, Samuel Mordecai delivered the oration.

He prospered. In 1817 Sam owned three slaves, two sheets, one clock, one gold watch and one piano. He was a man of substance. The "best" people in Richmond were his friends. He collected books and although he did not become wealthy he was known to have a "considerable" library. His Christian biographer describes Samuel Mordecai as "undogmatic and tolerant." He lived and died a Jew, but his funeral services were conducted by an Episcopalian clergyman. One of his relatives who was present wrote of the funeral: "I surmise that Dr. Mason improvised a service reading from the Psalms and selections from other books of the Bible."

It is of course possible that Dr. Mason officiated because there was no qualified rabbi in Richmond available. Samuel Mordecai died on the ninth of April in 1865—the day of Appomattox!

Because in his youth Samuel traveled rather widely, he wrote a few interesting letters. One of his letters was written from Havana, February 21, 1814. It shows that although he was a Southerner his sympathies were aroused by the abuses of the slave trade. He writes:

> The slave trade is still continued here and those concerned in it are much incensed at the interruption given them by the British. Several cargoes have arrived since I have been here. (He continues with a description of "the poor naked wretches") . . But I will leave the discussion of this subject to the Abolition Societies, who have my best wishes for their success.

He did his share of military duty, and, like his father, cherished literary ambition. He wrote *Virginia, Especially Richmond in Bygone days*. It was at first published anonymously in 1856. By 1860 it appeared under his own name. His was a goodly life and packed with diverse experiences.

But it is when we turn to the *Autobiography of Alfred Mordecai* that this history becomes more than a mere chronology and genealogy and takes on sociological significance. For we see the children of the old, patriarchal, Hebrew-loving Jacob Mordecai become marginal men and women. They are on the fringe of the Judaism he cherished. They are on the outer periphery of Christianity. We see the two magnets pulling in opposite directions. We see how the host culture, because of weight of numbers, because of social prestige, because of intermarriage, makes inroads into the ranks of the clan of Mordecai. Here is the process of social osmosis traced through the biographies of some of the Mordecai women, as recorded by their brother.

Mordecai always had the best teachers that he could procure in French, music (both vocal and instrumental), painting, drawing, and plain and fancy sewing. Of these teachers Miss Ellen (Mordecai) became the best known. Her "History of Hastings" in manuscript was a masterpiece. As she never married she went with her father to his farm near Richmond and often visited Warrenton. Late in life she became an Episcopalian, before she died at a seaside resort in October, 1884, at the age of ninety-four. She wrote a book on the great spiritual conflict through which she passed before she left her Jewish faith. She was a woman of wonderful character, marked intelligence and attractive personality.

Rachel Mordecai married a certain Lazarus, of Wilmington, North

Carolina and removed to that city. She remained true to her faith, but became a Christian on her death-bed.

Caroline Mordecai married Achilles Plunkett in 1820. He was a teacher of French in her father's academy. He was a Roman Catholic but late in life his wife became a Unitarian. Plunkett was born and reared in Santo Domingo. In the uprising of the slaves there three loyal slaves warned them, which enabled them to escape with these three slaves and a few pieces of silver and nothing more. Jacob Mordecai opposed his children marrying gentiles for he was very loyal to his native faith.

Of their home life we get many intimate glimpses. Some of the home tabus were definitely adopted from their Protestant neighbors. Says Alfred: "Cards were never seen in my father's house & when I left there I did not know one card from another." But there was an abundance of books and reading was a major recreation. "Although I was a healthy & sufficiently active boy, it was often with great reluctance that I laid down 'Miss Edgworth's Tales,' or 'The Arabian Nights,' &c, to join my young companions in playing at Marbles, Hop-Scotch & mumble-the-peg, or to shoot robins & other small birds with arrows fired from the Mulberry bows which Old Cy, (Cyrus) used to make for us, in the intervals of his occupation of running a country Mill." It was a busy, happy, carefree childhood.

There was evidence of great family pride. Certainly their attainments were remarkable for any age. The high school curriculum as we know it today was apparently absorbed by children before they were in their teens.

I was not twelve years of age at this time, but I had no doubt that my intellectual development, as regards knowledge acquired under the assiduous instruction of my indefatiguable teachers was a good deal in advance of my years—*My* brothers & sisters & myself had no instructors, except in French, out of our own family; yet, when I ceased to receive it at the age of fifteen, I was well versed in the English language & literature, in geography & history & arithmetic, knew something of geometry & trigonometry, & had completed a great part of the collegiate course of Latin & Greek; having read in the latter language the whole of the Iliad—I could read French fluently & write it pretty well.

They traveled extensively in those days. For there were relatives in many cities to be visited and life was so leisurely, its tempo so placid as to allow for the nursing of friendships through long letters and extended visits. When in 1828 Alfred paid a visit to Washington he was an accomplished visitor. The amenities of social life were known to him. He suffered neither from shyness or awkwardness nor discrimination. He was "on an easy and pleasant footing" with every one he met.

This sense of social ease which characterized the Mordecai family, this feeling of assurance and complete poise, stood Alfred in good stead when he was a student at West Point. He was freely accepted by his associates and seemed to feel that his fellow cadets practiced a tacit censorship in order not to embarrass him.

Perhaps you may expect me to say something on the subject of religious differences among so many associates—I have often thought, with some surprise, of the fact that, by some sort of silent consent, in our meetings, when we were cadets, that subject was never broached, & the same reticence was observed among our companions as officers; unless it may have entered indirectly in the free talks I sometimes held with Capt (afterwards General) Hitchcock, on *philosophical* themes, to the study of which he was much addicted.[24]

There is still much to be added to this Mordecai mosaic. We could write, were this a romance instead of a history, of how Sarah Ann Hays, daughter of Samuel and Richea Hays and niece of Rebecca Gratz, married the handsome young officer, Alfred Mordecai on June 1, 1827. We could trace the events, blessed and otherwise, in the Alfred Mordecai ménage. "Sara is a devoted Mother," writes her doting Aunt Rebecca, "and rarely has her little Laura out of her arms, it is a sweet little babe—she is going to take it to Richmond to receive a grand fathers blessing—the family are all called together to see perhaps for the last time the venerable old man."

It was the end of an age.

CHAPTER X

The Last Frontier

⇢⟫⟫   *Als Pilgrim wag' ich. . . .*

—from *Das Licht von Zion*[1]   ⟪⟪⬳

FROM THE backwoods to the urban areas change was in the air. The outposts were developing their own folkways and mores. Pride in place was the new creed. A generation of "native sons" had grown up. There was an awareness of an emerging American personality, yet the plainsman, the Western farmer, knew that his interests differed from those of the Southern planter and the New England shipbuilder. Now each region had its spokesman. It was a group of men to be proud of—men of talent, of character, of vision. Clay. Calhoun. Webster. Jackson. Magic names. To American Jews these leaders were more than abstractions. Some were friends. Others were political associates. Some were casual acquaintances. Henry Clay, whom she knew well, is mentioned forty-three times in the *Letters of Rebecca Gratz.* Andrew Jackson is mentioned fifteen times. Webster and Calhoun not at all.

The agrarian West was in the news at home and abroad. The fertile river valleys were magnets which drew settlers from the East and from across the Atlantic. The stagecoach was still in use when John Quincy Adams took his oath of office, March 4, 1825, The Concord Coach appears in the newspaper advertisements in the 1830's and 1840's and the 1850's. But river traffic increased during those years. Ditches and canals became important highways. Often towns and settlements owed their origin to a waterway. The Jewish settlement of Shalom owed its short existence to the opening of the Delaware and Hudson Canal in 1837.

There was an intensive period of canal construction which ended in 1845. Gradually, with pride and lofty satisfaction, Americans took to the railroads. The "Best Friend," first locomotive built for rail-road use, made its debut in 1831. In the same year the Mohawk and Hudson Railroad of New York proudly carried passengers up and down its wooden rails. The Baltimore and Ohio whisky bottle reading, "Success to the Railroad," was used in many a roaring toast.

The age of Andrew Jackson was at hand. The West had come into its own. "The man who could write" was supplanted in the White House by "the man who could fight." Men and women of status and rank everywhere shook their heads decrying the turn of events. The proprieties were flouted openly. Rebecca Gratz complained in one of her letters at this time that, "Politicks no longer interests me—I am offended at seeing Mrs. Eatons name in every print—What ever she may deserve—the decencies of domestic life ought not to be violated as they have been." For gossip was rife and it touched many of Jackson's intimates.[2] Harvard could bestow its coveted honorary doc-torate upon the new Chief of State, but nothing would make a polished gentleman of Old Hickory. And Rebecca Gratz and her sheltered friends disapproved heartily of the new era. So grave were party dif-ferences that Calhoun could answer a toast of Jackson's, "To our federal Union—it *must* be preserved!" by a ringing challenge: "Liberty dearer than Union!"[3] The issues that were to split the Union were shaping up. Men were taking sides with a vengeance. Alfred Mordecai, on visiting Hartford, Connecticut, in the 1830's, heard "the first low mutterings of a storm" when he attended a lecture of William Lloyd Garrison.

No matter what ideological differences might be found, no matter how high party feeling ran, no matter what the American hardships that letters sent back to relatives in Europe might have described, still to the harassed, driven, submerged, legislated-against Jew of Central Europe, America looked good. Among the educated the idea of freedom became cherished. The poets sang of it, the journalists described it. There were clubs and societies devoted to the study of America and to the desirability of emigration.

In 1825, while Mordecai Manuel Noah was playing at his great role of savior of the Jews in America to a sympathetic audience, social pressure in Germany compelled Heinrich Heine to accept conversion to Christianity. And the statue which his birthplace, Düsseldorf, rejected, eventually found a resting place in New York. America became a symbol and a haven for the persecuted Jews of Europe. Migration began en masse with the application of the cruel marriage laws of Bavaria in 1835. It was a desperate period for the

Jews who had borne anti-Jewish uprisings since 1819 in Germany, who were to taste the bitter brew of the Damascus ritual murder accusation in 1840. All eyes turned westward.

In 1823, Mordecai Aaron Ginzburg, a native of Salant transplanted to Vilna, wrote the first nonreligious Hebrew book to be published in Russia. It was called the *Discovery of America*. It was in Vilna that Max Lilienthal, who spent six years in Russia and who was to become an editor of the *American Israelite*, met Ginzburg.[4] The kinship of ideas between Jews of Europe and Jews of America persisted.

England had its Bevis Marks Jews. They were the rich and the mighty. Wealth always seeks its level. So the affluent Sephardim chafed at restrictions, fought for equality. Some who found the social aversion of Christians coupled with the stringent laws of the synagogue, too hampering and galling, left the Jewish fold. David Ricardo, famous disciple of Adam Smith, married a Christian and severed his connections with his people. Still he could not, as a friend of Jeremy Bentham, do less than support Jewish emancipation in 1823. Isaac D'Israeli was stung by a fine imposed by his congregation for refusing to serve as warden. So Judaism knew him no more. Yet Benjamin Disraeli, like Ricardo, was a champion of Jewish rights as were Christians like Macaulay and Russell. By 1830, John Elijah Blunt found that some disabilities were no longer operative.

America had become a laboratory where full participation of Jews in national life was being tested. Not a government in Europe but was aware of it. Not the most isolated hamlet but knew the importance of the American system of citizenship. In the halls of Parliament reports on the great experiment were eagerly followed. Macaulay in his famous speech advocating Jewish emancipation reminded his colleagues that "it is an undoubted fact that, in the United States of America, Jewish citizens do possess all the privileges possessed by Christian citizens." Another advocate of the removal of Jewish disabilities, Joseph Hume, said that he had received a letter from John Quincy Adams, "stating that there were not better citizens than the Jews, and expressing the hope that ere long the whole of Europe would see the justice and wisdom of freely conceding to them the fullest political privileges."

A decade later English liberals of all denominations stood shoulder to shoulder in their determination to solve the Jewish problem. The Damascus affair was the catalytic agent. At the forefront was Moses Montefiore who in the year of Queen Victoria's accession to the English throne, 1837, became sheriff of London. He had made his first pilgrimage to Palestine in 1827 and was to make six more! Two Scots, Andrew Bonar and Robert M. M'Cheyne were chosen by the General Assembly of the Church of Scotland to go to Palestine for the same purpose.

"The question of the restoration of the Jews to Palestine had meanwhile become a matter of sufficient importance to occupy considerable space in the periodical press. *The Times,* as the leading newspaper of the country, in particular devoted much attention to this subject," writes Hyamson.[5] In the London *Times* of March 9, 1840, reporting the mass indignation which the false, foul charges of ritual murder at Damascus had aroused—indignation which was voiced in Parliament, in *Diaries* and *Letters,* in the periodical press—a solution not unlike the Balfour Declaration of a later date was recommended.

England had her Montefiore. France had her Adolphe Crémieux. He too enlisted in the cause of clearing the Jewish name of the slander which stemmed from Damascus. But where Montefiore had an aroused England with him, Crémieux had official French opposition to fight. Undaunted, he carried on. He knew, as Jews were to learn to their sorrow a century later, that the destiny of Jews does not exist in vacuum. A false charge hurled at his brethren in Damascus was slander leveled at Jews everywhere. Nevertheless it was as an international spokesman in the antislavery crusade that Crémieux impressed American Jews. In 1840, Crémieux speaking in French before an English Antislavery Convention said:

I feel great pleasure in joining this Convention, because I am a descendant of those Hebrews who were first to proclaim the abolition of slavery; and I this day only repeat what the Jews have always admitted in principle. . . . The slavery of man by man is a perpetual crime against humanity.[6]

What echoes did his words find in American Jewry? How did vested interests line up for or against slavery? The record will show that it was sectional, economic and personal interests that determined the reaction of Jews of America to the institution of slavery. Conscience ran a poor second to the pocketbook. But the importance of the Crémieux speech, of his impassioned stand, goes deeper than the surface meaning of his words. It shows again that there was a rhythm of common interest on both sides of the Atlantic. The swing of the cultural pendulum now touched the eastern, now the western shore of the Atlantic. Both groups were aware of each other, more aware than they themselves realized. Jews in America were among the slave-

owners. The still small voice of conscience spoke out of the aroused
emotions of a French Jew. Later, much later, it would find many an
echo here. Later young American Jews would offer their lives for
the sake of preserving the Union.

We know that Jews were associated from the earliest days with the
general opening and development of the West. Indian outposts, stock-
ades, frontier villages, little struggling pioneer communities each had
their Jewish pioneers. In Michigan, for example, Jews were found
before the beginning of the nineteenth century. When German Jews
began to settle in the United States in large numbers, the entire
Northwest Territory saw little Jewish communities mushrooming in
the clearings. Not all came as itinerants or peddlers. Augusta Levy
pioneered with her family in La Crosse, Wisconsin.[7] She and her
English-born husband, John Levy, managed to enjoy life, to make
friends, to maintain harmonious relations with neighbors, to trade
amicably with Indians, in a little log cabin that did not keep out the
rain, in an area so infested with mosquitoes that they had to be
smoked out periodically. There was the picturesque role of stowaway
in which Edward Kanter came to New Orleans, and then working his
way north on the tramp steamers of the Mississippi, finally reached
Michigan. In Kentucky, Jews felt so much at home, that most of
them like Benjamin Gratz intermarried. Their descendants are for the
most part no longer Jewish. "Whoever came, came singly," writes
Lewis N. Dembitz of Kentucky, "found no one to pray with, and . . .
no one to mate with." In the little city of St. Louis in 1844, there
were about forty or fifty Jews, who limited their Jewish practices to
keeping a *shochet* and observing the high holidays. But otherwise,
writes a contributor to the *Occident*, "they live not as Jews."

A Kansas Jewish pioneer records his early days there in these
words:

About August 1, Benjamin returned from St. Louis. He had brought
along a good two-horse wooden axle-wagon, a good yoke of five-year old
oxen, a two-barrel shot-gun, and lots of provisions and tools, and a hired
man to assist in putting up a good lot of hay. Including myself we were
five men. I continued as cook, Benjamin to keep the breaking plough
going and the hired man, Klein and Fox to start and keep at haying, to
mow, rake. . . . Every man did valiantly perform his share of the work
assigned to him.

So in breaking land under the plough Jews like others had their
share.

These were the conditions in Iowa and in Illinois. Iowa has early Jewish associations. When La Salle visited Iowa in 1680, he had a man among his followers named Moses de Leon. And Pike, who visited Iowa in 1804, had Jewish solaiers in his company. During its territorial days, there was a handful of Israelites there. When Des Moines was Raccoon Forks and there were not more than twenty white settlers, William Krause, a Jew, was one of that group. In the *Lee County Democrat*, on July 8, 1843, there appeared an article on the Jews which is typical of the generally friendly attitude displayed toward them in the Middle West:

The present physical, moral and social condition of the Jews must be a miracle. . . . A Jew walks on every street, dwells in every capital, traverses every exchange, and relieves the monotony of the nations of the earth. . . . The race has inherited the heirloom of immortality, incapable of extinction or amalgamation.

Chicago Jewish history begins in 1841. In that year four Jews sought out this village on Lake Michigan, and opened their little stores here. In 1846 came Michael Greenebaum. He was followed by two of his brothers in 1848. Their numbers were gradually and steadily augmented. By 1847 "The Congregation of the Men of the West," *Kehillah Anshe Mayriv*, was a reality. Chicago Jewry was fortunate to have as one of its early pioneers, Dr. Bernhard Felsenthal, a distinguished scholar and teacher. Indeed the entire community of Chicago Jews, like those of St. Louis, seems to have been outstanding in having recruited to its ranks an unusually high type of early settler.

Henry Mayer was the first Jewish farmer in Cook County, Illinois.[8] He bought 160 acres of land from the government and took up the agricultural life in earnest. There were also peddlers and tailors, tobacco dealers and scholars among them. The occupational diversity of this latest group of Jewish pilgrims to America was in its way as striking as that of the earlier immigrants. An analysis of occupational patterns of one community, Easton, Pennsylvania, may serve as a blueprint for others. They range from agent to watch-maker. They include gentlemen and casual laborers. Among them is found a lens-grinder and a brewer, a letter carrier and a teamster. There are tailors and milliners, shoemakers and cattle dealers. There is a cordwainer and a lawyer, a boatman and a mail agent. In short, there is diversity.

The prevailing patterns are dynamic, ever changing. Society, the major social institutions, man himself, all are in a constant state of flux. Within the occupational capsule of Easton Jews, as in the great

society, there is movement up and down. The casual laborer becomes
an artisan. The peddler becomes a merchant. The speculator may lose
his substance and the rag dealer may become a man of means. Vertical
mobility is a movement in two directions.

"It was in 1842 when the first contingent of German Jews settled
in Boston," writes one chronicler. From Boston to San Francisco,
from Prairie du Chien to St. Louis to Austin, Texas—everywhere
Jews, along with other Americans, were on the move. So great was the
number of men who solved their problems through emigration that it
does not surprise us to find that a small prayer book was prepared for
the use of German Jewish immigrants in 1842. The Jewish traveler
compelled to leave his fatherland was given one measure of security.
He was to be kept in close contact with the otherworldly domain of
his faith. Not all his ties with the past were permitted to be severed.
Yet fortified with a prayer book or not, the surgery was painful. "O,
how very much have I sacrificed; how I have renounced everything
that was dear to me, separated from my mother, perhaps (O horror!)
never to see her again," laments one Jewish pilgrim in 1847.[9] Bitter
to a man of pride is the insecurity that awaits him. "Here I must go
peddling and cry 'Do you want to buy?' sweat and carry my basket."
From the diary which this traveler kept, we know how galling to his
manhood, how soul-searing was the experience he was to undergo.
Again and again he had to support his flagging spirits with pious
admonitions. "I will not think," he resolves. "God will guide everything for the best." To a sensitive, devout Jew the greeting of the
Sabbath is an act of consecration, a ceremony of dignity and solemnity.
How painful then for our diarist to record on a Friday evening: "The
day is about to end. Unshaved, in week-day clothes, I must greet
Shabos." It was a bitter journey not only because of physical hardship
but because of the tearing asunder of the cherished mores, the separation from the beloved and accustomed folkways of his youth. Yet the
journey was inevitable. There was no choice.

In the meanwhile active groups in Europe advocated mass migration. In Vienna, in 1848, a Jewish journal frequently published articles
encouraging Jews to emigrate. On May 14, 1848, a committee composed of Dr. Engel, Dr. Ludwig August Frankl, Dr. Ignaz Von Hof-
mannsthal, Dr. Matzel, and Isidor Bush was formed for the furthering
of emigration. This ended abruptly in 1849, when Isidor Bush, one
of the most energetic advocates of immigration, came to America.
There was a decided change in the type of German Jewish immigrant
after 1848. The more cultured, and better educated, the professional

men, the scholars are found in the roster of immigrants, not only from Germany, but also from Bohemia and Austria.

To this group belonged such men as Dr. Max Lilienthal, Dr. Abraham Bettman, a pioneer Cincinnati physician, and the Rabbis, Bernhard Felsenthal, Isaac M. Wise, Liebmann Adler. They gave a stimulus and impetus to various Jewish movements, religious and philanthropic, which sprang up like mushrooms wherever these men took root. It was among them that the leaders of the reform movement were to be found.

There were culture areas in the United States in places like Chicago, New Orleans, Easton and St. Louis which bore the imprint of these strong personalities. Here, for example, is Isidor Bush.[10] His great-grandfather was the first Jew to become a member of the nobility in Austria. His childhood was spent with men and women of education and means. His father was owner of a printing house, where Isidor was employed. He was a young man of twenty-six with a number of publications to his credit when the Revolution of 1848 cut short his hopes and his work. He joined thousands of other migrants and almost penniless landed in New York. Here he opened a little book store and soon plunged into the publishing business. *Israel's Herold*, the first German-Jewish weekly in America, was his brain child. It lived for three months. Then, penniless and insecure, he turned toward St. Louis in 1849. He was a storekeeper in Carondelet. He was a landowner by 1851. At that time he bought a hundred acres of land in Jefferson County which he called "Bushberg." He raised grapes and so expert did he become that his grape manual, published in 1868 as the *Bushberg Catalogue*, was translated into many languages. He was by turns vintner, railroad freight agent, grocer, hardware merchant, bank president. He served as secretary to General Frémont, having from childhood suffered a physical disability which prevented active soldiering. He held a number of civic posts and vigorously lent his talents to the cause of abolition of slavery. The trauma of transplanting he took in his stride. He was a member of the Board of Education, of the Library Committee, of the City Council, of the German Immigrant Aid Society. By the time the hour of decision came for Missouri, he was a leader of the forces mobilized for the preservation of the Union. In 1861, his was one of fifteen names proposed for the Union party ticket. In March of that year he introduced a resolution endorsing union and deploring "dismemberment." But he did more than introduce resolutions. He became a forthright champion of "*speedy emancipation*."

In 1863, Isidor Bush delivered his most eloquent abolitionist speech. "I pray you," he cried with passion, "have pity for yourselves, not for negroes. Slavery demoralizes, slavery fanaticism blinds you. It has arrayed brother against brother, son against father. It has destroyed God's noblest work—a free and happy people." The accent may have been foreign, the sounds guttural, but the sentiments were in sound keeping with the best in American tradition.

It was not long before other foreign accents than German could be heard among the immigrant Jews of America. For even before the 1880's, going back to the time of Haym Salomon and long before that to Gaspar Judeo, Polish and other non-German Jews were among the Jewish pilgrims. In Buffalo, in 1847, Jews met to celebrate Passover. By 1850 there was a rift in the community. It was the usual one, resting on the distaste and aversion which German Jews felt for their brethren who came from Russia and Poland.

The Polish liturgy being used in the worship of this society, its services could not give satisfaction to the German Israelites. Hence, eleven of them called a preliminary meeting, which was held November 14th, 1850, and followed by another, November 27th, at which a congregation was organized according to the German liturgy.[11]

"In respect to nationality," writes Falk, who chronicles the beginnings of the Jewish community of Buffalo, "the Israelites are English, French, Germans, Hollanders, Austrians, Hungarians, Polanders, and Russians."

By 1852 there were enough Russian Jews in New York City to establish a congregation of their own. It struggled, as such groups do, with makeshift leaders and shabby quarters. "Their first place of worship was in the garret of No. 83 Bayard Street, paying eight dollars rent a month," writes Eisenstein. For years they attempted to bring about a union of all orthodox congregations in America. It was finally accomplished when they imported a scholarly resident of Vilna, Rabbi Jacob Joseph and appropriated an annual stipend of $500 for his maintenance. They were a tight little cultural unit. The synagogue was within walking distance of all the worshipers. It was an agency for strict social control. Every member was under the watchful eyes of the pious and his morals and manners were under constant scrutiny. But when the pull toward outlying areas coincided with greater earning power, matters changed. The history of this group shows "that out of a total of nearly 200 members in 1888, more than half, especially the elder members, have since moved up town.

The members of the congregation have now almost entirely lost the picturesque characteristics of the Russian-American pioneers."

It was not always easy to serve God alone. Mammon lived around the corner. The pittance on which congregations expected their ministers to flourish and rear numerous offspring may have served to maintain life, but could hardly have sustained a family in health and security and fun. The rabbi standing before his congregation could cast his scholarly eyes over many an ignoramus who made money hand over fist. Conscience and necessity fought constant bouts. Here is a case in point. It concerns the vacillating fortunes of Rabbi Ash, head of this Russian-American religious community. Poverty dogged his footsteps. It was his ever-present companion. Could he not branch out a bit, he asked his nagging conscience? His wife and children had some rights. So:

Rabbi Ash, about the time of the Civil War, became engaged with a partner in the manufacture of hoop skirts, then the rage of fashion in which business he accumulated nearly ten thousand dollars. He then changed the Rabbinate for the more dignified office of *Parnas*, and instead of receiving a stipend, contributed liberally towards the expenses of the congregation. Later he lost his money and had to resume the Rabbinate. In 1876 he took up the business of importing *Kasher* wine from Los Angeles, California. Fate, however, decided against him, and in 1879, in spite of all his endeavors, he was obliged to resume his religious functions in the congregation, his salary then being 25 dollars per month, till his death, May 6, 1887.[12]

But peace eluded the Forsyth Street Israelites. How could there be harmony within the ranks when two factions struggled for control and their ideologies miles apart? For the Hassidim believed in serving God through joy, through song and ecstatic prayer and mysticism. The Misnagdim frowned on such deviations from traditional observances, stressing the importance of learning and conformity.

Poverty stalked not only the hoop-skirt manufacturer and rabbi, but every communicant as well. Yet those good people managed out of their open hearts and hard-earned pennies to carry out the precepts of hospitality and charity. "Deserving cases were also taken care of out of the daily penny collections after the week-day's service, and larger collections for more urgent needs. Some of the newcomers were invited into the houses of the more wealthy members to partake of their meals on Sabbaths and festival days." The crowded tenements had rubber walls. The pot of soup was bottomless. The stranger was housed and fed and plied with advice, and turned loose with his basket of sundries to sell and coached in the singsong calls which proclaimed to the world that another itinerant was starting out in business. Each evening the footsore peddler returned to his swarming habitat to sip a glass of tea, to tell his adventures, to sigh a bit as he recalled with nostalgia the lanes of home and the familiar faces separated from him by the miles of ocean and land.

These bonds of memory united immigrants. The men and women of Pinsk, of Odessa, of Riga formed clubs and fraternal organizations to help each other over the rough periods of adjustment. To recall together the scholarship of this good rabbi, the wonder-working accomplishments of that one. To sing the folk songs they had known. To laugh at the old jokes. To repeat the folklore of childhood. To remind each other that they had biographies. That they were men. That life had once been different and would some day be again. That they were part of a world of kinsmen. The native Americans whom they met during the day might shrug and scoff and turn away from them. But here they were not strangers. The Gaon of Vilna and Reb Israel Salanter and the Baal Shem Tob were names they knew and loved. They were their imperishable monuments. So they forged those precious ties of friendship in America out of the gossamer fabric of their memories of vanished youth. New culture areas sprang up in America reminiscent of the old. Old World stews bubbled in American pots and pans. And on Friday nights the aroma of gefilte fish on Henry Street was indistinguishable from the same remembered odors in Warsaw lanes.

These were the differences which marked the Jewish community and set it apart from the non-Jewish cultural areas. But it is well to note that the twin processes of adjustment and differentiation which were at work here among Jews were also in motion in areas where the Czechs and the Greeks and the Armenians lived. Acculturation decimated the ranks of the newcomers. Nostalgia fought a losing war with American plumbing. The synagogue was a magnet whose pull lost its strength as diffusion of population replaced clustering in one area. The night school was in competition with the *landsmanschaft*. The Hyman Kaplans and the Nussbaums of America were casting sheep's eyes at *Webster's Dictionary*. The period of transition, arduous or ludicrous, tragic or laughable, was the bridge that led to new neighborhoods, better jobs, greater affluence. New culture traits were imperceptibly acquired. It was a dynamic process in which each individual traveled from the known past to the greener pastures of the unknown future, stumbling hurriedly over the pitfalls and hazards of each day. In his haste to reach his new destination the traveler often discarded his most priceless possessions—inner stability, kinship and memory.

In varying degree, with modifications imposed by geographic or economic conditions, this was the pattern all over the land. Transplanting. Traumatic interlude. Gradual acculturation. Bicultural ties. Severance of the old. Acquisition of new culture traits. Examples too numerous to cite are available. On May 6, 1849, in Montgomery, Alabama, Polish and German Jews formed Temple Beth-Or. On the plains of Texas, along the Pacific coast, in the lake region, along the great river basins, congregations were formed by groups of ten men or more.

The first manifestation of group consciousness may well have been in the acquisition of a cemetery. The second usually concerned itself with a place of worship. Then numerous other needs asserted themselves. The struggle for food, clothing and shelter was a drama of persistence, of courage and of heartbreak. Out of these needs many group affiliations grew. Within these groups were the many social institutions which were necessary to their perpetuation—the unions, the aid societies, the culture clubs, the *landsmanschaften*, the women's societies, the Hebrew schools, the hospitals, the theaters, the restaurants specializing in Old World foods, the foreign-language press, the lending libraries, the mutual insurance societies—all the diverse groups which make up the community.

In widely separated places, there was similarity in the growth and development of Jewish institutions. In Texas. In California. . . .

Long before Texas was admitted to the Union, an early settler, Samuel Isaacs, came there with Stephen Austin's colony of three hundred men. The year was 1821. Isaacs received a grant of land. He served in the Texan army in 1836-37 and was given an additional land bounty of 320 acres for his military service. At Velasco, near Galveston, there was a little settlement of Jews. Another little Hebraic community existed in Nacogdoches. One of the pioneers of this place was Adolphus Sterne who came to Texas in 1824. Sterne was a friend of General Sam Houston. He was a linguist and an able scholar, as well as one of the first Masons of Texas. As Alcalde, or Mayor, of Nacogdoches he is now remembered. Other Jews left traces of themselves on early Texan history. Kauffman County in that state honors a Jewish pioneer. Also "Kauffman's Good Faith Law." For David S. Kauffman framed the law calling for compensation to settlers for bona fide improvements on their land. So many Jews fought with Texan troops that it is impossible to begin to list them. A number of them were intimate friends of Sam Houston. They fought in the Battle of San Jacinto. They died at Goliad. They were slaughtered by Indian hordes. They were wounded at Neches. They distinguished themselves at Buena Vista. They met heroic death at the Alamo. It is a magnificent record.

So many exotic and interesting personalities were drawn to Texas that a long, well-documented volume could scarcely do them justice. How contain them in a few meager paragraphs?

Can we omit to mention Dr. Moses Albert Levy, Surgeon General of Houston's army during the Texas-Mexico War? Shall we ignore Dr. Isaac Lyons, Surgeon General under General Tom Green? Or Michael De Young of France who rendered such outstanding service to the Texan army as victualer and provisioner that the Lone Star Republic rewarded him out of her cornucopia by a gift of vast stretches of land? May we not add the romantic Sam Maas who came to Texas in 1836 and found a bride on a visit to Europe, no less a person than Isabella Offenbach, sister of the famous composer of the *Tales of Hoffmann*, Jacques Offenbach?

There were the brothers De Cordova, Phineas and Jacob, who came to Texas from Spanish Town in Jamaica. There was Simon Weiss, who came from Germany to Texas in 1836 and settled on the Neches River at a place now called Weiss Bluff. Typical of the mobility of Jews of this era was Albert Emanuel. He had traveled widely in the Old World and the New.

There was the Moravian immigrant who eventually became president of the National Bank of Texas and president of the Gulf, Colorado and Santa Fe Railroad. Moritz Kopperl made a long journey in terms of both horizontal and vertical mobility. Another example of social mobility was German-born Isidore Dyer who made Galveston his home from 1840 on. It was under Dyer's roof that the first religious services were held. Colonel Leon Dyer, his brother, once served as acting mayor of Baltimore. He joined the Army and rose to the rank of major, becoming a member of General Scott's staff. In 1846 Leon Dyer was one of a group of men who made the long journey to Texas to fight for her independence. President Van Buren appointed this erstwhile immigrant as a special envoy to the land of his birth. It was a good record he left behind.

A distinguished resident was Henry Castro, the European portion of whose biography and antecedents mark him as a man to be remembered.

Henry Castro, the pioneer of that portion of western Texas situated west of the city of San Antonio, was born in France in July, 1786, of rich parents, and was descended from one of the oldest Portuguese families (the Marrano family of DeCastro), one of his ancestors, João of Castro, having been fourth viceroy of the Indies for the King of Portugal. In 1805, at the age of nineteen, he was selected by the Prefect of his department (Landes) to welcome the Emperor Napoleon on the occasion of his visit to that department. In 1806 he was one of the guard of honor that accompanied Napoleon to Spain.[18]

In 1842, Henry Castro undertook a project at the request of the President of the Republic of Texas. He was to secure settlers for an ambitious colony. Houston appointed Castro Consul-General to France. From this vantage point Castro was able to send five thousand German immigrants to Texas between the years 1843-46. This was the first emigration plan undertaken by Texas in its brief history as a republic. Castro threw himself heart and soul into this assignment. He even spent one hundred and fifty thousand dollars of his personal funds to further the plan. His publicity campaign for his beloved Texas involved the publishing of maps and promotional pamphlets to advertise the land. To lure future settlers this literature was printed in both French and German. The immigrants came. They settled the town of Castroville and three other communities. A county in Texas also honors this indefatigable adopted son who served his State so well.

These were the individuals. Let us next examine the group patterns. First, usually the cemetery, as in Houston in 1844; next, within the decade, a synagogue. "Other cities established cemeteries and congregations in the following order," writes Rabbi Cohen: San Antonio—cemetery, 1854; congregation, 1872. Austin—cemetery, 1866; congregation, 1876. Waco—cemetery, 1869; congregation, 1881. Dallas—cemetery, 1872; congregation, 1876. The pattern is repeated in every city.

The pilgrims made sure that their wanderers had a place prepared for journey's end. The challenge of organizing and building for the living came later.

California was the last frontier. This land of promise began luring numbers of settlers of all faiths in the year of the gold rush. Before that Spain had owned the land inhospitably. There were numerous border incidents. Captain Frémont occupied Sonoma in 1846 and participated in the Bear Flag Rebellion. In 1848 by the Treaty of Guadalupe Hidalgo we acquired that vast stretch of Pacific shore and its "golden" era began soon after. California had hoarded its secret wealth deep within its bowels. It was a gift she would release at the proper time. But long years before the golden treasure was discovered, Andrew Jackson "had envisaged the acquisition of the Californias by a Texas which one day would become a part of the Union." It was an ambition shared by many. The events in Texas, the agitation by Southerners, the hope of adding another slave State to the Union, the numerous military incidents, were within the familiar pattern of the arithmetic of acquisition. As Mexico weakened, American pressure mounted. Did the handwriting on the wall spell out Manifest Destiny? The ink was not yet dry on the papers being drawn up in Mexico City when a worker in Sutter's sawmill found gold. The news spread by every method of communication then known to man. The gold rush was on. Men came over land and over water. "On the score of safety there was little to choose," say the Beards.[14] Many ships never reached their destination. Cholera, scurvy and tropical fever often decimated the passengers of ships that were able to complete the voyage. The overland journey was beset by many dangers. Preyed upon by Indians and by robber hordes, vanquished by thirst and conquered by sheer distance, many a hopeful migrant met death on the way. Like others, Jews joined the bands of westward travelers.

On January 29, 1849, Rebecca Gratz writes that her nephew Edmund Moses "sails on the Falcon for California—he has the gold mania and means to adventure there." By 1854, news of disasters en route were commonplace. Rebecca writes on January 8 of that year:

Tell Hyman we are grieved & shocked at the fate of an old favorite of his, Valeria Merchant—who with all her family are passengers on the ill fated steamer San Francisco—on her passage to California—as it is feared she perished in the late storms at sea—the steamer was seen in such peril—that scarcely a hope remains of her escape—and 800 troops & passengers the officers wives & families who accompanied them it is feared are lost.[15]

But high adventure sang its siren song. Dazzling dreams of wealth blotted out all thought of danger. Migrants continued to pour into California. The first Pacific Mail steamer to reach San Francisco, February 26, 1849, had Jews aboard. On Yom Kippur of that year in a tent pitched by Louis Franklin of San Francisco, services were held. A small group of worshipers also met in a room over a store of that mushrooming metropolis. In 1850 there were two congregations. Polish and English Jews banded together to form "Shearith Israel," while "Emanuel" consisted largely of German and other Jews from various parts of the country. "Mining congregations" dotted the State. Cemeteries were acquired. Synagogues were established. There was a Hebrew Benevolent Society in 1852 in Marysville. In a town named Jesu Maria there was Jewish group life in 1852. Fiddletown and Shasta had Jewish communities in 1857. Rabbi Coffee estimates that at least one hundred Jews were in San Francisco in 1850. There was the same occupational diversity that we have noted elsewhere. Merchants, brickyard and lumberyard owners, fur traders, miners, fruit and poultry farmers, Alaskan traders in fur, bankers and shopkeepers. One man, Isaac Friedlander, became known as a grain king. There were cattlemen and vintners, dealers in wool and drygoods. One far-sighted pioneer, Daniel Meyer, developed a system of irrigation. Others entered the field of politics. There were aldermen, mayors, legislators and judges among them.

Alexander Mayer, an immigrant from Germany, a prospector and an early entrepreneur, was eventually caught up by the chamber of commerce spirit long before it came into being. "It's a great country," he exults, despite many previous gloomy descriptions. Others join with him in these exuberant sentiments. California inexorably exerts her blandishments on her new settlers. When we analyze the record of many of Alex Mayer's coreligionists, it is understandable that they found cause for rejoicing. The mayor of San Francisco in 1849 was Lieutenant Washington Bartlett, whose mother was a Jewess. One of the first justices of the Supreme Court of California was a Jew, Henry A. Lyons. A noted civic leader and one of the first aldermen of San Francisco was A. C. Labatt, whose earlier history was not without interest. Rabbi Cohen summarizes his biography for us:

Abraham Cohen Labatt was born in Charleston, South Carolina, in 1802. He was one of the forty-seven Israelites who, in 1825, organized the first reformed Jewish congregation in the United States. The movement aroused such intense opposition in the orthodox congregations of the world that, for the time being, it was abandoned. In later years reform met with better success. In 1831 Mr. Labatt removed to New Orleans and followed a merchant's calling. He was one of the founders of the first Jewish congregation in Louisiana, as well as of the first fireman's charitable association in that state.[16]

The county treasurer and the federal port appraiser were Jews, as was Isaac Cardoza, who was a member of the State Assembly. One of the most successful of men was Adolph Sutro, whose four-mile tunnel led to the Comstock Lode. He made millions in his mines. He dispensed his wealth freely. As the Populist mayor of San Francisco at a later day he attained considerable distinction.

Finally there were the Heydenfeldt brothers, Elkan and Solomon. Elkan served in the first California Legislature. Solomon Heydenfeldt was born in Charleston, South Carolina, in 1816. He studied law and practiced it in Alabama. His talents and character won recognition. By 1840 he was a judge in Tallapoosa County Court. But his conscience and humanitarian principles were at odds with the institution of slavery. He became an outspoken foe of slavery and wrote a pamphlet advocating the limitation of importation of slaves into Alabama. This was not what the Alabamans wanted to read. He ran headlong into the wall of prejudice with which the Southern slaveowner surrounded himself. It took Heydenfeldt just one year to move to San Francisco. This transplanted idealist soon made a niche for himself in the raw pioneer community. Law and order was the first and most urgent need in those days of lawlessness and disorder. Heydenfeldt had courage and integrity. By 1851 his talents and character received the voters' accolade. He was elected justice of the Supreme Court of California, the first Jew to be elected by the voters of California. He served for six years and then entered private practice. This he continued for some years until again his conscience dictated another course of action. In 1862 he found he could not take the rigid oath required of lawyers during the Civil War. He gave up pleading cases in court and continued such services as he could render in an advisory capacity. But there were so many ways in which he could serve. "With Felix Adler, of New York, and Julius Jacobs, he founded the first free kindergarten in San Francisco. Above all, he was a man of wide philanthropy," writes Friedenberg.[17] But philanthropy was not enough. He was capable of deep moral indignation. He was aroused over the kidnapping of little Edgar Mortara of Bologna, Italy. He was not alone. The flagrant child-snatching, the forceful conversion, the open defiance of all fairness, decency and humanity, the affront to mankind by the Pope who boasted that he "snapped his fingers at the world"—all made for a cause to rally justice-loving men. "At the time of the Edgar Mortara episode, the Jews of San Francisco held an indignation meeting in Music Hall, Saturday evening, January 15, 1859, 'for the purpose of publicly expressing their feelings upon this grievous wrong.' Heydenfeldt was the presiding officer." Here was work to be done. Solomon Heydenfeldt, native of South Carolina, knew that the theft of a Jewish child in Italy concerned him and all Jews everywhere. It was another demonstration of Jewish solidarity such as had been shown over the Damascus slander, such as had been shown in the centuries past and was to be demonstrated in the tragic century that was to come.

The pattern of communal organization in California was like that found in other States. There were regional variations and minor changes to be noted. In Stockton the synagogue preceded the cemetery by four years. Could that have been due to the magical climate of California which banishes thoughts of death? In Sacramento two other institutions preceded the organization of a synagogue—the Hebrew Benevolent Society was founded in 1850 and its female affiliate in 1855. Los Angeles had a half dozen Jews in 1850 and services in 1852. Several years later Carvalho, who had been a member of John Charles Frémont's party of exploration to the upper Mississippi and Missouri River basins, proposed the establishing of a Hebrew Benevolent Society. With the help of Rabbi Joseph Newmark this was done. The Society performed a triple function. It replaced the burial and funerary committees. It dispensed philanthropy. It provided fellowship, religious and social. It was a social institution which evolved from current needs and was in every sense a cultural invention which would repay further study.

Solomon Nunes Carvalho was a man who typified a mobile people, a man who had the courage to adventure, to strike out over unblazed trails in the direction of the setting sun, who made the overland journey—at what a cost!—and who then became one of the prime movers of a group in California geared to meet the challenge of life in a crude society.[18]

Charleston during the War of 1812 was a city of romance. One of the war brides in 1814 was Sarah D'Azevedo, a family name which is familiar to the reader. Her husband was David Nunes Carvalho. Her son, born a year later, was named for his grandfather. By the time he was twenty, young Solomon was a portrait painter of reputation. Two of his well-known portraits were of Thomas Hunter, who headed Normal College, and of the eminent Isaac Leeser, editor of the *Occident*. He painted such religious subjects as "Moses Receiving the Tablets of the Law," for which he received a medal from the South Carolina Institute, and the interior of the Charleston synagogue. He wrote a book on religion titled *The Two Creations*. He married a Sunday School teacher, Sarah Solis, who had taught under Rebecca Gratz.

These are the skeletal facts. But we know him far better than that. He is as dashing a hero as the conquest of the American frontier produced. He has revealed himself in his *Journal* and *Diary* with much candor and artlessness. He was impulsive, warmhearted, loyal, compassionate, sentimental, adventurous, hardy. His mind was open. His allegiance once given was irrevocable. He was tender-minded and tough of spirit. He was gregarious and yet he knew and enjoyed to the full the uses of solitude. Because he was a man of such lovable contradictions, he is human and dear to each succeeding generation that will trouble to make his acquaintance. The key to Carvalho may be found in a book he wrote. The book has a ponderous title. We should know it.

Incidents of Travel and Adventure in the Far West; With Col. Frémont's Last Expedition Across the Rocky Mountains: Including Three Month's Residence in Utah and a Perilous Trip Across the Great American Desert, to the Pacific. By S. N. Carvalho, Artist to the Expedition. N.Y. 1857[19]

His life was changed in one day—the day he met John Charles Frémont. It was on the twenty-second of August in 1853. Carvalho admits frankly that he joined the expedition on an impulse at first meeting with Frémont. Although they met as strangers Frémont's accomplishments and personal charm were widely celebrated. His discoveries had already made him a national hero. Carvalho succumbed easily. And why not? Here was a man but two years older than Carvalho and a Southerner to boot. Not only that—he was a graduate of Charleston College and so knew well Carvalho's birthplace. Besides, what literate American had not thrilled to the accounts of Frémont's discoveries and explorations? From 1838 on, this intrepid American had doggedly added to our knowledge of our land. He explored the upper Mississippi and Missouri Rivers. Thomas Hart Benton sponsored his explorations in the Des Moines River region. With Kit Carson he journeyed to the Oregon country. In 1845 he headed an exploring party overland to California. He defied the Mexican regime there and helped Commodore Stockton wrest California away. As a reward he was made governor of the region. In the change of authority, Frémont repudiated Kearney, supported Stockton, was court-martialed, found guilty, pardoned by President Polk. Gold was found on his land and his personal fortune skyrocketed. He married a gifted author, Jessie, daughter of Senator Benton. He became a champion of the Free-Soil party and was chosen one of the two first senators from California. By 1856, shortly after the journey which Carvalho records was completed, he was chosen as the first Presidential candidate of the newly born Republican party.

It was to his blandishments and to his magnetic personality that Solomon Nunes Carvalho succumbed almost in the twinkling of an eye. Less than a month after that historic meeting, Carvalho was headed west.

I left New York on the 5th September, 1853, having in charge the daguerreo-type apparatus, painting materials, and half a dozen cases of Alden's preserved coffee, eggs, cocoa, cream, and milk, which he sent out for the purpose of testing their qualities.

There were eighteen men in the party. Among them were ten Delaware chiefs and two Mexicans. Carvalho liked his Indian companions. He says: "Today we met our Delawares. . . . A more noble set of Indians I never saw. . . . They became very much attached to Col. Frémont, and every one of them would have ventured his life for him."

The fact is Carvalho liked everybody in the party. When Colonel Frémont was ill he was deeply concerned for his health. When after an absence necessitated by an acute illness Frémont rejoined his men, Carvalho was jubilant. "No father who had been absent from his children, could have been received with more enthusiasm and more real joy." His enthusiasm for his leader overflowed to Frémont's wife, for the second edition of Carvalho's book reads: "To Mrs. Jessie Benton Frémont, This book is, by permission, most respectfully dedicated."

Neither cold, nor hunger, nor danger dimmed this wonderful sense of confidence and loyalty to his chief. It overflowed like a bubbling fountain out of a nature as generous as it was rare. Nevertheless as their expedition progressed and their troubles multiplied, as exhaustion and starvation threatened life, the men were sorely tried. Still Carvalho's spirit was dauntless. His determination to carry on the work of sketching the terrain they discovered was undiminished.

While suffering from frozen feet and hands, without food for twenty-four hours, travelling on foot over mountains of snow, I have stopped on the trail, made pictures of the country, repacked my materials, and found myself frequently with my friend, Egloffstein, who generally remained with me to make barometrical observations, and a muleteer, some five or six miles behind camp, which was reached only with great expense of bodily as well as mental suffering. The great secret, however, of my untiring perseverance and continued success, was that my honor was pledged to Col. Fremont to perform certain duties, and I would rather have died than not have redeemed it. I made pictures up to the very day Col. Fremont found it necessary to bury the whole baggage of the Camp, including the daguerreotype apparatus.

He saw the vast new land not only as an artist whose duty it was to record for his fellow countrymen the great sweeps of valley, the majestic heights of mountains, the tortuous river beds, the dense forests. He saw it with the sensitive eyes and warm heart of the descendant of a long line of pilgrims for whom there had never been any room in the world since the black day when they had lost Palestine.

As the miles dragged out and the road they blazed seemed never-ending, as food supplies dwindled and one by one the men showed marked signs of emaciation, Frémont and his second in command, Carvalho, became acutely worried. Spirits sank and bodies were dragged along with difficulty. The pack animals were slaughtered one after another and in this way hunger would be staved off for a few days. A beaver shot by a sentry made a meal for the starving men. A porcupine made another meal. Soon their mounts had to be sacrificed to feed them. Carvalho's own pony was killed for meat. "I shed tears when they shot him down," Carvalho wrote.

On New Year's day they had "horse steaks fried in tallow Candles and Blanc Mange for dessert." That dessert was a triumph for Carvalho, and a testimony to his unselfishness for it was made out of some arrowroot leaves which Mrs. Carvalho had given him to be used in an emergency. Like a schoolboy who has contrived a feast out of hoarded sweets, Carvalho surprised his party with the blanc-mange of his own making and with characteristic naïveté he records the way his companions rejoiced at the treat.

But soon there was so little food of any kind that all the men were asked by Frémont to swear an oath that they would all die together like men. On a previous occasion, years before this expedition, Frémont had sent a band of starving men off to get help for their stranded party and they had eaten one of their own. This was not to be repeated. The men solemnly swore that they would "stand by one another to the end."

Conditions grew worse. They ate grass seed and gnawed cactus. Fifty days passed in this way. Even their indomitable leader was failing in strength and could no longer hide the ravages of malnutrition and the corrosion of hopelessness. Around them were mountains and snow and more snow. It was trail's end for all of them, or so they thought.

Carvalho, dragging himself along with Colonel Frémont and the others, was completely spent. His hands were frostbitten. His fingers split at the joints. He, like all the others, was suffering from scurvy and diarrhea. He was emaciated. His tattered clothes hung in shreds on his worn body. And what worried this fastidious soul was that he was unkempt and unwashed. But miraculously help was at hand. They neared a little Mormon outpost. Later Carvalho and his friend Egloffstein were both moved to Salt Lake City. Here he gradually regained his health. When food and rest had worked their miracle, he found himself a welcome and much-desired addition to Mormon society. He was in demand as an artist and as a guest.

I received a good deal of marked attention from his excellency, Governor Young; he often called for me to take a drive in his carriage, and invited me to come and live with him, during the time I sojourned there. This invitation I refused, as I wished to be entirely independent to make observations. I told Brigham Young that I was making notes, with a view to publish them.

At last he was himself again and able to complete the overland journey. He joined a group of Mormons and, keeping a careful, daily record of their safari, completed the undertaking.

There was little that escaped the artist's eye. He found possibilities for industrial development and for colonization. "From San Bernardino to Los Angeles, a distance of forty-five miles, the road lay over one continuous field of wild mustard, covering the whole breadth of the valley." Not a bad idea, he suggests, to build a mustard mill.

He notes the manners and customs of the Mormons, discusses their vagaries and shows the manifest unfairness of their system to the women in their midst. The crudeness of the new communities in California, the lack of morals, the abandonment of all customary restraints, were noted sadly. The San Francisco area was the cesspool of California morality. "Alas! for the morals of the people at large . . . almost every night while I was there, one murder, at least, was committed." In Los Angeles he found opportunity to put his organizing ability to work. He promoted a Hebrew philanthropic society. Throughout California he found wealthy patrons who welcomed his talent. He was commissioned to paint the portraits of many native Spaniards and of some newcomers. He made friends and enhanced his reputation.

Finally Solomon Nunes Carvalho returned to his wife and to his children. Both in Baltimore and in Philadelphia where the Carvalhos lived, he and his wife were active in Jewish communal life. He was a dashing, handsome fellow. He could write and he could paint and he had thousands of anecdotes to relate. What an addition he must have been to the social gatherings which he graced and how he must have delighted in his audience!

Hinton Helper's book, *The Land of Gold*, "unveiled" California, Carvalho's described its crudities. How different were the founding fathers of our Western outposts from those who had first hewed their homes from the virgin lands along the Eastern seaboard! Where were the prayers and the devotions, the theocratic societies and the sense of impending doom? Within the far-flung boundaries of the expanding nation, there were vast contradictions. It was hard to reconcile them. Solomon Nunes Carvalho had made a long journey across the land—and a longer one on the road that led to unraveling its mysteries. The nation was emerging from adolescence. And the men who had traveled across the length and breadth of it were helping the country to grow up. Carvalho was of this select group.

CHAPTER XI

"Father Abraham" Achieves
an Honorary Membership

-》》》　　 I will say of the slave . . . humanity recognizes no color,
mind recognizes no color; pleasure or pain, happiness or
misery, life or death recognizes no color.
　　　　　　　　 —ERNESTINE ROSE, *speaking*
　　　　　　　　　 in Boston in 1855　　《《《-

THERE COMES a time in the history of every nation when subtly
but persistently ideas and principles become all-engrossing. Peaceful
men and home-loving women are willing to die for them. It is difficult
to say with assurance just when and how latent feelings crystallize,
hidden strata of thought crop out, deep inner emotions come to the
surface unleashed with wild fury. Sometimes the contagion of ideas
spreads like an epidemic infecting one area, skipping another. At
other times the moral forces are restrained or let loose by the exigencies of the pocketbook. On occasion an event or an incident will
startle complacent people out of their lethargy. A book, a sermon,
an idea may set off the moral forces which create violent social
change. There are some citizens who quicken with moral indignation.
Others accept conditions as the Will of Providence. Rebecca Gratz
and Judah Touro failed to be emotionally aroused by slavery. To
some of their friends and neighbors the enslavement of the Negro
was becoming the most engrossing social problem of their generation.
　　It would be wrong to forget that part of the silence of compassionate, altruistic, normally warmhearted and responsive Jews on the
subject of slavery may have been due to an unwillingness to stir up
latent hostility to themselves. In even the most sheltered and protected Jewish biography there were memories of slights and hostilities, of snubs and aggressions. We know of the duel which Rebecca
Gratz so feelingly described to a member of her own family, a duel
which would not have occurred if the term "Jew" had not been used

as an epithet.[1] A minority group walks warily, constantly aware of threats to its security and status. Unconsciously, in the minds of both oppressor and oppressed there are categorical reactions based on loose, inaccurate thinking. The intuitive knowledge that resides in all of us lives cheek by jowl with primitive, inaccurate ideas. From 1661 to 1906 this psychological association of the relationship of minority groups like Jews and Negroes may be found in American records.

There were, however, positive antislavery leaders, bold, assured spokesmen among Jews. When we examine the record, we find it clear, incontrovertible, legible.[2] We do not know whether there were Jews in the Society for Promoting the Abolition of Slavery founded by Benjamin Franklin in 1775. We cannot tell how many Jews subscribed to *The Emancipator*, to *The Genius of Universal Emancipation*, to *The Liberator*. But we know of Jews who spoke and wrote with eloquence for abolition, who pleaded and expostulated, who cried out as fearless champions of abolition.

Writing during the Civil War, Rabbi Felsenthal in *Die Juden und die Sclaverei* insisted that the majority of American Jews were antislavery in sentiment. He found its supporters in a minority. It is difficult to summarize a social attitude of a group as scattered as were the Jews of America. It is impossible to state categorically what they felt without relating the issue to geography, economics or social contacts with non-Jews. Kohler is right when he calls our attention to the absence of Jewish agencies which could speak with authority and without fear of contradiction. "As there was, however, no Jewish synod in America, no declaration was presented by the Jews as such, *pro* or *con*, on this question."

We may say with assurance: in the age of the gathering storm, in the time before the War, there were Jews who faced the issue squarely, forthrightly and without flinching. The record is eloquent. Kohler writes:

We learn from a Jamaica correspondent's letter to the *Allgemeine Zeitung des Judenthums*, published in 1838 (vol. II, p. 443) that a Jewish resident of Jamaica was the first one on the island to liberate his slaves, for he celebrated Queen Victoria's Coronation Day, on June 28, 1838, by assembling his slaves, and forthwith giving them their freedom.[3]

Of far greater significance was the contribution made by Adolphe Crémieux. To him emancipation meant emancipation for all and enslavement was a degradation for all who were associated with it. Kohler writes:

In 1840, at the Anti-Slavery Convention held in London, at which Garrison, Birney, Jay and other leaders of the American movement joined with Clarkson, Brougham and the other famous English leaders in their endeavors to abolish slavery throughout the world and particularly in the United States, a noble champion of human liberty stepped forward to espouse the holy cause on behalf of Israel, and in earnest, moving language which fortunately has been handed down to us, Adolph Crémieux proclaimed that the Jews must needs be the enemies of human slavery, and that a Jewish sect, the Essenes, had been the first abolitionists.[4]

Crémieux spoke as "an Israelite." Did he, perhaps, also speak for many Israelites in America?

Yes, all persecutions are akin to one another, and this was well understood by that venerable Bishop Grégoire, who, while he raised his voice in favor of the emancipation of the blacks, at the same time demanded the emancipation of the Jews. . . . The slavery of man by man is a perpetual crime against humanity. Cast far from you those absurd accusations which would degrade one part of creation. Persecutors are ever fertile in arguments to give a color to their oppression.[5]

Unfortunately we have no way of checking on American-Jewish response to the impassioned words of Crémieux. But we know that his eloquence bore fruit in his native land. "Closely in line with this, is the emancipation of the slaves effected by the French Assembly of 1848, in France's colonial possession," adds Kohler.

There were some American Jews however who were the active foes of slavery, men and women who labored openly to abolish an institution they viewed with loathing and with abomination.

Rebecca Gratz may have been inscrutable. Ernestine Rose was not.[6] Judah Touro may have been tentative. Moritz Pinner was not.

A native of Poland, born in 1810, Ernestine left her home at seventeen, revolting "against the religious fanaticism of her environment." To her father, an orthodox rabbi of distinction, she left her few possessions asking him to distribute them to the poor. She who had been a "pattern of piety" now turned her back on all religion of orthodoxy and became a servant of the religion of humanitarianism. She met Robert Owen in England in 1832. She married an English abolitionist and with him went to America. She warmly espoused his social philosophy. From her teens to her death she was an unswerving champion of the underdog. One writer quotes a correspondent to The Liberator, May 23, 1856, who salutes Ernestine as an advocate of "Woman's Rights, Anti-Slavery and Religious Liberty," as one who "has earned a world-wide celebrity." It is true that she had won international acclaim. In 1834, just two years after her meeting with

Robert Owen, she presided at the first meeting of an organization which staggered under the name of "The Association of All Classes of All Nations, Without Distinction of Sect, Sex, Party Condition, Or Color." It was a forerunner of the World Republic.

From 1836 to 1869, Ernestine Rose was to fight for these ideas in the United States. Her title was "Queen of the Platforms." She was to urge the rights of labor, to champion women's rights. She lost no time. At a meeting held in New York to discuss improvement in schools she heard the Reverend Robert Breckenridge of Kentucky attack, instead, the radical element in this country who would abolish slavery and who dared advocate women's rights. She publicly reproved the speaker for departing from the subject under discussion, saying that those who fought free education also opposed emancipation and the rights of women. This almost caused a riot. That a foreigner, a Jewess, a woman, would dare take issue in public with a clergyman was a thing unheard of. There were cries of protest. There were shouts urging her forcible ejection from the hall. But Ernestine could take it. She refused to budge and delivered a speech which won her the resounding cheers and acclaims of those who had just recently booed her. She had found her work and she loved it! From then on she became a circuit rider, traveling from barn to meeting hall to plead her many causes—a female Don Quixote tilting at many windmills. She must have had a tough time of it again and again. It was not a woman's work, not seemly, not proper. She knew it. In 1852 at a meeting in Syracuse, New York, she referred to herself as a universal voice for freedom, "a daughter of . . . the downtrodden and persecuted people called the Jews." In Boston, in 1855, she said that she had been antislavery all of her life. "I will say of the slave . . . humanity recognizes no color, mind recognizes no color; pleasure or pain, happiness or misery, life or death recognizes no color." That was her creed, restated again and again wherever she could find men to hear her. It was not easy to be a woman and to face hostile crowds. To be a Jewess and a foreigner made matters worse. Many newspapers attacked "this Polish propagandist." They said she was subsidized by England to promote a revolution in this country. The usual campaigns of slander and vilification dogged her wherever she went. But she kept right on. Every challenge was a boomerang. She wrote to the *Albany Register*, in answer to a blistering attack, that "no true soul will ever be deterred from the performance of a duty by any criticism." She had her friends too. How the Seneca Falls coterie must have adored her. For she was cut after their pattern. The members of the National Women's Suffrage Association elected her as one of their delegates to the Women's Industrial Congress held in Berlin in 1869. Had she not almost single-handed forced the adoption of women's suffrage in Wyoming in that very year? They were in truth grateful and could do no less for Ernestine.

Her co-workers all thought her beautiful. Her portrait shows her to be a rather plain woman with large eyes and a wide mouth and rows of little sausage curls framing her face. But the impression the photograph conveys is of a person of tremendous discipline and vitality. She was a human dynamo, of unlimited energy. She made many warm friends. When Susan B. Anthony felt that the time had come to storm the nation's Capitol, she "gathered up Ernestine Rose and went to Washington."

The complacent, native American Jewess was redeemed by the fiery immigrant from Poland. American life was once more enriched by the gift of a pilgrim. The "ardent Ernestine" had made a permanent niche for herself in the United States.

But men of conscience were among the immigrants as well as women. Kohler states that "Moritz Pinner . . . became an active abolitionist worker in Missouri as early as 1856. The idea of starting an abolitionist paper in the Southern district where he was living appealed so strongly to him that he repaired to Boston, the headquarters of the leading abolitionists of the day, for advice, and there formed personal acquaintanceship with Theodore Parker, Wendell Phillips, William Lloyd Garrison and others."[7] Pinner was one of a committee of thirty-nine which undertook the free distribution of ten thousand copies of *The Impending Crisis*. This book by Hinton R. Helper of North Carolina had first appeared in 1857. It proved by an array of incontrovertible statistics that slavery was an economic millstone to the South. This thesis, as well as the distribution of Helper's book, was heartily espoused by Moritz Pinner. In 1859 Pinner began a stormy period as the editor of the *Kansas Post*, an uncompromising abolitionist paper. The following year, his adopted State, Missouri, chose Pinner as its delegate to the National Republican Convention. It was the convention that nominated Lincoln. Lincoln offered Pinner a post in Honduras in 1861. This Moritz Pinner declined, choosing to join the Union Army instead. He was a captain of the United States Volunteers and served as a brigadier quartermaster and a member of General Kearney's personal staff.

The record of Jewish participation in the abolitionist movement now becomes impressive. The participants are often German immigrants inured to revolution, veterans of the fight for freedom. The abandon and enthusiasm with which they espouse the cause of emancipation is a credit to them. For had they not once had poverty and prejudice to fight? Did they not need to learn a language, to seek means of earning their daily bread? Again and again they risked their lives to advance an idea. Incidents like the following are not uncommon.

In Chicago, as early as 1853, a mob interposed in favor of a poor fugitive slave who had been arrested by the Federal authorities, and liberated him. The mob was led by Michael Greenebaum, and a mass-meeting was held that evening to ratify this act. Others followed, the first official call for a German mass-meeting in Chicago to join the Republican party being signed by George Schneider, Adolph Loeb, Julius Rosenthal and Leopold Mayer, four of the five signers having been Jews.[8]

Typical of the articulate and the aware among these new immigrants was Bernard Felsenthal who came to Madison, Indiana, to act as the rabbi of its little community. After three years there, he journeyed in 1858 to Chicago, then a young and sprawling town of hardy pioneers. Here his clarion voice was heard again and again voicing the conscience of American Jewry. Ardently antislavery in sentiment, his humane spirit shines through his published works. He was an early Zionist. He was an early advocate of unity in Israel. He was much in demand as a speaker before German Republican clubs.

Many of the agitators used their native tongue, perforce. Some plunged into the English language like hardy divers, long before they were ready. We can only imagine with sympathy how they must have struggled to be understood. Their voices left no record. But their pens did. Here is one confused letter composed under conditions that threatened that writer's serenity and elevated his blood pressure:

BOSTON May 5 1862

Hon J C Crittenden M C—
Washington, D. C.
WORTHY SIR!
History has no instance on record where so much patriotism has been rewarded with such much indignities and malice as *you* and those Gentlemen from the "loyal Border States" ever since this notorious Congress is in Session. . . .

I never was in a slavestate do not personally know a "Slaveholder" but by the eternal God, befor I would yield to mobbish majorities to dispos of my inherend right in my property, I would rather assamble in Hell and meet with the Devils befor I would remain one hour longer with those who under the Garb of Liberty would make ME their servant *and slave*

Thank God! I have told you my sentiments
truly yours SAMUÉL STERN

Not all Jews attacked Crittenden. Some were his friends and warm admirers. One of them, who also knew Lincoln well, was Abraham Jonas of Quincy, Illinois. He wrote:

QUINCY ILLS—March 22/58

Hon. J. J. Crittenden
  Washington
MY DEAR SIR
  Permit an old friend to express his satisfaction and delight, at reading your recent able speech on Kansas affairs—the sentiments therein expressed are just such as I should have expected from the John Crittenden of my past recollections, and I am quite sure had Mr Clay been alive and by your side in the Senate, he would have spoken as you did—I am more than gratified, that the only surviving leader of the Glorious old Whig party should stand before the Country, the advocate of just and Constitutional principles—I had never doubted the correctness of my own course, *here in Illinois*, in meeting with the Republican party, but since reading your speech, I am sure I am right—The old Kentucky Whigs, living in this part of Illinois and we are very numerous, are all as much delighted as I am—May God bless and prosper you, is the prayer of
Your old & devoted friend
A. JONAS

send me a pamphlet
copy of your speech[9]

Jonas' letter must be read with a full knowledge of the events to which he refers—for it is an important document. Four years before he wrote that letter, Jonas and others had followed with tense interest the plans for Kansas and Nebraska Territories. Stephen A. Douglas of Illinois was responsible for a compromise measure which, in effect, repealed the Missouri Compromise. In 1854, Congress decided that each Territory was to determine whether it wished to be admitted as a free or slave State on the basis of "squatter sovereignty." Against Douglas, Seward, Sumner, Everett had thundered and pleaded. It was in vain. The South had resolved to recognize no boundaries to slavery. It won its point. A few weeks after the Kansas-Nebraska Bill was passed, the antislavery forces in the North were galvanized into action. The Republican party was born in Jackson, Michigan, in July, 1854. But the Free-Soilers knew that it was a time for concerted action as well. The New England Emigrant Aid Society was formed to assist new settlers who would hold the territory for the antislavery forces. By March of 1855, the establishment of Lawrence, Kansas, was tangible evidence of their intentions. Now the South organized armed bands of men known as "border ruffians" who overran Kansas at election time, tampered with ballots, enacted laws favorable to slaveholders. "Bloody Kansas" became a battleground. In 1856, Lawrence was raided. Its printing presses were destroyed. Its dwellings burned. The nation was aroused. Lincoln and Douglas held their historic series of debates in Illinois. And John Brown imbued with a messianic complex took the law into his own hands. There were Jews among the soldiers of emancipation.[10]

"Prominent among these free state men were three Jews, Theodore Weiner, a Pole, Jacob Benjamin, a Bohemian, and August Bondi, a native of Vienna. Weiner was about thirty-seven years of age, while the others were considerably younger. Bondi was eminently fitted to become an associate of John Brown," writes Hühner. The Bondi manuscript, "With John Brown in Kansas," gives us considerable information about the early Jewish settlers not only in Kansas but in the surrounding country. These men emerge as personalities. It may be because of the abundance of records they left behind. It may be because their portraits are accessible and their historic homes have been photographed and preserved and made into patriotic shrines. The tree-shaded home at Salina, Kansas, where August Bondi lived is a constant reminder of his share in Kansas history.

Bondi lived for a while on the Mosquito branch of Pottawatomie Creek. He was associated in business with Benjamin and Weiner, for whom Weinersville is named. But that was of secondary importance. Abolition, John Brown, driving out "the border ruffians" —these matters came first. They were in the fight up to the hilt.

For Bondi and his friends, "bloody Kansas" was but a proving ground of courage. He and many of his fellow Jews lost no time in donning a uniform. In 1861, Bondi joined the Fifth Kansas Cavalry and was first sergeant of Company K for more than three years. Every battle of his company, every military engagement, found Bondi with his men. He survived and in 1866 moved to Salina. His old home had been burned to the ground while he was away serving in the Union Army. The one object that was saved in the fire was a flintlock musket which "the old man," John Brown, had given him. This he turned over to the Kansas State Historical Society, one of whose directors he had become. He lived a full life after the War. He was by turns a farmer, a lawyer, a real estate broker, a township trustee, a clerk of the district court and a land office clerk. It was not a bad record for an immigrant, an erstwhile soldier of the Vienna Academic Legion, and a friend and associate of Louis Kossuth of Hungary and John Brown of Kansas.

Some men like Rabbi Samuel M. Isaacs were expedient and, though they took part in antislavery activities, refused to preach antislavery sermons. Others like Dr. Sabato Morais were not. "In Philadelphia itself, Rev. Dr. Sabato Morais uttered burning words of protest against slavery on behalf of orthodox Judaism, in spite of the pro-slavery sentiments of some of his congregation, who for a time even prevented him from speaking. He was tendered the position of Jewish chaplain during the War, but declined." Here was a Jew of Livorno, Italy, who belonged to a family whose zealous participation in the Italian democratic movement made them marked men. Sabato Morais, while supporting his family, devoted every spare moment to acquiring an education. He became a Biblical scholar and linguist. He received the appointment of Hebrew teacher in a Jewish orphanage in London. Those were happy years, years of association with Sir Moses Montefiore and Mazzini. The liberation of Italy formed a close bond between Morais and Mazzini. In 1850 Isaac Leeser, of whom more later, resigned as rabbi of Mickvé Israel. The following year Rabbi Sabato Morais was chosen to succeed Leeser. He continued at this post until his death in 1897. From 1851 until the outbreak of the War, despite protests against Morais' antislavery sermons, despite actual attempts to silence him, despite congregational mutterings and averted faces, he preached what he felt to be right.

He was one of a brave fraternity. There were others. Their biographies should be known. To defy the ethos is to fly in the face of convention. It is to court ostracism, to invite isolation. It is to swim against the current.

In spite of all these deterring influences, Jewish pulpit and press were destined . . . even before Lincoln's inauguration, to proclaim on behalf of Judaism that negro slavery should not endure. The pioneer among Jewish pulpit leaders in this cause, and the one destined to bring the greatest sacrifices in its behalf, was Rev. Dr. David Einhorn.

After a stormy rabbinical career in Germany, made more difficult by his flying in the face of authority both lay and secular in his revolt from orthodoxy, David Einhorn came to Baltimore to head the Har Sinai Congregation. Here he took a dynamic rather than a passive role. He edited a magazine in German, *Sinai*, in which he courageously wrote exactly what he felt. In the pulpit too he was forthright. Word of his sermons spread throughout the city. There were ugly mutterings against him. He was undeterred. There were plots against him. He went on preaching, writing, taking sides against slavery. His life was threatened. The crisis came the night of April 22, 1861

Soldiers, policemen and friends all warned Einhorn that his name was on the list of those proscribed and fixed upon by the mob. Friends came and begged that he, too, display the rebel flag from his house-tops, but he indignantly refused. So serious were matters becoming, that a volunteer guard of young men belonging to his congregation remained in his home, ready to shield him against the threatened assault. Then at length he yielded to the entreaties of the officers of the congregation to remove his family from the scene of danger, and silently home and belongings were abandoned in a flight from the city to a point of shelter, Einhorn insisting on returning as soon as his family was placed in safety. After a long and dangerous drive, Philadelphia was reached, but return to Baltimore was prohibited under martial law.[11]

David Einhorn did not choose the easy path. His is a record of rugged courage, of willing martyrdom. Once again the voice of an immigrant spoke for the conscience of American Jewry.

"There have always been two opposing forces operating on American life and character," wrote James Truslow Adams. Just so it was with the Jews of America. There were enough Southern Jews and spokesmen for slavery in the North to permit the popular press to jump to any conclusion. Editorial writers could seize on a sentence or a paragraph and twist it in any direction. Generalizations are the ready tools of the demagogue and rabble-rouser. But a man's opinion is related to his physical and social environment. Opinion often is molded by the pocketbook, yielding to moral suasion only if the voice of conscience is in harmony with the voice of the investment counselor. There were Jews who bought and sold slaves and Jews who were active in the Underground Railroad helping Negroes escape northward. Perhaps Morris Jacob Raphall may serve as a case in point.[12] Did the fact that his father was the banker to the King of Sweden constitute a major reason for his later opinions? It would certainly seem so. He was born in Stockholm in 1798. He was a delicate youth, sheltered and protected by his devoted father. His education for the rabbinate took him to Denmark, Germany and England. He was a popular interpreter of matters Jewish to the non-Jewish world. When he came to New York in 1849 to head B'nai Jeshurun Congregation, he was voted a very liberal salary which enabled him to continue a life free of financial worries. He preached with the assurance of the fortunate. One of his sermons openly justified slavery as part of God's plan. Dipping into the Bible, he came up with literal evidence to buttress his oratory. The sermon found immediate acclaim in the plushy circles of certain rich New York merchants who published it and gave it wide circulation. It was referred to with approval in the *American Israelite* and admired in the *Occident*. But it aroused a storm of indignation among the antislavery Jews. They railed against such a perversion of Jewish religious views. Einhorn wrote: "Why should we, in America, keep silence when a Jewish preacher plays such pranks? Those Jews only who value the dollar more than God and their religion, can give it their consent and approval." A Polish Jew, Michael Heilprin, a man warm of heart, gifted of pen and thoroughly learned in Hebrew lore and tradition, effectively answered Raphall's arguments. It was well that he did so for many Christians had been misled by Rabbi Raphall into thinking that he spoke for all Jews. So fickle is the populace that the heroic men who followed John Brown with valor were quickly forgotten and the merchants who stood to profit from slavery became symbolic of Jewish opinion. Sabato Morais, David Einhorn, Adolph Bush, Moritz Pinner might never have been.

Fortunately the views of Michael Heilprin carried considerable weight. Two years after coming to this country, his scholarship had won him the position of associate editor of Appleton's *Encyclopaedia of American Biography*. Here was a man who could read eighteen languages and speak eight of them, a man whose memory was inexhaustible and whose reputation as a friend of liberty and co-worker of Kossuth had preceded him to this country. He was a welcome contributor to the *Nation* and translated David Einhorn's prayer book into English. It was Raphall's word against Einhorn's or Heilprin's.[13]

Lincoln's election in 1860 changed everything. Jews as well as other Americans could no longer straddle the issue. The choice was simple now—preservation of the Union or secession. The time for decision was at hand. "I hope . . . that our beloved Union may survive the dangers that threaten," wrote Rebecca Gratz on the thirteenth of December, 1860. "The seceders are bringing ruin on their own heads as well as the deepest distress on the whole country," she wrote a month later. The *Occident* carried "A Plea for Union."[14] In August of 1861 in discussing partisanship and political parties, an editorial in the *Occident* pointed out that among Jews differences in opinion on all questions were always tolerated and that perfect agreement was neither possible of attainment, nor to be desired if it could be had. In September, 1861, one correspondent writing on "The American Crisis" states flatly that when the American flag is in jeopardy "the Jewish heart sympathizes with this trouble."[15] Yet it was a bitter choice men had to make—to take up arms against their siblings, to cut themselves off from their dear ones, to know that the cherished fabric of Jewish family life in America must be torn, possibly for all time.

"Dear, dear Ann," wrote Rebecca to her sister-in-law in September of 1861, "what changes have taken place in our once happy country. One can hardly realize they are *at home*—in the U. S. of America— and are at war with each other—I have been reading loving letters from some so near to me in blood & affections whose arms are perhaps now raised against the hearts at which they have fed—this I cannot but lament as among the horrors of war." The tragedy of war lashed out at her own family as she was writing that very letter. She received the tragic news that her young nephew, Cary Gratz, was killed in the battle of Wilson's Creek, in Missouri, August 10, 1861.[16] The bell tolled North and South.

A man well known to us was to live out within his own person the drama of a civil war. It was a long and bitter battle he waged. His beginnings in Warrenton, North Carolina, were auspicious. His student days at West Point were happy. So was the time spent at his alma mater as assistant professor. His record as a military engineer was brilliant. Yet Alfred Mordecai, when confronted with the Civil War issue, felt he could not face it. He writes in his *Autobiography*:

In the spring of 1861, when the first gun was fired in that Calamitous Conflict, I was with some other Ordnance officers, at Fort Monroe, making trials of a sea coast gun carriage. I had taken your mother & Laura with me to Richmond, & being ordered to return immediately to my post, I hastened back with them to Watervliet Arsenal—When Civil War became inevitable, unwilling to engage in it, for reasons peculiar to myself, I resigned my commission in the army, (being then a Major in the Ordnance Department) & retired with my family to Philadelphia, which has been their home ever since.[17]

The man who had been valedictorian of the class of 1823 at West Point and had served his country with all of his talents since then was a person of deep loyalty to the place of his birth. He could not forget his happy childhood at Warrenton, North Carolina. He was bound by a thousand ties of memory and affection to the South he loved so well. It had been hospitable, friendly, warm to the clan of Mordecai. To fight against it? He could not bring himself to do it. They were his friends!

He stepped aside, and with a heavy heart continued his research work in engineering. That his peace of mind was forever destroyed is patent from his letters. His son and namesake, who had followed in his father's footsteps, chose to fight for the Union. The year of Alfred Mordecai, Sr.'s, resignation, 1861, was the year that Alfred Mordecai, Jr., graduated from West Point. As second lieutenant he served in the Manassas campaign and took part in the Battle of Bull Run. His rise thereafter was rapid. He was brevetted lieutenant colonel in 1865. He remained with the Army, becoming brigadier general, retiring in 1904. What did it cost the father to part company with his son? Here is a fragment of a letter written in 1865 which speaks volumes:

Havanna Thursday, June 29/65

. . . Friday, June 30th Our son Alfred's birthday—I trust he is well, & that God has softened his heart towards his fellow countrymen & relatives of the South—Mine bleeds daily to think of them—let me try not—[18]

"Except for the critical years 1775-1789, in which our nation was formed," writes Muzzey, "no other period in our history can compare with the great Civil War of 1861-1865." He then mentions the overwhelming number of official documents, running to 130 volumes, the thousands of source and secondary works available to the scholar or student which cover these four years. It is not our purpose here to review the military campaigns. Nor is it necessary to follow the major events of the War. Our task is to evaluate the contribution of Jews both to the Confederacy and the Union. It is to select the data which are pertinent. It is to present the record and to introduce a few of the leading Jewish characters in the drama of civil war in such a way that without distortion and fanfare, they can be known as people and their performance recalled with justifiable pride.

The Union forces numbered three hundred sixty thousand men killed in combat. The Confederacy lost two hundred fifty-eight thousand.[19] How many more on the home front died of secondary wounds, heartbreak and anguish, we can only imagine. How many more lived thereafter as if in death, only the understanding heart can apprehend.

The casualties on either side exceeded the total number of Jews in the United States in 1860. In 1848, it was estimated by most authorities that there were some fifty thousand Jews in the United States. The years before the conflict saw many immigrant Jews swell the census of the North and border States. "Two hundred thousand Jews held to their ancient ritual," says Carl Sandburg in discussing population figures at the outbreak of war. Population statistics have been variously estimated. Says Markens:

> The Jews of the United States formed but a small portion of the population in Lincoln's time. The President of the Board of Delegates of American Israelites, their representative organization, estimated their number in the loyal States near the close of 1861 at not less than 200,-000, which figures are now regarded as excessive. The Rev. Isaac Leeser as late as 1865 could not figure the entire Jewish population of the United States as exceeding 200,000, although he admitted that double that number had been estimated by others.[20]

The fact that they were relatively few in number should not hinder the narrative. Even the autobiography of one person, a bundle of letters of another, can add to our general knowledge. Sometimes the mind becomes dulled to mass phenomena and yet can grasp the total scene from the vantage point of one diarist. The separation of the two Alfred Mordecais, father and son, is revealing of the pain of separation. The loss of Cary Gratz in combat brought sorrow to one family. There were nearly six hundred thousand such tragedies. To know one is to know all. There are so many ways to tell the story of Jewish participation in the Civil War. An over-all picture may be presented based on statistical estimates. The War may be told from the distinguished service records of the Jewish soldiers who were decorated for valor. Seven of them received the Congressional Medal of Honor. It may be reconstructed from the letters and papers of the men who knew Lincoln or Jefferson Davis. It may be pieced together from sources such as the *Portfolio* of Colonel Moses, which is preserved in the archives of the American Jewish Historical Society. It may be told as a fight for recognition—and that would not be far from wrong. It may be interpreted from the pages of the contemporary Jewish press. Together, all of these approaches would cover many volumes. Singly, none is satisfactory. The most that can be done is to give a few biographical glimpses, show the emergence of Jewish communal sentiment, indicate group response, North and South, cull a few letters here and there, show the impact of the War on individuals and of individual Jews on their times.

Lincoln's election touched off the flame. As soon as the news reached Charleston, South Carolina took steps to secede from the Union. In a matter of weeks six other States followed her lead. On February 4, 1861, the Confederacy was organized. A month later Abraham Lincoln was sworn in as President of the United States. Fort Sumter was fired upon and Lincoln promptly issued a call for troops. Now events followed each other at a dizzy pace. The North, united behind the President, responded to Lincoln's call with enthusiasm at fever pitch. Immediately four more Southern States joined the Confederacy. Kentucky and Missouri were on the fence. But while Kentucky remained precariously within the Union, there was fighting in the streets of Baltimore and in the cities of Missouri. On the sea and on the land, along the seaboard and in the Mississippi Valley, campaign followed campaign, victory alternating with defeat.

North and South, the Jews rushed to the colors.[21] Geography determined allegiance. Let us not blink at the facts. There were twenty-four Jewish staff officers in the Confederate Army. At the apex was Judah Philip Benjamin.

Upon the organization of the Confederate Government, President Jefferson Davis immediately called Judah P. Benjamin into his Cabinet, first as Attorney-General, on February 25, 1861, to which was added the position of acting Secretary of War on September 17, 1861. On November 21, 1861, he became regular Secretary of War, resigning the Department of Justice portfolio. He retained this position till March 17, 1862, when he became Secretary of State, which position he retained till the collapse of the Confederacy in 1865. Throughout, he was Jefferson Davis' most intimate and most influential adviser, and was constantly described as the "brains of the Confederacy.[22]

Benjamin's leadership in the Confederacy, his apparent influence on the course of events, his prestige in the South, had for some time been noticed and reviled in the North. He was a Jew and so was a legitimate target on that score to many a newspaper Haman, to many a rabble-rousing partisan. He became a symbol to his enemies.

This type of mob reasoning is not new to the Jew of any land. As far back as 1856, the *Occident* had decried the practice of lumping all Jews into loose categories on the basis of the opinions or performances of a few individuals. For the Jews, the editor insisted, are no longer a unit in opinions and practices, in matters lay and secular. The following year the editor inveighed against the zeal and intemperance shown by Jews on both sides of the slavery question. Astutely he pointed out that "the system of education to which the leading men of these opposing parties have been subjected from their infancy" had shaped their thinking. How could any one be other than he was? The editor wisely proposed to show "the effect which early training and usage have on the formation of our judgment, in instances where it would be wrong to impute dishonest motives or sinister intentions to either of the contestants." To the hotheaded allegations of demagogues that Jews were leading the public down one or another road with which the critics were not in agreement, the editor of the *Occident* answered that on the whole the influence of Jews was "slight."

In October, 1858, the editor of the *Occident* called attention to the latent dislike which some people invariably harbor toward Jews. He repudiates the popular legends which attribute great wealth to Jews as a people. He pleads again for the unbiased view, for dispassionate judgment. But the impassioned years bring matters to a crisis. The calm tenor of the editorial page changes. The War and its demands invade the pages of the *Occident*. The editor deplores the exclusion of Jews from the chaplaincy. In summarizing a year of war, in the issue of April, 1862, the editor laments that "the present deplorable war" has made serious inroads in his circulation. In December of that year, the *Occident* hotly repudiates charges that were made in a Tennessee newspaper that Jews were speculating in cotton. In 1863, General Grant's infamous anti-Jewish decree is excoriated. The editor wants to know whether it is fair to tar a class or a sect for the faults of an individual. "We think not," he adds sadly, pointing out that there are thousands of non-Jewish transgressors, and yet let a Jew be apprehended and the crowds rush to condemn the entire group. In 1864, a news item headed "Something about Jews in the United States Army" stresses the need for accurate statistics on the number of Jews in military service. The editor declares that, "We take no pleasure in war, and studiously avoid alluding to it—but facts are facts—and, by the way, not a single Israelite has as yet held the rank of General."[23]

Two things continue to worry the editor of the *Occident*. The mounting fury of devastation that it has brought to the South, and the growth, in spite of Jewish heroism on the battlefield, of anti-Jewish sentiment which crops up like a noxious weed in the wake of war. In November of 1864, under the heading of "Religious Prejudices" we read:

During the continuance of the unfortunate war which desolates the South of the Union and brings mourning and distress to almost every household at the North, a spirit of intolerance has gradually been developed which seeks to wreak its spite on our defenceless heads. Efforts have already been made to Christianize the Constitution of the country and that man is bold indeed, who will maintain that success cannot attend the labors of the agitators. . . . Newspapers . . . have aided some military satraps to spread a spirit of personal dislike against us.

The subject had long been a matter of preoccupation to the writer of this article but he admits that he preferred to gloss over it in silence for fear of making matters worse.

No doubt some worthless creatures who have been born Jews have done unworthy things during the war . . . and thus disgraced by their shameful conduct the noble name of Israel. But we venture to assert that in all the dealings which the government has had with Jews, they have acted on the whole as honorably as the same class of other persuasions.

He marshals the facts. He recalls the many Jews who volunteered for military service. He reminds his readers of the wounded Jews crowding the hospitals. He recalls with sadness the many who met their death on the battlefield. "Officers and privates are among the slain, prisoners, and missing, and we have drained the same cup of sorrow as all others." In view of the overwhelming facts, in view of the proud record, he cannot see how some members of the press dare attack Jews for their own private ends.

Is it therefore fair that political journals should hold us up as a class to public odium? That Israelites do not all profess to be adherents of the administration is no crime in them; in this they exercise their privilege as citizens to judge of the acts and measures of their rulers to sustain them if they deem proper, and reprove them if they think it best to do so.

Jews are greatly outnumbered. There are many opportunities to mold public opinion into channels which tend to emphasize religious differences to the detriment of the Jew. Agitators are doing their utmost. The masses may succumb to "The United onslaught." Jews must be alerted to the dangers which threaten them.

Jewish protests pour in upon men in public life as our patriots beat their heads against the stone wall of indifference.

It is the old story. Senator Wade sneered at "Israelites with Egyptian principles." Major Alfred Mordecai goes into voluntary retirement as if to prove the point. His son performs acts of heroism far above and beyond the call of duty in the Union Army. But that proves nothing. The editor of the *Occident* bemoans the havoc wrought in the South. The *Jewish Messenger* hammers away at the justice of the Northern cause. Isaac Leeser regretted the war. Samuel Meyer Isaacs was an antislavery zealot. He rejoiced at Northern victories even as he bemoaned the loss of Southern readers. "We want subscribers," he wrote, "but we want much more truth and loyalty."

This contrast is ever prevalent. The South had a Jewish surgeon general, David Camden DeLeon. The North had its Jonathan Phineas Horwitz, who rose to a similar position.[24] Horwitz was the son of Dr. Jonas Horwitz, who received his M.D. in 1815 from the University of Pennsylvania. He enlisted for service in the Mexican War, acting as surgeon to a volunteer corps of Baltimore Jews. Father and son then both rendered medical service to the nation at the same time. Young Dr. Horwitz was a native of Baltimore (1822) and was educated at the University of Maryland and the Jefferson Medical College in Philadelphia. In 1847 he was made assistant surgeon in the United States Navy. During the Mexican War he was in charge of a naval hospital. At the outbreak of the Civil War, Horwitz was made assistant to the United States Bureau of Medicine and Surgery. At the close of the War Congress unanimously commended him for his efficiency in administering this department. In 1865 he was appointed chief of the Bureau. Owing largely to his efforts the Naval Hospital was built in Philadelphia. Dr. Horwitz administered pension funds to disabled veterans and to those who were beneficiaries of slain soldiers.

His name was a familiar one to the bereaved of the nation. Such a person was Rebekah Hyneman.[25] She was just one of the anguished survivors of the three hundred sixty thousand who died to preserve the Union. Rebekah had a Jewish father and a Christian mother. She was brought up a Christian. But there was a pull toward the faith of her father which she could not resist. As an adult she embraced Judaism. She became a writer. Her prose and poetry won her an admiring audience. Yet like many of her generation she was the victim of "untoward circumstances which sorely tried her faith." Her faith survived but her sons did not. "One of her sons, who had inherited his mother's natural enthusiasm, enlisted in the Union army during the late Civil War, and died in the rebel prison at Andersonville from sheer starvation." What could the chief of the Bureau of Medicine and Surgery, Dr. Horwitz, have written to the grief-stricken mother? "The Surgeon General regrets. . . ." Another son died. Her sister Sarah followed shortly after. "Still the bereaved woman arose above gloom, and turned her mind to the task of communicating to others her godly sentiments." "Who calls for help in that wild surging sea?" she wrote in "Miriam's Song." Her own unavailing cries for help fell on deaf ears. Yet with a fortitude which few could emulate she kept on writing, turning out prose and poetry, including "some beautiful delineations of the Women of the Bible and the Apocrypha." She lost her own children. Yet within her depths she found the strength to write for other women's children. Her *Tales for Children*, —written at what a cost!—became popular.

It was for mothers like Rebekah Hyneman that Dr. Jonathan Phineas Horwitz was to act as government official. . . .

David Camden DeLeon was like Dr. Horwitz the son of a physician, Dr. Abraham DeLeon. His father, who was a native of Charleston, had served as surgeon's mate in the War of 1812. His son David was graduated from the University of Pennsylvania medical school in 1836. Two years later he joined the Navy as surgeon. He served in the Seminole War and in the Mexican War. At the Battle of Chapultepec he distinguished himself by assuming command when the combat officer was disabled. He led several cavalry charges against the enemy with such high courage that he later received Congressional commendation. He was thereafter known as "the fighting doctor."

When the Civil War tore the nation apart, Major David Camden DeLeon resigned his commission in the United States Army. He did not believe in secession. Yet he felt that his services belonged to his native State and to the Confederacy. He was given the task of organizing the medical services for the Confederacy and offered the post of surgeon general.

It was a strange coincidence which placed the welfare of the wounded soldiers of both sides in the hands of Jewish doctors.

Southern Jews were ardently loyal to the South and to the Confederacy. They gave of their brains and talents and brawn and life. At the top was Judah Philip Benjamin, Secretary of War for the

Confederacy. Max J. Kohler wrote of him: "I venture to describe Judah P. Benjamin as the most distinguished statesman, orator and lawyer, that American Jewry has produced.[26]

He was born in St. Thomas, in the Virgin Islands, in the year 1811. His parents were English Jews who led a nomad life, moving from place to place, leaving but faint traces of themselves. Young Judah grew up with a wall of reticence around his antecedents. Was this a deliberate "policy of mystery"? He made a fetish of destroying papers and records that might be tools for the reconstructing of his past. When he was five, the Benjamins moved to Charleston. Then they moved on to Warrenton, in North Carolina. A philanthropist of Charleston, Moses Lopez, paid his tuition in a preparatory school. Two years at Yale followed. His record was brilliant, his funds inadequate. He left in his junior year. By this time the wandering Benjamins were living in New Orleans, where Judah studied law, worked at odd jobs, and tutored the daughter of a wealthy Creole planter whom, according to the formula in French novels, he subsequently married. He was handsome, mysterious, reticent, gifted. His prospects were unlimited.

He published a legal handbook which he had compiled with his friend, Thomas Slidell. By the time he was in his early thirties he was considered a brilliant success in the law, was earning a hundred thousand a year, and was the proud owner of a magnificent plantation, Bellechase. His wife and daughter lived there for a few years, but when the child was five years old Mrs. Benjamin and Ninette moved to Paris. Thereafter, Benjamin was a commuting husband, making a summer trip to France annually.

Since matrimony was only a part-time relationship and Benjamin a man of great energy, politics became both outlet and sublimation. His State conferred a number of honors upon him. He was a member of the State Constitutional Convention. He was a member of the senate of Louisiana. Here he made a notable contribution to his State. He was instrumental in improving judicial procedure. He helped draft a law abolishing imprisonment for debt. He helped accomplish another pet project—the establishment of a State university. Had he not been compelled to leave Yale for want of funds? So brilliant was his record that before the year had passed his colleagues elected him to the United States Senate. President Pierce, against whom he had campaigned actively, now offered him a place on the Supreme Court. Benjamin chose to remain in the Senate where he felt his voice was needed as a spokesman for the South. It was this "Israelite with Egyptian principles" who delivered the summation of the Southern point of view on the question of slavery. Slaves were property. Abolitionists were robbers who would deprive owners of what was legally theirs. The aroused opponents of slavery had a ready channel of attack. They could have attacked the logic. They chose to center their vituperation on religious grounds.

Says Kohler:

But though Benjamin was little more than a race Jew all his lifetime, his race was throughout his career a target of attack upon him, on one hand, and on the other, led to most unjustified identification of Jews with the pro-slavery cause in the public mind.[27]

He gave some cause for being identified with Jews, however. For it is important to recall that four years before his eloquent speech of March 11, 1858, in which without qualm or scruple he defended slavery, he had introduced a petition for the protection of American Jews abroad. It was one of his rare moments of concern for his own people.

Yet his colleagues willy-nilly respected him. Charles Sumner considered him the most brilliant orator in America. This in an age when brilliant orators dominated our political life. He was a statesman of brains and of vision. His organizing ability was exceptional. He had a grasp of the law second to none. On the fourth of February, 1861, he bade his Senate colleagues good-by in a speech which argued with brilliance for the right of secession. It was not lost on Jefferson Davis, who became Benjamin's stanch supporter in good times and in bad. When reverses in war brought popular wrath down upon "the hated Jew," Davis was adamant in his belief in Benjamin's ability and his services to the Confederacy. The two remained loyal friends through every stage of war, through defeat and heartbreak. Even after Lee's surrender, Benjamin continued his companion, hiding with Jefferson Davis in Virginia, North Carolina and Georgia. Then the two men parted, Benjamin, after many a thrilling adventure, including a month in the swamps of Florida, set out for the Bimini Islands. Their small craft carrying sponges exploded. Benjamin, like Robinson Crusoe, survived—only with him were three men "Friday," for by a curious trick of fate this defender of the theory that human beings were chattel was saved with three Negro shipmates. A British warship picked up these four survivors. His adventures were not over. At last, after experiencing a fire at sea, he managed to reach England. Disraeli, Gladstone and Tennyson welcomed the penniless veteran of misfortune. He was admitted to the bar and became Queen's Counsel. His success as an English barrister was nothing short of phenomenal. His retirement in 1882 marked the first time that a public banquet was tendered to a British barrister. Lord Chief Justice Coleridge was present and delivered a toast saluting Benjamin as an Englishman, which is probably the finest compliment within the repertoire of a Britisher. It was a signal honor to be paid a pilgrim whose wanderings were occasioned by his adherence to a lost cause, whose abilities far outshone his handicaps.

On both sides of the conflict there were multiple enlistments by members of the same family. North Carolina had six Cohen brothers. Mississippi had five brothers of the Jonas family, of whom one fought for the Union in the Fiftieth Illinois Infantry. The others wore the gray uniforms of the Confederacy. Charles H. Jonas became a major. In South Carolina five Moses brothers were in uniform. Georgia had a father and three sons of the Moses family. Arkansas had three Cohen brothers. There were three Goldsmith brothers from Georgia and South Carolina. Virginia and Louisiana each had three Levy brothers. The ubiquitous clan of Moses also had three brothers in the Alabama ranks. Wolf accounts for this plural enlisting, particularly by Southern Jews, by reminding us how long and how closely they were allied with the development and the history of the South. The North had more Jews of the unattached, immigrant type who came over here singly. There were fewer multiple enlistments. Still in the Union ranks were five Wenk brothers. There were a father and three sons named Levy. There were the three Feder brothers. Pennsylvania sent the three brothers Emanuel to the front. Ohio had three Koch brothers.[28]

Serving the Confederate Congress was the son of Moses Elias Levy, an early Florida pioneer. David Levy was a weak character, yet an able one. His marriage to a Miss Wickliffe induced him to change his name. He became David Levy Yulee and later dropped his middle name altogether. But it was as David Levy that he served the Territory of Florida and as David Levy that he was elected to the United States Senate for the newly admitted State in 1845. Thus he became the first Jew to be elected a member of the United States Senate. He took no part in military action during the War. After Lee's surrender the Governor of Florida sent Yulee to Washington to secure the readmission of Florida. He was captured en route and spent a year in prison. He severed his contacts with Judaism and later retired from public service. With his Christian wife and children he lived the life of a gentleman planter at Fernandina, Florida. As president of the Gulf Railroad he may have achieved his goal—the search for status.

A South Carolina newspaper summarized the Jewish record well when it said:

The list of South Carolina Jews who remained true to their country and to their country's cause in the darkest hours and who proved their fidelity and patriotism by laying down their lives upon the field of battle could be greatly extended. Their names are graven upon a monument throughout the land, and their prowess in arms is a part of the military glory of the country. As Montaigne says, the virtue and valor of a man consist in the heart and in the will, and by this rule the Hebrew soldiers of South Carolina may be fairly judged. . . . When the history of South Carolina's part in the great struggle is written . . . the Hebrew soldiers of this State, who wore grey will have their full meed of praise.

This tribute to the valor of Confederate Jews will do for Jews of the Union Army as well.

Space does not permit nor does the plan of this book warrant a detailed study of each of the Jewish staff officers in the Confederate Army. The Secretary of War and the Surgeon General of the Confederacy were Jews. Dr. DeLeon's Assistant Surgeon General (Dr. I. Baruch) was also Jewish. The Quartermaster General and the Assistant Adjutant General were Jews. The record is impressive and distinguished. For these men were fighting for what they held dear— their homes and loved ones. Private and officer, navy captain or gunner, their courage was indomitable, their spirit gallant. Their individual records were valorous, heroic. There was Dr. Marx E. Cohen, Jr., of Charleston. He was the only son of a planter and the grandson of Mordecai Cohen, one of the earliest Jewish settlers of the South. The family was well-to-do. Dr. Cohen's father was educated in Scotland, as were so many sons of Southern planters, graduating with high honors from Glasgow University. On his return home he led the life of amenity and leisure which went with freedom from financial worry. He married Armida Harby, daughter of Isaac Harby of Charleston. He held a number of civic posts, met reverses due to the Civil War, sold his plantation and lived vicariously in his only son, for whom he had high hopes, the gifted and able youngster who had completed his medical studies by the time he came of age.

During the agonizing battles of the War they hoped and prayed as all parents do whose spirits march with their soldier-sons. The War was nearly over. At the Battle of Bentonville highly explosive shells were thrown into the Confederate lines. It was necessary to remove them without delay. The captain of Hart's Battery called for volunteers to hurl the shells aside. Three men volunteered. Young Dr. Cohen was one of the volunteers. The soldiers managed to remove the shells and were returning to their own lines when all three were killed by enemy gunfire.[29]

Joseph Frankland rose from private to assistant provost marshal. Randolph Mordecai also rose from private to assistant adjutant-general. Colonel Raphael J. Moses was on the staff of General Longstreet. He was called the "honest commissary," a title he earned when serving as chief commissary of the State of Georgia. At the end of the War he turned over a gold surplus of $30,000 to General Molyneux, exacting the promise that the money be used for Confederate hospitals and for the rehabilitation of Confederate soldiers. His request was carried out.

Nor was the Confederate Navy without Jewish representation. The greatest service was rendered to the Confederacy by a civilian, an inventor of the ancestor of the modern torpedo boat. It was the *Little David*, which was designed by the Jewish architect of Charleston, David Lopez. It was this vessel which sank its teeth into the *Ironsides* of the North. It is strange that its inventor should have been the artist who designed the beautiful Charleston synagogue. From blueprint to finished building, the structure of Beth Elohim pays tribute to his genius. It was a curious talent which permitted so ambivalent a record of accomplishment. Yet the *Little David* made its signal contribution—as well as the synagogue.

There was a midshipman who enlisted at fifteen, Louis P. Levy from Virginia. He served on the gunboat *Chicora*. Another midshipman, Randolph Lyons, was detailed as signal officer on blockade running. There were familiar names like Isaac Moïse and Perry De-Leon. The *Merrimac* had a Jewish officer aboard, Lieutenant R. J. Moses, Jr. There was Captain Levi M. Harby, who resigned his commission with the United States Navy to join the Confederate ranks. He commanded the Neptune and later a fleet of gunboats on the Sabine River, rising to the rank of commodore.

They were men whom their fellow countrymen could respect for their zeal, their valor, their disregard of personal safety. Simon Wolf renders a great service in providing "Lists of Jewish Soldiers in the Union and Confederate Armies During the Civil War." Whether our protagonists wore the blue or the gray uniform, they acquitted themselves as patriots, willing to die for a cause they believed in and for the homes they cherished and held dear, willing to stand up beside their Christian neighbors and to be counted!

When a record like the following turns up we do not ask ourselves on which side the "modern Maccabean" fought. We are glad to know that he is remembered as a man with "the heart of a lion."

THE BLOODY ACUTE ANGLE.
AN INTERESTING CHAPTER OF THE CIVIL WAR.
THE GRAND, TERRIFIC, SUSTAINED FIGHTING IN THE
"ANGLE OF LIVID HELL AND DARKSOME
DEATH."

. . . I cannot forego the mention of one individual. Fronthall, a little Jew, though insignificant in appearance, had the heart of a lion. For several hours he stood at the immediate point of contact, amid the most terrific hail of lead, and coolly and deliberately loaded and fired without cringing. After observing his unflinching bravery and constancy, the thought occurred to the writer—I now understand how it was that a handful of Jews could drive before them the hundred kings; they were all Fronthalls!

(Signed) A. T. WATTS.[80]

If the biographies of the Jews who fought with distinction in the Confederate Army are too numerous for easy summary, it becomes overwhelmingly difficult in the Union Army. The North was more populous. More than six thousand Jewish soldiers wore the Union blue. The population of the North had grown by leaps and bounds, swelled by tough young survivors of the revolutions in Europe. A man who has fought once is always ready to enlist in a good fight. Such a man was Leopold Blumenberg, a veteran of the Prussian-Danish War. He became sated with Prussian antisemitism and emigrated to the United States. The attack on Fort Sumter spurred him to enlist. He organized the Fifth Regiment of Maryland Volunteers. He was appointed major. He took part in the Peninsular Campaign and commanded his regiment in the Battle of Antietam. A non-Jewish friend wrote of him:

I was intimate with General Leopold Blumenberg . . . you and others of his friends are familiar with the deserved encomiums passed upon that gallant and kind-hearted American Jew, who received terrible wounds in leading his regiment on the battle-field of Antietam, and of which wounds he died after having served in several important positions in Baltimore.

The "several important positions" refers to his duties as provost marshal of the Third Maryland District, a post to which President Lincoln appointed him when he was no longer able because of injuries to take an active part in military campaigns. President Johnson later appointed him Brevet Brigadier General, U.S. Volunteers. Another Jewish soldier who was given the same rank was Jonas Frankle of Massachusetts who was promoted from major.

In 1861 General John C. Frémont commanded the Western theater of the War with headquarters in St. Louis. He invited Isidor Bush to become a member of his staff. Bush became his aide-de-camp with the rank of captain. He was but one of many Jewish citizens whose talents were enlisted at the outset of hostilities.

We have met Rebekah Hyneman. Consider now the young son whom she mourned. Elias Leon Hyneman, Sergeant, Company C, Fifth Cavalry was a volunteer. He fought from Bull Run to Gettysburg. He was an impetuous youth, "always eager for active service, distinguishing himself in several battles, and being one of twelve skirmishers who advanced on the enemy in the Battle of Gettysburg." He had many a close call. His mount was shot from under him in the Battle of the Wilderness, and he finished the engagement on foot. He was known among his comrades for his unfailing courage. By 1864 he had fought in many a bloody campaign. His term of enlistment expired. His zeal and patriotism had not. He re-enlisted. Shortly after his re-enlistment, in June of that year, he took part in a cavalry sortie near Petersburg. He noticed that one of his comrades was wounded and had been dismounted. He hurried to offer his help. The enemy was closing in. Disregarding his own safety, young Elias dismounted and placed his wounded comrade on his horse and so helped him to escape. He was trying to get back to his own lines, when he saw another comrade who was barefoot and bleeding. He took off his own boots and pressed them on the injured soldier. But he was captured. After great privation and suffering he finally died in prison, a victim of neglect and abuse.

This was just one story out of thousands. One of the undecorated and forgotten heroes.

Among the remembered heroes were many officers and enlisted men whose cool courage, absolute disregard for personal safety, ability to accept with extraordinary adaptability the most grueling conditions of battle and hazardous campaigns—all make this chapter of American Jewish history a cherished legacy for all Americans.

There was Leopold C. Newman, whose wounds at Chancellorsville proved fatal and who died with President Lincoln at his bedside. And Brigadier Max Einsfein, who helped cover the retreat of the Union Army after the first disastrous Battle of Bull Run. And Private Joseph B. Greenhut, whose exploits as a soldier won him a series of promotions. And Lieutenant Max Sachs, who met his death at Bowling Green, Kentucky, after holding off the enemy until re-enforcements could be obtained—"one of the most heroic deeds of the war."

There were the Congressional Medal of Honor recipients, whose recorded accomplishments are an indelible part of American history.

There was Sergeant Leopold Karpeles of the Fifty-seventh Massachusetts Infantry. He was wounded at the Battle of the Wilderness and decorated, "he having saved a part of the army from being captured during a retreat in disorder, by rallying troops around his colors." Benjamin B. Levy was sixteen when he enlisted as a drummer boy in the First New York Volunteers. His quick thinking and prompt action saved the steamer *Express* when it was attacked by the Confederate *Seabird*. Abraham Cohn, who enlisted as a private and was gradually promoted to adjutant, received the coveted medal because of "conspicuous gallantry displayed in the Battle of the Wilderness, in rallying and forming disorganized troops, under heavy fire; also for bravery and coolness in carrying orders to the advance lines under murderous fire in the Battle of the Mine, July 30, 1864." David Obranski of the Fifty-eighth Ohio Infantry was decorated "for distinguished bravery and coolness under heavy fire at Shiloh, Tennessee, and at Vicksburg, Mississippi." Henry Heller, Sixty-sixth Ohio Infantry, for daring bravery at Chancellorsville. Abraham Grunwalt, One hundred and fourth Ohio Infantry, for valor at Franklin, Tennessee. Corporal Isaac Gans, Second Ohio Cavalry, for capturing an enemy flag.[31]

There were the naval heroes too. Men like the sailor William Durst, who was aboard the *Monitor*. The Commander of that vessel was twice the recipient of a vote of thanks from Congress. Yet Admiral John Lorimer Worden insisted that Durst was worthy of recognition by Congress for his courage displayed during the historic engagement with the *Merrimac*, on the ninth of March in 1862.

Long after the War between the States was over, one of its non-Jewish officers, General Oliver O. Howard, wrote to Simon Wolf in recalling the war:

I had a Jewish Aide-de-Camp, one of the bravest and best, in the first battle of Bull Run; he is now a distinguished officer of the army, a man of high scientific attainment. I had another aide who was killed at the battle of Chancellorsville, a true friend and a brave officer. . . . So many of the German officers and men, the Poles and the Hungarians, were of Jewish lineage that I am unable to designate them.

The historian too is "unable to designate them." And unable to explain them as well. How explain an immigrant boy like Abraham Hart, who came to the United States when he was eighteen years old? He enlisted in 1861 at the age of thirty-one, serving in the Seventy-third Regiment of Pennsylvania Infantry. His rise from the ranks was rapid—lieutenant, captain, adjutant general. He volunteered to lead a squadron of picked men around the encampment of General "Stonewall" Jackson in order to ascertain the strength of the enemy at the Battle of Cross Keys. On another occasion he managed to rescue several hundred captured Union soldiers. "But perhaps Captain Hart's most important service was done at the second battle of Bull Run." For three heartbreaking days his Brigade fought back the heavy onslaughts of the enemy. The Brigade suffered cruel losses, among them their commanding officer, Colonel Koltes. It was then that Abraham Hart, German immigrant, loyal citizen, intrepid soldier, earned the respect and affection of the men with whom he fought. His leadership under fire was heroic.

And so the record reads. . . .

For five years the spirit of Lincoln brooded over the fate of the land he loved. From the time of his election until the unhappy hour of his death in a stranger's home, in a room so small that one wonders how it could have contained so great a soul, everything that happened near to or far from Washington, was in a measure related to him.

Lincoln was a man to capture the imagination of the Israelites of America. He was self-made. By his own efforts he rose above the handicaps which many of them knew, poverty and lack of status. He became the Moses of an enslaved Negro people. His words were the words a prophet would use, simple and strong, revealing a great heart, an understanding, gentle soul. He was compassionate as are those whose souls have been sorely tried. He was the champion of the underdog. He was the voice of the oppressed. He was the hope of the enslaved. So the Jews of the North who were on the side of the Union and who were antislavery zealots loved him—men like Bondi and Einhorn and Isaacs.

But we know that there were others. To make sweeping generalizations, to attempt to portray all Jews as enjoying a sweet unanimity of feeling, to write with wishful thinking and hindsight dictating conclusions, is as fatuous as it is inaccurate. *There was no unanimity.* We know men died both to preserve the Union and to save the Confederacy. They fought to free slaves and to keep them chattel. They were abolitionists and secessionists, and they sacrificed and suffered because of their beliefs.

The historian is no myth-maker.

There were Jews active in politics in Lincoln's day. There were electors who voted for him. There were rabbis who advocated his cause with fervor. Lincoln would have been less than he was—an astute politician, a capable organizer, a cautious statesman—to have overlooked his supporters no matter what their religion. He had his ear to the ground. When he blundered he could hear the rumblings of protest. He was human enough to bask in approbation. When in a speech made at Lafayette, Indiana, Lincoln referred to his principles as bound to Christianity, Jewish patriots protested. The *Israelite* mildly apologized for Lincoln saying that he had not yet mastered the "precise" use of words.[32]

Sandburg's *Abraham Lincoln* quoted the editor of the *Israelite* as saying:

Mr. Lincoln received the heaviest vote of infidels ever given to any man in this country. We do not believe there is a German infidel, American eccentric, spiritual rapper or atheist in the North States who did not vote for Mr. Lincoln. Let us see how much benefit he will derive from their Christianity. . . . He does not care for words. By and by he will learn the precise use and import of terms.

Again and again the same verbal slip occasioned indignant rejoinders from vigilant Jews. It was part of the greatness of Lincoln that he could and did learn to take into account the sacrifices and the zeal of the non-Christian minority in America.

When on the eleventh of February in 1861 Lincoln began his journey at Springfield, Illinois—a fateful journey which was to terminate forever in 1865—he received a present from Abraham Kohn of Chicago. It was a flag of the United States bearing across the face of it a Hebrew inscription from Joshua. Years later, another of our leaders destined for martyrdom, William McKinley, spoke feelingly of this gift and of its implications:

What more beautiful conception than that which prompted Abraham Kohn of Chicago . . . to send Mr. Lincoln, on the eve of his starting to

Washington . . . a flag of our country, bearing upon its silken folds these words from the first chapter of Joshua: "Have I not commanded thee? Be strong and of good courage." Could anything have given Mr. Lincoln mor' cheer, or been better calculated to sustain his courage or to strengthen his faith in the mighty work before him?

Perhaps this gift from one Abraham to another was symbolic. For did it not call attention to the common source of strength which the Christian Abraham and the Jewish Abraham shared? When in the bleak days of 1863 our Civil War President proclaimed a day of fasting and prayer, he declared only such sentiments as Americans of every faith could accept. And he valued the prayer no matter where spoken, in church or in synagogue. We owe to a chance visit which Adolphus S Solomons paid to the White House, one of the most precious of Lincoln anecdotes.

The day that Lincoln issued one of his early war proclamations I chanced to be at the White House with a distinguished New York Rabbi, Dr. Morris J. Raphall, who came to Washington to ask for the promotion of his son Alfred, from a second to a first lieutenancy in the army. The White House was closed for the day when we got there, but upon sending up my card we gained admittance and after Lincoln had heard the Rabbi's request he blurted out, "As God's minister is it not your first duty to be at home today to pray with your people for the success of our arms as is being done in every loyal church throughout the North, East and West?" The Rabbi, evidently ashamed at his *faux pas*, blushing made answer: "My assistant is doing that duty." "Ah," said Lincoln, "that is different." The President then drew forth a small card and wrote the following upon it:

"The Secretary of war will promote Second Lieutenant Raphall to a First Lieutenancy.

A. LINCOLN."

Handing the card to the Rabbi he said, with a smile all his own: "Now doctor, you can go home and do your own praying."[33]

Lincoln's friendship for still another Abraham is eloquent proof of his ability to rise to greatness while retaining enough "practical" qualities to redeem him from being a paragon and to endear him to us for being frail and full of human failings like ordinary men. Abraham Jonas was born in Exeter, England, in 1801. He died in Quincy, Illinois, a year before his friend in Washington. "A typical pioneer, he wandered from one frontier settlement to another." His wanderings prove him a restless, roving, adventurous spirit. Three years after his brother Joseph settled in Cincinnati, Abraham followed him there in 1819. Together they worked for the establishment of the Congregation of Beth Israel, the first in the West. He assisted in the cemetery-purchasing project. Jonas had itching feet. He moved on to Kentucky, where he served in the State Legislature and became the Grand Master of the Masons of Kentucky. Then Illinois beckoned. He moved to Quincy, studied law and supported himself meanwhile by running a store. In 1842 he was elected to the Illinois Legislature and the following year was admitted to the bar. He was the first Grand Master of Masons in the State. Three Presidents, Taylor, Fillmore and Lincoln, appointed him as postmaster of Quincy.

Jonas had long known Lincoln. They met in 1834 when the opponents of Jackson were becoming vocal and when their opposition was crystallizing into the new Whig party. They met again in 1842 in Springfield as fellow legislators. From the first, Jonas was Lincoln's ardent admirer. In 1856 he worked hard to have his friend nominated as the Presidential candidate of the Republican party. Failing in that, Jonas followed Lincoln throwing himself heart and soul into the Frémont campaign. It was Abraham Jonas who presided at the meeting in Quincy which was one of the chain of the Lincoln-Douglas debates. Whenever Abe Lincoln chanced to be in Quincy he made himself at home in the office of Abe Jonas, and it was to him that he wrote a lengthy explanation of his stand on the Know-Nothing movement. "The Know-Nothing party was the most curious development in our political life," says Muzzey. "It originated in 1852 as a protest against foreign influence in our politics. It was more like a lodge, or secret order, than a political party." It had been nurtured in the hotbed of political confusion. Men joined "because they had no other place to go. Thus that queer secret society actually carried several states in the elections of 1854 and 1855." But Jonas was touchy on the subject and with good cause. He wrote to his friend in Springfield demanding an explanation. Here it is:

Confidential

SPRINGFIELD, ILLS. July 21, 1860

Hon. A. Jonas

MY DEAR SIR

Yours of the 20th. is received. I suppose as good, or even better, men than I may have been in American, or Know-Nothing lodges; but in point of fact, I never was in one, at Quincy, or elsewhere. I was never in Quincy but one day and two nights, while Know-Nothing lodges were in existence, and you were with me that day and both those nights. I had never been there before in my life; and never afterwards, till the joint debate with Douglas in 1858. It was in 1854, when I spoke in some Hall there, and after the speaking, you, with others, took me to an oyster saloon, passed an hour there, and you walked with me to, and parted with me at, the Quincy-House, quite late at night. I left by stage for Naples before day-light in the morning, having come in by the same route, after dark, the evening previous to the speaking, when I found you waiting at the Quincy House to meet me. A few days after I was there, Richardson, as I understood, started this same story about my having been in a Know-Nothing lodge. When I heard of the charge, as I did soon after, I taxed my recollection for some incident which could have suggested it; and I remembered that on parting with you the last night, I went to the Office of the Hotel to take my stage passage for the morning, was told that no stage office for that line was kept there, and that I must see the driver, before retiring, to insure his calling for me in the morning; and a servant was sent with me to find the driver, who after taking me a square or two, stopped me, and stepped perhaps a dozen steps farther, and in my hearing called to some one, who answered him apparently from the upper part of a building, and promised to call with the stage for me at the Quincy House. I returned and went to bed; and before day the stage called and took me. This is all.

That I never was in a Know-Nothing lodge in Quincy, I should expect, could be easily proved, by respectable men, who were always in the lodges and never saw me there.

An affidavit of one or two such would put the matter at rest.

And now, a word of caution. Our adversaries think they can gain a point, if they could force me to openly deny the charge by which some degree of offence would be given to the Americans. For this reason, it must not publicly appear that I am paying any attention to the charge.

Yours truly

A. Lincoln[34]

The friendship was unimpaired. It was a mark of Lincoln's greatness that the knowledge that the Quincy postmaster had sons fighting for the Confederacy did not lessen his esteem. To be sure, Edward Jonas fought with the Fiftieth Illinois Infantry. But the other sons were all arrayed against the Union. Did that hasten the death of Abe Jonas of Illinois? It would not be farfetched to suppose that it did. When Abe was dying in Quincy in the final months of the war, he kept calling for his son Charles. Charles H. Jonas had fought with the Twelfth Arkansas Regiment and was a prisoner of war. Mrs. Jonas sent a telegram to the President pleading that Charles be allowed to visit his father. Lincoln immediately acceded. The official order reads:

Allow Charles H. Jonas now a prisoner of war at Johnson's island a parole of three weeks to visit his dying father, Abraham Jonas, at Quincy, Ills.

June 2nd 1864.

A. LINCOLN[35]

It was one of many compassionate acts. It must have gratified his Jewish admirers. They were numerous. There was Rabbi Sabato Morais. There was Rabbi Liebman Adler of Chicago, whose only son was fighting in an Illinois regiment. There was Abraham Arnold of the Maryland Republican Committee. There was Michael Heilprin. There was Rabbi Bernhard Felsenthal. There was Philip J. Joachimsen, who secured the first conviction for slave-trading while serving as assistant district attorney of New York.

Now that so many young Jews were fighting in the ranks, the time surely had come for them to have a chaplain of their own faith to minister to them in their last rites of passage on the battlefield and in the hospitals and over their graves in the military cemeteries. The Cameron Dragoons, a New York regiment with many Jewish soldiers in its ranks, was selected for particular attention. In 1861 the Secretary of War was confronted with an application from Rabbi Arnold Fischel, who had been for five years in the service of the Congregation Shearith Israel, asking for a chaplaincy.[36] The law was explicit. Chaplains must be clergymen. The application was denied. The vigilant Board of Delegates of American Israelites lost no time in rushing to the defense of so righteous a cause. Both the President and Congress were speedily memorialized. Their claims were set forth. There was so little time to be lost. The casualty lists played no favorites. Dr. Fischel was busy at the bedside of many a wounded soldier. He was working by the side of Christian chaplains. He was writing reports.

But this was not enough. Rabbi Fischel went to Washington to call on the President. He was armed with letters of introduction and high purpose. The cause was just. He met the President. Here is his description of that meeting:

Having obtained important letters of introduction to Senators, I started for Washington, where I arrived on Tuesday evening, and went at once to work to obtain an interview with the President. . . . I called this morning at ten o'clock at the White House, where hundreds of people were anxiously waiting for admission, some of whom told me that they had been for three days awaiting their turn. I was, nevertheless, at once invited to his room and was received with marked courtesy. After having

read the letter of the Board and delivered to him several letters of introduction, he questioned me on various matters connected with this subject and then told me that he fully admitted the justice of my remarks,
that he believed the exclusion of Jewish chaplains to have been altogether
unintentional on the part of Congress, and agreed that something ought
to be done to meet this case.[87]

But Lincoln was not content with verbal assurances. He gave the
subject his careful consideration and then wrote to Rabbi Fischel on
December 14, 1861.

EXECUTIVE MANSION, Dec. 14, 1861

Rev. Dr. A Fischel.

MY DEAR SIR.—I find there are several particulars in which the present law in regard to chaplains is supposed to be deficient, all which I
now design presenting to the appropriate Committee of Congress. I shall
try to have a new law broad enough to cover what is desired by you in
behalf of the Israelites.

Yours truly,

A. LINCOLN.[88]

On the twelfth of March, 1862, Congress amended the law to permit Jewish as well as Christian clergymen to serve as chaplains.

The next issue which once more united the Jews of the Union was
far more involved, more drawn out, more acutely painful to consider.
It left great repercussions. Like every smear campaign it tarred all
within its range. It involved smugglers and blockade-runners and war-
speculators of whom a few were Jews.

Wars breed great heroes. Men rise to unsuspected heights of courage and sacrifice. Life is held less precious than valor. Privation and
suffering are willingly endured. Danger and capture are faced for
the sake of an injured comrade. But war also breeds hatred and
prejudice. In its wake profiteers spring up like toadstools. Great
fortunes are made while some men die and the survivors' hearts are
broken. Mankind is an instrument on which both harmony and dis-
cord may be played. There is the sound of marching feet walking to
glory. There is the furtive clang of gold as it passes at night from one
trembling hand to another. There is the sibilance of whispered plots
of profiteers. In high places and in low, in Washington and on the
fringes of military establishments, the vultures and the carrion crows
await the feast. The evidence of greed and corruption is abundant
and nonsectarian. In the pages of *The Rise of American Civilization*,
a brilliant and exhaustive study in which the Jews are accorded but
microscopic recognition, we find the following astute summary:

The armed combat which called forth so much heroism and sacrifice was accompanied by all those darker manifestations of the human spirit that always mark great wars: corruption in high places, cold and cynical profiteering, extravagance and heartless frivolity. Before six months had passed, the air of Washington was murky with charges of fraud. . . . An eminent authority estimated that from one-fifth to one-fourth of the money paid out of the federal treasury was tainted with the tricks of swindlers.[89]

The Northern blockade was repeatedly violated by cotton traders. It was easy to recognize the Jews among them. Many were newly arrived. Their language and manners and clothing often made them conspicuous. In November of 1862 Grant wrote two letters. This was followed in December by an official order. Here are the documents.

LA GRANGE, TENN., November 9, 1862

Major-General Hurlbut, Jackson, Tenn:

Refuse all permits to come south of Jackson for the present. The Israelites especially should be kept out.

What troops have you now, exclusive of Stevenson's brigade?

U. S. GRANT,
Major-General

LA GRANGE, TENN., November 10, 1862

General Webster, Jackson, Tenn.:

Give orders to all the conductors on the road that no Jews are to be permitted to travel on the railroad southward from any point. They may go north and be encouraged in it; but they are such an intolerable nuisance that the department must be purged of them.

U. S. GRANT,
Major-General

General Orders,   )   HDQRS. THIRTEENTH A. C. DEPT.
     No. 11.   )   OF THE TENN.

HOLLY SPRINGS, December 17, 1862

The Jews, as a class violating every regulation of trade established by the Treasury Department and also department orders, are hereby expelled from the department within twenty-four hours from the receipt of this order.

Post commanders will see that all of this class of people be furnished passes and required to leave, and any one returning after such notification will be arrested and held in confinement until an opportunity occurs of sending them out as prisoners, unless furnished with permit from headquarters.

No passes will be given these people to visit headquarters for the purpose of making personal applications for trade permits.

By order of MAJ.-GEN. U. S. GRANT.

JNO. A. RAWLINGS,

Assistant Adjutant-General[40]

To say that the Jews of the Union were aroused is to put it mildly. The fathers and mothers of the boys in uniform, Christian and Jew, were indignant. The *New York Times* called it "one of the deepest sensations of the war." November and December were black months for the Jews of the North whose hearts and whose sons were with the Union. There were meetings of protest. There were resolutions, letters, speeches of indignation. Captain Ferdinand Levy of the New York Volunteers wrote to the *Jewish Messenger* that General Grant should be compelled by Lincoln to apologize or be forced to resign from the service. The Jews were vocal. They took their pens in hand and deluged those in high places. So one Israelite was to write during the course of the war a defense not only of American Jews but of their coreligionists abroad who had been accused of favoring the Confederacy.

And now, General, permit me to go over a little broader ground, and show the influence Israelites abroad have exercised for the benefit of our beloved Union. Loving liberty as their very life, the Jewish "bankers and merchants" of Europe have, without exception, stood by the Union. It does not require a vivid imagination to portray the extent of the injury the cause of the Union must have sustained, had the Jewish capitalists turned a friendly ear to the importunities of southern statesmen, ambassadors and agents, and assisted the Confederates *in that which was their greatest strait*—the supply of money.[41]

The clergy were as one in this. Rabbi Isaac Mayer Wise was burning up the pages of the *Israelite* with righteous indignation. The Jews of Ohio and Kentucky were aroused when these orders were put into effect. The matter reached Congress. Markens submits the following summary of the *Congressional Globe's* account of the proceedings:

Mr. Powell, according to the *Congressional Globe*, then addressed the Senate. He had in his possession, he said, documents that would go to establish the fact beyond the possibility of a doubt that some thirty Jewish gentlemen, residents of Paducah, were driven from their homes and their business by virtue of this order of General Grant. They had only the short notice of four and twenty hours. The Jewish women and children of the city were expelled under that order. Not a Jew, man, woman or child was left, except two women who were prostrate on beds of sickness.

"If we tamely submit to allow the military power thus to encroach on the rights of the citizens we shall be setting a bad and most pernicious example to those in command of our Army."[42]

The Jews of Paducah were mobilized in a passionate unit of moral indignation. For in Kentucky venerable Jewish pioneers had lived and reared families. Michael Gratz, father of Rebecca was no stranger there. Benjamin Gratz, her brother, whose son Cary had died in combat, was a citizen of this State. Benjamin Gratz was the second president of the Kentucky Railroad. Vast landholdings and stately mansions had conferred status and rank, dignity and prestige on these men. So close was the co-operation and so frequent was intermarriage that fewer States in America show the phenomenon of assimilation, absorption and obliteration so strikingly put into practice. Not all, however, were among the bankers and the landed gentry. In 1832 there was the ubiquitous Benevolent Society in lieu of a formal religious group. In 1836 Polish and German Jews lacking the social graces and the wealth of their native coreligionists came to Kentucky. They settled in Louisville, elevated a *shochet* to the leadership of the newly formed rabbinate. In 1843 the Congregation Adas Israel was established. But a military order is no respecter of bankrolls or of rolling acres. It is resented as hotly at the cobbler's bench as at the counting house.

The Jews of Paducah next memorialized Lincoln:

PADUCAH, KY., Dec. 29, 1862

Hon. Abraham Lincoln, President of the United States.

General Order No. 11 issued by General Grant at Oxford, Miss., December the 17th, commands all post commanders to expel all Jews without distinction within twenty-four hours from his entire Department. The undersigned good and loyal citizens of the United States and residents of this town, for many years engaged in legitimate business as merchants, feel greatly insulted and outraged by this inhuman order; the carrying out of which would be the grossest violation of the Constitution and our rights as good citizens under it, and would place us, besides a large number of other Jewish families of this town, as outlaws before the world. We respectfully ask your immediate attention to this enormous outrage on all law and humanity and pray for your effectual and immediate interposition. We would especially refer you to the post commander and post adjutant as to our loyalty, and to all respectable citizens of this community as to our standing as citizens and merchants. We respectfully ask for immediate instructions to be sent to the Commander of this Post.

D. WOLFF & BROS
C. F. KASKEL
J. W. KASKEL[43]

They elected a champion appropriately named Cesar. Cesar Kaskel, one of the signers of the appeal to the President, was a member of the "gentry." He was the vice-president of the Paducah Union League Club. He was fortified with numerous letters of introduction, one of them from Rabbi Max Lilienthal. Cesar Kaskel reached Washington on January 3, 1863. He saw the President the same day. Lincoln listened thoughtfully, with his customary patience and with the twinkle in his eye that was so characteristic of him said, "And so the children of Israel were driven from the happy land of Canaan?"

Cesar Kaskel bowed to the President. "Yes. They have come to Father Abraham's bosom to seek protection."

Father Abraham came through magnificently. "And this protection they shall have." He seated himself at his desk and picking up a pen drafted an order revoking the blanket indictment of a brave minority.

The following day from the offices of the War Department a letter went out to Grant.

WAR DEPARTMENT,
WASHINGTON, January 4, 1863

Major-General Grant,
   Holly Springs, Miss.

A paper purporting to be General Orders, No. 11, issued by you December 17, has been presented here. By its terms it expels all Jews from your department.

If such an order has been issued, it will be immediately revoked.

H. W. HALLECK,
General-in-Chief

The same channels which had been utilized to carry the calumny now were used to carry the retraction. It was a victory brilliantly executed. It showed the innate fairness of the people of America and their complete awareness of the technique of the deserved apology.

Circular.

HDQRS. THIRTEENTH A. C., DEPT OF THE TENN.

HOLLY SPRINGS, Miss., January 7, 1863.

By direction of General-in-Chief of the Army, at Washington, the general order from these headquarters expelling Jews from the department is hereby revoked.

By order of MAJ.-GEN. U. S. GRANT.

JNO. A. RAWLINGS,
Assistant Adjutant-General[44]

But the matter did not end here. The outraged pride of American Israelites once ruffled continued to look out for slights, overt or covert. Christians in every walk of life were the recipients of letters which explained, cited, enumerated the merits of the Jewish case. Lincoln had objected to Order Number 11, said Halleck, because it is "in terms [which] proscribed an entire religious class, some of whom are fighting in our ranks." It was a good thing for the country. For it brought the minority and majority face to face and caused each to appraise the other. In 1864 the highhanded General B. F. Butler was a party to such a correspondence with M. S. Isaacs. The General had used the term "Jew" loosely. It called forth quite an avalanche of definitions.

I regret to find so grievous a misconception or rather conflict of ideas as to the meaning of the term "Jew." I do not propose trespassing upon your patience by argument or illustration, farther than this: I am a native American, and proud of it—I attend Synagogue, and believe in the principles of Judaism, and am therefore a Jew in the sense that you are a Christian; yet I am an American in nationality. . . . In literary and scientific circles, you find the Israelite as well as the Christian. The army, navy and marine corps, have a fair representation of Israelites, some of them distinguished, earnest and patriotic. One of our regiments, which served first as militia, then as a three-year regiment, and is now home on furlough to return to the field a veteran organization, is composed mainly of Israelites. If, at any time, you should desire to be informed of the extent of your error with regard to the occupations of the Jews, I should be most happy to furnish you with details.[45]

Nor did the matter end for Ulysses S. Grant. Order Number 11 was to dog him all of his life. The *New York Times* had said editorially:

The order, to be sure, was promptly set aside by the President, but the affront to the Jews conveyed by its issue, was not so easily effaced. A committee of Jews took it upon themselves to *thank* President Lincoln at Washington for so promptly annulling the odious order. Against the conduct of this committee the bulk of the Jews vehemently protest. They say they have no thanks for an act of simple and imperative justice— but grounds for deep and just complaint against the Government, that General Grant has not been dismissed from the service.[46]

Grant himself was hard put to it to explain his action. The good old American game of passing the buck was played, with the responsibility shifted from one pair of shoulders to another. Grant recalled that he had many Jewish friends. He let the fact be known. He appealed to them for corroboration.[47] Had he not always been scrupulously impartial as a man and as an officer? Was there the slightest evidence in his record to prove that he was anything but a friend of the Jews? He wrote to Congressman Morris of Illinois in 1868, still explaining, still protesting his friendship for the Jews and claiming his impartiality as an officer:

At the time of its publication, I was incensed by a reprimand received from Washington for permitting acts which Jews within my lines were engaged in. There were many other persons within my lines equally bad with the worst of them. . . . The order was issued and sent without any reflection and without thinking of the Jews as a sect or race to themselves, but simply as persons who had successfully (I say successfully instead of persistently, because there were plenty of others within my lines who envied their success) violated an order, which greatly inured to the help of the rebels.

Give Mr. Moses assurance that I have no prejudice against sect or race, but want each individual to be judged by his own merit. Order No. 11 does not sustain this statement, I admit, but then I do not sustain that order. It never would have been issued if it had not been telegraphed the moment it was penned, and without reflection.[48]

Years later when Simon Wolf, author of *The American Jew as Patriot, Soldier and Citizen*, met President Grant, after his first election, and the two were engaged in a cozy fireside chat, the subject came up again. It was "a long and interesting conversation," says Wolf. It seems that the report really came from

General Sherman, who had complained that there were a large number of citizens, especially Jews, who were violating the rules and laws of war in running the blockade and in purchasing cotton contrary to law, and that it was demoralizing and proving very injurious to the service, in consequence of which, in the absence of General Grant, the order was made by one of the staff officers, but, unfortunately, bore the name of General Grant, and he never would state the facts as here given, simply because he did not wish any one, as he stated, to suppose that he was seeking public applause; he would rather suffer in silence.[49]

"Father Abraham," in whom the Jews had found an unfailing friend, was shot by an assassin on the fourteenth day of April in 1865. The Jews of the land mourned him as they would a father. Seven thousand Jews of New York City marched in solemn columns in the procession which numbered fifty thousand mourners of all faiths. The Masons were there in full regalia. So were the members of B'nai Mosheh and B'nai B'rith. But it was the Free Sons of Israel whose mournful placard told the story of their loss and of their devotion:

> The Father of his Country is Dead,
> The Nation Mourns him.
> LINCOLN
> He is not dead but he still lives in
> the hearts of the Nation.[50]

On the sabbath following his death, April 15, in the oldest synagogue in North America, Shearith Israel, the *Hashkabah*, the Sephardic prayer for the dead, was recited for the first time for one not of the stock of Abraham. "Father Abraham" had achieved honorary membership in the clan. It was the deepest oblation. It was the highest accolade.

CHAPTER XII

An Age of Titans
and Anonymous Men

-»» The course of instruction comprises, Religion; the Hebrew, the English, the German and French, Languages, in
all their branches; the Ancient and Modern History of the
World; Geography, Mathematics, Book-keeping, Composition, Writing . . . also Drawing, Music and Dancing, when
required.
*The Reverend Dr. Lilienthal advertises a "Hebrew and
Classical Boarding School . . . for the instruction of
Jewish Youth."*

—*Asmonean*, October 24, 1851[1] «««

JEWS OF America were part of the total scene. But they also wove
their own patterns.

"The fortunes of the pilgrim people scattered in all the countries
of the civilized world are organically connected with the fortunes of
the most representative nations and states, and with manifold tendencies of human thought."[2] Thus Dubnow. It is of these fortunes and
these tendencies that we would now write. They are mirrored in several publications. From the pages of the *Asmonean* and the *Occident*,
we may glean the main harvest which relates us not only to the Jews
of America, but to all Americans.

American Jewish journalism has an interesting history in the nineteenth century. In the year 1823, *The Jew*, the first American Jewish
periodical, saw the light of day. For two years it carried on a sturdy
campaign designed to keep Jews safe from the blandishments of missionaries. Its editor was Solomon H. Jackson, who was related to
Mordecai Manuel Noah. Another short-lived journalistic venture was
Israel's Herold, which lasted for three months in 1849. The twelve
numbers of *Israel's Herold*, published in German, were a valiant attempt on the part of Isidor Bush to transplant some of the brave new

296

ideas of the days of the revolutions in Europe. Its general theme was to be the dissemination of "truth," particularly as it applied to revealed religion. A secondary purpose was the establishment of harmony in Judaism. "Just as there are no two faces exactly alike, so are there also no two types of thinking alike," said Bush, attempting the impossible, the achievement of ideological harmony in the ranks of Jewry in spite of deep cleavages. These were but the forerunners. Other publications soon followed. Rabbi Samuel M. Isaacs began the publication of the *Jewish Messenger* in 1857. *The Hebrew Leader* was begun two years later. The *Jewish Record*, founded in 1862, was an orthodox paper. It devoted considerable space to news of clubs and fraternal organizations. It was later merged with *The Hebrew Leader*. During the Civil War *The Hebrew* in California was begun contemporaneously with the *Jewish Record* in New York.[3]

American Jewish life was constantly renewed and revitalized by European Jewish scholarship. There was Rabbi Max Lilienthal, whose ambitious advertisement for scholars appears in the pages of a New York periodical, the *Asmonean*. His boyhood was spent in Germany. As a student he was exposed to the scholarly Jewish weekly published in Germany, the *Allgemeine Zeitung des Judenthums*, founded in 1837.[4] The paper became very influential in Central and Western Europe. It had been in existence three years when Lilienthal was summoned to Russia. There he was to work with Nissan Rosenthal in Vilna and other cities, their purpose to reorganize the Jewish schools. The educational reform mission met with indifferent results. So our pilgrim wended his way to New York, and a private school for boys.

Other intellectual pilgrims, similarly influenced, came to America, some to found schools, some to occupy pulpits, others to become editors of Anglo-Jewish weeklies—all of them more or less modeled on the successful *Allgemeine Zeitung des Judenthums*. It was no accident surely that all the founders and editors of the Anglo-Jewish periodicals had been immigrants, that all of them had come from Europe. The Jewish members of the writing craft before the coming of immigrant journalists were people like Noah, Harby, Penina Moïse, Carvalho, the last three born in Charleston, the first in Philadelphia.[5] Totally different in background and experience was English-born Robert Lyon, founder of the *Asmonean*, the first major weekly of Jewish interest. Isaac Leeser, editor of the *Occident and American Jewish Advocate* was born in Germany. Samuel Myer Isaacs, editor of the *Jewish Messenger*, came from Holland. Isaac Mayer Wise, of the *American Israelite*, was a native of Bohemia.

Robert Lyon[6] was born in London in 1810. He was meant to be a merchant but from the first it was writing that fascinated him. He was a man of parts. In addition to being treasurer of the synagogue in Maiden Lane, he was elected by his congregation to accompany Baron Goldsmid to wait on Queen Victoria and present her with the felicitations of the synagogue on the occasion of her marriage. The reasons for his leaving England for America are obscure. There are many gaps in the biography. His personality was pleasing. He was "irreproachable in his private character, cultured and refined," writes Morais. His weekly, begun in 1849, was sprightly, well written, honest in point of view. It had decided character, marked with the traits of its founder, with "dignity and ability." It was humane, alert, responsive. For nine years Robert Lyon also edited the New York *Mercantile Journal*. Then his untimely death cut short both publications. To posterity, he left the *Asmonean*. To its pages we now turn. It is the crystal pool which reflects the life and manners, anecdotes and opinions, folkways and mores of a vanished generation.

The *Asmonean* describes itself as "A Family Journal of Commerce, Politics, Religion and Literature, Devoted to the Interests of American Israelites." Part of its usefulness lies in its advertising columns. Consider the issue of October 10, 1851. The "New Mourning Store" advertises its somber wares. Adams & Co. announces its schedule for the Great Western & Southern Express. Jewelry is offered for sale. Musical instruments are purchasable. A "Day and Boarding School" has room for additional pupils. The editorials and articles offer diversified reading. For the intelligentsia there is an article on "The American Indian." For the pious, a discussion of the "Efficacy of Prayer." The subject of religion is one of constant concern. On November 9, 1849, there is a letter from Rabbi Wise praising the editor for his offer to co-operate with Isaac Leeser in the cause of Jewish unity. There is some speculation about Heine's return to Judaism. There is a summary of the activities of Jewish Philanthropic Societies. News of Jews abroad is given considerable space. Prayer books are offered for sale. Current events are summarized. Finally excerpts from non-Jewish periodicals in which there are references to Jews, are given.

On December 6, 1850, there is an appropriate quotation from Byron, one which may well be the theme song of the Pilgrim People:

Tribes of the wandering foot and weary breast,
How shall ye flee away and be at rest?
The wild dove has her nest, the fox his cave,
Mankind their country,—Israel but a grave!

There are articles on "Hebrew Poetry in the Middle Ages." On "Talmudical Ethics." On "Biblical Astronomy." They are for the "elite." For the average reader, other fare. Hats and clothing and patent medicines and smoked meats are advertised. Also "Lyon's Magnetic Powder." The issue of February 22, 1850, offers varied reading. "The Position of Israel's Women" is explored. "Intolerance in the 19th Century" is analyzed, perennial subject with endless variations. Furriers, clothiers, confectioners and bakers proclaim their wares. The following year reduced rates to California entice the readers of the *Asmonean*. Watches and drygoods and harps are offered for sale. So are furniture, life insurance and pill boxes. Importers of European goods are much in evidence. Discreetly Miss R. Lazarus announces her qualifications as "Teacher of Piano Forte." Readers are exposed to many nostrums, salves, ointments and sundry drugs: "All-Healing Ointment," "Beal's Hair Restorative," "March's Superior Pain Reliever," "Hutching's Dyspepsia Bitters," "Canton Chinese Hair Creme," "H. U. Bush's Celebrated Renovating Aromatic Cordial," "Professor Alexander C. Barry's Tricopherous or Medicated Compound." Advertisements occupy increasingly greater space; soon they are found on the first page.

A Mr. Rosenfeld of 240 Bleeker Street, wants "a young lady of good address to attend a Lace and Trimming Store. Also a Miss from 12 to 15 years of age, to learn the business, a German preferred."

Education is very much in the foreground. The Reverend Dr. Max Lilienthal proclaims his school, "The Hebrew Commercial and Classical Boarding School," with a flourish. His pupils are required to speak the language of their English, French and German teachers. They are given many opportunities to acquire polish and the social graces. Nor are girls neglected, thanks to the indefatigable Misses Palache, who proudly announce that since 1841 they have conducted a "Boarding and Day School for Young Ladies of the JEWISH FAITH," at 97 Thompson Street.

Could Robert Lyon have been writing with an eye to the future when he issued this announcement to his advertisers?

Not only is the Asmonean, The Organ of the 200,000 Jews of America, but it includes among its subscribers, a large and increasing body of Unitarians, besides a great number of the German Citizens of the United

States. Our Journal therefore presents an unusually eligible medium for Advertisements of a Commercial, Literary, Musical, Theatrical, and Miscellaneous character.

Reluctantly we are compelled to deduce that Mr. Lyon's readers were by nature a race of hypochondriacs. For they are worried about falling hair. They need the bolstering effects of "celebrated renovating cordials." They are addicted to trusses. They are offered "A Balsam so curative that it has Death and Doctors Baffled." A Dr. Tobias turns out to be a savior, for his Venetian Liniment has actually cured 10,000 Persons!

What did our ancestors do before the techniques of psychoanalysis were perfected? They went to phrenologists. Not just the gullible ones had their cranial bumps analyzed, but men like Charles Dickens, women like George Eliot. It is not surprising that the readers of the *Asmonean* are told by a phrenologist that, "These mental portraits are becoming almost as common and indispensable as a daguerreotype of the outer man, while as a guide to self-improvement and success in life, they are invaluable."

On December 26, 1851, a subscriber would find the editorial content of the *Asmonean* stimulating. There is a summary of a damage suit headed "The Modern Inquisition Foiled." "Is the American Eagle Asleep?" asks the editor? He is referring to "the atrocious outrage perpetrated by the Spanish authorities" on the person of an American citizen. There is an article on California which would shock its much-publicized chamber of commerce. We learn that, "California has now come to be looked upon as not only a habitable but a desirable place of residence."

The editor decries "Cliquism" in Jewish circles. For the Sephardim do not mix with Ashkenazim. He objects with vigor to "every prejudice of country so rife among the Hebrews of New York." He says astutely, "We knew of no difference between Poles—Bavarians—Hollanders—Englishmen or Frenchmen." It is a lesson the Jews of America have yet to learn. A century later it still divides and separates them!

The Hebrew Congregation of Mobile is looking for a "minister and Teacher." The Congregation Rodoph Shalom is looking for a *shochet*. The Congregation B'nai Israel offers for sale "a set of five handsome bronzed chandeliers." Salem Fields Cemetery advertises Family Burial Plots. A Jewish Dispensary is being readied for patients at 31 Bleeker Street. Dr. M. L. M. Peixotto and a group of other physicians have joined "for the Gratuitous Medical and Surgical treatment of sick and destitute Israelites."

In October of 1852 an employment agency advertises "Good servants," adding that "the best of Irish help is always on hand."

In the fall of the year Robert Lyon discusses "The Judaism of the Future." The Jew, writes the astute editor, was able to sustain ancient suffering because of his conviction of the justice of his cause. It is possible that "centuries of miseries and oppressions had almost caused the Jew to forget the eternal truth" of the tenets of his faith. Rabbi Wise contributes an article advocating the shortening of services. For rabbis are overtired. Proper decorum can be better maintained with shorter services.

In late summer of 1853, distant places beckon. The *Fly Away* and *Heloise* are sailing for Australia. The *Onward, Wide Awake, Siam* and *Sweepstakes* are scheduled to depart for San Francisco. The Broadway Theater announces that Mr. Forrest, the American Tragedian, will "perform one of his Favorite Characters Every Evening this Week." In November 1853, *Othello* and *Richard III* are to be performed at the Broadway Theater. There is a description of Jews in China. An Englishman "lately arrived . . . wants a position as Chazan-Teacher."

The Jews' Hospital of New York is scheduled for a cornerstone laying ceremony on Thanksgiving Day. The President of the Hospital is Sampson Simson. The Secretary is Theodore F. Seixas. On March 24, 1854, an editorial compares the two interesting rites of passage for adolescents—confirmation and Bar Mitzvah. A biography of Moses Mendelssohn by G. M. Cohen is announced. Gradually the infiltration of German-speaking Jews is recognized by the appearance of an occasional article in German. The position of Jews in Palestine is not overlooked by the editor. There is another article on Heinrich Heine. The Laws and Customs of Israel are constantly expounded. A lottery is advertised. Food for the ailing and the gullible, the dull and the bright. . . .

In May, in the year 1824, a young man of eighteen arrived at Richmond, Virginia. Isaac Leeser, recent graduate of the Münster Gymnasium, an earnest, pious youth taking a serious view of the world, of the plight of Jews and of himself, came to work for his uncle, in what was euphoniously called a "mercantile establishment."[7] His days were spent there but it was "mental culture" he wanted. So his evenings were devoted to "literary pursuits." He immediately identified himself with the leaders of the little Jewish community. He taught without charge "the younger portion" of the congregation, serving as assistant to Rabbi Isaac B. Seixas. He read omnivorously.

So it was that he came across a series of articles in the *London Quarterly Review*. These "slanderous productions" defaming the character of his people and his faith so aroused our protagonist that he submitted a rebuttal to the local paper. It was quite a feat for someone who had but a four-year knowledge of the English language. "The circumstance related," writes Morais sadly, "clearly indicates the state of religious learning in America, when the defence of Judaism had to be assumed by an obscure young man." As a result of the "vindication," the "obscure" young man was discovered by the Congregation Mickvé Israel of Philadelphia. He was modest and not sure of himself. But his uncle and his many friends prevailed on him to accept the post of Hazan and minister. He had energy, ideas and the courage to try the new—the preaching of sermons in English. He continued studying and writing. One of his books, *The Jews and the Mosaic Law*, was a collection of some of his antidefamation articles. He published a Catechism and edited the works of Grace Aguilar and Hesther Rothschild. Nothing could tempt him from his work. He published textbooks, translated prayer books, edited his sermons. He translated the Bible from the Hebrew into English. He helped Rebecca Gratz begin a Sunday School. It is to her sprightly and facile pen that we are indebted for our best description of Isaac Leeser and to our knowledge of the reasons for the absence of any romantic interludes in his biography.

He must have been a grievous disappointment to the young women of the fashionable Philadelphia synagogue. In a letter dated November 4, 1829, Rebecca writes of

our young pastor who is certainly more attractive to those who are indifferent to the *outer Man*—there is a witticism on record of a mean looking sage, who in reply to a high born damsels remark on the freak of nature in placing so much wisdom in so ugly a creature, demanded what kind of vessel her father kept his wine in—she said a common earthen, for wine kept in precious metal became sour—he observed wisdom is safest with ugliness—for there are fewer provokatives to *vanity*—which is an enemy of wisdom—this anecdote is mostly applied to Mr. Leeser—who is ugly & awkward—but so sensible & pleasant as well as pious—that all the old ladies are charmed, while the girls are obliged to persuade themselves to be pleasant.[8]

Rebecca was nearing fifty when she wrote these lines. Her objectivity may be trusted as she could look on and laugh at the pious enthusiasm of the old women and the forced politeness of the young.

Providence continued to treat Mr. Leeser like a stepchild. His outward appearance, always unprepossessing, now was made worse. To a shy, sensitive person like Leeser it must have been a crushing blow. Rebecca writes in 1834:

There is another evil under the sun that has been making havoc in our city varioloid—poor Mr. Leeser is one of its present subjects, his attack has been unmitigated small pox, and tho his life & eye sight have been spared I am told his countenance will bear many marks of his ravages— he has always been so sensitive on the subject of personal disadvantages —that his former humility will appear like vanity to his present state— and unless some Desdemona shall arise to see his visage in his mind—all his future expectations must be confined to solitary studies.[9]

Her predictions were correct. He must have compensated for his lack of social charm by ceaseless hard work, for only so may we account for the energy and productivity of his ensuing years. He often worked himself to the point of sickness. Leeser developed a great eloquence in the pulpit. He traveled widely all over the United States, "everywhere *exhibiting his eloquence,* obviously to the spiritual advantage of his hearers."

Since he could not found a family, he founded clubs, societies, committees, a college, a periodical. The Hebrew Education Society, the Board of Hebrew Ministers, the Jewish Hospital, the Maimonides College, the Board of Delegates of American Israelites, the American Jewish Publication Society—these are some of the causes he helped to promote.

There may have been times when he must have thought himself, like Job, especially singled out for trouble. "In the previous fire poor Mr. Leeser lost several thousands of dollars in books," writes Rebecca Gratz. He heard of a convert to Christianity, and "the novelty of a Jew preaching the Gospel is irresistible," wrote Rebecca. Isaac Leeser went to hear him only to be plagued by the consequences. It seems that Mr. Leeser "was simple enough to write him a note in hebrew, pointing out some misquotations . . . which he turned to good account, by reading from his pulpit as from a Rabbi, wishing him to retract."

Rabbi Leeser had many friends and admirers. "Indeed, few persons can bear comparison with him who is revered for his self-sacrificing devotion and unremitting labor." For seven years Leeser was, by his own choice, without a pulpit. In 1857 some of his friends persuaded him to head another synagogue in Philadelphia. His ceaseless activities alternated with "spells of sickness." But his zest for work was undiminished until the end. He died February 1, 1868. "Thus, the

Hebrews of America were deprived of a bold champion, a staunch friend, and a great benefactor," wrote one of his contemporaries, about a decade later. The record he left may be read in the pages of the *Occident* and *American Jewish Advocate*, an enduring, imperishable monument of twenty-six volumes.

From the first issue our attention is aroused. Julius Stern, a German Jew, "being convinced that the Israelites of Germany do not enjoy the full privileges of citizens," suggests that a number of them emigrate to America, there to "found a colony in some of the western territories."[10] In the same issue there is an unsigned editorial, refuting Stern's impassioned arguments. It would be neither practical nor expedient. Jews had better form communities, not States, for "the equitable laws of the United States and the freedom of opinion, equality and protection guaranteed by the Constitution, must satisfy us." There are other controversial problems. The editor objects to "the foolish attempts at conversion" made in New York and elsewhere. "The American Society for Meliorating the Condition of the Jews' gets a thorough going-over. Later the same subject is pursued with vigor. Missionary efforts are perennial at home and abroad, "under the specious guise" of helping the Jews.

A Sunday School "for Religious Instruction of Israelites" is the answer to such proselyting activities on the part of Christians. On the 19th of March, 1843, "a truly surprising number" of participants were present for the fifth anniversary examination of the Sunday School. Synagogues are consecrated. Schools spring up in many cities. That is the positive answer to the program of conversion and "melioration."

In the previous year, Rabbi Samuel M. Isaacs had established "The New York Talmud Torah and Hebrew Institute." Now in May, 1843, the progress of the school is considered and its merits are weighed. The record is good. The purpose, to teach both English and Hebrew, is being accomplished. The school maintained at a cost of $1,500 per annum, now has eighty scholars. In June another Jewish institution is appraised. The "Cheap Jewish Library, dedicated to the Working Classes" is found to be somewhat wanting. The characters described in its series, purporting to be "short moral stories, based upon Jewish life and manners," are found "not Jewish enough" to please the editor. In the July issue, the "Jewish female" comes into her own. An address is reported which was delivered in Charleston. Female benevolence is extolled. Woman's growing influence on society is noted. She is "one of the most powerful and efficient causes of its progress in refinement and civilization." In the same issue "Religious

Prejudices" are analyzed. A contributor who signs himself "Abraham" decries the fact that those who are best qualified to defend the Jews against the prejudices of non-Israelites, have remained silent.

In August, the editor welcomed a new Jewish weekly, *The Israelite*, which appeared in German, its editor none other than Julius Stern. The reason: "so many Israelites . . . are now spread over the entire Union from the banks of the Hudson to the Mississippi, and from the Atlantic to the Missouri," whose only language is German.

In September, 1843, Mordecai Manuel Noah proposed the establishment of a "collegiate institution" for Jewish children from the age of six on.[11] There is a grave need for such a school, for "Every reflecting Israelite must long since have been cognizant of the evil tendency of sending his children to Christian boarding schools, or to colleges in towns where there are no Jews, for their education." Mordecai Noah had found "an eligible situation" for such a college at Poughkeepsie. He argued the need for a classical education, for instruction in Hebrew, for having pupils live in conformity to Jewish customs, for the need of acquiring a liberal knowledge of the principles of the Jewish religion.

October, 1843, found the Congregation of Shanarai Chasset of New Orleans asking for financial help. Object—the erecting of a synagogue. There were some 125 families in that city wanting a place of worship. The congregation at Charleston proudly reviewed its history. It stressed its unity with the older congregations of London and Amsterdam. It noted with pride that it follows the "Minhag Sephardim" as its rule and guide.

December saw still another controversial idea discussed in the pages of the *Occident*: "Jewish Children Under Gentile Teachers." The reader is warned that it is a "dangerous tendency" to have the tender mind exposed exclusively to Gentile teachers. Young children were particularly susceptible. It was too much to ask of a young and unformed mind to swallow one set of doctrines at home, another at school. Do not school children hear prayers recited "in which the name of a mediator" is invoked?

The following month Rabbi S. M. Isaacs further pursued the subject. In a forthright discussion of "Religious Education" he insists that the question is not "whether Jewish children shall be taught by Gentiles, but whether Jewish souls shall be lost through the criminal neglect of parents, and the apathetic slumber of Hebrew ministers." Parents are alerted. They must be on the lookout for so "pernicious" a system. Again and again Isaacs excoriates "the apathetic state of ministers on the subject of religious education." Not only are ministers "apathetic." The "Disjointed State" of American Jews is deplored in January, 1844. What is wanted is religious union. One community will support several synagogues of "different denominations." Too many individuals pursue private aims, neglecting matters of spiritual welfare. Geographic as well as doctrinal divisions are current. It is imperative to have a "union of action." It is urgent to reconcile the differences between "the different classes." What are the stumbling blocks to union? Some Jews are native, others are newcomers. Some are rich, others poor. Some "profess love" for the German Minhag, others for the Polish or Portuguese. Some are adherents of reform, others refuse to make even the smallest concession to the new conditions under which Jews in America live. "With the prevalence of a better state of feeling toward us, with the enjoyment of perfect liberty in this land, why should we so soon learn to despise each other, and thus justify the conduct of Israel's enemies towards us?" It is a knotty point, this difference of Minhag, or custom, of the various synagogues. It is time for a federated union. For are not "modern heresies" being brought here on every boat from Europe. The land is overrun with the godless who defy ancient usage, profane the Sabbath, head un-Jewish households, intermarry with Christians.

Who is the aggressor? Surely not those who wish to uphold the customs of their fathers. . . . The system which we have so long lived under . . . is surely one which has the sanction of wise and eminent men, and we cannot surrender it blindly to the tender mercies of those who ask us to help them pull down, before they have shown us a fair specimen of what they mean to build up in its stead.

The "lovers of ancient usages" are not enemies to improvements. They do hope, however, that reform should not be accomplished in haste. Let gradual amelioration be brought about by education.

In August Mordecai Manual Noah's "Plan for a Hebrew College" is again endorsed with the hope that the project need not be too long deferred. The editor lashes out attacking "The Reform Agitation," complaining of the laxness in matters of orthodoxy, of the neglect of the Sabbath and of dietary laws. He finds "the indifference one of supineness, not of an aggressive nature." He laments that a new race has come upon the scene—"Israelites learned in worldly things," but imperfectly acquainted with Jewish matters. It is high time for the "Rabbins" to speak out in no uncertain terms. Silence is inexcusable. When they emerge from their deep silence, they issue their manifestoes in Hebrew. While the reformers in a state of perpetual loquacity bombard their hearers in German, French or English. It is leadership that is wanting, not new practices.

Judaism could flourish in "vigor and beauty" if the ministry were better qualified, more zealous, more alert to actual needs. How then to acquire "a proper ministry"? The difficulties are enormous. For there is "no school either in England or America, where a Jewish student of theology could be educated." Why are Jews so blind to this need? Christians "strain every nerve to have an intelligent and virtuous ministry."

Among the Literary Notices is a review of Grace Aguilar's *Records of Israel*. The work is first discussed in the July issue. The book needs, in the opinion of the reviewer, "a little more habitual caution in the gifted author's exposition of what are, in reality, Jewish principles and opinions." In a subsequent number the reviewer relents. He goes back to a closer scrutiny of Grace Aguilar's stories and decides that since the Jewish public is small in number, all possible encouragement should be given those who choose to labor in that field. Grace Aguilar was a frequent contributor to the pages of the *Occident*. Her pleasant poetry and impassioned historical prose fascinated its readers and filled its pages with the type of reading considered most suitable for the feminine mind. She was preoccupied with the martyrdom motif in Jewish history.

In 1845, Isaac Leeser seriously belabored intermarriage. Beginning with the January issue, when, he prophesied that "in nearly all, if not all, cases, the result must be that regret will spring from the mixed marriages," he attacked the spread of mixed marriage. He deplored "the tendency to seek matrimonial alliances" outside the fold. Public opinion, he pleaded, must be mobilized. Always such "matrimonial connections prove detrimental in the highest degree to the religion of the weak party—to wit, the Jews."

Other troubles crowd the question of intermarriage. For now in South Carolina, Governor James H. Hammond has offended the Israelites of his State by urging that Thanksgiving Day be celebrated "in the Christian spirit." This exclusion of Hebrews from celebrating Thanksgiving violates the spirit of our Federal Constitution. How can any governor of any State ask his people "to pray to God through any mediator?" asks the editor.[12] A petition is drawn up and signed with one hundred names. A meeting of Israelites is called at Masonic Hall of which Michael Lazarus is Chairman. The Governor replies in detail to the protests and the petition: "Whatever may be the language of

Proclamation and of Constitution, I know that the civilization of the age is derived from Christianity, that the institutions of this country are instinct with the same spirit, and that it pervades the laws of the State as it does the manners and I trust the hearts of our people."

This was not the answer the Committee of South Carolina Hebrews hoped to receive. They note that the tone of Governor Hammond's letter contains "languages which they deem calculated to excite the worst of feelings in our country." The government of South Carolina, like that of the United States "is a government of *equal rights* in religious privileges, as in all other things, and not as his excellency infers, a *government of tolerance*, enabling rulers to give or to withhold."

Other matters are brought to the fore. The dissolution of the Pennsylvania Society for Evangelizing Jews is noted. But for one such society that expires several others spring to life. Nantucket has an "auxiliary" society and there is one each at New Bedford, Edgartown, and Bristol, Rhode Island. There were some inroads made by Christians. But only one well-known Christian who became a Jew.

Warder Cresson was born in Philadelphia in 1798. His people were well-known, well-to-do Quakers. He was a religious zealot who saw good in a number of sects and went through a series of conversions. At a critical and uncertain period in his life, Warder Cresson met and cultivated the acquaintance of Isaac Leeser. They became fast friends. In 1844, Cresson was appointed Consul to Jerusalem. Here his early leanings toward Judaism sprouted. He was captivated by Jerusalem and easily fitted into Sephardic communal and religious life, became a great friend of its Rabbis. After four years he decided to become a Jew. He was strenuously opposed by the very people whom he sought to join. But he overcame their objections, and taking the name of Michael Boaz Israel, he returned to Philadelphia to wind up his affairs in America. His family believed him insane and his son secured a commission of lunacy in court. Cresson carried the case to a higher court where they reversed the decision. On his return to Palestine, Michael Boaz Israel sought to put his experience as a successful, practical farmer to use. He decided to establish an agricultural colony in the valley of Rephaim. It was on the soil of Palestine, he felt, that the oppressed people of Israel could be re-established and rehabilitated. Agricultural colonies would relieve their immediate economic wants. Here Israel would be reborn.

Prominent Jews were enlisted in support of this project. Isaac Leeser offered Cresson space in his journal. So did Dr. L. Phillipson of Leipzig. His contributions appeared both in the *Occident* and the

Allgemeine Zeitung des Judenthums. Judah Touro, Sampson Simson, and many of their friends furthered the cause of Palestinian colonization. Moses Montefiore, Adolph Crémieux and others saw merit in his projects.

Always there was much favorable publicity given to men and women who became Christians. None was judged insane like Cresson. Leaflets and tracts describing the miracles of these conversions were commonplace. One such book may serve as an example. *The Memoir of Maria, The Converted Jewess* went through four London editions and was published in New York in 1847. The Sunday School Union of the Methodist Episcopal Church in New York sponsored its publication.

A distinguished contributor, S. M. Isaacs, writes "On the Violation of the Sabbath." He asks poignantly, "What is all profession of Judaism, if the Sabbath continues to be publicly violated and profaned?" Things have come to a pretty pass when men wear the mantle of Judaism carelessly or cast it aside altogether, expecting their wives and children to pay *"their oblations at God's shrine* while they go to discharge their *obligations* at the stock exchange, the counting house, the auction mart, and the public store."[13] A valued contributor to the pages of Leeser's journal was Abraham De Sola. He was one of the group of intellectual immigrants. A whole series of literary productions on Jewish subjects came from his pen. He was a devoted collaborator of Isaac Leeser. It was De Sola who later bought the plates of Leeser's books for reissuance. Both men were concerned with making available to their public suitable reading of all kinds. Again and again the question of inexpensive books for Jewish readers was discussed. This is a pet project of the editor's. He is glad to announce that "a few friends of religion," generous of heart and open of purse, have undertaken to inform and educate the public on Jewish matters by arranging "for the publication of a series of works in a cheap packet form, calculated to diffuse information on our religion." The first work is one of fiction titled *Caleb Asher*. Readers of the *Occident* are exhorted to assist the Provisional Publication Committee which seeks to establish institutions to be known as "the American Jewish Publication Societies." There are to be branches of this group in all American cities.[14]

There are times when the editor pauses for a bit of stock-taking, for self-appraisal, for a chummy aside to the reader. On one of those occasions the reader is told that, "We have honestly sought to give our readers an impress of the events and doctrines of Judaism, as far as they came within our knowledge." He is modest, well aware of his own limitations and those of his journal. He regrets that he is largely cut off from foreign publications, "which is so much desired both for our readers and our own person." He laments the small number of subscribers. He notes with some satisfaction that every month has seen an increase in circulation. He requests his few *reform* readers to bear with the periodical patiently, "not to excite themselves with a useless anger at what may occasionally be written by us."

Other matters involving adherence or departure from orthodoxy continue to plague the readers of the *Occident*. In New York there is an ecclesiastical schism. The Elm Street Synagogue is having trouble with a dissident group called "the seceders." In July, after brawls and disputes in which some of the pious took matters into their own hands and "employed physical force," Rabbi S. M. Isaacs resigned from the synagogue. Rabbi Isaacs is constrained to reply to his critics who cast aspersions on his conduct "in the painful contest." But if the situation in New York is dark, the one in Charleston is rosy. An examination of students of "The Society for the Instruction of Jewish Doctrine" is a brilliant occasion. Some fifty-five children, aged from four to fifteen years, showed themselves to be saturated in orthodoxy. They were a credit to Mrs. Henrietta Hart, President of the institution.

During that year a threefold program had been presented to the readers of the *Occident*. It called for:

1. The establishing of a competent ecclesiastical authority.

2. The establishing of schools for religious and general education.

3. The promotion of harmony and "a concert of action" among all Jews scattered over the Western Hemisphere.

By this time the publication has made it plain to its readers that the *Occident* is a journal with an avowed mission, that its editor is a person of definite bias, tempered with vision and imagination, that he is a man of adamant will and of strong personality. The Argus-eyed editor records many meetings. The New York Hebrew Benevolent Society dines at the Apollo Saloon to celebrate its twenty-fourth year of existence and the event is duly recorded. A Hebrew is arrested for Sabbath-breaking and an impassioned article pleads his rights. There are other matters, however, showing our esteemed protagonist, Isaac Leeser, to be tarred with prejudice. Here is an urgent request for an augmented police force on Sundays and holidays, when "a vicious population of slaves and free negroes are let loose upon the community in idleness." Leeser's humanitarian fight is very limited. Its scope is quite restricted. Leeser is a bundle of contradictions. He provides moral sentiments for his readers. He keeps sentimentality bright and untarnished by welcoming Grace Aguilar to his pages as often as possible.

The year 1846 opens with an attack on reform and reformers. Reform, if it comes, must be lawful, universally demanded, gradual, arrived at by democratic processes. In other matters time seems to stand still. Sunday legislation is a moot point, as it has been for years. The clergy is underpaid as always. There is need for better trained ministers. The American Jewish Publication Society closes a year's activity with a cash balance of $267.27. Four books have already been published providing Israelites with such reading "as will not chill in them the ardour of their faith."

Leeser is gallant toward women. Of course, there are lengths beyond which he does not propose to go. We may assume that the review of Grace Aguilar's *Women of Israel*, by S. Solis, has his tacit approval. Solis in general agrees with Miss Aguilar but he does not see the need of "insisting so often, and so strongly, upon the perfect equality of woman with man, as a moral and accountable being." However, her "Communings with Nature" and "Sabbath Thoughts" strike no controversial note.

The agitation for reform soon grew into an organized movement with a formal program and militant leadership. It is historically important to notice the first formal report in the *Occident*, titled "Proceedings at the Meeting of the Beth-Din in New York." A momentous step in the direction of reform was taken. Prayers according to American needs (Minhag-America) are advocated:[15]

Rabbi Wise (of Albany) . . . proposed a *Minhag-America* for divine service. He had been charged with such a work, because experience teaches that in most places different congregations are set up and the strength of the Israelites is divided, because every emigrant brings his own Minhag from his home, and the German will not give way to the Polish, nor he to the English, nor the latter to the Portuguese Jew. Such a cause for dissension would be obviated by a *Minhag-America*.

Toward the end of 1847 Isaac Leeser was still optimistic about "Synagogue Reforms." He is ready to compromise, to adjust, to yield a little. The reason is simple. He had met Isaac Mayer Wise. The two men had found much in common. They parted with a sense of mutual esteem. While he still views "with apprehension" the inroads of "un-Jewish manners," he is ready to go along in the direction of some innovation, for "it would argue but little good sense to exclude every improvement, for fear of further changes, which are not sanctified by our laws and customs." The editor is willing to be reasonable: "We see everywhere, especially in this country, a demand for instruction, a craving for a well-regulated public worship . . . that we believe that the sincere Israelite is justified in predicting a better state of things before the passing away of this generation."

But there are other matters of interest to readers of the *Occident*. Rabbi Lyons of Shearith Israel has called a meeting for the relief of the famine victims in Ireland. Surely a most worthy cause. From England comes the happy news that "Jewish liberal partisans" acclaim the election of Baron Lionel Rothschild to Parliament— they are "almost intoxicated with joy at their victory." Philanthropy is examined and the methods of disbursing relief in Jewish circles is given close scrutiny.

In November of 1847 there falls to the editor of the *Occident* the unhappy task of writing the obituary notice of one of his cherished contributors—Grace Aguilar. She had in the past year sent in her usual welcome contributions: "The Jewish Year," "Address to the Ocean," "Sabbath Thought." In Charleston, South Carolina, they held a memorial meeting for the English Jewess whose writings they had loved. The *Occident* commented sadly on her passing: "There has not arisen a single Jewish female in modern times who has done so much for the illustration and adornment of her faith as Grace Aguilar." Sorrow at her death is universal.[16]

The year 1848, the year of great upheaval in Europe, came in quietly for the Jews of America. The enforcement of Sunday laws in South Carolina worried one contributor. In September, the case of the City of Charleston *vs.* Sol. A. Benjamin was reviewed. A previous protest signed "American Jew" had produced one salutary effect. "Judge O'Neale himself has thought that some apology was due to our people." The Judge's letter was published in the *Occident*. He defended his decision in the case and asserted that no thought of offending the Jews or depreciating their religion entered his mind while considering the legal aspects of the lawsuit. "*The Bible is a part, and a large part of Christianity.*" In asserting Christianity to be the only standard of good morals, "*the Bible* was of course *as much that standard* as the New Testament. . . . How I, *not born a Jew*, could say otherwise . . . is hard for me to conceive." To which the editor added drily that as long as Judge O'Neale recognized the Jews' Bible, "he might have easily seen that they had as good a standard

as he has." It was a fight that was to be waged for many years to
come with many variations.

In 1856, a Jew was fined five dollars for working on Sunday in
Iowa. Ohio's Court of Common Pleas ruled that "a person of any denomination, who conscientiously keeps one day holy" may dispense
with Sunday observance. In Virginia Jews and Seventh Day Sabbata-
rians were relieved in 1845 of compulsory Sunday closing. The vigilance of the *Occident* was one of the factors which must be counted as
carrying considerable weight. In November, the Governor of Pennsylvania issued a Thanksgiving Day proclamation to all denominations of Christians. This time, however, Christians were quick to
point out how unfair "to exclude the Israelites from an invitation
meant to embrace all the worshippers of God in a common call."
The Governor apologized stating that the omission of Jews was
"certainly accidental."

Reform is more and more on everyone's mind. There are certainly glaring faults which should be corrected. "Synagogue Reforms" analyzes the current situation. Good manners and decorum
and a spirit of reverence are lacking. Worshipers arrive late, leave
early, or are irregular in attendance. Christians hurry to be on time
for services. Jews drop in at the synagogue "before or after the
commencement of the service, as it may suit their taste or convenience." Four rules are suggested, involving punctuality, silence, and
"not to permit anyone whether Israelite or Gentile visitor, to quit
the Synagogue before the meeting is over." Finally, "not to allow any
children to be brought in who are too young or unruly to remain
during the whole time of worship." Even the most orthodox at this
time were never completely oblivious of the impression they made on
their Christian neighbors. Much of the writing at this time seems
slanted toward Christians. When William Jacobs published in 1848
The Jews Reason For Believing in One God Only, he was not writing
for a Jewish audience.

At the end of the year and at the beginning of 1849, the tempo
of social change becomes accelerated. An article titled "On Association" rehearses the need for the union of all Jews in America. Jews
are isolated—"Every community is uninfluenced by and without
influence on others." Statistics are lacking. Information on communal
organization is difficult to obtain—"In brief, no data whatever on
which to found a general movement, or to concert a plan for the
advancement of the public good." A meeting of representative
ministers of congregations might well take place in New York,

between Passover and Pentecost. A "Call to Israelites" by Rabbi Wise is issued.[17] For it behooves the Jews "to be united as one man; to be linked together by the ties of equal views concerning religious questions—by uniformity in our sacred customs." The editor reports that the "Call to Israelites" has received a warm response. Cincinnati has already started to appoint congregational delegates.

In December of 1849 a welcome is extended to a new paper devoted to Jewish interests, the *Asmonean*. An article in its third issue written by Dr. Wise is singled out for particular attention.[18] It stresses again the need for union among the Israelites of America. Rabbi S. M. Isaacs writes to the *Occident* endorsing the need for concerted action. The "poor of Palestine" are introduced to the readers as worthy recipients of American relief funds. Heinrich Heine's return to Judaism is discussed. It proves that, "Our religion is something so entirely in concert with our nature, that its eradication becomes absolutely impossible."

So the *Occident* continues to exhort, to admonish, to praise, to persuade. It welcomes new congregations and clubs and newspapers. Sadly and respectfully it comments on the exits of great men and women. Through its pages life ebbs and flows. "A Funeral Panegyric to the Memory of the Late M. M. Noah, Esq." gives us pause.

A contributor who signs himself S. N. C. writes on "The Congregation Beth Elohim of Charleston." Could the author be our old friend Solomon Nunes Carvalho of that city? A new synagogue is consecrated at Syracuse, New York, "this capital of the poor." The Hebrew Education Society's School is flourishing after only six weeks of life. Finally, Isidor Bush of St. Louis contributes a paper on "The Task of Jews in the United States." This critical analysis of the position of the Jew in the United States, of the problems that confront him, of the means of solving them, is a valuable contribution to a study of the cultural scene a century ago. Here we have a yardstick by means of which we may measure social change, as well as resistance to change.

Leeser became a circuit rider. For sixteen weeks, from November 9, 1851, to February 27 of the following year, he traveled through the South and West. His purpose was "to urge in person the claims of his work, among others, on the attention of the Jewish public." He visited twenty-five congregations "from the shores of Lake Erie to the Gulf of Mexico." From his trip he brought back the impression "on the state of *isolation* in which all our communities exist." His original opinions about the "inefficiency of Jewish ministers" were re-enforced. For this the congregations are to blame: "Synagogue affairs are not well managed." There is another glaring fault: "Want of knowledge of the language of prayer is a frightful source of want of devotion." On this point Leeser is eloquent. "We ought to have, of right, a dialect of our own, which will distinguish us everywhere as Israelites." To be effective, Hebrew must be a living speech "readily understood, and universally calling up *thoughts* in the hearts of those who pray." His dream is to restore Hebrew to its people, "by which means our own would cease to be a dead tongue, and take its rank among those called living languages." He continues his advocacy of Hebrew in the following issue, "inasmuch as it is the vernacular of Israel, and the bond which unites the most distant dispersions of our people into one homogeneous whole." He pleads again for "a federal union" of all American congregations. He wants to see a college established for the proper training of ministers and teachers. There is need for "a college of Rabbins." "Traveling Missionaries" are needed by our people to "examine into the conduct of local ministers and teachers." The Jewish Publication Society should be given every material aid, "to encourage Jewish men and women of approved talents to devote their leisure to the production of useful and learned works illustrative of our religion, history, literature, or whatever can benefit our cause."

Palestine begins to worry Leeser. "The deplorable condition of its residents" is a matter of concern. Should it be but an asylum for the poor and the aged? "Is it right to continue the system of alms-sending, which has utterly failed to remove the direful load of poverty?" The Association for Promoting Jewish settlements in Palestine is discussed under a London dateline. And from Jaffa in Palestine, there comes a communication describing an agricultural colony there. It is the duty of American Israelites "to restore the poor of Palestine to an honorable feeling of self-dependence and self-support." The editor further insists that his people must incur "the guilt of neglect" if they leave their "suffering brethren there to linger in hopeless misery."

Rabbi Wise contributes a paper titled "Gross Invectives." This is a review of a book Wise dislikes and a challenge to enemies of Israel who "write and publish invectives against Israel, their pens being wielded by fanaticism, ignorance, and ill will." Incidentally Rabbi Wise's pen when dipped into a well of moral indignation writes many an invective on its own. Now an important journalistic event is noted. Isaac Mayer Wise, whose greatest efforts were expended in the founding of Reform Judaism, adds to his activities. He is the founder of the *American Israelite* which dates from July 15, 1854. It is a vehicle through which to preach his doctrines of reform. For the time had come to attempt an integration of Judaism and Americanism. It is noteworthy that this devotee of religion should have said, "We are first Americans and then Israelites." A new and indigenous American Judaism emerged in the *American Israelite*. Max Lilienthal and Gotthard Deutsch were among the contributors to this periodical, which is the oldest extant publication devoted to Judaism in America. Wise was at the helm of the *American Israelite* from the day of its founding until his death on the twenty-sixth of March, 1900. For a number of years the pages of the *Occident* and those of the *American Israelite* were to reflect parallel ideas on Judaism—ideas that seemed destined not to meet. Yet they often agreed on their estimates of the great men whose passing both editors mourned. Judah Touro's death is a news item in the *Occident* and the many eulogies of his friends are included. There is an interesting essay on "Superstition." Here the editor warns his readers "against the new superstition which is just now spreading over the land, under the name of 'spiritual manifestations,' or whatever else may be the names by which this deception is known."

Sometimes to protect his sanity, Leeser deliberately chose to be thick-skinned. At other times he vibrated with passion, lashing out at all who were glib, inaccurate, unscientific. He abhorred the smug and the righteous. Yet, he was not above being a little of each.

Still the *Occident* flows along, covering the banquets, the meetings, the books, the needs of the Jewish community. The unwary reader is occasionally swept off his feet by unexpected fireworks. A simple book review may set off an explosion. Solis' "Remarks on Dr. Wise's History of the Israelitish Nation" is such an item. How Rabbi Wise must have fumed when he saw his work called "a case of Biblical Defamation," when he read, "If the Bible is true, Dr. Wise's history is a farce." This called forth an avalanche of mail, including a rejoinder by Isaac M. Wise, an explanation by Isaac Leeser and loud and angry protests by other contributors. One angry critic wrote that it was a presumptuous review which was based on "a casual perusal" and which managed to avoid "quoting a single passage to justify your opinion. . . . This was imprudent, if it was nothing else." Leeser is accused of being prejudiced against Wise because of their "former controversies." The editor mildly admits that he was perfectly conscious that he was raising a storm when he published the short notice of Wise's *History*. But he defends himself by saying that the work "was calculated to do mischief." He drops the controversial subject. But here and there, by innuendo, there are further attacks on the rising tide of reform and reformers. When Dr. M. Mayer preaches a sermon at Charleston on "The River of Reform," condemning it as a perversion of Scripture, Leeser is jubilant. Religions must be nothing if not "fixed, certain and reliable." Reform "is uncertain, its limits undefined, its ground constantly shifting." Isaac Leeser soon throws all editorial restraint to the winds. Things have come to a pretty pass, writes Leeser, and all brought about "by men who have somehow slipped into the teacher's chair." His language crackles with anger. Reformers "endeavour to uphold every crooked doctrine they propound by the show of some great authority, uniformly incorrectly quoted." What makes matters worse, says Leeser, is that "no two of them reform on the same principle." By October of 1854, Leeser feels forced to warn his readers that the reformers have pushed matters into an acute crisis. He calls upon these radicals to pause before adherents of the true faith will cut them off irrevocably "from the parent stem of Israel." Some of these agitators are already "beyond the pale," and the faithful will not tolerate much more. Reformers "must not complain, nor speak of illiberality and persecution, if the faithful dissolve all connection with them." So for more than a year the Charleston sermon continues as fuel for the flame of Leeser.

Politics become a matter of some interest. In 1855 the formation of the "New American Party" is noted. Leeser believes "that the Jews of America as such, should never form a separate political organization." Political equality has Leeser's blessing. Senator Cass's letter is quoted which refers to the treaty with Switzerland: "The invidious distinction contained in the treaty with Switzerland, between American citizens, granting rights to Christians which are withheld from Jews was not ratified by the Senate; such a principle will never receive the sanction of this body." But international affairs are driven out when intolerance bares its fangs in California. The Speaker of the California Legislature slandered the Jews and the news had hardly reached Leeser when he reacted vigorously, lashing out at the offender. With the same zeal he attacks legislation in Pennsylvania which is "tinctured with the spirit of persecution." He refers to the "Sunday Laws."

The word "reform" has become to its opponents "so hateful, savors so much of radical change and gentile innovation," that the ranks of American Jews are hopelessly divided. The *Occident* accuses the despised innovators of wanting "to render religion more acceptable to the wealthy." Reform arguments are demolished. Individuals are singled out for criticism. The battle waxes hotter as the opposition musters greater strength. Leeser has his hands full. But as if that were not enough, he is apparently under some pressure to state his opinion on the slavery question. He tries in 1857 to be judicious, to straddle the issue. He accuses both factions of "zeal and intemperance," curiously forgetting his own. Judiciously he maintains that a man's thoughts are from infancy conditioned by his environment. He cannot impute "dishonest motives or sinister intentions to either of the contestants." This sounds strange coming from a man who imputed base motives to those who differed from him on matters of orthodoxy.

Controversy in some form or other is not long absent from the pages of the *Occident*. Now it is the subject of "post mortems" which is argued pro and con. Jews in America being divided, they appeal to the Chief Rabbi of London "whether post mortem examinations under *any circumstances*, should be allowed in the hospital." Rabbi Adler gave a somewhat Delphic answer which was, on the whole, opposed to the practice. Immediately a staff member of the New York Jews' Hospital objected on the grounds that "reason and humanity . . . unite in sanctioning any effort to progress in a knowledge so useful and practical as surgical science."

In 1857, the *Occident* surveys the national field and finds that the influence of Jews over the entire country is slight. A few families are highly respected. But the rank and file exercise "but little perceptible influence." There is a moral here and Leeser does not lose the opportunity to point it out: "It is the want of cohesion, the want of a unity of purpose, the want of mutual toleration, the absence of a public spirit, the want of an active sympathy with each other's sorrows, joys, and pursuits." At present the various "nationalities repel each other." What then is to be done? "We must learn to look on each other more as equals, as men of Israel who have the same aspirations."

One can almost hear the sigh of relief as our worthy protagonist turns from controversy to reviewing a book titled "Prayers and Meditations for Every Situation and Occasion in Life." This work is translated and adapted from the French by Hesther Rothschild. Here is a collection of "devotional exercises" to gladden the hearts of the righteous. The reviewer points out that again it is a *Jewess* who brings us the fruits of her labor, "much to the shame of the *men* of Israel . . . [who] have done so little to adorn their faith."

The Jewish community gives birth to other Jewish periodicals. Leeser surveys them with a jaundiced eye. Here are more faggots to feed the flame of his moral indignation. Here also is something new to write about, to take issue with, to comment on with smug righteousness and Olympian approval. The *Israelite* for September 26, 1856, carries an article written by "the peaceful associate editor," whose restraint and calmness Leeser finds a welcome departure from that of the editor of the *Israelite*—"and we are pleased to notice that there is a prospect at length of having a discussion on religion, without the danger of being overwhelmed by torrents of abuse." The *Israelite* article refers to the *Occident* claims that the Rabbinical group is "holy and inviolable." To which Leeser tartly responds that the *Piutim* [orthodox] have been upheld by the chief rabbis of Great Britain and France. Leeser likes the company he keeps. Still rival papers keep Leeser busy. He is seldom at a loss for subjects. He finds it necessary to survey the situation in "The Press and the Pulpit." He draws up a set of rules for "the Press." Editors of Jewish religious papers should endeavor:

1. To promote good-will and unity among all Israelites.

2. To remember as a general rule that "the *conduct* of the advocates of any opinion is not the legitimate subject of public animadversion."

3. To bear in mind that "no editor writing in America should forget the comities of life, and deal in hearsay falsehoods to slander the character of his opponents."

4. It would be well "not to venture on subjects which they do not thoroughly understand, nor to mystify those with which they are familiar."

These are excellent rules. But our scribe has not exhausted the subject. In religious discussions, "though we be certain that our opponent is wrong, it should . . . be the duty of all controversialists not to lose sight of the sublimity of the subject." Censure can be qualified. Fault-finding can be done with discrimination. Praise need not become fulsome flattery.

Another series of articles running from June through November of 1857 deals with the provocative subject, "Jew or not Jew." Here Leeser undertakes to answer the question raised by the proposed *Minhag-America*, as introduced by Isaac M. Wise. Is it right, asks Leeser, to assume that "a change of time and country can of right work a change in religion?"

Now "The Swiss Treaty" is again under discussion. Readers are urged to write letters to the President and the Senate protesting its "odious," discriminating clause. The editor advises protest meetings. He is in favor of a delegation calling on the President and offers himself as the "medium of communication." The December, 1857, number of the *Occident* reports that such a committee waited on the President, who "made a courteous reply. The Secretary of State also promised his aid to remove the grievances."

Other welcome noncontroversial subjects keep turning up. There are the poor whom we have always with us. Here Leeser's naïveté is colossal, childlike and unbelievable. He seems unaware of Adam Smith, of Malthus, of Ricardo, of Marx, of Jeremy Bentham. He recognizes the existing economic inequalities but maintains that a system might be contrived to obviate the great disproportion between the rich and absolutely poor! What he wants is "to bring the latter within the closer supervision of the former, and thus prevent them from sinking to so low a level that there is no resort for them, except the poorhouse, when they find themselves unable to work or to obtain employment in time of pecuniary depression." The Micawber formula.

As one of the constructive plans for the Israelites of America Leeser suggests "Agricultural Colonies." He has the imagination to dream of the time when the Jews of the land will have "to resort to other modes of earning a livelihood than the branches of business now pursued by them." Commerce is now their major occupation. Why not handicrafts and agriculture? asks Leeser. The time to change is now. Later it will not be so easy. What is needed is a system of trade and agricultural associations. Plan now, he urges, for a large-scale agricultural settlement in the West.

Volume XVI of the *Occident* covers the crowded year between April of 1858 and March of 1859. It was the year of the unhappy Mortara case. Leeser was busy and with good cause. Sunday Laws continue to agitate the editor. Rabbi Wise's prayer book raises his blood pressure. "Religious Prejudices" annoy him no end. Minhag-America has invaded Baltimore. The editor unhappily reports that, "It is mortifying that our neighbors should have cause to suppose that a change in the religious sentiments of our people is taking place." He quotes from a news item in the *Baltimore Sun* which innocently describes the "Important Movement Among the Israelites." He consistently rejects reformers. He is still unyielding, still adamant in his total aversion to religious change.

As the years roll on and as the volumes of the *Occident* become familiar companions, the endless repetition becomes wearisome. Were there moments when Rebecca Gratz yawned a little as she read the latest number of her friend's journal? Did she long for a little humor and sprightliness? She was so nicely blessed with both. But the fare does not vary. "A Plea for Union." "Radical Reform in Cleveland." "Parties and Partisans." This question is debated from August to November of 1861. Should we allow "to mingle the blood of Jacob, in hallowed wedlock with that of foreign races?" It is all the fault of the opponents of unity of action, of persons who labor for their own elevation, who turn their back on time-honored custom and revered ritual.

The War crowds in, elbowing aside the trivial, the transitory interests. "The American Crisis" is discussed in a series of articles. Slavery is at last seriously considered, now that men are dying to abolish the institution. Some fancy tightrope walking is indulged in and many evasive phrases are invoked to keep from taking sides. Slavery, writes one contributor, is not a sin like blasphemy. This is the essential error of abolitionism.

It is responsible for "the terrific hatred" between North and South. He assigns slavery to the same category as polygamy, evils which are gradually coming to an end. Emancipation need not, therefore, be immediate. Slavery need not continue in perpetuity. This double-talk did not raise a storm of resentment. Readers were either too busy fighting the War, or waiting for news from the front, or too indifferent.

The Board of Delegates of American Israelites submits its annual report. In its two years of existence it has managed to acquire enemies, opponents and detractors.

This organization was the sounding board of American Jewry for a generation—1859-78. Samuel Myer Isaacs was the first secretary of the group, then in 1876 its president. Isaac Leeser was its vice-president until his death in 1868. Isaacs was a stanch, forthright, vigorous champion of the North and of its ideology. His editorial in his paper, the *Jewish Messenger*, dated April 26, 1861, called "Stand By the Flag," left no doubt in the minds of his subscribers as to where his sympathies were. It was widely reprinted. It was greeted with favorable editorial comment in the Christian press.

Then stand by the Flag! What death can be as glorious as that of the patriot, surrendering his life in defense of his country . . . to live forever in the hearts of a grateful people?

The *Jewish Messenger* was begun in 1857. It fought with vigor the new forces of reform which were then becoming vocal. It attacked slavery. It thundered against injustice in whatever guise it reared its head. Both Leeser and Isaacs were teammates on the Board of Delegates.

The organization grew out of a need that long antedated the kidnapping of a little Italian Jewish boy, Edgar Mortara. As far back as the Damascus affair of 1840, American Jews had felt the need for concerted action in intervening when Jewish rights were threatened. What was needed was a group to register disapproval and secure intervention in behalf of persecuted Jews everywhere.

Like a snowball gathering momentum, was the championing of Jewish rights in Switzerland and other countries. Isaac Mayer Wise entered the fray. *The Israelite*, founded by him in 1854, climbed on the bandwagon. By 1857 every propaganda technique was being exploited to arouse popular action. Front-page editorials in 1857 were carrying the plea.

American Jewry had come of age. It had tasted the heady wine of group action. It was an important lesson, dearly learned. In this setting and at this time, the Board of Delegates of the American Israelites began an institutional existence which was to last for almost a score of years. Its vigilance was felt almost from the start.

One of the purposes of the organization was to serve as a fact-finding body. The inaccurate methods of arriving at estimates of the Jewish population had long been a matter of concern to its leaders. Aware of the existence of an unsynagogued contingent in every State in the Union, they had long been dissatisfied with census methods which were based on the counting of tombstones in cemeteries or seats in synagogues. Between the two extremes there was room for a considerable floating population which had not yet found permanent asylum in a cemetery nor yielded permanent allegiance to a religious institution.

There were thirty-six congregations covered in the statistical report. Here is a summary of the first four on the list, which shows something of the nature of information sought.

A new issue shapes up on the horizon. The question of army chaplains agitates the community of Israel. Jews have borne their full share of danger. Is it just or reasonable that their soldiers should be deprived of religious solace in the field? The Board of Delegates had petitioned Congress, December 10, 1861, for the appointment of Jewish chaplains. The agitation continues. We are familiar with the results.

STATISTICAL REPORT OF JEWISH CONGREGATIONS OF U. S. TO BOARD OF DELEGATES (1860–61)

Place	Name	When Founded	No. Members Males	Females	Total	Rabbi or Chazan	Officers	Miscellaneous
Boston, Mass.	Ohabei Sholom	1845	123	214	337	Rev. Benjamin E. Jacobs	B. Nelson, Pres. S. Reinstein, Vice-Pres. L. Anthony Isaac Adams G. Philips } TRUSTEES S. Stern B. Hart A. Louis, Sec.	Free school: 60 pupils; Hebrew and English taught; 2 instructors; 9 sessions per week. Reports three other congregations in same city: Adath Israel; Mischkan Israel; Beth El; 44 births, 7 deaths for year.
Brooklyn, N.Y.	Beth Elohim	1859	65	—	65	N. Gotthold, Reader	Adolph Baker, Pres. Gabriel Weinberg, Vice-Pres. S. Kaufman, Sec. Cornelius Rose, Treas. T. Bernheim I. Eiseman Lippman List } TRUSTEES Maurice Adler Moses May	School: 40 pupils; 2 instructors; 6 sessions per week; another congregation in Western District reported.
Charleston, S.C.	Beth Elohim	1791	40	65	105	Rev. Abraham Harris	Major Joshua Lazarus, Pres. Phillip Cohen, Vice-Pres. Colimyer Jacobs Hon. M. C. Mordecai } TRUSTEES B. D. Lazarus Philip Wineman Aaron I. Moses Joseph E. Esdra, Sec. & Treas.	School: about 25 pupils; 10 instructors; 1 session; 5 births, 11 deaths for year.
Charleston, S.C.	Shearith Israel	1843	12	83	95	Rev. Henry S. Jacobs	Sam Hart, Sr., Pres. Jacob Cohen, Vice-Pres. Nathaniel Levin E. Sommers } TRUSTEES Charles H. Moise S. Valentine, Sec. & Treas. Mrs. E. Minis, Pres. of Sunday School	Hebrew school: 51 pupils; 4 instructors; 1 session. Reports also a Polish congregation "numbering a few foreigners" and a reform congregation composed of native Israelites; 7 births, 5 deaths, 2 marriages.

In April, 1862, "Our Twentieth Volume" is saluted. It is an occasion and a literary landmark. The editor can look back with justifiable pride on his accomplishments. He looks forward too. He has ambitious plans for the future. The present he finds grim due to "the present deplorable war." It has proved a serious drawback to the circulation of the *Occident*, while causing "mercantile derangements" throughout the country. He cannot foresee a large number of new subscribers in the North. Had the editor been inspired by "pecuniary interest solely," he would not have continued with the publication of the *Occident*, "at least not until the return of more tranquil times." Nevertheless he intends to go on as before along his usual editorial policy. "We shall endeavor to point out the cause of our want of spirituality, to defend the principles of orthodox Judaism, and to rebuke the spirit of sectarianism which would, if left uncombated, bring disunion in our midst, and render us a reproach and by-word to our neighbors." *To point out—to defend—to rebuke* . . . it is an excellent summary of the first nineteen volumes.

The Third Annual Report of the Board of Delegates is reviewed. Jewish chaplains are appointed.[19] "Suffering Jews in the Holy Land" have their claims presented. The Hebrew Orphan Asylum has a cornerstone laying ceremony. From December of 1862 on, "Illiberal Comments" about Jews receive increasing space. The editor is at his best here. His prose is inspired by moral indignation. It crackles and sparkles as he hurls imprecations at the enemy. This is "a vulgar spirit" which threatens the good name of the Jew. When General Grant issues his ill-starred order expelling Jews, Leeser can hardly contain his anger. The article "Persecution" is a classic Jeremiad.

The War walks with heavy feet through the hearts of America. The young go off to fight, rise to undreamed-of heights of valor and are seen no more. Their kin remain heavy of heart and broken in spirit and the leaden days follow each other bringing no respite, no hope.

The bachelor editor feels no personal pull at his heartstrings. He does not follow the battle lines with beating heart. The funeral bells do not toll for him. April, 1863: Hebrew-American literature languishes. May, 1863: Parents are becoming indifferent to Jewish education. July, 1863: Jewish religion is best served by "the exclusive devotion of its followers." There is again a crying need for "Union of Israelites." August, 1863: "The Lunacy Trial of Warder Cresson" is discussed in great detail. October, 1863: Jewish meetings in Italy and France are covered. February, 1864: Jews have been profaning the Sabbath day by going to the theater. "Ladies' Seats" in the new temple in Cincinnati are introduced as evidence of noxious reform. These little things were paramount to Isaac Leeser in the bleak days, the solemn, heart-searing days.

But the War was real to his readers.

In every city in the North Jewish enthusiasm rose to fever pitch. What happened in Buffalo is an example. Let it be recalled that the hiring of substitutes was at this time a commonplace procedure. Even Lincoln had one.

The Hebrew Union Benevolent Association originated from a meeting, which was held July 15th, 1863, in the house of Samuel Kohn on Batavia street, for the purpose of raising funds to buy substitutes for every Israelite who might be drafted into the army of the United States. But the waves of patriotism ran so high on that occasion, that instead of raising funds, the formation of a Jewish company of volunteers was reported; thirty-two names being subscribed for membership. Of the signers, nine actually enlisted in different regiments. Instead of furnishing substitutes, a benevolent society was started on the same day with the formation of the military company; and funds were secured, by subscription, for the efficient assistance of our Jewish home poor, and worthy Jewish travelers.[20]

By 1864, the *Occident* calls attention to the need for accurate statistics as to the number of Jews in the United States Army. The editor reminds his readers that he "has studiously avoided alluding to the war." But facts are facts and he would like to publish them. There is no question but the War is increasing prejudice and race antipathy. In a discussion of "The Civil War and Intolerance" the influence of demagogues upon the masses is astutely analyzed. The establishing of a Jewish Chaplaincy in United States hospitals is approved by the editor. "Jewish Ladies and Their Charities in London" are described. A Jewish hospital for Philadelphia is urged. The B'nai B'rith Convention had already favorably considered the measure. "A hospital is a necessity to rescue our suffering poor from the annoyances attendant on leaving them exposed to Gentile charity and treatment."

There now begins a series of articles on *Rishuth* (prejudice). The anatomy of prejudice is described. The discussion is precipitated by a movement to amend the Constitution in such a way as to stipulate that we are a Christian nation. This, according to our protagonist, is an attempt made to destroy liberty of conscience and "to burden the limbs of *free* America." The writer does not "apprehend that the attempted treason will succeed." But he warns that the "conspirators" will continue to recruit followers—"and no man is wise enough to fix a period when they will cease."

He has the answer ready. Let all Israelites

endeavor to demean themselves so as to give their opponents no cause to charge them with any acts unbecoming their holy ancestry, and to call into being institutions which will dignify their name, and be an honor to their religion, and to see to it that they train representative men who will be able to seize the pen in the hour of need and to utter the living word, when occasion calls on us to defend the cause and fair fame of Israel.

Could anything have better expressed Leeser's inner ambition? Certainly he had so charted his life as to be the champion and the spokesman of the people to whom he belonged, whose past he revered, whose folkways and mores were so dear to him that he wanted to preserve them unaltered and unchanged. He was consistent. He had chosen the road he would walk. He would not be lured from his path.

On April 14, 1865, our nation lost Lincoln. Stricken alike with grief were the Jews and Christians of the land. In May of 1865 a moving tribute to our martyred President was included in the *Occident*. But of far greater interest to us is a sermon which Isaac Leeser delivered in the Synagogue in Washington, D.C., on the following Sabbath morning, April 22. "How to Mourn" was the subject of his address, which stressed the goals which those who mourn must seek in honoring the departed. For Isaac Leeser could rise to great heights on occasion.

The year also marked for Leeser the publication in London of his translation of the twenty-four books of the Bible. That too was a labor of love which Leeser laid before his beloved people.

The war was over. The chaplains were mustered out of the Army. Rabbi Jacob Frankel, who had served as hospital chaplain, was especially singled out for praise. Leeser was inordinately proud of Rabbi Frankel's zeal in getting the soldiers "to attend public worship." Gradually all references to war and its aftermath grow faint in the pages of the *Occident*. Only the crop of postwar acts of intolerance, prejudice and illiberality cause anguish to the editor. He notes an increase in hostility throughout the land. Everywhere Jews are blamed for whatever happens to be wrong. In the South they are accused of not having been ardent enough in the War. In the North, "It has been the fashion to call all who were engaged in smuggling or blockade-running, as it was termed, Jews." What price heroism in battle? Valor?

Casualty lists? "But the greatest sin committed by Israelites, in the estimation of the friends of abolition, was that with many . . . the freeing of the slaves was not a fundamental principle." This strikes home with Leeser. His reticence on the subject was well known. But the trouble goes deeper than that. It is the resentment which is based on envy. Some Jews have done well in the land. In some cities they have stately homes, occupy positions of importance, have achieved a measure of security. This our enemies can not tolerate. "While we are poor and unsightly, we may be tolerated; but let us only look up, and become the social equals of our neighbors, and their ire will be at once roused, that we should dare to enjoy the blessings of the earth, which are justly due solely to the members of the only saving church."

The twenty-eighth anniversary of the Hebrew Sunday School in Philadelphia gives Leeser a chance to pay tribute to a remarkable woman: "The name of Miss Gratz has been the watchword among Jewish women. . . . Yes! whenever or wherever a project was suggested for the good of her people, her name was a guarantee that it not only was excellent in itself, but that it would be judiciously planned and admirably executed."

The Board of Delegates meets again for the first time since the outbreak of the Civil War. Leeser advocates "A Rabbinical College." He urges denominational hospitals in addition to the ones already in existence. But not all leaders of American Jews are in agreement. One of the most astute and most lovable of his colleagues, Rabbi Bernhard Felsenthal, takes issue with Leeser. A letter from Rabbi Felsenthal is published under the heading "Some Remarks on Jewish Hospitals." It differs radically on every point. Magnanimously the editor offers to let his readers judge between Felsenthal and himself. Rabbi Felsenthal considers a Jewish hospital "a superfluous and costly luxury." Besides he is opposed to such exclusiveness: "Let the Israelites of the respective cities arrange matters so that they will have in the hospital one or more rooms under their own control, and let them have their own cook, and provide *Kosher* food, and thereby this scruple will be quieted." But Leeser insists on a rejoinder. He stresses "the inexpediency of putting ourselves under the direction of any other association, and to be thus compelled to follow their rules instead of our own." This reply is characteristic of our protagonist. He liked to play the game according to his own rules.

The year 1866 is in many ways remarkable. The Board of Delegates happily reports that their intention "has not been directed to a single instance of intolerant legislation or public action affecting the tranquility of the Jewish community of the United States." If Leeser's vigilant ear and eagle eye detected nothing of the sort then conditions were truly on the mend. War hatreds were dying. Men were becoming more tolerant. There are other happy omens. In Switzerland Jews are now "accorded equal rights with other residents." Israelites of America have been extremely generous to their brethren in Palestine. The Jews of Charleston, for many years torn by internal strife and differences based on innovations in religious practices, have now patched up their quarrels. The Executive Committee of the Board of Delegates was very happy "to announce that the restoration of peace throughout the union has enabled them again to communicate with congregations in all sections, and has been signalized by the return of representatives of communities separated and estranged during the four years of war." Signs of the times! It must have been also a matter of some satisfaction for Leeser to record that the Philadelphia Jewish Hospital Association was to be ready for patients on August 6, 1866. The movement was progressing. The Jewish Hospital Association of America was a functioning organization. But success in this field did not limit Leeser's ambitions. He wanted a Hebrew college. A circular was issued by the Board of Delegates with respect to this educational institution.

Sir Moses Montefiore's report to the Board of Deputies of British Jews on Palestine is discussed in several successive numbers of the *Occident*. One of the most interesting recommendations is the one pertaining to Palestine.

> We cannot avoid calling . . . attention to the statements we have frequently made, that the system of alms giving pursued hitherto towards the poor of Palestine is worse than useless, leading to no practical results; and this is now confirmed by the request made to the philanthropic baronet on the part of the chiefs of the Israelites of Jerusalem, if their wishes are fully carried out—We shall not hear in the future so much nor so frequently of poverty and distress in the old land of our fathers.[21]

Nothing pleases the editor so much as a subject he can sink his teeth into, one which can be continued over several months. His style, dignified, a bit stilted, and always earnest and serious, does not lend itself to terseness, to pithy condensation. Such a series, Leeser finds, can be extracted from the general subject of "The Ministry." There is a shortage of qualified clergymen. Those who are in the ministry are woefully underpaid. The editor deems it his duty "to call again the attention of the public to our defective arrangements for supporting the persons engaged in our ministry." Congregations should, of right, place their ministers beyond want *"and never compel them to experience an emotion of envy when contrasting their poverty with the wealth and elegant appointments of their constituents."* Leeser has just completed "a rapid tour through the seaboard cities . . . as far south as Savannah." This tour left him more convinced than ever "of the poor policy hitherto pursued" by congregations toward their ministers. Formerly salaries offered were inadequate and ministers were regarded as "a sort of genteel servants." Now the salaries offered are much larger "but the candidates for these lucrative posts are wanting. It is time we had an American-trained ministry. European rabbis who do not speak English cannot satisfy the public wants fully. Can strangers know the characters of the people, and the circumstances which surround them?"

His vigor is undiminished in the last two years of his life. He brings the same zest to his editorial job. He flays the same dragons as ever. He is just as interested in his fact-finding jaunts. In "Our Stand-Point" he sadly concludes that there is no real improvement in the condition of society. It is his earnest opinion that, "It is love of ease, interest, ambition, avarice or unbelief which underlie the action of so many modern Jews, who are so unlike their forefathers in everything, and all to their disadvantage in comparison. . . . We ask in all seriousness 'Could not a higher worldly training be combined with a strict conformity?' We think it can." He does not feel that "the progress of society demands us to change our mode of worship, and to re-model it on the basis of any other Church save our own. Nor do we see that Jewish men and women have received a qualified dispensation to do away with our dietary laws on any plea they may be able to present at the bar of divine justice." Then, in case his readers have not guessed that he is still of the same mind on every issue as before, he adds that he began the twenty-fifth volume with the same sentiments as he had the first. Is this an admission of the bareness and paucity of his personal life?

The views he held with such tenacity as a young man have not been hammered away, mellowed, rounded off by the daily contacts with reality and with family which other men knew. He had not changed and so—for him—life had not changed. He takes a winter trip in 1867 and records unhappily that, "Everywhere there is a *looseness of dietary laws*." He visits the war-ravaged South. His reaction is just what we might expect Isaac Leeser to have. "All over the South the war has played sad havoc with conformity—the inability to procure lawful food in many instances, has persuaded some formerly strict people to yield to temptation, and the return of peace has not yet persuaded them to revert to their former good practices."

He is grieved because in all of North Carolina there is not one Jewish congregation. There are some 120 Jews in Wilmington: "It is perhaps the only place in the world where so many Jews live without a union." But that was in April. Whatever the drawbacks of his personality, his zeal was contagious. On September 29 an orthodox synagogue was organized in Wilmington. It was in more ways than one a tribute to Isaac Leeser, although in all modesty—and that too was characteristic of the man—he does not point out the connection between his visit and the creation of a synagogue. He could have many times during his active and creative life pointed to the geography of his days by showing how often a synagogue flowered where once he walked. That he did not say it or write it is one of the most lovable traits of the editor of the *Occident*.

As the sands in his hourglass begin to run low there is more sadness and less brimstone in his strictures on reform. He denies "the incompatibility of modern times and our religion." Long before Professor Clark Wissler analyzed the universal culture scheme of religious practices—ritualistic forms, treatment of the sick, treatment of the dead, their proper place in the general scheme of culture patterns —Isaac Leeser had grasped these principles intuitively and elected himself the custodian for the preservation of the old, the time-honored customs which were invested with the symbols of authority and with the mantle of the Prophets. What Leeser wanted was to arrest social change, to preserve the old without innovation, to hurl himself against the tide of modernity, to stop the evolutionary process. It was the way of heartbreak. For the goal he had in mind was unattainable. He stood for isolation and remained a solitary figure of a man. He lived in an age of transition. The torrential tides of change swirled about him. He was stationary. He resisted change with all his strength and gradually his strength was departing.

But if he is frustrated by the inevitability of social change, he is gratified by the growth of those institutions which he advocated. So the establishment of the Jewish Hospital in Philadelphia, which is the only private hospital in the city offering free medical service to the "afflicted" of every nation, delights and rewards him.

Another of his long-advocated pet projects is born in 1867. It is Maimonides College. A circular issued by the trustees announces that the new college will open the fourth Monday in October. Regulations concerning admission of students, tuition fees, scholarships, and the names of the professors are given. The "Hebrew College of Philadelphia" is a tangible and visible tribute to the man who has so ardently worked for its establishment. How many heartaches and rebuffs Leeser experienced in founding the first college in America for rabbinical and Hebrew education, it is impossible for us to know. He had enlisted powerful friends to help him. The Board of Delegates of American Israelites, the Hebrew Education Society of Philadelphia whose moving spirit he was, supported the institution. Isaac Leeser was president of Maimonides College. Among the members of the faculty were Aaron S. Bettelheim, Marcus M. Jastrow and the wise and gentle and scholarly Sabato Morais. Leeser was to live but three months as head of an institution that was "the darling of his heart." The college lasted only until 1873, when lack of financial support made its further existence impossible.

In the *Atlantic Magazine* for August there is an article by a Christian writer lauding Rabbi Wise, his associates, the reform movement. Leeser points out "with what pleasure the gentile critic speaks of the revolutionary Rabbis; he knows of no others; they are his ideals of Judaism, and he encourages them to go on." How this salute to a rival must have grated on Leeser's sensibilities we may well guess. When the Christian author described "the happy way" in which Cincinnati Jews "are mingling . . . with their fellow citizens," Leeser must have squirmed. When he read of the exchange of pulpits between Rabbis and Christian clergymen his indignation was great. And what must his resentment have been when he read of Rabbi Wise, "whose mission it is" to assist in delivering his people from the tyranny of ancient superstitions! Rabbi Wise to be hailed as the emancipator of his people! Leeser groaned in angry protest and threw himself heart and soul into the work he loved.

The Reverend Isaac Leeser, Provost of Maimonides College, Professor of Homiletics, Belles Lettres and Comparative Theology, now turned to his classes with a will. There were six professors on the faculty, counting Leeser. There were but four students, three from Philadelphia, one from Dubuque, Iowa. Four members of the faculty worked gratuitously, "but still money is needed for everything else." The Hebrew Education Society shared its building with the College. But how meager was the response of American Jews! "Shall it be said that the poorest Christian sect in America can have its high school, but that Jews are too poor-spirited to maintain one of their own, though it cost next to nothing?" Apparently that was the way things were to go with his brain-child. It was a time of heartbreak. It finally wore down his strength. Isaac Leeser died February 1, 1868. His own *Occident* sadly recorded his passing.[22] There were the usual tributes. There was a brief biography. His life's accomplishments were ably summed up in one sentence. He was, said the *Occident*, "more widely known than any other Jewish minister in the country, acquainted with more persons in different portions of the union than probably any clergyman in the land, he had, by his speeches, his writings, and his presence, interwoven himself into the whole system of American Judaism."

In the final, twenty-sixth, volume of the *Occident*, the new incumbent, Mayer Sulzberger, pledges that the spirit of its founder will not be violated. "It will, in every way, endeavor to foster and promote ancient Judaism." It is a deserved oblation to the memory of a great man. The task of continuing the *Occident* was undertaken at Leeser's own request. "We did not deem ourselves at liberty to leave unheeded a darling wish of the greatest of American Israelites."

Now other tributes pour in, sincere, heartfelt expressions of grief and respect. There are group responses such as an "Isaac Leeser Lodge" of the B'nai B'rith in Philadelphia. Measures are undertaken by the trustees of Leeser's estate to establish a Jewish Publication Society as a tribute to Leeser's memory. Eighteen years had elapsed since the original society established for publishing books of interest to Jews was compelled to suspend operations.

It was reserved for its original projector, the Rev. Isaac Leeser, to take the initiative towards recalling it into life. In his will . . . he directed that there should be formed, incorporated, and put into operation in the city of Philadelphia or New York, within five years after his decease, a Jewish Publication Society.

He left books, many books. For Leeser's library "was in its day one of the best Hebrew libraries in America." When he was not quite twenty, Cyrus Adler, as a labor of love, catalogued this library. "I must say that this collection contained some very interesting and rare books," writes Adler. "I have always kept this library in mind, and when the Dropsie College was established arranged for its permanent deposit there, so that off and on I have had this collection under my eye for fifty years." Leeser was not completely without an heir.

In December of 1868, Dr. J. L. Levison of London sent in a tribute to "The Late Reverend Isaac Leeser." Soon after that the *Occident* ceased publication.

In his "Valedictory" published March, 1869, the new editor throws in the sponge. He could not carry the Herculean load which his predecessor had borne for a quarter of a century. Isaac Leeser's shoes were too big for him. So he explains his position. It was the desire of Leeser that he assume "the literary and mercantile supervision" of the *Occident*. He undertook the task despite his many misgivings. The difficulties were insuperable. One of his greatest handicaps was lack of contributors. Whereas "the great monthlies and quarterlies require the utmost discrimination to select judiciously from the abundance of articles struggling for admission, our magazine has had the assistance of but few pens." Circumstances do not permit the present editor to continue. He hopes that some one will be found who can make of the *Occident* "a pecuniary and literary success."

No such person was found.

It was a strange time, a time of growing up and of integration. An age of acceptance and of rejection. A period of involvement in communal affairs and of stark personal loneliness. It was an era of moral grandeur and of compromise. The leaders were men of stature. Their names were known. Their affairs were celebrated.

But there were nameless Jews then. These anonymous ones found their way deep into the interior. They lived on the fringe of communities. They existed in the borderlands. They departed like ghosts leaving faint footprints behind them. Still they are a part of the narrative. Somehow their past must also be apprehended.

A nameless Jewish peddler was murdered in his little log cabin on the outskirts of Bishop Hill, in Illinois. What business he had with the religious community founded by Erik Jansson and his Swedish emigrés, we do not know. The anonymous one had a rascally associate whose name is preserved. John Root was an adventurer from Sweden who married the cousin of the founder of Bishop Hill.

He was opposed to serious labor and spent his time in the chase. . . . But tiring even of this employment, he sought new adventures as interpreter and guide to a Hebrew peddler. The Jew was never heard of again; but a few years after, the decomposed body of a murdered man was discovered under the floor of a deserted cabin some miles from Bishop Hill.[23]

A hundred years later, on April 14, 1946, the writer found a Torah scroll in Bishop Hill, a tattered, mildewed, frayed, rodent-nibbled but still beautiful roll of leather on which a seventeenth-century Hebrew virtuoso had carefully and lovingly inscribed the Book of Deuteronomy.

It was a symbol of the anonymous Jews of a vanished age.

CHAPTER XIII

The "Songs of a Semite"

→≫≫
　　　　　"In Exile"
Freedom to love the law that Moses brought,
To sing the songs of David, and to think
The thoughts Gabirol to Spinoza taught,
Freedom to dig the common earth, to drink
The universal air—for this they sought
Refuge o'er wave and continent. . . .
　　　　　　　　—EMMA LAZARUS,
　　　　　　　　　Songs of a Semite[1]　　≪≪

THE BITTER harvest of war was reaped in the dark unhappy days following Lincoln's death and the end of hostilities. Hate dies hard. Anguish lingers in the hearts of men. Devastation presents its bill. Creatures who during the tragic era crawled into dark places seeking their personal safety emerge like slugs. The demagogue struts and shouts while the hero digs in the rubble.

Andrew Johnson of Tennessee succeeded Abraham Lincoln, came within one vote of being impeached and was, in turn, followed by Ulysses S. Grant. But before he turned over his office to his successor, Johnson had a brief tussle with the Senate over the appointment of a Jew as Minister to Mexico. The man involved was Marcus Otterbourg. Otterbourg was born in Germany in 1827. He emigrated to America and became a newspaperman in Milwaukee. He was an ardent Republican and came to know Lincoln. As a reward for his political exertions, Lincoln appointed Otterbourg in 1861 as Consul to Mexico City. He was an interested witness of the Maximilian drama and made himself useful and acceptable to all factions. When he wrote his reports to Washington, his journalistic talents proved useful. His letters to the State Department were sprightly, informative, vivid. He earned the respect of his chief, William H. Seward. Ill health and overwork forced him to consider resigning his post. Seward would not hear of it. Nevertheless Otterbourg went to Washington and presented his resignation to the State Department. It was not accepted. He returned to Mexico City. He tried with all his energies to save the life of the Emperor Maximilian. In the meantime Seward was urging Otterbourg's promotion from Consul to Minister. One of Seward's associates wrote in his diary:

The President is disinclined to appoint Otterbourg, the German, or German Jew, Minister to Mexico, although Seward is very persistent for him. Randall (Postmaster General) originally proposed Otterbourg and would be pleased to have him promoted, but seeing the President's hesitancy, does not press it. Seward, however, holds on vigorously.[2]

Johnson eventually succumbed to pressure and sent Otterbourg's name to the Senate as Minister to Mexico. It was just one of the many requests of Johnson's that the Senate refused to honor. In the few months he continued as unconfirmed Minister to Mexico, Otterbourg protected not only American citizens but other foreigners whose safety was threatened. He fed the hungry. He watched over the insecure. Otterbourg was one of the men who negotiated with Diaz for the surrender of Mexico City. When he returned to the States he could point with pride to his years of honorable service in behalf of his country.

Not only in the Senate, where Otterbourg's appointment was debated, but all over the land the fact of a man's being Jewish was enough to arouse comment, to cause debate, to bring out latent prejudice. Jews were one way or another in the news. The *Nation* in 1868 was writing with scholarly detachment on a number of aspects of Jewish affairs. There were sympathetic references to the plight of Jews in Europe, to the irrational persecution which dogged them, to their age-old suffering. On June 18, 1868, "The Reform Movement Among the Jews" traced the history of enlightenment and the development of a secular learning. The works of Wessely, editor of *Measseph* (*The Gatherer*), and other great Hebraists were cited as proof of emancipation. The contribution of the Kantian philosopher, Bendavid, was analyzed with insight. His proposal to do away with all ceremonial Judaism, which Bendavid called "a dead weight on pure Mosaic monotheism," was brought to the attention of American readers. During Johnson's administration readers of the *Nation* were introduced to Jost, Zunz, Reggio, Luzzato and many other great Jewish luminaries.[3]

Among American Jews Leeser and Wise were Olympians. They

were engaged in a contest whose implications are clear. Yet the reform movement over which they fought so passionately was older than
both men. The issue was destined to survive them.

In their years of wandering the Pilgrim People had made of their
ancient law and of their way of life a rock to which they could cling
for safety and security. They had made of their great men their
cherished monuments whose memory they carried in their hearts.

Now new ideas beckoned. Freedom was a siren. Contact with great
minds, rationalist, Christian, lured Jews into the great community.
Change was their destiny. Some Jewish writers compare the reform
movement with the Protestant Reformation. It was a protest against
the rigid hand of the past which still clutched the garments of the
modern Jew, restraining the freedom of his movements. Whether the
new way led to spiritual extinction or was the promise of a more
integrated and more vital Judaism is still a moot question. Certainly
some Jews who listened to the voice of reform were lost to Judaism.
But so were many who had adhered to orthodoxy. What was obsolete?
Who was to decide?

Even before the great migration began, a native reform movement
indigenous to the new land had sprung up.[4] In 1824, a group of
Charleston radicals rebelled against the long services, the exclusive
use of Hebrew and some of the traditional ceremonies. They knew
of the beginnings of similar tendencies in Germany. Their first memorial summarizing their history and origin mentions it. "It cannot be
claimed that Isaac Harby was the originator of the modern reform in
Jewish worship. All scholars know how difficult it is to trace any great
idea to its original source," writes Harby's biographer. Forty-seven
of these malcontents, led by Isaac Harby, petitioned the trustees for
some concessions to change. They were denied. David Nunes Carvalho became the first reader of the seceding group. The credo of the
Charleston reform movement stated that each adherent believed in
God as the Creator and Governor of the universe; that he believed in
the unity and in the incorporeality of God. That he accepted with a
"perfect faith" that God was to be adored and worshiped. He accepted
belief in the immortality of the soul and assumed that God rewarded
the righteous and punished evildoers. The Ten Commandments were
the "foundations of piety," God was the "true Redeemer of all His
children." The reformers were snubbed by the pillars of tradition
from the first. Later the schism was somewhat healed. When Rabbi
Gustavus Poznanski came to Charleston in 1836, however, the reform

group gained an able ally. For two years the battle raged and the community was split in two while some members clamored that an organ be built into the new synagogue, a building which had been beautifully and lovingly designed by David Lopez. The organ was included. Forty members seceded and erected in 1847 a synagogue known as Shearith Israel. The organ was but a symbol. Other controversial issues continued to divide American Israel.

Philipson sees the reform movement begun in Charleston as a cultural adaptation, its innovations as the result of adjustment to social pressure.[5] "With the exception of the Charleston congregation, there were no steps taken anywhere in the country in the interest of the reform movement before the year 1840."

The Jews of Charleston had looked to Germany. Now English Jews looked to Charleston.[6] England had its reform leader in David Woolf Marks. By 1840 there had been a number of attempts made in England by various dissident Israelites to shorten the services, alter the ritual and in general to achieve in atmosphere and decorum a closer conformity to prevailing Christian practices. The West London Congregation of British Jews was formed and began to conduct services in January 1843.

Gradually there developed, in London particularly, two types of Judaism—the "vigorous" religion of the East End Jew and "shadowy faith" of his West End coreligionist.

In America this dichotomy became more in evidence with the passing years. Isaac M. Wise had been hard at work for a long time on his new book, *Minhag America*.[7] It was to be his contribution to the reform movement of his adopted land. He had originally summarized his point of view on reform in two English lectures, which he meticulously wrote out. One of his friends asked to see the manuscript and sent it without Wise's permission to Isaac Leeser.

Before I had given any further thought to the manuscript, I saw it, to my astonishment, published *verbatim et literatim* in the *Occident*, accompanied by long notes from the pen of the highly incensed editor. In addition to this, I was called to account for having introduced a mixed choir into the synagogue. . . . I wrote a very drastic letter to Leeser.

I wrote in an exceedingly pedantic and excited strain, and . . . asked Leeser how it happened that of all the Jews who had emigrated to these shores between 1620 and 1829 there were not 200 families left that belonged to congregations, while the great majority had disappeared among the masses. Leeser never answered this question, and the orthodox party owes me the answer still.[8]

So the battle raged. In 1842 the Har Sinai Congregation of Baltimore had been established along the lines laid down by the Hamburg Temple movement. Three years later Emanuel Congregation in New York joined the parade of reform. The reform movement may have actually been founded in Germany. But it flowered in America.[9]

A group of German Jewish immigrants of Cincinnati in the year of the founding of the Baltimore Reform Congregation organized the Congregation Bene Jeshurun. The election of Rabbi Isaac Mayer Wise in 1854 gave them a leader as well as an organization. The geographical pattern of the reform movement is obvious. It followed the pattern of mobility of the German immigrants.

In 1858 a dissident group of Chicago Jews resigned from the Congregation Anshe Maarab and formed a *"Reformverein."* Its secretary was Rabbi Bernhard Felsenthal, who was to become the first Rabbi of the Congregation. On the historic occasion of the formation of the group Rabbi Felsenthal paid tribute to the minority of Jews who "will not permit the work of their fathers, that has existed thousands of years, to be destroyed." Eventually this unit became Sinai Congregation of Chicago, which was formally organized in 1860.

Philipson's *Reform Movement in Judaism* lists the following men as its leaders: Max Lilienthal, Isaac M. Wise, David Einhorn, Samuel Adler, Bernhard Felsenthal, and Samuel Hirsch.

What was their philosophy? What their beliefs? Most ably summarized by Rabbi Philipson, who lets each one of the leaders state his own ideological concept of reform, here are brief credos from the writings of these religious leaders. Wise said:

Judaism has become a set of unmeaning practices, and the intelligent Jew either mourns for the fallen daughter of Zion or has adopted a course of frivolity and indifference. . . . All unmeaning forms must be laid aside as outworn garments. The internal spirit of Judaism must be expounded, illustrated, and made dear again to the Jew.

Lilienthal said:

We are tired of seeing men violating the Sabbath until they have accumulated an independent fortune, and calling themselves orthodox nevertheless; we are disgusted at seeing men transgressing every religious ceremony in public life, and yet clothing themselves with the halo of sanctification; we wish to see this contradiction solved.

Samuel Hirsch said:

The ceremonies became meaningless . . . no symbol can hereafter pass as Jewish which prevents the Jew from participating. . . . He may not be a mere spectator of the work of the modern age.

Einhorn said:

There is at present a rent in Judaism which affects its very life, and which no covering, however glittering, can repair. The evil which threatens to corrode gradually all the healthy bone and marrow must be completely eradicated.

Bernhard Felsenthal was the father of the reform movement in Chicago. His *Kol Kore Bamidbar* was an uncompromising defense of the need for reform. He pleaded for the discarding of "all heathenism and foolishness," all outworn customs and outdated observances.[10]

Reform made its inroads into one community after another. Sometimes peacefully, sometimes with violence and bitter vituperation, but inexorably and inevitably it took its place in Jewish communal life. Everywhere but in Philadelphia. There orthodoxy was unassailable. Says Philipson:

The city of Philadelphia was, in the fifth and sixth decades (of) the century, the stronghold of Orthodox Judaism, owing largely to the prestige and influence of the Reverend Isaac Leeser. . . . Any effort at reform in that community naturally met with the greatest obstacles, and the pages of the *Occident*, the organ of Mr. Leeser, present a vivid picture of the opposition superinduced by any step toward reform anywhere in the country.[11]

The first conference of the "reform school" of Judaism was held in Philadelphia in November, 1869. Leeser had departed the scene of his labors the previous year.

It was Leeser against Wise while the former lived. Not only the cumulative evidence in the *Occident*, but the narrative of his early struggle for recognition in America as told by Wise himself, is a subtle tribute to that doughty soldier of Orthodoxy, Isaac Leeser. Some of the most perceptive comments on the editor of the *Occident* came from the pen of Isaac M. Wise. Here were two dynamic adversaries, each imbued with passion and fire, each convinced of the righteousness of the cause he advocated, yet each grudgingly and unwillingly admiring the other. Leeser is familiar. What of Wise?

Isaac Mayer Wise was born in Bohemia in 1819. He studied in Prague, became a member of the rabbinate, emigrated to America in 1846. His first glimpse of America was disappointing. Like so many others who came to America at this time, he had expected more.

He experienced the deep unhappiness of seeing the waste, the exploitation, the ruthless assumption that the immigrant is fit only for the menial task:

I found in a basement, a number of young fellow-countrymen of culture transformed into factory hands, cigar-makers, and peddlers, who, like a lot of political quidnuncs, uttered absolute and decided opinions about the Mexican War which was then in progress.[12]

He wandered about the city making gloomy observations, meeting rebuffs and slights with which the immigrant is all too familiar. He had many a black hour. He tried to support himself by teaching others but he was not much of a pedagogue. People gave him the usual advice—peddle or learn a trade. "I was disgusted." Then came the first happy experience. He made a friend. "Doctor Lilienthal was the first one to encourage me and inspire me with hope, and at that time this was of prime importance and significance for me." He gathered impressions for his future work, albeit unconsciously. He visited the Polish synagogue and didn't care for it, for to hear "some individual sniffle through a bit of *Rashi* in so pitiably ignorant a manner" filled him with revulsion. Wise was always fastidious to a fault. He lacked the warm, intuitive understanding, the imagination which would make even a poor, shabby place like a Polish synagogue partake of the magic transformation with which simple faith and unquestioning belief gilds everything. Yet he called himself a dreamer and visionary. "We idealists are perfect builders so long as only air castles are to be erected. . . . We imagine everything to be charming and easy of accomplishment." He could scarcely conceal his contempt for some of his brethren. New York was, for him, a desert and he was a parched soul. In 1846, he writes, that with the exception of Lilienthal and Merzbacher, "there was not one leader who could read unpunctuated Hebrew." He found only "three men in private life who possessed any Jewish, or any Talmudical learning."

He found much in America that was wanting. He could justly criticize many archaic usages, much usurpation of power by the laity. This latter abuse particularly was more than he could stomach. "A correct conception of the power and autocracy of the *parnass* in those days can be formed from the following occurrence; Isaac Leeser who was the *lumen mundi* of American Jewry at that time, was not permitted to preach in his own synagogue without the permission of the *parnass*."

The grudging respect which each of these two rival religious leaders accorded the other is developed at length in Wise's fascinating *Reminiscences*. Leeser infuriated Wise. Wise frustrated Leeser. Wise resented criticism. Leeser was unsparing of it. When Wise received a critical letter from Leeser he could hardly contain his anger.

Upon perusing this letter, I grew very angry at the thought that a man who could not read unpunctuated Hebrew presumed to direct Jewish affairs in the rôle of editor and guardian. I intended to write him this in plain, unvarnished terms . . . but I thought it was a pity to waste the paper, since it was impossible to effect any change.

He decided to plunge into the study of English so that he could best his rival in his own field, American journalism. Eventually he, too, edited an English publication, the *American Israelite*. He also published *Die Deborah* in German. He had a brilliant mind, a retentive memory and inflexible purpose. Leeser was the grain of sand to Wise's oyster. We may thank Leeser for the pearls.

Wise soon became convinced that he could not long defer the hour of "public and decisive combat." Some of his articles had appeared in the *Occident*. But his enemies had multiplied. "Leeser had introduced me to the American Jewish public. Every reader knew where and how to find me. My opinions had not been kept secret. . . . The *Occident* furnished these enemies with ever fresh material and a storm was brewing whereof I had no inkling."

Eventually the two met. Wise described their dramatic meeting simply:

One morning late in the autumn of the year 1847 a lean, pock-marked, clean-shaven little man clad in black stepped into my study. The sparkling eye and the black hair betrayed the Jew. The rapid enunciation designated the foreigner, and the readiness and unrestraint denoted the intellect.

"Whose acquaintance have I the honor of forming?"

"My name is Isaac Leeser."

"I am happy to make your personal acquaintance."

Explanations followed and in one-half hour we understood each other thoroughly. Leeser seemed to me a man worthy of respect. . . . I treated Leeser very respectfully. He seemed to appreciate being treated thus by an opponent. He informed me of his sufferings and his struggles. And in a few hours we were very friendly.[13]

Both men emerge enhanced. Leeser, lonely, recently ill, driven by his restless nature to unceasing work, denied the comfort of a family circle, was a pathetic figure of a man. This Wise was quick to note.

He was a compassionate and astute host. Wise analyzed the circle of readers for whom Leeser labored so prodigiously:

The *Occident* was published for native-born, English, some Polish and Dutch Jews. The latter were Talmudically Orthodox. The native Jews were, if I may say so, tinged with Christian thought. They read only Christian religious literature because there was no Jewish literature of this kind. They substituted God for Jesus, unity for trinity, the future Messiah for the Messiah who had already appeared, etc. There were Episcopalian Jews in New York, Quaker Jews in Philadelphia, Huguenot Jews in Charleston, and so on, everywhere according to the prevailing sect.[14]

The following year found Wise restless. He followed the news of the revolutions in Europe with keen interest. He was by nature a fighter. It was hard to be so far away. He read all the bulletins, even had services interrupted whenever there was news. Never does Wise appear more lovable, more heroic, than in his boyish enthusiasm for the cause that was to emancipate a continent. "At the same time that I entertained these patriotic and revolutionary ideas, and constructed air castles for liberated humanity I was exchanging letters with Isaac Leeser relative to a plan for unification and elevation of American Jewry."

Leeser and I had agreed that a gathering of the representatives of the congregations would be a strong impetus. No matter what they might do at the first meeting, it could not but be a clear gain for Judaism. . . . It was therefore resolved that Leeser should advocate the project personally in Philadelphia and in the West and South, and that I should make propaganda for it in the East, particularly in New York.[15]

Their ambivalent relationship was nourished by their many common interests. Latent hostility goaded each man. Still they had a common goal, to bring about union between the various factions among America's Jews.

New threats menaced. Societies for converting Jews were making headway. Isolated Israelites cut off from religious and educational sustenance were ripe for conversion. In 1849 a brilliant young Presbyterian clergyman was imbued with the idea of converting Jews en masse. As secretary of the Presbyterian General Assembly, he and a number of associates issued a manifesto to the Jews inviting them to enter the Presbyterian Church as a unit. Wise, who was a sound scholar, promised Leeser to write a series of articles for the *Occident* on the subject of the New Testament. He wrote as a rationalist. The articles aroused heated discussion. His rationalism was impartial. Wise tilted with Orthodox Jews as well as Christians. "Miracles were not wonderful or marvelous for me," writes Wise. Likeminded Christians, Theodore Parker among them, became his sincere admirers. "Chief-Justice Wood danced about like a mischievous boy with my articles in his hand . . . and sent them to all his friends." It was an age of rationalism and honest inquiry for Christians. Why not for Jews also?

But this glow of accomplishment soon yielded to personal tragedy and ill health. In 1850 Wise was in a state of deep melancholia. "Weariness of life overcame me. I was sick, hypochondriacal, and surrounded by foes." He went traveling. Gradually the black mood was dissipated. The therapy of contact with likeminded friends began its healing work. Gratification at progress made alternated with a sense of failure always. Wise was spurred on by his friends and cast down by his critics. "A terrible fate has condemned me to be the scapegoat of an era in contradiction with itself," he concludes. In other matters this sharp critic of society records his disillusionment. He became a member of B'nai B'rith. "The ritual seemed to me colorless, the people commonplace, and the proceedings unbearably wearisome and trivial. The whole thing seemed to me childish tomfoolery, and made so disagreeable an impression on me that I thought immediately of plans of improvement."

His sphere of influence widened. Personal success attended many of his undertakings. In 1854, he was launched on his literary career. *The Israelite* (later *American Israelite*) made its debut. It is still published. Success brought new problems.

Leeser and Wise had many grievances in common. They shared many common goals. Over the years their differences sharpened and tension between the two became more marked. Wise believed that Judaism needed him and his gifts. He was ready to wage the fight as long as his powers lasted. He was fortunate. His life was lived until 1900. He realized many of his dreams. He saw the reform movement become solidly established. He was one of the founders of the Union of American Hebrew Congregations in 1873. He founded the Hebrew Union College two years later. In 1889 he helped create the Central Conference of American Rabbis. He wrote a number of enduring, scholarly books. He infused much of himself into his many students. He left an enduring impression on his age.

At Jacksonville, Florida, on December 6, 1944, the *S. S. Isaac Wise* slid proudly down the ways. In 1946 the centennial of Wise's landing in America was celebrated. It was a good life, long to be remembered.

These two—Leeser and Wise—long dominated the American Jewish scene. Both men made a passionate identification with America. To one the destiny of America's Jews was of deep personal concern. It was the wife he did not have, the children who were not born to him. It was his fireside and his fantasy, his fulfillment and his purpose in life. He died in the midst of battle. The other protagonist served the same master with an intensity of concentration and an enthusiasm which were the fruits of a happy life. Leeser died with his "darling" projects just begun. Wise lived to see his ambitions realized and his dreams fulfilled.

The intervening years have perpetuated these differences and contributed little to their solution. The *Nation* in 1868 discussed the growth of the reform movement in America in terms that are applicable today. The *Allgemeine Zeitung des Judenthums* many years later, on January 24, 1896, devoted its leading editorial to a subject familiar to the readers of the *Occident* half a century before—the causes of prejudice. On October 30, 1896, the editor of the *Allgemeine Zeitung* protested his patriotism and loyalty in almost the identical words that Isaac M. Wise had used in America. While in the pages of the *Jewish Quarterly Review*, Julia Richman was writing of the Jewish Sunday School movement in the United States, founded by Isaac Leeser and Rebecca Gratz a generation before.[16] The pages of the *Jewish Quarterly Review* took up the subject which the *Occident* had once discussed. Leeser was not altogether forgotten.

The quill was passed from hand to hand. It seems but a moment from the *Jewish Quarterly Review* of 1890 to the *Christian Century* of 1942, where Reform Judaism was discussed. The same subject is analyzed in the same terms, as if the sun and the moon and the stars had stood still since the days of Isaac Wise and Isaac Leeser. A recent issue of *Liberal Judaism* speaks of this "recurrent" theme. In a conference on "Judaism and American Democracy" held in Cincinnati October 18, 1945, the same principles were enunciated as we found in the last report of the Board of Delegates of American Israelites. Are we "first Americans and then Israelites," as Wise described us? It would seem that we are. "This conference," said the assembly of rabbis which met on the occasion of the seventieth anniversary of the Hebrew Union College, "declares anew that in American democracy and in Judaism, and very clearly in reform Judaism, there exists a natural synthesis. . . . We are certain that this spiritual reciprocity will endure."

Emile Durkheim, an astute student of the universal patterns of religious life, once said that, "There is something eternal in religion which is destined to survive. . . . There can be no society which does not feel the need of upholding and reaffirming at regular intervals the collective sentiments and the collective ideas which makes its unity and its personality."[17] The truth of these words is manifest when we consider the persistence of the problems which divided American Jews a century ago and to this day. All of the issues which divided Leeser from Wise still separate their spiritual heirs. But there is this difference. The century has been prolific. It has added variations and magnified differences. It has introduced new philosophies and perpetuated the old schisms. The history of the Jews of America for these past hundred years could well be written as a history of theological diversity. The days when there were two camps in Jewish ranks are elementary in their simplicity. Did Leeser hurl an editorial at Wise, Wise could dash one off with equal ease. Each could give as well as he got, and beneath it all a deep liking, an ineradicable affection lingered. But now? Personalities still clash. Ideologies still separate. Judaism in America is a chromatic scale beginning with strict orthodoxy, embracing the conservative, the Reconstructionist, the Zionist and non-Zionist, the reformer, the ethical culturist, the rationalist, the synagogued nonbeliever, and the believing unsynagogued. Religion in the days of yore was a fellowship of likeminded. The ministry, as one of our modern sages wisely said, was once dedicated to comforting the afflicted and afflicting the comfortable. Now it comforts the comfortable and afflicts the afflicted. Huge buildings are erected. Style of architecture is a moot question. There are differences and divagations. . . .

"There were those in our Congregation who wanted a Greek Temple. There were others who wanted a New England Meeting House," wrote one scribe in 1944.[18] The Jewish clergy is busy campaigning for bigger buildings, pleading for followers for this cause or that. The little man is swallowed up. He is menaced by bigness. Science overawes him and undermines the foundations of his faith. He wants sanctuary. It is easy enough to look nostalgically to the past. "Traditional Judaism possessed a well knit social structure." But the modern man wants tools adequate to meet his present daily problems. What solved his dilemmas in the past will not solve them today. There is discontent among American Jews. "If any of the current versions of Judaism, if neo-Orthodoxy, Reform or Zionism, enabled us to cope with our problems and difficulties, there would be no occasion to express discontent with Judaism as it is. But unfortunately all these versions fail to reckon fully with our needs," writes Professor Mordecai M. Kaplan advocating his own solution—Reconstruction.

Jewish life in America continues fluid. It is still constantly being debated and assessed and reassessed.

"American Jewry has long been a composite of three well-defined groups," wrote Dr. David de Sola Pool, rabbi of historic Shearith Israel, in 1942.[19] It was the Orthodox synagogue that held the Jewish community together, he avers. Sephardic Jews have by and large remained loyal to the Orthodox tradition. But with increase in East European immigration, with geographic dispersion, with closer association with nonconformist neighbors the bonds that tied Jews to their synagogues were loosened. In the eighteenth century the synagogue was the dynamic center of religious, philanthropic, educational, social activities. In the nineteenth century, "the synagogue lost its position of centrality in American Jewish life."

There are about 5,000,000 Jews in the United States today, although according to the latest *American Jewish Year Book*, "accurate and up-to-date statistics of the Jewish population of the United States are not available." In the past century, 1850-1950, the Jewish population has grown from fifty thousand to its present size. Essentially, American Jews may be divided into four categories: Orthodox, Reform, Conservative and unaffiliated. "Orthodoxy, the main stream of historical tradition, has been the Judaism of the overwhelming majority of Jews in the United States," declares Rabbi Pool. "It clings to Hebrew as a sacred tongue, to the Hebrew Bible as its ultimate authority, to the Law of Moses as a way of life, to the admonitions of the Prophets for its ethics, to the outpourings of the Psalms for much of its liturgy." The Reform movement may be described as essentially stressing the relaxation of orthodox practices, as largely substituting Sunday for Sabbath services, as rejecting both Talmudic authority and ceremonial law. "The unresolved, recurring question at every convention was: what is Conservative Judaism?" wrote Rabbi Davis in his summary of "Religious Life and Institutions in America." "All Conservative Jews accepted the formula that Judaism is a changing and developing religion," continues Rabbi Davis. "The advocates of the theory of obsolescence argued that Catholic Israel will itself determine what laws are to be abrogated and what laws retained in the permanent system of Judaism. Others, who could not suffer the steady disintegration of Jewish legal sanction, proposed immediate collective revision of the ritual law. A third group counseled that both these viewpoints be incorporated into an organic Judaism . . ."

These divisions in the ranks of American Jewry merely prove that it is still dynamic, evolving, changing. Advocates of Reform Judaism feel themselves challenged on many fronts. The adherents of tradition reject reform because "it does not have the sanction of the masses . . . it has failed to unite Israel." These words were not spoken by Leeser. They were written a century later.

Rationalism and enlightenment inevitably led to reform. Isaac Mayer Wise and his confreres challenged the stronghold, attacked the ancient folkways, demanded a restatement of Judaism in terms of progress. The vigor of the attack left orthodoxy reeling. It is still under siege.

American Orthodoxy is making conscious and vigorous attempts to save itself. More and more one hears of a modern American Orthodoxy, an Orthodoxy which blends with the American scene. . . . The status of the orthodox rabbi has been happily raised in the last generation. He no longer belongs to a Jewish social and cultural type that is passing.[20]

The ancient folkways, the time-honored mores persist in the orthodox synagogue. But the din and clamor of its critics penetrate the walls and demand to be heard.

Conservative Judaism is comparatively recent. It owes its beginnings to Solomon Schechter. One of its advocates has defined it as follows: "Conservative Judaism is resolved not only to perpetuate our great heritage, but to make it function as a vital and creative factor in Jewish life and, through Israel, in human civilization as a whole."[21]

Solomon Schechter, native of Rumania, received the best instruction that Europe had to offer. He absorbed it like a sponge. His radiant personality, deep erudition, aptitude and scholarship brought him an invitation to England. Here his writing interpreted to a wide audience the essentials of Judaism, of the Talmud, of Jewish history. He gained international fame when he discovered priceless manuscripts belonging to the Genizah of the synagogue in Cairo, Egypt. The hundred thousand manuscripts were brought to England and presented to Cambridge University by Schechter and the Christian scholar, Charles Taylor. Schechter was a member of the faculty of

Cambridge from 1892-1902. He became president of the Jewish Theological Seminary of America, an institution which owed its inception to Sabato Morais and H. Pereira Mendes. The great legacy which Schechter, like Leeser, left behind him, concerns itself with the "catholicity" or universality of Judaism, of a faith resting on the consensus of the people it represents, perpetuated by their implicit acceptance of its principles. Something of this point of view was expressed by the head of the Jewish Theological Seminary, who is a disciple of Solomon Schechter. Rabbi Louis Finkelstein wrote in the *Jewish Quarterly Review* what amounts to an appeal to all those of any faith who believe in God, to come together in a common cause— the perpetuation of the God-idea, for the disappearance of the God-concept "would be an unqualified catastrophe."[22]

As to relative numerical strength, a recent scholar, Rabbi Robert Gordis, gives the following estimate: "In 1940 there were 4,000 congregations in the United States. Of these 307 belonged to the Reform group. 275 were Conservative. The rest were Orthodox.

In 1920, Mordecai M. Kaplan wrote a paper for the *Menorah Journal* titled "A Program for the Reconstruction of Judaism." Since then his philosophy of Judaism has been developed and enlarged in his *Judaism as a Civilization* and *The Future of the American Jew*. This is a frank attempt to restate the folkways and mores of Judaism in terms acceptable to the sociologist, anthropologist and psychiatrist as well as to the religionist. Says Kaplan:

Reformist Judaism represents the first deliberate and organized effort to adjust traditional Judaism to the exigencies of modern political and economic conditions and to reckon with the modern world-outlook.[23]

Reconstructionist philosophy seeks to make of Judaism a creative relationship. It tackles definition and obligation, creed and deed. Judaism, it is stressed, is a way of life. "The predominant teaching has been that the Jewish people owed the prerogative of salvation entirely to the particular way of life to which it had dedicated itself." Judaism is a civilization, unique and indestructible. Reconstructionism seeks a formula for creative Jewish participation in American life. It recognizes the social conflict and the inevitability of social change by stressing that "there is the need for correlating the struggle for Jewish survival with the social conflicts upon which the attention of mankind is at present focused." Reconstructionism is an integrated acquiescence to all of man's needs on every level of his behavior. The Reconstructionist can say with Edmund Fleg, "I am a Jew because the faith of Israel demands no abdication of my mind."

"The Reconstructionist Platform" defines Judaism, correlates Judaism with American democracy, advocates unity through federation of communal organizations, stresses the importance of Jewish studies, seeks to make ritual meaningful as folk art, enumerates the goals of social justice, defines God in terms "free from superstition," seeking integration of religion with all that is new in science and in social science.[24]

It is a century since Isaac Mayer Wise issued a "Call to Israelites" in the pages of the *Occident*.[25] One hundred years ago he pleaded for all Jews "to be united as one man." That utopia has not come about. There is no "uniformity in our sacred customs." There are no common goals. There is no unity. It is almost a century since Isidor Bush wrote his thought-provoking paper on "The Task of Jews in the United States." His seven rules for the guidance of the Hebrews of America are still applicable.[26]

The subject is endless and relentlessly pursued. Since religion is a part of life and life is fluid, there is no answer to the questions which depressed Leeser and troubled Wise. The issue survives its ablest protagonists.

When Grant became President in 1869 the malevolent oppression of Jews in Rumania was the nightmare of their coreligionists the world over. Simon Wolf, whose friendship with President Grant is a matter of record, persuaded the President to call a special Cabinet meeting to consider the news of the expulsion of Jews from Russian Bessarabia. Heading our State Department was Hamilton Fish. He upheld the Department's humanitarian tradition. Mr. Fish exerted himself valiantly in behalf of the victims. "The people of this country universally abhor persecution," he wrote in one of his communiqués. President Grant then appointed Benjamin Franklin Peixotto to "the important, though unremunerative, position of United States Consul to Rumania." The choice was a happy one. No more humane —nor more capable person could possibly have been found.[27]

It was a generation of great men and great activity. The appointment of Peixotto could very well have been due to the influence exerted by Simon Wolf on President Grant. Simon Wolf, friend of the President, was born in 1836. He came to the United States at the age of twelve. He started as an office boy in a small Ohio town. But he was ambitious. He began an arduous program of night study. He studied for the bar in Ohio and was admitted to practice in 1861, and became an immediate success. From 1862 on, Simon Wolf headed a law firm in Washington. He became the friend and associate of many men prominent in American life. Wolf was an ardent Republican. It was General Grant's impetuous and ill-fated "Order Number 11" which turned Simon Wolf into a champion for the Jewish cause. From then on he spoke often and vigorously in behalf of Jewish rights wherever challenged.

Simon Wolf was active in the affairs of the Board of Delegates of American Israelites. He was chairman of the Council of the Union of American Hebrew Congregations in 1876. Always interested in the affairs of B'nai B'rith, he presided at their Chicago Convention in 1874 and their Philadelphia Convention in 1879. His research in behalf of the American Jew was indefatigable. His accumulations of data were to prove of inestimable value in establishing the Jew as a patriot, as a daring and self-sacrificing soldier, as a citizen to be cherished.

Peixotto, whom Simon Wolf knew and admired, was born in New York in 1834. He was the son of Dr. Daniel L. M. Peixotto. He chose law as a career and prepared for the bar by working in the offices of Stephen A. Douglas. He supported Douglas in the Presidential campaign. He espoused the Union cause during the War. Wolf states that Peixotto "severed the affiliations of an active political career and took an earnest part in arousing the patriotic sentiments of the people." In 1863, Peixotto took a major step in the direction of affiliation with his coreligionists. He joined the B'nai B'rith and became president of the Supreme Lodge of that fraternal organization. The "Sons of the Covenant," or B'nai B'rith, was then twenty years old. It had been founded in New York by twelve German Jews who called themselves *Bundes Brüder*. Among its founders were Rabbi Leo Merzbacher, friend of Isaac M. Wise, Joseph Ochs and Mosley Ezekiel, father of the sculptor. The growth of B'nai B'rith was little short of phenomenal. When the first English-speaking lodge was formed in Cincinnati, a major step in the direction of integration and effectiveness was taken. Peixotto's active leadership for the four terms that he served as president channeled the organization toward many philanthropic activities. One of the first social service goals he recommended was an orphanage for Jewish children whose fathers had been killed in combat. This plan eventually developed into the Cleveland Jewish Orphanage.

It was his diplomatic mission however, which insured Peixotto a permanent place in the affections of his people. His letters aroused the conscience of the State Department. He was alert, humane, morally responsive.

Three International Jewish Conferences were held in Europe partly at Peixotto's insistence. The inclusion of the Jewish question at the Congress of Berlin of 1878 was also partly the result of his efforts. The situation of Rumanian Jews was desperate: "They had suffered for ten years from a succession of barbarous persecutions and mob outrages, which had reduced them to the utmost misery and had excited the official protests of the Great Powers, and the outspoken indignation of the civilized world."

A report from our legation in Vienna in 1878 to Mr. W. M. Evarts, Secretary of State under President Hayes, is eloquent testimony to American concern for the Jews of Europe.

There is little conception in America of the tenacity of the prejudice against that race in Roumania, and of the contempt and occasional violence and wrong to which this prejudice leads, as well as to the legal deprivation of the ordinary privileges of good citizenship.

It would be to the honor of the United States Government if it could initiate a plan by which at once the condition of American Hebrews resident or travelling in Roumania, and the conditions of natives of the same race, could be ameliorated and their equality before the law at least partially assured.[28]

Such letters continued to nurture the policy of humane concern so early established by this country. James G. Blaine carried on the Seward-Evarts-Fish policy. Oscar Straus, writing from the American Legation in Constantinople to his chief in Washington in 1889, assures Mr. Blaine that American intervention has again been effective.

T. F. Bayard, John Hay, Elihu Root continued to uphold and preserve the traditional policy, which was consistent with the alerted conscience of the land. The protection of its own citizens was the entering wedge. Coupled with it there was the steady insistence on Jewish rights in the case of American Jews traveling abroad and gradually on their non-American coreligionists.

Out of the thousands of documents, of letters and papers concerned with American diplomatic history one case emerges which arrests our interest.

The central character in this international drama is a heroine whose biography is so brief and whose personality is so shadowy that she is almost an anonymous figure. All the known facts about her are chiseled in stone in a Jewish cemetery in Richmond, Virginia. Her tombstone biography reads:[29]

Rebecca Davis
Born October 30, 1840
Died July 27, 1915

She was the center of one of the most exciting episodes in American diplomatic history.

The Keiley incident was precipitated by intermarriage. It was an unequal affair. For we know everything about the hero, nothing of the heroine except that she was a Jewess. How a woman could have lived so long and been involved in a life of such intense drama without once asserting herself as a person or emerging as a definite personality, is a mystery which only some student of self-effacement can explain. For Mrs. Anthony M. Keiley succeeded in leaving a vacuum as her memorial. The most thorough search through newspaper and periodical files has yielded nothing. There is not a letter or a scrap of paper that survived Rebecca Davis Keiley. There is no photograph. There is no recorded opinion. The newspapers are as silent as during her lifetime she herself must have been discreet. Her relatives have recorded her birth, her existence and her demise and, having ignored her marriage on her tombstone, considered her past buried with her bones. And there Rebecca and her case rested— until students of American diplomacy disinterred Mrs. Keiley and left her unsolved mystery on the historian's doorstep.

There is a woodcut of Anthony M. Keiley.[30] There is a biographical sketch in the *National Cyclopaedia of American Biography*. There are many other references to this dashing, colorful hero. He was born in New Jersey in 1835 and educated in Randolph Macon College in Virginia. He became a journalist and founded and edited the Norfolk *Virginian* and the Petersburg *Index and News*. At the close of the War Keiley ran afoul of the law. "The newspapers had their share of trouble. A. M. Keiley was put in Castle Thunder for several days for an editorial the military commander did not like." But the voters of Virginia liked him. He was chairman of the Virginia State Democratic Committee. He rose to the rank of major. He became city attorney. In 1870 he was elected mayor of Richmond on the Conservative ticket.

The following year the Catholics of Richmond met at St. Peter's Cathedral on January 12, "to protest against the occupation of Rome by King Victor Emmanuel and the Italian Government, and the subse-

quent deposition of Pope Pius IX from the throne of St. Peter."
Keiley was one of the speakers at that meeting.[31]

When news of the Chicago fire reached Richmond, Mayor Keiley
recalled a similar disaster that befell his own city. He promptly
called a meeting of Richmond citizens to raise money and express
sympathy to the stricken city. He was equally ready and responsive
when news of the famine in Ireland reached him. With exemplary
zeal he collected funds for the relief of the starving Irish.

He must have known some of the Jews of Richmond well. He
admired a Mrs. Frances Levy, calling her "one of the brightest
women in the city." The details of his meeting with Rebecca Davis,
daughter of George Davis, are not known. Her father was a former
resident of Petersburg, where Keiley had founded and edited its
Index and News.

In the year 1885, in the month of May, President Cleveland appointed Anthony M. Keiley Minister Plenipotentiary to Austria-
Hungary. T. F. Bayard wrote the usual note bespeaking "that favorable reception at Vienna which is due to his merits as an American
citizen of great ability and character.[32]

The fireworks started immediately. But Mr. Keiley happily unaware of what was ahead took passage (presumably with his wife)
for Europe. He was to go first to Paris and then to Vienna. While he
was somewhere on the Atlantic, Secretary Bayard received the following message through the usual diplomatic channels:

> We regret the nomination of Mr. Keiley as minister plenipotentiary
> and envoy extraordinary to the imperial court and his sudden departure
> from America, as here, too, like in Rome, *prevail scruples against this
> choice. . . .*
> The position of a foreign envoy wedded to a Jewess by civil marriage
> would be untenable and even impossible in Vienna.
>
> COUNT KALNOKY[33]

The Austrian message to Bayard is interesting for two reasons.
First, it calls attention to the fact that Rebecca and Anthony had
been parties to a civil marriage. Second, it refers to Mr. Keiley's
curious experience with a previous appointment.

The Italian incident referred to has been briefly summarized by
W. A. Christian in his *Richmond:*[34]

> Hon. A. M. Keiley had been appointed United States Minister to Italy,
> and before his departure the citizens gave him a banquet April 22nd at
> Sänger Hall. . . . Keiley left for Italy but was not received because he

was not acceptable to King Victor Emmanuel. It will be remembered that when Victor Emmanuel was made King of Italy a meeting was held in St. Peters (sic) to protest against his occupying the domain of the Pope, and at this meeting Keiley spoke. This was remembered against him and he had to return.

Bayard's reply to Count Kalnoky dated May 18, 1885, is a masterful statement of American policy:

It is not within the power of the President nor of the Congress, nor of any judicial tribunal in the United States, to take or even hear testimony, or in any mode to inquire into or decide upon the religious belief of any official, and the proposition to allow this to be done by any foreign Government is necessarily and *a fortiori* inadmissable.

To suffer an infraction of this essential principle would lead to a disfranchisement of our citizens because of their religious belief. . . . Religious liberty is the chief cornerstone of the American system of government, and provisions for its security are imbedded in the written charter and interwoven in the moral fabric of its laws.

Anything that tends to invade a right so essential and sacred must be carefully guarded against, and I am satisfied that my countrymen, ever mindful of the suffering and sacrifices necessary to obtain it, will never consent to its impairment for any reason or under any pretext whatsoever. . . .

It is not believed by the President that a doctrine and practice so destructive of religious liberty and freedom of conscience, so devoid of catholicity, and so opposed to the spirit of the age in which we live can for a moment be accepted by the great family of civilized nations or be allowed to control their diplomatic intercourse.

Certain it is, it will never, in my belief, be accepted by the people of the United States, nor by any administration which represents their sentiments. . . .

Into the religious belief of its envoy or that of any member of his family, neither this Government nor any officer thereof, as I have shown you, has any right or power to inquire, or to apply any test whatever, or to decide such question, and to do so would constitute an infraction of the express letter and an invasion of the pervading spirit of the supreme law of this land.[35]

This is a document to be cherished by all liberty-loving Americans. It enunciates the principles held dear by the first pilgrims who ever sought sanctuary here. It proclaims with dignity, assurance and pride, our unswerving determination to cherish and defend religious liberty. It would have made Thomas Jefferson glow with pride and would have warmed the heart of Tom Paine!

Bayard was inflexible. Cleveland was adamant. Viennese diplomats could no longer base their rejection on the sole fact that Mrs. Keiley was a Jewess. They used the Italian episode as a face-saving pretext, claiming Keiley's "want of political tact evinced on his part on a former occasion." Also they pleaded that "his domestic relations preclude a favorable reception by Vienna society." It fell to our American Ambassador in Paris to break the news to Mr. Keiley just as he was boarding a train for Vienna that he must wait in Paris until matters were adjudicated. In the meanwhile European papers got hold of the story. It became a *cause célèbre.*

Mr. Bayard reviewed the case in a long letter to John M. Francis, the American Minister in Vienna whom Keiley was to have replaced. When Mr. Francis left, James Fenner Lee took over the negotiations in Vienna. Baron Schaeffer left Washington. Mr. Lee wired Secretary Bayard that Mr. Keiley would under no circumstances be accepted by Austria-Hungary. Mr. Bayard did not pull his punches. He refused to accept the evasive double-talk of the Austrians.

His excellency avers that his intention was to have had his views stated verbally to me by Baron von Schaeffer. I can only say, as to this, that whatever may have been his private intentions, the full copy of his telegram to Baron von Schaeffer, of May 8, was by the latter carefully translated and handed to me in writing, and that the objection to the religious faith of Mr. Keiley's wife, which appeared in that telegram, was the main point of discussion between Baron von Schaeffer and myself, and was insisted upon by him against my earnest remonstrance and objection that the President could not withdraw Mr. Keiley on such grounds. A month later, on the 11th of June, Baron von Schaeffer, in writing, communicated to me Count Kalnoky's declaration "that his objections to said nomination remain in full force."[36]

Not only was Bayard indignant because of the manifest unfairness to Mr. Keiley and because of the affront to our nation. He was outraged because of the violation of the principles he and his fellow Americans held dear.

It is a cause of astonishment that in an era of advanced civilization in which musty prejudice and illiberal discrimination among religious sects and races of mankind are giving such gratifying proofs of their rapid extinction, when throughout the wide world the death of the venerable and philanthropic Montefiore is so genuinely mourned, when the council of highest rank and most exclusive privilege of the British Empire is glad to enroll in its peerage a member of the noted house of Rothschild, that from so enlightened a Government as that of Austria-Hungary should proceed the declaration that "proximate Semitic descent" will be sufficient to proscribe individuals of admittedly blameless and virtuous personality from appearing at that court clothed in the representative character of a friendly power.[37]

Anthony M. Keiley returned to America—presumably with Mrs. Keiley. He immediately sent his resignation to President Cleveland and refused any form of compensation for his expenses during the four months of travel and waiting. Keiley's letter to Secretary Bayard does not mince words. He knew that the crux of the matter was that Mrs. Keiley was a Jewess.

This objection, thus announced with a certain bluntness, disdaining even the affection of respect for modern ideas of freedom, is, as we shall see, repeated at every step of this correspondence with a persistence which discloses either the purpose of a deliberate and gross insult to the American people or a desire to mask under a false reason avowed though disreputable, a true reason too disreputable to be avowed. I say an insult to the American people, because in this, its first form of state- ment, as ever throughout this correspondence, it is proclaimed that in the official regard of Austria, Hebrew blood brands as with a leprosy, not only excluding all tainted with it from high honor at Austria's hands, but disqualifying beyond remedy even the agents of other Governments who may have business with Austria, so fatal indeed, that even a mar- riage connection with it by a citizen of whatever blood or belief, unfits him for the representation of a foreign and friendly power at this im- perial and royal court.[38]

Keiley steadfastly refused to accept another post because he did not wish to appear as a perennial office-seeker. That Bayard and Keiley and Cleveland saw the matter eye to eye is most gratifying. Bayard's answer to Keiley reads in part:

I will not believe that the people of the United States will ever con- sent to the creation or enforcement of such tests as have been insisted upon by the government of Austria-Hungary as conditions precedent and qualifications for the selection of their representatives in foreign courts by the United States. Such action must naturally cause widespread amaze- ment, coupled with indignation and resentment, when the history of the case is made public, nor do I believe that these sentiments will be con- fined to our own country, but that, wherever religious liberty is valued and respected, a common judgment will be formed.[39]

For two years the United States had no minister in Austria. The matter did not cease to interest the diplomats, the newspapers, or Jews the world over.

The *Allgemeine Zeitung des Judenthums* made numerous references to the Affair Keiley.[40] It praised Secretary Bayard's eloquence and courageous defense of religious freedom. *"Die Keiley—Angelegenheit kommit nicht zur Ruhe,"* reads one of its editorial comments on the case. It compares and contrasts Old World attitudes with the New World ideas, showing how religious freedom is cherished in America. As proof it summarizes the Bayard letters. Sadly it states that, "Mr. Keiley was not accepted because his wife was a Jewess."

In 1886, President Cleveland appointed Anthony M. Keiley to the "International Court of First Instance" at Cairo, Egypt.[41] There he served his country with dignity and honor. Presumably Mrs. Keiley was with him. He met with a fatal accident in Paris, January 24, 1905. She died a decade later.

A generation after Keiley's death, in November of 1933, another United States Minister to Austria, Mr. George H. Earle saw the bloody handwriting on the walls of Vienna. Solemnly he warned the Austrians that such a course on which that nation had embarked would alienate American good-will. He told newspapermen after making a tour of the country that he could not condone antisemitic measures:

As an American, I am interested in this question (anti-Semitism). It is well known [that] 90 per cent of Americans either came or are descended from persons who came to escape racial or religious persecution. Americans therefore would have no sympathy for a country where such persecution is carried on.

It is the right of any country to frame its own racial policy. It is equally America's right to refuse its sympathy to a country with whose policy towards the Jew or other races it should disagree.[42]

Anthony M. Keiley cast a long shadow. His wife was buried with her kin in Richmond. She is like a candle that once gave a light, briefly, and then sputtered out. . . .

The second half of the nineteenth century was a creative period in the ranks of European Jewry. It was also a time when tentative efforts are discernible toward a solution of the Jewish problem through federation, through organization, through large-scale planning. The impact of both creativity and genius of European Jews upon their kinsmen in America cannot be measured. Refreshed and strengthened by contact with the effulgence of men of scholarship and wisdom, American Jewry borrowed ideas and embellished them. The Isaac Leeser versus Isaac M. Wise situation is paralleled in Germany, with Samson Raphael Hirsch championing orthodoxy and Abraham Geiger advocating reform. It was the period of Moses Hess, who was a precursor of the Zionist movement. During that creative period Rabbi Israel Lipkin, or "the Salanter," as he was called, founded a mystical movement which numbered thousands of adherents. These "societies for the propagation of ethical principles" stressed the goals of self-perfectibility and moral discipline through asceticism and self-renunciation. It was at this time that three great Jewish historians labored zealously for their people: Heinrich Graetz, Moritz Steinschneider, Meyer Kayserling.

Hirsch or Heinrich Graetz lived between the years 1817 and 1891. His great contribution is encompassed in his monumental *History of the Jews*, which despite his evident bias and prejudice remains to this day an imperishable classic.

Moritz Steinschneider was born in 1816 and died in 1907. A great present-day Jewish scholar, Dr. Alexander Marx, wrote of him:

> Moritz Steinschneider, the greatest Jewish scholar of our time, one of the founders of Jewish science together with Zunz and Rapaport, devoted all his energies for seven decades with untiring enthusiasm to the elucidation of Jewish literature in its relation to general culture. At the age of almost 91 years he passed away in the middle of his work. There is hardly any Jewish scholar to-day who does not consider Steinschneider his teacher. There are not many departments of mediaeval Jewish literature for which he has not laid secure foundations.[43]

Students of American Jewish history are familiar with the name of Kayserling. It is a name which every Jew should be proud to pronounce, because he worked and lived and was impelled by one overpowering ambition—that was to go back to the sources, to comb them for evidence of every fact. He too was one of the great men born in the early years of the nineteenth century.

While great scholars labored in self-imposed obscurity, two Jewesses found fame at this time. Henriette Hertz, linguist and beauty, whose brilliant salon was the bright spot for the elite of Germany, had died a convert in 1847. Now two loyal Jewish women outshone her in the next generation. Adah Isaacs Menken was born in New Orleans in 1813 and died in Paris in 1868. "*La Belle Menken*" became a legend from her youth. To her is ascribed the intellectual feat of translating Homer's *Iliad* at the age of thirteen. This apocryphal anecdote is dwarfed by her substantiated accomplishments. She contributed poems to Wise's *Israelite*, urging Jews to respond to the plight of their persecuted kinsmen. She proclaimed herself a Messianic emissary. She rushed to the defense of Baron de Rothschild, who was then making his campaign to be admitted to the seat in Parliament to which he was elected. Gratefully Rothschild dubbed her "Deborah." She became a friend of Charles Dickens and Charles Reade, of Gautier and Dumas the elder. She dedicated a book of poetry to Dickens. She fascinated thousands of people on both sides of the Atlantic by her histrionic verve. Once when a newspaper notice displeased her for its omissions of pertinent data and for its pert references to herself, she wrote a letter to the editor summarizing her essential biography. She wrote:

The biography of my humble self seems written in that light and flippant tone, as of a woman who, with all her advantages, had lived on the surface of life. This is wrong. I am a *thinking, earnest* woman. And in that light alone I wish to be spoken of. My biographer has also taken several liberties with his knowledge of facts, the most serious of which is that I *embraced* the Jewish religion. I was born in that faith, and have adhered to it through all my erratic career. Through that pure and simple religion, I have found greatest comfort and blessing. . . . My first name is spelt "Adah" and is a Hebrew name.[44]

In her death her friend Baron Lionel de Rothschild did not forget his erstwhile friend. He found her grave at Montparnasse and there placed a monument in tribute to her memory.

Far greater of fame, more enduring, and more precious to us than la Menken, was Emma Lazarus, whose life began in the year that Isaac Leeser founded the Hebrew Education Society, 1849. Her life ended when the Jewish Theological Seminary of America was one year old, 1887. She is the synthesis of all the best traits of her land and of her faith, a combination of heart and lyrical sentiment, of compassion, of wisdom, of the most creative strain of American Judaism. She was a passionate pilgrim in a moment of history charged with drama. The year before her birth saw the historic feminine assembly at Seneca Falls, New York, and witnessed the publication of the "Declaration of Sentiments," in which women proclaimed their just grievances to the world. Thoreau had but recently emerged from seclusion at Walden. It was a time of national pride. "Every one thinks that he is better than his neighbor," an astute French observer Alexis de Tocqueville had said a few years before in summing up his American travels. At the time of Emma's birth her native land was beginning to assume the characteristics of diverse regionalism. Around geographic nuclei separate cultures were taking shape. "Geographical conditions and the stocks from which the people sprang are the most fundamental factors in shaping sectionalism," wrote Frederick Jackson Turner in *The Significance of Sections in American History*.

Both of these factors are clearly in evidence in the pattern of Jewish life in America. Already Jews of the South and those of the East and West differed radically from each other. The differences were to become more marked as economic and political ideologies began to assert themselves. The Jews of Missouri and the Jews of Louisiana were not at all in accord. Within each section or community there were additional sharp cleavages based on Old World origins and practices. Over the temples and the synagogues was "the shadowy image of the European nation." A Jewish traveler who spent three years in America was careful to note the European origins of the religious communities he visited. So in Boston he found on the eve of the Civil War four religious groups, mainly consisting of German, English, Polish and Lithuanian Jews.

What was the background of the years of Emma's life? What major currents are discernible in the American-Jewish community between 1849 and 1887? First and foremost was a deep concern, a tender compassion for the Jewish victims of persecution, oppression and pogroms. There was a sense of kinship in adversity which stretched from San Francisco to Damascus, which embraced the little kidnapped boy in Italy and the terrified masses in Rumania, which concerned itself with diplomatic slights like the Keiley incident, with acts of major aggression in Bessarabia, with legal disabilities in North Carolina and in Switzerland.

"Day long I brooded upon the Passion of Israel. I saw him bound to the wheel, nailed to the cross, cut off by the sword, burned at the stake, tossed into the seas. And always the patient, resolute martyr face arose in silent rebuke and defiance," wrote Josephine Lazarus, Emma's older sister. This tender brooding etched itself into the consciousness of the Jews of America just as an ailing, frail child will by its very weakness bind with bonds of love those who cherish and care for it.

A second major current in American Jewry is found in the psychic awareness of Zion. In England it expressed itself through men like Sir Moses Montefiore and his Ashkenazic wife, Judith Cohen Montefiore, whom he married against the usage of the land. For "intermarriages were avoided; a Portuguese deeming it derogatory to his standing." Lady Judith and Sir Moses made a number of pilgrimages to Palestine. Her *Notes of a Private Journal of a Visit to Egypt and Palestine* is a shining record of her latent love of Zion. His deeds are token of the same deep absorption with the ancient homeland and its then existing possibilities and opportunities. In America, the love that Isaac Leeser bore for Zion was demonstrated again and again in the *Occident*. Gradually through the minds and hearts of many Americans who were his subscribers and readers, the same idea took root.

The third motif discernible in America was a return to Hebraism. In her thirty-fourth year Emma Lazarus began her study of Hebrew. For a long time her friend, Ralph Waldo Emerson, had pointed out to her that the way to creative writing lay not in imitation but in discovery—discovery of her genius as a lyric voice of Hebraism. But it took the infamous pogroms and the May laws of Russia to strike her as lightning strikes. Her songs became *The Songs of a Semite.*

We now turn to a closer study of the life and work of Emma Lazarus, to see whether the threefold motif of the middle years of the nineteenth century—*kinship and compassion for all Israel, the affinity for Zion* and the *revival of Hebraism*—are to be found in her poetry and in her prose.

Emma Lazarus was born in New York City on the twenty-second of July in 1849. She died November 19, 1887. Her family was very well-to-do. She was given every opportunity which a devoted father and mother could shower on her. Her parents were Sephardim of status. Her father supervised her education. The bond between them was remarkable. He died in 1885. Her own health began to fail immediately thereafter. She survived him by only two brief years. To those who have read her works the grace of her diction, the charm of her imagery are well known. She was richly endowed. She was precocious. She had the rare ability of apprehending emotion and translating it into such form that it remained a crystallized, lasting, lyrical expression of a mood. Her first poetry was classical. It was far removed from her later work. She was influenced by Tennyson and other English poets. So she wrote at first not out of the inner depths of her nature but out of her surface reactions to life. When in 1871 *Admetus and Other Poems* was published she was hailed as a talent of first rank in England and America. The *Westminster Review,* the *Athenaeum,* and the *Illustrated London News* were extravagant in their praise. The *Boston Transcript* wrote: "Miss Lazarus, if not the best of our living poetesses, is among the best.'

The early Hellenist became in her maturity a Hebraist. In considering the influences which molded and changed her, we must not forget the one correspondent who came closest in spirit to Emma. That was John Burroughs. He, like Emerson, pointed out that the strength in Walt Whitman and in Carlyle was the strength of the Hebraic influence. So Miss Lazarus was ready, having been urged by men she admired to look to herself as a Jewess and at her people as subjects for inspiration. She visited Ward's Island. There her heart was wrung by the unhappy sight of people who once were men, who had been reduced by persecution and evil destiny to frightened, cringing creatures waiting patiently for admission to a land which was to give them an opportunity to live again as men.

Now she found her subject and her genius. Now she began to write not gifted imitations of the works of others, but deep, searching cries for justice and for understanding for a people who were her own. Never was a change so marked and so astonishing. It was as if she had opened wide the door of her subconscious self and let all the imagery and beauty of a sensitive soul shine forth. Now she knew. Now she could write. And what she wrote and how she wrote is something to make every Jew in America proud.

In 1882 in the pages of the *American Hebrew* there began a series of prose articles titled "Epistles to the Hebrews." Emma Lazarus was the first in America to suggest the importance of industrial training for Jews. She suddenly found within her sensitive and retiring nature the strength and the ability for public leadership. She organized meetings of Jews. She helped create the Hebrew Technical Institute of New York. In 1883, Emma Lazarus wrote "The New Colossus," a sonnet which was engraved twenty years later on a plaque at the base of the Statue of Liberty. She has become the symbol of the spirit of America welcoming each new pilgrim to her native shores.

"Yes, Whitman is Hebraic; so is Carlyle, so are all the more vital literary forces of our century."[45] Thus her friend, John Burroughs, wrote to Emma Lazarus, March 20, 1885. She was influenced by the great Christians of her day, men and women whose concern for Jews was both genuine and absorbing. But she qualified her sense of obligation by saying, "Eternally grateful as all Jews must be to such Christians as George Eliot and Laurence Oliphant, they neither should nor need seek outside of their own ranks their guide or their spokesman. They who in our own generation have led the Conservatives of England, the Liberals of Germany, the Republicans of France, can surely furnish a new Ezra for their own people." She herself discharged her obligation as gracefully as any one could. *The Dance to Death* is a historical tragedy which Emma Lazarus dedicated as follows: "This play is dedicated, in profound veneration and respect to the memory of George Eliot, the illustrious writer who did most among the artists of our day towards elevating and ennobling the spirit of Jewish nationality."

In "The Jewish Problem," which appeared in *Century Magazine,* is found the quintessence of Emma's philosophy about her people.[46] She realized that man pitied can never be regarded as an equal. She knew that the driven, persecuted, homeless Jew must attain a fixed address, status, security, to be accepted by others. So she wrote:

Neither we nor our immediate descendants can hope to see humanity at that point of perfection where the helpless and submissive victim will, as such, be respected. Existence continues to be a struggle in which the fittest can survive only through the energetic assertion and constant proof of superiority. The idea formulated by George Eliot has already sunk into the minds of many Jewish enthusiasts, and it germinates with miraculous rapidity. "The idea that I am possessed with," says Deronda, "is that of restoring of political existence to my people; making them a nation again, giving them a national center, such as the English have, though they, too, are scattered over the face of the globe. That is a task which presents itself to me as a duty; * * * I am resolved to devote my life to it. *At the least, I may awaken a movement in other minds such as has been awakened in my own.*"[47]

Thus Emma Lazarus, American Hebrew prophetess, wrote of the crying need of her own people for a solution to their millennial quest.

There were times when Emma, modest though she was, seemed to sense her own greatness. She richly earned the right to say:

My song I have inscribed on the forehead of Time,
They know and hate it—for it is lofty.

She wrote again in "Exultation":

The world is his who can withhold it rightly,
Who hears the harmonies of unseen angels
Above the senseless outcry of the hour.

Her translations of Ben Ezra, Gabirol, and Halevi show not only a thorough knowledge of Hebrew but an ability to identify herself in mood and in passionate experience with these ancient authors. Her "Longing for Jerusalem" is reminiscent of Halevi:

> Oh, city of the world, with sacred splendor blest,
> My spirit yearns to thee from out the far-off West,
> A stream of love wells forth when I recall thy day,
> Now is thy temple waste, thy glory passed away.
> Had I an eagle's wings, straight would I fly to thee,
> Moisten thy Holy dust with wet cheeks streaming free.
> Ho, how I long for thee! Albeit thy King has gone,
> Albeit where balm once flowed, the serpent dwells alone.
> Could I but kiss thy dust, so would I fain expire,
> As sweet as honey then, my passion, my desire!

The tenor of her major work was heavy with unshed tears. She knew grief, anguish, moral indignation. She knew the taste of ashes and the weight of sackcloth. So she wrote of "Grief":

> There is a hungry longing in the soul,
> A craving sense of emptiness and pain,
> She may not say nor yet control,
> For all the teeming world looks void and vain.
> No compensation in eternal spheres,
> She knows the loneliness of all her years.

She was at the peak of her talents when she found rest beneath the cypress trees she had so often described. Then her friends could well recall her "Wine and Grief" and chant the lines she had written:

> With heavy groans did I approach my friends,
> Heavy as though the mountains I would move. . . .
> Ye laugh but silently the soul weeps on;
> Ye cannot stifle her sincere lament.[48]

Recently Professor Ralph L. Rusk of the English Department of Columbia University edited a volume of *Letters* addressed to Emma Lazarus. This is an important addition for the student of American literature. There were more than a score of letters from Ralph Waldo Emerson. There were six letters from John Burroughs, the great naturalist. Two each from Henry George and Edmund Clarence Stedman. There was one letter from William James and one from Tourgeneff. There were two letters from James Russell Lowell. There were seven letters from William Morris and one from Robert Browning. Edmund Gosse wrote to her and Charlotte Cushman and Lidian and Ellen Emerson. Finally there was a letter from Laurence Oliphant written from Haifa, Palestine.

"You are young and hold a facile pen," Emerson once wrote Emma, inviting her to write to him often and pleading his advanced years for not writing as much as she deserved.[49] Henry George warned her that he did not suggest that she write for *her* people, but for *the* people. Browning in writing to Emma used Hebrew which they both knew. Oliphant urged that America sponsor the entry of Jews into Palestine. Lowell said that he liked Emma's poem "The New Colossus" better than the Statue itself: "Your sonnet gives its subject a *raison d'être* which it wanted before," he wrote in 1883.

The single sheet of paper on which Emma Lazarus wrote her poem is preserved in the American Jewish Historical Society. "The New Colossus," which many pilgrims have lovingly spelled out, belongs to all Americans. It bears repeating:

> Not like the brazen giant of Greek fame,
> With conquering limbs astride from land to land;
> Here at our sea-washed, sunset gates shall stand
> A mighty woman with a torch, whose flame
> Is the imprisoned lightning, and her name
> Mother of Exiles. From her beacon-hand
> Glows world-wide welcome; her mild eyes command
> The air-bridged harbor that twin cities frame.
>
> "Keep, ancient lands, your storied pomp!" Cries she
> With silent lips. "Give me your tired, your poor,
> Your huddled masses yearning to breathe free,
> The wretched refuse of your teeming shore.
> Send these, the homeless, tempest-tost to me,
> I lift my lamp beside the golden door!"

So this gentle, warmhearted, richly endowed woman held out both her hands to welcome the newcomer. She pleaded his cause. She urged his welcome. Yet even in her day "The Jewish Problem" worried her. She saw injustice prevail. She saw the latent gifts which every immigrant brought to America wasted and rejected. She wanted to erase all prejudice. So she wrote:

And yet here, too, the everlasting prejudice is cropping out in various shapes. Within recent years, Jews have been "boycotted" at not a few places of public resort; in our schools and colleges, even in our scientific universities, Jewish scholars are frequently subjected to annoyance on account of their race. The word "Jew" is in constant use, even among so-called refined Christians, as a term of opprobrium, and is employed as a verb, to denote the meanest tricks. In other words, all the mag-

nanimity, patience, charity, and humanity, which the Jews have mani-
fested in return for centuries of persecution, have been thus far inadequate
to eradicate the profound antipathy engendered by fanaticism and ready
to break out in one or another shape at any moment of popular excitement.

Even in America, presumably the refuge of the oppressed, public
opinion has not yet reached that point where it absolves the race from the
sin of the individual. Every Jew, however honorable or enlightened, has
the humiliating knowledge that his security and reputation are, in a
certain sense, bound up with those of the meanest rascal who belongs
to his tribe, and who has it in his power to jeopardize the social status
of his whole nation. It has been well said that the Jew must be of gold
in order to pass for silver.[50]

In 1882, in the *American Hebrew* there appeared sixteen articles
from the pen of Emma Lazarus. She had written largely to a Christian audience in the *Century Magazine*. She now proposed to address
herself exclusively to Jewish readers. Her *Epistles to the Hebrews*
present a sound program for social reconstruction and for the need
for industrial training for Jews.

Now American Jews found a new leader. They were called on to
lead constructive lives, to integrate their activities with America's
needs, to cherish and welcome the immigrant and the gifts he brought
to the land and to its people. What the effect was on readers of the
Century Magazine and of the *American Hebrew,* it is impossible to
tell. Time has not dulled their meaning nor diminished their significance.

Toward the end of her life in preparing a paper on "Renan and the
Jews" she wrote, "My interest in the culture and improvement of
American Jews, makes me anxious to serve their cause to the full
extent of my ability." This purpose she accomplished magnificently.

While Emma Lazarus was pleading the Jewish case before America, one young boy of whom she was not even aware was bent on
becoming an anonymous hero. She was working feverishly in her
study, writing her *Epistles to the Hebrews*. He was in the frozen
Arctic. It was as if he tried by his fine gift of courage to prove that '
his people had in them great depths of sacrifice and deep wells of
patriotism, a quiet willingness to offer their lives for their country,
and never to count the cost.

The year was 1881. A young boy named Edward Israel is the
unsung hero.[51] Had she known about him, Emma would have been

the first to acknowledge him, but few knew him in his short lifetime and all have forgotten him now.

Edward Israel was born in Kalamazoo, Michigan, in 1859. He graduated from the University of Michigan. His interest in mathematics and in the sciences led him to join the Signal Corps of the United States Army. When General A. W. Greely organized the Lady Franklin Bay Expedition in 1881, Edward, then twenty-two years old, volunteered as astronomer and mathematician for the party of exploration. He helped in 1882 to find an overland route to Hazen Land in Greenland. He made the mathematical calculations, recorded the scientific data and although the youngest member of this group of explorers, he won the esteem of all his associates. His courage was boundless. His good spirits were inexhaustible. His sense of fair play was unassailable. When he became seriously ill, although urged by his fellow explorers to accept more than his share of the dwindling rations, he refused them and to the last would take no more food than the others.

So he died before he could return home. But while he lived, he had lived magnificently. And in the meanwhile, Emma Lazarus pleaded with inspired eloquence for justice and acceptance for others like him. And sorrowed for the generation of "those who were brave to act, and rich enough their actions to forget." Surely Edward Israel was of that number!

Everything depends on the eye of the beholder. A man may appear a bearded patriarch akin to the prophets to one person. He may seem a ragged pariah to another. Emma Lazarus found inspiration in the crowded East Side streets of New York. To her America was "the mother of exiles." The people she met at the gates were "the tired, the poor, the huddled masses yearning to breathe free."

A contemporary of Emma's, a man six years her senior, saw only wretched squalor where she found inspiration. His nostrils twitched. His overbred face wore a mask of repugnance. Henry James in *The American Scene* describes the crowded streets of New York where Jews lived, as if he were a botanist who set out with net and notebook to record the movements of a strange and disagreeable species of fauna.

The ghetto was to him "a vast sallow aquarium in which innumerable fish, of overdeveloped proboscis, were to bump together, forever, amid heaped spoils of the sea." This man could write with sympathy and imaginative insight about every kind of human tragedy. He could transform evil incarnate into a charming poltergeist. His heart could ache and throb with anguish over fictional tragedies of his own devising. But in the midst of transplanted poverty he was the effete aristocrat with a queasy stomach. In 1881 there had been pogroms in Russia and mass emigration had begun. It meant nothing to Henry James. Nor had the years brought freedom from care to the Jews of Central Europe. Sir William Osler in a letter dated May 1, 1884, could speculate of the time when another Moses would arise and preach a Semitic exodus from Germany. Many followed their unhappy history with an awareness of its serious implications. Still there were some who could neither feel with compassion nor react with justice. Emerson and Hawthorne had understood and defended the New England Irish. George Eliot had done the same for the Jews she knew. *Daniel Deronda* was published in 1876. The gifted authoress knew and was influenced by the personality of Emanuel Deutsch, the great Talmudic scholar of her day. "The period of George Eliot's girlhood corresponded with the early stages of the controversy over the Jewish Disabilities Bill, and it is possible that she followed the speeches of Lord Macaulay, Lord John Russell, John Bright and others in support of the measure," says Modder.

Disraeli had written widely about Jews and Jewish nationalism. Since 1831, when as a traveler he first beheld Zion, Disraeli had been an ardent believer in a revived state. He wrote of his dreams in *Alroy* and *Tancred*. He had written: *"A race that persists in celebrating their vintage, although they have no fruits to gather, will regain their vineyards."*[52]

Charles Dickens had described a Fagin. But he also had saluted a Mr. Riah. The one was a villain, the other a paragon. Dickens was quick to see the unfairness of his first Jewish character and eager to correct the unfortunate impression he created at a time when the Jews of England were putting up a stout fight for their civil rights. There are extant interesting letters which passed between Charles Dickens and Eliza Davis. Mrs. James P. Davis was "a prominent Jewess" whose husband bought Tavistock House from Charles Dickens when the famous author moved to Gad's Hill. Eliza Davis did more than enlist Dickens' sympathy. She bespeaks for the "wanderers" his overt friendship. She writes:

Fagin I fear admits only of one interpretation; but [while] Charles Dickens lives the author can justify himself or atone for a great wrong on a whole though *scattered nation.*

Charles Dickens tried to make amends handsomely. He had Mr. Riah say:

Men say, "This is a bad Greek, but there are good Greeks. This is a bad Turk, but there are good Turks." Not so with the Jew. Men find the bad among us easily enough—among what peoples are the bad not easily found?—but they take the worst of us as samples of the best; they take the lowest of us as presentation of the highest.

Presumably Henry James, who had written *A Passionate Pilgrim* and the *Pilgrimage of Henry James* and who settled in England in 1869 and became a British subject, knew of the attitudes of Dickens and George Eliot toward the Pilgrim People. He might even have heard F. W. Farrar deliver a speech at Mansion House in London February 1, 1882, in the course of which he said, "It is to the Jewish nation that humanity owes the deepest debt of gratitude, and it is on that nation that humanity has inflicted the deepest wrongs." But if he knew and read and heard, it made no difference to Henry James. His distaste and aversion for Jews placed a gulf between himself and the disinherited.

Disraeli found the magic formula in his travels. Emma Lazarus was awakened by the prodding of her friends and by the suffering of immigrants which she witnessed. There were men and women in her generation with eyes that saw and hearts that understood, who had the magic of insight within themselves. Such people could find romance in the ghetto streets. They could see in its tattered denizens the descendants of a proud old people.

There were many such editorials and books. Often they were written by Christians. There were brave and forthright words uttered in accents no one could mistake. When John Hay said in a speech in Washington, D.C., June 15, 1903, "Nobody can ever make the Americans think ill of the Jews as a class or as a race," he spoke for a large segment of his fellow countrymen. Jacob A. Riis wrote his *Children of the Poor* with a benevolent pen. He saw "the sweaters' shops" in all their malodorous squalor. He knew the abuses. He saw the little children growing up in streets where harlots vied for clients. He saw the pathetic little pushcarts and the dusty sidewalk stores, all the noisy, gritty, smelly, ugly tempo of ghetto life. "Except for the patriarchal family life" of the inhabitants the moral degradation was boundless. "It is that which pilots him safely through the shoals upon which the Gentile would have been inevitably wrecked," wrote Riis. This Christian social worker describes a Friday night in a poor Jew's home. The candles are lit. The festive family circle gathers. Pathetic efforts are made at Sabbath finery. "Their light fell on little else than empty plates and anxious faces; but in the patriarchal host who arose and bade the guest welcome with a dignity a king might have envied I recognized with difficulty the humble pedlar I had known only from the street."

It is not an idealized picture. There is nothing praiseworthy in a Hester Street *Cheder* (Hebrew school). Such schools were an unhappy contrast to the public schools. The Cheders were usually "dark and inhospitable dens." Their teachers were haggard, tattered, slovenly men who ruled by force and taught by rote. They were medieval in practice and in theory. It was the transplanted world of Sholem Aleichem. Every new outburst of pogrom and persecution sends "hordes of destitute emigrants" here. In 1892 the United Hebrew Charities had 23,571 calls for its services out of a total of 52,000 immigrants who came that year. More than forty-five per cent of the transplanted population needed assistance. In the same year, 46,678 persons who lived in the country two years or more had recourse to philanthropic aid.

Sights and sounds and smells offended the visitor. Displaced persons who leave their possessions behind and flee for their lives with just the clothes on their backs eventually reach a point where their clothes need mending, laundering or discarding. If they disgust the beholder, how must they seem to themselves who once knew a better life, who were not strangers to some of the amenities? Once there were homes and fields and gardens. Now only the stench of the gutter, the filth of the sidewalk, the noise and clamor of the street vendor. The old and the young, the sick and the well, the depraved and the virgin, all immersed in one caldron waiting for the miracle of deliverance. Sometimes the miracle took place. Sometimes the forces of humanity triumphed. Christian insight and American fair play rose above the dregs and the refuse, the tatters and the wasteland, saw the resurgence of talent and dignity, of reconstruction and recovery.

Such a miracle took place in May, 1902, when *Harper's Weekly* published an editorial on "Race-Patriotism." The editor chides those of his contemporaries who are now trying to substitute "race-patriotism . . . for the old fashioned notion of humanity, once the ideal of high-thoughted men." There are those who are self-constituted elite, the self-chosen autocrats. They dream of elevating their class above all others. "As for that dream of universal Anglo-Saxon Empire, it is a cheap and vulgar hallucination." The writer concludes on a prophetic note, pleading that, "The federation of the world, in which every nation shall be equally a power, is the only solidarity which we can safely hope for." That was the humane voice of America.

Opinions based on fact and not on bias, judgments judiciously considered, words and ideas used as tools by honest investigators—these are to be welcomed. Whether a man attempts to describe a distant part of the universe or a corner of Hester Street, it is well to remember that what he is describing is a joint phenomenon of the observer and the observed. The same street may be viewed by an Emma Lazarus or a Henry James—and what a world of difference in their reporting. Sounds may become savage assaults on the ear or rhapsodies. Old men in shabby coats have made subjects for beautiful portraits for Rembrandt. Peddlers were patriarchs for Jacob Riis. Byron heard "Hebrew Melodies." Browning loved the wisdom of Rabbi Ben Ezra. Hans Christian Andersen's heart, which loved little children, had room in it for the Jews of the world. García-Granados thrilled to Jewish accomplishments in Palestine. An open mind, a listening ear, a warm heart, a quest for truth. These are the essential ingredients.

Joaquin Miller felt these truths. So he sang his "Songs of the Hebrew Children." Addressing an audience of persecuted Jews in Russia with overflowing heart and brimming eye, he offered them "God's inheritance" in America. In "To Rachel in Russia" he appeals to

> Rise up and come where Freedom waits
> Within these White, wide ocean gates. . . .
> Forsake that savage land of snows;
> Forget the brutal Russian's blows;
> And come where Kings of Conscience dwell.
> Oh come Rebecca to the well!

And so they came—the Rebeccas and Isaacs and Abrahams.

Now the night schools became crowded. Men, women and children, fired by a zeal for knowledge, became part-time pupils in public and private schools. Some of them had been educated in Europe. There were Talmudists and graduates of gymnasia among them. Not a few had acquired the equivalent of a university education. Some were professional men. But what they desperately wanted now was to master the language, to learn the laws, the history and constitution of their adopted land. They wanted to be citizens.

There were men and women in America who were eager to help the immigrants, to establish schools, to teach in their classes. One of these women was the beloved Henrietta Szold, eldest daughter of Rabbi Benjamin Szold of Baltimore. In 1889 she suggested to the members of a Hebrew Literary Society the necessity for establishing such a school in Baltimore. In November of 1889 this young woman destined to become one of the immortals of her race, began to teach on the second floor rear of a store on Gay Street. The location belied the name. The scholars, thirty Russian Jews, were anything but gay. They were an earnest, sorry, shabby group. They soon brought their cousins and their uncles and their aunts. Miss Szold was swamped. Larger quarters were needed. Two additional women volunteered their services. The school was a success.

The total registry of pupils, before the close of the classes in 1898, was over 5000 men, women and children. A few old men came, as did many middle-aged men with their wives, likewise children; but those of school age were almost from the start not received; above 14 years they were deemed wage-earners, whose help was needed at home. The seven classes were all graded, only experienced school teachers being placed in charge; the highest class in charge of the superintendent was given over to instruction in American history, and encouragement given thereby to look to naturalization. English alone was used as a vehicle of instruction, and it was never found necessary to depart from this rule.[53]

The education of the Hyman Kaplans had begun in the land.

While they were trying to acquire the idiom of America, they kept alive the cultural treasures they had brought with them. Here were no escapist Jews tossing overboard everything they had once known and loved. These were men and women who cherished their memories, who made much of their kinsmen, who remembered and perpetuated through countless *Vereins*, and *Arbeiter Ring* associations the cultural heritage of their youth and origin.

The Russian Jews had fostered a Hebrew and a Yiddish press in America. Out of poverty—cultural riches. The Hebrew periodical press in the United States goes back to 1870.

According to Fannie M. Brody, who has made a thorough bibliographical study of the subject, many Hebrew readers forsook the ancient tongue as soon as they had mastered English.[54] But there was always a small group that tended the flame. Since 1871, some 125 Hebrew periodicals have been published in America. Some of these journalistic ventures were short-lived, others sturdy. The *Hadoar*, still extant, serving Zionism, is a weekly established in 1921, the longest continuous Hebrew publication in the United States.

The Yiddish press in the United States had its birth in 1872 when

Henry Gersoni founded *Die Jüdische Post*. Another paper was founded in New York in the same year by K. H. Sarasohn. It soon had a rival paper, *Yiddisches Tageblatt*, founded in New York in 1885. The *Jewish Daily Forward* was established twelve years later. Its editor, Abraham Cahan, was a man of parts. He was of the Russian intelligentsia, steeped in Socialism, a member of Socialist societies in Europe and America. Under his leadership the twin causes, the championship of the economically oppressed and of the rising labor movement, were made the purposes on which his newspaper achieved stability and success. He gained considerable fame as a novelist when his *The Rise of David Levinsky* was published. The *Forward* still has a loyal following despite the drop in immigration. The other Yiddish newspapers follow a more orthodox line and have a more limited circulation than the *Forward*. There are in all fourteen periodical publications in Yiddish with a more than twenty-year record of existence. Of these one is published in Pittsburgh, two in Chicago, including the Chicago edition of the *Forward*. The rest have their home in New York.

Yiddish is more than a language. It is the vibrant record of a people in exile. It throbs with meaning. It bristles with power. It is for those who speak it packed with the cargo of past ages and past places. It is memory in action. It is the universal conversational coin which is legal tender in Poland and Rumania, along the Vistula and on the banks of the Hudson. It was an integrating force for the migrating masses who were dumped unceremoniously on American shores and who, speaking no English, turned to Yiddish as a means of orientation and communication in a new and frightening world. So the immigrant clung to it. So his children heard it spoken. So gradually it has made its way into strange places. Little Abner has a Yiddish frame of reference. Thousands of Americans daily, involuntarily, accept its riches and smile at its nuances. The census of the United States in 1940 indicates the survival of Yiddish. Nearly two million Jews in America were bilingual, using Yiddish at home and English in the great community. In 1925 a group of scholars founded the Yiddish Scientific Institute in Vilna. The same year saw an American branch of this society come into existence. Popularly known as Yivo, it has staked out an ambitious research program in the social sciences as pertaining to the Jews. Eminent scholars like Jacob Lestschinsky have made notable sociological contributions to the understanding of Jewish folkways, culture and history. In 1939 the American branch of Yivo became the center of training and research in this field. A Jewish Culture Congress held in New York in 1948 based its program on the permanence and continuation of Yiddish culture in America. The consensus of opinion was that Yiddish "seems to have no intention of dying."

Perhaps Yiddish survives because as one of its advocates has succinctly put it, "It is a language with a policy." It is also a language in action!

These were the years of great social change the land over. In 1880 James A. Garfield was elected President. Within a few years American historians were to note the passing of the American frontier. The vast agricultural domain was no longer inexhaustible. Now laborers were needed to tend the machines, to build the railroads, to work the mines and factories. And as the land seemed to shrink, the Jewish population of America faced its own problems, problems made crucial by growing numbers. On February 12, 1882, the chairman of a committee "to devise ways and means of receiving and caring for Jewish refugees" was reporting that instead of the five hundred expected immigrants at the port of New York in January, two thousand three hundred had already reached New York. An attempt was made by the committee to dispatch these refugees to other cities. Some one hundred of them were sent to Philadelphia.

So men and women and children fled the terror and the nightmare of mass murder in Europe. They became refugees and displaced persons. They turned their faces toward the promised land. They crowded the harbors and the ships and spilled over into many American cities. An arduous apprenticeship awaited them. Men rapacious and evil exploited them. They were worked like slaves. The deep morass of the sweatshops swallowed them. How they survived, what courage drove them on, how they managed to create order and stability, to bear and educate children, to evolve a law-abiding society, to sing and read and even laugh a little, to found theaters and newspapers, clubs and labor unions, is one of the miracles of history.

They believed in themselves and in their future. They dreamed good dreams. Here and there they found friends like Emma Lazarus and Henrietta Szold and Lillian Wald. And journalists like *Harper's Weekly* editorial writers. And greathearted statesmen. That helped to accomplish the miracle of their survival. That and destiny. For no man can escape his fate.

In 1882, the Hebrew Foreign Mission Society, which sought to help Russian Jews settle on the land, noted with approval that the New

Orleans Jewish Community with the co-operation of the Governor of Louisiana, Samuel D. McEnery, offered 160 acres of fertile land to each family of settlers. A constitution to govern this agricultural colony was drawn up. Every contingency was provided for. The project was saluted far and wide. One Jewish orator speaking in New York called this venture "a piece of Jewish history." But many of the colonists sickened and some died as malaria laid them low. Then the heat came. Mosquitoes plagued them. Finally the Mississippi River rose up and with a total disregard for the plans and the constitution and the hopes of the agrarian community, overflowed its banks, "sweeping everything away."

So there came to an end the "Experiment of the Sicily Island Colony." The settlers scattered. The farms were obliterated. The river had triumphed.

And over the swamps and the mist which covered everything, the shade of Elias Stultheus may have brooded. For between the year 1720 and the year 1882 there was not so much difference in time. The river had not changed. Nor had the pilgrims. The song of hope had been the same. Now it was stilled.

As the years piled up, as the nineteenth century was drawing to a close, a beloved American author, Mark Twain, attended a meeting of the City Council of Vienna. The year was 1898. He heard Dr. Karl Lueger, Mayor of Vienna, discuss the Jewish question. It was an address friendly to the Jews. As Mark Twain heard the words a passionate resolve was born in him. He too would lay his garland! So the seed for his essay "Concerning the Jews" was planted. Jews everywhere soon read it and rejoiced in their hearts. For who in his generation came closer to the soul of America than Samuel Langhorne Clemens?

CHAPTER XIV

The Antisemite and the Philosemite in America

→>>

The pedigree of honey
Does not concern the bee.
For every clover is to him
Sheer aristocracy.
　　　—EMILY DICKINSON

<<<

SOMEWHERE IN each man there lurks prejudice. There are people and ideas he dislikes. It is a form of psychic allergy. The organism reacts with antipathy toward an unlike object. Custom, habit and association play a powerful role in determining our race attitudes.

Prejudice may be expressed by a scornful look, an averted face, a shrug of the shoulders. It may mount in intensity resulting in restrictive covenants, commercial boycotts, incendiary speeches, attacks in the press, exclusion from employment, bodily violence, expulsion, confiscation of property, concentration camps and gas chambers. It is a question of degree and of intensity of hatred. This applies not alone to Jews but to all minorities. All of them have experienced some form of the disease. The Jew has known it always because in every generation on some spot on earth there have been self-appointed apostles of hate to see to it that he is despised, reviled, discriminated against, lampooned, pushed around, persecuted.

Many students have sought to analyze and to explain, to advance reasons of all sorts seeking to rationalize the irrational. Xenophobia has been cited. So has the herd instinct. Everything but the real reason. Deep within the hearts of most men there lodges the knowledge that man has always failed himself. Always he looks to others for alibis for his failures. The Jew has been selected by many as the universal scapegoat for the failure of our civilization. Those who nominated and elected him to this position were the frightened, the befuddled, the failures among mankind. Often they have been in the majority. From

376

the stables and the beer halls and the asylums for the insane their leaders have been recruited. The masses followed these Pied Pipers like the rats of Hamelin.

The subject is perennial. From the street corner and saloon to the university classrooms where "social distance" tests are given, the debate goes on. Lines are drawn for religious, economic, social reasons. Nor is it limited to Jews versus Christians. For among the latter there are philosemites. There always have been. Jacques Basnage, intrepid Calvinist divine who settled in Rotterdam where he wrote his *Histoire des Juifs*, was such a man.[1] Henri Grégoire, French Revolutionary and onetime Bishop of Blois, who wrote *Histoire des Sectes Religieuses* was another. So was the unknown wit who said, "Half of Christendom worships a Jew and the other half a Jewess." So were Reuchlin and Grotius, Leroy-Beaulieu and George Eliot. And many others.

In America the student of philosemitism has a fertile field to till. There were men like David Longworth, an early American publisher who from 1797 to 1821 published many books, but deleted prejudicial paragraphs or made friendly annotations to hostile references to Jews. He recalls the long and honorable list of Presidents and statesmen, clergymen and teachers whose letters and speeches made their position clear and unblemished. From the days of the founding of the nation when men like Ezra Stiles of Yale University befriended Jews to our time when Professor Ellsworth Huntington of the same university asserts, "The Jews are probably the greatest of all races," Jews have not wanted for champions in America.

So Jews made enemies, but they also made friends. The list is long and honorable. Madison C. Peters wrote *Justice to the Jew*. John Spargo wrote *The Jew and American Ideals*. Ada Sterling wrote *The Jew and Civilization*. There were many, many others. The periodical literature of America bulges with articles written by philosemites.

The reasons for espousing the Jews range from the sublime to the ridiculous. They rest on logic or caprice. Sometimes a single factor may be magnified or isolated and a superstructure erected on it, as when Mencken writes:

The Jews fastened their religion upon the Western world, not because it was more reasonable than the religions of their contemporaries . . . but because it was far more poetical. . . . For the Jews were poets of a truly colossal eloquence, and they put their fundamental superstitions into dithyrimbs of such compelling loveliness that they disarmed the common sense even of skeptical Romans . . . To this day no better poetry has ever been written.[2]

Long ago Spinoza had pleaded, "not to laugh at the actions of men, nor yet to deplore or detest them, but simply to understand them." That is the historian's formula in discussing antisemitism.

American antisemitism is the child of Europe. The black-robed friars who sleuthed through the pioneer settlements seeking to discover Jews in the New World were educated, indoctrinated and briefed in Europe. So were the agents of the Holy Office who transported the Inquisition to the Western Hemisphere. It was they who forced the earliest Jewish settlers in America to migrate and pioneer as New Christians. When Peter Stuyvesant blustered against "the obstinate and immovable Jews"; when in 1722 Harvard compelled its Hebrew teacher to undergo conversion; when young Minis fought a duel in 1832 because a Christian suggested that he name his horse Shylock and called him a "damned Jew"; when Grant issued his infamous "General Order No. 11" against Jews—they were acting in the European tradition, conforming to the prevailing patterns of many centuries.

There has been anti-alienism here in various forms, such as the "Know Nothing" movement. The Jew came in for his share of it. There was some social discrimination. There were some overt acts of hostility. Still there were no professional antisemites. Between 1880 and 1914, however, more than two million European Jews entered the United States. Following the First World War, there were enough Jews to make a good target and enough crackpots to do something about it.

It is inaccurate to state categorically that, "The first overt manifestation of anti-Semitism in the United States took place in 1877." It is obviously an oversimplification of the facts. But it is correct, and Carey McWilliams does it brilliantly, to associate antisemitism with increase in immigration and with "the corrosion" which the expanding industrial era had wrought.

Between 1818 when Mordecai M. Noah estimated the Jews in the United States at 3,000 and the closing years of that century when David Sulzberger estimated their number at 937,800, the situation had altered radically. And just as the situation had changed so had the climate of public opinion. In summarizing the cultural scene at the close of the nineteenth century, Volume 37 of the *Publications* of the American Jewish Historical Society observes that prejudice in some form had always existed. It was possible for any American with a spare dime to buy in 1879 a twenty-four page pamphlet titled *Hell for the Jews*. In 1888 a scribe whose name was Telemachus T. Timayenis was bitten with the virus of antisemitism and borrowing from a European master, E. A. Drumont, wrote a novel to prove that Jews lack "Aryan" virtues which Timayenis as the watchdog for Aryanism was prepared to defend to his last pencil. Again in 1899, an anonymous magazine article attempted to prove the usual canards, perversions of fact, malicious slanders.

When in 1877 Judge Hilton and an associate chose to deny to Joseph Seligman the hospitality of the Grand Union Hotel at Saratoga Springs, New York, the public was dramatically aroused. This noisy rejection gave their enemies a chance to gloat and their defenders the opportunity of restating the basic concepts of American democracy. Henry Ward Beecher denounced the incident in a famous sermon titled "Jew and Gentile." Oliver Wendell Holmes and Mark Twain and Robert Ingersoll took issue with the innkeepers. Americans were groping for a native formula and a democratic program.

In Europe the witch's brew was bubbling, stirred by many hands. In the United States George William Curtis from his "Easy Chair" in *Harper's Magazine* was gratefully contemplating "What We Owe to the Jews." William Cullen Bryant was pleading that we "do justice to the grandeurs of the Jewish race." That the issue had wider implications than those that grew out of industrial and economic conflicts may be glimpsed from an article in the *Journal of the Knights of Labor* written by T. V. Powderly, a railway shop worker whose talents and acumen elevated him to the leadership of the Knights of Labor. "Flings at the Jews," he wrote, "are flying about promiscuously at every hand, and it seems to me that this practice is neither just nor manly."

In the years immediately preceding the Spanish-American War, the first president of Cornell University was struggling valiantly as Minister to Russia to mitigate the desperate situation of Russia's Jews. Some years before, Andrew Dickson White had served as an attaché of the American legation. He had witnessed Russian brutality and sadism toward its Jews. Writing from the Legation of the United States in St. Petersburg, July 6, 1893, he says:

I have been accustomed in discussing the subject with the Russians, to point to such examples of the truest love for human kind as those shown by Judah Touro in the United States, Sir Moses Montefiore in England, Nathan de Rothschild in Austria, James de Rothschild and Baron Hirsch in France, and multitudes of other cases, citing especially the fact . . .

that the first considerable contribution to the Russian famine fund came from a Jewish synagogue in California, with the request that in the use of it no discrimination should be made between Jews and Christians.

Two years later an infamous import from Germany, a rabble-rouser named Ahlwardt, arrived in the United States to organize an anti-semitic movement. The alert police commissioner of New York City at once assigned Jewish policemen to maintain order at his meetings. The name of that vigilant police commissioner was Theodore Roosevelt.

The *American Jewish Year Book* records the following events as the peaks of interest to American Jewry in the year 1903-04: In September of 1903 there were pogroms in Russia. In October the Reverend Dr. Kaufman Kohler was installed as President of Hebrew Union College. In November the trial of the Kishinev rioters began. In January of 1904 antisemitic riots broke out in Limerick, Ireland, to be followed shortly thereafter by "disturbances" directed against Jewish laborers in Wales, to be succeeded by anti-Jewish outbreaks in Morocco. In that year of history four synagogues in America were destroyed by fire. But these misfortunes were technically known as "acts of God." Finally on the twenty-third day of May, in the year 1904, the first synagogue since their expulsion in 1497 was prayerfully dedicated by a handful of Jews in Lisbon.

It had taken more than four centuries to complete the circle.

The bells that tolled for massacred Jews resounded mournfully in Christian ears. When news of the massacres at Kishinev reached the mayor of Galesburg, Illinois, he issued an indignant proclamation and a fervent appeal to conscience. Said Mayor George Shumway: "Not only the Jewish people but the civilized world stands aghast at the horrors of Kishineff." A mass meeting was called at the Galesburg YMCA, "to arouse sentiment against such outrages." From New England to Portland, Oregon, in every corner of the land, such protest meetings were called. The deep moral indignation which was voiced served to unite Americans of every faith in bonds of fellowship.

Depressions and economic reversals breed antisemitism. Social disorganization follows hard on the heels of economic breakdown. During 1933-40, the years of depression and great social unrest, 121 antisemitic organizations were spawned. Of these eleven were intensively studied by Donald S. Strong in his *Organized Anti-Semitism in America*. They are:

German-American Bund
Silver Shirts

National Union for Social Justice
Defenders of the Christian Faith
Edmondson Economic Service
American Vigilant Intelligence Federation
Industrial Defense Association
James True Associates
American Christian Defenders
Order of '76
Paul Reveres

These groups employ the customary propaganda techniques. They use meetings, books, periodicals, newsletters and the radio to reach their audience. They sound the warning note, alert their followers to "danger." They play on the baser emotions. Facts are distorted. The truth is of no moment. What counts is the inculcation of an anti-image, furnishing the public with an object to despise and revile. Membership is recruited from the ranks of the earlier immigrants' descendants. The common prevalence of English names is no indication of ancestry. For name-changing has been frequent in American history. The malcontents of any origin are potential antisemites.

"While the older immigrants were considering themselves heroes, the newer ones were being viewed as a problem," wrote Professor Hansen in *The Immigrant in American History*.[3] The logic of other groups seemed not to apply to Jewish immigrants. Even contemporaneous migrants, claiming no priority in time of arrival, somehow arrogated to themselves the airs of dragomen of the native tradition when in contact with the Jewish immigrant. The Jew was considered a little more foreign, a shade less welcome than the peasants who made the Atlantic crossing with him. The sons of Erin felt they had a right to be here, to run our police and fire departments and political machines. But the sons of Aaron were trespassers! These groups were powerful enough to force through Congress laws in 1921 and 1924 revising immigration procedure according to a quota system which almost succeeded in eliminating Jewish immigration. Between 1931-36 only 26,402 Jews entered the United States—a little more than 4,000 a year. And this during the nightmare years in Germany when Nobel Prize winners had to await their turn while the crude and ignorant, classified as "Anglo-Saxons," could enter almost at will!

There are other conditions which favor and abet the enlistment of recruits of antisemitism. The possibility of war and the reluctance of cowards to fight for principles will make them lash out at the "international" Jew who they claim is "the cause of it all." There is social contagion too. Antisemitism in one part of the world is like the bubonic plague in one harbor. It spreads. Ideas can not be quarantined. Just as literature and the arts and religion spread throughout the world, so do hate and malevolence and aggression. There is no single factor. There are countless reasons, but most of them are due to failure—failure of self and failure of groups to meet the challenge of reality successfully.

The *American Mercury* in January of 1945 published Philip Wylie's "Memorandum on Anti-Semitism." Here Wylie summarized the haphazard thinking of those who think they can recognize Jews by their appearance. "Mr. Johnson, the typical man in the street, thinks in clichés and exudes bromides with his sweat. So he is convinced that people who differ from him or are non-Johnson are therefore inferior creatures or sub-Johnson." What Mr. Johnson is looking for is a happy world full of Johnsons. What he wants is for every mirror in the universe to reflect his own image. His fantasy life is as limited as his intellect. Mr. Johnson wants quite simply to "succeed." He wants to do away with all obstacles to his progress. When he is told that Jews are his only stumbling blocks, he wants to eliminate them. "To be an anti-Semite is to repudiate our Constitution and to deny every syllable of meaning in the story of America," writes Wylie.

If the antisemite succeeded in his dearest wish—the elimination of the Jew—we would lose the Constitution and its Bill of Rights. We would give up our security, liberty, and self-respect, and our immortal souls. "This," says Wylie, "is a truth known by me, Philip Wylie, a sixth-and-seventh generation, Scotch-Irish-Presbyterian-American. It is written by me of my own free will in the great, freedom-loving land, because I too love liberty and justice and truth."

Words are flung about casually. Their meanings are obscure even to those who mouth them. We talk of democracy, of freedom, of equality, of prejudice. Vocabularies will not solve the problem. What is wanted is reorientation in thinking, an approach founded on reality and truth.

In analyzing the *Roots of Prejudice*, Professor Gordon W. Allport and his associate, Bernard M. Kramer, make a synthesis of the ethos of countermeasures:

There are important ethical implications . . . we are saying that prejudice will be prevented only if the philosophical mold of one's life is sound. A sound mold requires a basic trust of mankind, freedom from the jungle-outlook, from rigid categories, from the paranoid inability to take blame upon one's self, or to adopt the point of view of the other fellow. A sound mold requires one to know the extent of one's own hostile attitudes, to feel some shame in having them, and to understand their probable roots.[4]

What is wanted is wholeheartedness, an earnest desire for social progress, the determination to introduce scientific methods into human relationships, an unswerving belief in social telesis.

The chronology of antisemitism in America may begin with the door-slamming incident at Saratoga Springs, where a New York politician and an Irish-born immigrant drew the line at admitting a German-born Jew to their hostelry. Joseph Seligman, friend of Abraham Lincoln, banker-financier of the Civil War, admirer of Ulysses S. Grant whose appointment to the supreme command of the Union forces he had advocated with the President, had a long and honorable service record in the land of his adoption. Carey McWilliams in discussing Seligman's financial services to the Union cause says, "The historian William E. Dodd has characterized the successful fulfillment of this mission as scarcely less important to the Union cause than the Battle of Gettysburg." In the year of his ejection from the New York summer resort, Joseph Seligman had performed an outstanding service to the Navy Department by renegotiating a loan. Thereafter, with the exception of the years when Cleveland was President, his firm continued to serve as fiscal and naval agents of the United States Government. President Grant counted Seligman among his intimates. As token of his esteem he offered Joseph Seligman the post of Secretary of the Treasury. This post Seligman refused, but continued until his death in 1880 to serve his country with unflagging zeal.

In the same year of the summer resort incident, 1877, the New York Bar Association refused to admit an attorney to membership because he was a Jew. The "Nativist spirit" was flourishing. In the following year, 1878, a Jew dying in San Francisco, Michael Reese, left his fortune impartially to Jewish and Christian philanthropies. So Jews managed to make the headlines from coast to coast. Both phenomena continued. Rejection competed with philanthropy for the headlines. Toward the close of the century, in 1895, the Philadelphia *Times* mourned the passing of a Jewish citizen, Simon Muir, in its editorial columns. "He was an example . . . to many a professing Christian," wrote the editor in extolling Muir's Jewish virtues.

It was an eventful decade for the Jews. Alfred Dreyfus was retried and released. Another war was fought. Some four thousand Jews served in the Spanish-American War. Fifteen Jews were among the crew of the *Maine* when it blew up. Thirty were officers in the Army and twenty in the Navy. Teddy Roosevelt had a Jewish lieutenant and six enlisted men in the Rough Riders. A sixteen-year-old boy, Jacob Wilbusky, was among them. He was mortally wounded in his first battle. There were many citations for gallantry. The first man to meet his death in combat in the Battle of Manila was Sergeant Maurice Juster, a California Jew. Sergeant Morris J. Cohen captured the first flag from the enemy in the Philippines and died later in combat. Dr. Joseph M. Heller, assistant surgeon, a member of the expedition into northern Luzon, was cited for "great courage in ministering to the wounded under fire." Private Morris Schamberg became acting assistant surgeon and was promoted to lieutenant for the work he carried on in the Spanish Military Hospital at Ponce. Private Nathan Levy distinguished himself at the Battle of Manila. Irving Peixotto was one of the first group of American soldiers to reach the top of San Juan Hill during the bloody engagement for its capture.

The naval record of participation was equally distinguished. Lieutenant Joseph Strauss began his notable career of service then, rising eventually to the rank of rear admiral. Lieutenant Commander Edward D. Taussig, who occupied Wake Island and was the first American officer in charge of the island of Guam, also rose later to the rank of rear admiral. Lieutenant Commander Adolf Marix, who had commanded the battleship *Maine* until a few weeks prior to its loss, was cited for heroism in two naval engagements off the coast of Cuba. He too was to become a rear admiral.

So they continued to pile up citations and encomiums on the battlefields while frightened, frustrated civilian propagandists dug in behind their desks to "expose" their coreligionists. Hilaire Belloc did not wear a uniform. He was born in France, naturalized in England. Never threatened by bullets, he still managed to convince himself and his readers that he was besieged by Jews. He had a persuasive pen and managed to endear himself to quite a few readers in America. Also to a few writers who plagiarized him because they admired his style and content. Belloc maintains, like all of his ill-informed fraternity, that the Jews are an alien body within the society they inhabit. This he considers the chief cause of social friction. He refers to Jews as if they were a cinder in the eye of Christianity. He has a simple definition of the antisemite. "The anti-Semite is not a man who hates the modern Arabs or the ancient Carthaginians. He is a man who hates the Jews. . . . *He hates Jews in themselves.* . . . He detests the Jew as a Jew and would detest him wherever he found him."[5] Nothing could be more open and more direct. Here the patron saint of the Ku Klux Klan and the Silver Shirts is speaking. Here is the inspiration of the hacks who perpetrated the *Dearborn Independent*.[6] Who are these men? The answer is simple: *They are the men who hate Jews in themselves.*

It is one of the paradoxes of history that the forces of antisemitism and those of philosemitism are always in a state of acute imbalance following war. The fraternity of the trenches is forgotten. The fellowship of facing death together, the unity won under shell and mortar fire, the kinship which knits men at the graves of their fallen comrades—these binding sentiments crumble and decay in the days of peace, of reunion, of thanksgiving for having been recalled to life. The courageous combatant is absorbed by complacent civilians. Soon, but for the faint blur of memory, the ordeal of fire might never have been.

A few years after the Spanish-American War, the Jews of the land celebrated the two-hundred-and-fiftieth anniversary of their settlement within the boundaries of what is now the United States. It was an occasion greeted with appropriate fanfare and rejoicing. It gave many Americans of all faiths and all professions the opportunity of saluting a long and honorable record. Newspaper stories and editorials throughout the land greeted their fellow citizens of Jewish ancestry in terms of warm approbation. The centuries from the days of Jacob Barsimson to the days of Sam Dreben (who was preparing for his magnificent performance in the First World War by soldiering south of the border) were reviewed with warm admiration. American Jews basked in the warmth of approval and duly collected the cream of these salutations in a volume entitled *The Two Hundred and Fiftieth Anniversary of the Settlement of Jews in the United States.*

But a few brief years separated American Jews from the postwar epidemic that was soon to be let loose upon them. In Europe *The Protocols of the Elders of Zion*, lies forged in Russia in the year of American celebration, 1905, were spread like poison gas. They were carried across the Atlantic. The Protocols now donned American dress. Borrowing from the London *Morning Post* the sweepings of antisemitism which had appeared serially as "The Cause of World Unrest," professional Jew-haters laid their garlands of poison ivy impartially on the doorsteps of the living and the tombs of the dead. They found an "angel" in Henry Ford. Antisemitism in America was launched.

In the pages of the *Dearborn Independent* is found the asylum of the Jew-hater. The antisemite who peddles bromides and dispenses clichés lives there. He requires no knowledge, no education, no information. All he needs is hate. "Though Americanism is yet unfinished, Judaism has been complete for centuries," its editor writes and does not pause in his self-appointed task of driving nails into the coffin of the Judaism he buries. He is the sleek, smug undertaker who wants to expedite the funerary ceremonies and make sure that the "corpse" dead or alive is really safe underground. There is no rhyme nor reason for these slanderous articles. There is only one purpose—vilification, destruction, annihilation of Jews. Any single copy will serve as a sample.

Here is the issue of March 5, 1921. It contains not one honest paragraph. There is not a sentence here to comfort or sustain or uphold anyone. Hate is what they advocate, hate for Jews and all of their friends. A legitimate target is anyone who is a friend to justice, or to Jews. The *Dearborn Independent* of this date attacks Woodrow Wilson, calling him a Jekyll-Hyde personality. The accusation against Wilson rests on "the fraud committed upon a trusting public by Woodrow Wilson." The fraud? On January 16, 1921, two former Presidents, Wilson and Taft, with more than a hundred of America's outstanding Christian leaders, had solemnly issued a warning and a protest titled "The Perils of Racial Prejudice." Against these men the peddlers of lies and the salesmen of forged documents now frothed and screamed. For the literary scavengers are busy men. They search the garbage dumps, empty wastebaskets, listen at keyholes, sniff gunpowder plots, examine droppings in quest of "material."

In an article titled "Jewish Jazz Becomes Our National Music," the music expert who despises what he calls "the moron music of the Yiddish Trust" laments that it is allied with the movies in spreading degenerate ideas. We read that "Popular music is a Jewish monopoly. Jazz is a Jewish creation. The mush, the slush, the sly suggestion, the abandoned sensuous notes, are of Jewish origin." This refers, no doubt, to Gershwin, Romberg, Kern, Copland, Bernstein. "Jewish Infection in Our Music" is decried with much shedding of tears and anguished wringing of hands.

When Jews protested the introduction of religion into our public schools, the hate-sheet in Dearborn began to beat its war drums. "Mass Meetings Well Staged," read one news item.

When the philosophers of Dearborn, Michigan, discovered that there were Christians who liked Jews, they tried desperately to explain the phenomenon. They found the word antisemitism in common usage. But there was no well-known, acceptable antonym. So they coined "pro-Semitism," meaning philosemitism.

Sometimes these frustrated crusaders start tilting at windmills— and lo! they disappear. The enemy has resorted to the countermagic of name-changing. This is a familiar escapist technique used by all minority groups in adjusting their names to the more accepted forms in vogue in the host culture.

This is an unhappy subject. It is discussed at great length in *Aspects of Jewish Power in the United States,* authored by the brain trust. It covers the compulsory measures requiring Jews to take family names in Europe. If a Jew failed to choose a name, one was forced on him. The names were based on: 1. precious stones, like Goldstein; 2. places, like Berliner; and 3. adding the word "son" to the father's name, as in Isaacson. This they do not like at Dearborn, Michigan. But name-changing is anybody's prerogative. The Battenbergs become the Mountbattens and Hanovers the Windsors. So the Schneiders become Taylors and the Holzmans the Woods, and Mr. Katz becomes Mr. Filene by a translation and a slight reversal of vowels. "The Mandansky brothers will henceforth be known as May. The Levy family has been calling itself Lytton," lament the sages of Dearborn, gnashing their dentures as they decry "The Gentle Art of Changing Jewish Names."

There are other subjects. There is the Jew's aversion to "truth," at least the kind of "truth" the *Dearborn Independent* bought and sold. "The Jews have never in all their history feared the lies of their enemies; but they have feared the truth." The tragedy is, say these hirelings of Ford, that Jews have usurped power in America by techniques they did not themselves invent. "Jews rule, not by reason of their brilliance or their money, but by ideas which are not even Jewish, but Babylonian. They have captured the castle from within."

There is no impotence like that of hysteria. When ideas fail and the contaminated waters of inspiration run dry, then individuals become legitimate prey. Here we find a vitriolic attack on Rabbi David De Sola Pool of Shearith Israel of New York. He is accused of pleading for Jews to be brought up in a traditional atmosphere under conditions which are reminiscent of Jewish history and background, indoctrinated with awareness of the great Jewish past. That amounts to treason in Dearborn! They make much of such "subversive" teaching. There is an enemy lurking under every Murphy bed and antisemites refuse to go to bed without looking.

There is nothing the elder statesmen of Michigan love as much as a good quotation from the "enemy." The *Dearborn Independent* is as happy with a quote as a dog with a bone. So Justice Brandeis is quoted as saying that Jews tend to throw off ancient restraints which once exercised control over them as they lose contact with Jews and Judaism. When Brandeis pleads for moral restraint and greater respect for authority he waves a red flag. The *Dearborn Independent* is against Zionism and Brandeis is its advocate. He wants unwelcome European Jews to have a land where "they may lead a Jewish life." This will not do. European Jews are to be excluded from America. They are to be barred also from Palestine.

Apt students of Sombart are found in Michigan. Sombart's interest in the subject of *Jews and Capitalism* began with his study of Max Weber's analysis of capitalism and Puritanism, "especially as I felt that the dominating ideas of Puritanism, which were so powerful in capitalism, were more perfectly developed in Judaism." The accusations the Jews are confronted with in the Sombartian literature of antisemitism often amount to defamation. The purpose all too often is open incitement against Jews.

The student of history confronted by the fact that antisemitism is on the increase in America naturally asks himself why this is so. It is obvious as we recall the record of Christian-Jewish relationships in the early days of the founding of this nation that there was much more basic good-will at that time than there is now. One explanation is that the founders of our nation had moral values, that they were constantly inquiring into the state of their conscience. That they loved the Prophets, the Bible and justice.

The antisemites loudly proclaim that Jews have many faults. The Jew is too energetic. He is acquisitive. He is a capitalist, thrives under capitalism, or invented capitalism.[7] He is addicted to conspicuous consumption and to conspicuous leisure. His manners leave something to be desired. The list is long. Need we go on? Only if the subject has specific bearing on the history of Jews in America, or on American history. It has. Criticism is anyone's prerogative. It is part of the democratic tradition. The artist, the traveler, the diplomat, the reporter describes what he sees, good or bad. All that is required is that the reporter be honest and his intentions honorable. Again and again America has been described by foreigners. Americans have been analyzed, made fun of, charged with all manner of faults. Curiously, the faults that are universally ascribed to Jews by their detractors in the *Dearborn Independent* and similar publications are the same as are widely attributed to all Americans by many foreign observers. Frances Trollope was one of a group of English visitors to our shores who was repelled by the manners of her American hosts. She spent four unhappy years here and revenged herself by venting her spleen on her hosts. Her book was published in 1832. It was called *Domestic Manners of the Americans*. She accused Americans of being clannish and of displaying toward the outsider or stranger "malice, hatred, and all uncharitableness." They are braggarts, forever boasting of their virtues. Yet their stories make her "doubt if the speakers knew what honor and honesty meant."[8] As a matter of fact their "broad assumption of superior virtue" is not only offensive but is completely without foundation. In business they are grasping. As for the Yankees, they complacently admit and even boldly boast "that no people on the earth can match them at overreaching a bargain." They are money-mad. "This sordid object [money], forever before their eyes, must inevitably produce a sordid tone of mind, and worse still, it produces a seared and blunted conscience on all questions of probity. "Mrs. Trollope further states that no American conversation is ever complete without the word "dollar."

Their women, like American men, are guilty of bad taste. They overdress shockingly. They are vulgarly conspicuous and when it comes to cosmetics, they do not know where to stop. "They powder themselves immoderately, face, neck, and arms with pulverized starch: The effect is indescribably disagreeable by day-light, and not very favorable at any time."

She thinks American ethnocentrism is crass impertinence. Their arrogant assumption that they are the cream of humanity is very irritating to Mrs. Trollope. Americans consider themselves the Chosen People.

If the citizens of the United States were indeed the devoted patriots they call themselves, they would surely not thus incrust themselves in the hard, dry, stubborn persuasion, that they are the first and best of the human race, that nothing is to be learnt but what they are able to teach, and that nothing is worth having which they do not possess.[9]

It is by no means easy to give a clear and just idea of a Yankee. . . . In acuteness, cautiousness, industry, and perseverance, he resembles the Scotch; in habits of frugal neatness, he resembles the Dutch; in love of lucre he doth greatly resemble the sons of Abraham; but in frank admission, and superlative admiration of all his own peculiarities, he is like nothing on earth but himself.[10]

Nor did Charles Dickens paint a more flattering picture of Americans. His Elijah Pogram (and could the name be without significance?) was a coarse, uncouth fellow. "A man deliberately makes a hog of himself, and that's an Institution!" cries Martin Chuzzlewit in despair as he contemplates a "typical" American.[11] In his *American Notes*, Dickens was equally unsparing. Among America's faults he finds:

Another prominent feature is the love of "smart" dealing which gilds over many a swindle and gross breach of trust; many a defalcation, public and private; and enables many a knave to hold his head up with the best.[12]

The literature of anti-images is rich and redolent. It is not always directed against the same group. The dossier is interchangeable. Mrs. Trollope could with very few changes be copied by the antisemitic press—and none be the wiser.

Alexis de Tocqueville's *Democracy in America* is another work which finds much fault with the manners, folkways and mores of Americans. He criticizes their "restlessness and insatiable vanity."[13] (So does William James!) According to Tocqueville, good breeding is noticeably absent in America. Democracy separates men from the past and cuts them off from a sustaining sense of oneness with their ancestors. It all boils down to a want of breeding, laments Tocqueville, for "the manners of democracies, though often full of arrogance, are commonly wanting in dignity."

Bryce's *American Commonwealth* also lists many American faults. Like his fellow critics, Bryce finds their preoccupation with business and money-making as the chief trait of Americans. How often do the purveyors of antisemitism hurl the same accusation against the Jews! "In no country does one find so many men of eminent capacity for business, shrewd, inventive, forcible, and daring, who have so few interests and so little to say outside of the sphere of their business knowledge."[14]

Frances Trollope published her study of American life and manners in 1832. D. W. Brogan's *The American Character* was written more than a hundred years later, in 1944. Brogan describes a situation that has not greatly changed. The Jewish question, however, has now emerged as a major issue. That concerns us.

America is now the capital of world Jewry, and anti-Semitism is one of the problems that perplex the wise American, Jew or Gentile, and tempt the demagogue, lay or clerical. . . .

Whether American Gentile society is so rich in social talent, in artistic taste, and in intellectual power to be able to afford, in the long run, the snobbish exclusiveness of so many clubs and fashionable suburbs is open to question.[15]

What is the difference between the critics and the hate-mongers? The difference is in their purpose. The former hold up a mirror and describe what they see. The latter distort, pervert, perjure, incite. There is a wide gulf between incitement and propaganda. "Free speech, yes; free incitement, no!" wrote Lasswell in *Democracy Through Public Opinion*. Justice Holmes was eloquent on the difference between incitement and propaganda. So were many of his peers. The critics of America may look upon the land and its people and tell us what they think. So may the critics of the Jews if they are honest and, within reason, objective; if their purpose is to describe and not to defame.

There has never been a time in the history of our nation when books about Jews were not generally available. Basnage's *History of the Jews* was translated into English by Thomas Taylor in 1708. Hannah Adams early introduced the Jews and their history to her compatriots. Byron's "Hebrew Melodies," written for the cantor Isaac Nathan, were well known in America. Coleridge wrote three *Talmudic Tales* and translated two poems by his friend, Hyman Hurwitz, called "Israel's Lament" and "The Tears of a Grateful People." Coleridge was no stranger in America. Dickens and George Eliot and Disraeli were perhaps as well known in America as in England. Every writer of note was recognized as a friend or a foe. If a writer failed to make his stand clear, his correspondents were sure to write to him to find out where he stood. Robert Louis Stevenson was no exception. He wrote:

(Vailima, May 1891)

To Miss Adelaide Boodle

What a strange idea, to think me a Jew-hater! Isaiah and David and Heine are good enough for me. Were I of Jew blood, I do not think I could ever forgive the Christians; the ghettos would get in my nostrils like mustard or lit gunpowder.[16]

Periodicals, always a listening post for readers' preferences, opened wide their pages to authors, Jewish and Christian, who thought they had something to contribute on the Jewish question. It was to persuade the intolerant that Nina Morais wrote "Jewish Ostracism in

America" in the *North American Review* in the year 1881. The argument which Nina Morais poses is that the "untutored mind" dislikes those from whom it differs. She says that "the aversion to the foreigner is an instinct of the human heart." This she deplores. America has no reasons to dislike foreigners, insists Miss Morais, being almost wholly made up of foreigners. "America is the scrap-bag of the world," she says. Her argument endlessly repeats itself: "The American Revolution was a union of foreigners."[17]

Christians as well as Jews now began to write about Jews more objectively. They turned out many works, friendly and unfriendly. Anna Laurens Dawes's speculation on *The Modern Jew, His Present and Future* was one of numerous works dealing with this perennial subject.[18] She poses the question: "What is to become of the Jew?" She insists that the whole world is thinking about the Jewish problem. She is disturbed by the massacres of Jews. She is also worried by the large numbers who are coming to the United States, asking whether "a piece of ancient society [may] be thrown into modern civilization and survive?"

It is interesting that in 1886 a Christian woman in America should soberly discuss a return of Jews to Palestine. "Sentiment would induce all nations to favor a Hebrew State in the Holy Land, while as a neutral power with affiliations in every country, the balance of nations would be advantaged, not overturned. . . . Disgusted and over-Hebraized communities would eagerly welcome the relief afforded."

As Jewish troubles multiplied in Europe, more and more Americans gave expression to moral indignation toward the oppressors. Cardinal Gibbons, writing in December of 1890, expressed the opinion of many liberal Catholics whose hearts were stirred by the suffering of the Jews.

Every friend of humanity must deplore the systematic persecution of the Jews in Russia.

For my part I cannot well conceive how Christians can entertain other than most kindly sentiments toward the Hebrew race, when I consider how much we are indebted to them. We have from them the inspired volume of the Old Testament which has been consolation in all ages to devout souls. Christ our Lord, the Founder of our religion, His Blessed Mother, as well as the apostles, were all Jews according to the flesh. These facts attach me strongly to the Jewish race.[19]

The years brought increasing recognition of the plight of Jews and of the rising of antisemitism, as well as sympathy. In this vein Sidney

Whitman writes on the "Anti-Semitic Movement" in the *Contemporary Review* in 1893. This is but one of the many articles which the last decade of the century produced. The *Forum* in the same year was warmly defending the immigrant's contribution to America. George P. Parker considered "What Immigrants Contribute to Industry." The demands to put up bars to keep European immigrants out were a loud chorus. Still this was nothing new in America. Parker says, "It has been suggested and discussed by every generation since the thirteen struggling colonies were successful in forming a government for the conduct of their own affairs." The immigrant was needed. The immigrant was rejected. Always there was this dichotomy, the cry for cheap labor versus the opposition to its importation. "There is very little sentiment in the matter of immigration. It is purely a matter of business." Parker estimates that between the years 1789 and 1821 there were approximately a quarter of a million immigrants added to our population. Later years saw the tide swell to even greater proportions. His conclusion appeals both to logic and to sentiment.

That man must be cold indeed who cannot admire the unflinching courage of the sturdy young people of other lands who, leaving everything dear to them, come here to assist in subduing the earth. So long as they will come, so long as we need them—a question which cannot possibly arise for discussion until our population has multiplied ten- or twenty-fold—we cannot afford, either in fairness or in humanity to erect a single barrier against the flow of this tide of men.[20]

With the years the magazines of America became still more receptive to articles about Jews. Herman Cohen, writing in the *Fortnightly Review* of 1896 on "The Modern Jew and the New Judaism," makes a plea for greater tolerance and understanding.

A thoroughly able discussion is "Russian Jews as Desirable Immigrants" by Ida M. Van Etten.[21] "The Russian Jew seems to possess a dual character; to be the best of men and the worst, to practice the meanest vices and the most exalted virtues." The Russian Jew when he migrates looks upon his initial hardships as an apprenticeship to a good life. He means to stay. He is never lured back to the land of his origin. How could he be? It is that which makes him a good citizen. The wealth that he earns remains largely in this country. "Politically, the Jews possess many characteristics of the best citizens," concludes Miss Van Etten.

In 1896 *Israel Among the Nations* by Leroy-Beaulieu was made available in English. This was a work of a French philosemite whose book first appeared in his native land shortly before the Dreyfus affair. Within a few years of the appearance of the English translation of his work, its brilliant author was invited to lecture at Harvard and other American universities. Now they could hear the French philo-semite tell his American audiences that the Jew was admirable and unique.

Compare, indeed, this infinitesimal Jewish minority with the Christian majority; count the number of celebrated men who have issued from the ranks of Israel. There can be no doubt that the Jews, the so-called Semites, have given proportionately more men of talent to our Aryan civilisation than the so-called Aryans themselves.[22]

We know that William James gave him a ready ear. And many, many more! Leroy-Beaulieu said that the migrating Jew was not changing his country. He was in search of a country. He extolled Jewish virtues, explained their history, praised their women, their culture and tradition. He may be credited with having further spurred a philosemitic trend in the United States. Two years after his English translation appeared, a contributor to the *Review of Reviews* on January 15, 1898, was asking, "Are Jews Superior to the English?" and answering in the affirmative. The writer insisted that in brains and character the Jews surpass the English. "Clearly it is time that Christian England began to learn the elementary lesson of morality, intelligence and industry from the despised Hebrews."

The Dreyfus affair, the impassioned articles of Zola and Nordau filled our newspapers and periodicals. Now the conscience of many Christians became uneasy. *Harper's New Monthly Magazine* for October, 1899, carried an article by G. W. Stevens, titled "France As Affected by the Dreyfus Case." The impact of the affair Dreyfus on Americans was noticeable. Then Mark Twain spoke for America. His "Concerning the Jews," which appeared in *Harper's New Monthly Magazine*, was an answer to a correspondent who wrote, "Now will you kindly tell me why, in your judgment, the Jews have thus ever been, and are even now . . . the butt of baseless, vicious animosities?" Mark Twain was not a man to dodge a moral issue. His biographer quotes Mark Twain as saying, "The Jews he did consistently admire as a people and considered the most gifted race in the world."

"I can stand any society," wrote America's greatest humorist. "All that I care to know is that a man is a human being—that is enough for me; he can't be any worse." He was furious at the French for allowing the innocent Dreyfus to be pilloried. After examining his own opinions, he decided that he too was prejudiced, but against the French!

If they chafed and grieved over the antisemites, Jews could take heart at the encouragement from many of their notable friends. The number of philosemites was swelling and their recruits were the illustrious of our land.

Now it was 1900. Jews stood uncertainly on the threshold of a new century. In the past they had known the tragedy of being displaced and unwanted. What would the twentieth century bring them?

In *The Jewish Quarterly Review*, 1899-1900, Alice Lucas translated from the Yiddish a poem called "On the Ocean" by M. Rosenfeld. Just a metric conversation between two displaced persons on a storm-bound ship on the Atlantic. Hopeless. Anguished. They had been rejected by America and were being returned to Russia. The refrain is a sad one: "America drives us to Russia again." But it was a conversation that bore fruit, a lament that was not to be lost. The sad refrain, the heavyhearted lamentation was not dissipated by the biting wind and the hiss of waves on the Atlantic. Somehow the sad refrain found response in the hearts of many Americans.

One of the most interesting sources for the social history of American Jews at the dawn of the twentieth century is *Harper's Weekly*. In 1902, *Harper's Weekly* was attacking the urban concentration of Jews and urging them to scatter over the land rather than remain at the ports of entry. The issue of October 11 carried photographs of Hester Street and other congested New York areas as potent arguments for the evils of urbanization. Immigration between 1880 and 1890 was summarized as seventy-five per cent desirable immigration and less than eighteen per cent undesirable immigration. What was the nature of the other seven per cent, *Harper's Weekly* does not say. The editor proposes that Jews go West: "They would make, in time, valued citizens." The *Nation* for September 14, 1911, discussed Jewish composers. "It seems to be the fate of Jewish composers particularly to be over-rated during their life-time, underrated afterwards." The *Atlantic Monthly*, like its sister publications, was not averse to discussing Jews. In "The Problem of American Judaism" Ralph Philip Boas begins with an analysis of martyrdom. Persecution, he says, begets martyrdom, and martyrs, unfortunately, are very righteous people. Boas deplores not only the trend to righteousness which he confuses with orthodoxy, but Zionism as well. "No more insidious than persecution," says Boas, is "the gradual disintegration of race and religious consciousness within the faith." In the past the Jew was kept in line by persecution, poverty and discipline. Now that this threefold discipline no longer exists, each individual within the group must solve the problem for himself. Judaism in America, he pleads, must become articulately American: aware of the age in which it functions and of its current problems. American Jews can no longer "live on their ancestors." The country is deeply concerned with the Jewish problem, Boas maintains. It wishes the Jews to clarify "the issue" and to fulfill themselves.

On the long thread of periodical literature in America, like so many beads of a special color and design are articles about the Jews. They follow no pattern, no rhythm. They persist because the Jews persist. No social history can be complete without at least a quick look at them. For each discussion admits us into the mind of the writer of that time and indicates both editorial approval and popular interest. It makes us contemporaries.

In his commencement speech made at Harvard in 1903, William James said, "The day when Harvard shall stamp a single hard and fast type of character upon her children will be that of her downfall." That was the point of view then of some of the contributors to magazines. Then an editorial in *Harper's Weekly*, July 1, 1905 compares Jews with non-Jews and comes to the sad conclusion that these comparisons are always to the disadvantage of the group compared with the Jews. The editor comments on the *London Lancet's* study of physical conditions of the children of the slums of Leeds. "In every case the Jewish children showed a marked superiority in condition." The writer in *Harper's Weekly* feels that a comparable study in New York would show the same results. "That expectation is a remarkable tribute to something," adds the editor humorously. "Who is the American?" asks John Graham Brooks in *The Chautauquan* in October, 1907. The author believes that the traits for which Jews are most severely criticized are the very qualities for which the Yankees are extolled: thrift, mental alertness, adaptability, energy, driving toward success.

Now periodical literature on Jews in America swells to a mighty river. It is no longer possible to contain it. The historian suffers from an embarrassment of riches. The most provocative series of articles devoted to Jews in America and the most brilliant is by Norman Hapgood in *Harper's Weekly*. "Do Americans Dislike Jews?" asks the editor of *Harper's Weekly* in 1915. And stays to answer. A discussion on Zionism had just been completed in the summer issues. Many readers wrote letters to the editor expressing dislike or admiration for the Jews. Perhaps the single catalytic agent which precipitated the rush of articles at this time was the tragic miscarriage of justice known as "the Frank case." Here was America's Dreyfus case with a tragic ending. A young man of thirty-one of unblemished reputation, falsely charged with the murder of a little girl. Georgia enflamed by a rabble-rouser, Tom Watson, spewing anti-Jewish propaganda. A conviction on flimsy "evidence." The nation aroused. The yellow press fanning mob excitement. Appeals for justice and reason flooded the Governor's desk. Governor Slaton commuted the death sentence. A mob lynched Leo M. Frank, August 17, 1915. Later a confession by a criminal serving in Atlanta Prison on another charge exonerated the martyred Leo M. Frank. All that could be now done by the decent folk in Georgia was to give way to a sense of abject shame, to dedicate themselves to the abolition of lynch law. . . . There is still a long, long road to travel.

To Norman Hapgood, editor of *Harper's Weekly*, the Frank case was an unmitigated, rank miscarriage of justice. Spurred by this tragedy his articles assumed more than a reportorial and editorial tone. It was not enough to deplore and to decry. What was wanted was affirmation. Hapgood cited a long list of illustrious great—Bergson, Lombroso, Pinero, Georg Brandes, Nordau, Sidney Lee, Beerbohm, Bernhardt, Zangwill—and many, many more. He mentions great American Jews like Brandeis, who "circulate freely" in American society. He speaks of the valor on the battlefields of France in the war then raging, of the thousands of young European Jews who were dying for their countries—countries that had often abused them. How well do the Jews fight for our country where there is only "a misty barrier between them and us." He turns to the colleges where subversive forces are already at work against them. Says Hapgood, *"They honor our colleges."* If Jews were treated with complete equality and not kept perpetually on the defensive, would they not "show more of the qualities that marked Jesus, the greatest of all Jews?"

Intermarriage is approved by *Harper's Weekly*. In Denmark, Italy, Sweden, France and Australia there is considerable intermarriage. "In Denmark mixed marriages are much more than a third of the total in which Jews take part. . . . To the Gentile there can be no sound reason against marrying a Jew, and indeed a strong reason for it. He knows that such a strain, selected through several thousand years—able, persistent, patient—cannot but strengthen his stock."

Hapgood in speaking of this desideratum forgets that intermarriage means eventual extinction for the Jew. "Idealistic Jews think that to marry a Christian . . . is to lower a noble banner," says Norman Hapgood, philosemite. He greatly influenced the philosemitic trend. Before long others, like Hapgood, began to write of the Jew with sympathy, insight and dispassionate scholarship. The years of the publication of the *Dearborn Independent* saw books like Spargo's *The Jew and American Ideals* add their weight on the other side of the scales.

The seeds planted by Ford's paper in Dearborn were harvested in American colleges. The year 1922 witnessed many periodicals and newspapers taking cognizance of the growth of antisemitism in American universities. In the *Nation*, between July and December of 1922, there are a number of such articles and letters on this subject. The *Nation*, like other periodicals, is aware not only of the growth of antisemitism but of the more widely adopted but secretly practiced quota system which is used in many American universities. So a correspondent vents his spleen in the *Nation* in the heat of summer, in 1922: "The Jew problem in colleges is the farmer's stock problem: grade cattle or scrub cattle. . . . Some of my best friends are Jews, but not of the usual sort. . . . Christ was a Jew and told a lot of the truth about them." In September, there is a summary of "Harvard Student Opinion on the Jewish Question." The writer, William T. Ham, summarizes the findings which Professor Richard C. Cabot received in answer to a survey made in a course in Social Ethics. The question was: "Is a college ever justified in limiting students on the basis of race?" Eighty-three students at Harvard took the examination. Of these forty-one, or almost half, believed in race limitation in colleges; thirty-four emphatically said never; eight were on the fence. Eight of the eighty-three students had Jewish names. One of the Jewish students was uncertain about admitting other Jews to Harvard!

A flood of letters to editors followed. Victor Yarros (writing from Hull House) asks: "Is Americanism a hollow sham, and must we make the country safe for all the vices and hatreds that make reconstruction so difficult in Europe?" There is reassurance in the Middle West. Robert M. Lovett writes: "I beg to reassure you in regard to the status of Jews in the University of Chicago. They are received without question." One correspondent, Fay H. Babbe, of Philadelphia says: "I, for one, though a Gentile, would prefer placing my children under a Jacques Loeb or a Morris Jastrow, rather than wasting their time with the mediocre brains met with in the majority of faculties."

The chorus swells. Some voices clamor for exclusion. Others are for fair play. The mills of propaganda grind out their yield of words, written and spoken. The eyes and ears of America are bombarded. Lies skillfully planted here and there grow into dense, impenetrable jungles. Men labor mightily in the effort to keep them cut down, to let sunlight in. Darkness and light alternate in an inexorable rhythm. The Jews of America are dizzy on a pendulum which swings from social acceptance to social rejection. There are poverty-stricken Jews who struggle to send their children to State schools, undergoing heroic privations and hardships. There are rich Hebrews in America who want their sons at Harvard and their daughters at "finishing schools." Miss Lucy Madeira, head of a fashionable "exclusive" school, finds it necessary to accept Jews as students in the Madeira School only within a certain quota. "Madeira's, along with Walker's and Rose-Marie, is distinguished by this racial liberalism. Madeira's Jews run to Meyers and Warburgs."

The pattern of quotas is universal. Here is a sample. In 1946 a member of the North Shore Congregation Israel in Glencoe, Illinois, received the following letter from a private school for girls:

The application for your daughter's admission was brought to my attention. I will do my best to set forth our position in a letter.

For a good many years, we have been advising Jewish applicants to seek another school. We do it reluctantly and in the realization that, by so doing, we miss the opportunity of having a number of excellent students and desirable members of the student body from every standpoint. There have been several factors which have led us to the conclusion that our position is well taken. We have no place of worship for Jewish students in or near ———, and no Jewish members of the community. It is impossible, therefore, for Jewish students to fulfill our requirements of church attendance. Our dormitories are arranged for four girls in a room and when we had Jewish students they invariably drew one or more roommates who were prejudiced against Jews, or had parents who were. The result was considerable unhappiness all around. . . . The psychological scars caused by discrimination could be exceedingly harmful to a sensitive adolescent. For this reason, I feel that Jewish students should seek state or other public institutions, if they do not want to attend their own exclusive schools, where there would be a considerable group of persons of their own faith, so that their failure, if they do fail, to adjust to the whole group would be less distressing and would leave them less alone.

I hope you will believe that I am writing with the best interests of your daughter at heart and in a spirit of friendliness.[23]

Jews dig deep into their wallets. Liberal donations to universities pour in. Chapels and lecture halls are built with gifts from Jewish donors. The money is accepted. Gothic towers rise toward the skies in many parts of the land. But social amelioration cannot be bought with medieval architecture. The outstretched hand receives the gifts— but withholds the clasp of fellowship.

In 1936 the editors of *Fortune*, not unmindful of recent happenings in Germany, addressed themselves to a study of the position of the Jews in America, maintaining that "any man who loathes Fascism will fear anti-Semitism."[24] They define antisemitism as "the deliberately incited, affirmative racial phobia which has produced the social and economic and sometimes physical pogroms of modern Germany just as it produced the murderous pogroms of Czarist Russia." Every depression, every war, every major dislocation of the norms of life has bred the Jew-baiter and the Jew-hater. But it is not within the mores of America to practice this perverted doctrine. It is a product made in Europe. "The conclusion is inescapable that current American anti-Semitism is feeble." Popular antisemitic charges are examined. The crux of the rebuttal is that, "There is no basis whatever for the suggestion that Jews monopolize U. S. business and industry."

The Jews are negligible in heavy industry. Rubber is a non-Jewish industry, so are shipping and transportation non-Jewish. There is only one exception to Jewish control of an industry, the clothing industry. "By and large, then, the case for Jewish control of American industry falls pretty flat. But the little propagandists of the Shirts have another tune to their whistle. They contend that, whatever the facts about industry, the Jews control opinion in America through their control of newspapers, publishing, radio, the theatre, and above all the movies." This charge is then carefully examined and thoroughly refuted.

The editors of *Fortune* append a brief statement on the ownership and control of motion picture companies. Twentieth Century-Fox was largely controlled by the Chase Bank. In charge of production was Darryl Zanuck, the son of a Christian minister. Warner Brothers is a Jewish company. RKO is largely controlled by Jews, as is Loew's, Inc. Paramount is non-Jewish. Columbia is Jewish. Universal is largely non-Jewish. United Artists is both Jewish and non-Jewish. However, Jewish movie moguls have not used the movies to bolster their coreligionists. Instead, writes Ben Hecht, who knows the subject intimately:

These Jewish heroes of Hollywood put 100,000 churches in their movies—and nary a synagogue. They ride to the rescue of every wounded folk in their films, and glorify the valor of all oppressed people—except the Jews. For they have a mission. It is to convince the world that their Americanism is untainted by any special consideration for Jews.[25]

Even the casual moviegoer can confirm this fact.

Urban residents, according to *Fortune*, have greater opportunities for education than the rural population. So Jews benefit from proximity to great schools. "The Jews share with the Scotch and certain other peoples an almost morbid passion for higher education. But that passion would have been futile had immigrant Jews not remained in the larger cities."

Law and medicine are examined, for it has been charged that the Jews have crowded out the rest of the population in these two fields. The most important legal business in America, which is incidental to banking, insurance companies, railroads, investment companies, patents and the admiralty as well as some of the largest corporation matters involving the law, is in the hands of non-Jewish firms. There are many Jews in trial work. This is partly because Jews are able trial lawyers. But also because "non-Jewish lawyers tend to prefer the fat fees and regular hours and routine, solicitor-like labors of their office to the active combative practice of the law courts."

The occupational analysis is thorough and carefully appraised. The conclusion is very simple. Antisemitism makes a poor showing. "Ideologically the propaganda of all of them is repetitious, childish, and so far unsuccessful. . . . Anti-Semitism in America, judged by its exponents, is a very sick donkey."

Time changes all things. Institutions yield to pressure. Even rocks yield to erosion. But the "Jewish question" is endless, immutable. Just how much do articles on Jews, the Jewish question and race prejudice accomplish? The readers whose opinions are rigid, unyielding, inflexible, remain comfortably buried in their point of view. Those who are in the limelight and are sensitive are often wounded and sorely tried. The fact that these discussions are still current is an indication that there is considerable reader-interest in their content. Such articles are legion. Here is a laboratory sample, Waldo Frank's

"The Jews *Are* Different" in the *Saturday Evening Post* for March 21, 1942. Only the date sets it apart. The contents could have been penned two generations before. Waldo Frank repudiates the current antisemitic myths which have not changed from those current in the nineteenth century. They belong in the realm of demonology. The forgeries of the *Protocols of the Elders of Zion*, the flagrant lies in the pages of the *Dearborn Independent* are well known. Yet they must ever be denied over and over again.

In October, 1944, Knight Dunlap slays the same old dragon in the pages of the *Scientific Monthly*.[26] "The Great Aryan Myth" is held up to the sunlight and shrivels as always when exposed to scientific inquiry. "The Aryan myth is now completely discredited among scholars," says Dunlap in his brilliant analysis of the age-old subject. The assurance is welcome but the myth will not die. That hardy ghost still walks its beat in colleges and universitites, in clubs and summer resorts, as it walked in the days when Gobineau wrote his *Essay on the Inequality of Races* nearly a century before. Gobineau infected Wagner who gave the disease to the Germans. The medium was the *Bayreuther Blätter*. After the German composer died, the Gobineau Vereinigung was founded in Leipzig in 1894. Wagner's son-in-law, Houston Stuart Chamberlain, resuscitated the Aryan myth. Thickheaded burghers welcomed an idea they could grasp and understand.

Language is no indication of racial relationships, says Knight Dunlap. Nor is the cephalic index. Group association is paramount. Relationship is for the likeminded. The name "Aryan" has been in ill repute for fifty years and more. Since the Germans like the designation and nobody else wants it, the solution is simple, says Dunlap. Let the Germans and their friends be called Aryans. Then will this term of shame come home to roost.

Such articles may please the scholar, but they are not read in the slums of Boston or other cities. For even as Knight Dunlap was writing his logical, careful, well-documented article, Jewish heads were being fractured by young toughs in Boston, Jewish tombstones were being turned over in Chicago and synagogue windows were broken in New York. In the *Atlantic Monthly*, in an article titled "Who Persecutes Boston?" Wallace Stegner writes:

For the past two years vicious propaganda, much of it couched in the vein of raw humor has been circulated through the war plants, navy yards, barrooms, beauty parlors, and subway stations. Much of it is calculated to give the impression that all the heroes of this war are Irishmen, all the chiselers Jews.[27]

It is among the semiliterate that such propaganda devices achieve an immediate response. The dullards and the half-wits thrive on it. In vain do the educated, the enlightened and humane wrestle with the octopus. They collect evidence, present reports, vote resolutions. All to no avail. "The American Jewish Congress, The Anti-Defamation League of B'nai B'rith and the American Irish Defense Association have been collecting affidavits on such incidents for five years." But the saloon intelligentsia and the poolroom literati do not read official reports.

There were anti-Catholic riots in Boston and elsewhere in the nineteenth century. The Irish were exploited, resented, rejected, pushed around. "The miserable and driven Irish found reason to hate Bostonians almost as much as they hated the English. Boston found Irishmen useful as laborers and their wives and daughters useful as domestics." But the Irish knew how to organize and how to fight back. The Irish knew how to sing. They had all America singing the praises of dear old Ireland. Mother Machree was more celebrated than Whistler's mother. Says Stegner:

the Boston Irish, attacked on every side, developed a group consciousness hardly matched by any other group in the history of America. They had already had it when they came from persecuted and plundered Ireland. And their experience in America, far from levelling the old hatreds, built new ones on top of the old. From that time to the present two cultures with different premises and different traditions have lived uneasily side by side in Boston.[28]

The Irish can teach the Jews an important lesson in survival.

Survival depends on affirmation, not on negation. It rests on self-acceptance. It depends on being at ease with oneself. To be an "authentic Jew" (the phrase is that of Jean-Paul Sartre) is to be an integrated personality. It is to have an accepted set of values, a mores, a code of ethics which is related to the whole individual, biologically, historically and psychologically. To reject a part of the whole is to reject a part of oneself. The "authentic Jew" knows that he is different from others because all people are different from each other. So he does not shadow-box with his own image. He accepts it because it is his own and because each man must in the final analysis live with himself in stark, unmitigated loneliness. "Anti-Semitism," says Sartre, "manifests the *separation* of men and their isolation in the midst of the community. . . . In a society whose members feel mutual bonds of solidarity . . . it would have no place."

In ancient days Jews knew the flavor of solitude. For were they not doomed to the lonely highways of history? Their therapy lay in contemplation of their law. "He who journeys on the highway without companionship," said the Talmud, "shall lead his thoughts to dwell upon the Torah." The Jews of Boston and Chicago, of New Orleans and San Francisco have lost touch with that source of strength. They have no staff to lean upon. The solitary journey often becomes unbearable. . . .

Clocks often stand still for the Jews. It seems but a moment from 1898 to 1944. A brief look at their periodicals is convincing. The *Congress Weekly* discusses "The Anti-Semitism of Voltaire" just as the *Review of Reviews* wrote about antisemitism forty-six years before.[29] "We Jews have a right to be tired of being used—or rather abused—for one purpose or another." The pages of the *Congress Weekly* in the middle of the twentieth century, like all Jewish periodicals, resemble Isaac Leeser's *Occident* of a hundred years before. So Professor Kurt Lewin in "A New Approach to Old Problems" submits a program for eliminating race tensions. It is a problem, he feels, for the social engineer. Deploring the fact that accurate statistics are not available today, he also regrets that adequate tools for fighting the irrational forces of antisemitism are lacking. What is wanted is not the cultivation of tolerance, so much as the rejection of intolerance. "The last ten years have left us bewildered," says this eminent authority, casting about for a straw. What is needed is the help of social scientists in tackling these grave problems. The "Commission on Community Inter-Relations" proposes to establish "the peculiar circumstances under which various manifestations of anti-Semitism have developed in this country . . . and the methods by which they can . . . be uprooted." Max Levine, in "These Our Prejudices," finds the nativist groups manufacturing many antiforeign myths. "When a person discriminates against others, he makes it possible for others to discriminate against him. Intolerance is contagious," says Mr. Levine in a plea to his own people not to fall into the stupidities of prejudice in any way, shape or form. In the *American Scholar* in 1945, Rabbi Ephraim Frisch writes on "The Book and the People of the Book." The shibboleths he demolishes were the same ones that confronted Jews of America a century before.

Under the date of October 17, 1945, *PM* carries a story titled "Ford Asked Again to Disclaim Use of Name by Anti-Semites." Rex Stout, chairman of Friends of Democracy, urged Henry Ford to "stop the further publication and circulation of pamphlets and books containing copies of extracts from the *Dearborn Independent* articles. Repudiate . . . pamphlets and books quoting your endorsement of the *Protocol* . . . quoting other anti-Semitic statements of yours which presumably no longer represent your true beliefs. . . . Prosecute for libel any one who states you are anti-Semitic." Then *PM* comments on Rex Stout's demands: "These requests are not new; they were made of Henry Ford by the Friends of Democracy before Pearl Harbor in a booklet called *Henry Ford Must Choose.*"

Americans are becoming aroused. For they know that antisemitism is essentially a Christian problem. It must be stopped at the source. Laura Z. Hobson wrote *Gentleman's Agreement* because "Illness was in her, and shame for all of them." Dorothy Thompson wrote "The Lesson of Dachau" because "the revelation from the German concentration camps burst upon the world." Eleanor Roosevelt, in her column for September 18, 1946, thus analyzed the disease of race prejudice:

For a long time, I am afraid, the Anglo-Saxon race has taken it for granted that, by some peculiar dictum from on high, it was endowed with particular virtues. Our efforts must be bent in the future to giving all people an opportunity for development in the hope that, in that way, we can promote a safer and better world for all.

Church groups have reacted to the threat. The Home Mission Convention of North America, representing twenty-three Protestant denominations, solemnly issued the following warning: "Unless the Protestant and Catholic Churches of the United States launch a determined campaign to stop anti-Semitism, the United States will perish as did Nazi Germany." "Anti-Semitism is a curse against humanity. The whole Christian religion was founded on the Old Testament, a product of the Jewish spirit, and, therefore, anti-Semitism is completely an act of Anti-Christ," says Cardinal Faulhaber, Archbishop of Munich, in an interview with Bartley Crum and Frederick Leggett of the Anglo-American Inquiry Committee. Léon Bloy, who has induced many eminent converts to join the Roman Catholic Church, has recently been introduced to American readers. He who has been called "the Pilgrim of the Absolute" writes:

People forget, or rather do not want to know, that our God-made man is a Jew . . . that His mother is a Jewess, the flower of the Jewish race; that all His Ancestors were Jews; that the Apostles were Jews as well as all the Prophets; finally that our Holy Liturgy is entirely drawn from

Jewish books . . . anti-Semitism . . . is the most horrible blow yet suffered by our Lord in His ever continuous passion.[30]

John Haynes Holmes writing his column "Through Gentile Eyes" has given repeated proof of his friendship for his Jewish fellow Americans. The National Committee to Combat Anti-Semitism publishes a little paper called *Counter Attack*. Its purpose is to assail and expose antisemitism in any form. One of the most active agencies designed to combat prejudice was created by the B'nai B'rith in 1913. It is called the Anti-Defamation League. The work of the Anti-Defamation League is expanding because the current need is urgent. Its reports are given wide publicity. The *New York Herald Tribune* for May 7, 1947, carried the following story, "No Organized Anti-Semitism Is Found Here," summarizing the survey made by the Anti-Defamation League for 1946: In New England antisemitism had not increased. In Chicago and the Midwest it had decreased. In the Rocky Mountains it made no headway. In the South it was unabated.

To obliterate hate is the first step on the road to the Promised Land of fulfillment and realization. The great and the wise of all races have pointed the way. It may be that in the human experiment, the Jew is the touchstone. . . .

CHAPTER XV

Jewish Workers and Farmers

->>>
We only are desolate. Earth, cold and stern,
Begrudges us fiercely the home that we found.
We journey, but no one awaits our return.
O, tell us I pray of you, whither we are bound.
——M. ROSENFELD[1]   <<<-

"I wonder how many of us would be here if the founding fathers had been as nervous as we are about the oncoming hordes that threatened to starve them to death when they were not growing much more than they themselves could eat!" wrote Eleanor Roosevelt in her column, November 20, 1946.

More than fifty years passed between the dirge by M. Rosenfeld and the lines written by Eleanor Roosevelt. There has been revolution in industry, in ideas, in methods of living and in methods of mass murder. Two major wars were fought. Big, brave words have been spoken and dissipated into air. At Lake Success the United Nations in the role of little David tackled the Goliath born of war and hate and famine and aggression. Everything changed, including the role of the Jew in world history. A new nation has been added—Israel is reborn.

Are there American implications in the change of status of the Jew? Without a doubt there are. The historian who undertakes one hundred years from now to reconstruct American history from the front pages of our daily papers will have to deal also with Jewish history because our headlines and cartoons and editorials are surcharged with items concerning Jews.

Jewish arithmetic has changed violently. Between 1939 and 1946, it diminished from more than sixteen million six hundred thousand to some eleven million one hundred thousand. This loss of five and a half million Jews did not make the remainder any more loved

or welcome. America had its immigration quotas. Those Jews they
had "and their adoption tried" they were willing to keep. But there
were no welcome signs for their displaced cousins across the seas.
Had not American Jews demonstrated their worth sufficiently to be
allowed the privilege of bringing in their kith and kin? What of the
centuries of participation, of valor, of contribution? It seems as if
the country would say to them: "We would have more like you!" The
opposite happened. So as we wind up the story of the Jews in America—we seem to be completing a circle. The centuries between
Loronha and Lubin, between Barsimson and Brandeis, between
Carigal and Cardozo, were centuries of social change and of social
progress. There is much physical difference between a caravel and
a Constellation. But how much difference in the hearts of men?

In Middletown in 1937 the Jews were considered as "cultural
deviants." In Lima in 1537 they had another name for the Jew. He
was a heretic. What change had the centuries wrought?

The closing years of the nineteenth century saw a change in our
immigrants. The northern and western countries of Europe were no
longer the major source of the man-power reservoir. Southern and
Eastern Europe and Italy now sent their ragged thousands to our
shores. "A significant fact about Russian emigration is that it has
been chiefly non-Russian," writes Professor Davie in *World Immigration*. In 1899 the United States began its classification of immigrants according to race. Between 1899 and 1930, 1,905,561 Jews
were admitted to this country. Prior to that date it has been estimated
that there were a half million Jews in the United States. In that
period the Jews were numerically second in volume of entrants,
being exceeded by Italians, of whom twice as many came here.

Shortly before the American Revolution, the Russian Government
granted a measure of autonomy to its Jewish inhabitants. Between
the years 1772 and 1844 the Kahal was officially recognized as the
legal communal governing body. "The general tendency of the Jewish
law was to invest the Kahal with enough power to enable it to withstand outside pressure." When in 1835 Russia confined its Jews to a
restricted Pale of Settlement extending from the Baltic to the Black
Sea, she created a culture area within which there developed culture
traits, a language and literature, folkways and mores which influenced
the thinking and social behavior of its component members. Lithuania, Poland, the Ukraine were more than geographic expressions.
The movements of Jews to the rest of Russia were rigidly controlled.
Their lives were regulated and circumscribed. "They were violently

urbanized, torn away from agriculture and forced into fierce competition within their own ranks and with the non-Jewish city population and the landless peasantry flowing into the city," writes Davie.

Here they developed their own economy. They perfected their magically elastic language, Yiddish. They had their folklore. Their own literature. Their periodicals. Their theater. Within the Pale were the great masses crushed by poverty, then the insecure middlemen, and at the top the few wealthy families who owned the banks and helped develop the railroads, who owned the factories, the sugar mills and the textile mills. There were also students who went to foreign countries or studied within the schools in the Pale or managed to enter the Russian universities and gymnasia under a rigid quota system. These young men and women became the rebels. They rejected much of the orthodoxy. They resented the economic inequality. They were the spokesmen for the exploited and the malnourished, for the submerged and inarticulate.

When the mass migrations began, they drew off from the Pale not only the inarticulate. It was a movement that attracted the intelligentsia as well. To visualize this mass transplanting of population we must realize that it was a pyramidal movement involving all but the very apex of the social pyramid. It was not a planned exodus. There was nothing orderly about it. It was flight from terror. Savage massacres involving bestial acts of cruelty, lust, pillage, fire, murder, rape began in 1881 and continued at intervals until 1906. The civilized world was aroused. Christians with conscience were enraged. Jews formed a solid phalanx of sympathy. New words were added to the vocabulary of mankind. "Pogrom." "Black Hundreds." There were new and tragic lessons in geography. Kishinev. Homel. Zhitomir. Troyanov. Now Bialik cried aloud to God charging that he had betrayed his people. Men forsook faith. They turned instead with tenderness and brotherly love to believe in the tortured folk itself. Their finest and most creative minds began to plan, to work, to sacrifice, to chart a new destiny for a weary, old, battered people. They looked to the East and Zionism was born. They looked to the West and the migrations began.

The *London Quarterly Review* in 1882 described the conditions prevailing in Russia as characterized by "the most cruel outbreaks of race-hatred that has disgraced the annals of civilization." Disraeli, infuriated by the excesses and the bloodletting of the Russians, described the Caucasian races as "flat-nosed barbarians." He pleaded for immediate measures of rescue.

Everywhere outside of Russia the deepest moral indignation was registered. In the United States public-spirited citizens called protest meetings. President Theodore Roosevelt, warmhearted and forthright, thundered out his anger. America's women, traditionally humane, like Julia Ward Howe, cried out their wrath. Jacob Gould Schurman, president of Cornell University said at a mass meeting in New York, "O Christ! What crimes have been committed in Thy name against the race which gave Thee to the World!"

Perhaps some day the historian of the future will be wise enough to explain why Americans took the Jewish massacres of 1881-1906 to heart and not those of 1933-45.

Life was a dirge. It was a perpetual funerary procession. It had no dignity. It had no security or peace. It only held terror and flight. Endless terror. Never-ending flight.

Not all could run away. The very old, the sick, the little ones, often had to be left behind. Only the strong, those fit to labor, were wanted. Farewells were sad as deathbed partings. For there was no returning for these pilgrims once they said good-by. The journey was long and the steerage passage a nightmare experience. The awful uncertainty about admission to the United States made physical discomfort secondary. The immigrants who were allowed to enter were coming into a world of poverty and crowding, of exploitation and malnutrition, of long apprenticeship in insecurity.

Let us summarize briefly the types of opportunities open to an immigrant who joins any American Jewish community. His first concern is to find shelter. This he does in the area in which his kinsmen live. Failing kin, he finds people who came from the same town as he did or who speak his language. Once he is fitted into some crowded tenement, already bulging with occupants, his next concern is how to sustain himself. Here too he turns to his friends and kinsmen for advice and financial assistance. If he happens first to contact peddlers, he is likely to become one of them. If all his friends are tailors, shirt-makers, cobblers, then he becomes a member of these crafts. It is all haphazard, without regard for previous education, status or experience. There are many inequalities at the tailor's bench in background and education, but all are considered as members of the needle trades. After the immigrant becomes an earner, he next casts about for a place where he can pray. This is usually predetermined by his place of origin. The man who came from Rumania will be a little averse to praying with a Jew who came from Poland. He will be happier to chant the psalms and prayers in the presence of people whose accents are those of his childhood, where green memories may be evoked. So a place to live, a job to work at, and a place in which to offer up his prayers, may be said to be the primary searches of the immigrant. Next he picks up the threads of his old life by writing letters home, by saving his pennies for his relatives who are so eager to join him. It is not necessary to describe at length the teeming streets and tenements. Nor to draw pen portraits of the threshold citizens whose feet are planted on American soil and whose memories are of distant places.

In 1906 a group of American scholars under the auspices of the "Liberal Immigration League" made a study of *The Immigrant Jew in America*. The people associated with it were men and women of scholarship who were actuated by the finest motives of social service. While their work naturally lacks the statistical refinement which knowledge of recent methods has created as a tool, nevertheless the study has merit, if for no other reason than for purposes of comparison of data, of change in attitude and in status. Edmund J. James, president of the University of Illinois, led the research group. He says:

The conclusions reached by the investigators fully sustain the just appreciations of the character of the Jewish race and its certain advance in this country, which were so memorably furnished by ex-President Grover Cleveland, President Eliot of Harvard University, Bishop Lawrence, and others on the occasion of the commemoration of the 250th anniversary of the settlement of Jews in the United States. . . . President Eliot attributes the extraordinary power of endurance and survival to their religious faith and the singular purity, tenderness, and devotion of their family relations.

They had friends among those who took the trouble to become acquainted with them.

One thing which excites the wonder of the investigator is the vitality of the Jew in spite of living under the double curse of slum and Ghetto. . . . Hand in hand with the energy of the body goes an energy of mind which is equally challenging—as a description of the various forms of industrial and social activities plainly shows.

How zealously did they turn to night schools, to books!

The progress of the Russian Jew in this country is sure and constant, in spite of his poverty and distressful start. . . . In our public schools the Jewish scholars are, as a rule, bright, attentive, and studious. They excel in mathematics, English, and history. They show special aptitude for studies appealing to the imagination, and the enthusiasm of even the littlest children for the free flag that covers them is a sight to stir the heart of the most heedless scoffer at the immigrant.[2]

Whatever of concern, anxiety, sympathy or resentment the coming of the Russian Jews might have aroused, one thing is certain. It brought a revolution in the needle trades. It stimulated the development of the labor movement in America. From the days of Abraham Galanti, a sixteenth-century employer of labor who set a pattern for fair dealing in labor relations, many Jews have had a conscience responsive to the needs of labor. The long list of labor leaders in America attests to that. Samuel Gompers, Sidney Hillman, David Dubinsky and others.

Exploited immigrants managed to pull themselves up by their own bootstraps. Such a man was Samuel Gompers.[3] He was born in England of Dutch-Jewish parents in 1850. He came to New York as a boy during the Civil War days in 1863. It was but a step from the East End of London to the East Side of New York. He was an alumnus of the Jewish Free School which he attended from the age of six. The headmaster was a gentleman named Mr. Moses Angel! By the time he was ten his formal schooling was over. He went to work. But like so many book-hungry Jews he attended night school. "At night school," says Gompers, "I learned something of the Talmud. I was taught Hebrew—not the mongrel language spoken and written by many Jews of the present age—but that honorable language that unlocked a literature of wonderful beauty and wisdom."

Gompers never forgot those early lessons in Judaism and the wisdom of the fathers. He spoke and acted as a Jew. What he saw in ghettos, of poverty and of the misery and human degradation that follows in its wake, revolted him. So it had been in London. It was no different in New York. Poverty knows no fashion, no manner, no language but its own. The tenement-house system of making cigars, like the sweaters' system of making clothes in crowded basements, in dank railroad flats, in garrets that were firetraps, proved to be a breeding ground for disease and a ripe field for delinquency. "I failed to see how men . . . whether Christian or Jewish could profit through the misery of human beings," he said. In his effort to give expression to his social discontent he joined the ethical culture movement. If formal religion failed to improve society, perhaps social telesis was the answer.

So he labored with Adolph Strasser. First they organized the cigarmakers' union. Their first strike was a dismal failure. They now rebuilt their union on the British model. The rest of the story belongs in labor history. In 1886 he became the first president of the American Federation of Labor. He continued his activities, becoming more and more of a factor until the First World War, when he headed the War Committee on Labor. After the War he worked with the members of the Commission on International Legislation in an effort to arrive at an equitable world program for labor.

When the Jews of Eastern Europe began pouring into the United States in great numbers, Gompers, despite a tendency to give his first loyalty to the labor movement, could not help but become involved in the acute problems of his coreligionists. In spite of himself he became involved in the plight of the immigrants. Few of the newcomers had any industrial training. He found that Jewish workers could not be organized with workers of other nationalities. It was that clannishness of theirs which Henrietta Szold had noted when she wrote that "the Russian population carries the tendency to grouping to a fault." The men of Kovno and men of Vilna and men of Odessa "lead separate existences in the effort to perpetuate the home traditions."

Gompers had had a generation in which to become Americanized. He could well feel that these men who spoke Yiddish and had their noses ground into the direst poverty could have been turned over to their own leaders. He names their leaders: Abraham Cahan, Joseph Barondess, Gregory Weinstein and Henry Miller. But Gompers could not long remain a spectator. There was an acute problem to solve. There were urgent reasons for union. "Despite many difficulties, we organized several Hebrew trade unions. There was a racial emotionalism and aspiration that both helped and hindered unionism." By the end of a decade group tensions became more acute. In the nineties the racial problems in unionism could not be dodged. They became serious. There was considerable violence. European ideologies had been transplanted which had no relation to the situation in America. Nihilism and anarchism had sprouted in Russia, the unhappy harvest of a blind and cruel government. They had no business in America. Gompers wanted to act in terms consistent with the existing situation in America. He resented too great a partisanship which stemmed from exclusively Jewish affiliation. Gompers made his own point of view clear when he discussed David Lubin's aggressively Jewish attitude. He said: "Lubin insisted upon forcing upon all with whom he came in contact his pride in his Jewish ancestry. He stated upon any and all occasions that it was his greatest glory that he was a Jew. He really made himself obnoxious to delegates by thrusting his religion upon them." Gompers wanted moderation in all things, including identification with things Jewish.

The influx of cheap labor brought with it a new phenomenon, a Simon Legree known as the contractor. These men operated so-called "outside" shops. They undertook to have garments sewed by workers to whom they farmed out bundles to be sewed and delivered back to them. Often the owner of an "inside" shop—one where the labor was employed and the garments sewed on the premises—would supplement his factory output by farming out part of his output. The immigrants clustered in one area. They needed work immediately, could not finance an intermediate training period. They insisted on their Saturdays off. A sewing machine could be bought by paying a few cents a week to the agent who sold it. It could be squeezed into a corner of the dwelling. Women and even children could be taught to help out. Often there were times when a man had to carry his machine strapped to his back in search of work. He was required to furnish his own needles. He did not make a "living." He just managed to exist.[4]

By 1893 the factory inspector of the State of New York could write in his annual report that the needle trades are dependent almost wholly upon tenements and sweatshops.

One authority finds that some sixty per cent of the Russian Jews in this country in 1900 were engaged in manufacturing. More than a third of all gainfully employed Jews were turning out clothing, millinery, caps and other forms of wearing apparel. One-fifth were engaged in trade. There were some few in domestic and personal service, in clerical work, in the professions. There were some hackmen and teamsters.[5]

Jews are an urban people because they have been forcibly separated from the land. "They are the most urban people in the world," says Davie. Because of this, Davie maintains that East European Jews have succeeded in business, trade, and industry. "The Jews are probably the most successful of all the recent immigrants in gaining economic competence. . . . The sky-rocket careers leading from the peddler's pack to the banker's desk or the professor's chair testify to rare singleness of purpose."[6]

Not all immigrants ended up at the tailor's bench or as peddlers. The students had their own special biographies. Abraham Cahan may be considered a shining example of Jewish intelligentsia. He was born in a sleepy little village on the outskirts of Vilna in the year that

Abraham Lincoln was campaigning for the Presidency of the United States. He was the son of a poor *melamed*, a struggling schoolmaster who had also tried his hand unhappily at running a little store. Abe Cahan was graduated from the Teachers' Institute of Vilna and taught in the Jewish elementary school. Like many of his generation he became a member of the revolutionary underground. When his connection with the forbidden political movement became known, he fled to America.

Cahan believed in an articulate labor movement. He joined the Socialist party. He contributed to a number of periodicals. For three years he edited the *Zukunft*. In 1897 he became the editor of the *Forward*, which with a brief interruption he edited for the rest of his life. He wrote a history of America in Yiddish. Also several English novels. *The Rise of David Levinsky* was a case study of just such people as he knew and moved among during his transplanted lifetime. His autobiography is both a sociological case study and the dramatic record of a life packed with incident.

These are the skeletal facts. We cannot dismiss Abe Cahan without recalling that his name carried great weight in tens of thousands of homes in America. His editorials were widely quoted, discussed and debated. His opinions swayed the masses whose sage and household idol he became. The paper he edited was an instrument for Americanization. It served to promote the cause of unionism among its readers. It supported strikes and sought aid for strikers' families. Its adherence to the Socialist party was a major source of strength for that group. The fact that the *Forward* lent tacit support to Zionism was of inestimable value. Into the home of the transplanted Jew this newspaper brought education and discussion, pathos and humor. Its "Bintel Brief" column is crucial to the study of the social problems of immigration. It educated but it also lampooned a little. It introduced stereotypes like the shrew, the slattern housewife drowning in a sea of malapropisms, overwhelmed alike by the wisdom of Jewish sages which eluded her and English expressions which she never quite grasped. It exposed the rich ignoramus. It held up the summer hotel and the crowded street in the Jewish quarter to scrutiny, serious and profound, but also whimsical or humorous, always infinitely charged with pathos.

The history of this period can not be adequately told until the definitive history of the *Jewish Daily Forward* is written. Then the historian can have his fun and research both.

Now, numerous sister publications were born and lived their

truncated days. The intervening years have seen the rise and fall of many papers. They have constituted the cultural bridge between the past the immigrants knew and the present they had not quite assimilated. It is a story with an unfolding plot.

Stratification in the crowded urban settlements existed aplenty. There was no right and no wrong side of the tracks where most of the residents lived in concentric circles fanning out around the stores and cafés and factories, the poor and the rich stepping on each other's toes. But there was the aristocracy of learning, of talent, of the professions. While the rich man may have had his following, the many jokes that cluster about the dullard and his financial successes prove that the capitalist of the ghetto was not a very important fellow as people went. It was the men whose words were steeped in Hebraic lore and learning, the writers, the professional men, the labor leaders, who were the aristocrats of the Halsted Streets and Henry Streets of the New World.

The intelligentsia strutted. The rich stepped aside in deference. Such a man was Dr. Joseph Isaac Bluestone, an immigrant from Lithuania whose memoirs trace the narrative of his days from his childhood, through his student days in Russia. An autobiographical fragment discusses the fluctuation of his fortunes in those first hard days in America when he tried to be a storekeeper and longed to be a doctor. The wish triumphed. He finished his medical training at New York University and practiced his profession on the East Side of New York. But even in his struggling student days he nourished a dream and found kindred spirits who shared it with him. The dream was of prophetic quality. It is important because it reveals the spontaneous group fantasy which eventually blossomed into Zionism. For men must dream before they build.

Bluestone's aspirations were translated into a speech he delivered on the Fourth of July in 1882, when Emma Lazarus and countless others were wrestling with a formula to help Jews everywhere. He dreamed of Palestine rebuilt to serve as a bark for the drowning Jews of Europe. He dreamed of a Jewish State in Palestine whose effulgence would permanently sustain American Jews, keeping them safe from assimilation.

There was no conflict in the twin purpose. American Jews needed spiritual sustenance. Europe's Jews needed an address, a home, passports, the status which is conferred by citizenship. So with a group of loyal friends, the first group of *Hovevai Zion* (Lovers of Zion) was formed in New York City with Bluestone as one of its officers.

There were many other visionaries like him in those early days. He knew them as people or through their ideas. His diary is studded with luminaries. Sir Laurence Oliphant, the Christian Zionist, is described in these memoirs. And Moses Gaster. Kaufman Kohler and Solomon Schechter, Gustav Gottheil and Israel Schapiro and many, many more. He knew Herzl and Nordau. He met Bialik and Shmarya Levin. It was a life of rich content.

Just as Jewish life in America was not a matter of layers separate and unrelated to each other, so was its cultural life not lived in isolation.[7] Emma Lazarus of Sephardic stock found her genius when she unlocked her heart to Russian Jews. Lillian Wald became renowned when she left the security of her German-Jewish middle-class environment and cast her lot with the underprivileged on Henry Street. Born in Cincinnati in 1867, insulated from hardship, aloof from the major tragedies of the Jewish people, she found in a chance moment, on a professional nursing visit to an immigrant's home, the key to immortality. Lillian Wald and May Brewster offered their skill as trained nurses to clients desperately in need. Between Lillian Wald and the people she chose as her neighbors, there developed a beautiful relationship. It needed the outpouring of a rich personality and the gratitude of a neglected, struggling, but passionately loyal folk.

The slums were Pandora's box. Lift the lid and the smell of poverty rushed out and troubles by the millions were revealed. Sickness and privation, insecurity and deprivation, crowding and lack of sanitation. Mothers dying for want of adequate care in childbirth. Children dropping off from malnutrition. Older people living out their days in borrowed space. No security. No dignity. No amenity. No peace. Just a mad scramble for the bare essentials—a place to live and a place to die.

But there was magic in Pandora's box. There was wonderful talk. There was reading aloud of Peretz and Sholem Aleichim. There were endless hours of tea-drinking in cafés with solemn deliberations about the state of the world and the plight of the Jews. There were gay, warm, happy evenings in the theater, with the audience boisterous, sad, irreverent, or hushed into compassionate silence. There were the holidays and Holy Days when everything was turned out and scrubbed and polished. And the population of the slums rushed to the Turkish and Russian baths and emerged glowing with satisfaction.

There were the Sabbaths which were green oases in the midst of the drabness and the daily desolation. The candlelit magic Friday nights which every immigrant housewife like a genie wrought by her own labors. For by rubbing the little copper kettle and the pair of candlesticks she had brought from her European home, she became a veritable Aladdin. The dark railroad flat became a palace redolent of spices and ambrosia.

Among the transplanted folk there was emerging order and organization, the ability to build dignified, integrated industrial relations through co-operation with the newly created labor unions. And of the generation of transplanted leaders and visionaries we can name but a few. There were the Charney brothers, of whom one was known as Samuel Niger, writer and Zionist leader. There was B. Charney Vladeck whose managerial activities on the *Forward*, in labor ranks and in the Socialist party still left him time for study at the University of Pennsylvania. As a member of the Board of Aldermen of New York he advocated and urged slum clearance and municipal housing projects. Any one who has seen and marveled at the revolution in some of the crowded areas of New York has paid tribute to his vision and his genius. Mayor LaGuardia appointed him a member for the New York Housing Authority. Now posthumously a vast stretch of airy, clean apartment homes honor his memory. A number of times he was sent by his paper or by the American Federation of Labor in reverse lend-lease to help the Jews abroad in ORT rehabilitation work; to call on Sir Walter Citrine, leader of the British Trade Union movement. Together they launched the labor offensive against the Nazi and Fascist blight then threatening Europe. In his person the best of several cultures fused, creating a radiant personality whose humanity, integrity and vision are more enduring than the homes of brick and mortar that proudly bear his name.

Sidney Hillman was of this group. He was born in Lithuania, attended a rabbinical seminary where he studied for two years. But the outside world, the world of science and economics and political ideology, lured him. He dropped his religious studies for an apprenticeship in a chemical factory. Then like countless others he joined the underground movement, identifying himself with that band of ardent visionaries who, undaunted by the crushing weight of reaction in Russia, labored to move mountains. He was imprisoned for his participation in these forbidden activities and used the period of his prison sentence to obtain an education in the social sciences, reading Adam Smith and John Stuart Mill and Herbert Spencer. He migrated to England, to America, to Hart Schaffner and Marx.

Hillman was in Chicago just long enough to get settled and to take his bearings when the polyglot group to which he belonged rebelled against hours that ranged from sixty to seventy a week and wages that climbed from two dollars and fifty cents a week to four dollars a week. He joined and led the strike of 1910. Out of that strike came first an articulate presentation of grievances. Second, an arbitration plan which was to become the pattern for other groups. Four years later he was elected the first president of the Amalgamated Clothing Workers, which was to become in American labor history the very model of a model labor union.

The early history of the Amalgamated was also the personal biography of Sidney Hillman. For the two were truly one. He endowed the Union with his idealism. The Union gave him a rich field to till. His integrity and statesmanship, his ability to plan and to negotiate lifted the rank and file in the industry from chaos and exploitation, from insecurity and starvation to a planned group with a co-operative structure that benefits the worker, management and the public.

But this practical visionary had only begun. Now the Amalgamated opened its own banks in Chicago and in New York. It established co-operative housing projects. It used its vast buying power to buy and sell at a reasonable cost to its members, food and milk and electricity and laundry service. It operated busses. It expanded to include social service and nursing and medical counseling to its members. It added the creative arts to give its members the opportunity at group recreation and the development of talent, using many propaganda techniques very skillfully to enhance and motivate its songs and plays. Very soon it broke with the American Federation of Labor. Sidney Hillman became the head of the Textile Workers Organizing Committee of the CIO.

The social program of the New Deal coincided with the objectives of Sidney Hillman. In 1933 President Roosevelt named him to the Labor Advisory Board of the National Recovery Act. This was the first of a number of important government appointments. In 1940 when war threatened in earnest, Hillman assumed still more arduous duties. He was named as a member of the eight-man National Defense Advisory Commission. The following year he was appointed associate director-general of the Office of Production Management. He took over the full duties as director of the Labor Division of OPM. To him fell the task of feeding man-power to the expanding needs of the nation's war industries. His vision planned the orientation courses. His imagination anticipated an integrated program of adapting workers to the new jobs, of indoctrination and explanation, so that each man knew his relation to the whole, so that each worker could make a creative contribution to the nation's war efforts.

For twenty-four years Sidney Hillman was the conscience and the drive, the spur and the prophet of the Amalgamated. For more than a generation, this modest, gentle, self-effacing pilgrim from Lithuania repaid America for the asylum he had found here. More than any other man, Sidney Hillman illustrates the principle that the *help and the redemption of the exploited masses came from within.*

His heart was big enough to lend adherence to his people outside the labor scene. He served as a non-Zionist member of the Council of the Jewish Agency. He entered the political arena when he felt that the candidate in the field came close to the needs of labor. He did not spare himself any more than does any soldier in the field. And when he died he was mourned by countless thousands whose lives he had touched and by the tens of thousands who had cause to rejoice that such a man had lived.

The early history of David Dubinsky parallels that of Sidney Hillman. The childhood in Lodz, the rabbinical studies to the age of thirteen, the indoctrination of the ideologies of revolt, the arrest and imprisonment for antigovernment activities, the humble beginnings as an immigrant in 1911, the rapid rise in labor ranks due to native ability and vision. He became a major factor in the growth and development of the International Ladies' Garment Workers' Union and its president in 1932. He followed John L. Lewis into the CIO and like Moses led his union back to the AF of L in 1940.

The ILGWU led the way to a reconciliation between the culture the immigrant had brought to America and the one that had flowered here prior to his coming. The history of the recreational and educational activities of the Union makes rewarding study. Between 1890 and 1900 educational clubs mushroomed in all the large cities where the ILGWU held sway. Workers were exhorted to give up all "time-wasting" activities, to forswear saloons and card-playing and turn to Spencer and Darwin instead. The movement had all the earmarks of a religious crusade. Did not the Methodists and other religious groups exert social pressure to the same ends? Except that they urged their followers to read Wesley and Whitefield instead. Benjamin Schlesinger, who had been by turns laborer and labor leader, organizer and journalist and editor of the Chicago office of the *Jewish Daily Forward*, had urged at the 1902 convention that the development of the intellectual and educational areas was crucial to the unions. What was needed was workers with social vision beyond the range of the machine. So schools like the Rand School of Social Science began in 1906 series of popular lectures which attracted workers in their leisure time. Schlesinger's insistence on a "soul" as well as a body conferred status and a goal and trained leaders who could both moderate and mitigate the non-American aspects of the immigrant's cultural heritage. Gradually this work expanded into Unity Centers. This was a system of night school education with which the authorities in many cities willingly co-operated. In addition to courses in English, Civics, American History and kindred subjects, there were courses in public speaking and in leadership. Recreational activities were stressed. There was folk dancing and there were hikes and visits to museums and art galleries. There were summer vacation programs on large country estates bought by the Union. Gradually the orbits of life were extended. The worker was given glimpses of new horizons, new fields. The result was greater efficiency, greater stability, more integrated and intelligent participation in civic affairs.

At the dawn of the century, in the year 1900, the Jewish Agricultural and Industrial Aid Society was incorporated in New York. But earlier efforts to create agricultural settlements had been initiated without benefit of formal organization, for a number of years. In the early 1880's, "with an enthusiasm that often amounted to a creed," Jewish farmers tackled the meager soil of southern New Jersey, a terrain where only stunted pine and scrub oak and little else grew. Here idealists planned to undo the centuries which had separated through force and legislation the normal interaction of man and land. So Alliance and Carmel and Rosenhayn and Woodbine were wrested from the soil.

The Hebrew Immigrant Aid Society bought a tract of eleven hundred acres of land. Twenty-five families settled there in the spring of 1882. Alliance is about thirty-three miles from Philadelphia. The land had once been under cultivation but had long since been abandoned. It had reverted to its original state, a wilderness of stunted brush and trees. Now the land was to be cleared, roads laid, dwellings erected. It was a grueling task. The soil was anemic like the poor immigrants who had come to till it. Shelter was inadequate. There was not enough warm clothing. Provisions and supplies were scarce. Yet there was little grumbling, few complaints. "When the poor, wild soil did not yield, when willing hands failed to find work," there was just cause to despair. Some colonists were assisted by cash subsidies ranging from eight to twelve dollars a month. Others hired themselves out to neighbors. Still others opened tailor shops. Whatever could be done to supplement earnings was undertaken. When their produce came in and the harvest taken to market, they had to compete with the crops which experienced farmers had raised on the alluvial soil east and south of their tracts of land. The four colonies survived by establishing industries which could be operated during the winter. Cigar and shirt factories and clothing establishments were run on a part-time basis. But there was a unifying goal in which they all shared. There were common ideals. There was communal life. "Even the most ignorant settler was not a stranger to the sentiment of a common purpose," writes Dr. Lipman. Within a few years there emerged a new Jewish type in America, the Jewish farmer. Not since the days of the earliest agricultural settlements in South America, not since the days when Jewish vintners brought grape culture to North America, did the Western Hemisphere know the breed of the Jewish farmer. It was a leveling, democratic experience. The educated and the ignorant, the descendants of the scholar and the teamster were partners in the new venture.

Next to having Passover wine from Palestine, their American coreligionists relished that made from grapes that Jewish immigrants cultivated and processed. Dairying and canning and truck gardening —what a contrast to peddling, to being sweated in a dank basement or a cold ill-ventilated firetrap of an attic!

Now one man pitted his strength and his fortune against destiny.[8] He was Baron Maurice de Hirsch, born in Munich in 1831, died in Hungary in 1896. His grandfather was the first Jewish large-scale landowner in Bavaria and was ennobled in 1818. His father, banker to the King of Bavaria, was made a baron in 1869. His ancestors had been for generations people of honor and probity. Maurice was sent to school in Brussels when he was thirteen. There he remained for four years. Then, his education completed, he was recalled by his family to enter business. He became associated with a banking house which had branches in Brussels, London and Paris. He had the Midas touch, for everything he turned to prospered. His speculations in sugar and copper netted him great gains. He bought and shared in the development of many railroads in Austria and Turkey and the Balkans. But unlike the mythical character, his heart and his purse were ever at the call of those who needed his help. He was not merely a philanthropist who handed out bounty—although in that role he made fabulous history. He was a man of sound sociological concepts which were concerned with the rehabilitation and regeneration of the recipients of his bounty.

He married Clara, daughter of Senator Bischoffsheim of Brussels. She was a worthy partner and a gallant associate. Their personal life was tragic beyond words. They had two children, a son and a daughter, both of whom died before their parents. His son Lucien, whom he lost in 1887, he mourned gallantly. He wrote in answer to a letter of condolence: "My son I have lost, but not my heir; humanity is my heir." His first vicarious heir was the tragic victim of persecution in Russia. The year of the massacre of Starodub brought the golden-hearted Baron de Hirsch to the rescue of his coreligionists. He was already known as a princely donor. Twice he had given a million francs to the *Alliance Israélite Universelle*. To celebrate the fortieth anniversary of Francis Joseph's accession to the Austrian throne he gave five hundred thousand pounds for the purpose of establishing technical schools in Galicia and Bukovina. Now the plight of the Jews in Russia awoke in him a determination to establish their existence on a solid foundation. He believed in the therapeutic effects of manual labor and of farming. The Russian Government was willing to accept the lavish gift which Baron de Hirsch offered, but stipulated that the distribution of the funds was to be in its hands. Such a proposal was preposterous. A government which had connived at extermination, rape and pillage, was not to be trusted.

Now it chanced that a group of pioneers from Russia had settled in Argentina in 1889.[9] When the Baron learned of their heroic struggles and magnificent endurance, he consulted with Professor Guillaume Levental of Lausanne. A commission was sent to Argentina to study the land and its possibilities. In March of 1891 the group returned with its report. Hirsch undertook the large-scale purchase of land in Argentina. The report came in the nick of time. The mass flight from terror had already begun.

Large tracts of land were bought in the provinces of Santa Fé, of Buenos Aires and Entre Rios. Plans were drawn up for the mass colonization of thousands of immigrants. Refugees from the terrors of the 1890's trod the soil which the refugees from the terrors of 1492 had known. There were 135 families of recent Jewish arrivals already established in Argentina when the Jewish Colonization Association— known as the ICA—was established in 1891. The ICA had colonies prepared and to them the refugees turned. Hardships were many.

Some settlers managed to adapt themselves to the new land. Others went to the cities. Buenos Aires was the main point of settlement. Until 1914 a stream of Russian migrants continued to seek a haven there. From 1920 on there were between six and seven thousand Jews a year who came to Argentina. The population is now in the neighborhood of three hundred thousand of whom ten per cent are Sephardim and the rest Ashkenazim. To the three original provinces where Baron de Hirsch colonies were established, there have been added agricultural colonies in Pampa Central and Santiago del Estero.

In the same year, 1891, that Baron de Hirsch endowed the Argentinian experiment, he gave a vast sum of money, four hundred and ninety-three thousand pounds, for the creation of a trust fund for the benefit of Russian-Jewish immigrants to the United States. An agricultural school was established at Woodbine, New Jersey. Numerous agricultural scholarships were endowed by this fund. His total benefactions, which exceeded one hundred million dollars, were the sole prop of many of the victims of terror. The Jewish Agricultural and Industrial Aid Society was founded jointly by the Baron de Hirsch Fund and the Jewish Colonization Association. From Canada to Argentina there were farms and farmers and farm settlements that owed their existence to the warm heart and broad philanthropic vision of Baron Maurice de Hirsch and his wife Clara.

Events in a European country thus began a chain reaction that had its culmination in the Western Hemisphere. Persecution in Russia led to mass migrations creating major problems in the areas of first settlement. Ameliorative measures were manifold. First they came from native American Jews, like Emma Lazarus and Lillian Wald, whose compassion was awakened and whose finest talents were enlisted in behalf of the exploited. Next help came from within the ranks of the exploited. Leaders like Sam Gompers and Sidney Hillman began a crusade to achieve greater security and a dignified participation in production. Finally a financial wizard of Europe shared his vast fortune with the victims of terror establishing agricultural and industrial settlements which stretched from Canada and the United States in North America to Argentina in South America.

The Jewish Agricultural Society has remained the backbone of the back-to-the soil movement. This group was the outgrowth of a committee which Rabbi R. A. Levy formed in 1888. Incorporated in New York City in 1900, it had Baron de Hirsch as its fairy godfather. Its purpose, simply stated, is to act as a matchmaker between the American Jew and the soil of America. From the beginning it has been well planned and solidly established. Its machinery is as simple as its objective. It investigates land transactions and protects purchasers from fraud. It conducts an employment department assisting young men in obtaining positions which will train them for farm ownership. It extends loans for purchase of land on terms that are generous and easily met. It has a legal department which looks into titles and kindred matters.

By 1908 the Jewish Agricultural Society had listed 2,409 Jewish farm families, increased to 3,040 in the very next year. These families, comprising over 15,000 souls, were, in the opinion of the Society, only about half of the actual total Jewish farm population. A traveler journeying through the country from east to west and from north to south could have encountered Jewish farmers in thirty-seven states.[10]

The most successful colony up to 1909 was the one in Woodbine, New Jersey. Two agricultural schools for Jews were well organized and doing a fine job of training young men for agriculture. One was at Woodbine. The other at Doylestown.

Through its Extension Department the Society advises farmers as to the latest scientific methods in agriculture, conducts symposiums among farmers, sends trained workers into rural areas to advise farmers, maintains co-operative purchasing bureaus. It has the distinction of publishing the only Yiddish agricultural magazine in the world, *The Jewish Farmer*. Numerous scholarships are awarded to students interested in agriculture. One of the most valuable services of recent years has been that offered to refugees who have been afforded agricultural training on a farm settlement in New Jersey. Here for a nominal fee those who wish to train for rural life are given the necessary instruction. Synagogues and community centers have been erected through subsidies given by the Society. An open-door policy toward many social agencies has enlisted their co-operation. Together Jewish farmers and agricultural workers have been inducted into a new way of life, integrated and Americanized.

There is a long roll of distinguished Jews who have been trained in agriculture and who have made a signal contribution in their chosen field. Davidson lists among Jewish men of distinction in the agricultural field some of the following:

Jacob Joseph Taubenhaus and Bernhard Ostrolenk; Samuel Brody, Professor of Dairy Husbandry in the University of Missouri; Bruce Mayne, entomological expert of the United States Public Health Service; Abraham Miller, head of the American Bulb Company; Samuel Rudley, a prominent Philadelphia landscape architect; Ira J. Mills, a nationally known breeder of milk goats and president of the Delaware Valley Milk Goat Association; Julius Ulman, the owner of the well-known Ulman Dairies in Georgia; Samuel Kogon, landscape engineer in the New York City Department of Parks, and Robert Marshall, who at his premature death in 1940 was Chief of the Division of Soil Conservation in the United States Forest Service.

One of the phenomena apparent from the history of the "lowly" East European Jew is that he has the faculty of devising his own solutions to his difficulties. Much as friends and well-wishers have helped from the outside, the greatest leaders and the biggest progress have come from within. Just as the answer to mass exploitation of factory labor came from the ranks, so did the harassed agricultural workers have their David Lubin. His life is a romance of achievement, a brilliant record of unwavering idealism. One of his official biographers has subtitled the story of Lubin's life *A Study in Practical Idealism*. His life began in Galicia in 1848. It ended in Rome in 1919. The major interlude was American. The years were crowded with action and charged with accomplishment. With his half brother, Colonel Harris Weinstock, he operated a store in Sacramento, California. He did more than trade with the farmers. He learned to know them, to understand their problems, to sense the economic disadvantage under which they worked. He became a fruit-grower in 1885 and from that time forward identified his interests with those of other farmers. The Fruit Growers Convention in San Francisco dates from that year. He next went on to the organization of the California Fruit Growers Exchange. "This Exchange initiated a new chapter in the economic history of the West as well as in the marketing of farm produce."

Lubin's economic philosophy rested on the concept that the need for protection should be extended to agriculture as well as to industry. If we accept a tariff on imports, he argued, we must by the same token be ready to grant a government subsidy to farmers which would help equalize the burden of ocean transportation to foreign markets. The Republicans of California endorsed "Lubinism." Before long it became a national rallying point for all those who believed that the farmer was the forgotten man of our economic structure. By 1896 the plan had crossed the country. In that year fifty-five Philadelphia clergymen formed a "Lubin Club." His name had become synonymous with a practical program for the amelioration of the lot of the farmer. He was known from coast to coast for this and other projects designed to aid the farmer, not the least of which was the establishing of the parcel post service. For this plan also was designed with a view to helping the man on the farm who needed to reach the consumer as quickly and inexpensively as possible.

Perhaps it was owing to the fact that he had spent his impressionable childhood years in the depths of darkest Europe, perhaps it was because of a pilgrimage which he made to Palestine in 1884, perhaps because he was one of the truly great of heart who see a problem in its entirety. Certain it is that some leaven was at work in Lubin which distinguished him from other reformers. For he felt that all farmers the world over were faced with the same problems and labored under the same handicaps. The farmers of the world had a universe of discourse. Over-all conditions determined low farm prices. Farmers of one part of the world were engaged in competing with farmers in other parts, causing a downward price spiral which only made matters worse. After a number of years of intensive study in San Francisco, Lubin launched an international campaign whose object was the improvement of the farmer's lot no matter what soil he tilled. The United States, England and France rejected his plan for an International Institute of Agriculture. But help came from Italy. Under the sponsorship of King Victor Emmanuel III of Italy, forty governments met in Rome in 1905. Was this conference not in its way a step toward world peace and world government? It was a momentous and historic assembly which voted the establishment of the International Institute of Agriculture in Rome. From its inception until the year of his death, David Lubin, citizen of the United States, was the head of that great institution. This became the channel through which vital information was collected and then disseminated throughout the world. It became a beacon which pointed the way to co-operation on a world-wide basis.

Yet strangely, David Lubin who achieved international recognition, whose tomb in Rome was the scene of a touching pilgrimage on the twenty-fifth anniversary of his death when seventy nations sent representatives to honor his memory—this man who believed that it was the mission of the Jew to lead the world into the pathways of justice and economic fair play is well-nigh forgotten by the very people whose interests he served so zealously and with such selfless devotion.

In America and in England during the long years of the nineteenth century Palestine was considered as a geographic almshouse to which indigent Jews betook themselves to await bounty from their wealthy kinsmen. We have seen how Isaac Leeser and others of his generation pleaded for a more reasonable attitude. It was not in terms of statehood but in terms of philanthropy that Palestine of the nineteenth century was largely discussed.

What does a displaced person dream about? A permanent location, an address where he can be reached, a place that is familiar to the touch even in the dark, a little area with an imaginary circumference where he can expand his soul and stretch his limbs in utter relaxation. It is a place where the furniture of his mind and of his tangible home can be arranged to his own liking. It is a dwelling which no man may enter except at his own bidding. Such dreams have been the magnets of men of all faiths and of all races. Every wandering migrant has had such a destination firmly planted in his soul. The unwanted person has been doubly eager. For fantasy rather than place has sustained him.

Among the many theories to account for Jewish migration and their easy mobility is one cited by Professor E. N. Adler in his book, *About Hebrew Manuscripts*. Adler says that a Jew migrates easily because his faith is tied to a book rather than to a place.[11] A man may move with his ideological heritage more freely than one who is a landowner and weighed down by his possessions.

Americans, with the exception of the Indians, are all children of the transplanted. So they looked on with more than passing interest at plans for the settlement of Jews in a colony of their own. We are familiar with the dream of Mordecai Manuel Noah. Even after his Ararat project failed he did not wholly abandon the idea. John Quincy Adams referred to Major Noah with some asperity in his memoirs on September 7, 1830:

He has great projects for colonizing the Jews in this country and wants to be sent as Chargé d'affaires to Vienna for the promotion of them. He is an incorrect and very ignorant but sprightly writer and as a partisan editor of a newspaper has considerable power. He urges with great earnestness his merits in supporting the administration as a title to the president's favor.[12]

Here in America Emma Lazarus sang her Zionides with passion. Even her prose was charged with deep emotion and great moral indignation. Here Christians as well as Jews were ready to sympathize, to lend a helping hand to those who dreamed of Jewish colonies.

There are many examples of this shared dream of colonization. A

Protestant clergyman in Chicago, the Reverend William E. Blackstone, drew up a petition which was sent to President Benjamin Harrison. The petition asked that a conference be called forthwith "to consider the condition of the Israelites and their claims to Palestine as their ancient home." And among those who signed this petition were the following: Chief Justice Fuller, Cardinal Gibbons, John D. Rockefeller, J. Pierpont Morgan and Russell Sage.

Ideas concerned with the revival of a Jewish State in Palestine blew like thistledown from place to place. The diffusion of the Zionist dream was as erratic as the wanderings of the pilgrims who nurtured the dream. The society which called itself "Lovers of Zion," or *Hovevai Zion*, was pre-Herzlian. It began in Russia in the twilight era of 1880. It spread west, crossing the Atlantic. By 1884 the members of the New York Society had their hopes aroused by the incident revolving around the Sampson Simson legacy which left fifty thousand dollars to any society interested in Palestinian colonization. Then in 1896, stirred to a frenzy of moral indignation over the Dreyfus affair, Herzl published *The Jewish State*, advocating mass migration to Palestine and the rebuilding of a nation whose capital was Jerusalem. Like a bolt of lightning splitting a live oak, this clarion call rent Jews asunder. The dream of a Jewish State was violently rejected by some American Jews. In the hearts of others it found fertile soil.

From the first there were two trends discernible. There was a colonization movement. There was an ideological crusade. The one was materially aided by Baron Edmond de Rothschild. The other was created by Theodor Herzl.

Baron Edmond de Rothschild was born in France in 1845. His biography makes a fabulous narrative. Life unrolled a regal carpet before him. The world saluted him for his wealth and possessions. He was a banker, philanthropist, patron of literature and the arts, proud owner of the most famous private collection of paintings in Paris. Yet it was not for the Arabian Nights setting that he was admired by his fellow Jews—although he became a legend—but for the deep compassion with which he viewed the persecuted and unwanted of his people. When Emma Lazarus was shaken to her depths by the carnivals of blood and hate, she wrote her imperishable Zionides. When Baron Edmond heard of the pogroms of 1881 he at once established a committee to disburse relief.

From an unexpected quarter there came a new plan for rescuing the victims. General Lupéron, ex-President of the Republic of Santo Domingo, submitted a plan to Baron Edmond in which he offered to the survivors of terror the hospitality of his country. There was a warm welcome for them both on the land and in the hearts of his nation. Gratefully the Baron replied and a long correspondence ensued. But there were Jews to the North of Santo Domingo—in Cincinnati and New Orleans and San Francisco and New York—who were quick to demur and to dissuade. So the project failed; but the need for rescue persisted.

The story captures the imagination. Who can read of the Bilu movement without being deeply stirred? "House of Jacob, let us arise and go forth" was the magic Hebrew slogan of the exodus from Russia in 1882 from which the word "Bilu" was coined. But this narrative does not belong in the annals of American Jewry. It is enough to record that Baron Edmond de Rothschild became the greatest single factor in the development of modern Palestine. Many are the colonies whose very names are songs—Rishon le-Zion— which owed, if not their founding, their continued existence to the munificence of this benevolent Parisian Jew.

In 1896 Baron Edmond received a caller. Theodore Herzl. Here was antithesis. Herzl, the impecunious journalist, was born in Budapest in 1860. His profession took him to many lands. He was in Paris when Jews of the world were pilloried in the person of Dreyfus. Stung by the implications of this foul betrayal of justice, fired by the acute need for amelioration, Herzl cast about for ways of serving his people with whom he had but recently discovered kinship. Baron de Hirsch would have none of his plans. Baron de Rothschild too felt that Herzl was an impractical idealist. He did not wish to underwrite Herzl's daydreams. Now Herzl turned back to himself and his own talents. He could not sell his dream to the affluent. But the ragged and the disinherited subscribed to it wholeheartedly. Herzl became the prince of the tatterdemalions, the spokesman for the inarticulate, the ambassador for the landless, the plenipotentiary for the submerged, stateless Jews. In America Park Avenue rejected him, but Hester Street took him to its heart.

Then in Russia the Lovers of Zion lit a little candle of hope. Tenderly its votaries shielded the flame. It crossed the Atlantic with them. And while some of their kith and kin tended their newly planted vineyards in Palestine, a handful of Jews in America was spreading the gospel of regeneration and rebirth. They read Herzl's *Jewish State*. They contributed to the Jewish National Fund. They

debated and argued and organized. They sent delegates to the first
Zionist Congress at Basle, Switzerland in 1897. In that year of
history, in Chicago, three immigrant Jews, brilliant young idealists,
knights-errant of a new crusade, founded the Knights of Zion. And
the names of these three were Max Shulman, Bernard Horwich and
Leon Zolotkoff.

A year later under the leadership of Rabbi Gustav Gottheil, the
Federation of American Zionists was born.

Who were the leaders of this renaissance? What gave them the
vision and the strength to implement it? Whence this universe of discourse with the Jews across the Atlantic? The dedication? The intimation of things to come? The answer may be found in their individual biographies. It may be imbedded in the mass fantasy to which
thousands of American Jews subscribed. They had tasted the wine of
democracy and it had restored their faith in the future of humanity
and of the Jews. For every American Jew had either been born under
the Constitution and learned the Bill of Rights or had come within
its shelter by choice. Jewish experience in America had conditioned
them to optimism. The followers of Herzl were virile and vocal. But
so were the opponents. There were loud protests, written and vocal
from the dissenters of "the Zionist heresy." So the issue of Zionism
divided the Jews of America into disparate camps.

Isaac Mayer Wise continued to lash out again Zionism. In Montreal in 1897 he led those who repudiated Zionism at the Central
Conference of American Rabbis. Unanimity was as unattainable as
ever in the ranks of American Jews. The Zionist organization in
America was still in swaddling clothes when Rabbi David Philipson,
before the Union of American Hebrew Congregations, said, "We are
unalterably opposed to political Zionism. The Jews are not a nation,
but a religious community."

In the pages of the *Jewish Quarterly Review* in the year 1905 two
Titans, Lucien Wolf and Israel Zangwill, grappled with the Zionist
issue. Even as Theodor Herzl was dying, Wolf was reading proof on
"The Zionist Peril."[13] The note after the article carried the news of
Herzl's death. There was acrimony and recrimination. Lucien Wolf
refers with considerable heat to Zangwill's "attempted raid" on the
Hirsch millions. Zangwill had dubbed the Jewish Colonization Association a failure. It was Israel Zangwill's firm conviction that had
Baron de Hirsch lived he would have been a Zionist. How could
anyone be sure, asked the opposition? This is no time for dodging
behind philanthropic shades. "Zionism is . . . the . . . abiding ally of

anti-Semitism and its most powerful justification," thundered Wolf It violates the spirit of Judaism. Then Wolf concludes with a gloomy and inaccurate generalization: "History never repeats itself. . . Nothing that is once destroyed is ever really restored."

Zangwill picked up the challenge. In language charged with emotion and passion he scoffs at the "emancipation" which Wolf had so generously extolled. "The real Zionist peril is the searchlight Zionism brings to bear upon flabby thinking or feeble conviction," is Zangwill's rebuttal to Wolf's "The Zionist Peril."

For the non-Zionist Zangwill expresses an academic pity. The opponent is really the victim of circumstances with his "nerves ruined by hereditary Marranoism." When he looks at Zionism, Zangwill's heart is gladdened. "Zionism has uplifted the position of the Jews. . . . Humanity sympathizes with a strenuous aspiration."

That this battle was fought for Jews on both sides of the Atlantic is patent. There was more than an insular audience in mind. Wolf wrote for readers on the Continent and in America as well as in England. So did Zangwill. The latter carefully fortified himself with an official statement from that gallant friend of the Jews, the forthright and outspoken vehicle of the great American tradition, Secretary John Hay. Says Zangwill: "In America Secretary Hay permitted me to publish his view that Zionist work would in no way impugn the patriotism of the American Jew."

For Zionism had now become a universal topic charged with emotion. It had put on seven-league boots and was making great strides forward. In 1915 Norman Hapgood contributed a notable series of articles in which he showed how American was the concept, how congruous and how integrated. "Personally, I think Zionism is as creative an idea as there is extant today, and as apt to the moment." In discussing "The Future of the Jews in America," Hapgood is quick to point out that the opposition to Zionism is recruited from the ranks of the secure and the entrenched.

If we could but sing a song of leaders! Of prophets and seers, of men and women touched with the same greatness that inspired Amos and David and Deborah! Of judges and rabbis and teachers and historians, good Americans all, and greatly to be cherished, whose minds were big enough to serve their own country faithfully and well and yet who could also serve at the altar of an ancient shrine. They had nothing to fear, for their motives were pure and the boundaries of their hearts were elastic.

There had always been such men and women in every age and in every culture. These people had journeyed to the outermost parts of the world to diffuse their culture and to spread their beliefs. And the world had honored them. Had not the Society of Friends sent emissaries to the Indians? Had not the English, concerned for the spiritual welfare of American colonists, formed the Society for the Propagation of the Gospel in New England? In China and Africa and India there were American men and women who had dedicated their lives to an ideal, and none to question their loyalty to their native land.

Now there were American Jews who saw in Zionism a new way of life for weary, footsore pilgrims. They saw regeneration of the spirit for those of their brethren who only helped the noble experiment at a distance and thrilled vicariously to its accomplishments.

Their motives were mixed. Their intentions were not unanimous. But what does that matter? Some looked upon the land as a sanctuary for their declining years. Such a man was Solomon Schechter, pupil of Steinschneider, scholar of eminence in his own right who as President of the Jewish Theological Seminary of America and the investigator of the Cairo Genizah and the founder of the United Synagogue of America and the philosopher who conceived the principle of consensus as the dynamic process uniting Jewry, had surely crowded several lifetimes into one.

There were Americans, like Brandeis, who did not plan to leave their native land, but who lent the prestige of their illustrious names to the cause of Zionism. There were those, like Judah L. Magnes, who turned their faces toward the East forswearing ease and comfort and recognition, vowing a life of poverty and labor, of dedication and toil, closing ranks with their coreligionists from many other lands.

Gustav Gottheil and Stephen S. Wise together built the Federation of American Zionists in New York. Out of the heart of the great Middle West had come the sustaining breath of life breathed into the American Zionist Movement by men like Bernhard Felsenthal. And from Baltimore there came the transfusion which men like Dr. Aaron Friedenwald and Benjamin Szold could offer. From Louisville there came the support of Louis N. Dembitz and in New York also was the inspiration and the strength of Joseph I. Bluestone. Then a new generation rose up, of younger men who caught the vision and grasped the torch, carrying it down to our own day to the creation of the State of Israel.

Names became magical. Far-away leaders were the luminaries who would lead the scattered and oppressed among the Jews to the green pastures of Israel rebuilt. Max Nordau, who was one of the first colleagues of Theodore Herzl, was such a man. Nahum Sokolow, who worked all of his life with zeal and passion, who spent years in research in the British Museum (sitting next to Thomas Garrigue Masaryk engaged in a similar task) preparing the dossier which led to the issuance of the Balfour Declaration, was another. And finally there was Chaim Weizmann who nursed the dream of Zion restored, from the days of his childhood in a tiny village in the Pripet Marshes through the twin careers of brilliant research in chemistry and practical diplomacy, which led inevitably to the presidency of the state he had dreamed of as a boy.

Such a fairy tale was just the kind to appeal to American Zionists, who like all Americans loved a success story. Besides, Weizmann was a trans-atlantic commuter whose comings and goings they followed with vicarious pride. He became a familiar figure at Zionist meetings. His thin, ascetic face with its far-away look and detached expression was as familiar to American-Jewish audiences as was his precise and dynamic speech when at last he was called upon to speak. For Jewish meetings are notoriously interminable and Weizmann was always saved up for the rousing climax. So they looked upon their leader. They talked with him and shook his hand. They came to know and love him. And when the inevitable schisms arose, American Jews took sides with all the gusto and enthusiasm which strong leaders always evoke in their followers.

As the crisis in Europe was racing toward inevitable war in 1914, two historically important events transpired. In 1912 the Zionists of America secured their most noted convert—Louis D. Brandeis. In 1914 the creative center of Zionism moved to the United States. Central Europe, whence Zionist activities had radiated throughout the world, was now isolated by impenetrable barriers. Shemarya Levin, a member of the World Zionist Executive, was in this country. A conference was called. A Provisional Committee was created. Its chairman was the most brilliant and most dynamic figure American Jews had ever produced—Brandeis.

Three years later, on the second of November, in the year 1917, an historic letter was mailed from the British Foreign Office to Lord Rothschild. This letter conveyed the official British expression of sympathy with Jewish Zionist aspirations:

His Majesty's Government view with favor the establishment in Palestine of a national home for the Jewish people, and will use their best endeavors to facilitate the achievement of this object, it being clearly understood that nothing shall be done which may prejudice the civil and religious rights of existing non-Jewish communities in Palestine or the rights and political status enjoyed by Jews in any other country.

It was signed by Arthur James Balfour.

Behind the statement there was the prestige and authority and the tacit consent of Woodrow Wilson and of the French Government. It was subsequently endorsed by many other nations. Our Congress declared itself in favor of the Balfour Declaration and President Harding approved the Congressional Resolution on September 21, 1922.

This was the turning point. Zionism became more than a dream and an inspiration of a small group of Jewish idealists—it became world news. It moved over into the front pages of metropolitan dailies and found a berth on many an editorial page. It became part of the vocabulary of the world. It was discussed not only in parliamentary assemblies. Books and periodicals took cognizance of this aspiration which soon leaped into the agenda of world politics. Philosemites espoused it. 'Antisemites by turns sought to condemn it or to consider Palestine as a dumping ground for all Jews everywhere— an international wastebasket which was to become the receptacle not only for the displaced and unwanted and persecuted, but for all Jews no matter how integrated, or how reluctant.

The *Dearborn Independent* and Hillaire Belloc alike found grist for their mill in Zionism. Belloc in his book *The Jews*, published in 1922, urged that Jews should police and arm their own troops and not depend on England. Belloc unwillingly pays tribute to the Jews. "The Jew," he says, "cannot help feeling superior but he can help the expression of that superiority." His final argument is also worth recalling: "I repeat the formula for a solution: It is recognition and respect."[14]

The literature on Zionism grew by accretion and addition. Both the friends and the enemies of the Zionist aspiration were prolific in America. Noted for its continuing opposition to Zionism and to the Balfour Declaration was the Central Conference of American Rabbis, a group which numbered notables like Isaac M. Wise, David Einhorn, Kaufman Kohler and David Philipson. The latter vigorously makes it clear that Zionism is incompatible with Reform Judaism.

Jews in America are part of the American nation. The ideal of the Jew is not the establishment of a Jewish State—not the reassertion of

Jewish nationality which has long been outgrown. We believe that our survival as a people is dependent upon the assertion and maintenance of our historic religious role and not upon the acceptance of Palestine as a homeland of the Jewish people.

Under the inexorable pressure of recent events this attitude has yielded ground and made a compromise of sorts. The Columbus Platform in 1937 reversed the earlier position by affirming the need for the rebuilding of Palestine as a refuge for persecuted Jews and as a dynamic cradle for the renaissance of Jewish culture and learning. The Second World War brought even greater changes in the rank and file of adherents of reform. In 1945 a chaplain writing from the vast stretches of the Pacific theater of operations throws down the gauntlet to his congregation.

Chaplain Roland B. Gittlesohn, who was the Assistant Divisional Chaplain of the Fifth Marine Division, wrote a "Case History of a Reform Congregation." Rabbi Gittlesohn, on leave from Central Synagogue of Nassau County, Rockville Center, Long Island, New York, wrote this article "Somewhere in the Pacific." He sent it to members of his congregation at a time when they were being polled on their attitude toward Zionism and Palestine. His congregation is described as "an average Reform group." It is interesting that those members of the congregation who responded to the questionnaire were unanimously in favor of unrestricted Jewish immigration into Palestine. Eighty-three per cent of those responding were in favor of a Jewish Commonwealth in Palestine.

To me personally your decision will be a final test of my effectiveness as your religious leader for 9 years . . . if now, in the Valley of the Shadow of Death, faced with the greatest horror that has ever befallen a people well worn to horror, you turn your back to several million who are left, you will at the same time be rejecting one of the central themes of my own conviction and teaching as a rabbi.[15]

The Palestinian issue continued in the political arena, in the press, on the forums. When Senators Robert A. Taft and Robert F. Wagner united in a bipartisan plea to President Truman in support of Senate Joint Resolution No. 112, their plea was titled "The Case for a Jewish Commonwealth." Here among other facts they reviewed the historic official position of the American Government which since 1919 had agreed to support the policy of recognition of Palestine as a Jewish State. The two senators insisted that "Our country can only proceed on the assumption that the pledges given the Jewish people and embodied in international covenants shall be honored."

"The issue is not only moral; it is political . . . the Jews have a better claim than the British," wrote Edgar Ansell Mowrer, advocating that "the land of Israel go back to the people of Israel." "Jewish Homeland a Must Under United Nations Rule," insisted a great American statesman, Sumner Welles. "The Government of the United States is officially committed to the establishment of a Jewish national home in Palestine." Ralph McGill, brilliant editor of the *Atlanta Constitution*, after completing a firsthand survey of Palestine, after studying objectively the land and its settlers, pleads that we "remove the oil from the face of Palestine." He urges that we "shut out the power politics wrestling match." Its Jewish settlers are deeply rooted in the land. There is "a sharply-etched, living and breathing, hard-working and productive, deeply rooted Jewish life all up and down Palestine."

No one has stated the case more eloquently than Ralph McGill. He speaks with the voice of America which has been consistent and clear from the days of Ezra Stiles and Hannah Adams to the days of John Hay and Mark Twain and Norman Hapgood and Woodrow Wilson, and all the great Americans who placed conscience above other considerations. Palestine "could become the basis for a great renaissance of learning, of modern farming and industry to lift the standards of all the Middle East." He concludes:

There is room.
I have seen it. . . . It is one of the tragedies of the postwar world that Britain, which has so fine a record of defending liberty, freedom and human rights generally, should have traveled the road of appeasement, fear and moral wrong in Palestine.
Palestine is historically a Jewish nation. The Jews were there originally and they never left. . . . Justice and morality, I think are weary of waiting on fear and appeasement.[16]

American Jews by the thousands enrolled under the banner of Zionism. The rank and file continued to be recruited largely from the crowded areas of the cities. The opposition continued to be at home among the descendants of the well-to-do, the sons and grandsons of the department store owners. An ecological analysis of Zionism in America would show clearly that there was a correlation between amount of living space and adherence to Zionism. With dilution of population there was a corresponding separation from and concern for specifically Jewish problems.

What was true for the rank and file was not true for the leaders.

For they came from every stratum of society. Emma Lazarus belonged to the "elite." So did many other American Zionists who gave of their time and of their energies without counting the cost. It was the proud boast of Rabbi Gustav Gottheil of Temple Emanu-El of New York City that he had helped to turn the genius of Emma Lazarus in the direction of her people. Despite his background—he was born in Germany and was early identified with the reform movement —he could not be indifferent to the acute needs of East European Jews whose problems did not cease with migration. He had but to read the report of the First Zionist Congress in 1897 to be convinced that the Zionist program offered hope to the unwanted and persecuted Jews of Europe. He became a Zionist at that time and continued an active leader until the day of his death. In 1898 with Stephen S. Wise he founded the Federation of American Zionists. By the turn of the century more than fifty Zionist societies had been established in the United States.

Like Rabbi Gottheil, whose pupil he was, Stephen S. Wise brought to American Zionism echoes of the world of contemplation and scholarship. He had to discover Zionism through spiritual affinity rather than through cultural contagion found in the poverty-ridden areas of our larger cities. Born into a tradition of scholarship and piety—both his father and grandfather were noted rabbis—he lived in the United States from his second year on, received his secular training in New York, including a doctor's degree from Columbia University. His rabbinical training was secured under the private tutelage of some of the greatest scholars. When Temple Emanu-El invited him to become its rabbi he had already served his apprenticeship in other congregations and had made his position as a liberal unmistakably clear. Many innovations in congregational arrangements stemmed from his passionate belief in the need for applying democratic principles in synagogal affairs. He insisted on absolute freedom of speech in the pulpit. Louis Marshall, who headed the trustees of Temple Emanu-El, was equally adamant: controversial subjects were within the jurisdiction of the trustees. Rather than compromise with his principles, Rabbi Wise in 1907 founded the Free Synagogue. Here the rabbi was freed from surveillance and censorship. Here pews were to be unassigned, thus abolishing the ancient custom which had enabled the wealthy to purchase proximity to the Arc and pulpit during their devotions.

In 1922 Dr. Wise founded the Jewish Institute of Religion, a graduate school for the training of Jewish communal leaders. The

Institute has the authority to confer rabbinical degrees as well as degrees in Hebrew literature, law and kindred subjects. It often invites distinguished scholars to lecture and teach there. Israel Abrahams, Cecil Roth, David Yellin, Shalom Spiegel and Guido Kisch have been among the notables on its faculty. The Institute maintains its own press for the publication of scholarly works in the field of Judaica. After a quarter century of independent existence, the Jewish Institute of Religion in 1948 merged with the Hebrew Union College. Henceforth the college founded by Isaac M. Wise and the one established by Stephen S. Wise will make history as one institution.

The doughty fighter and silver-tongued orator, Stephen S. Wise, spoke his mind on every social issue without fear or favor. He endeared himself to the American labor movement by taking a stand for social justice, by pointing the finger of scorn at abuses in the steel industry, by insisting on amelioration for women workers in the canning industry, by attacking the malpractices in the needle trades. He won friends in all ranks and in every religious group. When he turned his dynamic abilities to Zionism, he poured his talents unstintingly in the direction of solving for all time the problem of finding a permanent address for the unwanted millions of Jews of Europe.

Wise was fortunate in many things—particularly in his marriage.

Often the mothers and wives of Jewish leaders are the forgotten folk of history. This may be a survival of the traditional Jewish attitude, which largely ignores women. So when a woman like Louise Waterman Wise comes along, it is a cause for satisfaction. For she was a personality in her own right as well as the wife of Stephen Wise. She was primarily a social worker. Among her good works were the founding of the Free Nurses Association of Portland, Oregon. She helped establish the Women's Division of the American Jewish Congress and worked valiantly among the refugees from German terror. She founded and directed a social agency for child placement, known as the Free Synagogue Child Adoption Committee. She was in addition an endowed painter whose works have been exhibited in the foremost galleries in the country. She found time to translate several important works from the French, among them Aimé Pallière's autobiographical account of his conversion from Catholicism to Judaism. Together with her husband she made contemporary history.

For fifty years the zeal did not waver, the energy proved unfailing. Stephen Wise has preached and written and fought and served on committees and as president of the Zionist Organization of America. He has dissented, seceded, and returned to the ranks. His differences were not mild. His angers were Jovian, his struggles Olympian. He was not unmindful of his role and of his contribution to his people. Sometimes his followers chafed under his authoritarian father-role. But the rank and file lavished its affection upon this man as toward a father. For a sense of stability was conferred with the authority that Wise wielded.

Among his friends at least two non-Jews must be singled out. Toward John Haynes Holmes he was as David had been to Jonathan. His friendship with President Woodrow Wilson was of historic significance. Wise had Wilson's ear. He was an eloquent man. Wilson was responsive. So it came about that Stephen Wise was appointed to look after Zionist interests at the treaty of Versailles. A generation later with undiminished eloquence and ardor, his voice joined in the celebration of the creation of the new State of Israel.

It was because of his faith in the masses that Wise created the American Jewish Congress, thus instituting a democratic process for consultation on Jewish problems and giving the rank and file a chance at self-determination in the organization of philanthropic activities and the control of their institutions.

The crusader-iconoclast-clergyman-politician was not content. To his protean interests he was to add two more fields, journalism and education. In 1931 Wise became one of the editors of *Opinion*. So still another vehicle for reaching the Jews of America was to be made available to Wise. The fiftieth anniversary of his ministry in the Free Synagogue was utilized by American Jews everywhere as an opportunity to do Wise honor. This seasoned trouper was undaunted and in that year graced countless pulpits with his oratory untarnished, his sense of humor undiminished, his energies seemingly inexhaustible. His death on April 19, 1949, was mourned by millions.

There was a time when the American Jewish community depended on leaders trained abroad to bring the fruits of their learning to them. Generations of men and women grew up under such tutelage. But as the dynamic center of Jewish life shifted to the western shores of the Atlantic, as the matrix was transplanted and took root here, the concentric circles of influence began to reverse the trend. Then the influence went out of America unto the farthermost corners of the world. It was a spiritual reverse lend-lease which sent San Francisco born Judah Leon Magnes to Palestine. The road he traveled eastward was one of striving toward an ideal which he approached as

unerringly as if drawn to it by a magnet—a magnet which was for
Magnes as it had been for Halevi, the pull of the land of Israel.

Between 1877, the year of his birth, and 1900, the year of his
graduation from Hebrew Union College, his story was the usual growing up to maturity followed by countless of his colleagues. But somewhere there was a leaven at work which influenced him to depart
from the preconceived pattern. The years of his coming of age were
the years of maturation of American Jewry. The storm and stress of
the earlier period had been outgrown. There was room in the America he knew as a student for the Judaism of Isaac M. Wise and that
of Isaac Leeser. There was room for the Hebrew Union College and
for the Jewish Theological Seminary, for Dropsie College, for Kaufman Kohler and Solomon Schechter.

On a sensitive youth growing up in America the impact of European tragedies must have struck a series of violent blows. He was
a bridge in spirit between the two worlds which were so interwoven
and so interrelated. But Magnes, like Emma Lazarus, insisted on but
one world. His sympathy was ready and his response came from
an overflowing heart. So he could give to Zionism an allegiance and
an understanding which made of it a rare gift. He helped found and he
headed the New York Kehillah (from the term *Kahal*, meaning the
organized Jewish community). From 1909 to 1922 he headed that
institution. With Mordecai Kaplan he organized the Society for the
Advancement of Judaism. He helped found the Joint Distribution
Committee. Then his ebullient spirit helped to create the dream which
became a vibrant reality—the Hebrew University in Jerusalem. In
1925 he was appointed chancellor of the university. A decade later
he became the president of an institution whose creative achievement
was one of the miracles of the renaissance of modern Hebraism.

It was in Zionism that the greatest American Jewess found her
vocation. Henrietta Szold was born in 1860, when Emma Lazarus
was eleven years old and Rebecca Gratz was beginning the last
decade of her life and Penina Moïse still had a score of years to live.
So that her lifetime is a bridge between the generations which produced the most gifted women in American Jewish life. In many ways
her biography is linked with diverse elements, not only in time but in
ideologies. She was receptive to all shades of opinion, yet was able to
transmute the crudest differences into the noblest principles. Her
name was one to conjure with. For in the macrocosmic Jewish scene
of the last two generations she constituted the center of agreement

and consensus. There lies her contribution and significance. She was both a symbol and an oblation. She was a symbol of unity. She was the gift par excellence which the Jews of America offered up on the altar of Israel.

Henrietta Szold was born in Baltimore. Her father was Rabbi Benjamin Szold, veteran of barricade battles in Vienna in 1848 and a doughty champion of the underdog in America, the Negro and immigrant. She was the eldest of five daughters and very close in spirit to her pious mother and her erudite father. She studied Hebrew, knew the Bible intimately, became a student of the Talmud, translated a number of scholarly works from the German. One of her most exacting tasks was the preparation of the index volume for the Graetz *History of the Jews*. For a quarter of a century the quiet, retiring, scholarly woman served as secretary of the Jewish Publication Society. Through her capable hands there passed countless works that enriched the cultural life of the Jews of America. Upon her frail shoulders had fallen the mantle of Isaac Leeser.

The year of calamity, 1881, which tolled in the news of Russian pogroms and drove thousands of Jews to America, confronted American Jews with the need for facing the sociological problems which poverty in numbers always brings. There were two alternatives. One was aloof detachment. The other was active participation. Henrietta Szold, like Emma Lazarus and her sister Josephine, chose to identify herself with the needs of immigrants. Not so, many of the sheltered, comfortable, entrenched generation whose immediate antecedents were Central European. "Prosperity," she once wrote, "has something vulgar and repugnant about it. I feel very much more drawn to these Russian Jews than to the others—a prejudice as vile, doubtless, as the contrary one. Nor do I mean only the suffering Russian Jews. I mean those, too, who are earning a competency. There is something ideal about them. Or has the suffering through which they have passed idealized them in my eyes?"

In 1905, Charles S. Bernheimer undertook to have a group of Jewish scholars survey the new immigrant. The result was *The Russian Jew in the United States*, a symposium to which Henrietta Szold contributed the leading essay. Peter Wiernik, the pioneer historian of Jews in America, was among the contributors, as was Abraham Cahan, the eminent journalist and novelist.

Henrietta Szold founded the first night school in America for immigrant adults, just as Rebecca Gratz had helped to found the first Jewish Sunday School in America. But all through the years, years of research and writing and social service, there was a ferment at work. She was not satisfied with mere palliative measures. What was wanted was a permanent solution. So she faced the issue. Now a brilliant collaborator came forward to help her. He was Dr. Harry Friedenwald of Baltimore. Together with her night school pupils whom she had come to love and to respect, they formed in 1893, a society known as the *Hebras Zion*, Society of Zion, thus anticipating the contribution of Theodore Herzl by three years. Through the years that followed, these two continued their creative concern for the Russian Jewish victims of sadism and aggression. Perhaps it was no accident, but rather the fruition of an ideological partnership, that when Henrietta Szold was ready to take a major step in the direction of Palestine, it should have expressed itself in the project whose motto is: "The healing of the daughter of my people." Years later Dr. Friedenwald was to hail the opening of the Rothschild-Hadassah University Hospital as "a national creative act" of utmost significance.

In many ways Henrietta Szold's passionate dedication to her people was expressed again and again. As early as 1895, in a speech in her native Baltimore, she urged the study of Judaism and the importance of knowing Hebrew. She wrote and edited and read proof on books which would educate the indifferent and enlarge the educated. She did not spare herself. Her labors were indefatigable. But they were still in their initial stages.

There came a day when Miss Szold decided to visit Palestine. That visit was historic. Dormant ideas sprang to life. Tentative remedial plans were crystallized. European Jewry was mortally sick. Miss Szold conceived a plan of healing. That was woman's work. So the Daughters of Zion came into being. Then at a Purim Festival honoring Queen Esther the name was changed to Hadassah, the queen's Hebrew name.

The year was 1912. The group comprised a handful of women. The following year two nurses were dispatched to Palestine to begin a health service. It was a first step in one of the greatest women's crusades in all history. The War came and needs for medical services became acute. In 1917 the World Zionist Organization turned to Hadassah for help. The American Zionist Medical Unit, consisting of forty-four medical specialists augmented by trained nurses, came into being. In 1918 hospitals and dispensaries were established in Jerusalem and other cities to serve the sick of Palestine without regard to creed or nationality. The work expanded. Phenomenal strides were made in the control of trachoma and the war on malaria.

Dedicated personnel worked heroically, disregarding personal health and danger. Preventive as well as curative therapies were employed. In May of 1939, the Rothschild-Hadassah University Hospital and Medical School on Mount Scopus became the tangible symbol of Hadassah's service. It is the finest medical center in the Near East. Honoring its founder is the Henrietta Szold School of Nursing.

Magnificent as was this accomplishment of the scholar from Baltimore, it does not begin to summarize her life's labors. For her biography, which began in the days of the Civil War, was to contain within its span the greatest tragedies that ever befell the Jewish people. The anti-Jewish excesses which followed the First World War were but the beginning.

The war was barely over when Henrietta Szold became a commuter between Palestine and the United States. In 1933, the black year of the accession of the Nazis, she took into her aging but still capable hands the rescue of the children. A children's crusade to Palestine, known as the Youth Aliya, rescued thousands of young victims from the bloodstained clutches of the Germans. Now the tempo of murder and destruction accelerated. And the heart, responsive and overflowing, that had once in its youth grieved over the victims of the pogroms of 1881, knew the anguish of deepest mourning for the millions who died in the crematoria and concentration camps of Germany. The work went on. The planning for the victims who managed to escape from the death chambers continued.

This was the summary of her days until February 13, 1945, when this gallant, indomitable crusader, who fused within her person all that was best in America with all that was finest in renaissant Judaism, ended her labors.

What shall we write of a great American whose character and personality still linger as if he were with us? How shall we describe one whom a nation delighted to honor? He has been the subject of a definitive biography by Alpheus Thomas Mason.[17] His papers have been collected and edited and are a running critique on the age he lived in. His friends who knew him, like Justice Holmes and Morris Ernst, paid tribute to Louis D. Brandeis in countless ways.

He was a child of forty-eighters. His father, Adolph Brandeis, was a frustrated chemist. Early nineteenth-century Prague was not the environment to encourage that ambition. So he studied agriculture at the local technical training school, graduated, fell in love with a neighbor's daughter, migrated, first to England and then to America.

By 1849 Adolph could write to Fredricka to whom he was engaged, "I already love our new country." The young enthusiast settled in Madison, Indiana, the Mecca toward which Rabbi Felsenthal was also journeying. His enthusiasm was contagious. A year later, twenty-six people of the Brandeis and Dembitz and Wehle families migrated to America. Adolph Brandeis met them in New York. By barge up the Hudson, this party sailed, impressed by the beauty of the granite hills which line that dreamy and majestic river, exclaiming over the purple mists cradling the distant scene and rejoicing in the churning foam and the sibilant lapping of the gray waters. Through the Erie Canal to Buffalo. Thence by boat across Lake Erie. Then by train to Cincinnati. Dickens described a similar journey. Could they have felt as he did?

On September 5, 1849, Fredericka Dembitz and Adolph Brandeis were married. The Brandeis and Wehle families started a factory for the conversion of corn into starch. But the starch mill did not prosper and in 1851 they moved with their little daughter Fannie to Louisville. Here on November 13, 1856, Louis D. Brandeis was born. He was the youngest of four children, auspiciously born. For the move to Louisville brought material prosperity to the clan of Brandeis. It brought recognition and success in the professional fields for the numerous cousins and uncles. With his partner Charles W. Crawford, Brandeis owned a flour mill, a tobacco factory, a river freighter called the *Fannie Brandeis* and a farm of more than a thousand acres.

Young Louis played the violin, attended school and found many congenial playmates. Among them was young Abraham Flexner who became a name to conjure with in American medicine. These good times lasted until 1872. Then Adolph Brandeis, foreseeing the crash ahead, dissolved his partnership and took his family to Europe to travel, study and look up relatives. But America looked good to them when the homesick travelers disembarked with gratitude. Louis, verging on nineteen, entered Harvard Law School, a period in his life which he was to recall as "the wonderful years."

In a real sense his entire life span may be characterized as the wonderful years. Was he not "the people's attorney"? Did not the years of his life from 1856 to 1941 constitute such a measure of achievement and service as is vouchsafed to few men? His life was a cornucopia of friends, family, battles for people and causes, of ideas tumbling over each other in his fertile brain, of leadership in humanitarian undertakings, of dreams for Zion rebuilt. So many incidents come to mind that his chroniclers may say wistfully, "There was a man!" And the writer recalls gratefully the memory of his gentle face brooding over his judicial robe of black.

Louisville is not far from Washington as distances in this country go. But what a road of achievement it became.

In 1878, Brandeis was admitted to the bar, in St. Louis. Between 1879 and 1897 he practiced law in Boston as a member of the firm of Warren and Brandeis. In 1889 he was admitted to the bar of the United States Supreme Court. Two years later he married Alice Goldmark.

Alice, judging from an early photograph, was a comely young woman. She was his second cousin, daughter of Dr. Joseph Goldmark, an eminent scientist and Viennese Revolutionary of 1848. They were well mated. Sam Warren, Brandeis' partner, wrote to Alice Goldmark of her future husband that "his courage is high, his fidelity perfect, and his sense of honor delicate." When they were planning their first home and Alice deferred to Louis in everything, he wrote her that she must exercise "the prerogatives of a partner— to doubt and to criticize." A creative partnership their marriage proved to be. Theirs was a simple formula according to Professor Mason: "Brandeis and his wife arranged from the beginning to live simply but well."

In many ways Brandeis was unique. Often great men know how others should live. Great preachers deliver eloquent sermons—but fail to apply their philosophies. Not Brandeis. With his wife and two daughters he led a life graced with all the amenities, warmed by many friendships. There was time for outings with his wife and children, for horseback rides and canoe trips, for tennis and swimming. Time to teach carpentry to Susan and swimming to Elizabeth. Time to read aloud from wonderful books like Stevenson's. "Brandeis took a vacation whenever he felt he needed one. The test was the frame of mind with which he approached the day's work. If he could not look forward to it with pleasure, he knew a vacation was overdue."

"When he married Alice Goldmark in 1891," writes Charles A. Beard in his biographical introduction to *The Social and Economic Views of Mr. Justice Brandeis*, "he explained to her that by continuing his frugal habits he would be able hence-forward to devote himself to many aspects of public life in which he was already interested." His biographical record is studded with such entries as would prove that he held steadfastly to his philosophy of gratuitous service:

1897—1911 People's Attorney for Public Franchise League and Massachusetts State Board of Trade.

1905 Unpaid Counsel for the New England Policy-Holders' Protective Committee.

1907—1913 Unpaid Counsel in New Haven merger controversies.

1907—1914 Unpaid Counsel for the State in defending hours of labor and minimum wage statutes of Oregon, Illinois, Ohio, and California.

But this is not all of the record. He gained renown as a mediator.

With Norman Hapgood he formed a dynamic relationship in the world of ideas. So in 1906 he wrote to Hapgood, then editor of *Collier's Weekly*, suggesting that his publication lead the movement in advocating insurance for workers. This Hapgood did a few weeks later with such results that reprints were demanded by the hundreds and permission given to newspapers all over the country for their use. A few years later the roles were reversed. It was Hapgood who advocated the appointment of Brandeis as legal spearhead of the Ballinger investigation. Brandeis came to New York to work on the case in the seclusion of the Harvard Club, "seeing no one but Hapgood." On October 8, 1913, Norman Hapgood, now editor of *Harper's Weekly*, announced a new series of articles by Brandeis. Of these articles, Professor Mason writes: "Brandeis's fame as publicist and prophet rests, probably more than anything else on a series of articles called 'Breaking the Money Trust' which appeared in *Harper's Weekly*."

Again and again their intimate friendship proved fruitful. There was spiritual rapport, there was harmony and understanding, as well as exchange of most confidential data between these two men. During the struggle over Brandeis' appointment to the Supreme Court each man knew what the other was thinking, each trusted the other with intimate disclosures. Is it too much to ascribe Norman Hapgood's emergence as a noted advocate of Zionism to the conversion which Brandeis underwent at the same time? Brandeis had joined the Zionist movement in 1912. Their friendship persisted to the end, as when Brandeis wrote to Hapgood in 1934 giving his opinion of the NRA. "The dominant strain in Brandeis," writes Mason, "was an urgent zeal for freedom." In a letter to his friend Hapgood, Brandeis wrote in 1935 that the ultimate goal which no man will surrender is freedom.

In his own life and in his own person Brandeis proved the advantages of personal organization. He managed in his lifetime to crowd in so many kinds of activities, to produce such a stupendous amount of work, as to astonish businessmen, social workers, jurists and journalists, financiers and politicians. "All these talents combined in one of the most masterful legal minds in the country!" exclaims his biographer. How did he do it? By applying "scientific management to his own life and work." His time was carefully budgeted. His energies husbanded. He insisted that between a man's output and his abilities there was sometimes a difference of one hundred per cent. His days often began at four in the morning. He worked until five in the afternoon. The evenings were devoted to friends and family. His day ended at ten. Brandeis was cheerful by nature, even in the face of reversals. He simply refused to worry. He was indifferent to possessions and was spartan in taste. It was a life that hewed to a chosen line. Happily that line was one of great social usefulness, of great personal accomplishments, a record of integrated living.

In addition to his great services in the interpretation of the law, there were his signal achievements in the field of labor arbitration. But that story, important as it is, belongs elsewhere. What concerns us here is what Professor Mason, his biographer, highlights as "International Justice and the Jews."

Until 1912 Brandeis is described as "a typical American assimilationist." To Jewish vicissitudes he brought only "tenuous sympathy" at first. It was when he was fifty-four that his opinions underwent a dramatic change. The year was 1910. Brandeis had been drafted to settle a strike of New York garment workers. The men he came to know, the wretched conditions under which they worked, their fragile dreams for the future were then fully revealed to him. They struck a responsive chord in Brandeis, the liberal. The seed was planted. He met Jacob De Haas, an English Jew who had once been secretary to Theodor Herzl. His affiliation with American Zionism was announced at the Cleveland Zionist Convention in 1912. This was no half-hearted conversion. Brandeis now gave generously to the cause, both of his time and talents. He was forthright, consistent. Meeting criticism in many quarters, he straddled no issue, dodged no inquisitive reporter. When war broke out in 1914 and Brandeis was asked to assume the leadership of the Zionist movement in America, he accepted the call. He was aware of his lack of preparation for the task, calling attention to the antecedent years in which he had been "separated from Jews."

He became a circuit rider known on many platforms. His classic speech "Zionism and Patriotism" was heard by thousands, reprinted, read by thousands more. His open profession of faith brought down a hornet's nest of critics. He was involved and embroiled. He had left the scholar's study for the arena. He wrote his brother on one occasion that he had declined to speak in Cincinnati because he wished to avoid public controversy with Rabbi Philipson, but it was not often that he avoided controversy. In April of 1915, speaking from Stephen Wise's pulpit, Brandeis declared that, "The Jewish Renaissance has come—the nation is reborn."

It was a thorny path. For he was repeatedly challenged. He was asked to "reconcile" what opponents of Zionism insisted was the irreconcilable dichotomy between Americanism and Zionism. The Los Angeles Times described him as "a high grade opportunist," dubbed him "the Boston butter-in," suggested that he open a real estate office in Jerusalem "and stay there, above all, stay there."

In the midst of battle, Brandeis' name was catapulted into the news. On January 28, 1916, President Woodrow Wilson precipitated a domestic crisis by submitting the name of Louis D. Brandeis for a vacancy in the United States Supreme Court. The act was unprecedented. Wilson was challenged on every front. Yet surprising though the choice may have been to the nation, it had for Woodrow Wilson an inevitable logic. Brandeis and Sam Gompers had been among the first friends he had made on his initial political junket. He had previously thought of offering a Cabinet post to Brandeis and been dissuaded. When he decided on Brandeis for the Supreme Court the chorus of opposition could not sway the President. The nominee took the name-calling and opprobrium in his stride. Having found his relationship to matters Jewish through Zionism, Brandeis explained to his brother that he attributed his ability to withstand hardship to "eighteen centuries of Jewish persecution." This was strange reasoning from one who for more than fifty years had known little of such hardships and thought even less about them. When Justice Brandeis assumed his new duties, he had already won from the Jews of America their everlasting affection, respect and loyalty. His elevation to the Supreme Court was of symbolic importance. It vested him with authority. It lifted him above controversy. It was the perfect accolade to a favorite son. It was a triumph for the Jews of America as well as a victory for American democracy.

On June 5, 1916, Louis D. Brandeis took the oath of his high office. For nearly twenty-three years, this good and faithful servant served his country and his conscience unswervingly. He remained a great liberal. In preparation for his donning of the judicial robes of office, Brandeis had divested himself of his contacts with special interest groups. He resigned from the National Economic League, the Utilities Bureau, the Conciliation Council for the Garment Trades. Nevertheless his membership in the Zionist Organization was maintained. There was no ideological conflict involved.

To Brandeis was vouchsafed not only the planting, but the harvesting as well. His years of crusading, his decades of dissenting opinions, when with his distinguished colleague Oliver Wendell Holmes he stood firmly for what he saw to be the right, were years of accomplishment. He lived long enough to see these dissenting opinions become the law of the land. Professor Mason summed up the fruitful years well: "The dissenter had in his own time, become the prophet of the living law."

In Palestine a colony was established which proudly bears the name of *Kfar Brandeis*; in Waltham, Massachusetts, a university.

In America, the nation had recently honored the memory of Isaac M. Wise by naming a ship for him. The Jews of America in 1948 honored the memory of their greatest leader by naming a university in his honor.

The institution and the man belong together. Both are unique in the American Jewish chronicle. Have not American Jews always loved learning?

Now history and biography had come the full circle. And time and leadership and an ideal were interwoven in order that the Jews of America could point with pride to their continued love of learning, to their kinship to Louis D. Brandeis, to their fulfillment by the founding of a university on American soil dedicated to the belief that "education is a precious treasure transmitted—a sacred trust to be held, used, and enjoyed, and if possible strengthened, then passed on to others upon the same trust."

Those were the words of the man whom the Jews of America delighted to honor.

In one way or another Zionism was indigenous in America. From the days of Loronha's caravel named the *Judea*, from the early settlement in South America named Cananéa, from the time when Rabbi Carigal awakened in the Jews of Newport an interest in Hebron, and Mordecai Manuel Noah dreamed of a new Ararat and Isaac Leeser promoted the welfare of Palestine—the two worlds were aware of each other. Now the forests that bloom in the Judean desert, the colonies like *Ain Hashofet* (Eye of Justice) celebrating Justice Brandeis—all point to the indissoluble tie between the two worlds.

One phase of Jewish history in America came to an end on May 14, 1948 with the creation of the State of Israel. Another which had its beginnings with the discovery of America is still continuing. It is the period of participation, of integration, of sharing. . . .

CHAPTER XVI

American Jews Rescue
the Remnant of Israel

➤➤➤   A Jew who abandons the customs of his people and
close associations with his own people in the United States
today, if he is a deeply thinking man, must have a certain
guilty feeling that he is helping to destroy his historic race.
— NORMAN HAPGOOD in *Harper's*
Weekly, August 21, 1915   ⫷⫷⫷

THE AMERICAN Jew faced the twentieth century with the experience of four centuries of life in the Western Hemisphere. From the
dawn of discovery through the days of pioneering and early settlement, through war and peace, he had been on the American scene.
He had been present at every major event in American history. He
had built his own institutions and evolved his cultural compromises.
He had maintained his identity and produced his own leaders. Assimilated in some areas, he survived in others. Often this survival
depended upon the replenishing springs of immigration. Jewish group
life was dynamic and fluid. For through a kind of social osmosis there
was a visible, more or less continuous, loss of component members
who through intermarriage or social pressure were absorbed by the
host group.

Such centrifugal trends were decried by the faithful and deplored
by the impregnable. Anxiety and insecurity are related phenomena.
American Jews considered themselves the custodians of a good and
beautiful legacy which had been handed down to them through the
ages. The cost of survival could not be measured. For its price had
been beyond life itself. From 1881 on, Jews had been in a state of
siege in one part of the world or another. They held the citadels—but
not without developing the accompanying symptoms of combat
fatigue. As the position of the Jew became untenable in some parts of
Europe, tension mounted everywhere. Defeatism and hopelessness

afflicted those on the periphery as well as those who were under attack.

The problem was not new to the Jews of America. It had been one of the justifications for the introduction of *Minhag America* by Rabbi Isaac M. Wise and his confreres. It had been one of the reasons a generation later for the searching of the religious processes in American Jewish life by Mordecai Kaplan. "The world's hostility . . . is beyond their control," writes Kaplan, insisting that to compensate for this hostility "the Jew must make his Jewishness as richly significant to himself as he can."

In summarizing the year 5707 (1946-47), the *American Jewish Year Book* notes that such defections are of major concern to the leaders of the American Jewish community.[1]

A lively controversy was stirred up in the Jewish press and in Jewish religious circles by a public statement of Dr. Louis Finkelstein, president of the Jewish Theological Seminary of America, to the effect that American Jews are deserting their faith and streaming into the fold of Christianity by wholesale conversions. The general reaction to this statement was that it was alarmist and defeatist and did not accurately portray American Jewish life.

The tendency of marginal members of minority groups to escape inevitable social pressure, social ostracism, rejection, exclusion, denial of equal rights, disfellowship, is too well known to need enlarging here. "The ultimate hope of American Jewry rests with those whose being is rooted in Jewish life, and who cannot contemplate the disintegration of Judaism without a deep sense of frustration," insists Kaplan.[2]

For the historian this is hardly an academic problem. For there comes a time when he must determine by definition what constitutes a Jew. The question of identity touches upon the intent of the individual concerned, yet it cannot altogether rest upon his choice alone. For to make good his separation from his group two factors are needed: the severance of all ties with kin and siblings, and the recognition by society that the surgery has been effective. It is possible for an escapee to take radical steps to accomplish his separation, involving change of name and physiognomy, of address and religion, without successfully removing from the popular mind the association with his former cultural or religious environment. Disraeli and Karl Marx are two examples. Both had undergone conversion in childhood. Yet neither accomplished full psychological severance from his ancestors.

In American annals there are many cases of frustrated intent. Judah Monis of Harvard protested his sincerity even from his tombstone. United States Senator David Levy Yulee trusted to a metamorphosed name and his non-Jewish wife and children to establish his separation. The sixth governor of Georgia (1801), David Emanuel, is included in Jewish reference works as a Jew although he was a Christian by intent. There is a record of the baptism of "David Emanuel, a Jew" and there are numerous clues left behind by him indicating his purpose of disassociating himself from his Jewish antecedents.

In approaching such psychic factors as grow out of personal insecurity and imbalance, the historian forsakes his true domain. While the psycho-social environment is an integral part of history, its divagations may be noted only in passing. The problem of the marginal Jew must be considered as a study in cultural adaptation which is germane to the analysis of all minority groups. Attention has been focused on certain practices within the marginal Jewish group which are stressed as if they were unique and applicable to that group only. One example will suffice—that of adapting names to the new environment. A recent news dispatch carried the story of a Czech refugee who on arrival to the United States changed his name from Vacla Vaclavik to Randolph Williams. Such changes are legion. Yet the practice is inveighed against as if it were limited to the descendants of Aaron. Whenever two cultures meet, adjustment and accommodation must follow. It has been argued that forced segregation and isolation lead to beneficial results. Others stress the importance of melting-pot fusion. One sociologist asks: "Can it be said that the scoundrels joining the Know-Nothings, the American Protective Association, or the modern Ku Klux Klan contributed more to American culture than the disciples of the melting pot?" Another stresses the transitional aspects of minority groups. Such searching sociological studies have greatly illumined the task of the historian. Closer rapprochement between the social sciences will tend to uncover new trends and new directions. The time is fast approaching when historians will discard "the Anglo-Saxon myth."

The question of identification is for the historian no mere academic discussion. It poses a problem with a series of repercussions. The contribution of Louis D. Brandeis to American Jews was inestimable. Yet it began when he was well past the middle of life. The antecedent years were crowded with the impact of problems of moment to all Americans. As Brandeis was evolving as a social reformer, a jurist, a leader in industrial peace, he was making a contribution from which the entire nation was the beneficiary. Yet as a worthy associate, Justice Felix Frankfurter, has astutely pointed out, it was Brandeis' connection with Zionism which brought him "understanding and happiness." Brandeis could have missed personal happiness and understanding by failing to respond to the vibrant dream of the masses, Zionism. He would then have been a great American of Jewish parentage who had by-passed his cultural heritage. It was a subject to which Justice Brandeis himself gave careful consideration.

Brandeis could not have chosen a better time and place to discuss "True Americanism" than at Faneuil Hall in Boston, on July 4, 1915.[3]

The new nationalism adopted by America proclaims that each race or people, like each individual, has the right and duty to develop, and that only through such differentiated development will high civilization be attained. Not until these principles of nationalism, like those of democracy, are generally accepted will liberty be fully attained and minorities be secure in their rights.

That is cultural pluralism in a nutshell.

Thirty-three years later, Professor Kaplan was constrained by the nagging persistence of the same problems to investigate the causes for the estrangement between the Jews of America and their luminaries. In "The Key Persons in Jewish Life," Kaplan asks why it is that the opinion-molders, the great Jewish entrepreneurs, the executives and financiers, the philanthropists, the writers, artists, poets, critics, have stepped aside from Jewish folkways and mores, have disassociated themselves from their ancient heritage? Even the openhanded philanthropists who give with both hands to Jewish institutions, distribute their largesse as if to a lost cause or to an expiring recipient. Sadly the integrated Jew contemplates the one who has disinherited himself. Their successful men wield tremendous power, for they have reached the heights of eminence. "At worst, they disdain to have anything to do with the Jewish people; at best, they regard it as an anachronism which, for the good of all concerned, they think should be liquidated. Indeed, one or two more generations of such Jews, and American Jewry will be a thing of the past."[4] Thus Kaplan.

Since such self-annihilative tendencies exist, they must be regarded as related to the over-all destructive trends to which the twentieth century is obviously committed. The first half century already has witnessed two major wars and countless minor conflicts. It has seen the reduction of a continent, genocide, rampant sadism, the collapse of civilization and the perfection of atomic warfare to facilitate total annihilation of mankind. Man has declared war on himself. He is both aggressor and the thing destroyed. It is against this frame of reference that the phenomenon of the Jewish escapee must be noted. The vitality of Jewish life in America rests on affirmation. Negation is akin to death.

As the historian approaches the contemporary scene, he leaves behind the relative security of indisputable data and enters the realm of the tentative, the debatable, the speculative, the controversial. Even the study of demography, mathematical, impersonal, is circumscribed. The most recent studies of population problems involving Jews deplore the difficulties of obtaining accurate statistics and the misleading results obtained with the present methods. One scholar in this field writes: "Any comparison of the various techniques of estimating the Jewish population raises the question of how to define the designation 'Jew.'" Here at least the dilemma of the statistician is shared by the historian.[5] Unfortunately no satisfactory definition exists to describe the unaffiliated Jew. That is the crux of the matter. "Jews," according to *Columbia Encyclopedia*, is a "term used synonymously with Hebrews and Israelites to indicate the descendants of the tribes of Israel, followers of Judaism." "But what makes the Jewish identity?" asks Rabbi Steinberg seeking to define the term. The Jews are a religious body, a culture, and a people. "There are Jews aplenty alien to the religion and civilization alike. To be sure, it is a very exceptional Jew who is not in some way, shape or manner touched by being Jewish. At the very least he is likely to belong to some Jewish association or to support some Jewish cause," concludes Steinberg. Tenuous definitions of phantom beings!

It was a distinguished American Jew who made an important stride in the direction of clarification of this dilemma. Adolph S. Ochs, son-in-law of Isaac M. Wise, made possible, at a cost of a million dollars which he underwrote, the publication of the *Dictionary of American Biography*. Cincinnati-born, his was the typical career of a self-made journalist.[6] He served a four-year apprenticeship as a printer's devil in Knoxville, Tennessee. He worked on the Louisville *Courier* and was the prime mover in the founding of the Southern Associated Press. In politics he became known as an opponent of Bryanism. When he reached New York in 1896, he found that the *Times*, a newspaper barely seven years older than Ochs, was in financial trouble. The rest is history. How he made over that paper and how he made journalistic history while he headed the *Times* is an exciting narrative in the heroic tradition. Declaring war on yellow journalism, choosing slogans like "All the News That's Fit to Print" and "It Does Not Soil the Breakfast Cloth," cutting the price to a penny, Ochs made his newspaper the most respected in America. When he had reached a half century of achievement, Chattanooga honored Ochs with the title of "Citizen Emeritus" and in a two-day civic festival celebrated his continuous ownership of the Chattanooga *Times*. He received honorary degrees from Columbia, Dartmouth, Yale and other universities. He was hailed by Nicholas Murray Butler as "the master mind of the outstanding triumph of modern journalism."

This uncompromising crusader for clean journalism made his mark as a Jew also. Two women influenced him greatly, his mother Bertha Ochs and his wife Effie Miriam Wise. Both were well grounded in the content of Judaism. Both were well-integrated women. In countless ways this chivalrous son and husband became the instrument of these two women. As when he headed the five-million-dollar campaign for the creation of an endowment fund for Hebrew Union College. Or when he built a temple and community house in Chattanooga honoring the memory of his parents. Or when he served as trustee of Temple Emanu-El of New York. Or when he presented two bronze menorahs to the Cathedral of St. John the Divine in New York—a symbol of interfaith good-will to which both women were devoted, as well as to their own cherished faith.

When the *Dictionary of American Biography* appeared, biographies of notable American Jews emerged as part of the over-all pattern. It permitted comparative studies to be undertaken. Professor Leo Shapiro contributed to *The Reconstructionist* an excellent analysis of these data.[7] Of the well over two hundred articles dealing with Jewish subjects, many describe men and women familiar to the reader— Samuel Gompers, Emma Lazarus, Isaac Leeser. The two most extensive biographies are concerned with Judah P. Benjamin and Samuel Gompers, the latter written by no less an authority than John R. Commons. However, Professor Shapiro is quick to point out that such biographical studies "are useful on an elementary rather than on an advanced level."

"The treatment in the DAB of Jewish personalities is of limited value for other reasons than skimpiness. Readers will miss certain people in the DAB and wonder why they were not included." Among those omitted were Isaac Franks, David Salisbury Franks, Adolph Kraus and Judah Touro. "How sad that there should be room for Arthur Flegenheimer (better known to the police as Dutch Schultz) and for his non-Jewish confrere John Dillinger," and not for the many, many others who made a notable contribution to American history.

There is a twenty-one-column essay in the "Supplement" on Oliver Wendell Holmes, written by Felix Frankfurter. "Frankfurter's essay is, in more than one respect, the high point of the volume." Other biographies in the "Supplement" deal with Felix Adler, Morris Hillquit, Belle L. Moskowitz, social worker, Max J. Kohler, who did so much for the cause of American Jewish historiography.

There is an embarrassment of riches. Reference works, encyclopedias, necrologies, books, magazine articles. Here is one example. *Distinguished American Jews* is a recent book which contains a dozen biographical sketches. Among these are biographies of Charney Vladeck, one of the heroes of the American labor movement; Carl Laemmle, a pioneer in the motion picture industry; Felix Adler, founder of the Society for Ethical Culture; Joseph Goldberger, heroic physician who dedicated his life to fighting pellagra; and Charles P. Steinmetz, distinguished scientist. As such data multiply beyond the limits of any single book, defying condensation, the words of Maimonides console the overwhelmed chronicler. "No intelligent man will require and expect," wrote the author of the *Guide for the Perplexed*, "that on introducing any subject I shall completely exhaust it." A few guideposts may be erected, a marker put up, the boundaries faintly traced. Then the reader, like the hero of a fairy tale for whose benefit pebbles were dropped, picks up the trail.

The Encyclopedia of Jewish Knowledge begins its alphabet of accomplishment with Agriculture and David Lubin. Biology recalls Jacques Loeb's inestimable contribution in parthenogenesis and his association with two leading American universities, as well as the Rockefeller Institute whose division of physiology he headed with distinction. And so on down the list. The *Universal Jewish Encyclopedia* in its ten volumes goes into far greater detail. Contributions of Jews to art, astronomy, athletics, chess, chemistry, education, finance, industry, journalism, literature, mathematics, medicine, music, military service, philosophy, physics, public service, travel and exploration, are only a few of the fields covered. The countless names of the leaders in each field belong in *Who's Who*. Each branch of knowledge acknowledges its own peculiar indebtedness.

Among the lists of great Americans that have been compiled is one Franklin D. Roosevelt made in one of the most critical moments of American history.[8] Aboard the Presidential yacht on a muggy Friday evening in June of 1940, the President of the United States and a representative of beleaguered France, René de Chambrun, met to discuss the urgent needs of France. The enemy had already crossed the Seine. They were marching toward the Loire. The President mentioned twenty-three names of indispensable Americans, jotted them down on a cablegram blank and said to René de Chambrun: "These are the people to see." Four of the twenty-three names were of American Jews: Morgenthau, Hillman, Frankfurter, Baruch.

Henry Morgenthau, Jr., was the distinguished son of a famous father. Henry Morgenthau, the father of the man on Roosevelt's list, was born in Germany four years before the Civil War. He came to the United States as a boy of nine and was educated in New York City, receiving his law degree from Columbia in 1877. His success in business was phenomenal and by 1912 he had enough money and leisure to devote himself to politics. The political philosophy of Woodrow Wilson attracted him. It was more than lip service that he gave. He became treasurer of the Democratic party and a valuable campaigner. He was rewarded for his services by being appointed Ambassador to Turkey. Among the duties with which President Wilson charged Morgenthau was that of ameliorating the situation of Turkish Jews, pointing out that such concern "will reflect credit upon America." His devotion to President Wilson during the dark days of the War, his active sponsorship of the League of Nations, his valiant labors in behalf of the International Red Cross, his attempts to find ways of rehabilitating postwar Polish Jewry, his ready availability as adviser and consultant on problems in the Near East, were but a few of his major services. In 1923 he was named chairman of the Refugee Settlement Commission of the League of Nations. For his statesmanlike strategy in solving the problems arising from the transfer of populations in the Balkans and Near East, he was voted honorary citizenship by Athens and Salonika. He continued his brilliant career of humanitarian service both at home and abroad. Not the least of his many benefactions was directed toward his underprivileged coreligionists on the teeming East Side of New York. And in the evening of his life—he died in 1946—he could glow with pride at the accomplishments of his son.

The first Jewish name on President Roosevelt's list belongs there by virtue of many spectacular accomplishments. To the fact that Henry Morgenthau, Jr., was his father's son—the honorary Athenian citizen—he owed his initial advantages—exceptional home influence, education in the best private schools and Cornell University. It gave him a diversified background so that he could sum up his occupations as farmer, publisher, financier and public servant. His fortunate antecedents relieved him of the need of earning a living and so released his vast energies for the public good. Born in 1891, when his father had already established a sizable fortune and was able to indulge his inclination as a gentleman and public benefactor, young Henry studied agriculture at Cornell as a prelude to a useful life on the land. His Dutchess County farm embracing one thousand five hundred acres of land became a laboratory of diversified farming. But he had acquired other skills growing out of his experience as a volunteer and resident social worker of the Henry Street Settlement. He served as his father's secretary in Turkey. He was one of the directors of a camp which took boys from the streets of New York to summer vacations in the country. Morgenthau enlisted in the Navy, serving as a lieutenant junior grade. After the war, he worked toward popularizing the League of Nations and campaigned for a Dutchess County neighbor, Franklin D. Roosevelt. He edited a farm paper, worked for agricultural reform, became a director of the Jewish Agricultural Society. When his former neighbor was elected President, Morgenthau, the farmer, was appointed chairman of the Federal Farm Board. Here Morgenthau distinguished himself both as an administrator and as a social planner. When on January 1, 1934, he was appointed Secretary of Treasury, he was one of the youngest men in the country to hold so important a post. It was a grueling task that he faced. His decisions had world-wide repercussions. To all major social problems with which he was confronted, he brought some of the insight he had gained as a resident at the Henry Street Settlement. So it was that the Public Health Service then administered by the Treasury Department not only made a study of nutritional habits in the low income groups, but worked out a program in co-operation with the Department of Agriculture for supplementary diets through a system of food stamps. His service to his country during the war and after its close is too important to be summarily condensed here.

The *Morgenthau Diaries* are a guide to his life of humanitarian service. Here his social philosophy and his deep sense of kinship with all mankind are blueprinted. Here too are his passionate preoccupations with surplus humanity, the tragic, unwanted Jewish alumni of concentration camps. In vain had Morgenthau sought to rescue the sacrificial victims in the days before the War. Our government knew from August of 1942 on, that the Nazis planned to murder all the Jews of Europe. For eighteen leaden months the State Department buried this information within its entrails and did absolutely nothing!

Secretary Hull, who administered this department, "was not set up for rapid action or for humanitarianism." It was, as far as the Jews were concerned, a Circumlocution Office of the worst order. Social amenities preceded humanity. Information about Nazi atrocities was suppressed. "Officials dodged their grim responsibility, procrastinated when concrete rescue schemes were placed before them." There was no moral indignation, no compassion. Only delay—endless, unfeeling, callous torpor! "Hull's indulgence of such men as Breckenridge Long, who did not harass him with perplexing policy problems and with whom he could relax socially, was one of the Secretary's major weaknesses." History had its precedents. Nero fiddled. Hull relaxed socially.

So the War Refugee Board was created. "The agonizing cry" which prompted the creation of this board was long overdue and came as a result of a "dramatic White House interview." Morgenthau suggested the name of Wendell Willkie to head this new commission. But the President demurred. John Pehle however, made an excellent administrator. Of the work of this group Morgenthau says:

It did a magnificent job. But think what it might have done had it begun work a year earlier! As a result in part of the delays in beginning a serious rescue program, only one out of seven European Jews is alive today.

The narrative ends with praise for President Truman and Secretaries Byrnes and Marshall. And then Morgenthau recalls a statement which President Roosevelt made at a Cabinet meeting on March 18, 1938. "America," said the President, "was a place of refuge for so many fine Germans in 1848. Why couldn't we offer them again a place of refuge at this time?"

Would American hospitality have been invoked if these doomed people had been billed as Germans and not as Jews? It is a moot question for the historian of the future.

In an editorial titled "Giants In Our Time," on March 22, 1947, *Collier's* salutes two great Americans.

Somebody remarked a while ago that in the person of Winston Churchill we had all been privileged to see greatness in our time. We agree with that estimate. But we'd like to add to the list of present-day greats the names of two Americans, at least—Bernard M. Baruch and Secretary of State George C. Marshall.

Here, too, is a famous son of a renowned father. Like the elder Morgenthau, Simon Baruch, father of Bernard was a transplanted American. By the time he was twenty-two, in 1862, he was graduated from the Medical College of Virginia. He then enlisted in the Confederate Army, serving as assistant surgeon in the Seventh Carolina Battalion and surgeon of the Thirteenth Mississippi Regiment. After the war he practiced medicine in the South. He established a hospital, became active in medical circles, was elected president of the South Carolina Medical Society, became chairman of the State Board of Health. In 1881 he moved to New York where his numerous hospital and institutional connections gave him even greater scope for service. He was the pioneer exponent of hydrotherapy in the United States. The two books which he wrote on the subject became medical classics. *Uses of Water in Modern Medicine* was published in 1892 and *Principles and Practice of Hydrotherapy* in 1898. It was due to his efforts that free municipal bathhouses were established first in Chicago, then in New York and later in more than one hundred other cities.

To Dr. Simon Baruch goes the credit for first diagnosing and successfully operating upon a patient with a perforated appendix and for the development of surgical techniques in appendectomy. He made a thorough study of the incidence of malaria in the temperate zone and summarized his studies in a series of articles which were later corroborated by Sir William Osler. Next Dr. Baruch developed a method of cold water therapy for the treatment of typhoid fever. He became a professor of hydrotherapy in the New York Post-Graduate Medical School and attending physician in the New York Juvenile Asylum.

In many ways his name and influence persist. In the hospital which serves as his memorial in Camden, South Carolina. In Baruch Park in New York City. In the memorial fellowships which his son endowed after the Second World War in memory of his father. These fellowships permit physicians, many of them veterans of the last war, to study and apply the principles of physical medicine—water, heat and massage. At the University of Iowa, at the Mayo Clinic, at Johns Hopkins University, at the Institute of Rehabilitation and Physical Medicine of New York University Medical Center and other schools, physicians are studying the therapies advocated by this farsighted medical pioneer.

"You must understand," said Bernard M. Baruch in 1948 as he was reminiscing about his life which began in 1870, "that my mother was a remarkable woman. She was very beautiful, and she had a pure and serene heart. She always endeavored to instill into her children lessons of tolerance and kindliness. . . . She was active in all kinds of charities. . . . Whether it was for a Jewish or Protestant or Catholic organization made no difference to Mother so long as she felt she was doing some good . . . the people who used to work with her on these charities called her *la Grande Duchesse*." Of his father he adds, "He was a remarkable person, too."9

It was his proud boast that on his mother's side there were seven generations of Americans of Spanish and Portuguese descent behind him, so that he was a lineal descendant of the Sephardim. His father was of German birth, "partly of Polish descent." Indeed *Columbia Encyclopedia* so lists Simon Baruch's birthplace. Bernard Baruch recalled a conversation with Clemenceau in which the great Frenchman said to him, "The Polish Jews are very great people." From both his parents he inherited a profound faith in social progress. "We *can* fix the world," he said. "We've got to believe we can, and then we will."

Although he was phenomenally successful in making money, he insisted that he didn't care about it. He recalled the days of his youth when he "grew up a poor boy." He remembered the attic of a boarding house at 144 West Fifty-seventh Street where the family lived in those early days. He attended City College and recalled the fact that he was not elected to membership in a Greek-letter fraternity. "I don't think it was because I was disliked. I think it was because I was a Jew." He managed to compensate for that by becoming a successful member of the New York Stock Exchange.

"President Wilson was my first hero," said Bernard Baruch, still smarting from his sense of rejection as a college student. "He became my hero long before he was President, because of his policy of democratizing the eating clubs at Princeton." The sentiment of cordial admiration must have been reciprocated, for President Wilson gave Baruch his first opportunity at public service by appointing him a member of the Council of National Defense in 1916. Here Baruch was at his best. His thorough knowledge of national resources, his ability to tap them, his aid in mobilizing resources and man-power, proved invaluable. When in recognition of his administrative genius, Wilson named Baruch Chairman of the War Industries Board, the man and the job were well mated. The industries of the entire nation were mobilized by Baruch and put to work to facilitate the winning of the War. So well did he carry out his assignment that at the end of the War he was awarded the Distinguished Service Medal by President Wilson.

Other honors piled up. France, Belgium and Italy decorated Baruch. Seven universities bestowed their honorary doctorates on him. Groups of all sorts tripped over each other trying to do him honor. He kept his head. A homespun philosophy sustained him. If he was to be known as an "expert," he was determined to be a modest one. "I've noticed that these noisy experts never have two nickels to rub against each other," he said a little smugly. Much of the money he earned he gave away in liberal contributions. The causes he espoused had far-reaching programs for education and social amelioration, like the Williamstown Institute of Politics. He subsidized many research projects, including a study of the causes of war.

Maxims, proverbs, admonitions, float on the surface of his conversations. He spoke with the prestige of authority. "Woodrow Wilson used to call me Dr. Facts," he recalled with pride. "People believe in me. . . . They think I am honest and they listen to my advice. They think I am always right. That's the greatest satisfaction I've had in life—being right." "The children of famous men generally have a hard time. They remain in the penumbra of their fathers." Was that an unconscious reflection on his own relationship with his own father? "I've been in all walks of life and I've seen men under temptation. . . . But I've never lost faith in human beings." Here perhaps is the essence of his philosophy. "You've got to be ready for anything and fearful of nothing. I believe I can say I am afraid of nothing. . . . I'm not afraid of death. . . ."

To Baruch, the dauntless, many adventures have been vouchsafed. President Franklin D. Roosevelt relied on him for counsel and guidance. Some of the social legislation of the Roosevelt Era is known to have been distilled in fireside chats at the White House, for which Baruch was always available. The National Industrial Recovery Act of 1933 is attributed to Bernard Baruch. The tense, uneasy years which led inexorably to war, called for wisdom and planning. Baruch's forte! So he was often summoned by Roosevelt and later by President Truman.

In 1935 Baruch had advocated *Taking the Profits Out of War*. The war profiteer, the business tycoon who fattened on the consumer, the exploiter of labor, the rent gouger—on all of these enemies of his country, Baruch waged unceasing war. He had enlisted in his youth, and on the threshold of fourscore years his sleeves were still rolled up and he was still fighting the good fight.

And now, quoting Horace on the impartiality of death, which seeks out rich and poor alike, Baruch awaited death calmly, stoically, until it took him on June 20, 1965, and marked his exit after an unforgettable performance.

The last of Roosevelt's quadrumvirate of great American Jews is Felix Frankfurter.[10] Henry Morgenthau and Bernard Baruch were natives. Sidney Hillman and Felix Frankfurter were transplanted Americans. But the life Felix Frankfurter charted was peculiarly his own, unlike that of any of his contemporaries or associates. In a carefully weighed evaluation of Frankfurter's career, Adolf A. Berle, Jr. has called it "one of the most brilliant careers of the present generation." Felix Frankfurter's contribution to the American scene still remains to be told. It touches too many contemporary events and personalities, it reaches into too many corridors of current history, it involves too many still debated issues, to be assayed with detachment or seen in its entirety. All that can be done is to summarize a few of the incidents which led to Frankfurter's appointment to the Supreme Court, an appointment which Matthew Josephson calls "canonization this side of paradise." The same writer describes Frankfurter as "the little Keeper of the Conscience of the Nation," and "a whole institution in himself."

Felix Frankfurter came from a family which for three centuries prior to his birth in 1882 had numbered rabbis among them. How that knowledge shaped his thinking and what it contributed to his ambition, formed in childhood, of dedicating his life to public service, it is impossible to say. It must have been deeply interwoven with his childhood fantasies of leadership, with a feeling of dedication, with the conviction of belonging to the Chosen People, of wearing the mantle of the Prophets. When he was twelve his family, headed by a gentle, vague, impractical father and a practical, levelheaded mother, left Vienna for New York. By 1906 he had graduated from the sidewalks of New York where he sold newspapers, from the New York public schools, from the College of the City of New York and from the Harvard Law School. It was not a bad record of achievement for the second twelve years of his life.

Harvard gave him the best of opportunities. For here he was admitted into the dazzling world of men of great character and intellect. Oliver Wendell Holmes and Louis D. Brandeis and Henry L. Stimson were more than names to him because of Harvard. His first major opportunities in the life of service he had chosen came to him through his association with Stimson, whose influence in President Theodore Roosevelt's administration and that of his successor, President Taft, was considerable. Henry L. Stimson became Secretary of War under President Taft. In 1911, Frankfurter was on the staff of the Bureau of Insular Affairs which was attached to the War Department. His next appointment was that of professor at the Harvard Law School. This coincided with the beginning of the Wilson era of liberalism. The campaign to create a Federal Trade Commission which was one of President Wilson's early undertakings won Frankfurter's untiring support. Like Brandeis he was from the first interested in labor problems. He brought the full vigor of his mental energies and his teaching skills to the task of training hundreds of young men in careers of public service. His students nicknamed their mentor "Foxy Felix." But once under his spell they were committed to a point of view and an attitude which was not unrelated to his. So he has amounted to "an Institute for Shaping and Guiding Public Opinion." Yet he remained unobtrusive and comparatively unknown until 1939.

With his wife, the daughter of a Congregational minister, he lived a quiet, busy life. His friends, colleagues and students made his social orbit. "Frankfurter's attitude toward his students was paternal. In addition to trying to inspire them, he all but adopted his favorite pupils into his childless family. He became absorbed in their private lives and their ambitions." His mother used to visit her son at Harvard occasionally and he would proudly introduce her to his colleagues. "They admired and used to repeat her original, common-sense maxims, which she delivered in a strong Austrian accent." He had time to work and to write books.

Frankfurter was co-author of *The Business of the Supreme Court* and author of *The Public and Its Government* and *The Labor Injunction* and a number of other studies interpreting government and law. His passionate belief in social justice impelled him to forsake his study and turn himself "into a Zola" when he espoused the cause of two penniless immigrant laborers charged with the murder of a paymaster in South Braintree, Massachusetts. The arrest and conviction and ultimate execution of Sacco and Vanzetti turned the clock back in Massachusetts to the days of witch-hunting and burning. It was a crushing blow to Frankfurter. President Lowell of Harvard headed a committee whose findings were against the two condemned men. Posthumously history exonerated Sacco and Vanzetti. Frankfurter's *The Case of Sacco and Vanzetti* is a masterful summary of the evidence in their favor. He insists that the men were innocent and that their execution was murder.

Felix Frankfurter has been described as "a vaguely humanitarian liberal" and as one whose emotions were rigidly controlled by his intellect. His life was well integrated. His goals were clearly charted.

His sentiments have influenced his major affiliations. In 1918 he served as assistant to the Secretary of Labor and as chairman of the War Labor Policies Board. With the eclipse of Wilsonian liberalism, Frankfurter concentrated during 1920-28 on his teaching and writing. "His ambition even then was to end his career as a justice of the United States Supreme Court, and he set about it methodically, studying the work of the Supreme Court, teaching and continuing to liberalize administrative law, and supporting from time to time various liberal causes." Under President Hoover, Henry L. Stimson had become Secretary of State. Through the years, Stimson's and Frankfurter's friendly contacts had been maintained. It was now possible to suggest as appointees to various governmental posts some of Frankfurter's students in whose careers he was interested and whose talents qualified them for public service. The election of Franklin D. Roosevelt gave to the Frankfurter coterie of young liberals still greater opportunities. The rapport between President Roosevelt and Felix Frankfurter grew. Frankfurter was frequently consulted by President Roosevelt and by his former students in key government positions.

Felix Frankfurter was appointed Justice of the Supreme Court in 1939, a post which he filled with distinction until his retirement in 1962.

Benjamin Nathan Cardozo was the third Jewish member of the United States Supreme Court, the second to be appointed.[11] To write even a condensed biography of this man and his antecedents is to review the history of Pilgrim People in America. For within his person he was the epitome of American-Jewish history. His character was the reflection of all that was good and beautiful in the American-Jewish tradition. Frankfurter was a naturalized citizen. Brandeis was the son of immigrants. Cardozo was descended from pre-Revolutionary pioneers and from Revolutionary War soldiers.

Here was an American hero whose forebears had made history and forged a tradition. The name of Cardozo appeared on the Inquisition rolls. The American branch of the family was founded by Aaron Nunez Cardozo, who came to the colonies around the year 1752. We are told that Benjamin Cardozo belonged to a clan consisting of a select group of Sephardim who intermarried among themselves and constituted a universe of kinship. The Peixotto, Seixas, Nathan, Hart, Frank, Levy, Hendricks, Phillips, Gomez, Lazarus families were interrelated. Soldiers and officers of the Revolutionary War and the War of 1812 and every war fought since, were among Cardozo's kin. The affairs of the Congregation Shearith Israel of New York were "in almost unbroken succession" in the hands of members of the clan.

It was a distinguished record stretching from the days of the patriot rabbi of the Revolution, Rabbi Gershom Mendes Seixas, to the present time. In his own day, Benjamin Cardozo could call Emma Lazarus his cousin, as well as Robert Nathan, the novelist, and Maud Nathan, pioneer social worker, and Captain N. Taylor Phillips, who served in the First World War.

It was a proud, untarnished history but for one name. Justice Albert Cardozo, father of Benjamin, was the first Jew named a justice of the Supreme Court of the State of New York. He lost caste through his association with the notorious Boss Tweed and resigned his office while he was under investigation. "Lawyers who have gone deep into the study of the proceedings are of the opinion that he never accepted any money bribe from the Tammany boss, but they agree that the evidence is strong of his having taken orders." He based his resignation on the fact that "his value on the bench had been largely destroyed by reason of the accusations at the hearing." Although Benjamin was three years old at the time, this shattering of the father-image was perhaps the strongest single traumatic incident in his entire life. His life thereafter was lived as if he tried to atone and to compensate for his father's involvement with Boss Tweed, for the doubts that were raised whenever Albert Cardozo's name was mentioned. The father went back to his legal practice. His friends stood by him loyally. He was elected one of the Grand Sachems of the Tammany Society. But the son, sensitive, abnormally shy and retiring, never forgot.

Perhaps if his mother had lived, things might have turned out more happily for young Benjamin. He lost his mother when he was nine. It was a sad, bleak household, in which his sister Ellen valiantly tried to take over the mother role. Such a relationship can become tyrannical as well as tender. In later years, when Nellie, as he called her, was a confirmed invalid, she exacted from her then famous brother many compensating attentions for the ones she had lavished on him in his infancy. "The man who felt such deep concern over his sister's illness disregarded as far as possible ill-health of his own. When she died, he was bereft. His most cherished letter was one which Justice Oliver Wendell Holmes wrote to Cardozo on the subject of grief. Holmes was then deeply mourning his wife. Cardozo, the last of his family circle 'was still sorrowing for Nell.' " "There was in the letter," writes a cousin of Cardozo, "a remarkably beautiful expression of grief . . . there emanated from the pages an exquisite realization of the fugitiveness of all Life . . . a quiet regret at the little it was possible to accomplish in even a long life."

At home the strictest orthodoxy prevailed. Membership in the Congregation Shearith Israel was not to be taken lightly. Besides Albert Cardozo was vice-president of the congregation and a brother-in-law of its rabbi. Close ties were maintained with the synagogue. At thirteen young Benjamin was confirmed by Rabbi H. Pereira Mendes, a scholarly, dynamic, forceful figure in Jewish life. Rabbi Mendes left a lasting impression on Benjamin Cardozo. When he died in October, 1937, his former pupil wrote of Rabbi Mendes:

What can I say, save that I have loved and honored him? His sweetness was unique and beautiful. Now that the life is finished it is that personal phase of it which is uppermost in my thoughts. The larger achievements will be measured by the world.[12]

It was a sustaining and wholesome relationship for the orphaned boy. How deeply ingrained was this sense of orthodoxy and conformity to traditional Judaism which he learned from Rabbi Mendes, may be seen from an incident in Cardozo's later life. In 1897, when Cardozo was twenty-seven years old, Shearith Israel moved from its Nineteenth Street location to Central Park West, where it is now. At that time dissident factions proposed a modification of some of the traditional observances and practices, such as the wearing of hats, the segregation of women, the chanting of prayers in Hebrew. The debate had been heated.

Young Benjamin Cardozo . . . was the only speaker. He talked for an hour or more, pleading for continuance along the old lines which had been followed for centuries. He was appealing to sentiment; and then he left sentiment behind. He denied the right of the congregation to go against the stipulation of its own constitution.

He won his point.

One of the happier aspects of young Cardozo's growing up had to do with his tutor. Albert Cardozo, in order to keep his children's orthodoxy untarnished, decided against sending them to public schools. Instead he engaged a tutor namer Horatio Alger! Here was "a roly-poly little man, shy, and not at all forceful," who loved boys and who had become a teacher after some years of being "an ineffectual young minister." When Ben Cardozo applied for admission to Columbia, the sole educational reference that he could muster was that his preparation had been the work of Horatio Alger. Whatever his educational shortcomings, he was indoctrinated in his impressionable years by one who believed in the fairy-tale pattern of life—that success was possible to any American boy who really set his mind to it. Cardozo did. He was known as "Nathan the Wise" at Columbia.

The academic honors he won—he was a member of Phi Beta Kappa and valedictorian of his class—were but a prelude to a life of recognition and accomplishment. Prophetically he chose as his commencement address, "The Altruist in Politics." It was the keynote of his life.

Benjamin Nathan Cardozo was the quintessence of Americanism. He was a quiet, gentle, ascetic, self-sacrificing, altruist. His brilliant mind was dedicated to the highest social purposes. His accomplishments as a "lawyer's lawyer" brought him deserved eminence. After twenty-two years in private practice he was elected on a Fusion ticket to the New York Supreme Court in 1913. In 1926 he was nominated by both parties and chosen Chief Justice of that court. He was indefatigable in his efforts to simplify the law. He found time to sum up his legal philosophy in his books. *The Nature of the Judicial Process, The Growth of the Law, The Paradoxes of Legal Science* were notable contributions to American jurisprudence. Yet the pattern of his life remained consistent. He was a solitary man, a simple, dedicated public servant, a quiet, contemplative, modest, retiring scholar. Now great honors came to him. His alma mater conferred the honorary doctor of laws degree. Then Yale. Then Michigan. And Harvard. Other universities vied with each other in saluting the gentle scholar— State universities of New York, Massachusetts, New Jersey, Pennsylvania, Brown University, Chicago, Williams, Yeshiva College. Cardozo considered himself "a mere plodding mediocrity." The president of St. Lawrence University saluted him as a

modest and cultured gentleman at home in the world of art, philosophy, and literature, but especially distinguished as the legal scholar and jurist whose written opinions are models of substance and style, universally trusted as a man of wisdom, equity, and mercy, lover and friend of mankind, whose character, personality, and authority inspire confidence and give a sense of security in these troublous times.[13]

Surely not in his one hundred or more novels did Horatio Alger produce a greater hero than this pupil of his. It is a strange paradox, but one that needs to be recorded, that the life of Alger was published in 1928 under the title *A Biography Without a Hero.* The year before, Alger's former pupil had been offered by President Coolidge the signal honor of becoming one of the American members of the International Permanent Court of Arbitration at the Hague, whose other American members were Charles E. Hughes, Elihu Root and John Bassett Moore. Cardozo declined in order to continue serving the people of his State. Could Alger's life have been totally devoid of a hero?

The ultimate promotion was offered in 1932 to Cardozo, a Democrat, by President Hoover, a Republican. It was an appointment "hailed by every section of the country." He had reached the apex of a noble career. On his sixty-first birthday, May 24, 1931, just prior to the culminating honor of his life, Cardozo summed up his life's philosophy in a lecture at the Jewish Institute of Religion. It was altogether fitting that he should accept the invitation of his good friend, Stephen Wise, to deliver the commencement address. He spoke on "Values." With searching candor he examined his personal faith. He had long since replaced with a rationalist deism his former adherence to orthodoxy. He came close to adopting Huxley's philosophy stressing the correlation of ethics and biology, particularly referring to Huxley's *Lay Sermons and Addresses.* Cardozo spoke of Tycho Brahe, astronomer of Denmark, and of his City of the Heavens where he charted the stars. "The submergence of self in the pursuit of an ideal, the readiness to spend oneself without measure, prodigally, almost ecstatically, for something intuitively apprehended as great and noble, spend oneself one knows not why—some of us like to believe that this is what religion means."

He had been appointed to fill the place of Justice Oliver Wendell Holmes, who had always been Cardozo's hero and model. No more fitting successor could have been found in the entire nation. Certainly none who had more revered Holmes, deferred to him, studied him, emulated him.

When Governor and Mrs. Herbert H. Lehman called on Cardozo to congratulate him on the great honor that had come to him, they found that

His whole attitude was of deep humility and modesty. He seemed to care nothing for this great honor and distinction which had been conferred on him. His only thought reflected a desire to serve the people of the country to the best of his ability.[14]

For six brief years he served his nation on the bench of the Supreme Court. For him justice was "the synonym of an aspiration, a mood of exaltation, a yearning for what is fine or high."

His picture always stood on Justice Brandeis' desk. Pointing it out to a friend two years after Cardozo's death, Brandeis said, his voice breaking with emotion, "You know that man, Justice Benjamin Cardozo. He was my very dear friend, a beautiful character. His work raised the standard of the New York Circuit Court of Appeals, and even of our Court. We were very close."

Nature cast him in a perfect mold. Who that was privileged to see him can ever forget him? The fine features, the gentle, sensitive eyes, the fleeting smile, the air of seeming to listen both to what was said and to an inner voice, so that he appeared to be simultaneously in reverie and actively participating, spectator and performer, the one who was to pass judgment and the one on trial before the court.

Praise can become fulsome. Words are inadequate. Cardozo was the apex of Jewish performance in America. It took almost two centuries to produce him. It needed the perfect fusion of two traditions to create his personality. It required a life of stern sacrifice, unswerving idealism, constant sublimation, intuitive mysticism, perpetual devotion and ceaseless self-imposed discipline to achieve the synthesis. The miracle was in the achievement.

We approach now a creative period in American history which for the Jews may be summarized by one word—participation. The creativity of American Jews defies condensation. There is no field, from athletics to zoology, that does not have its Jewish votaries, its adherents and luminaries. In teaching and research, in creative arts and literature, in industry and invention, in war and in peace, Jews are carrying their share of the burden. And that is an obvious understatement. The record is proud and honorable.

There are those who are so intimately identified with American culture as to have disinherited themselves from their contact with Judaism and the Hebraic tradition. There are some who are always wistful immigrants, overcome with nostalgia, steeped in indelible memories that go back to their childhood days under European skies. Still others there are whose natures are crucibles in which the two are inseparably intertwined. What matters is not their fantasy life but the labor of their hands and the fruits of their creative talents and the altar at which these are reverently laid. It is good to have it so.

Even a random selection of the daily press and the periodicals of importance today brings countless Jews within the spotlight of public concern and points out clearly the extent of their involvement and participation in the fluid, current, contemporary scene. In the newspapers and magazines as they pour off the presses, there is overwhelming daily evidence of the extent and the intimacy of the sharing, the partaking and participating of Jews in their times and in their land.

The history of Jews in America has become a part of the history of America. Separation is impossible. To speak of Brandeis and Cardozo is to speak of American jurisprudence. To speak of Damrosch and Gershwin is to speak of American music. It is not so much that the Jew is losing his individuality or his specific identity as it is that he is fusing with once strange elements to form something new.

Here is *Time* Magazine for February 24, 1947. The entire first page is devoted to David E. Lilienthal, "Public Servant," native of Illinois, graduate of the Harvard Law School, head of the TVA and of the Atomic Energy Commission. Surely one of the men in our times in whose hands the greatest powers are concentrated. Writing in the *Menorah Journal*, this man who had been under bitter attack in Congress because he is a Jew, stated in 1948 his belief in "Democratic Faith in Man." It is an American credo: "I speak of the substance of things. I am asserting that the vitality of our distinctive institutions . . . depends . . . upon . . . ethical and moral assumptions and purposes."[15] Is not this consistent with the spirit of Thomas Jefferson and the dedicated founders of the American nation?

So Albert Einstein is saluted by the *New York Post* for his kindness and gentleness as well as for his mathematical genius. The *Saturday Evening Post* examines the services of Isador Lubin, President Roosevelt's "favorite economist." "The Legacy of Jerome Kern" is acclaimed in *Liberal Judaism* and is saluted by Lloyd Lewis in the *Chicago Sun*. Ben Cohen is celebrated in *Time* as a "quiet, unstuffy . . . key figure in the State Department." He is denounced in the *Chicago Tribune*, in a blistering editorial headed "Renounce the Lies." Reviewing a speech of Ben Cohen's before the American Philosophical Society, the editorial states: "Now, quite naturally, Cohen wants to commit the nation eternally to this whole series of lunacies." The reference is to the bipartisan foreign policy of the United States. "If they and Cohen had their way the country would be committed in perpetuity to the New Deal policy." "The Faith of a Jew" is discussed in *Time* in connection with Franz Werfel, "a Jew who writes so much like a Christian." Jewish owners of department stores have their day in the *New Yorker*. Bernard M. Baruch gives the keynote speech in 1948 at the *Herald Tribune* Forum. In identifying him the paper states that Baruch "drew up a plan for the most powerful agency on earth, tied the atomic-control plan which bears his name to a scheme to police the world for possible violations." Morris Raphael Cohen, an "irritating" philosopher who was always making his students think, is discussed in *Time* magazine. This iconoclast who warred on "petrified complacencies" is skeptical, but he has a faith of sorts: "that man is fallible and should therefore be humble, tolerant of other people's ideas." Cohen was a philosopher whose influence touched many facets of American life. "Though a layman, he has influenced Frankfurter and many another jurist. In his writings, he is unsparing of friends like Holmes, Brandeis and Einstein as he is of his enemies."

A Milwaukee schoolteacher received a fanfare in *Harper's Bazaar*. Mrs. Golda Myerson is described at length as "Envoy Extraordinary of Israel." President Truman paid public homage to Oscar Straus and his brothers, Nathan and Isidor. Said the President:

> I wish we could have the same tolerance today to meet the situation with which we are faced as we had in 1852 and 1854, when the Straus family came to this country. . . . This great man stood for tolerance and reason. He did more for the Christians in Turkey than all the ambassadors we had there up to that time. . . . Oh, that we had more like him! I wish we could raise some more of the same stock.[16]

"During the war I met only one admiral in the Navy Building, who didn't act, think and talk like a stuffed shirt," writes Edwin A. Lahey in the *Chicago Daily News*. "He was Rear Adm. Ben Moreell, head of the Bureau of Yards and Docks." The reference is to the Utah-born Jewish officer who has had a distinguished record in the Navy since his enlistment in the First World War. A Boston rabbi, Joshua Loth Leibman, wrote a book in 1946 which made the best seller lists for two years, and was translated into eleven languages. In his personal quest for *Peace of Mind*, he evolved a synthesis between psychoanalysis and religion which satisfied the needs of people of many religions in his own and other countries. When he died Boston closed its public schools and little children were "among those who listened to the services."

The United Nations Charter was signed in 1945 by Sol Bloom, among others. Once Tammany's choice for Congress because he was "an amiable and solvent Jew," he became in 1938 chairman of the Committee on Foreign Affairs, at a time in his nation's history when foreign affairs determined much of American history. The parents of Meyer Levin were present when the portrait of one of America's greatest war heroes was unveiled in the Hall of Fame in the Pentagon. Then Meyer Levin's father, Samuel Levin, a naturalized American, said to Secretary of Defense Forrestal that he was glad "we gave something fine to our country." Herbert H. Lehman received from workers in the garment industry the 1948 medal for "Interfaith in Action."

In the postwar years, Americans could view the paintings of Marc Chagall. They could see and discuss the sculpture of New York born Jacob Epstein. They could admire Jo Davidson's massive sculpture-portrait of Gertrude Stein. They could and did pay homage to the "Nation's Number One Melody Man," Irving Berlin. They could pay tribute to the memory of the gifted critic, Paul Rosenfeld. He was a man whose life was an "astonishing history of single-minded devotion to the arts in America." He approached the work of others "with so little envy and so much love . . . yet through his lifetime he carried deep within him the traditions of a German-Jewish household of the early 1900's that gave all their hopes to Culture." He fused within himself what was best in that home and best in America, and so became one of "the real princelings of criticism."

There are several categories of participation. First, there is the group which makes its total identification with specifically non-Jewish concerns and affairs, stressing severance rather than kinship. Second, there is the segment of society which admits relationship but minimizes its importance, maintaining a shoulder-shrugging attitude toward Jewish problems and needs in America and elsewhere. Third, there is the rank and file, embracing numerically the largest group, which is able to lead a threshold life, permitting an easy relationship in both Jewish and non-Jewish circles. Finally there is the group which maintains and perpetuates those elements in its life which are strongly reminiscent of European antecedents. Within each group leaders have evolved who speak for their followers. From the days of the creation of the Board of Delegates of American Israelites in 1859 there has been a continuing effort to devise techniques for unification and cohesion. In the ensuing ninety years numerous other agencies have supplanted the Board of Delegates. The oldest and most representative group, embracing many strata of American Jewish society, is the B'nai B'rith, which anteceded the Board of Delegates by sixteen years. The American Jewish Committee, the American Jewish Congress and the Jewish Labor Committee are offspring of the twentieth century.

To the integrated American Jew, many names are part of his universe of discourse which are less known in the great community. Except for the fraternity of scholars in the social sciences, the average non-Jewish Americans are unfamiliar with them. The scholars like Solomon Schechter and Louis Ginzberg; the philosophers like Horace M. Kallen and Mordecai M. Kaplan; the historians like Alexander Marx and Max J. Kohler; the sociologists like Jacob Lestschinsky and

Nathan Goldberg; the administrative leaders like Cyrus Adler and Louis Marshall; the full-time volunteers in social work involving co-ordinated leadership in America and directing of large-scale medical programs in Israel, like Rose Jacobs and Tamar de Sola Pool; the rabbis upon whom has devolved the mantle of leadership, like Solomon Goldman and David de Sola Pool. These are some of the names. . . . Also words which have special meaning to the Jews of America, which, like nicknames within a clan, tend to unite them by common acceptance and understanding—words like HIAS, YIVO, ICA, ORT, names of important social institutions in Jewish life.

So with the development of their own leaders, communal organizations, vocabularies, there were forged new links in American-Jewish life, uniting and integrating culture traits, welding scattered groups into unified patterns of activity. There are diverse culture areas in the structure of American-Jewish life. But there is also an over-all pattern to which Jewish communal life conforms. Sociologists are beginning to recognize this fact. Indeed one of the foremost Jewish sociologists, Arthur Ruppin, noted this factor when he described the "ascendancy of American Jewry" to a position of leadership among the Jews of the world. "The influence of American Jewry is marked even in the cultural life of East European Jews," wrote Dr. Ruppin in 1934, on the eve of the decade of destruction and annihilation. "They have founded and maintain schools, orphanages. . . . Consciously or unconsciously they impress on the East European Jews the superiority of their own outlook, and American-Jewish influence penetrates into the remotest Jewish communities of Eastern Europe." The forces of accommodation and assimilation are, according to the same authority, rapidly carrying the American-Jewish community closer to the culture patterns of the majority, away from the differentiating customs and practices which once served to separate Jewish folkways and mores from those of the larger group. As cultural pluralism in America shows signs of weakening, there are many astute students, Christians and Jews, who note this tendency with regret.

So a struggle began—a titanic contest for survival—in which the forces for accommodation and assimilation struggled for supremacy with those of survival through participation. At this moment, the victory is to those who have solved their personal conflict through greater involvement both as Jews and as Americans.

The record of participation assumes vast dimensions. In a postscript chapter to four centuries of Jewish life on the Western Hemisphere, it is obviously impossible to do more than to point to the peaks of the icebergs.

The ultimate test of a man's participation in his country's life is his willingness to die in combat for his country's sake. There is no greater test and no higher sacrifice. The record of Jews as soldiers transcends words. For they have grasped this ultimate truth, hugged it to their hearts, and quietly, magnificently, heroically demonstrated their faith on every battlefield, for every land that offered the Jews sanctuary. In 1915 a Jewish soldier who called himself "Litvak" wrote a letter. It was written on the sixteenth of May, just before the battle in France in which he met his death. He wrote:

... I know that we shall fight well, and that we shall die facing the enemy, and we will show every one that the Jews know how to die proudly.

Death has no terrors for us when we think that it will not be unperceived, and that it will benefit our persecuted Jewish race. And we shall show France that the Jews know how to die for a country which makes no difference between her sons. ... I feel myself a Jew and a soldier. In an hour we shall be marching, and we shall die for France, for the Jews, for the emancipation of all the Jews. Vive la liberté, vive la République, vive la libre, noble et démocratique France![17]

It was a simple East European Jew who left us this priceless legacy. Beside him there stand the ghostly armies of his fallen comrades in two world wars.

It is a woefully incomplete record, the story of Jewish participation in its recent wars. "The full record of American Jewish participation during a great war has not been made public." This was the serious charge made—and justly—by Dr. Joshua Bloch on March 26, 1943, of a war fought a generation earlier. "What has happened to the more than 150,000 individual records of American Jews who served their country in a great war? ... Now that almost a quarter of a century has passed since the demobilization, it is in order to ask that these records be made available."

Some quarter of a million American Jews served in the armed forces of the United States in the First World War, enough men to man eight full divisions. Of those who died in combat or as result of being wounded in combat there were three thousand five hundred men. So three per cent of the population accounted for five per cent of the combat dead. About twelve thousand Jews were wounded in battle. Praise was showered upon those who never returned and upon those who did by the heads of the American Expeditionary Forces from General Pershing down. One of the outstanding units of the AEF was the Seventy-Seventh Division. Lieutenant Colonel Douglas Campbell said of this group, which had the highest concentration of Jewish soldiers of any American division, "The Jewish boys of the 77th Division were the best soldiers on earth." Of the twenty-five hundred Jews who enlisted in the Marine Corps, more than a hundred became commissioned officers. There were close to ten thousand commissioned officers in the United States Army in the First World War. Since relatively few of them were West Point graduates, most of these men received their promotions at the front, often in the midst of battle. There were men like Brigadier General Charles H. Lauchheimer of the Marine Corps, who was awarded the United States Navy Distinguished Service Medal; Brigadier General Milton J. Foreman, commanding the One Hundred and Twelfth Field Artillery, who received the Distinguished Service Medal as well as French and Belgian decorations; Brigadier General Abel Davis, who received the United States Distinguished Service Medal and the French Legion of Honor Medal. Rear Admiral Joseph Strauss, who bottled up the German U-boat bases, commanded the mine force of the Atlantic Fleet and was decorated for his magnificent record—laying a fifty-seven-thousand-ton mine barrage in the North Sea. He served forty-four years as a naval officer before his retirement on his sixty-fourth birthday, having graduated from Annapolis in the class of 1885. His experiences on active duty in the Spanish-American War proved most useful in his World War I assignment. He was an inventor of note. Ten years after his graduation from Annapolis, he invented the suppressed turret system for mounting battleship guns. He invented the first spring-recoil gun mount, was a pioneer in smokeless powder improvement and designed a disappearing mount for submarine deck guns. In addition to the decorations which his own government conferred on him, he was made a Knight Commander of St. Michael and St. George by King George V and a member of the Legion of Honor of France. In 1937, despite his advanced years, he was recalled to duty by Secretary of the Navy Claude H. Swanson to serve on an advisory board in the planning and preparation of battleship construction. Commander Walter F. Jacobs was awarded the Distinguished Service Medal for commanding a division of mine sweepers in the North Sea. Admiral Joseph K. Taussig escorted convoys through submarine- and mine-infested waters. A number of Jewish officers commanded submarines, many of them besting the enemy in his own waters under extremely hazardous conditions. There was a radio operator who became a hero in an encounter with an enemy submarine. He was Ensign L. W. Freedman, who was cited "for distinguished and gallant conduct. . . ."

The Air Force was then young. It numbered many Jews. There were more than three thousand Jews in service, of whom 374 were commissioned officers. Some of the officers flew behind the German lines returning with invaluable information. Others gave cover to our photographic planes. Still others attacked German aircraft and submarines. The Distinguished Service Cross and the Croix de Guerre were awarded to a number of these fliers.

There were six Jews who won the Congressional Medal of Honor in the First World War. Two hundred Jewish soldiers were awarded the Distinguished Service Cross. There were many other citations, awards, decorations.[18]

There are so many feats of heroism!

Captain Robert S. Marx reorganized his battalion after its ranks were decimated. Wounded severely, he led an attack on the enemy and "displayed highest quality of courage and leadership in the face of a murderous artillery and machine gun fire." In Belleau Wood, the Germans held an impregnable position, their guns concealed by rocks and shrubs. Lieutenant Jacob H. Heckman aided by three sergeants crept forward to capture the enemy outpost. Against their spitting machine guns, he held only a pistol in his right hand. He rushed the enemy. The Germans offered violent resistance. Heckman came back. Before him with upraised arms and heavy feet walked a German officer and ninety other prisoners. Young Arthur Biesenthal was a private. He carried wounded comrades to safety from a forward dressing station until he was hit by a shell fragment and was no more. This form of heroism was marked among Jews. Of the one hundred and ten men who met death giving aid to the wounded in the AEF, sixty-four were Jews. Of the sixty-three men who volunteered as runners and dispatch-carriers between outposts under fire, thirty-seven were Jews. When the Lost Battalion was fighting its last ditch stand, surrounded by the enemy, outnumbered, its ranks depleted, when one after another dispatch runner was killed while attempting to get help, it was Abraham Krotoshinsky who made it back to American headquarters and so saved the heroic remnant. Jacob Levi's company was surrounded on three sides by the enemy. He was killed when he volunteered to carry a message to headquarters calling for help. When Sergeant Abraham Cohen coolly took charge of a battery of dummy guns in an open field in Chateau-Thierry in order to attract enemy fire, "he drew intense enemy shelling and prevented the enemy from locating the real American guns." Sergeant Martin Beifus met his death in combat, refusing to be evacuated although critically wounded. He rallied his men keeping up their morale and spirits until the last.

A Brooklyn youth, Lieutenant Louis Cohen, was perhaps as decorated a soldier as the War brought forth. He was awarded the French Croix de Guerre with six citations, the Belgian Croix de Guerre with palm, the Cross or St. Stanislaus, the Order of the Bey of Tunis and a Medal from the French Minister of Interior. There was a certain Jewish family in New York:

Mrs. Gustave Jacobson had seven sons and a daughter. Shortly after the declaration of war her eldest son, Gustave A. Jacobson, enlisted in the army. Then Harry and Samuel joined the Signal Corps. Simon signed up with a gas contingent. Benjamin joined the 305th Artillery. Jacob enlisted in the aviation branch of the service. Of her seven sons, only Daniel, not yet 15, remained home. Within a year Mrs. Jacobson received word that Harry had been killed, Simon had been wounded and promoted to a sergeant, and Jacob had been injured in an airplane crash.

Suddenly, the boy Daniel, disappeared. A police search for him proved fruitless. He seemed to have dropped completely out of sight. When the Armistice came, five of the six sons Mrs. Jacobson had sent to the army returned, two of them wounded. And one Sabbath eve Daniel returned, too. He had gotten himself accepted in the Marine Corps by changing his name and falsifying his age.

A generation later, a Jewish family of Opelousas, Louisiana, where Elias Stultheus, *"le juif,"* had first trod American soil, had the distinction of contributing six children to the armed forces of their country. The children of Julius B. Stander and his wife were:

Major Lee H. Stander
Lieutenant Lloyd Stander
Lieutenant (j.g.) Otis B. Stander
Corporal Alvin Stander
Private Bernard Stander
Seaman Esther Stander (a Wave)

"I know that we shall fight well, and that we shall die facing the enemy, and we will show every one that the Jews know how to die proudly."

The long armistice was like a trench between two raging fires. The Second World War was the inevitable climax of the Black

Decade. The bells tolled all over Europe for the tortured and impaled, the frail, the persecuted victims of the bestial Nazis. The dirge that sounded the knell of civilization penetrated every isolationist hideaway. The islands on which the secure dwelt became fortresses under attack. It was a plague that could not be quarantined, a contamination that spread its deadly germs, a pox that killed.

Now young Jews, like crusaders of old, rushed to their standards. There were five hundred and fifty thousand of them. They enlisted in every branch of service. Boys too young to be called up bullied and cajoled their parents into signing those precious papers which would enable them to get into uniform and overseas. Sensitive young men put away slide rule, notebook, microscope, and lined up at enlistment centers. They put aside their baseball bats and amateur radio sets and model airplanes and learned how to operate tanks and shoot guns of every caliber. They flew the planes and shot the cannon and drove the Sherman tanks. They died on every battlefield from Iwo Jima to the Roer River. They knew how to die.

"If there must be rubble," wrote one soldier in his teens from Normandy, "then I am glad that our country is spared."

So they added another chapter in Jewish participation in American life, in the Second World War.

They began with Pearl Harbor to write an imperishable record in the annals of American valor. Again it was Brooklyn that gave them their first hero. Lieutenant Commander Solomon Isquith received the Navy Cross for directing the rescue of the crew of the *Utah*. There is a destroyer named for a young Minneapolis boy, Ensign Ira Jeffery, who was killed while keeping the ammunition supply going on the battleship *California*. And Private Louis Schleifer, who met his death while trying to rescue his plane at Hickam Field. At Bataan and Corregidor there were many dead and missing in action and some who were taken prisoner. A soldier from Los Angeles, Lieutenant Henry D. Mark, was killed in combat, throwing hand grenades at close range at a Jap tank! Radioman David Goodman was awarded the Silver Star and the Oak Leaf Cluster for helping bring General Douglas MacArthur out of Corregidor, himself to be reported missing in action. A machinist's mate on a submarine, Murray Weinrub, added "another brilliant saga to the feats of the Navy's undersea vessels."

The bombardier of Colin Kelly's plane was Sergeant Meyer Levin of Brooklyn, who added a brilliant chapter to American military heroism, twice sinking enemy ships in the Pacific and being twice decorated. He died in action in 1943.

At Iwo Jima, where so many brave young lives were snuffed out, Lieutenant Roland B. Gittelsohn, Chaplain of the United States Marine Corps, spoke these words over the fresh mounds of earth where America's heroes had just been buried:

Here lie men who loved America because their ancestors generations ago helped in her founding, and other men who loved her with equal passion because they themselves or their own fathers escaped from oppression to her blessed shores. Here lie officers and men, Negroes and whites, rich men and poor—together. Here are Protestants, Catholics and Jews—together. Here no man prefers another because of his faith or despises him because of his color. Here there are no quotas of how many from each group are admitted or allowed. Among these men there is no discrimination. No prejudices. No hatred. Theirs is the highest and purest democracy.

So in words worthy of being enshrined in the hearts of all Americans spoke a young American Jew, the first Jewish Navy Chaplain to become attached to the Marine Corps. He found the strength in Iwo Jima on the Pacific to comfort men of all faiths. But the source of his wisdom and compassion had stemmed from the Prophets of old and he had learned about them at the Hebrew Union College in Cincinnati.

They fought and died in Europe and Asia, on the Pacific and the Atlantic. They went down with their ships and in burning planes and in blazing tanks. Doctors died in forward dressing stations, like Dr. Jacques Saphier, who met death while caring for wounded marines at Guadalcanal. Chaplains met their death, like Rabbi Alexander Goode, who with three Christian chaplains went down with his ship February 26, 1943, after having given up their life preservers to enlisted men. Reporters died in action, like Lieutenant Morris B. Penner, formerly of the *San Antonio Express*, who exploded like a meteor with his plane flying over England.

Of the valorous Armored Command, whose symbol is one half of the Star of David, but two men are to be singled out, a general and a private. Both died in combat. Major General Maurice Rose, son of a Denver rabbi, has been named "one of America's greatest soldiers." "Although Maj. Gen. Maurice Rose's body reached Padderton on a litter atop the hood of a jeep, his spirit and brain had enabled his 3d Armored Division to accomplish one of the greatest surprise dashes in all military history." Thomas R. Henry who talked with General Rose shortly before his death writes:

We found the former cavalry officer, who was the son of a Denver Rabbi, a tired man. . . . For two weeks, since crossing the Rhine at Bad Godesburg, his division had been constantly on the roads and under fire. Only the day before, with two aides and two privates, he had fought a close-up battle in a cemetery against twenty German soldiers who were firing from behind gravestones. They had killed ten of the enemy and captured the others, and had brought their prisoners back to headquarters in the general's jeep. . . .

Possibly there was some vague presentiment of approaching death in the tired man's melancholy tones the night we talked to him. . . . He talked of his hope that the war would soon be over. . . . He was eager for that day to come when he could play with his four-year-old son, whom he had left as an infant. But, as he told of his hopes, his voice seemed to lack conviction.

General Rose had helped liberate Belgium. It was a brilliant campaign. "With this enemy army slaughtered or captured, General Rose, who had taken over the 3d Armored several weeks before, made a quick turn northeastward and during the next eight days helped to liberate Belgium." The victorious Armored Command continued its spectacular campaign.

General Rose was the first army commander since Napoleon to invade the Reich from the west. . . . But the tanks had been almost constantly on the move and in action for more than two months. The big steel machine was running on nerve and mechanical miracles. Tanks were tied together with bailing wire. The 1st Army was short of gasoline. The men had been pushed to the limit of human endurance.

There followed a moonlight battle for the city of Marburg.

This is recognized as one of the most critical actions of the war. It is referred to in War Department reports as "the battle of the Rose pocket," in memory of the leader who fell there. After that, everything was anticlimax. The 3d Armored continued westward. . . . It liberated the terrible prison camp of Nordhausen . . . the men of the 3d Armored found 1500 bodies of slave workers in piles like cordwood.

That was the general.

And now for the private who also fought with the Armored Command of the First Army. He was the youngest soldier in his company. Ben Hecht wrote of him: "He was one of the young knights who went forth to bring the sky back to us. . . . I shall always remember his young, clever face turned fearlessly toward the enemy." That was David R. Lebeson, a private of the 743rd Tank Battalion whose motto is: "We keep the Faith." He volunteered at a critical moment to ride through the snow-banked Ardennes Forest, to round up the men in his unit whom, because of their performance on the battlefield, the enemy had dubbed "Roosevelt's Storm Troopers." The men of the 743rd were in rest areas after heavy engagements with the enemy. American forces had been surprised by the fury unleashed by the enemy in the Battle of the Bulge. Every man was needed at his station. The commanding officer calling for a volunteer added that the assignment meant almost certain annihilation.

The scenic beauty of the Ardennes is a tourist's delight and a soldier's terror. No battleground is beautiful to the man who must fight upon it. The narrow hinterland roads that climb and descend through strands of trees, skirting streams and cliffsides, might look well on an artist's canvas, but wet and slippery they are a dangerous stretch of hazards for the man at the controls of a tank—particularly at night, when he had to guess where the road stopped and a drop down the mountain side began.

Young David volunteered for the job, carried out his assignment, and was killed several battles later, in combat February 27, 1945.

That is the chapter which Jews in America wrote in the Second World War.

"Shall we give you glory?" asks a poet in an elegy, "To the Jewish Dead,"

> Or shall we search, below the trumpets,
> In the mute, unyielding dust, to find the star
> You followed, the dream-America
> So worth the cost, the young not coming home?[19]

"And the sons of Israel have kept faith with the Land of the Free. And they loved the Land of Liberty which upheld the worth and the dignity of man."[20] In these words in the fourth decade of the twentieth century does a psychiatrist sum up the role of Jews in America. They loved the land and shared in its vicissitudes and fought its battles and took the nation's troubles to their hearts. In addition to general reverses—and in the years of the depression they were not inconsiderable—Jews had a private and special anguish of their own. They were condemned to stand helpless while their kinsmen were decimated. It had begun at the end of the First World War. On March 8, 1922, there was an article in the *Nation* calling attention to the appalling loss of Jewish life in Europe. "The Murder of a Race" was described and pogroms of appalling proportions were noted. Of 694 pogroms in the Ukraine, 38 were by Poles, 54 by Petlura gangs, 509 were carried out by miscellaneous gangs, many of them under Petlura's influence.

Jews were unhappily in the news. It was a solemn decade, paving the way for the more tragic decade of the thirties. In 1920 the American Jewish Committee and other Jewish organizations had issued a formal denial of the lies being circulated as the *Protocols*. Attempts were made to link Jews with Communism. This too led to vigorous denials. The following year, 119 leading Christians issued a vigorous plea for fair play, denied the flagrant falsehoods which were disseminated by antisemites, pointed out the "Peril of Racial Prejudice." John Spargo collected the signatures for this document. The names of two former Presidents of the United States headed the list—Taft and Wilson. The Federal Council of the Churches of Christ in America passed resolutions condemning antisemitism. But the Ku Klux Klan was waxing stronger in many parts of the country. Meretricious journalists were available to spread untruths and calumnies. Against them Christians and Jews labored valiantly seeking to expose the lies, to tell the truth as the facts would prove. Max J. Kohler laboriously collected supporting data and early in 1923 they were published in Anglo-Jewish periodicals. Norman Hapgood was indefatigable, refuting perversions of truth. His series of articles also appeared in 1923. On the twenty-third of April, 1923, the trustees of Harvard University rejected President Lowell's formula for the Aryanization of Harvard by voting to adhere to "its traditional policy of freedom from discrimination on grounds of race or religion." Four years later, having been sued for libel by Aaron Sapiro, Henry Ford presented to Louis Marshall a complete retraction of his defamation of Jews together with an apology to the Jewish people for the campaign of vilification which he had sponsored. "The Ford apology brought to an end the only systematic anti-Jewish agitation in the United States until that time."

American Jews shared vicariously the evil times that had befallen their coreligionists in Europe. But they were not spared indignities of their own. On the eve of Yom Kippur in September, 1928, in Massena, in the State of New York, a little girl wandered away from her parents. The rabbi of the community was led by a state trooper to the mayor's office for questioning. The mayor wanted to know whether among the Jews the custom of human sacrifice prevailed!

The child was found. But the shocking, appalling assumption by a mayor of an American community that such a thing was possible left a deep scar on the Jews of America.

In 1930 Rutgers University was charged with limiting the admission of Jewish students. Again the untiring Max J. Kohler presented a brief for the Jews in an oral statement before the State Board of Regents of New Jersey. A public statement by Rutger's University disclaimed the practice of the quota system. Two years later *The Army and Navy Register* printed an anonymous attack on the patriotism of American Jews. The editor was compelled by public protests which poured in to retract these vicious lies. The Secretary of War, Patrick J. Hurley, denounced the scurrilous attack. Nevertheless, overt and furtive antisemitic practices continued. But such troubles were relegated to the background as the news of anti-Jewish excesses in Germany began to supersede troubles at home. The age of violence and extermination had begun for the Jews. The era of degradation and death chambers was here.

The war was fought and won. American soldiers who helped to liberate enslaved Europe came back with indelible memories. The Jews in their ranks who had fought and bled every inch of the way with their Christian comrades saw the piles of dead bones stacked like cordwood and vowed that they would never forget the sight. They saw the handful that remained reduced to rags, bereft of dignity, stripped of everything they held dear, the orphaned survivors of the world's greatest disaster. The rescued wept. And the rescuers. The age of unreason had ended. More than six million Jews had been sacrificed to perpetuate a myth—the myth of Aryan supremacy. Now the Jews of America were united as never before. They would save the tragic remnant of Israel. They would rehabilitate the victims. They who had been so cruelly robbed of their past would be given a future. That was the blueprint of rescue. Now the Zionists worked harder than ever to speed the return of the homeless to a land which had belonged to their ancestors. Even the opponents of Zionism were more concerned with rescue than with ideology. But the solution was not yet in sight. There were to come years of added anguish, of heartbreaking disappointment, of cruel rejection.

It was so simple and yet so involved. Nobody wanted the remnant of Israel but their kinsmen in Israel. They could not go back to the cemeteries that once had been their homes. They could not remain in Germany to rebuild that land of wickedness and iniquity, of murder and foul deed. They had to take to the roads again. They had to go underground again. They had to steal their way to the seaports of the Mediterranean and smuggle their way back to Zion. They became people without passports, without addresses, without shelter. They were the stepchildren of their age, outcasts of every doorstep. The land that claimed them and prepared a brother's welcome for them, Palestine, was now snarled with foreign intrigue and surrounded with bristling British bayonets and ringed with a cordon of warships and patroled in the sky with swift planes. The scene was set for the greatest manhunt in history. The remnant of Israel on its final exodus was pursued, not by a handful of Egyptian hirelings, but by one of the mightiest nations of modern times—the sons of the Magna Carta, the descendents of liberty, the defenders of human rights. Now the gallant men of England, led by the indomitable Winston Churchill, were mowed down by a scythe wielded by a burly hater of Jews, Bevin. Even as they revered the memory of General Wingate who had been their true friend, so Jews added to their Haman lists their enemies who called them interlopers in their ancient land that they had reclaimed with blood, sweat and tears.

And in Palestine in the midst of the strife and the bitter dissension Jewish settlers paused to honor a British officer, Major General Orde Wingate. There, at the foot of Mt. Gilboa overlooking the plain of Esdraelon, a forest was planted in memory of a gallant Christian, a member of the sect of Plymouth Brothers, "a profound and reverent student of the Bible." Palestinian Hebrews called him *Ha'yedid*, the friend. While serving in Palestine he studied Hebrew and became an ardent Zionist. He was killed in Burma. But his friends in Palestine keep his memory green and lovingly tend a forest in his memory.

Long after the politicians who play games with human destiny are forgotten this gallant Englishman will live in the hearts of the people whose frail destiny and battered victims he espoused. And the forest of Esdraelon will remind them. . . .

Now the presses in America were rolling. Books and magazines and newspapers tackled the Jewish problem. Poets wept and even coldblooded reporters could not keep the moral indignation from seeping through their dispatches. The great heart of America was aroused. The men and women in America who were faithful to American democracy began to write letters to editors. Clubs passed resolutions. Congress was memorialized. The clergy led a campaign of re-education. They discovered kinship between the displaced wandering family of the year 1—for whom only stable-room could be found—with those sleeping under open skies, in the ditches of Europe and the wire cages of Cyprus. It became the fashion to talk about the Jews, their past and their future, reversing the old adage "ever since God forsook the Jews, it has not been good form to discuss them."

Then the Jews of America began their pleas for reason's sake. They became eloquent campaigners for justice for their kin. They bought pages in the daily papers so that they could reach their fellow Americans and touch their hearts and their minds. Long, long ago, one of their noblest sages, Maimonides, had said:

If men possessed wisdom . . . they would not cause any injury to themselves or to others; for the knowledge of truth removes hatred and quarrels, and prevents mutual injuries.

They told the truth. They shouted it from their housetops. They "advertised" their displaced Uncle Abrahams and their disinherited Aunt Saras. They publicized the stark grim reality, stripping their own pride to the raw. They clamored for justice. And when they could not get it, young American Jews went to war again. They joined groups of "Samson's Foxes" who were fighting to liberate Palestine and to open its gates to the caged citizens from Cyprus.

Karl Shapiro said what millions of American Jews were thinking when he wrote of "Israel":

When I see the name of Israel high in print
The fences crumble in my flesh; I sink
Deep in a Western chair and rest my soul.
I look the stranger clear to the blue depths
Of his unclouded eye, I say my name
Aloud for the first time unconsciously.[21]

And here is what another American Jewish writer wrote years before:

There is something absolutely startling in the world's sudden awakening to the probable destiny of Israel. To judge from the current literature of the day, as represented by the foremost European periodicals, it has been reserved for Christians to proclaim the speedy advent of that Jewish triumph for which the Jew has hoped against hope during his prolonged agony of twenty centuries.[22]

Prophetic words written by Emma Lazarus in 1883 to mark the end of the era of "prolonged agony" which had still to be endured for sixty-five long years!

The vigor with which Jews were asserting their will to live was only matched by the indomitable will which kept the displaced persons alive while waiting for admission to Palestine. A hundred thousand Americans saw Ben Hecht's pageant, "We Will Never Die." Millions of Americans were given graphic descriptions of the urgency of the case of displaced Jews. The *Saturday Evening Post* gave half a page to a photograph of a kosher kitchen in Bratislava maintained by the American Joint Distribution Committee, one of the illustrations for a story titled "The Second Exodus of the Jews." In the *American Scholar*, Robert Gordis was pleading for "The Jews —a Problem That Cannot Wait." John McDonald was asking, "What Road to Zion?" in *Fortune. Collier's* was describing the last stand of the Jews under the title "They'll Never Run Away." Henry Wallace on a fact-finding mission to Palestine cabled the *New Republic*: "I've learned a new . . . and powerful argument for the support of Jewish efforts in Palestine," saluting "the conquerors of the Negev." Christians became aroused and most deeply concerned over the obvious miscarriage of justice. Bartley C. Crum wrote *Behind the Silken Curtain.* Sumner Welles discussed our moral obligations in Palestine in *We Need Not Fail.* García-Granados, a member of the United Nations Committee on Palestine, described *The Birth of Israel* in terms of glowing sympathy. The columnists attacked the problem with vigor. Walter Lippman was loud in calling for "Clarification in Palestine." Anne O'Hare McCormick wrote that, "The British are leaving behind them a power vacuum which only the Zionists are prepared to fill." Eleanor Roosevelt, writing as "an outsider, a simple citizen of the United States," called attention to "the miserable, desperate people" in Cyprus, insisted that something had to be done for them. Sumner Welles wrote that, "It is by now an open secret that American volunteers are training and directing the Jewish Army."

For American Jews who had just put off their uniforms could not stand idly by. They could not read of the victims of the underground who, like Eliza, were pursued by baying hounds and were finally run down and imprisoned like animals in a zoo behind the barbed wire of a British detention camp in Cyprus. They had not fought the war for such a solution. Not for that were their comrades forever laid to rest under the Crosses and the Stars of David. Now there were new casualty lists in American newspapers. More obituaries.

Dov Seligman, twenty-five, formerly of 1465 Grand Concourse, the Bronx, was killed Monday in Palestine by Arab snipers, his family was informed by cable yesterday from Palestine. This announcement followed by two days the disclosure that another American, Mosheh Pearlstein, a Brooklyn youth, had been slain by Arabs in the Holy Land.

Mr. Seligman is reported to have been ambushed while driving a tractor on a collective settlement. . . . The settlement is operated by Hashomer Hatzair, a Zionist youth movement with an office at 305 Broadway. . . . Mr. Seligman, who changed his name to Dov when he became active in the movement, was known as "Tiny" because of his size. He stood 6 feet 2 inches and weighed 200 pounds. . . .

In November, 1942, he enlisted in the United States Army and was sent to the Pacific theater in 1944 as a sergeant in the ground crew of an Air Transport Command Unit. . . . He was mustered out in January, 1946.[23]

Dov Seligman was but one of many young Americans who went from uniform to uniform. Their war was somehow not to be counted finished until the last displaced person was provided with an address.

A full newspaper page was devoted to honoring the memory of William Bernstein, "young American hero, first mate of the Haganah ship *Exodus 1947* who was killed on the high seas by British forces while bringing his Jewish brethren home."

There was the day that was called "Colonel Marcus Day." Sunday, October 10, 1948, was set aside to honor a Brooklyn hero. A playground was dedicated which henceforth would bear the name of David Marcus.

Yesterday was observed in Brooklyn as Colonel David Marcus Day in memory of the Brooklyn veteran of World War II who was killed June 10 last while leading Israeli troops near Jerusalem. He was at the time supreme commander of Jewish forces in Jerusalem. Formerly he was New York City Commissioner of Correction.

On the memorial plaque which was unveiled in his memory was this simple statement: "Liberty and equality for all men were more precious to him than his life."

The perfect accolade for this hero came from President Truman, who wrote that the life and death of Colonel Marcus "symbolize all that is best in the unending struggle for liberty."

When Jacob Barsimson reached New Amsterdam in 1654, his arrival was top-level news spread from burgher to burgher by word of mouth. Now in 1948, almost three centuries later, Jews were again in the news. A new state was being created across the seas in Israel. The Jews of America were keeping step with historic events. Forty thousand Jewish War Veterans paraded down Fifth Avenue, April 4,

1948, in "one of the largest pro-Zionist demonstrations in the city's history." A quarter of a million spectators lined up to watch the veterans parade. "About 100,000 of the spectators crowded into Madison Square Park to hear pro-Zionist speakers declare that it is not too late for the United States to rally again to the support of Palestine partition." The Chief Police Inspector of New York said that it was "the biggest crowd ever in the park." They marched with military precision, these veterans of the war. They chanted as they marched. The burden of their chant was "A Jewish State in '48." Their Christian comrades marched with them, chanted with them. The American Legion was there and the Veterans of Foreign Wars and the Catholic War Veterans. . . .[24]

Jews made the news columns and the cartoons and the editorial columns.

Acclaimed in some cities, they were in hot water in several of our seaport towns where their participation in Israel's struggle for life involved them in arms traffic. Under a Miami, Florida, dateline we read that nine men were indicted for smuggling arms into Palestine—an act that is somewhat reminiscent of certain patriot activities in 1776. The nine men were residents of California and Connecticut, of Florida and New York. Among the "arms" shipped to Israel were three B-18's, and a Lockheed Constellation. But if they sent aircraft, American Jews also sent medical supplies, tractors and jeeps. One boat that left the United States in July of 1948 carried among other items: 4 ambulance interiors, 1,291 cases of dried milk, 1 hypo needle sterilizer, 1 obstetrical table and mattress, 3 cases of streptomycin, 1 case of vaccines and vitamins. One organization, the B'nai B'rith of Chicago, sent a truck, a trailer, an ambulance and four carloads of food. The Minister of Defense of Israel, in acknowledging the contribution of materials for Palestine, wrote that Israel was indebted to American Jewry for much help extended the new nation in a critical hour of its history. One incident is eloquent testimony of what American help accomplished in the battle for creating the new state. At two o'clock one morning an American ship docked at Haifa. Aboard were forty-two jeeps. A battle was in progress. "The jeeps were taken off the boat at once, gassed up and loaded with troops who reached Ramleh in time to support the attacking forces and turned a doubtful battle into a spectacular victory." Did not the taxi drivers of Paris once turn the tide of battle in the First World War?

For the Jews of America it was the busiest of times. They were deeply involved in events in Palestine. They felt the urgency of rescuing the Jews in the Displaced Persons Camps and on Cyprus. These men and women had to be clothed and their meager diet had to be supplemented. Their morale had to be kept up. Three years had passed since "liberation" and the end of the War. Yet the first victims of Nazi aggression were still herded together in barracks and in former prison camps. Medical supplies were needed and clothing for babies born in detention camps and "in the bleak, bare Limbo of Cyprus." Now the Jewish men and women of America addressed themselves to the job. Shiploads of supplies were sent. Social workers were recruited. Training schools were set up for the re-education of the remnant of Israel. Teachers were sent from America to teach new skills to musicians whose artist hands were blunted by slave labor and to professors whose once creative minds were dulled by the Beasts of Belsen. . . . Occupational therapy was wanted. It was supplied. The camps had to be emptied. Laws passed in the twenties imposed barriers to immigration. They had to be re-examined in the interest of fair play, because of the record which Jews in America had established. Testifying before a Senate Judiciary Committee, Edward Corsi, State Industrial Commissioner of New York and former United States Commissioner of Immigration, branded our immigration laws as obsolete.

It is a quaint relic of a racist attitude which we have just fought a war to defeat. Our laws express a brusque and summary judgment of the peoples of the world, and the lightness with which our inherited policy dispenses its insults can almost be measured. In large part they are entirely gratuitous, and no practical objective is served.

Corsi added that while from 1900 to 1917, approximately one million immigrants arrived in this country each year, this number had dropped to sixty thousand annually since the quota system was enacted. He foretold a critical labor shortage if such legislation remained on our statute books. Then he added, "Within ten years there will not be a tailor in the city to make a suit." A sociologist writing for the *Reconstructionist* astutely pointed out that the DP Admission Act of 1948 was akin to the discriminatory bill of 1924. The law is notorious for "Admitting Pogromists and Excluding Their Victims." The branded, the tattooed, the scarred Jews were rejected. Many of their oppressors made themselves at home in America. The blighted lives on Cyprus continued a reproach to civilization. An American woman flew to Cyprus to report conditions. In August,

1948, Ruth Gruber wrote that, "The spirit of the people today is even more hopeless, bewildered and explosive than last year . . . the mood was of a desperation close to the breaking point."

An indignant Montclair, New Jersey, correspondent wrote a letter to the editor of the *New York Herald Tribune,* calling for "a little more good will and a little less hypocrisy on our part," urging the adoption of the Stratton Bill. On the Fourth of July, 1948, in Pittsburgh, Pennsylvania, American Zionists heard their friends, Senator Claude Pepper of Florida and Dr. James G. McDonald, head of the American Mission to Israel, urge the American Government to help the struggling new State of Israel. Senator Pepper insisted that it was the duty of the American Government to ship arms to Israel. James Wellard, under a Rome dateline, wrote: "One hundred thousand Jews are waiting in Europe to move into Palestine after May 15. . . . There are 40,000 trained Jews in Italian DP camps alone." From Tel Aviv Richard Mowrer wrote:

No one here pays much attention any more to the floundering deliberations of the United Nations at Lake Success, N. Y. A Jewish state is being created, the war of independence is on, and the Jews have not much time to waste. At Lake Success, they are still trying to put the chicken back into the egg.

American Jews and their kinsmen would mark well the date in their history books—the fifth day of Iyar, 5708. On May 15, 1948, the State of Israel was born. It was a consummation two milleniums overdue. From all the corners of the earth, from every hiding place and hovel, from the reeking barracks and the teeming basements, from the converted prison camps and the rat-holes of Europe, Africa, Asia—the word went out that the unwanted ones were coming home. They had found an address at last!

For the Jews of America this was the turning point. The patient at whose bedside they had watched and agonized, whom they had supported and helped to rescue from certain death, was going to recover. He was on his own. American Jews could rejoice that the infant state had drafted its Constitution "in the spirit of the United States." It was altogether fitting and proper that their country at whose birth they had been present in 1776, whose honor and existence they had protected so loyally in the intervening years, should set a precedent to the newest republic on the earth. When they opened their newspapers and read the headlines: "Israelis Draft a

Constitution on U. S. Model," they could be proud and rejoice.

Subtly the tenor of the stories changed. For now there were Jewish victories on the front pages of American newspapers. Bold black headlines telling of battles won against overwhelming odds. Within a few brief months the miracle of world-wide acceptance had come to pass. Status had been achieved. Instead of pogroms there were triumphs to record—the kind of triumphs that all Americans love to read about, like Lexington and Bunker Hill and Yorktown. "Israeli Army Wins Control of All Galilee." "Israel's Negeb Victory." For thousands of years the Jews had been reciting every Passover the story of their flight from the Egyptians. Now suddenly and dramatically the historic roles were reversed. "The Jewish victories turned the tables on the Egyptians. Instead of the Jews being dependent on Egyptian good will to get supply convoys through the lines, it was now the Egyptians who were dependent on Jewish good will to get supplies through to their advance forces or what was left of them," wrote Marcus Duffield in the *New York Herald Tribune.* "Current Palestine Scene Is Characterized by Change. Israel Is Held To Be a Solid State but in Transition" is the page one headline over a story by Anne O'Hare McCormick in the *New York Times.* "Sea Battle Fought Off Tel Aviv, Israel Repels Egyptians. Planes, Corvettes Pursue Attackers. Israelis Threaten To Raid Cairo If Egyptians Try New Assault on Capital." That was still another page one story. "Samson's Foxes," comprised of the youth of the land, were winning skirmishes with the Arabs. Air and sea battles were waged and won.

It was a turning point in Jewish history.

The Jews of America are on the threshold of a renaissance. From the days of Haym Salomon they have shown concern for their indigent relatives in the little towns and villages which once were home to them. They formed associations and *Landsmanschaften,* philanthropic devices for raising money and maintaining contact with Pinsk and Vilna and Odessa. Now these communities of Jews have ceased to exist. Those who are left have Israel as their goal or have already reached it. Soon they too will be self-supporting and independent. So the Jews of America will have to revise their philanthropies, re-evaluate their institutions, redirect their thinking. They will undertake research projects to facilitate the evolution of a creative, vibrant Jewish life in America. They will have to find the moral equivalent for philanthropy. Already searching questions are being asked. Such an inquiry is that of a sensitive, gifted American-Jewish novelist, Irving Fineman, who asked the question: "Where Do We Stand Now?"

I ask of you here in America only that you rouse yourselves to the task of reviving the afflicted Jewish spirit—of strengthening it for its own preservation. . . . If you are concerned about the fate, not merely of the Jewish people, but of all humanity, study and learn what has been stored up for you in ages past.

In a magazine published by the American Jewish Committee, *Commentary*, "The Situation of the Jew" is critically examined by Jean-Paul Sartre. The American scene is surveyed by competent observers and social scientists. The *Menorah Journal* undertakes to analyze "Goals for Jewish Living." In its pages Rabbi Jacob Agus had issued a ringing call for a return to religion and the synagogue. Lee M. Friedman, President of the American Jewish Historical Society, agrees that, "Jewish leadership must stem from the synagogue . . . it is to American Jewry itself, rather than to Palestine, that we must turn for the hope of Jewish survival here." That this attitude ignores the irreligious Jew, unsynagogued as well as the synagogued, is the opinion of Professor Louis Gottschalk. A social worker, Harry L. Lurie, contends that, "The spiritual problem of American Jews in many respects is the problem of all Americans." It all points to an awareness of a crossroads dilemma. "Judaism must not be viewed as a burden, something imposed from the outside on the back of the American Jew. It must represent an enrichment of his life, directed towards his needs as a human being and as an American." That is the gist of the point of view stressed by Agus. "Is Religion a Flight from Reality?" asked Rabbi Abraham Cronbach in a searching analysis of the current social situation, finding that in the place it assigns to the father-image and to mutual aid, religion serves an indispensable role in the cultural life of American Jews. It remained for the late Rabbi Joshua Loth Liebman to summarize the situation of the Jew in the current American scene:

American Jewry is in the process of Becoming; it is not a static reality, rigid and arteriosclerotic. Part of the confusion of American Jewish life is due to our character structure as an adolescent compelled to assume the responsibilities of adulthood. Faced with the problem of maturity, some among us are mature enough to assume our historic role of Jewish destiny. Others would like to flee to some Shangri-La of uninvolvement and Jewish unrelatedness.

To Liebman there was no ideological conflict involved in a creatively dynamic Jewish life in America. Nor does a withdrawal from Judaism "make for a closer symbiosis with Americanism." In cultural pluralism is the secret of integrated participation in the national life of America.

To describe and place in their proper setting the hundreds of organizations which function within the framework of American Jewish society is the task of a sociologist. There are thousands of groups, representing many fragmentary aspects of cultural activities. They range from the little known to the familiar. They represent many types of needs, from the search for inner security to large-scale philanthropy. One might begin by mentioning one of the least known of these associations, the Jewish Theosophists of America. They had at one time their own publication, *The Jewish Theosophist*. Henry C. Samuels, one of the founders of the fellowship, describes the history of the group as follows:

During the Jubilee convention of the Theosophical Society, held at . . . Adyar . . . India, in 1925, a number of Hebrew members of the Theosophical Society have organized into an Association of Hebrew Theosophists. . . . It does not seem to me that I am a "Hebrew Theosophist, but rather a member of the Theosophical Society who is of the Hebrew faith. Also, being a Hebrew it is my sacred duty to make the best of my faith.

In *The Jewish Theosophist* one may find the hand of fellowship extended by Annie Besant and Krishnamurti to Jews and Christians as well as to the followers of the older religions. "Last year I had the pleasure of laying the foundation stone of a Hebrew synagogue on the Theosophical Society's estate at Adyar, and in our daily Act of Worship a Hebrew Theosophist chanted a Hebrew prayer," wrote Annie Besant in 1926. "The Message of Judaism" was interpreted in *The Jewish Theosophist* by Jinarajadasa in December of that year.

It was a strange departure—that American Jews should have sought to transfer the religious matrix of their spiritual association from Jerusalem to Adyar. This modification of traditional attitude, the pull toward peripheral contacts, toward derivative philosophies, needs closer scrutiny on the part of the sociologist. There are many such cultural deviations in American-Jewish life. The historian bows to the social psychologist, the anthropologist, the psychiatrist in interpreting human divagations. "Historians for centuries saw nothing but the surface motivations," is the bolt hurled by Dr. Franz Alexander

in a recent study. For the historian is the cartographer of the cultural
landscape. He notes the main rivers and also the tributaries. Another
such tributary organization, marking a departure from the main
stream of American Jewish thought, is the Freeland League. An
editorial in the *Ladies Home Journal* in September of 1948 called
attention to a "proposed Home For the Jews." Suddenly, dramatically, the clock and the calendar were turned back three hundred
years! For the Freeland League had fixed upon Surinam as a refuge
for homeless Jews of the twentieth century, a place where Jews had
sought shelter and sanctuary in 1639. So the *Joden Savanne* (Jewish
Savannah) which had once sheltered Jewish pioneers among its green
mansions would once more welcome the displaced wanderers.

These are examples of the fragmentary aspects of Jewish life in
America. The basic structural patterns of Jewish group life are
related to the basic needs of the group. They grow out of the religious, the social welfare, the recreational, the educational needs.
They are influenced by density of population, by proximity to metropolitan areas, by the cultural resources within the community, by
the presence of qualified leaders. Of all of these the most difficult area
to ascertain and to summarize is in the field of demography. While
certain generalizations are permissible and numerous excellent studies
have been published dealing with population trends, it is the con-
ensus of opinion that accurate analytical studies cannot be made at
he present time. "America has today the largest community of Jews,
perhaps the largest that ever existed, not excluding ancient Palestine," writes one scholar. Yet for all that it remains "a vast, demographic dark continent, regarding its past, present and possible
future," adds another scholar. The *Statistical Abstract of the United
States* summarizes the census of religious denominations, giving
number of congregations in the United States, listing "heads of families, seat holders and other contributors, but admittedly incomplete."
These data have been analyzed and interpreted by outstanding
scholars—Nathan Goldberg, Jacob Lestschinsky, H. S. Linfield,
Sophia M. Robison. "As you probably know from your correspondence with the various agencies in your search for population
figures for Jews, there are no really reliable statistics. All that there
is available are the very tentative estimates of total Jewish population," writes the author of *Jewish Population Studies*. There are
nevertheless significant studies of population trends, as well as qualified interpretations of distribution of Jewish population. The past
century saw a radical shift of population to the Western Hemisphere

as a result of immigration. "Accurate facts about migration are available only for the past century," writes Ogburn, describing the general
situation. Briefly summarized, the demographic picture of the Jews
in the United States, shows the following salient aspects: "The Great
Jewish Migration" began in 1881 and by the close of the century
more than a half million Jews had entered the country, more than had
migrated to this country in the preceding two centuries. By the outbreak of the First World War the total number of Jewish immigrants
rose to approximately two million. In 1947, the *American Jewish
Year Book* estimated that there were approximately 5,756,000 Jews
in the Western Hemisphere, of whom some five million lived in the
United States. Canada had some 176,000 Jews. Argentina accounted
for 350,000. Brazil had about 100,000. Other Latin American countries had smaller Jewish communities.

In 1906 there were 1,152 Jewish congregations—the statistics
being "admittedly incomplete." Thirty years later there were 3,728
congregations, with a claimed membership of 4,641,184.

In the *American Jewish Year Book* for 1947, Dr. Linfield summarizes the figures as follows: There are in the United States three
communities having more than 100,000 Jews out of a total for the
country of 967 Jewish communities. There are seven communities
in the country with a population range of 50,000 to 100,000 Jews.
There are thirteen communities of 20,000-50,000. There are thirty-
five communities of 8,000-20,000 and seventy-six communities of
2,000-8,000 Jews. The preponderant numbers are urban or living
in close proximity to metropolitan areas.

Earlier concentration along the Eastern seaboard has given way
to a marked westward movement. Urban concentration is reflected
in a declining birth rate which is characteristic of all city dwellers.
Also native American-Jewish families are smaller than immigrant
families. Hostile legislation restricting the entry of Jews coupled with
a declining birth rate forecasts a downward trend in population
figures. Another significant factor which should be noted and which
accounts for decrease in population is that the rate of exogamous
marriages has increased.

One scholar reports that forty-seven per cent of the Jewish students
at Yale, in 1944, believed that intermarriage between Christians and
Jews should not be discouraged. About one-fifth of the Jewish students at Yale had no opinion on the subject. Thirty-four per cent
did not approve of intermarriage. Approximately four-fifths of the
Jewish students at Cornell felt that exogamous marriages were work-

able. The rate of intermarriage is one of the major factors in downward population trends.

First, a relatively large number of such marriages end in divorce or separation; second, such couples usually have a low birth rate; third, some of their offspring do not identify themselves with the Jewish group. The growth of the Jewish population will therefore vary inversely with the trend of intermarriage.

One qualifying aspect does exist. For every Jewish Barkis who is "willing" there are many Christians who take a definite stand against intermarriage. The Jews may therefore owe to Christian reluctance to intermarry with them the retarding of the trend toward assimilation and consequent reduction of their numbers. But "Jewish men have a higher intermarriage rate than Jewish women. . . . And, finally, Jewish men and women are more likely to marry Protestants than Catholics." Depletion in the ranks of American Jewry is also due in some measure to the fact that conversion to Christianity has made additional inroads. Dr. Louis Finkelstein, President of the Jewish Theological Seminary of America, deplores "the stream of conversion from Judaism." He notes that in mixed marriages the tendency is to join the church of the Christian partner. At times the lack of Jewish education and complete ignorance of the tenets of Judaism drives Jews to seek religious solace in Christian churches, under the impression that religious therapy cannot be found in the synagogues and temples to which these converts are complete strangers. To meet this crisis in America an integration is needed to be fused through an ancient institution, the *Kehillah*, an authoritative body in whom administrative powers are vested. "A union of Jews ready to identify themselves with what is historically Jewish can lay the basis for an American version of the historic *kehillah*." Perhaps then will the tendency to seek shelter from slights and rejections be met with vigorous, positive countermeasures permitting Jews to take a definite stand rather than to flee from a menacing reality.

Another aspect of population studies in which there is much uncertainty is in the analysis of occupational patterns of American Jewish society.

The pattern of Jewish economic activity in the United States has changed markedly since the first wave of Jewish immigration from Eastern Europe in the 1880's. . . . The economic life of Jews is highly sensitive to the political and social climate in which they live. . . . As long as Jews are handicapped in their struggle to earn a livelihood because they are Jews, so long will there remain a specifically Jewish pattern of economic activity.[25]

In this way Dr. Goldberg summarizes the evolving patterns of economic life in America. The Jewish immigrants who came to the United States between 1900-1925 were largely artisans and skilled workers with a large sprinkling of men experienced in commerce. "A general survey of the occupational distribution of Jews in the United States reveals that it is similar to the occupational distribution of Jews as it existed before the war in most countries in Europe," writes Lestschinsky, adding that the percentage of American Jews in the liberal professions is somewhat higher than it was in the lands from which the Jews migrated. In addition to the influence exerted on Jewish immigrants by previous occupational patterns, the new environment exerts inevitable pressures upon them. Geographical location, and other ecological factors enter into the picture. Since 1900 the movement of Jews has been away from the factory in the direction of stores and offices. One-eighth of the gainfully employed Jews in sixty-one communities studied during the 1930's were in manufacturing. Nearly half of the group studied was in commerce. About fifteen per cent were clerical workers and almost twelve per cent were in the professions. The children of immigrants tend to turn to commerce, clerical work and the professions. An appraisal of "The Jewish Labor Movement in the United States" made in 1948 corroborates the difficulties of making scientific deductions from the data available. Also it shows the extent of integration and participation in the general scene. "Jewish labor on the North American continent is now so intimate and integral a part of the general American labor community that it is not possible to trace its outlines with precision and determine where its borderlines begin and end." Jews are found in appreciable numbers in the needle trades, in the leather industry and in food processing. They are beginning to enter the building industry in larger numbers. Labor unions serve to protect the workers and furnish social contacts and mutual benefits such as health services and group insurance and in some cases housing.

On the periphery of labor unions are auxiliary organizations like the *Arbeiter Ring* (Workmen's Circle). This group, organized in 1892, serves as a social club to its members. It provides recreational and educational facilities. It extends aid in sickness and death, maintaining a sanatorium in Liberty, New York, for its members who are stricken with tuberculosis. Ideologically the group is identified with

Socialism. It has attempted to bridge the gap between immigrant parents and native-born children by maintaining schools for children where both linguistic and ideological differences may be resolved. In 1948 the organization had 713 branches and a total membership of 70,000 in the United States and Canada. Other groups which stem from immediate needs, from political philosophies and from identification with Zionism have combined likeminded Jewish workers into closely knit organizations. The Jewish National Worker's Alliance and the Jewish Labor Committee are notable examples. The last-named organization was formed in 1933 pursuant to a call issued by B. Charney Vladeck. The Committee represented many labor organizations. They sought to alert America to the menace of Nazism. They advocated a boycott of German goods which was heartily endorsed by all American Jews. The group has maintained an active interest in the rise of the State of Israel and has joined hands fraternally with the *Histadrut*, the Labor party of Israel.

Group life in American Jewish circles revolved around the synagogue. It also grew out of the daily needs for fellowship, for contact, for interaction. It combined mutual interests growing out of economic needs as well as from the needs for education and recreation. To the urban dweller in a crowded tenement, relaxation was possible only away from home. So the café and the night school became extensions of the home. The wealthy Jews had their city and country clubs. But that was not enough. Synagogues developed recreational and social programs. Labor groups had their lyceums and recreational centers. Communities undertook programs for the integration of Jewish youth activities. Young Men's and Young Women's Hebrew Associations and Community Centers developed to satisfy many needs. These institutions are affiliated with the National Jewish Welfare Board, which in more than thirty years has expanded to include many areas of social and communal service. It was the major Jewish co-ordinating agency during both wars. It has added the sponsorship of the American Jewish Historical Society as one of its projects. It takes an active part in furthering Jewish education, maintains a research bureau, a lecture bureau, as well as a music and book council.

In 1906, the American Jewish Committee was organized. The Russian pogroms gave rise to a mass feeling of horror and the need became urgent to create a single agency to safeguard the rights of Jews wherever threatened and to assist the victims of the massacres and of discrimination. Among its leaders have been noted Jewish philanthropists—Judge Mayer Sulzberger, Oscar S. Straus, Jacob H.

Schiff, Louis Marshall, Julius Rosenwald, Cyrus Adler. "There was a dual leadership in communal life: the paternal, philanthropic leadership of the wealthy, Americanized, English-speaking Reform Jews of German origin . . . and the leadership of the Yiddish-speaking community, then just beginning to assert itself." The split between the two factions occurred at a time when a united front was most needed. A movement for an American Jewish Congress with a broad democratic base was initiated and supported by Louis D. Brandeis and other nationally known leaders. It became a reality in 1917. This was only a partial step in the direction of unity. There were a number of other agencies within the orbit of American-Jewish life. Social pressure in the direction of unity was repeatedly exerted. The Anti-Defamation League of B'nai B'rith was founded in 1913. The Jewish Labor Committee in 1934. These groups, together with the Union of American Hebrew Congregations, Jewish War Veterans and Jewish Community Councils, joined in 1944 to form the National Community Relations Advisory Council. The American Jewish Conference had been organized the year before, in 1943, to formulate immediate plans to rescue European Jewry, to help in solving postwar Jewish problems in Europe, to safeguard Jewish rights in Palestine. The attempt to take an active Zionist line created a schism, culminating in the withdrawal of the American Jewish Committee from the Conference. The United Jewish Appeal has constituted a cohesive force within the ranks of American Jews. Under its aegis three fund-raising agencies, the Joint Distribution Committee, the United Palestine Appeal and the National Refugee Service, have combined their efforts. Henry Morganthau, Jr., headed the UJA in 1947 and 1948; during that time $270,000,000 to meet current needs was raised. Since its inception in 1939, the United Jewish Appeal has raised more than $500,000,000. The money was used for refugee aid, overseas relief, aid to Israel and the resettlement of three hundred and fifty thousand homeless Jews. This is in itself a staggering achievement. But more than that, it contributes a documentary note to the age—an age which specialized in uprooting, displacing, exterminating Jews. That American Jews rose to a challenge which does not have its equal in all of human history, is their greatest achievement and triumph. For into their hands was thrust the role of ransoming, rescuing, restoring and re-educating the remnant of Israel. They accomplished the heroic task.

One of the most vigorous of institutions on the American scene in recent times has been Jewish education. The early attempts of

East European immigrants to preserve the Hebrew language and to instil the rudiments of religion into the young were pathetic, crude and thoroughly inadequate. The *heder* (Hebrew school) was a lamentable travesty on education. Reluctant children were compelled to attend after-school classes in converted stores and basements or dragged from the streets to their homes where the itinerant Hebrew teacher made his rounds when classes were not feasible. "The unsanitary, uninviting physical surroundings, the unpleasant associations which pupils connected with Jewish schooling, the identification of Jewish study with a mechanical repetition of meaningless words and phrases by rote did much to alienate the products of these hadarim [schools] from Jewish life."[26]

Vigorous measures were taken to remedy the situation. The New York Bureau of Jewish Education was established at the behest of the New York Kehillah. Dr. Samson Benderly was appointed as head, textbooks were prepared, expanded and modernized schools were set up. Hebrew Teachers' Colleges were established. Congregational schools were created. Sunday School teaching was strengthened in the Reform congregations. Institutions of higher learning attracted students who wished to specialize in Jewish education and community organization and group work. Gratz College in Philadelphia was founded from a bequest by Hyman Gratz in the closing years of the nineteenth century. The Teachers' Institute of the Jewish Theological Seminary was founded in 1909, and in the same year Dropsie College for Hebrew and Cognate Learning came into existence. The Jewish Institute of Religion founded in 1922 had the training of teachers as one of its purposes. Yeshiva University of New York has a graduate division for teachers. The National Council for Jewish Education publishes a magazine, *Jewish Education*, which seeks to interpret the needs of the American Jewish Community in terms of creative participation and integration of Jewish youth, to enable them: "to live bravely and affirmatively, to accept the realities in good cheer without illusion; to stand up and not yield, vindicating the integrity of his Jewish being according to the democratic rule of equal liberty for all men." An important agency for transmitting Jewish culture to America as it was once known in the European culture areas, is the Yiddish Scientific Institute, popularly known as Yivo. Disavowing all religious bias and political idealogy, this group sees itself as carrying on sociological research "essential for our healthy survival." A growing library of noteworthy studies has been published in both Yiddish and English. The Hillel Foundations of American

Universities have stressed courses in Jewish-leader training. The Jewish Chautauqua Society has brought into sparsely settled areas, speakers and information about American Jewish folkways and mores. Women's clubs and sisterhoods have furnished audiences and organized numerous educational and cultural forums. All indications are that the movement to foster Jewish education is growing by leaps and bounds.

Yet leaders of American Jewry are far from satisfied. A recent graphic appeal issued by Rabbi Louis Finkelstein of the Jewish Theological Seminary categorically asserts that only one-fourth of the Jewish children in America attend religious schools and that "there is a dearth of adequately equipped teachers." He foresees a "lost generation" growing up in America, cut off from needed knowledge and sustaining contact with fellow Jews and "therefore, failing to win the respect of their fellow Americans." Five million American Jews are served by one thousand two hundred rabbis. A comparable number of Presbyterians have nine thousand ministers.

The trend is in the direction of more intensive Jewish education in America. As philanthropic activities abroad tend to lessen, as American Jews have greater opportunities to examine their own institutions more carefully and support them more generously, there will in all likelihood be a revival of interest in Hebrew and Hebraism and a renaissance in Jewish education.

There are ceremonials, portentous and awe-inspiring, when at the base of a building or a monument, a few objects are solemnly consigned to the earth so that the generations of some future day will find them and marvel, saying, "Thus and so did they live long, long ago." Now a period in Jewish history which began with the quest for a utopia by Eldad the Danite ends with the realization of an age-old dream—the creation of Israel. The American chapter of Jewish history began with an exodus and ends on the threshold of a renaissance. What will the historian of the future find in the annals of American-Jewish history as he turns the pages of yellowed newspapers and ragged magazines of the middle of the twentieth century?

There will be much to remind him of the past. In 1946 an American Jewish synagogue of a congregation that was founded in 1658 was made a national historic shrine. The oldest synagogue building in the United States was dedicated in 1763 and beautifully designed by Peter Harrison and named for the Touro family which was so closely identified with the congregation. President Truman in the closing years of his first term of office acclaimed "the commemoration of the founding of the Union of American Hebrew Congregations seventy-five years ago by the late Dr. Isaac M. Wise, a happy event for all Americans, be they Christian or Jew."

The most popular work of fiction was a novel dealing with antisemitism, *Gentleman's Agreement*. At the head of the nonfiction list was Rabbi Liebman's *Peace of Mind*, a record of a quest for therapy which was acclaimed by Christians as well as Jews. In the New York art galleries the work of a Vilna native, transplanted to Brazil was creating a major sensation. Lasar Segall's exhibit of paintings dealing with "War," "Pogrom" and "Survivors" was symbolic of the age.

A college class walked out of a university classroom because the instructor was an antisemite. The director of the Hillel Foundation of the Uptown branch of the City College of New York upheld the students in their protest. Both Jewish and non-Jewish students joined in the demonstration, demanding the removal of the offending professor. The *Key Reporter* of Phi Beta Kappa noted that "Discrimination Exists in Private Institutions." And the New York Board of Rabbis protested the showing in this country of the English movie "Oliver Twist." The *Reconstructionist* congratulated the rabbinical group on their opposition to "this dangerous film." Eleanor Roosevelt wrote in her column of January 17, 1949, that, "At the present all of us are breathlessly watching developments in Palestine." The editorial page of the *New York Herald Tribune* the day before devoted fifty-two inches of newsprint to subjects of interest to Jews: "British Policy on Israel" and "Justice Brandeis as a Zionist."

The Jews have been for two thousand years a Pilgrim People. Their pilgrimages have taken them to every corner of the earth. Their intellectual quests—pilgrimages no less—have led them down every highway of inquiry. They came to America as refugees in the Exodus of 1492. They have continued to come, fleeing terror and persecution. "Instead of taking jobs from Americans, the refugees have increased job opportunities and been an economic asset to the country," writes Professor Davie in his recent study about *Refugees in America*. Of the one hundred and two refugees listed in *Who's Who in America*, there are thirty known Jews, beginning with Maurice Abravanel and ending with Stefan Zweig. Of the two hundred and twenty refugees listed in *Men of Science*, ninety-seven are known to be Jews. There are at least two Nobel Prize winners—Albert Einstein and James Franck.

An important book titled *The Universe and Dr. Einstein*, reporting the adventure of "The Mind of Man Taken on Cosmic Grand Tour Following Revolutionary Theories of Great Physicist," has just made its appearance. Perhaps that will be the ultimate symbol to the historian of the future. That a twentieth-century pilgrim to America should open the door to new concepts "far beyond the mere relativity of space and time and the equivalence of matter and energy"—is that not a gift to be prized above all else? Is it not to be compared to that solemn moment in history when the lookout for Columbus spied a new land?

From the Eastern seaboard to the shores of California the magic carpet unrolls. And the life of Jews in America ebbs and flows in the same basic rhythms as the rest of the population. There is continuity. There is regional diversity. The land, climate, cultural institutions work their inevitable changes in men. American Jews participate in American life with zest and ardor. Their response is ready to appeals from abroad. They are wholehearted in everything they do. Their sensibilities are easily aroused. They are "joiners" and form a bewildering number of lodges, clubs, societies. They are both amenable to institutional controls and heartily indifferent to them. Attitudes and habits are built up within the group which are vital to its preservation and continuation. Collective opinions express themselves through customs and folkways, traditions and beliefs. The group transmits its cultural heritage. Problems too complex and too difficult for individual solution are delegated to specially created social agencies.

From the first American Jews have had to face the problem of acculturation and adjustment to their environment. That is true of all cultural minorities. They have adapted and modified to their own needs many of the customs which they found here. To their own institutions for which, being gregarious, Jews had a penchant, they added many more variations native to the American scene. Their summer camps had Indian names. At least in one case the Indians on an Indian Reservation in Colorado reciprocated by naming some of their buildings for Jewish notables—there was a Yehuda Halevi Lodge, a Theodor Herzl Recreation Hall, a Max Nordau Guest House, a Chaim Nachman Bialik Library. The Indians explained the names on the basis of reciprocity. That is what happens when two cultures meet.

Inexorably both conflict and accommodation continue. Generations of Jews, native sons and immigrants, carry on their activities, now seemingly impervious, now highly vulnerable to the environment in which they function. They consider their accomplishments and are proud. Their detractors raise the old hue and cry of undue influence, of spreading control and monopolies, and the Jews of America are sunk in gloom.

The age of migration is over. No more will the entrenched and wealthy Jews be vexed by the influx of large numbers of impoverished immigrants. There will be less to do in the area of philanthropy and service for immigrants. For the reservoirs of potential immigrants will have dried up. The remnant of Israel that is left wants to return to the land of Israel. America no longer beckons to them. The tide of mobility flows to the East, toward the river Jordan and to Jerusalem—the places which once were the centers of the world to the Jewish cartographers who lavished their finest skills in drawing maps of a world that refused them sanctuary.

So there will be fewer immigrants. But because of that there will be no replenishing of scholarship and genius. Where will the Jews of America find their leaders and teachers and interpreters of the Law? Where but within their own ranks, in their seminaries and colleges and institutes?

Their strength will come from within.

"I am concerned with the fate of the five million Jews in America and with others whom we might bring to our country for refuge," wrote Judge Ulysses S. Schwartz of the Superior Court of Cook County, Illinois. "I find myself too bound up with the hopes and the dreams which I have for our own country to share in the prospect of of a revived past. . . . All I ask is that they join in the preservation of our American community. . . . We must find a formula for union. . . ."[27]

This is the credo of a twentieth-century American Jew for whom the problems of America—here and now—are paramount. Perhaps it points the direction for the history of Jews in America in the centuries to come.

"The Pilgrims had faith, we should have it," Brandeis once said, "for the Pilgrims had the indomitable spirit."

Faith . . . indomitable spirit . . . these words from the man whom President Franklin D. Roosevelt called "Isaiah" sum up the narrative of the Pilgrim People in America.

CHAPTER XVII

A Rebirth in Our Times

"The Pilgrims had faith, we should have it, for the
Pilgrims had the indomitable spirit."
—Louis D. Brandeis

IN A TIME OF enlarged horizons, in an era of the deepest probing of
the human psyche, of social change and social revolution, of human
grandeur and self-abasement, of devastation caused by war and
hatred, the historian, alone and overwhelmed, seeks answers and solutions for the present anxieties, for the building of a future for the remnant of Israel, and for the regeneration and amelioration of all mankind.

Being human he is fallible. Being mortal he is insecure. Being
myopic his vision is blurred. Overwhelmed, he turns to greater souls
whose faith is steadfast and whose vision pierces the unknown tomor-
rows. Upheld by memories of prophetic vision and of heroic valor, of
moral grandeur and steadfast faith, he borrows from the past as he
confronts the uncertain future. He lifts his pen.

A long time ago—in the first century of our present calendar—a
wise man wrote: "Do not ask for the City of God on earth, for it is
not built of wood and stone; but seek it in the soul of the man who is
at peace with himself and is a lover of true wisdom." The author of
these lines was Philo Judaeus.[1]

It is nearly twenty centuries since these words were written. Others
have said them in countless ways. The philo-Semite, Edwin Markham,
wrote in "The Pilgrim":

> Man comes a pilgrim of the universe,
> Out of the mystery that was before
> The world, out of the wonder of old stars . . .
> His feet have felt the pressure of old worlds,

508

And are to tread on others yet unnamed,
Worlds sleeping yet in some new dream of God.[2]

The cornucopia of history continues to spill its contents. Observers trained as historians, diplomats and newsmen continue to pour out their observations in an unending stream. Expanding means of communication bring information, commentary, cinematic records of new developments. The traumatic exposés, the congressional hearings, inflation, unemployment cut a wide swath affecting hundreds of thousands of lives. For many life is a precipice of insecurity. Memories of the past are bathed in roseate hues. The future is unpredictable—and often the present seems unbearable to the bewildered protagonists. So history unrolls.

American involvement is global. We woo our former enemies and compromise on many fronts. Yet solutions are uncertain, and all plans seem tentative.

"Who Lost the Yom Kippur War?" asks Drew Middleton in *The Atlantic* in March 1974. Writes Middleton: ". . . men have died for lands more desolate than the Sinai where, in October of last year, the greatest armored battle since World War II was fought. The battle was the climax of the fourth Arab-Israeli war, a war which neither side won. . . ."[3]

There is a river of books which gladden the heart. Books which unravel the past and tie their strands to events of more recent years. They are written by Jews barely at home in America and those who are native. They are also written by Christians who are eager to erase the evils of the past and to help Jews to aid the Israelis to build a future in the land of its ancestors. So Paul Tillich writes in the *Dynamics of Faith*—"When there is faith there is an awareness of holiness." And later: "The divine law is of ultimate concern in old and new Judaism. It is the central content of faith." He urges his readers that "sin is the estrangement from one's true self."[4] He has many dedicated followers.

Jews in free lands were inundated by books, articles, sermons, and speeches. They learned that to live on borrowed thoughts was not enough. To face the tragedy that had befallen their fellow Jews each person had to go down deep into the well of self, dredge up faith and strength and courage to share of his substance with the deprived surviving victims. And "Niemand"—the baby born in a ditch while its parents fled the Nazi horror had to be given another name. The little "Niemands" of this age of atrocity could no longer be nameless.

Alfred Kazin, in a perceptive essay, wrote: "There are experiences so extreme that, after living them, one can do nothing with them but put them into words. There are experiences so terrible that one can finally do nothing with them but forget them."[5] The Jewish experience under the black Nazi years makes this rule applicable.

"Holocaust literature," writes Cyrt Leviant in reviewing Elie Wiesel's *A Soul on Fire*, "which deals with the most cataclysmic event in Jewish history, speaks in many tongues. . . . Whether the works have been in Hebrew, Yiddish, English or various European languages, the artist's basic problem has been how to objectify the tragedy's emotional impact into purely literary terms—for no fiction concerning genocide can outimagine the fact. . . . Elie Wiesel has realized the terror of the holocaust and its equally painful aftereffects by poeticising autobiography via symbol, legend and philosophical speculation. . . . A person who enters the world of Elie Wiesel's tales can never be the same again."[6]

The reader must agree with Abba Eban: "Jewish thought is bound to be influenced by the traumatic experience of the holocaust. Never in history has any people borne a memory such as this. . . . Jewish history in this generation is dominated by a fantastic transition from tragedy to consolation, from the European slaughterhouse to the position of a sovereign state established within the international family."[7]

The calendar of events and the nuggets of scholars revolve constantly. Divergent views and geographic differences make a strange yet powerful involvement where one common factor unites Jewish settlers returning to their ancient heritage. It has been well summarized by Simon N. Herman in his study titled, *Israelis and Jews: The Continuity of an Identity*. He said: "Israelis are not . . . an entirely new people. The majority of the Israelis . . . see themselves linked to the Jewish people and to its past. The thread of historic continuity has not been snapped. . ." He concludes: "There are Israeli *Jews* for whom the Jewish element is primary, and Jewish *Israelis* with whom the Israeli component is dominant."[8]

Writing on the memory of the Holocaust, he adds: "Despite the fact that the Israeli War of Independence was fought only a few years after the Holocaust, and the Six Day War twenty years later, the indications are that the consciousness of the Holocaust was even more strongly present in 1967 than it was in 1948. . . . the memory of the Holocaust moved before the Israelis as a 'pillar of fire' and steeled their determination when they joined battle with the Arab armies in the Six Day War."

In May 1948 the Jewish State of Israel was proclaimed. President Truman announced its recognition. Three days later came the de jure nod from the Soviet Union. "Not since the days when the exiles of Babylonia were led back to the homeland had such great and over-whelming revolution occurred in Jewish life. The Psalm which was sung by the returnees in the sixth century B.C. leaped to life again."[9] It was Psalm 126.

Life-saving campaigns in the United States proliferated. In a forth-right discussion of the service rendered to Jews and other minorities by the American Jewish Congress, there are some facts to be noted. First, it took courage to take the stand they did—and "its leaders and its members sensed and understood their duty not only to their broth-ers abroad but also to themselves as free citizens of America. They recognized that if they were silent or timid because they were Jews, they were . . . imposing on themselves a second-class citizenship."[10] It took moral courage and the leaders of the American Jewish Con-gress had it. Despite opposition and fiscal cutbacks, "The national officers . . . under the leadership, since 1951, of Dr. Israel Goldstein, have not swerved. . . . They are deeply committed to the belief that, as citizens of America, Jews must continue to play their full part in shap-ing its affairs." This dynamic group "has been seeking ways in which fuller understanding of Jewish traditions and Jewish values can become part of the Jewish community . . . it published *Congress Weekly* . . . and *supports Judaism* . . ."[11] It is grateful for "its years of lonely leadership," significant, valorous, and uncompromising.

The mood of American Jews as the tragic postwar statistics unfolded was bleak and anguished. The horrors and mass deaths which their kinsmen experienced, the skeletal survivors—bereft and homeless—that were to be somehow restored to life, the postwar establishment of the state of Israel which had announced its willing-ness to absorb the homeless victims—these were daily press dis-patches and their impact was not lost upon their kinsmen in America. The tragedy in Europe found an echo in each heart. The safe and the secure responded with warmth and generosity. So did the poor. There was an outpouring of funds which brought the total contributions to UJA to over $1,400,000,000 by the end of 1962. There were many reasons for this. First of all there was in this country greater economic security, as more children of immigrants joined the ranks of the pro-fessions, or became skilled workers. The numbers of Jewish students in colleges increased as well as their future economic opportunities. The areas of "first residence" in crowded tenements were being replaced by homes in suburbia. "The creation of the state of Israel had certainly served to raise the public dignity of Jewish identity . . ."

Synagogue membership increased and many houses of worship were built. The Conservative movement developed to meet the needs of the formerly Orthodox. "It is not too much to say that the *Minhag America* of the East European second generation was Conservative Judaism . . ." It was assumed that the future of American Jewry rests "in the grandchildren and the great-grandchildren of older settlers."[12] All the splinter movements to which American Jews gave allegiance or lip service prior to the Holocaust were obsolete. The "general disenchantment" led to a search for new ideologies. "Attitudes were quite diverse and motivations differed. . . . Some thought that the long and rich Jewish tradition provided an abundant source of the mythic and non-rational attitudes which could form the basis of a fresh approach to the problems of the 'human condition,' while others . . . in David Riesman's phrase moved from a 'vindictive and aggressive and contemptuous attitude towards tradition [to] a honeyed and sentimental one.' "

A pertinent question was raised: "Will the account of American Jewish religious life to be written a generation hence be a tale of great historic success . . . or will it be an elegy?" For ". . . the dominant response of Jewish intellectuals to the cumulative experience of the depression, fascism, the Soviet betrayal of democracy and socialism, the extermination of European Jewry, and the war itself was part of a thorough re-evaluation by western intellectuals . . . of the liberal culture of the past one hundred years." Sadly it is averred that "the misery, terror and destruction that had been visited upon the world since the beginning of the twentieth century were such that intellectuals became profoundly convinced that liberal culture itself was at fault."[13]

The American Jewish Year Book continued to explore new and hitherto little known ideologies in current American Jewish life.[14] Under the title "Folk and Elite Religion in American Judaism," the subject is discussed. Awareness of new trends is important—even given the state of change in which the newly described ideologies are presented to the reader. Here is one point of view which bears examining: "Reconstructionist ideology is an articulation of the folk religion of the American Jews. Orthodoxy, Conservatism, and Reform represent the three *elitist* ideologies of the American Jewish religion. . . . What, we may ask, is the difference between folk religion and denominationalism. . . . Folk religion is not self-conscious; it does not articulate its own rituals and beliefs. . . . Therefore, in the eyes of the elite religion, folk religion is not a movement, but an error . . . shared by many people. . . . Folk religion is not necessarily more primitive than elite religion. . . . Hence folk religion can develop ceremonial responses to new needs which may then be incorporated into the elite religion . . ."

The differences may be semantic, a matter of mere definition. They are cited to indicate the many divagations there are—and the innumerable explanations!

Nevertheless, the role of American Jews was expanding. International problems depicting the desperate plight of Jews in Soviet Russia continued to agitate the Jews of America, many of them having had the experience of reminiscing grandparents and parents whose indelible memories of persecution under Czarist and Communist Russia provided a background of anguish to the narrators and their young listeners. "America's compassion is no recent phenomenon."[15] The United States had shown its concern for the repeated offenses of the Russian government. "At the outset, the United States, like Israel, was mild in voicing criticism . . ." but as evidence of Russian anti-Semitism piled up, increasing tension was evident.

Many trends in group relations underwent marked changes. Catholics in small and gradually growing numbers showed a disposition to reverse themselves in their contact with Jews.

In *The New York Times*, on October 24, 1971, Seton Hall University, a Roman Catholic institution, purchased $250,000 in Israeli bonds ". . . as a demonstration of its confidence in the future of this democratic state in the Middle East." Monsignor Thomas G. Fahy, president of the South Orange, New Jersey University, called attention to the University's Institute of Judeo-Christian Studies "to advance Catholic-Jewish relations."[16]

A very important book is *The Anguish of the Jews: Twenty-three Centuries of Anti-Semitism* by Edward H. Flannery. It is dedicated "To all who suffer persecution." Father Flannery is editor of the *Providence Visitor*, "one of the liveliest diocesan newspapers in the United States"—and a contributor to *The Bridge*, a yearbook of Judeo-Christian studies. From the preface, by Monsignor John M. Oesterreicher, Director of the Institute of Judeo-Christian Studies at Seton Hall University, we read: "This is a book that is filled with pain; the pain of events and the pain of their narrator. *It is probably the first history of anti-Semitism written by a priest* . . . . Father Flannery seems to unmask the wrongs done . . . to the Jewish people."[17]

"Our history is a tale of horror . . . we have followed Pope St. Gregory the Great that great sixth-century defender of Jews who urges us to give priority to truth over the avoidance of scandal. In the end . . .

truth will abolish scandal." Later, "From the first literary strictures against Judaism in ancient and early Christian times . . . a crescendo in violence has unfolded."[18]

He writes of "an ascent in horrors" and discusses the progression from the Crusades through the Nazis. The Holocaust was "the ultimate of disasters." Under Hitler, asphyxiation and extermination were the solution. *Now silence is a crime.*[19]

"Anyone who still believed the American brand of racial anti-Semitism to be a benign growth was painfully disillusioned when a young Jew, Leo Frank, on the flimsiest evidence, was convicted of the murder of a fourteen-year-old-girl in Atlanta, Georgia, was lynched . . . at his lynching a shudder ran through the nation.

"This rabid anti-Semitism has failed . . . to catch on in America." But here "the Jew is destined to suffer more discrimination than others. . . .

"Today, a score of years after Hitler's murder of six million Jews, the anti-Semitic devil still roams the world."[20]

There was self-criticism in Jewish ranks: " . . . the ideological posture of Jewish intellectuals is also inadequate. Their criticisms of the established Jewish community and their own ideological investigations are of considerable value and serve to point up the hollowness of much of organized Jewish life in the United States."[21]

Acculturation etched many changes in American Jewish communal life. "Two generations ago, the image of American Jewry was that of an immigrant enclave with transplanted institutions, ideologies, customs and mores which appeared to have little relevance to American life. Today, the Jews are integrated into the American economy, extensively involved in the processes of American government and at home in the American milieu. In dress and appearance, in language and education, in fashions and recreation, conceptions of status and material values they conform to the prevailing norms of the predominant culture . . . they have become acculturated. . . . All this and other factors have created the image of homogeneity . . .

"Since 1933 . . . the financial philanthropic burdens of American Jewry have been overwhelming. Rescue of Jews from Germany and other Nazi-occupied countries, relief and assistance during World War II, post-war rehabilitation and migration, development of Israel, and . . . Jewish social services in America have required funds of staggering magnitude. . . . The *raison d'etre* of Jewish communal life itself has become fundraising . . ."[22]

Turning the pages of periodicals of the past generation is looking into a reflecting mirror which spurns time. Preoccupation with the past is part of the Jewish tradition. It is in evidence today. Articles facing present dilemmas and unresolved problems alternate with nostalgic glimpses of the past. There is an overriding sense of the intertwining of clock and calendar. The Jew is never detached from his roots—and even the runaways and changelings show the strength of their attachment by the elaborate disguises they assume.

For the purpose of summary *Congress Weekly* is our reflecting pool for two decades of time. In the Chronicle of Events for April 1951, the first recorded item is that the American Jewish Congress issued a joint report with the National Association for the Advancement of Colored People "charging both Houses of Congress with making a 'political football' of the civil rights issue . . . " It is the handwriting on the wall—presaging an era of black anti-Semitism as unfair as it was unexpected. For the weeds of that disease are even today regrettably in great evidence, estranging erstwhile friends and allies from each other. Non-Jewish students at the University of Maryland blocked the erection of a new building to house the B'nai B'rith Hillel foundation. "Approximately 50 members of fraternities and sororities appeared before the county commissioner and said that they did not want the Hillel building erected near their fraternity and sorority houses because they feared the Jewish students would make too much noise."[23]

The Book Issue in November 1951 begins with "The Creative Reader"—a salute to those rare souls who know how to read a book, how to enter into a viable partnership with its author. "What sets him apart is the relationship that he establishes with the ideas and with the author of the work he is reading and what he does with the information he has acquired from the printed page before him." Another critique deals with "the present trend toward preoccupation with mysticism . . . " In a survey of "Jewish Critics in America" Charles I. Glicksberg reaches a hortatory note. He urges the Jewish literary critic in America "to remain an eternal voice of prophetic protest, to exalt the creative life as opposed to the life of getting and spending." This is followed by statements of nine contemporary Jewish novelists expounding their literary credos.[24]

Jewish education is discussed in the December 1953 issue. The number of Jewish children attending all day schools is markedly increasing. New York City alone had tripled its Jewish day school enrollment since 1935. Seventy-five thousand children attended after-school or weekend religious classes. Eighteen thousand attended all day schools. There were other news items. The United States government, through Hadassah, made available for distribution in Israel, 1,169,000 pounds of surplus food. And Eleanor Roosevelt received the Histadrut Humanitarian Award for services to Israel.[25]

Increasingly Jewish students were asking many questions of themselves and each other. Thus, in 1955, a year after the Tercentenary celebration, one writer was trying to find the future of the American Jewish community by asking: "Are there seeds of disappearance and dissolution not planted deep into American soil? Will there be celebrants left in another three hundred years to mark the passing of the Jewish Calendar? . . . Where are the 'annointed' of the Lord?"[26] The answers elude us. Yet Israel Goldstein's "American Jewry Comes of Age" surveying the scene in depth faces both hope and defeat with objectivity. And in 1957, a dedicated historian, Rufus Learsi, grieving over lost millions accuses "our official religious bodies" of having "failed to rise to the occasion. . . . No effective proposal for keeping the memory alive has emanated from these groups." Learsi concludes: "We want all our people to remember. They owe it as a debt of honor and they owe it to their people's future and their own future as well."[27]

A new phenomenon is noted on the American scene in an article in January 1958 entitled "Writing about Jews" by Louis Falstein.[28] Happily announcing that "the coming of age of fiction dealing with Jews" has dawned, Dr. Falstein surveys the impact of this development by mentioning that *The Reporter* had noted a new kind of Jewish novel on the literary scene. Especially mentioned are *The Adventures of Augie March, Marjorie Morningstar, The Last Angry Man, Remember Me to God.* Falstein feels that the American Jew has done better in autobiographies than in fiction. He mentions Alfred Kazin's *A Walker in the City;* S. N. Behrman's *The Worcester Account;* Charles Angoff's *When I Was a Boy in Boston,* among others. Particularly saluted is Bernard Malamud for his "wise, compassionate novel," *The Assistant.*

In September 1958 there is an intellectual feast. Beginning with Abba Eban's brilliant analysis of "The Middle East: Its Nature and Destiny," it goes on to analyze "The Essence of Jewish Survival." This is followed by "Why Jewish Day Schools." Jacob Javits next discusses the plight of "Jews under Communism." The Venerable and Revered Martin Buber deals with "Israel and the Command of the Spirit." Buber notes that "the power of destruction . . . is only made possible through this inner disintegration . . ." which accompanies rampant power. He notes sadly that " . . . the Jewish people that were most cruelly afflicted through that victory of the subhuman over the human, the false teaching continued to prevail even when the subhuman was overthrown." He concludes with a plea for the preservation of the spirit in Israel, for "Only if it preserved the spirit as its leader could it hope to bring forth something greater than just one more state among the states of the world."[29]

So the pages turn and the years and the decades vanish into history. In the 1960s the old adage that the more things change the more they remain the same is verified again and again. A resolution condemning anti-Semitism was adopted by a UN subcommission. Jews from five continents meeting in Amsterdam deplored the situation of Jews in Russia. Chancellor Adenauer was a member of a pilgrimage to Bergen-Belsen and stated that he was "shattered by the memory of the misery that ruled here many years." IKE HITS "VIRUS OF BIGOTRY" IN MESSAGE TO AJ CONGRESS. And Rabbi Joachim Prinz preached in Cologne, Germany. It was his answer to the defacement of the synagogue on Christmas Eve "that touched off a wave of swastika-smearing across Germany and around the world."[30]

This brief survey will serve like the posthumous diary of an individual as a cornucopia of isolated facts—and yet it reveals clearly that change in human society is an inescapable fact. And that change is twofold: brought on by the individual's actions or totally unrelated to it by reason of the unfolding of a cosmic plot which mankind lives out without having had any conceivable share in the narrative.

The Anti-Defamation League of B'nai B'rith published *The Image of the Jews* to which noted scholars have made signal contributions. Here are to be found some of the cornerstones of Judaism and some of the challenges which recent times have caused Jews to grapple with. Here aspects of Jewish theology, tradition, and worship are explored. The position of the Jew in a host culture which outnumbers and often rejects him is analyzed. Jewish rites of passage are interpreted. The survival of Jews and their ultimate absorption are faced. Self-confrontation, the search for identity, commitment or detachment are examined. Man's search for God and God's relationship to man are considered in depth. So a noted scholar and author, Rabbi Eugene B. Borowitz writes: "Judaism has no dogmas. . . . And yet, in spite of this, there is a sense of unity to Jewish tradition . . . the Jew believed that there was something unified about the world in which he lived, and that this unity transcended all the divisions which can be found in life. It is this strong sense of the authority of one God . . . which lies behind what is often called the watchword of the Jewish faith, the Shema. . . ."[31]

The historian wears the garments of today. Yet he is attuned to the past. He has new insights which he owes to the dazzling new discoveries. Application of psychoanalytic insights, awareness of new directions in psychology—all of these have broadened his understanding, brought new awareness and new priorities. Man has changed as life on earth has changed. For the surviving victims of sadistic persecution, for the suffering experienced in concentration camps, for the indignities and degradations men and women underwent, for the exposure to death camps and mass extermination, for the impaling of little children before the eyes of their parents—there are no words. Evil was in the saddle, and arrogance of the ignorant criminals and contempt and brutality toward their victims are part of the unspeakable record.

On the positive side were the posthumous publication of Rabbi Milton Steinberg's "A Believing Jew" in 1951; Abraham J. Heschel's "Man Is Not Alone" which set forth his ennobling religious philosophy; Rabbi Philip Bernstein's "What the Jews Believe" which appeared in *Life* magazine eliciting the greatest number of letters from readers in its history.

And the posthumous poem of a great heroine—Hannah Senesh—was translated by Marie Syrkin. Hannah wrote: "Blessed is the heart with strength to stop its beating for honour's sake."

Six million hearts stopped beating. . .

When moments of repudiation and utter doubt assail the former believer, there is little he can do about it. For the records of bestiality have the effect of annihilation of faith. The former true believer refuses to pay homage to a formerly believed-in dispenser of love and concern for his chosen creatures. A devout and pious man, Rabbi Milton Steinberg, one of those committed to faith, has put it simply: "one of the great blunders of theologians in the past has been their quest after an absolute demonstration of the reality of God . . . the existence of God is not completely provable. It remains the conclusion of an act of faith."[32]

Professor Emil L. Fackenheim of the University of Toronto, a survivor of Nazi concentration camps, was credited with a moving moment of insight when he wrote: "Israel is collectively what every survivor is individually: A No to the demons of Auschwitz, a Yes to Jewish survival and security—and thus a testimony to life against death *on behalf of all mankind*."[33]

This survivor of Nazi murder camps states: "In the Nazi murder camps no effort was spared to make persons into living *things* before making them into dead things." He concludes with a question and an affirmation. "Why hold fast to the God of the covenant? Former believers lost Him in the Holocaust Kingdom. Former agnostics found Him." Each survivor "is a witness against darkness in an age of darkness. He is a witness whose like the world has not seen." The existence of the State of Israel testifies to this truth.

It was Martin Buber who said, "We know nothing of death . . . but I know that God is Eternity."[34] Maurice Friedman commenting on this affirmation of Buber's writes: "Buber's believing humanism . . . is faith as witness, as faithful testimony and response in the cruel as well as the gracious situations of life."[35] In an article by Michael A. Meyer entitled "Judaism after Auschwitz: The Religious Thought of Emil L. Fackenheim," we read: "Although the suffering of the righteous has always weighed heavily upon the religious man, the magnitude and proximity of the Holocaust makes the issue unavoidable for Jews in our generation. . . . Can it really be that God whom Fackenheim with Buber terms 'sole Power' should have allowed the destruction of one-third of the Jewish people and this same God has commanded Jewish survival? . . . As a faithful and believing Jew, Fackenheim has not allowed even Auschwitz to rob him of his transcendent faith."

On June 1, 1955, on the occasion of the closing assembly of the American Jewish Tercentenary, a noted American rabbi stated the "Credo of an American Jew" in words that found an echo in the hearts of his coreligionists. He said: "I believe that the American in me merges cogenially with my Jewish tradition. . . . I believe that the best hallmark of the Jew and his most valuable credential is his religion. . . I believe that the State of Israel has a special destiny as the natural habitat of Jewish survival, as a light to the nations. . . I believe that America is . . . to build here . . . a new heaven of human dignity . . . and that Jewish idealism can help keep America new and fresh. I believe that the exalted words of Isaiah . . . can find fulfillment both here and in Israel, 'for as long as the new heavens and the new earth which I make shall endure before me, saith the Lord, so shall your offspring and your name endure.' "[36]

The speaker was then saluted by Pierre van Paassen as a friend of some thirty years, as "a soul profoundly in love with justice."[37] In moments of public acclaim such encomia are heard. At other times, at social occasions and family celebrations other points of view often prevail. As witness the hundreds of antiestablishment jokes, the thousands of out of context anti-Miami Beach anecdotes. Ambivalence prevails. Introspection is lacking. It is a matter of logical orientation for a Mediterranean people to find a similar climate where temperature, vegetation, food crops, nourish ancient folk memories and feed bodies bred to such surroundings for thousands of years. Nothing strange in that. Yet, Jews have never completely come to grips with the idea. So it was with leaders, ideologies, promotional campaigns. Celebration and denigration were two sides of the same coin.

This dichotomy of alternating currents is nowhere more in evidence than in noting the history of Brandeis University. It was a dream in the minds of many. Credit has been claimed and assigned by many. The record is available in the book entitled *Two Generations in Perspective.*[38]

When Dr. Israel Goldstein had completed his presidency of the Zionist Organization of America and had met other pledged commitments, he felt free to undertake the founding of a Jewish-sponsored University in America. There were many critics. He was not discouraged. It was a "concept that was clearly etched in his mind, as a Jewish contribution to the American intellectual scene."

Negotiations had begun as long ago as January 7, 1946, for the possible acquisition of Middlesex University in Waltham, Massachusetts. "Dr. Goldstein persuaded the authorities of Middlesex University to transfer control of the institution to a small group of associates recruited by him." A number of distinguished members of the Jewish community were enlisted by him—the name of Albert Einstein led the list. Dr. Goldstein and four associates were now added to the trustees, five former members having resigned. The Albert Einstein Foundation for Higher Learning elected Dr. Goldstein as president, and plans were immediately determined for a financial campaign to make the dream a reality. After this came the choice of a name. There was one name which led all the rest—a name sponsored by the dynamic planner, Dr. Goldstein. Justice Louis D. Brandeis was "the greatest American Jew of his time, liberal in his Americanism and self-affirming in his Jewishness . . . whose noble life might well serve as an inspiration to American Jews." He next decided to mobilize support for the man he wished to head the new institution—Dr. Abram L. Sachar. But all was not unanimity, sweetness, and light. The rift came when Albert Einstein disassociated himself from the project. The reasons were many—the chief one being that Dr. Goldstein had made arrangements with Sachar "despite the tentative and provisional nature of the approach." Israel Goldstein withdrew from his official positions—and the plans were eventually consummated.

The second choice to head Brandeis University was Dr. Harold

Laski of England. This fell through. So once more, Sachar's name was introduced. Sachar secured the appointment and wrote to Dr. Goldstein: ". . . You are really the father of Brandeis University." The then acting president of the Board of Trustees of Brandeis University wrote to Israel Goldstein: "Had it not been for your fervor and enthusiasm in those early months, there would now be no Brandeis University . . ."

Many Jews have tried to balance their religious beliefs on the precarious scale of these conflicting attitudes. Many have failed. Some noble souls have made it. Let us consider one of "the saints in the land."

The prophets whom we met in the Bible spoke to God and for man. Traumatic centuries have separated us and their words still cherished seem far away. But the man whose recent life ennobled us and whose writings have upheld us and whose God-vision has illuminated us, walked among us, spoke to the multitudes, and to the solitary pilgrims who thirsted for his words. His voice is still heard. His concern for mankind still lingers. His message—still vibrant and viable—reverberates in our time. We are surrounded by his books, we hear the exhortations of his words, we recall his lectures and the times we met and talked together. The beneficent goodwill which he radiated, the notes and marginal comments which his dedicated readers scrawled in a continuing dialogue—all these are spiritual landmarks to be held in trust.

He was mourned by Jews and by Christians. In an issue of *America*, published by Jesuits of the United States and Canada and devoted to the memory of Abraham Joshua Heschel, 1907–1972, the editor, Donald R. Campion, writes " . . . the best instruction we Christians may receive concerning the continuing vitality and richness of the Judaic tradition in which we providentially share is the life and example of a Jew like Professor Heschel. . . . If he emerges from these pages, like those Jewish prophets he studied and emulated to call all of us to purity of religion, purity of motive and universal compassion, so much the better."[39]

Arthur A. Cohen, in discussing *"The Rhetoric of Faith: Abraham Joshua Heschel,"* calls Rabbi Heschel "Undoubtedly the most significant thinker which traditional Judaism has given to contemporary America." In Heschel he finds "the renaissance of belief" which has been hoped for, for centuries, and adds, "Perhaps the moment is now." Finding that both "the natural and supernatural Jew are joined in every Jew, he sees despair as the prevailing mood, for "destiny disappears for him and only the hard and implacable fatality of his life remains."[40]

Heschel's life was an unceasing dialogue with God. It was a familiarity which comes from intimate relationship and undeviating service to the Father of mankind. His book, *The Prophets,* is dedicated "To the martyrs of 1940–45." It is a portion of Psalm 44 which reads:

> All this has come upon us,
> though we have not forgotten Thee,
> Or been false to Thy covenant.
> Our heart has not turned back,
> Nor have our steps departed from Thy way . . .
> . . . For Thy sake we are slain . . .
> Why dost Thou hide Thy face?

"The prophet's task is to convey a divine view," says Heschel. "The prophet is not only a prophet. He is also a poet, preacher, patriot, statesman, social critic, moralist." He goes on: "The prophet is a man who feels fierccly. God has thrust a burden upon his soul, and he is bowed and stunned at man's fierce greed. Frightful is the agony of man; no human voice can convey its full terror. Prophecy is the voice that God has lent to the silent agony, a voice to the plundered poor, to the profaned riches of the world. It is a form of living, a crossing point of God and man. God is raging in the prophet's words."

The biography that will some day be written about Heschel as an authentic prophet of the twentieth century will be a record of this rage and sorrow and deprivation which in his lifetime he had seen and felt and inveighed against. And all mankind will profit for sharing in "the rage and sorrow and deprivation" which racked his soul.

To write about Abraham Joshua Heschel is an exercise in deletion. Memories of the books of his that were read and treasured, the shared conversations, the lectures heard, the research in libraries when the news came that he had left us, the urge to recall, reread, rethink the harvest we are heir to—all these things are overwhelming. For the thought persists that here was a prophet in our midst whose incandescent gifts to us—his contemporaries—were a legacy he shared with his brother-prophets. He has taken his rightful place with them. We are the gleaners. And a sentence of his comes to mind: "Rarely in our history has so much been dependent upon one generation. We will either forfeit or enrich the legacy of the ages."[42]

Those words were written in 1955. It was the year in which his book, *God in Search of Man: A Philosophy of Judaism,* was published. "The central thought of Judaism is the living God," he averred. "The craving for God has never subsided in the Jewish soul . . . worship, learning, and action: are the main aspects of Judaism. Among the many things that religious tradition holds in store for us is a *legacy of wonder.* . . . Indifference to the sublime wonder of living is the root of sin." "A return to reverence is the first prerequisite for a survival of wisdom. . . . The greatest insights happen to us in moments of awe."[43]

He next considers the meaning of his existence as a Jew. "And the more deeply I probe, the more strongly I realize the scope of the problem; it embraces not only the Jews of the present but also those of the past and those of the future, the meaning of Jewish existence in all ages." For Heschel "Judaism is not a chapter in the history of philosophy." It is a cherished legacy. "Bringing to light the lonely splendor of Jewish thinking, conveying the taste of eternity in our daily living is the greatest aid we can render to the man of our time." He continues, "Israel exists not in order to be, but in order to dream the dream of God. . . . We have not chosen God. He has chosen us. There is no concept of a chosen God, but there is the idea of a chosen people."[44]

The National Broadcasting Company presented an interview with Dr. Abraham Joshua Heschel who was then, as he had been for a number of years, Ralph Simon Professor of Jewish Ethics and Mysticism at the Jewish Theological Seminary. He was interviewed by Carl Stern. The first question Heschel was asked was "What was there in your life, especially your early life, that would give you the thoughts to fill so many books?"

The answer: "Hard work, training and a good environment. I was very fortunate in having lived as a child and as a young boy in an environment where there were many people I could revere, people concerned with problems of inner life, of spirituality, and integrity. People who have shown great compassion and understanding for other people." Heschel summarized his essential credo as follows: ". . . there are essentially three points. One, 'God in Search of Man,' to me, is a homily of all of the Hebrew Bible. Now it expresses the idea of Judaism about the position of man in the universe. . . . Man is very important to God." Asked Stern: "And the third point?" "The third point would be the nature of religion. . . . I think that God is more in search of man than man is in search of God. He gives us no rest. . ." And later in the interview, Heschel added: "The prophets are forgotten. No one reads the prophets. They have not touched the mind of

America." In winding up his almost posthumous message to a world he was soon to leave, Heschel added: ". . . remember the importance of self-discipline . . . study the great sources of wisdom (and) remember that life is a celebration. . ."[45]

Dr. John C. Bennett was president of the Union Theological Seminary of New York when Dr. Heschel was named Harry Emerson Fosdick Visiting Professor in 1965 and became its first Jewish faculty member. His published eulogy to Abraham Heschel was titled, "Agent of God's Compassion."

It began: "Abraham Heschel belonged to the whole American religious community." And Dr. Bennett ends his tribute with these words: "Always he lived in faithful wonder before God, and always he was an agent of God's compassion."

So Abraham Joshua Heschel lived. Those who were privileged to meet and know him, his coreligionists and other friends who cherished him, and in a time of rampant hate and war and prejudice "his works became the devotional reading of myriads of non-Jews." For he evoked "the depth of awe, wonder and mystery that life should evoke in all men."[46]

There are heroes sung and unsung in American Jewish history. The facts are known and were there room to give them due notice—which there is not—their biographies full of accomplishment and adventure would make a large and impressive volume. Space and time are limited, but now one other "giant in the land" will be saluted. He has been described in a recent magazine, *Upstate New York*, under his picture in his rabbinical vestments, as "the Irrepressible Rabbi Bernstein" and judging from the accumulated data that is no exaggeration.[47] The blurb reads: "Rabbi Philip Bernstein of Rochester's Temple B'rith Kodesh retires next June after 46 years of influence that has radiated from Rochester around the world," and the question is asked: "Whom else do you know who is on speaking terms with Al Capp, Yehudi Menuhin, Gen. Lucius Clay, and Golda Meir?"

"Bernstein's liberal views spring from his background. His parents were Eastern European Jews from Lithuania . . . he was raised in the orthodox tradition. . . . It was purely accident that . . . he bcame rabbi of the rich, radical German-Jewish temple in town." While in Israel with his bride, he met an influential member of B'rith Kodesh. She urged the congregation to engage him as assistant rabbi. The rest is history.

Philip S. Bernstein was a native son, born in Rochester, New York, and he left his mark upon that city which is indelible. He also managed to serve his fellow-Jews in countless dedicated ways in many distant parts of the world while maintaining his contact with the congregation which knew and cherished him from 1926 until his retirement from his leadership of Temple B'rith Kodesh of Rochester in 1973. An impressive list of academic degrees and honors were his One of the heroic tasks that he performed was during World War II. "It was my privilege," he writes, "to serve as Executive Director of CANRA (Committee on Army and Navy Religious Activities of the National Jewish Welfare Board) in World War II. . . . Mine was the functioning responsibility for all its activities. I had wider contact, direct and indirect, with Jewish military personnel than any other person." When the war years ended, he returned to his congregation in Rochester, having first completed his report on his "stewardship." This report was published in 1971—after twenty-five years of gathering dust in the files of the Jewish Welfare Board.[48]

His labors were indefatigable. His services to his coreligionists were unending. They still continue. He adopted causes and crusades which were dictated by conscience. His book, titled *The Fighting Jew . . . A Moral Dilemma*, is a testament to an imperishable faith.

Rabbi Bernstein has said, "Judaism is not a pacifist religion. I discovered this painfully when at one point in my pacifist period I was working on a thesis for a doctorate on Judaism and pacifism. After much effort, I just gave it up because I couldn't find support for my own views."[49]

In introducing Rabbi Bernstein's *Rabbis at War*, the American Jewish Historical Society which published this work stresses how the organized rabbinate, Orthodox, Conservative, and Reform mobilized for war, and established a world-wide program of ministration. Rabbi Bernstein states that "over six hundred thousand Jews served in the U.S. armed forces, the largest number in uniform in all Jewish history. More than half of the rabbis of the country volunteered for the chaplaincy. Three hundred and eleven were accepted and served in the various branches of the armed forces."[50]

After the war, Rabbi Bernstein was appointed adviser on Jewish affairs to the generals in command of the American-occupied zones of Germany. During 1946 and 1947, his work involved guiding the rescue of a quarter-million displaced Jews.

In the year that Israel was reborn, 1948, Temple B'rith Kodesh celebrated its Centennial—and Rabbi Bernstein came home for that celebration.

Of the work of Rabbi Bernstein, much has been written. ". . . Bernstein was expected to attempt to settle at least some of the refugees in places other than Germany and to do his best to prevent too large a flow of Jews to converge on the over-crowded zones in Germany and Austria. This policy . . . led the Army to support not only the attempts made to remove the refugees by legal means, but to connive illegal exit as well, as long as this was not done too blatantly.

"After his failure to achieve his goals with the various European Governments and the Pope, Rabbi Bernstein returned to the United States and was granted an appointment to see President Truman. . . . The interview was rather significant . . . Bernstein praised the top commanders of our Army in Europe . . . and the cooperation which they unfailingly offered. . . ." After a report in which details were transmitted by Rabbi Bernstein, President Truman said that the "Jews were good citizens of the United States and would be assets to any country. The rabbi then remarked that the world was sick and the attitude toward the Jews was a symptom of the sickness; Truman agreed."[51]

On January 2, 1974, *The Near East Report* carried a very important story on Rabbi Philip S. Bernstein.[52] He has been serving as Honorary Chairman of the American Israel Public Affairs Committee and his testimony before the Senate Committee on Foreign Relations was being considered in its debates on aid to Israel. Deputy Secretary of State Kenneth Rush had pointed out that if defense funds for Israel were not made available, the Israelis would feel that "their security is jeopardized. . . . There is no doubt [Rush continued] that the negotiating ability of the Israelis . . . to bring about peace very strongly depends upon Israel remaining secure and being militarily strong enough to defend herself." Russian efforts to keep the Arabs militarily supplied were noted. Rush said that "Israel needed substantial amounts to counterbalance the heavy flow of new and sophisticated weapons to Arab countries. There was no doubt in anyone's mind that Israel had been attacked suddenly and without warning during the recent fight."

It was at this point that the Bernstein testimony became crucial. He spoke for the many American Jewish organizations who favored continuing help to Israel.

"I knew and helped the Jewish survivors of the holocaust which had been brought about, in no small measure, by Europe's appeasement of Hitler. Most of them found sanctuary in Israel. I know that those who lead and defend Israel today will not permit Jews ever again to become the victims of appeasement or to be slaughtered with impunity."

He made it clear that Israel's needs are urgent and that there is an imperative need " 'to help Israel defend herself and to negotiate . . . a just and lasting peace.' " Senator Fulbright questioned Rabbi Bernstein about detailed plans. Rabbi Bernstein replied that " 'the best way to peace will be from positions of strength . . . rather than weakness. . . . It seems to me that the quest for a country like the United States and a country like Israel is survival . . . for survival, you have to be strong . . . to achieve a working relationship based upon mutual self-interest.' "

On November 4, 1973, *The New York Times* carried a half-page ad headed by the following: DECISIVE MAJORITIES OF THE U.S. CONGRESS SUPPORT AID TO ISRAEL. The honorary chairman of the nationwide campaign was Rabbi Philip S. Bernstein of Rochester, New York. This indefatigable leader of American Jews now raised his voice in behalf of Senate Resolution 189, which advocated help to Israel in these words: "It is the Sense of the Senate that the announced policy of the United States Government to maintain Israel's deterrent strength be implemented by continuing to transfer to Israel . . . Phantom aircraft and other equipment in the quantities needed by Israel to repel the aggressors." Also endorsed by Rabbi Bernstein and others was House Resolution 613 which noted that "the Soviet Union, having heavily armed the Arab countries with the equipment needed to start this war, is continuing a massive airlift of sophisticated military equipment to Egypt and Syria . . ."

It is a record of more than a quarter of a century of undeviating service to country and to coreligionists which Rabbi Bernstein has helped to achieve. It is a record to be enshrined in American Jewish history.

In the 1930s Jewish professors in all subjects numbered under five hundred and programs in Judaica were still centered in the Jewish rabbinical seminaries, only occasionally finding homes in the general universities. World War II, with its emphasis on research needs and trained personnel, encouraged Jewish students and increased the number of Jewish faculty members in all fields. Departments of Judaica began to appear in the universities and continue to grow in size and number, while more and more Jewish students are pursuing doctoral programs.

The renaissance of Jewish education in America is impressive. There is progress. There is quickened interest. There are new and impressive educational techniques. There is keen response from students on every educational level. "The Jewish educator is

aware of the progress and quickened interest in Jewish education, and
yet he remains depressed by frustration and dashed hopes. The unin-
formed faith of the parents in the Jewish school and the large enroll-
ments present challenges which he cannot meet under present conditions. Achievement in education is extremely difficult to measure . . .
the indispensable instruments are still in the experimental stage in
Jewish education, so that even what is measurable—progress in the
Hebrew language, for example—cannot be evaluated with precision."[53] Thus, a noted educator, Oscar I. Janowsky, deals with
"Problems and Needs" in this developing field.

"*The Jewish Book Annual* reveals the number of volumes appearing annually in the Jewish field and the high percentage of publications in the scholarly domain. Increasing, too, is the number of publishers issuing volumes on Jewish subjects, including commercial and
university presses . . . a book of Jewish interest or subject matter is no
longer dependent upon Jewish publishers alone."[54]

The Annual of the Thirty-eighth Issue of the *Yearbook of American Churches* devotes some space to Jewish congregations in America
for the year 1970, beginning with "churches": 4,700. "Inclusive
membership: 5,780,000." "Ordained clergy: 6,200." There are nine
"congregational and Rabbinical organizations"—all of them having
their national headquarters in New York. Heading the offices of president are some men whose professional work is outside New York,
among them Rabbi Roland B. Gittelsohn, president of the Central
Conference of American Rabbis, and Rabbi Ralph Simon, president
of the Rabbinical Assembly. There are nineteen educational and
social service organizations, all but four of them listing New York as
their national home office. Among the periodical publications serving
the nearly six million Jews in America, there are two Orthodox publications, four Conservative periodicals, three Reform publications, five
special interest publications, such as the *American Jewish Historical
Quarterly*, and educational and other special interest groups.[55]

The *American Jewish Year Book* for 1972 reported: "Estimates
for the United States Jewish population . . . total approximately
5,060,000. . . . The data, therefore, represent an annual growth figure
of 1.07 percent. . . . The proportion of the total resident population
estimated to be Jewish remained as 2.94 percent."[56]

On the first of March 1971, the newsstands of the United States
carried an issue of *Newsweek* guaranteed to attract the attention of
Jews, philo-Semites, and anti-Semites. The cover showed a Star of

David. Within it in large letters, THE AMERICAN JEW, and beneath it
NEW PRIDE, NEW PROBLEMS. Under the caption, THE AMERICAN JEW
TODAY, in the section on religion there was assembled a factual essay
buttressed by a Gallup poll study of a nationwide poll of American
Jews.[57] By a curious coincidence, the issue appeared on St. David's
Day.

"He is one American in 30, born to a people, a faith, a history
which he can embrace, reject or ignore, but cannot easily forget. . . .
Sociologists assure him that he, on the average, is wealthier than his
neighbors and far better educated. Historians remind him that he is
more secure today than his forefathers ever were over the last 2,000
years." The conclusion "many Jews [have] come to feel they have
entered a new phase in the perennial problem of coming to grips with
their identity." Many factors have been at work. Jews were faced with
the unpalatable fact that "many American liberals, including progres-
sive Christian churchmen" were unwilling to give ideological support
to Israel besieged and outnumbered. So the Gallup poll found that 95
percent of American Jews were pro-Israel. This seems to have given
the Jews of America "an enormous boost to their self-esteem." Their
generosity to Israel was spontaneous and overwhelming. "Within
weeks after the outbreak of the Six-day War in 1967, Jewish groups
raised more than $170 million in emergency aid for Israel." This help
in varying degrees is continuing.

Under a section titled, "Pride and Prejudice," the public opinion
poll tried to measure as with a psychic thermometer the increase or
decline of anti-Semitism in the United States. Sixty-one percent of
those queried acknowledged an increase in a sense of pride as a
group. To another query, "do you think anti-Semitism in the United
States has increased or decreased in recent years?" 34 percent felt that
it had increased. The third query dealt with the Jewish Defense
League. Seventy-one percent of American Jews disapproved of their
activities.

On the whole, the results stress "the achievements, cultural attitudes and ethical ideals that Jews can comfortably share with other
high-minded Americans."

Will Herberg writing on "Religious Trends in American Jewry"
calls attention to a revitalized and committed attitude of the American
Jew, especially of the younger, third generation Jew. "The return to
Jewishness, to self-affirmation as a Jew and to self-identification with
Jewry, is perhaps the most obvious sign of the times. The young
people . . . recognize and affirm their Jewishness in a way that would

have seemed unbelievable some thirty years ago, and to a greater or less degree this is also true of other sections of American Jewry . . . the events of the thirties and forties . . . served to heighten the sense of Jewish identification and self-affirmation among American Jews, as among Jews everywhere."[58]

Emil Fackenheim in an article in *Commentary Reader* discusses "The Dilemma of Liberal Judaism" and the dilemma—often unresolved—with which contemporary Jewry attempts to face this problem. "If Judaism is to continue to exist, there must be a sense in which the Jewish past has an altogether unique authority for the liberal Jew. But this is possible only if what speaks to him through it is not merely the voice of man, but the voice of God."[59] Fackenheim then defines traditional Judaism as "the living covenant between God and Israel. . . . To the mystic, revelation-as-commandment has always seemed an impossibility . . . how can he appreciate the gift of the Infinite, while himself remaining finite? Yet it is the innermost secret of Jewish faith and Jewish life that this 'impossibility' is actual . . . it is actual by virtue of divine love."

Fackenheim formulates his credo: "The past for traditional Judaism is not a dead past. Through it still speaks the God who gave it. He still speaks because He still lives, and because His covenant with Israel is still alive. And the Jew today, as the Jew of old, is enjoined to practice, not arid law, but living commandment. Hence the Midrash well says: 'All souls, even those which had still to be created, were present at the revelation of Mt. Sinai.' "[60]

Faith also shines through Leo Baeck's credo. It differs yet strangely agrees with Fackenheim's beliefs. Says Baeck: " . . . religion is not, in our case, a faith in redemption from the world and its demands, but rather . . . the assurance of reconciliation. All reconciliation is the reconciliation of the day with eternity, of the limited with infinity. . . . Reconciliation is the liberating assurance that even now, during our life on earth, while we are coping with what is given and assigned, we are related to God . . . it is possible for man to become certain of his origin as well as of his way, and so to turn back to devotion and to the task of his life—he can always return to himself."[61]

For the Jewish people the past does not die. It renews itself constantly. When present tragic events numb the heart and cause unceasing anguish and all hope seems lost—a news item appears which staggers the imagination, brings the long obliterated past, forgotten for erased millennia, into today's headlines—and a candle lights up and we are no longer in total darkness. We become the contemporaries of our recently discovered kinsmen and we become again (for a brief interlude) the Eternal People!

Here is one such avowal of allegiance to ancient kin and to their adventurous and committed past. We live again in them and in their deeds. The flickering hope of imperishable history lights our way again to the truths which are ablaze in our past, in our heroic past, which no enemy can forever obliterate.

The Eternal People lives!

NOTES

CHAPTER I

1. "The Travels of Rabbi Benjamin," in *A General Collection of the Best and Most Interesting Voyages and Travels in All Parts of the World.* Edited by John Pinkerton, 17 vols. (London: 1808-1814), vol. VII, 19 ff.
2. Fernão Mendes Pinto, *Peregrinação,* 4 vols. (Lisboa, Livraria Ferreira, 1908-1910).
3. Solidonio Leite, *Da Influencia do Elemento Judaico no Descobrimento e Commercio do Brasil (seculos XVI e XVII)* (Rio de Janeiro: Congresso de Historia Nacional, Instituto Historico Brasileiro, 1938). The early pages deal with Portuguese-Jewish history.
4. Charles G. M. B. de la Roncière, *La découverte de l'Afrique au moyen âge, cartographes et explorateurs,* 3 vols. (Cairo: Société Royale de Geographie d'Égypte, 1924-27), vol. I, 123-24, 126, 131, 136, 139.
5. Edgar Prestage, *The Portuguese Pioneers* (London: A. & C. Black, 1933), pp. 29, 205, 206. See also section titled "Maps and Scientific Geography Up to and During Prince Henry's Life" in Eannes de Azurara, *The Chronicle of the Discovery and Conquest of Guinea,* 2 vols. (London: Hakluyt Society, 1896-99); vol. II, cvi-cxvi, cxix.
6. Quoted by Prestage, *op. cit.,* p. 321. This book is not only an outstanding work of scholarship but is a most fascinating account of the history of Portuguese navigation, with many valuable addenda as to the role of Jews in Portuguese navigation and exploration.
7. Quoted by Friedenwald in *The Jews and Medicine.* Baltimore: Johns Hopkins Press, 1944. Vol. I, 303.

See also

Abraham ben Meir Aben Ezra. *The Beginnings of Wisdom; Astrological Treatise by Abraham ibn Ezra.* Edited by Raphael Levy and Francisco Cantera Burgos. Baltimore: John Hopkins Press, 1939. P. 152.

Abrahams, Israel. *Chapters on Jewish Literature.* Philadelphia, Jewish Publication Society of America, 1899. P. 115.

Adler, Elkan N. *About Hebrew Manuscripts.* London: H. Frowde, 1905. Pp. 117, 343.

Adler, Marcus N. "The Itinerary of Benjamin of Tudela," *Jewish Quarterly Review,* XVII (1905), 526. See also Pp. 132-41.

Azevedo, João Lucio d'. *Historia dos Christãos Novos Portugueses.* Lisbon: Livraria Clássica Editora de A. M. Teixeira, 1922. Pp. 20, 27, 446.

Baron, Salo W. *The Jewish Community: Its History and Structure to the American Revolution.* 3 vols. Philadelphia: Jewish Publication Society of America, 1942. Vol. II, 166-67. *A Social and Religious History of the Jews.* 3 vols. New York: Columbia University Press, 1937. Vol. II, 6 ff; vol. III, 78 (note on Benjamin of Tudela).

Bensaude, Joaquim. *L'Astronomie nautique au Portugal à l'époque des grandes découvertes.* Bern: M. Drechsel, 1912. Pp. 19 ff., 43 "Les tables du roi Alphonsine" (1252-56), 225 ff. See also Introduction in *Regimento do Astrolabio e do Quadrante.* Munich: C. Kuhn, 1914. P. 13, for reference to "baton de Jacob."

Bloch, Joshua. "Early Hebrew Printing in Spain and Portugal," *Bulletin of the New York Public Library,* XLII (1938), 371-75. See also "Venetian Printers of Hebrew Books," *Bulletin of the New York Public Library,* XXXVI (1932), 71-92.

Brav, Aaron. Review of Munz's "Jewish Physicians in the Middle Ages," *Jewish Quarterly Review,* XIV (1923-24), 375-77.

Cambridge Medieval History. 8 vols. in 16 vols. New York: Macmillan Co., 1911-36. Vol. VIII, 521.

Cantera Burgos, Francisco. "Notas para la Historia de la Astronomía en la España Medieval; el Judio Salmantino Abraham Zacut," *Revista de la Academia de Ciencias Exactas, Fisico-Quimicas y Naturales de Madrid,* XXVII (1931), 63-398, *passim.*

"Carta de Duarte da Paz Portugues Christão Novo," in Azevedo, *op. cit.*

Cirot, Georges. "Notes sur les 'juifs portugais' de Bordeaux," *Revista da Universidade de Coimbra,* XI (1933), 158-72.

Corrêa, Gaspar. *The Three Voyages of Vasco da Gama and His Viceroyalty.* From the *Lendas da India* of Gaspar Corrêa, translated by Henry E. J. Stanley. London, 1869. Pp. 17 ff., 21-25.

Cortesão, Jaime. "Le secret portugais des descouvertes," *Lusitania* (1924), 160-62.

Coudenhove-Kalergi, Heinrich J. *Anti-Semitism Throughout the Ages.* London: Hutchinson & Co., 1935. P. 132.

Durkheim, Emile. For a vivid discussion of the significance of "rites of passage," the reader is referred to his works.

Ecclesiastes.

Epstein, Isidore. "Judah Halevi as Philosopher," *Jewish Quarterly Review,* XXV (1934-35), 201-25.

Essays on Maimonides, an Octocentennial Volume. Edited by Salo W. Baron. New York: Columbia University Press, 1941. Pp. 3, 35, 282.

Fawthier, Robert. "The Jews in the 'Use of York,'" *Bulletin of the John Rylands Library,* V (Manchester, 1918-20), 381-85.

Finkel, Joshua. "An Eleventh Century Source for the History of Jewish Scientists in Mohammedan Land (Ibn Sa'id)," *Jewish Quarterly Review,* new series, XVIII (1927-28), 46, for reference to Ibn Sa'id (1029-70) who was a judge in Toledo.

Freyre, Gilberto. *Brazil. An Interpretation.* New York: Alfred A. Knopf, 1945. Pp. 5, 11.

Friedenwald, Harry. "Jewish Physicians in Italy: Their Relation to the Papal and Italian States," American Jewish Historical Society, *Publications*, XXVIII (1922), 133-211; *The Jews in Medicine.* 2 vols. Baltimore: Johns Hopkins Press, 1944. Vol. I, 23, 24, n. 26, 305; and Chapter III, "The Ethics of the Practice of Medicine from the Jewish Point of View," pp. 18-30.

Gibbon, Edward. *History of the Decline and Fall of the Roman Empire.* 6 vols. New York, 1880. Vol. II, 4; vol. VI, n. 38, 274.

Giddings, Franklin H. *Studies in the Theory of Human Society.* New York: Macmillan Co., 1922. *Passim.*

Goldman, Solomon. *The Jew and the Universe.* New York: Harper & Brothers, 1936. P. 55.

Halevi, Jehudah. "Israel's Duration," translated by Nina Davis, *Jewish Quarterly Review*, X (1897-98), 627.

Humboldt, Alexander. *Cosmos: essai d'une description physique du monde.* 3 vols. Milan, 1846-51. Vol. II, 195.

Jacobs, Joseph. *The Jews of Angevin England.* London, 1893. P. 29. *The Story of Geographical Discovery.* London, 1899. P. 66.

Kagan, Solomon R. *Jewish Contributions to Medicine in America, from Colonial Times to the Present.* Boston: Boston Medical Publishing Co., 1939. P. 625.

Katz, Solomon. *The Jews in the Visigothic and Frankish Kingdoms of Spain and Gaul.* Cambridge: The Mediaeval Academy of America, 1937. P. 54.

Kayserling, Meyer. *Christopher Columbus and the Participation of the Jews in the Spanish and Portuguese Discoveries.* New York, 1894. Pp. 5-6; *Sephardim, Romanische Poesien der Juden in Spanien.* Leipzig, 1859. P. 41.

Kimble, George H. T. *Geography in the Middle Ages.* London: Methuen & Co., 1938. Pp. 185, 227.

Komroff, Manuel, ed. "The Oriental Travels of Benjamin of Tudela, 1160-1173," in *Contemporaries of Marco Polo.* London: Boni & Liveright, 1928. Pp. 321.

Lecky, William E. *History of the Rise and Influence of the Spirit of Rationalism in Europe.* 2 vols. New York, 1886. Vol. II, 270-71.

Levy, Raphael. *The Astrological Works of Abraham ibn Ezra.* Baltimore: Johns Hopkins Press, 1927.

Lindo, Elias H. *The History of the Jews in Spain and Portugal.* London, 1848. P. 69.

Marcus, Jacob R. *The Jew in the Medieval World.* Cincinnati: The Union of American Hebrew Congregations, 1938. Pp. 185-88, 374.

Margolis, Max L., and Marx, Alexander. *A History of the Jewish People.* Philadelphia: Jewish Publication Society of America, 1938. P. 367.

Morison, Samuel E. *Portuguese Voyages to America in the Fifteenth Century.* Cambridge: Harvard University Press, 1940. *See* chapter on "The Policy of Secrecy."

Moses ben Maimon. *The Guide of the Perplexed of Maimonides.* 3 vols. London, 1881-85. Vol. III, 65-70.

Navarrete, Martín Fernández de. *Colección de los Viages y Descubrimientes que Hicieron por Mar los Españóles desde Fines del Siglo XV.* 5 vols. Madrid, 1825-37. Vol. I, ix. Refers to Benjamin of Tudela and his travels.

Neuman, Abraham A. "Some Phases of the Condition of the Jews in Spain in the Thirteenth and Fourteenth Centuries," A. J. H. S., *Publications,* XXII (1914), 67.

Newman, Louis I. *The Talmudic Anthology.* New York: 1945. Pp. 319-20.

Nordenskiöld, Niles A. E. *Periplus, an Essay on the Early History of Charts and Sailing Directions.* Stockholm, 1897. Pp. 54, 58-59.

Orta, Garcia da. *Colloquies on the Simples & Drugs of India.* Translated by Sir Clements Markham. London: H. Sotheran & Co., 1913. Introduction, pp. xiii, xiv.

Parkes, James W. *The Jew in the Medieval Community.* London: Soncino Press, 1938. P. 163.

"Pinto, Fernão Mendes." *Encyclopedia Britannica* (11th ed.). Vol. XXI, 629.

Pires de Lima, J. A. *Mouros, Judeus e Negros na História de Portugal.* Pôrto: Livraria Civilização, 1940. *Passim.*

Pool, David de Sola. *Jehuda Halevi's Defense of His Faith.* New York: The Union of Orthodox Jewish Congregations of America, c. 1925. Pp. 73-94.

Ravenstein, Ernest G. *Martin Behaim. His Life and His Globe.* London: G. Philip & Son, 1908. P. 9.

Robinson, James H., and Breasted, James H. *A General History of Europe.* Boston: Ginn & Co., 1921. Pp. 22 ff.

Roth, Cecil. *A Short History of the Jewish People, 1600 B.C.—A.D. 1935.* London: Macmillan Co., 1936. P. 298.

Russell, Bertrand. *A History of Western Philosophy.* New York: Simon & Schuster, 1945. Pp. 301 ff.

Sacchi, Federico. *I Tipografi Ebrei di Soncino.* Cremona, 1877.

Schleiden, Matthias J. *The Importance of the Jews for the Preservation and Revival of Learning during the Middle Ages.* London: Siegle, Hill & Co., 1911. P. 32.

Silber, Mendel. "America in Hebrew Literature," A. J. H. S., *Publications,* XXII (1914), 104.

Sivarama, Menon, Cherubala P. *Early Astronomy and Cosmology.* London: G. Allen & Unwin, 1932.

Sorokin, Pitirim A. *Social and Cultural Dynamics.* 4 vols. New York: American Book Co., 1937-41. *Social Mobility.* New York: Harper & Brothers, 1927.

Steinschneider, Moritz. *Die Hebraeischen uebersetzungen des Mittelalters und die Juden als Dolmetscher.* 2 vols. Berlin, 1893. *Eine unbekannte Incunabel mit Holzchnitten, 1490; der Buchdruck des 15 Jahrhunderts.* Berlin: 1929. Pp. xl and xli.

Stephens, Henry M. *Portugal.* New York, 1898. *Passim.*

Stevenson, Edward L. *Portolan Charts; Their Origin and Characteristics.* New York: Knickerbocker Press, 1911. P. 23. About 100 portolan charts prior to 1500 are preserved, p. 16.

Tout, T. F. "Medieval Forgers and Forgeries," *Bulletin of the John Rylands Library,* V (Manchester, 1918-20), 211. Speaks of the ease with which judges condemned Jews to death.

Trachtenberg, Joshua. *The Devil and the Jews. The Medieval Conception of the Jew and Its Relation to Modern Antisemitism.* New Haven: Yale University Press, 1943. *Passim.*

Wechsler, Israel S. *The Neurologists' Point of View. Essays on Psychiatric and Other Subjects.* New York: L. B. Fischer, 1945. P. 147.

Wedel, Theodore O. *The Medieval Attitude toward Astrology, Particularly in England.* New Haven: Yale University Press, 1920. *Passim.*

CHAPTER II

1. In Charles G. M. B. de La Roncière, *La carte de Christophe Colomb* (Paris: Les Editions Historiques, 1924), p. 2.

2. Fernando Colon, "The History of the Life and Actions of Admiral Christopher Colon, and of His Discovery of the West Indies, Called the New World, Now in Possession of His Catholic Majesty. Written by His Own Son Ferdinand Colon," in *A General Collection of the Best and Most Interesting Voyages and Travels in All Parts of the World.* Edited by John Pinkerton, 17 vols. (London: 1808-1814), vol. XII, 1-155. *See* p. 2.

3. Heinrich H. Houben, *Christopher Columbus: the Tragedy of a Discoverer* (London: G. Routledge & Sons, 1935), p. 12. *See* Chapter II, "The Riddle of Columbus."

4. Samuel E. Morison, *Admiral of the Ocean Sea: A Life of Christopher Columbus,* 2 vols. (Boston: Little Brown & Co., 1942), vol. I, 23, 73.

5. Charles E. Nowell, "The Columbus Question," *American Historical Review,* XLIV (1939), 802.

6. Abraham A. Neuman, *The Jews in Spain. Their Social, Political and Cultural Life during the Middle Ages,* 2 vols. (Philadelphia, The Jewish Publication Society of America, 1942), vol. II, 223.

7. Morison, *op. cit.,* vol. I, 137.

8. John Boyd Thacher, *Christopher Columbus*, 3 vols. (New York: G. P. Putnam's Sons, 1903-1904), vol. I, 459.
9. *Ibid.*, pp. 436, 514.
10. *Ibid.*, p. 462.
11. Elias H. Lindo, *The History of the Jews in Spain and Portugal* (London, 1848), pp. 284 ff. Italics mine.
12. Thacher, *op. cit.*, vol. I, 462 (has an important demographic note), 516, 521 n. 2, 524, 527 n. 2, 530; Salvador de Madariaga, *Christopher Columbus* (New York: Macmillan Co., 1940), p. 209; Morison, *op. cit.*, vol. I, 296, 298.
13. Thacher, *op. cit.*, vol. I, 530.
14. *Ibid.*, p. 560. The discovery of maize is reported in "Corn, Its Products and Uses," U. S. Bureau of Agricultural and Industrial Chemistry, *Bulletin* (Washington: February, 1947).
15. Samuel E. Morison, *Portuguese Voyages to America in the Fifteenth Century* (Cambridge, Harvard University Press, 1940), p. 108.
16. William B. Greenlee. *The Voyage of Pedro Álvares Cabral to Brazil and India* (London: Hakluyt Society, 1938), pp. 34 ff.
17. *História da Colonização Portuguesa do Brasil*, 3 vols. (Pôrto: Litografia Nacional, 1921-24), vol. II, 312.
18. William B. Greenlee, "First Half Century of Brazilian History," *Mid-America*, new series XIV (1943), 93-94.
19. *Ibid.*

See also

Abrahams, Israel. *Jewish Life in the Middle Ages.* New York, 1896. P. 399. Chapters XXIII and XXIV deal with "Personal Relations Between Jews and Christians."

Adler, Elkan N. *Auto de Fé and Jew.* London: H. Frowde, 1908.

Alguns Documentos do Archivo Nacional da Torre do Tombo. Lisbon, 1892. Pp. 408, 459, 460.

Amador de los Rios, José. *Historia Social, Politica y Religiosa de los Judios de España y Portugal.* 3 vols. Madrid, 1875.

André, Marius. "La véridique aventure de Christophe Colombe," *Revue de l'Amérique Latine*, XIII (1927), 1.

Anthiaume, Albert. *L'astrolabe-quadrant du Musée des Antiquités de Rouen.* Paris: G. Thomas, 1910.

"Atlas Catalan de Charles V, par Cresques le Juif." Photostat in the Edward E. Ayer Collection, from the original in the Bibliothèque Nationale, Paris, Ge CC54.

Azevedo, João Lucio d'. *Historia dos Christãos Novos Portugueses.* Lisbon, Livraria Clássica Editora de A. M. Teixeira, 1922.

Baldwin, Leland D. *The Story of the Americas, the Discovery, Settlement and Development of the New World.* New York: Simon and Schuster, 1943. Pp. 13, 18-19.

Ballesteros y Beretta, Antonio. *Cristóbal Colón y el Descubrimiento de América*. 2 vols. Barcelona: Salvat Editores, 1945. Vol. I, 203 ff., 207; also chapters on "La Patría," "El Colón Gallego," "El Colón Catalan," "Colón Portugues," "Colón Corso," "Colón Judio."

Baron, Salo W. *A Social and Religious History of the Jews*. 3 vols. New York: Columbia University Press, 1937. Vol. III, 94-95.

Beazley, Charles R. *Prince Henry the Navigator*. New York, 1895. Pp. 88-89, 161. "Prince Henry of Portugal and His Political, Commercial, and Colonizing Work," *American Historical Review*, XVII (1911-12), 252-67.

Bell, Aubrey F. G. *Gaspar Corrêa*. London: Oxford University Press, 1924.

Bensaude, Joaquim. *L'astronomie nautique au Portugal à l'époque des grandes découvertes*. Bern: M. Drechsel, 1912. Pp. 51, 59 n. 1, 92-95, 96 ff., 128 ff., 251-52, 255 ff., 281. *Histoire de la science nautique portugaise à l'époque des grandes découvertes*. Genève: Société Sadag, 1914. Introduction to *Regimento do Estrolabio e do Quadrante*, Munich: C. Kuhn, 1914. *Lacunes et surprises de l'histoire des découvertes maritimes*. Coimbra: Imprensa da Universidade, 1930.

Bloch, Joshua. "Early Hebrew Printing in Spain and Portugal," *Bulletin of the New York Public Library*, XLII (1938), 371-420. See pp. 402-406.

Cambridge Medieval History. 8 vols. in 16 vols. New York: Macmillan Co., 1911-36. Vol. VIII, 504, 521.

Cantera Burgos, Francisco. *Abraham Zacut*. Madrid: M. Aguilar, 1935. "Bibliografia," pp. 99-102. "Notas para la Historia de Astronomía . . . el Judio Salmantino Abraham Zacut," *Revista de la Academia de Ciencias Exactas, Fisico-Químicas y Naturales de Madrid*, XXVII (1931), 63-273. See especially pp. 69, 125, 151-236.

Carbia, Rómulo D. *La Carta de Navegar Atribuida a Toscanelli (1474)*. Buenos Aires, Imprenta de la Universidade, 1932. *La Investigación Científica y el Descubrimiento de America*. Buenos Aires, Tall. Graf. San Pablo, 1937. P. 12.

Centenario do Descobrimento da America. Lisbon, 1892. P. 32.

Cha Masser, Lunardo da. "Relazione de Lunardo da Cha Masser," *Centenario do Descobrimento da America*. Lisbon, 1892. P. 192.

Cirot, Georges. "Notes sur les 'Juifs portugais' de Bordeaux," *Revista da Universidade de Coimbra*, XI (1933), 158-72.

Collecção de Livros Ineditos de Historia Portugueza. 3 vols. Lisbon, 1790. Particular attention should be called to Document No. 22, vol. III, 461-62, titled "Detriminaçam d'El Rey com os do sur Conselho . . . acerqua dos Judeus que se filham no mar."

Colombo, Cristoforo. *Carta a Luis de Santangel de las Islas Halladas en las Indias 1493*; *Codice Diplomatico Colombo-Americano*. Genova, 1823.

Colon, Fernando. "The History of the Life and Actions of Admiral Christopher Colon, and of His Discovery of the West Indies, called the

New World, Now in Possession of His Catholic Majesty. Written by His Own Son Ferdinand Colon," *A General Collection of the Best and Most Interesting Voyages and Travels in All Parts of the World*, edited by John Pinkerton, 17 vols. London, 1808-1814. Vol. XII, 1-155. See p. 2.

Columbia Encyclopedia. Compiled by Clarke F. Ansley. New York: Columbia University Press, 1935.

Corrêa, Gaspar. *Lendas da India*. 4 vols. Lisbon, 1858. Pp. 23 ff. See also *The Three Voyages of Vasco da Gama and His Viceroyalty*. From the *Lendas da India* of Gaspar Corrêa, translated by Henry E. J. Stanley. London, 1869. Pp. 21-25.

Cortesão, Armando. *Cartografia e Cartografos Portugueses dos Seculos XV e XVI*. 2 vols. Lisbon: Edição da "Seara nova." 1935. Vol. I, 4; vol. II, 8.

Cortesão, Jaime. "Do Siglio Nacional Sôbre os Descobrimentos," *Lusitania* (1924), pp. 49-59. "Le Secret Portugais des Decouvertes," *Lusitania* (1924), p. 161.

Crone, Gerald Roe, ed. and tr. *The Voyage of Cadamosto and Other Documents*. London: Hakluyt Society, 1937. See especially João de Barros, *Da Asia*. Decada I, Livro III, cap. XI, 245-55.

Cumston, Charles G. *An Introduction to the History of Medicine, from the Time of the Pharaohs to the End of the XVIIIth Century*. London: K. Paul, Trench, Trubner & Co., 1926. P. 232.

Duhem, Pierre M. M. *Le Systeme du monde; histoire des doctrines cosmologiques de Platon a Copernic*. 5 vols. Paris: A. Hermann et fils, 1913-17. Vol. II, 263.

Eannes de Azurara, Gomes. *The Chronicle of the Discovery and Conquest of Guinea*. 2 vols. London: 1896-99. Vol. I, 12, 14-15; vol. II, cvi-cxvi, cxix, cxxvi-cxxvii, 334-35 (for note on "terrestrial paradise").

Eyre, Edward, ed. *European Civilization. Its Origin and Development*. By various contributors under the direction of Edward Eyre. 7 vols. New York: Oxford University Press, 1934-39. Vol. III, 575-76.

Fernandes, Valentim. *Reportorio dos Tempos*. Genève: Société Sadag, 1917.

Fernándes y González, Francisco. *Instituciones Jurídicas del Pueblo de Israel en los Diferentes Estados de la Peninsula Ibérica*. Madrid, 1881. P. 319.

Fontoura da Costa, Abel. *A Marinharia dos Descobrimentos*. Lisbon: 1933. Pp. 22-33, 34, 55, 80-86. "L'Almanach Perpetuum de Zacut," *IIIᵉ Congrès International d'Histoire des Sciences. Actas, Conferences et Communications*. Lisbon, 1936. Pp. 137-46.

Forjaz de Sampaio, Albino. *Historia da Literature Portuguesa*. 3 vols. Paris-Lisbon, 1929-32. Vol. I, 44-87; vol. III, 79, 83.

Freyre, Gilberto. *Brazil. An Interpretation*. New York: Alfred A. Knopf, 1945. P. 11. *Casa-Grande & Senzala; Formação da Familia Brasileira sob o Regimen de Economia Patriarchal.* Rio de Janeiro, Maia & Schmidt, 1933. Pp. 7 ff. "Some Aspects of the Social Development of Portuguese America," in *Concerning Latin American Culture.* Edited by Charles C. Griffin. New York: Columbia University Press, 1940. Pp. 79, 84-86.

Friedenwald, Harry. *The Jews and Medicine.* 2 vols. Baltimore: Johns Hopkins Press, 1944. Pp. 159, 429, 430 ff., 541.

Goff, Frederick. "The Letter of Christopher Columbus Concerning the Islands of India," The Library of Congress, *Quarterly Journal,* III (1946), 3-7.

Graetz, Heinrich H. *History of the Jews, from the Earliest Times to the Present Day.* 5 vols. London, 1891-1901. Vol. IV, 419.

Gravier, Gabriel. *La lettre et la carte de Toscanelli à Fernam Martins, et à Christophe Colomb d'après Henry Vignaud.* Rouen: E. Cagniard, 1902.

Greenlee, William B. "The Background of Brazilian History," *The Americas,* II (1945), 151-64. "A Descriptive Bibliography of the History of Portugal," *Hispanic American Historical Review,* XX (1940), 491-516. *The Voyage of Pedro Álvares Cabral to Brasil and India.* London: Hakluyt Society, 1938. Pp. xviii, lxvii, 10, 11, 12. See footnotes.

Halevi, Jehudah. "Israel's Duration," "Song of the Oppressed," "Where Shall I Find Thee?" translated by Nina Davis, *Jewish Quarterly Review,* X (1897-98), 117-18, 627, 628.

Hamy, Jules T. E. *Cresques, lo Juheu; note sur un géographe Juif Catalan de la fin du XIV siècle.* Angers, 189-P. 6, *passim.* "Jaffuda Cresques (Jaime Ribes). Commentaires sur quelques documents . . . publiés par D. Miguel Bonet sur ce géographe Juif Catalan," *Bulletin géographie historique et description,* année 1897, no. 3 (1898), 381-88. *Mecia de Viladestes, cartographe Juif Majorcain du commencement du XV siècle.* Macon: Protat frères, 1902. P. 5, *passim. Note sur la mappemonde de Diego Ribero (1529).* Paris, 1887. *Notice sur une carte marine inédite du cosmographe Majorcain Gabriel de Vallsecha,* 1896. Pp. 111-20. *Portolan Charts of the XVth, XVIth and XVIIth Centuries.* New York, 1912.

Harrisse, Henry. *Notes on Columbus.* New York, 1866. Pp. 186 ff.

Hirsch, S. A. "Early English Hebraists. Roger Bacon and His Predecessors," *Jewish Quarterly Review,* XII (1899-1900), 34-88.

História da Colonização Portuguesa do Brasil. 3 vols. Pôrto: Litografia Nacional, 1921-24. Vol. I, 36-60.

Houben, Heinrich. *Christopher Columbus: the Tragedy of a Discoverer.* London: G. Routledge & Sons, 1935. P. 12. See Chapter II, "The Riddle of Columbus."

Irving, Washington. *The Life and Voyages of Christopher Columbus.* 3 vols. London, 1877. Vol. I, 55-56.

Jacobs, Joseph. *The Story of Geographical Discovery.* London, 1899. Pp. 53, 210.

Jane, Cecil. Introduction to the Hakluyt Society volume titled *Select Documents Illustrating the Four Voyages of Columbus*. London, 1930. 2nd series, vol. XV, 1-cxli. "The Letter of Columbus Announcing the Success of His First Voyage," *Hispanic American Historical Review*, X (1930), 33-50. "The Question of the Literacy of Columbus in 1492," *Hispanic American Historical Review*, X (1930), 505.

Jervis, Walter W. *The World in Maps*. London: G. Philip & Son, 1936.

Jewish Encyclopedia, selected articles.

The Journal of Christopher Columbus (during His First Voyage, 1492-93). London, 1893. P. 186.

Katz, Solomon, *The Jews in the Visigothic and Frankish Kingdoms of Spain and Gaul*. Cambridge, The Mediaeval Academy of America, 1937.

Kayserling, Meyer. *Biblioteca Española-Portugueza-Judaica, Dictionnaire bibliographique des auteurs juifs*. Strasbourg, 1890. *Christopher Columbus and the Participation of the Jews in the Spanish and Portuguese Discoveries*. New York, 1894. Pp. 5-8, 12, 19, 70. *Geschichte der Juden in Portugal*. Leipzig, 1867. *Die Juden in Navarra, den Baskenlaendern und auf den Balearen*. Berlin, 1861.

Kimble, George H. T. *Geography in the Middle Ages*. London: Methuen & Co., 1938. P. 185.

La Roncière, Charles G. M. B. de. *La carte de Christophe Colomb*. Paris: Les Éditions Historiques, 1924. P. 2. *La découverte de l'Afrique au moyen âge, cartographes et explorateurs*. 3 vols. Cairo: Société Royale de Geographie de Égypte, 1924-27. Vol. I, 122, 126-29, 136; vol. II, 68-69.

Leite, Solidonio. *Da Influencia do Elemento Judaico no Descobrimento e Commercio do Brasil (seculos XVI e XVII)*. Rio de Janeiro: Congresso de Historia Nacional, Instituto Historico Brasileiro, 1938. Pp. 9, 16, 18, 23.

Lester, Charles E. *The Life and Voyages of Americus Vespucius*. New York, 1846.

Levy, Raphael. *The Astrological Works of Abraham ibn Ezra*. Baltimore: Johns Hopkins Press, 1927. P. 63.

Lindo, Elias H. *The History of the Jews in Spain and Portugal*. London, 1848. *Passim*.

Lopes de Mendonca, Henrique. *Estudos sobre Navios Portuguezes nos Seculos XV e XVI*. Lisbon, 1892.

Madariaga, Salvador de. *Christopher Columbus*. New York: Macmillan Co., 1940. P. 54. See also pp. 17-41, 90-93, 103, 119-35, 360-69, 410.

Marcus, Jacob R. *The Jew in the Medieval World*. Cincinnati: The Union of American Hebrew Congregations, 1938. Pp. 52, 382.

Minkin, Jacob S. *Abarbanel and the Expulsion of the Jews from Spain*. New York: Behrman's Jewish Book House, 1938.

Morison, Samuel E. *Admiral of the Ocean Sea: A Life of Christopher Columbus*. 2 vols. Boston: Little, Brown & Co., 1942. Vol. I, 23, 46-47,

51, 56-57, 85 ff., 92-93, 115, 133, 144, 243. *Portuguese Voyages to America in the Fifteenth Century.* Cambridge, Harvard University Press, 1940. Pp. 49 ff., 73.

Navarrete, Martín Fernández de. *Collección de los Viages y Descubrimientes que Hicieron por Mar los Españoles desde Fines del Siglo XV.* 5 vols. Madrid, 1825-37. Vol. I, 1-352.

Neuman, Abraham A. *The Jews in Spain, Their Social, Political and Cultural Life during the Middle Ages.* 2 vols. Philadelphia: Jewish Publication Society of America, 1942. Vol. II, 103-104, 221, 258-59. See particularly chapter on "The Rule of the Kahal" in vol. I.

Newton, Arthur P., ed. *The Great Age of Discovery.* London: University of London Press, 1932.

Nordenskiöld, Niles A. E. *Periplus, an Essay on the Early History of Charts and Sailing Directions.* Stockholm, 1897. Pp. 58-59.

Nowell, Charles E. "The Columbus Question," *American Historical Review*, XLIV (1939), 802.

Nunn, George E. *The Geographical Conceptions of Columbus; a Critical Consideration of Four Problems.* New York: American Geographical Society, 1924. P. 33.

O'Brien, George A. T. *An Essay on Medieval Economic Teaching.* London: Longmans, Green & Co., 1920. P. 216.

Orta, Garcia da. *Colloquies on the Simples & Drugs of India.* Translated by Sir Clements Markham. London: H. Sotheran & Co., 1913. Introduction, pp. xiii-xiv, 5.

Otero Sanchez, Prudencio. *España Patria de Colón.* Madrid: Biblioteca Nueva, 1922. P. 142. See also pp. 204, 225.

Pereira da Silva, Luciano. "A Arte de Navegar dos Portugueses desde o Infante a D. João de Castro," *História da Colonização Portuguesa do Brasil, op. cit.,* vol. I (1921), 29-104. *Astrolabios Existentes em Portugal.* Lisbon: Tip. dos Camos. de Ferro do Estado, 1917. "A Concepção Cosmológica nos 'Lusiadad,'" *Lusitania* (1925), pp. 265, 277, 284, 285, 286. "Kamal, Tabuas do India e Tavoletas Nauticas," *Lusitania* (1924), pp. 263-71. "A Propósito das Leituras do Infante," *Lusitania* (1924), pp. 23-27, 263.

Pirenne, Henri. *A History of Europe from the Invasions to the XVI Century.* London: G. Allen & Unwin, 1939. P. 540.

Prestage, Edgar. *The Portuguese Pioneers.* London: A. & C. Black, 1933. Pp. 20 n. 1, 29, 205-206, 218, 237, 317, 323.

Ravenstein, Ernest G. *Martin Behaim, His Life and His Globe.* London: G. Philip & Son, 1908. Pp. 12, 13, 19, 32-34.

Renard, Georges F., and Weulerasee, G. *Life and Work in Modern Europe (Fifteenth to Eighteenth Centuries).* London: Alfred A. Knopf, 1926. Pp. 1-7.

Roth, Cecil. *A Short History of the Jewish People, 1600 B.C.—A.D. 1935.* London: Macmillan Co., 1936. Pp. 233 ff.

Schleiden, Matthias J. *The Importance of Jews for the Preservation and Revival of Learning during the Middle Ages*. London: Siegle, Hill & Co., 1911. *Passim*.

Seignobos, Charles. *The Rise of European Civilization*. London: J. Cape, 1939. P. 182.

Sombart, Werner. *The Jews and Modern Capitalism*. London: T. F. Unwin, 1913. P. 30.

Sousa Holstein, Francisco de Borja P. M. A., *A Escola de Sagres as Tradições do Infante D. Henrique*. Lisbon, 1877. Pp. 34-35.

Sousa Viterbo, Francisco M. de. *Trabalhos Nauticos dos Portuguezes nos Seculos XVI e XVII*. 2 vols. Lisbon: Academia Real das Sciencias, 1898-1900. *Passim*.

Southey, Robert. *History of Brazil*. 3 vols. London, 1810-19. Pp. 24, 32.

Steinschneider, Moritz. *Die Hebraeischen uebersetzungen des Mittelalters und die Juden als Dolmetscher*. 2 vols. Berlin, 1893. *Passim*.

Stevenson, Edward L. *Christopher Columbus and His Enterprise*. New York, 1914. *Passim*. The quotations of the *Journal* used are those found in Thacher, *op. cit.*, vol. I, 512 ff. They are based on the abridged *Journal* which Bartolomé de las Casas made from the original holograph *Journal*, hence the use of the third person except for direct quotations. *Early Spanish Cartography of the New World, with Special Reference to the Wolfenbuttel-Spanish Map and the Work of Diego Ribero*. Worcester, Mass., The Davis Press, 1909. *Portolan Charts; Their Origin and Characteristics*. New York: Knickerbocker Press, 1911.

Thacher, John B. *Christopher Columbus*. 3 vols. New York: G. P. Putnam's Sons, 1903-1904. Vol. I, 176, 458-61.

Thompson, James W. *The Middle Ages, 300-1500*. 2 vols. New York: Alfred A. Knopf, 1931. Vol. II, 776, 778, 873-74, 1036.

Universal Jewish Encyclopedia. 10 vols. New York: Universal Jewish Encyclopedia, Inc. 1939-43. Vol. I, 108; vol. III, 53; vol. VIII, 606.

Varnhagen, Francisco A. *Historia das Lutas com os Hollandezes no Brazil desde 1624 a 1654*. Lisbon, 1872. P. 307.

Velho, Alvaro. *Roteiro da Primeira Viagem de Vasco da Gama*. Lisbon: Agência Geral das Colonias, 1940. P. 171 has a list of *degradados*.

Vignaud, Henry. "Columbus a Spaniard and a Jew," *American Historical Review*, XVIII (1913), 505-512. *Toscanelli and Columbus*. New York: E. P. Dutton & Co., 1902. Pp. 260-61.

Waddell, Helen J. *The Wandering Scholars*. London: Constable & Co., 1927. P. 106.

Waldseemüller, Martin. *Cosmographiae Introductio*. Deodate, 1507. See for interesting charts developed for navigators. Also section titled *Navigatio. The Cosmographiae Introductio . . . Followed by the Four Voyages of Amerigo Vespucci*. New York, United States Catholic Historical Society, 1907. P. 137.

Waxman, Meyer. *A History of Jewish Literature*. 4 vols. New York: Bloch Publishing Co., 1930. Vol. II, 319 ff. See chapter on "Original Works on Astronomy and Mathematics."

White, Lynn, Jr. "Technology and Invention in the Middle Ages," *Speculum*, XV (1940), 143.

Wroth, Lawrence C. *The Way of a Ship*. Portland, Me.: The Southworth Anthoensen Press, 1937. P. 25 says that the earliest account of the cross-staff was that of Levi ben Gerson. See also p. 30.

On Columbus the following may prove helpful: Herbert B. Adams and Henry Wood, *Columbus and His Discovery of America* (Baltimore, 1892); Armando Alvarez Pedroso, *Cristóbal Colón* (Havana; Cultural, s.a., 1944); Seraphim G. Canoutas, *Christopher Columbus, a Greek Nobleman* (New York: St. Marks Publishing Corp., 1943); Rómulo D. Carbia, *Origen y Patria de Cristóbal Colón* (Buenos Aires: Talleres Graficos, 1918); Candido Costa, *As Duas Americas* (Lisbon: J. Bastos, 1900); Maurice David, *Who Was "Columbus?"* (New York: The Research Publishing Co., 1933); Charles Duff, *The Truth About Columbus* (London: Grayson and Grayson, 1936); Enrique de Gandía, *Historia de Cristóbal Colón* (Buenos Aires: Editorial Claridad, 1942); Celso Garcia de la Riega, "Cristóbal Colón ¿Espanol?" *Boletin de la Sociedad Geográfica de Madrid*, XL, suppl. (1898), 1-43; Washington Irving, *The Life and Voyages of Christopher Columbus*, 3 vols. (London, 1877); Arthur Lobo d'Avila, *Cristóbal Colón* (Lisbon: Tip. da Emprêsa Nacional de Publicidade, 1939); Cesare de Lollis, *Cristoforo Colombo* (Rome: Fratelli Treves, c. 1923); Ernest G. Ravenstein, *Martin Behaim. His Life and His Globe* (London: G. Philip & Son, 1908); Patrocinio Ribeiro, *A Nacionalidade Portuguesa de Cristovam Colombo (The Portuguese Nationality of Christopher Columbus)*. (Lisbon: Livraria Renascenca, J. Cardoso, 1927); John B. Thacher, *Christopher Columbus*. 3 vols. (New York: G. P. Putnam's Sons, 1903-1904); Luis Ulloa, *El Pre-descubrimiento Hispano-catalán de America en 1477. Xristo-Ferens Colom, Fernando el Catolico y la Cataluna Espanola* (Paris: Librairie orientale et americaine, Maisonneuve freres, 1928); Henry Vignaud, *Toscanelli and Columbus. The Letter and Chart of Toscanelli* (New York: E. P. Dutton & Co., 1902); Edward P. Vining, *An Inglorious Columbus* (New York, 1885).

I am immeasurably indebted to Dr. William B. Greenlee, trustee of the Newberry Library, eminent scholar and author, for opening up to me the entire field connected with cartography, exploration, and discovery, with particular reference to Brazil. His reputation in this field is without a peer. He has generously shared valuable books, maps, and inaccessible information with the writer. To his published works and manuscript materials much credit is due. Without his guidance, this section could not have been written.

CHAPTER III

1. Gilberto Freyre, *The Masters and the Slaves* [*Casa-Grande & Senzala*] *A Study in the Development of Brazilian Civilization* (New York: Alfred A. Knopf, 1946), p. xli.
2. Charles E. Nowell, "The Discovery of Brazil—Accidental or Intentional?" *Hispanic American Historical Review*, XVI (1936), 317.
3. William B. Greenlee, "The First Half Century of Brazilian History," *Mid-America*, new series, XIV (1943), 107. The quotation is on pp. 118 ff.
4. João Lucio d'Azevedo, *Historia dos Christãos Novos Portugueses* (Lisbon: A. M. Teixeira, 1922), pp. 20 ff.
5. Herbert I. Bloom, "A Study of Brazilian Jewish History, 1623-1654, Based Chiefly upon the Findings of the Late Samuel Oppenheim," American Jewish Historical Society, *Publications*, XXXIII (1934), 74-75.
6. Johan Nieuhof, "Voyages and Travels into Brazil," in *A General Collection of the Best and Most Interesting Voyages and Travels in All Parts of the World*. Edited by John Pinkerton, 17 vols. (London: 1808-1814), vol. XIV, 753.
7. Quoted by Bloom, *op. cit.*, p. 94.
8. Gilberto Freyre, "Some Aspects of the Social Development of Portuguese America," in *Concerning Latin American Culture*, edited by Charles C. Griffin (New York: Columbia University Press, 1940), *passim*.

See also

Adler, Cyrus. "A Contemporary Memorial Relating to Damages to Spanish Interests in America Done by Jews of Holland (1634)," American Jewish Historical Society, *Publications*, XVII (1909), 50. "Original Unpublished Documents Relating to Thomas Tremino de Sobremonte (1638)," A. J. H. S., *Publications*, XVII (1909), 27-31. "Trial of Jorge de Almeida by the Inquisition in Mexico," A. J. H. S., *Publications*, IV (1898), 77.
Adler, Elkan N. "The Inquisition in Peru," A. J. H. S., *Publications*, XII (1904), 5-37.
Alguns Documentos do Archivo Nacional da Torre do Tombo, acerca das Navegações e Conquistas Portuguezas. Lisbon, 1892. Pp. 197-206, 408, 458-60.
Almeida Prado, Jorge da. "Inquisition in New World, Denunciation Against," A. J. H. S., *Publications*, IV (1896), 68. *Pernambuco e as Capitanias do Norte do Brasil (1530-1630).* 4 vols. São Paulo: Companhia Editora Nacional, 1939-42. Vol. II, 104-109 ff.
Amador de los Rios, José. *Historia Social, Political y Religiosa de los España y Portugal.* 3 vols. Madrid, 1875. Vol. III, 547.

Azevedo, João Lucio d'. *Historia dos Christãos Novos Portugueses*. Lisbon: Livraria Clássica Editora de A. M. Teixeira, 1922. P. 20. "Noticias de Portugal de 1578-1580," *Lusitania* (1924), pp. 33-39.

Baldwin, Leland D. *The Story of the Americas, the Discovery, Settlement, and Development of the New World*. New York: Simon and Schuster, 1943. P. 264.

Beals, Carleton. *America South*. Philadelphia: J. B. Lippincott Co., 1937. *Passim.*, especially pp. 172-173 ff.

Bensaude, Joaquim. *L'astronomie nautique au Portugal à l'époque des grandes découvertes*. Bern: M. Drechsel, 1912. Pp. 62-63, 126 ff., 133 ff., 253-54. Introduction to *Regimento do Estrolabio e do Quadrante*. Munich: C. Kuhn, 1914. Pp. 7, 11, 13, 14, 17.

Bloch, Joshua. "Early Hebrew Printing in Spain and Portugal," *Bulletin of the New York Public Library*, XLII (1938), 375.

Bloom, Herbert I. "A Study of Brazilian Jewish History 1623-1654, Based Chiefly upon the Findings of the Late Samuel Oppenheim," A. J. H. S., *Publications*, XXXIII (1934), 45-46, 83. *The Economic Activities of the Jews of Amsterdam in the Seventeenth and Eighteenth Centuries*. Williamsport, Penn.: Bayard Press, 1937. P. 129. "The Dutch Archives, with Special Reference to American Jewish History," A. J. H. S., *Publications*, XXXII (1931), 7-21.

Boletim da Sociedade de Geografia de Lisboa, series 46ª, no. 7-8 (1928), p. 175.

Bradley, Edward S. *Henry Charles Lea*. Philadelphia: University of Pennsylvania Press, 1931. P. 339.

"Brasil," *The South American Handbook*. London, 1942. P. 207.

Calmon, Pedro. *História da Civilização Brasileira*. São Paulo: Companhia Editora Nacional, 1935. P. 14. *Historia do Brasil*. São Paulo: Companhia Editora Nacional, 1939. "O Brasil e Portugal de 1500," *Meneario do Jornal de Comercio* (1939), pp. 555-65.

Caminha, Pedro Vaz de. *A Carta de Pero Vaz de Caminha, com um Estudo do Jaime Cortesão*. Rio de Janeiro: Livros de Portugal, 1943. Pp. 40, 260.

Camoens, Luis de. Quoted in *Time* (July 22, 1946), p. 30.

Campos, Agostinho. "Sobre a 'Decadência' e a 'Ignorância' da Espanha," *Lusitania* (1926-27), pp. 399-408.

Canabrava, Alice P. *O Comércio Português no Rio da Prata (1580-1640)*. São Paulo: Universidade de São Paulo, 1944.

Cantera Burgos, Francisco. *Abraham Zacut, Siglo XV*. Madrid: M. Aguilar, 1935.

Catálogo da Libraria Portugália. Lisbon, 1947(?). P. 116. Has four items under heading *Sôbre Judeus*. See also p. 328.

Cha Masser, Lunardo da. "Relazione de Lunardo da Cha Masser," *Centenario do Descobrimento da America*. Lisbon, 1892. Pp. 47, 52, 53,

61-63, 68-69, 71, 73. See also "Relazione di Leonardo da Ca' Masser," *Archivo Storica Italiano*. Firenze, 1845. Appendix, pp. ii, l.

Church, George E. *Aborigines of South America*. Edited by Clement R. Markham. London: Chapman and Hall, 1912. Pp. 16-38.

Cirot, Georges. "Notes sur les 'Juifs portugais' de Bordeaux," *Revista da Universidade de Coimbra*, XI (1933), 168.

Columbia Encyclopedia. New York: Columbia University Press, 1935. See "Antonio José da Silva."

Conway, George R. G. "Hernando Alonso, a Jewish Conquistador with Cortes in Mexico," A. J. H. S., *Publications*, XXXI (1928), appendix 26-31.

Corrêa, Gaspar. *The Three Voyages of Vasco da Gama and His Viceroyalty*. From the *Lendas da India* of Gaspar Corrêa. London, 1869. Pp. 17-25, 50, 59, 400, 422. *Lendas da India*. 4 vols. Lisbon, 1858. Vol. II, 134.

Cortesão, Armando. *Cartografia e Cartografos Portugueses dos Séculos XV e XVI*. 2 vols. Lisbon: Edição da "Seara nova," 1935. Vol. I, 144; vol. II, 316.

Crone, Gerald R., tr. and ed. *Voyages of Cadamosta and Other Documents*. London: Hakluyt Society, 1937.

Diffie, Bailey W. *Latin American Civilization: Colonial Period*. Harrisburg, Penn.: Stackpole Sons, 1945. Pp. 636, 700, 512.

Dutertre, Jean Baptiste. *Histoire générale des Antilles habitées par les François*. 4 vols. Paris, 1667-71. Vol. II, 122-25.

Ellis, Alfredo Junior. "Alguns Paulistas dos Seculos XVI e XVII Subsidio para a Historia de S. Paulo," *Revista do Instituto Historico e Geographico Brasileiro*, tomo especial, III (1927), 409, 437. ("Notas sobre João Ramalho" on pp. 410-11.)

Entwistle, William J. "The 'Lusiads,' Da Gama and Modern Criticism," *Lusitania* (1927), pp. 69-88.

Fernández y González, Francisco. *Instituciones Jurídicas del Pueblo de Israel en los Diferentes Estados de la Península Ibérica*. Madrid, 1881.

Ficalho, Francisco Manuel Carlos de Mello. *Viagens de Pedro da Covilhan*. Lisbon, 1898. P. 107.

"Find Quaint Sect of Jews in Mexico," *Chicago Sunday Times*, November 4, 1945. P. 16.

Fontoura da Costa, Abel. *A Marinharia dos Descobrimentos*. Lisbon, 1933.

Freitas, Jordão de. "O Descobrimento Pre-Colombino da América Austral Pelos Portugueses," *Lusitania* (1926), pp. 315-27. The writer has had this article translated.

Freudenthal, J. "On the History of Spinozism," *Jewish Quarterly Review*, VIII (1896), 17-70.

Freyre, Gilberto. *Brazil. An Interpretation*. New York: Alfred A. Knopf, 1945. *Passim. Casa-Grande & Senzala; Formação da Familia Brasileira sob o Regimen de Economia Patriarchal*. Rio de Janeiro: Maia and

Schmidt, 1933. *Passim. The Masters and the Slaves [Casa-Grande & Senzala] A Study in the Development of Brazilian Civilization.* New York: Alfred A. Knopf, 1946. P. 9. *Mucambos do Nordeste. Algumas Notas Sobre o Typo de Casa Popular mais Primitivo do Nordeste do Brasil.* Rio de Janeiro: Ministerio da Educação e Saude, 1937. *Sobrados e Mucambos; Decadencia do Patriarchado Rural no Brasil.* São Paulo: Companhia Editora Nacional, 1936. Pp. 396-97. "Some Aspects of the Social Development of Portuguese America," in *Concerning Latin American Culture.* Edited by Charles C. Griffin. New York: Columbia University Press, 1940. Pp. 81-87, 94-95.

Friedenberg, Albert M. "Brazil," *Universal Jewish Encyclopedia.* "Wätjen's Colonial Empire in Brazil," *Jewish Quarterly Review,* new series XIV (1923-24), 379-83.

Friedenwald, Harry. *The Jews and Medicine.* 2 vols. Baltimore: Johns Hopkins Press, 1944. Vol. I, 282.

Gama, Vasco da. *Diário da Viagem de Vasco da Gama.* 2 vols. Pôrto: Livraria Civilização, 1945. (Alvardo Velho, supposed author.)

Garcia, Rodolpho. "Os Judeus no Brasil Colonial," in *Os Judeus na História do Brasil.* Rio de Janeiro: U. Zwerling, 1936. Pp. 16-17.

Godbey, Allen H. *The Lost Tribes a Myth; Suggestions Toward Rewriting Hebrew History.* Durham, N. C.: Duke University Press, 1930. P. 709, n. 21.

González Obregon, Luis. *The Streets of Mexico.* San Francisco, G. Fields, 1937.

Graetz, Heinrich H. *History of the Jews, from the Earliest Times to the Present Day.* 5 vols. London: D. Nutt, 1891-1901. Vol. V, 95, 109.

Greenlee, William B. "The Captaincy of the Second Portuguese Voyage to Brazil, 1501-1502," *The Americas,* II (1945), 4, 8-9, 10-11, 12. "The First Half Century of Brazilian History," *Mid-America,* new series, XIV (1943), 94-97, 115. *The Voyage of Pedro Álvares Cabral to Brazil and India.* London: Hakluyt Society, 1938. Pp. xv-xviii, 35, 143, 200.

Guimarães, Argeu. "Os Judeus Portuguezes e Brasileiros na America Hespanhola," *Journal de la Société des Américanistes de Paris,* new series, XVIII (1926), 297-312.

Halevi, Jehudah. "A Love Song." "Song of the Oppressed." "Where Shall I Find Thee?" *Jewish Quarterly Review,* X (1897-98), 117-18, 627, 628. All translated by Nina Davis.

Herculano de Carvalho e Araujo, Alexandre. *História da Origem e Estabeleciemento da Inquisação em Portugal.* 3 vols. Lisbon, 1885. *History of the Origin and Establishment of the Inquisition in Portugal.* Translated by John C. Branner. Stanford University, 1926. (Gives an impartial recital of the struggles between João IV and the Jews.)

Higby, Chester P. *History of Europe (1492-1815).* Boston: Houghton-Mifflin Co., 1927. P. 11.

História da Colonização Portuguesa do Brasil. 3 vols. Pôrto: Litografia Nacional, 1921-24. Vol. I, 238-39; vol. II, 50, 75, 100-106, 192-93, 214, 278, 294, 324-30.

Inman, Samuel G. *Latin America. Its Place in World Life.* Chicago: Willet, Clark & Co., 1937. Pp. 34-35.

Jacobs, Joseph. *The Story of Geographical Discovery.* London, 1899. Pp. 100-101.

Jayne, Kingsley G. *Vasco da Gama and His Successors, 1450-1580.* London: Methuen & Co., 1910.

Os Judeus na História do Brasil. Edited by Uri Zwerling. Rio de Janeiro: U. Zwerling, 1936. P. 10.

Julius Caesar, Act III.

Kampen, Nicolaas Godfried van. *Geschichte der Niederlande.* Hamburg, 1831-33. P. 608.

Katz, Solomon. *The Jews in the Visigothic and Frankish Kingdoms of Spain and Gaul.* Cambridge: The Mediaeval Academy of America, 1937. P. 35.

Kayserling, Meyer. *Biblioteca Española-Portugueza-Judaica. Dictionnaire bibliographique des auteurs juifs.* Strasbourg, 1890. P. xxi. "The Earliest Rabbis and Jewish Writers of America," A. J. H. S., *Publications,* III (1895), 13-20. *Sephardim. Romanische Poesien der Juden in Spanien.* Leipzig, 1859.

Kimble, George H. T. *Geography in the Middle Ages.* London: Methuen & Co., 1938.

Kohut, George A. "Jewish Heretics in the Philippines in the Sixteenth and Seventeenth Century," A. J. H. S., *Publications,* XII (1904), 154. "Jewish Martyrs of the Inquisition in South America," A. J. H. S., *Publications,* IV (1896), 77, 111. "The Trial of Francisco Maldonado de Silva," A. J. H. S., *Publications,* XI (1903), 167-70, 173, 177.

Kuhn, Arthur K. "Hugo Grotius and the Emancipation of the Jews in Holland," A. J. H. S., *Publications,* XXXI (1928), 173-80.

Laet, Joannes de. *Iaerlyck Verhael van de Verrichtinghen der Geoctroyeerde West-Indische Campagnie (1624-1626).* S'Gravenhage: M. Nijhoff, 1931-37. Pp. 73-74, 104, 148-51, 161.

Lafitau, Joseph F. *Histoire des découvertes et conquestes des Portugais dans le nouveau monde.* 4 vols. Paris, 1736. Vol. I, 157.

Lazarus, Emma. "The Jewish Problem," *The Century Illustrated Monthly Magazine,* XXV, new series III (1882-83), 606-607.

Lea, Henry C. *The Inquisition in the Spanish Dependencies.* New York: Macmillan Co., 1908. P. 194.

Lebeson, Anita L. *Jewish Pioneers in America, 1492-1848.* New York: Brentano, 1931. Pp. 38, 40.

Leite, Solidonio. *Da Influencia do Elemento Judaico no Descobrimento e Commercio do Brasil (Seculos XVI e XVII).* Rio de Janeiro: Congresso de Historia Nacional, Instituto Historico Brasileiro, 1938. Pp. 23, 39-40.

Lewin, Boleslao. Review of "Los Leon Pinelo; la Ilustre Familia Marrana del Siglo XVII," *Hispanic American Historical Review*, XXIII (1943), 531.

Lindo, Elias H. *The History of the Jews in Spain and Portugal*. London, 1848. P. 267.

Manuel II, King of Portugal. *Livros Antigos Portuguezas*. 3 vols. London: Maggs Brothers, 1929-35. Vol. I. No. 36 deals with Pedro Nunez (pp. 543-565). Pp. 614-15 mention the King's (João III's) bookseller, Luis Rodriguez. P. 621 reads: "Portugal created a Renaissance, and though this superhuman effort may have exhausted the energies of the Country and made her bleed, we can never forget that the light she kindled was so brilliant that it still casts a glow upon the history of Portugal." [And not bled by the Inquisition? A. L. L.]

Marchant, Alexander. "The Discovery of Brazil: A Note on Interpretations," *The Geographical Review*, XXXV (1945), 296-300.

Marcondes de Souza, Thomas O. *O Descobrimento da América e a Suposta Prioridade dos Portugueses*. São Paulo: Editorial Brasiliense, 1944. P. 89.

Mello, Francisco M. de. *Espanáforas de Vária História Portuguesa*. Coimbra: Impr. da Universidade, 1931.

Michaëlis de Vasconcellos, Carolina. "Uriel da Costa, Notas Suplementares Relativas a sua Vida e sua Obra," *Lusitania* (1924), p. 9.

Minutes of the Congregation Tsur Israel.

Miscelânea de Estudos em Honra de D. Carolina Michaëlis de Vasconcellos. Coimbra: Imprensa da Universidade, 1933.

Nachod, Oskar. "Die Älteste Äbendländische Manuskript-Spezialkarte von Japon von Fernão Vaz Dourado 1568," *Atti del X Congresso Internazionale di Geografia, Roma, MCMXIII*. Rome, 1915. Pp. 1360-61.

Navarrete, Martín Fernández de. *Colección de los Viages y Descubrimientes que Hicieron por Mar los Españoles desde Fines del Siglo XV*. 5 vols. Madrid, 1825-37. Vol. III, 293 ff., 475.

Netscher, Peiter M. *Les Hollandais au Brésil, notice historique sur les Pays-Bas et le Brésil au XVII siècle*. La Haye, 1853.

Newton, Arthur P. *The Great Age of Discovery*. London: University of London Press, 1932. P. 65.

Nieuhof, Johan. "Voyages and Travels into Brazil, and the East Indies," in Awnsham Churchill, compiler, *A Collection of Voyages and Travels*. London, 1704. P. 4. "Voyages and Travels into Brazil," in John Pinkerton, editor, *A General Collection of the Best and Most Interesting Voyages and Travels*. 17 vols. London, 1808-14. Vol. XIV, 13, 753.

Nowell, Charles E. "The Discovery of Brazil—Accidental or Intentional?" *Hispanic American Historical Review*, XVI (1936), 316, 336.

Oliveira, Miguel de. *História Eclesiástical de Portugal*. Lisbon: União Gráfica, 1940. Pp. 41, 157 ff.

Oppenheim Collection, VI, no. 56.

Peixoto, Afranio. "Israel Continuara," *Os Judeus no História do Brasil.* Pp. 14, 97. (This and other translations made for *Pilgrim People.*)

Pereira da Silva, Luciano. "A Concepção Cosmológica nos 'Lusiadas,' " *Lusitania* (1925), pp. 263-89.

Pierson, Donald. "The Brazilian Racial Situation," *The Scientific Monthly,* LVIII (1944), 227-32. *Negroes in Brazil, a Study of Race Contact at Bahia.* Chicago: University of Chicago Press, 1942. Pp. 4-5.

Pirenne, Henri. *A History of Europe, from the Invasions to the XVI Century.* London: G. Allen & Unwin, 1939. Pp. 501, 511, 549.

Portugal. Agência Geral das Colónias. *Os Sete Unicos Documentos de 1500, Conservados em Lisboa, Referentes a Viagem de Pedro Alvares Cabral.* Lisbon: Agência Geral das Colónias, 1940.

Priestley, Herbert I. *The Coming of the White Man, 1492-1848.* New York: Macmillan Co., 1929. Pp. 5, 7.

Rae, George M. *The Syrian Church in India.* London, 1892. P. 131.

Raffalovich, I. "The Condition of Jewry and Judaism in South America," Central Conference of American Rabbis, *Yearbook* (1930), p. 416.

Ravenstein, Ernest G. *Martin Behaim, His Life and His Globe.* London: G. Philip & Son, 1908. P. 37.

Renard, Georges F., and Weulerssee, G. *Life and Work in Modern Europe (Fifteenth to Eighteenth Centuries).* London: Alfred A. Knopf, 1926.

Rios, Fernando de los. "Spain in the Epoch of American Civilization," *Concerning Latin American Culture,* pp. 25-48, especially, pp. 37-41.

Robinson, James H. *The Ordeal of Civilization; a Sketch of the Development and World-Wide Diffusion of Our Present Day Institutions and Ideas.* New York: Harper & Brothers, 1926. Pp. 9-10, 284.

Rodrigues, José H., and Ribeiro, Joaquim. *Civilização Holandesa no Brasil.* São Paulo: Companhia Editora Nacional, 1940.

Roth, Cecil. *A History of the Marranos.* Philadelphia: Jewish Publication Society of America, 1932. *The House of Nasi: Doña Gracia.* Philadelphia: Jewish Publication Society of America, 1948.

Scholem, Gershom G. *Major Trends in Jewish Mysticism.* New York: Schocken Books, *c.* 1946. Pp. 240-43.

Seignobos, Charles. *The Rise of European Civilization.* London: J. Cape, 1939. Pp. 223 ff., especially p. 258.

Sérgio, Antonio. Review of "Episódios Dramáticos da Inquisição Portuguesa," by Antonio Baião, *Lusitania* (1924), p. 447.

Sombart, Werner. *The Jews and Modern Capitalism.* London: T. F. Unwin, 1913.

Southey, Robert. *History of Brazil.* 3 vols. London, 1810-19. Vol. I, 10, 450-51, 566, 655.

Souto Maior, Pedro. *Fastos Pernambucanos.* Rio de Janeiro: Imprensa Nacional, 1913. P. 34.

Stevenson, Edward L. Introduction to *Facsimiles of Portolan Charts Belonging to the Hispanic Society of America.* New York, 1916.

Sweet, William W. *A History of Latin America*. New York: Abingdon Press, 1929. P. 54.

Teixeira, Pedro. *The Travels of Pedro Teixeira*. Translated and annotated by William F. Sinclair and Donald Ferguson. London: Hakluyt Society, 1902. P. ii.

Thompson, James W. *The Middle Ages, 300-1500*. 2 vols. New York: Alfred A. Knopf, 1931. Vol. II, 1036.

Toro, Alfonso. *La Familia Carvajal. Estudio Histórico sobre los Judios y la Inquisición de la Nueva España en el Siglo XVI*. 2 vols. Mexico: Editorial Patria, 1944. Vol. I, 41; vol. II, 91. "Era la más fanática de todas las Carvajales doncellas, Doña Mariana. . . ." P. 99 has pictures of Jewish utensils: beakers, mortar and pestle, sharp knife (and other objects I cannot identify), and refers to a report of "El Professor Judio Jac Bachbín . . . (illustrations very important: "El Valeroso Luis de Carvajal el Viejo," "La Circuncisión," "Luis de Carvajal el Mozo, Versificador Mistico"). *Los Judíos en la Nueva España; Selección de Documentos del Siglo XVI, Correspondientes al Ramo de Inquisición*. Mexico: Talleres Graficos de la Nacion, 1932.

Varnhagen, Francisco A. *Examen de quelques points de l'histoire géographique du Bresil*. Paris, 1858. See map opposite p. 706.

Velho, Alvaro. *Roteiro da Primeira Viagem de Vasco da Gama*. Lisbon: Agência Geral das Colónias, 1940.

Waldseemüller, Martin. *The Cosmographiae Introductio . . . Followed by the Four Voyages of Amerigo Vespucci*. New York: United States Catholic Historical Society, 1907. P. 137.

Yule, Henry. *Cathay and the Way Thither; Being a Collection of Medieval Notices of China*. 4 vols. London: Hakluyt Society, 1913-16.

The writer has had access to the famous Ayer and Greenlee Collections of the Newberry Library and has consulted every pertinent source in her field. It is impossible to document all of these sources for each would be a bibliography, rather than a footnote. Dr. Greenlee's "Descriptive Bibliography of the History of Portugal," *Hispanic American Historical Review*, XX (1940), 491-516, contains a detailed analysis of the source material. He it was who went over much of the material with the writer and generously placed the accumulated results of his scholarship, to which he has devoted a lifetime, at her disposal.

The section on the later history of Brazil is based on the writer's study of the Oppenheim Papers, which are in the possession of the American Jewish Historical Society. To the late Samuel Oppenheim a salute is due from all who use his papers for his indefatigable labors in this field. The writer wishes to acknowledge her sense of personal indebtedness to this fine Jewish scholar. The materials have been ably summarized in Rabbi Herbert I. Bloom's "A Study of Brazilian Jewish History 1623-1654, Based Chiefly upon the Findings of the Late Samuel Oppenheim," A. J. H. S., *Publications*, XXXIII (1934), 43-125. Because some of the papers were illegible, the writer carefully checked her own conclusions with those of Rabbi Bloom, whose excellent study makes this phase of Brazilian Jewish history readily available to all readers.

The writer has had translated for her use the poems and proverbs of Sephardic Jews collected as a labor of love by that great Jewish Scholar, Professor M. Kayserling, in his *Biblioteca Española-Portugueza-Judaica*. The translator, Mr. David G. Luna, also performed a labor of love, for he was so intrigued by his task that he went over each poem and proverb many times, submitting numerous versions, using every known dictionary. The most important dictionary that he used was that published by the Academia Española, *Diccionario de la Lengua Castellana*. 6 vols. (Madrid, 1726-39). The writer wishes to express her warm appreciation of Mr. Luna's assistance in preparing these translations.

CHAPTER IV

1. Photostated from the original document by permission of the Folger Shakespeare Library.
2. Samuel Oppenheim, "An Early Jewish Colony in Western Guiana, 1658-1666; and Its Relation to the Jews in Surinam, Cayenne and Tobago," American Jewish Historical Society, *Publications*, XVI (1907), 107; "An Early Jewish Colony in Western Guiana: Supplemental Data," A. J. H. S., *Publications*, XVII (1909) 58 ff.
3. *Ibid.*, 62-63, 66, 100.
4. Oppenheim (same as notes 2-3). See also Packet IV, no. 13 and Packet V, Oppenheim Collection, in American Jewish Historical Society Library. Microfilmed by permission of the Society.
5. Oppenheim, "An Early Jewish Colony in Western Guiana, 1658-1666," *op. cit.*, 154; Herbert I. Bloom, "A Study of Brazilian Jewish History, 1623-1654," A. J. H. S., *Publications*, XXXIII (1934), 43-125.
6. "Documents Relating to the History of the Jews in Jamaica and Barbados in the Time of William III," contributed by Frank Cundall, N. Darnell Davis, and Albert M. Friedenberg, A. J. H. S., *Publications*, XXIII (1915), 27.
7. *Ibid.*, p. 28. See also Samuel Oppenheim, "A List of Jews Made Denizens in the Reigns of Charles II and James II, 1661-1687," A. J. H. S., *Publications*, XX (1911), 109-113.
8. Oppenheim, "An Early Jewish Colony in Western Guiana, 1658-1666," *op. cit.*, 158.
9. *Ibid.*, 159.
10. The following quotations are taken from a document in the Oppenheim Collection, Egerton MSS2551, folios 152^b–158^b.
11. *Ibid.*

See also

Abrahams, Israel. "Isaac Abendana's Cambridge Mishnah and Oxford Calendars," Jewish Historical Society of England, *Transactions*, XVIII (1918), 99. "Joachim Gaunse: A Mining Incident in the Reign of Queen Elizabeth," J. H. S. E., *Transactions*, IV (1903), 88-89.

————, and Sayle, C. E. "The Purchase of Hebrew Books by the English Parliament in 1647," J. H. S. E., *Transactions*, VIII (1918) 63-77.

Abrahams, Lionel B. "The Condition of the Jews of England at the time of Their Expulsion in 1290," J. H. S. E., *Transactions*, II (1894-95), 76-105. "The Economic and Financial Position of the Jews in Medieval England," J. H. S. E., *Transactions*, VIII (1918), 171-88.

Adair, James. *The History of the American Indians.* London, 1775. *Passim.*

Adler, Cyrus. "Jews in the American Plantations between 1600-1700," American Jewish Historical Society, *Publications*, I (1893), 105-108.

Adler, Elkan N. *About Hebrew Manuscripts.* London: H. Frowde, 1905. Pp. 76-77. "A Letter of Menasseh ben Israel," J. H. S. E., *Transactions*, V (1908), 174-83.

Adler, Michael. "History of the 'Domus Conversorum' from 1290 to 1891," J. H. S. E., *Transactions*, IV (1903), 16-75.

Amaral Gurgel, L. *Ensaios Quinhentistas.* São Paulo: J. Fagundes, 1936. Pp. 110-13.

Azevedo, João Lucio d'. *História dos Christãos Novos Portugueses.* Lisbon: Livraria Clássica Editora de A. M. Teixeira, 1922. P. 436. Italics mine.

Bacon, Francis. *New Atlantis.* Edited with introduction and notes by Alfred B. Gough. Oxford: Clarendon Press, 1915. P. 119.

Bethencourt, Cardoza de. "Notes on the Spanish and Portuguese Jews in the United States, Guiana, and the Dutch and British West Indies during the Seventeenth and Eighteenth Centuries," A. J. H. S., *Publications*, XXIX (1925), 7-38.

Biet, Antoine. *Voyage de la France equinoxiale en l'isle de Cayenne, entrepris par les François en l'année MDCLII.* Paris, 1664. Pp. 315-320.

Bloom, Herbert I. "The Dutch Archives with Special Reference to American Jewish History," A. J. H. S., *Publications*, XXXII (1931), 11 ff. *The Economic Activities of the Jews of Amsterdam in the Seventeenth and Eighteenth Centuries.* Williamsport, Penn., Bayard Press, 1937. Pp. 6-7 ff.

Blunt, John E. *A History of the Establishment and Residence of the Jews in England: with an Enquiry into Their Civil Disabilities.* London, 1830.

The Cartwright Petition of 1649. Facsimile, published by the Sutro Library Associates. San Francisco, 1941. Pp. 1-2.

Coleman, Edward D. "The Jew in English Drama," New York Public Library, *Bulletin*, XLII (1938), 827.

Davis, N. Darnell. "Notes on the History of the Jews in Barbados," A. J. H. S., *Publications*, XVIII (1909), 120-148.

Felsenthal, Bernard. "The Jewish Congregation in Surinam," A. J. H. S., *Publications*, II (1894), 29-30.

Freyre, Gilberto. *The Masters and the Slaves [Casa-Grande & Senzala]. A Study in the Development of Brazilian Civilization.* New York: Alfred A. Knopf, 1946. P. 229.

Friedenberg, Albert M. "Wätjen's 'Colonial Empire in Brazil,'" *Jewish Quarterly Review*, new series XIV (1923-24), 382.

Friedman, Lee M. "Gabriel Milan, the Jewish Governor of St. Thomas," A. J. H. S., *Publications*, XXVIII (1922), 213-21. "Moses Michael Hays," A. J. H. S., *Publications*, XXXV (1939), 294.

Gaster, Moses. "Yiddish Literature in the Middle Ages," Royal Society of Literature, *Transactions*, new series VII (1927), 105-131.

Godbey, Allen H. *The Lost Tribes a Myth; Suggestions toward Rewriting Hebrew History.* Durham, N. C.: Duke University Press, 1930.

Gottheil, Richard. "Contributions to the History of the Jews in Surinam," A. J. H. S., *Publications*, IX (1901), 129-42.

Harvey, Gabriel. *The Prototype of Shylock, Lopez the Jew, Executed 1594.* Harrow Weald, Middlesex, 1927. P. 1.

Henriques, Henry S. Q. *Jews and English Law.* London: 1908. Pp. 82 ff.

Hilfman, P. A. "Notes on the History of the Jews in Surinam," A. J. H. S., *Publications*, XVIII (1909), 179-207. "Some Further Notes on the History of the Jews in Surinam," A. J. H. S., *Publications*, XVI (1907), 7-22.

Hirsch, S. A. "Early English Hebraists. Roger Bacon and His Predecessors," *Jewish Quarterly Review*, XII (1899-1900), 34-88.

Hollander, J. H. "Documents Relating to the Attempted Departure of the Jews from Surinam in 1675," A. J. H. S., *Publications*, VI (1897), 9-29.

Jacobs, Joseph. "Aaron of Lincoln," *Jewish Quarterly Review*, X (1898), 629. *Jewish Contributions to Civilization.* Philadelphia: Jewish Publication Society of America, 1944. P. 124. *The Jews of Angevin England.* London, 1893. "The Typical Character of Anglo-Jewish History," *Jewish Quarterly Review*, X (1898), 217-37.

Kohler, Max J. "Dr. Rodrigo Lopez, Queen Elizabeth's Jewish Physician, and His Relations to America," A. J. H. S., *Publications*, XVII (1909), 9-25.

Kohut, George A. "Who Was the First Rabbi of Surinam?" A. J. H. S., *Publications*, V (1897), 119-24.

Lee, Sidney L. "Elizabethan England and the Jews," New Shakespere Society, *Transactions*, series I (1887-92), 158. "The Original of Shylock," *The Gentleman's Magazine*, CCXLVI (1880), 185-200.

Leite, Solidonio. *Da Influencia do Elemento Judaico no Descubrimento e*

Commercio do Brasil (Seculos XVI e XVII). Rio de Janeiro: Congresso de Historia Nacional, Instituto Historico Brasileiro, 1938. Pp. 49-52.

L'Estrange, Harmon. *Americans no Iewes, or Improbabilities That the Americans Are of That Race.* London, 1652. Pp. 25-26.

Levy, S. "John Dury and the English Jewry," *J. H. S. E., Transactions,* IV (1903), 76-77.

A Library of the World's Best Literature, Ancient and Modern. Edited by C. D. Warner. 45 vols. New York, 1897. Vol. XXVI, 10260.

"London Jews' Petition to Oliver Cromwell, March 24, 1656." Contents: Permission to buy a burial ground and asking further protection. *J. H. S. E., Transactions,* X (1921-23), plate 2.

McKenny, Thomas L., and Hall, James. *History of the Indian Tribes of North America.* 3 vols. Philadelphia, 1848-50.

Mallery, Garrick. *Israelite and Indian. A Parallel in Planes of Culture.* Salem, Mass., 1889.

Manasseh ben Joseph ben Israel. *The Hope of Israel.* London, 1651. Last page. *Menasseh ben Israel's Mission to Oliver Cromwell.* Edited by Lucien Wolf. London: Published for the Jewish Historical Society of England by Macmillan & Co., 1901. Pp. 78, 79, 80, 87, 149.

Michaëlis de Vasconcellos, Carolina. "Uriel da Costa. Notas Suplementares Relativas a Sua Vida e Sua Obra," *Lusitania* (1924), pp. 5-22.

Modder, Montagu F. *The Jew in the Literature of England to the End of the 19th Century.* Philadelphia: Jewish Publication Society of America, 1944. Pp. 18, 32.

Oliveira, Miguel de. *História Eclesiástical de Portugal.* Lisbon: União Grafica, 1940. P. 159.

Oppenheim Collection, Egerton MSS2551, folios 152ᵇ–158ᵇ.

Oppenheim, Samuel. "The Early History of the Jews in New York, 1654-1664. Some New Matter on the Subject," *A. J. H. S., Publications, XVIII* (1909), 24-25. "An Early Jewish Colony in Western Guiana: Supplemental Data," *A. J. H. S., Publications,* XVII (1909), 58. "Jewish Owners of Ships Registered at the Port of Philadelphia, 1730-1775," *A. J. H. S., Publications,* XXVI (1918), 235-36. "A List of Jews Made Denizens in the Reigns of Charles II and James II, 1661-1687," *A. J. H. S., Publications,* XX (1911), 109-113.

Rabinowitz, L. "Literary Connections Between Abravanel and England," *J. H. S. E., Transactions,* XIV (1940), 131-39.

Roos, J. S. "Additional Notes on the History of the Jews of Surinam," *A. J. H. S., Publications,* XIII (1905), 127-36.

Roth, Cecil. "The Challenge to Jewish History," *J. H. S. E., Transactions,* XIV (1940), 1-38. *A History of the Jews in England.* Oxford: Clarendon Press, 1941. Pp. 154 ff. *A Life of Menasseh ben Israel, Rabbi, Printer and Diplomat.* Philadelphia: Jewish Publication Society of America, 1934. "New Light on the Resettlement," *J. H. S. E., Transactions.* XI (1928), 112-42.

Silber, Mendel. "America in Hebrew Literature," A. J. H. S., *Publications*, XXII (1914), 107, 110, 112.

Simon, Mrs. Barbara Anne. *The Ten Tribes of Israel Historically Identified with the Aborigines of the Western Hemisphere*. London, 1836.

Sisson, C. J. "A Colony of Jews in Shakespeare's London," *Essays and Studies by Members of the English Association*, XXIII (1938), 50.

Stokes, H. P. "The Relationship Between the Jews and the Royal Family of England in the Thirteenth Century," J. H. S. E., *Transactions*, VIII (1918), 153-70.

Thorowgood, Thomas. *Jewes in America, or Probabilities, That Those Indians Are Judaical, Made More Probable by Some Additions to the Former Conjectures*. London, 1660.

Universal Jewish Encyclopedia, vol. VII, 558-59.

Wolf, Lucien. "American Elements in the Re-Settlement," J. H. S. E., *Transactions*, III (1899), 76-100. "Jews in Elizabethan England," J. H. S. E., *Transactions*, XI (1928), 1-91. "Status of the Jews in England After the Re-Settlement," J. H. S. E., *Transactions*, IV (1903), 180-81.

CHAPTER V

1. Samuel Oppenheim, "The Early History of the Jews in New York, 1654-1664. Some New Matter on the Subject," American Jewish Historical Society, *Publications*, XVIII (1909), 3.
2. *Ibid.*
3. John F. Jameson, ed., *Narratives of New Netherland, 1609-1664* (New York: Charles Scribner's Sons, 1909), pp. 392-93.
4. *Ibid.*
5. Oppenheim, *op. cit.*, p. 75.
6. *Ibid.*, p. 25.
7. *Ibid.*, p. 35.
8. Charles A. and Mary R. Beard, *The Rise of American Civilization*, 2 vols. (New York: Macmillan Co., 1929), vol. I, 76.
9. N. Taylor Phillips, "A Landmark," A. J. H. S., *Publications*, I (1892), 91.
10. *Ibid.*, p. 92.
11. Abraham S. W. Rosenbach, "Notes on the First Settlement of Jews in Pennsylvania, 1655-1703," A. J. H. S., *Publications*, V (1897), 191-92.
12. Morris A. Gutstein, *The Story of the Jews of Newport; Two and a Half Centuries of Judaism, 1658-1908* (New York: Block Publishing Co., 1936), p. 27.
13. A. J. H. S., *Publications*, VI (1897), 167.
14. Samuel Oppenheim, "The Jews and Masonry in the United States before 1810," A. J. H. S., *Publications*, XIX (1910), 11.

15. Gutstein, *op. cit.*, p. 27.
16. *Records of the Colony of Rhode Island and Providence Plantations in New England*, 10 vols. (Providence, 1856-65).
17. N. Taylor Phillips, "The Levy and Seixas Families of Newport and New York," A. J. H. S., *Publications*, IV (1894), 191-92.
18. Sheftall Papers, no. 293. In the manuscript library of the American Jewish Historical Society, New York.
19. From the original manuscript in the Lopez Papers in the American Jewish Historical Society, New York.

See also

Andrews, Charles M. *Colonial Folkways: a Chronicle of American Life in the Reign of the Georges*. New Haven: Yale University Press, 1919. P. 149.
Cohen, Henry. "A Brave Frontiersman," American Jewish Historical Society, *Publications*, VIII (1900), 69.
Connecticut (Colony). *The Public Records of the Colony of Connecticut, 1636-1776*. 15 vols. Hartford, 1850-90. Vol. II, 6.
Cooley, Charles H. *Sociological Theory and Social Research*. New York: Henry Holt and Co., 1930.
Daly, Charles P. *The Settlement of the Jews in North America*. New York, 1893. P. 76.
Dyer, Albion M. "Points in the First Chapter of New York Jewish History," A. J. H. S. *Publications*, III (1894), 41-60. "Site of the First Synagogue of the Congregation Shearith Israel of New York," A. J. H. S., *Publications*, VIII (1900), 25-41.
Egerton MS. Reprinted in Lucien Wolf, "American Elements in the Re-Settlement," Jewish Historical Society of England, *Transactions*, III (1899), 83.
Freund, Miriam K. *Jewish Merchants in Colonial America; Their Achievements and Their Contributions to the Development of America*. New York: Behrman's Jewish Book House, 1939. P. 39.
Friedman, Lee M. "Cotton Mather and the Jews," A. J. H. S., *Publications*, XXVI (1918), 202. "Rowland Gideon, an Early Boston Jew, and His Family," A. J. H. S., *Publications*, XXXV (1939), 27.
Giddings, Franklin H. *Studies in the Theory of Human Society*. New York: Macmillan Co., 1922.
Hollander, J. H. "Some Unpublished Material Relating to Dr. Jacob Lumbrozo, of Maryland," A. J. H. S., *Publications*, I (1892), 25 ff.
Hühner, Leon. "Asser Levy. A Noted Jewish Burgher of New Amsterdam," A. J. H. S., *Publications*, VIII (1900), 9-23. "Isaac de Pinto. A Noted European Publicist and Defender of Great Britain's Policy during the American Revolution," A. J. H. S., *Publications*, XIII (1905), 118-19. "Jews in Connection with the Colleges of the Thirteen Original States Prior to 1800," A. J. H. S., *Publications*, XIX (1910), 115.

"The Jews of Virginia from the Earliest Times to the Close of the Eighteenth Century," A. J. H. S., *Publications*, XX (1911), 85-105.

Jones, Charles C., Jr. "The Settlement of the Jews in Georgia," A. J. H. S., *Publications*, I (1892), 11.

Kohler, Max J. "Civil Status of the Jews in Colonial New York," A. J. H. S., *Publications*, VI (1897), 81-106. "Jewish Activity in American Colonial Commerce," A. J. H. S., *Publications*, X (1902), 47. "Phases of Jewish Life in New York Before 1800," A. J. H. S., *Publications*, III (1894), 85.

Korn, Harold. "Receipt Book of Judah Hays, June 20, 1759, to December 23, 1762," A. J. H. S., *Publications*, XXXIV (1937), 121-22.

Massachusetts (Colony). *The Colonial Laws of Massachusetts.* Reprinted from the Edition of 1672 with the Supplements through 1686. Published by order of the City Council of Boston, under the supervision of William H. Whitmore, Boston, 1887. Pp. 53-55.

Miller, George J. "James Alexander and the Jews, Especially Isaac Emanuel," A. J. H. S., *Publications*, XXXV (1939), 183.

Muzzey, David S., *An American History.* New York: Ginn and Co., 1925. P. 39.

Oppenheim, Samuel. "The Early History of the Jews in New York, 1654-1664. Some New Matter on the Subject," A. J. H. S., *Publications*, XVIII (1909), 1-91. "The First Settlement of the Jews in Newport: Some New Matter on the Subject," A. J. H. S., *Publications*, XXXIV (1937), 7. "More about Jacob Barsimson, the First Jewish Settler in New York," A. J. H. S., *Publications*, XXIX (1925), 39-52.

Phillips, N. Taylor. "Items Relating to the History of the Jews of New York," A. J. H. S., *Publications*, XI (1903), 150. "The Levy and Seixas Families of Newport and New York," A. J. H. S., *Publications*, IV (1894), 191-92.

Rhode Island (Colony). *Records of the Colony of Rhode Island and Providence Plantations in New England.* 10 vols. Providence, 1856-65.

Roth, Cecil. "The Challenge to Jewish History," J. H. S. E., *Transactions*, XIV (1940), 12.

Sheftall Papers. No. 292.

Solis, Elvira N. "Some References to Early Jewish Cemeteries in New York City," A. J. H. S., *Publications*, VIII (1900), 135-40.

CHAPTER VI

1. John Locke, "Letter Concerning Toleration," in his *Works*, 3 vols. (London, 1740), vol. II, 273; "Two Treatises of Government," *ibid.*, 110 ff.

2. Isidore S. Meyer, "Hebrew at Harvard (1636-1760). A Résumé of the Information in Recent Publications," American Jewish Historical Society, *Publications*, XXXV (1939), 149.

3. Lee M. Friedman, "Cotton Mather and the Jews," A. J. H. S., *Publications*, XXVI (1918), 207. Abraham S. W. Rosenbach, "An American Jewish Bibliography Being a List of Books and Pamphlets by Jews or Relating to Them, Printed in the United States, from the Establishment of the Press in the Colonies until 1850," A. J. H. S., *Publications*, XXX (1926), 3, 4, 11.

4. Massachusetts Historical Society, *Collections*, V, Fifth Series, "Diary of Samuel Sewall" (Boston, 1878).

5. *Ibid.*

6. Abraham S. W. Rosenbach, "Notes on the First Settlement of Jews in Pennsylvania, 1655-1703," A. J. H. S., *Publications*, V (1897), 196.

7. Hyman B. Grinstein, *The Rise of the Jewish Community of New York, 1654-1860* (Philadelphia: The Jewish Publication Society of America, 1945), especially chapter IV, "Synagogue Government," pp. 58 ff., 60-68.

8. "The Earliest Extant Minute Books of the Spanish and Portuguese Congregation Shearith Israel in New York, 1728-1786," A. J. H. S., *Publications*, XXI (1913), 1-171.

9. *Ibid.*, pp. 71 ff., 85 ff., Leon Hühner, "Jews in Connection with the Colleges of the Thirteen Original States Prior to 1800," A. J. H. S., *Publications*, XIX (1910), 108 ff. and Meyer, *op. cit.*, pp. 145-79.

10. "The Earliest Extant Minute Books, etc.," *op. cit.*, p. 54.

11. Anita L. Lebeson, *Jewish Pioneers in America, 1492-1848* (New York: Brentano, 1931), has an extensive account of the founding of the Jewish community in Newport.

12. See Hühner, *op. cit.*

13. David de Sola Pool, "Hebrew Learning Among the Puritans Prior to 1700," A. J. H. S., *Publications*, XX (1911), 31-83.

14. Anita L. Lebeson, "Hannah Adams and the Jews," *Historia Judaica*, VIII, no 2 (October, 1946).

15. Henry Necarsulmer, "The Early Jewish Settlement at Lancaster, Pennsylvania," A. J. H. S., *Publications*, IX (1901), 30; Soloman R. Kagan, *Jewish Contributions to Medicine in America, from Colonial Times to the Present* (Boston: The Boston Medical Publishing Co., 1939), *passim*; Harry Friedenwald, *The Jews in Medicine*, 2 vols. (Baltimore: Johns Hopkins Press, 1944), *passim*.

16. The writer is indebted to the Rev. Dr. David de Sola Pool, Rabbi of Congregation Shearith Israel, for permission to consult his manuscripts and for calling her attention to Walter J. Judah.

17. The Lopez Papers in the manuscript collections of the American Jewish Historical Society are invaluable. See also *The Literary Diary of Ezra Stiles*, edited by Franklin B. Dexter, 3 vols. (New York: Charles Scribner's Sons, 1901), *passim.*; Meyer, *op. cit.*, pp. 139-43;

Newport Historical Society, *Early Religious Leaders of Newport* (Newport, R. I.: The Newport Historical Society, 1918).

18. Edmund H. Abrahams, "Some Notes on the Early History of the Sheftalls of Georgia," A. J. H. S., *Publications*, XVII (1909), 167-68, n.; see also Lebeson, *Jewish Pioneers*, pp. 165-71.

19. Barnett A. Elzas, *The Jews of South Carolina* (Charleston: The Daggett Printing Co., 1903), p. 48; "Publications Received. Publications of the American Jewish Historical Society. Number 9, 1901," *The South Carolina Historical and Genealogical Magazine*, III (1902), 62-63; Leon Hühner, "Francis Salvador, A Prominent Patriot of the Revolutionary War," A. J. H. S., *Publications*, IX (1901), 108 ff.; John Drayton, *Memoirs of the American Revolution*, 2 vols. (Charleston, 1821), vol. II, 348.

20. David E. Heineman, "The Startling Experience of a Jewish Trader during Pontiac's Siege of Detroit in 1763," A. J. H. S., *Publications*, XXIII (1915), 32.

21. Baron Marc de Villiers du Terrage, *Histoire de la fondation de la Nouvelle-Orleans, 1717-1722* (Paris: Imprimerie Nationale, 1917), 51 ff.

22. For the use of the document the writer is indebted to Dr. Stanley Pargellis of the Newberry Library.

23. Villiers, *op. cit.*, p. 73.

24. *Ibid.* Italics mine.

25. J. Hanno Deiler, *The Settlement of the German Coast of Louisiana and the Creoles of German Descent* (Philadelphia: Americana Germanica Press, 1909), pp. 50-51.

26. *Ibid.*, p. 125

27. *Ibid.*, pp. 36-37.

See also

Abrabanel, Solomon. *The Complaint of the Children of Israel.* London, 1736.

Blunt, John E. *A History of the Establishment and Residence of the Jews in England.* London, 1830. P. 16.

Byars, William V. "The Gratz Papers," American Jewish Historical Society, *Publications*, XXIII (1915), 1-23.

Cochut, P. A. *Law, son système et son époque.* Paris, 1853.

Deiler, J. Hanno. *The Settlement of the German Coast of Louisiana and the Creoles of German Descent.* Philadelphia: Americana Germanica Press, 1909. P. 21 n. 6.

Friedenwald, Harry. "The Ethics of the Practice of Medicine from the Jewish Point of View," in his *The Jews and Medicine.* 2 vols. Baltimore: Johns Hopkins Press, 1944. P. 18.

Friedman, Lee M. "Aaron Lopez's Family Affairs from 'The Commerce of Rhode Island,'" A. J. H. S., *Publications*, XXXV (1939), 295-304.

Gayarré, Charles. *History of Louisiana.* 3 vols. New York, 1854. Vol. I, 195-230.

Grande Enciclopédia Portuguesa e Brasileira. 20 vols. Lisbon: Editorial Enciclopédia, 1935.

Hanotaux, Gabriel. *Histoire des colonies françaises et de l'expansion de la France dans le monde.* 6 vols. Paris; Société de l'histoire nationale, 1929-33. Vol. I, 301 ff.

Hart, Gustavus N. "A Biographical Account of Ephraim Hart and His Son Dr. Joel Hart of New York (1747)," A. J. H. S., *Publications,* IV (1894), 215-18.

Kagan, S. R. *Jewish Contributions to Medicine in America, from Colonial Times to the Present.* Boston: Boston Medical Publication Co., 1939. *Passim.*

Kohler, Max J. "The Jews in Newport," A. J. H. S., *Publications,* VI (1897), 61-80.

Korn, Harold. "Documents Relative to the Estate of Aaron Lopez," A. J. H. S., *Publications,* XXXV (1939), 139-43.

La Harpe, Bernard de. *Journal historique de l'établissement des français à la Louisiane.* New Orleans, 1831. P. 234.

Lebeson, Anita L. *Jewish Pioneers in America, 1492-1848.* New York: Brentano, 1931. *Passim.*

Le Conte, Rene. "Les Allemands à la Louisiane au XVIII° siècle," *Journal de la Société des Americanistes de Paris,* new series, XVI (1924), 7, 16.

Margry, Pierre, ed. *Découvertes et établissements des français dans l'ouest et dans le sud de l'Amerique Septentrionale (1614-1754).* 6 vols. Paris, 1876-86. Vol. V, 575-76.

Newberry Library. *Bulletin,* no. 5. Chicago, September, 1946. Pp. 6-8. For a number of sources on Louisiana's early history the writer is indebted to Dr. Ruth Lapham Butler, custodian of the Ayer Collection of the Newberry Library.

Newport Historical Society. *Early Religious Leaders of Newport.* Newport, R. I.: Newport Historical Society, 1918.

Stiles, Ezra. *The Literary Diary of Ezra Stiles.* Edited by Franklin B. Dexter. New York: Charles Scribner's Sons, 1901. *Extracts from the Itineraries . . . with a Selection from His Correspondence.* Edited by Franklin B. Dexter. New Haven: Yale University Press, 1916.

Thiers, Adolphe. *The Mississippi Bubble.* New York, 1859. P. 142.

Villiers du Terrage, Baron Marc de. *Histoire de la fondation de la Nouvelle-Orleans, 1717-1722.* Paris: Imprimerie nationale, 1917. Pp. 51 ff.

Willner, Rev. W. "Ezra Stiles and the Jews (1727-1795), A. J. H. S., *Publications,* VIII (1900), 119-26.

CHAPTER VII

1. Thomas Paine, "Age of Reason," in *Basic Writing of Thomas Paine* (New York: Willey Book Co., 1942), p. 29.
2. Haym Salomon Letter Book. MS. in American Jewish Historical Society Library.
3. Leon Hühner, "Some Additional Notes on the History of the Jews of South Carolina," American Jewish Historical Society, *Publications,* XIX (1910), 155.
4. Thomas J. Wertenbaker, *American People: a History* (New York: Charles Scribner's Sons, 1926), p. 81.
5. Simon Wolf, *The American Jew as Patriot, Soldier, and Citizen* (Philadelphia, 1895), p. 51.
6. Leon Hühner, "Some Notes on the Career of Colonel David S. Franks," A. J. H. S., *Publications,* X (1902), 167.
7. Oscar S. Straus, "New Light on the Career of Colonel David S. Franks," A. J. H. S., *Publications,* X (1902), 101; Max J. Kohler, "Incidents Illustrative of American Jewish Patriotism," A. J. H. S., *Publications,* IV (1894), 82-83.
8. Charles P. Daly, *The Settlement of the Jews in North America,* edited by Max J. Kohler (New York, 1893), p. 75, n.; Max J. Kohler, *op. cit.,* p. 96; Leon Hühner, "The Jews of South Carolina from the Earliest Settlement to the End of the American Revolution," A. J. H. S., *Publications,* XII (1904), 46-56.
9. Max J. Kohler, "The Jews in Newport," A. J. H. S., *Publications,* VI (1897), 75.
10. Leon Hühner, "The First Jew to Hold the Office of Governor of one of the United States," A. J. H. S., *Publications,* XVII (1909), 187.
11. MS. in the American Jewish Historical Society; italics mine.
12. Translated for A. J. H. S., *Publications* by Dr. Joshua H. Neumann.
13. Max J. Kohler, "Phases in the History of Religious Liberty in America with Particular Reference to the Jews. II," A. J. H. S., *Publications,* XIII (1905), 29.

See also

Abrabanel, Solomon. *The Complaint of the Children of Israel.* London, 1736.
Abrahams, Edmund H. "Some Notes on the Early History of the Sheftalls of Georgia," A. J. H. S., *Publications,* XVII (1909), 182.
Adler, Cyrus. "Jews in the American Plantations Between 1600-1700," A. J. H. S., *Publications,* I (1892), 108.
Alvord, C. W. *The Mississippi Valley in British Politics.* 2 vols. Cleveland: Arthur H. Clark Co., 1917. *Passim.*

Beard, Charles A. and Mary R. *The Rise of American Civilization.* 2 vols. New York: Macmillan Co., 1929. Vol. I, 225, 229, 241.

Byars, William V. *B. & M. Gratz, Merchants in Philadelphia, 1754-1798.* Jefferson City, Mo.: Hugh Stephens Printing Co., 1916. *Passim.*

Calendar of the Sheftall Papers, MSS. Collections of the A. J. H. S. (3,172 items; 328 entries), prepared by the Historical Records Survey. New York, 1941.

Sheftall Papers: Five Classes
1. Commissarial activities of Mordecai Sheftall.
2. Post-Revolutionary mercantile ledger.
3. Continental paper money.
4. Privateer papers of the Schooner *Hetty* (Sheftall's Schooner).
5. Sheftall family letters.

Coleman, Edward D. "Plays of Jewish Interest on the American Stage, 1752-1821," A. J. H. S., *Publications*, XXXIII (1934), 182.

Croghan, George. Letter to David Franks dated Ft. Pitt, December 25, 1770. MS. in Ayer Collection of the Newberry Library.

Cumberland, Richard. *The Jew*, Act III, Scene ii, p. 29.

Feuchwanger, Ludwig. "Reflections on Anglo-Jewish History," *Historia Judaica*, IX (1947), 119-36.

Friedenwald, Harry. *The Jews and Medicine.* 2 vols. Baltimore: Johns Hopkins Press, 1944. P. 734.

Friedenwald, Herbert. "Jews Mentioned in the Journal of the Continental Congress (1774-1788)," A. J. H. S., *Publications*, I (1892), 65-89. "A Letter of Jonas Phillips to the Federal Convention," A. H. J. S., *Publications*, II (1893), 108. "Memorials Presented to the Continental Congress," A. J. H. S., *Publications*, II (1893), 123. "Some Newspaper Advertisements of the Eighteenth Century," A. J. H. S., *Publications*, VI (1897), 58.

Hühner, Leon. "The Jews of Georgia from the Outbreak of the American Revolution to the Close of the 18th Century," A. J. H. S., *Publications*, XVII (1909), 97.

Jastrow, Morris, Jr. "Documents Relating to the Career of Isaac Franks," A. J. H. S., *Publications*, V (1897), 32-33, 35.

Kagan, Soloman R. *Jewish Contributions to Medicine in America, from Colonial Times to the Present.* Boston: Boston Medical Publishing Co., 1939. Pp. 18-19.

Kohler, Max J. "Incidents Illustrative of American Jewish Patriotism," A. J. H. S., *Publications*, IV (1894), 84, "The Jews in Newport," A. J. H. S., *Publications*, VI (1897), 75. "Phases in the History of Religious Liberty in America, with Special Reference to the Jews," A. J. H. S., *Publications*, XI (1903), 69.

Lebeson, Anita L. "Hannah Adams and the Jews," *Historia Judaica*, VIII (October, 1946), *passim.*

London, Hannah R. "Portraits of Jews Painted by Gilbert Stuart," Daughters of the American Revolution, *Magazine*, LX (1926), 213-216.

"The Lyons Collection," A. J. H. S., *Publications*, XXI (1913) and XXVII (1919). Shedding light on the Revolutionary War, it occupies the two entire volumes.

Macaulay, T. B. *Essay and Speech on Jewish Disabilities.* Edinburgh: Ballantyne, Hanson and Co., 1909.

"The Minis Family." By the Genealogical Editor. *The Georgia Historical Quarterly*, I (1917), 45-49.

Morais, Rev. Sabato. "Mickvé Israel Congregation of Philadelphia," A. J. H. S., *Publications*, I (1892), 13-24.

Neumann, Joshua N. "Some Eighteenth Century American Jewish Letters," A. J. H. S., *Publications*, XXXIV (1937), 75 ff.

Oppenheim, Samuel. "The Jews and Masonry in the United States before 1810," A. J. H. S., *Publications*, XIX (1910), 9. "Letter of Jonas Phillips, July 28, 1776, Mentioning the American Revolution and the Declaration of Independence," A. J. H. S., *Publications*, XXV (1917), 128-131. "Two Letters of Solomon Bush, a Revolutionary Soldier," A. J. H. S., *Publications*, XXIII (1915), 177.

Phillips, N. Taylor. "Rev. Gershom Mendez Seixas," *American Jewish Year Book* (1904-1905). Pp. 40-51.

Phillips, Rosalie S. "A Burial Place for the Jewish Nation Forever." A. J. H. S., *Publications*, XVIII (1909), 102.

Rosendale, Simon W. "A Document Concerning the Franks Family," A. J. H. S., *Publications*, I (1892), 103.

Roth, Cecil. "A Jewish Voice for Peace in the War of American Independence. The Life and Writings of Abraham Wagg, 1719-1803," A. J. H. S., *Publications*, XXXI (1928), 33-75.

Rubens, Alfred. *Anglo-Jewish Portraits.* London: The Jewish Museum, 1935.

Sachse, Julius F. "Jacob Philadelphia, Mystic and Physicist," A. J. H. S., *Publications*, XVI (1908), 80.

Shpall, Leo. "The Sheftalls of Georgia," *The Georgia Historical Quarterly*, XVII (1943), 339-349.

Solis-Cohen, Solomon. "Note Concerning David Hays and Esther Etting, His Wife and Michael Hays and Reuben Etting, Their Brothers, Patriots of the Revolution," A. J. H. S., *Publications*, II (1893), 69-70.

Solomon, Haym. In her preparation of this section the writer has utilized the extensive source and secondary collection on Haym Solomon in the Library of the American Jewish Historical Society, the *Publications* of the A. J. H. S., Max J. Kohler's *Haym Solomon* (1931), an excellent summary. The article in the *Universal Jewish Encyclopedia*, IX (1941), 322 and 324, and the writer's account in *Jewish Pioneers in America, 1492-1848* (New York: Brentano, 1931), were also summarized. But by far the most valuable single manuscript source is Haym Solomon's *Letter Book*, which is invaluable. For permission to quote from this collection of letters, the writer is greatly indebted to Mr. A. S. W. Rosenbach, former president of the American Jewish Historical Society.

Straus, Oscar S. "New Light on the Career of Colonel David S. Franks," A. J. H. S., *Publications*, X (1902), 105.

Veen, Harm R. S. van der. *Jewish Characters in Eighteenth Century English Fiction and Drama*. Groningen, Batavia: J. B. Wolters' uitgevers-maatschappij n.v., 1935. P. 264.

There are among the manuscript collections in the American Jewish Historical Society many treasures. The *Letter Book* of Haym Solomon, the Sheftall Papers, the Lopez Papers, the Oppenheim Collection are some of the sources utilized in the preparation of this chapter. The *Publications* of the Society from volume I, with its article by Herbert Friedenwald titled "Jews Mentioned . . ." to volume XXXV, contain many articles on this subject. To cite but one example, the article by Frances Dublin titled "Jewish Colonial Enterprize in the Light of the Amherst Papers (1756-1763)" is but a segment of new data giving the background for the Revolution (A. J. H. S., *Publications*, XXXV (1939), 1-25).

CHAPTER VIII

1. Charles A. and Mary R. Beard, *The Rise of American Civilization*, 2 vols. (New York: Macmillan Co., 1929), vol. I, 447-49.
2. Max J. Kohler, "Civil Status of the Jews in Colonial New York," American Jewish Historical Society, *Publications*, VI (1897), 106.
3. Max J. Kohler, "Phases in the History of Religious Liberty in America, with Special Reference to the Jews," A. J. H. S., *Publications*, XI (1903), 69.
4. Lewis Abraham, "Correspondence Between Washington and Jewish Citizens," A. J. H. S., *Publications*, III (1894), 88.
5. N. Taylor Phillips, "Family History of the Reverend David Mendez Macado," A. J. H. S., *Publications*, II (1893), 55.
6. Abraham, *op. cit.*, 88 ff, 94.
7. Max J. Kohler, "Notes," A. J. H. S., *Publications*, IV (1894), 221; Leon Hühner, "Jews in Connection with the Colleges of the Thirteen Original States Prior to 1800," A. J. H. S., *Publications*, XIX (1910), 104.
8. Max J. Kohler, "Unpublished Correspondence Between Thomas Jefferson and Some American Jews," A. J. H. S., *Publications*, XX (1911), 11-12.
9. Cyrus Adler, "A Political Document of the Year 1800," A. J. H. S., *Publications*, I (1892), 111-15.
10. Jacob I. Hartstein, "The Polonies Talmud Torah of New York," A. J. H. S., *Publications*, XXXIV (1937), 123-41.

11. Nathaniel F. Moore, *Diary. A Trip from New York to the Falls of St. Anthony in 1845*. Edited by Stanley Pargellis and Ruth Lapham Butler (Chicago: Published for the Newberry Library by the University of Chicago Press, 1946).

12. In the Library of the Jewish Theological Seminary is an old Bible with this legend, "The first Bible used by our dear Father, From Aunt Richea to Joshua I. Cohen." The dates 1712, 1782, 1819 are written in it, together with numerous biographical and genealogical notations. See also, Aaron Baroway, "The Cohens of Maryland," *Maryland Historical Magazine*, XVIII (1923), 357 ff.

13. *The Lyons Collection.* "Miscellaneous Items Relating to Jews in New York," A. J. H. S., *Publications*, XXVII (1919), 396.

14. Max J. Kohler, "Jewish Rights at the Congress of Vienna (1814-1815), and Aix-la-Chapelle (1818)," A. J. H. S., *Publications*, XXVI (1918), 33-125.

15. *Ibid.*, p. 67.

16. Mosheh R. Ringel, "Further Information Concerning the Colony 'Sholam' on Yageville Hill, Ulster County, New York," A. J. H. S., *Publications*, XXXV (1939), 307.

17. Leland D. Baldwin, *The Story of the Americas. The Discovery, Settlement and Development of the New World* (New York: Simon and Schuster, 1943), pp. 504-505.

18. This section based on many important MSS. in the American Jewish Historical Society. Among them:
    1. Handbill, dated May 26, 1773, signed Bernard Gratz, offering two parcels of land, one of 9,000 acres and one of 25,000 acres.
    2. Land patent—311 acres to Issac Franks in Pennsylvania.
    3. Land transactions between Issac Franks and Benjamin Rush, M.D., in 1787 and 1792.
    4. Memorandum from Robert Morris to Aaron Levy, November 3, 1792. Levy surveyed a parcel of land (about 200,000 acres) for Morris.

19. David Philipson, "The Jewish Pioneers of the Ohio Valley," A. J. H. S., *Publications* VIII (1900), 47; David Philipson, "The Cincinnati Community in 1825," A. J. H. S., *Publications*, X (1902), 97-99.

20. Leo Shpall, "The First Synagogue in Louisiana," *The Louisiana Historical Quarterly*, XXI (1938), 518-31.

See also

Atherton, Gertrude. *Adventures of a Novelist*. New York: Liveright, 1932.

Dunbar, Seymour. *A History of Travel in America*. New York: Tudor Publishing Co., 1937.

Emden, Paul H. "The Brothers Goldsmid and the Financing of the

Napoleonic Wars," Jewish Historical Society of England, *Transactions*, XIV (1940), 225-46.

Friedenwald, Herbert. "Jacob Isaac and His Method of Converting Salt Water into Fresh Water," American Jewish Historical Society, *Publications*, II (1893), 112.

Hackenburg, William B. "Outline of a Plan to Gather Statistics Concerning the Jews of the United States," A. J. H. S., *Publications*, XII (1904), 157-61.

Jastrow, Morris, Jr. "Documents Relating to the Career of Isaac Franks," A. J. H. S., *Publications*, V (1897), 23.

Kohler, Max J. "Jewish Rights at Vienna (1814-1815), and Aix-la-Chapelle (1818)," A. J. H. S., *Publications*, XXVI (1918), 103. "Unpublished Correspondence between Thomas Jefferson and Some American Jews," A. J. H. S., *Publications*, XX (1911), 11-12, 29.

Lebeson, Anita L. "Hannah Adams and the Jews," *Historia Judaica*, VIII (October, 1946), *passim*.

Liebmann, Walter H. "The Correspondence between Solomon Etting and Henry Clay," A. J. H. S., *Publications*, XVII (1909), 81.

Philipson, David. "The Cincinnati Community in 1825," A. J. H. S., *Publications*, X (1902), 97-99. "The Jewish Pioneers of the Ohio Valley," A. J. H. S., *Publications*, VIII (1900), 43-57.

Roper, R. C. "Thomas Paine: Scientist-Religionist," *Scientific Monthly*, LVIII (February, 1944), 101-111.

Wallach, L. "The Beginnings of the Science of Judaism in the Nineteenth Century," *Historia Judaica*, VIII (April, 1946), 33-60.

Wright, Richardson L. *Hawkers & Walkers in Early America*. Philadelphia: J. B. Lippincott Co., 1927. P. 254.

CHAPTER IX

1. Morris U. Schappes, "Toward the Biography of Judah Touro," *Jewish Life* (April, 1947); Leon Hühner's biography, *The Life of Judah Touro, 1775-1854* (Philadelphia: The Jewish Publication Society of America, 1946); Simon Wolf, *The American Jew as Patriot, Soldier, and Citizen* (Philadelphia, 1895), p. 71; Max J. Kohler, "Judah Touro, Merchant and Philanthropist," American Jewish Historical Society, *Publications*, XIII (1905), 96-103; "Death of Judah Touro," *Occident*, XI (March, 1854), 589-602; "Funeral of the Late Judah Touro," *Ibid.*, pp. 595-96; "Will of the Late Judah Touro," *Ibid.*, pp. 596-602.

2. Henry S. Morais, *Eminent Israelites of the Nineteenth Century* (Philadelphia, 1880), pp. 335 ff.

3. David Philipson, *Letters of Rebecca Gratz* (Philadelphia: The Jewish Publication Society of America, 1929).

4. Anita L. Lebeson, *Jewish Pioneers in America, 1492-1848* (New

York: Brentano, 1931), summarizes Rebecca's biography at some length.

5. Joseph Jacobs, "The Original of Scott's Rebecca," A. J. H. S., *Publications*, XXII (1914), 53-60; David Philipson, "Some Unpublished Letters of Rebecca Gratz," A. J. H. S., *Publications*, XXIX (1924), 53-60, *passim*.

6. Morais, *op. cit.*, p. 112.

7. These letters are found in Philipson, *Letters of Rebecca Gratz, passim*.

8. Lebeson, *op. cit.*, pp. 268-83; George A. Kohut, "A Literary Autobiography of Mordecai Manuel Noah," A. J. H. S., *Publications*, VI (1897), 113-21; Albert M. Friedenberg, "The Correspondence of Jews with President Martin Van Buren," A. J. H. S., *Publications*, XXII (1914), 71-72, 79-87; Sampson Falk, "A History of the Israelites in Buffalo," Buffalo Historical Society, *Publications*, I (1879), 289-304.

9. Mordecai M. Noah, Address delivered at Grand Island, New York, in September, 1825, A. J. H. S., *Publications*, XXI (1913), 230 ff. Isaac Goldberg, *Major Noah: American-Jewish Pioneer* (Philadelphia: The Jewish Publication Society of America, 1936).

10. Lucius C. Moïse, *Biography of Isaac Harby* (Columbia, R. L. Bryan Co., 1931); Max J. Kohler, "Isaac Harby, Jewish Religious Leader and Man of Letters," A. J. H. S., *Publications*, XXXII (1931), 39 ff.

11. Moïse, *op. cit.*, p. 51.

12. Barnett A. Elzas, *The Jews of South Carolina* (Charleston: The Daggett Printing Co., 1903), chapters VIII and IX.

13. Based largely on research on Penina Moïse summarized in Lebeson, *op. cit.*, and Moïse's contributions to *Occident*.

14. Introduction to Alexis C. de Tocqueville, *Democracy in America*, 2 vols. (New York, 1898), vol. I, 11-12.

15. Samuel Oppenheim, "The Question of the Kosher Meat Supply in New York in 1813: with a Sketch of Earlier Conditions," A. J. H. S., *Publications*, XXV (1917), 33-35, 38.

16. *Ibid.*

17. Albert M. Friedenberg, "Calendar of American Jewish Cases," A. J. H. S., *Publications*, XII (1904), 87-88.

18. Richardson L. Wright, *Hawkers & Walkers in Early America* (Philadelphia: J. B. Lippincott Co., 1927), p. 91.

19. Soloman R. Kagan, *Jewish Contributions to Medicine in America, from Colonial Times to the Present* (Boston: The Boston Medical Publishing Co., 1939), pp. 10, 18-19.

20. Henry Berkowitz, "Notes on the History of the Earliest German Jewish Congregation in America," A. J. H. S., *Publications*, IX (1901), 123-125.

21. David de Sola Pool, "Gershom Mendes Seixas' Letters, 1813-1815, to his Daughter Sarah (Seixas) Kursheedt and Son-in-law, Israel Baer Kursheedt," A. J. H. S., *Publications*, XXXV (1939), 189-205.
22. Philipson, *Letters of Rebecca Gratz, passim.*
23. Alfred Mordecai, "The Life of Alfred Mordecai as Related by Himself," edited by James A. Padgett, *North Carolina Historical Review*, XXII (1945), 58-108; Alfred Mordecai, "Life of Alfred Mordecai in Mexico, in 1865-1866, as Told in His Letters to His Family," edited by James A. Padgett, *North Carolina Historical Review*, XXII (1945), 198-227; Gratz Mordecai, "Notice of Jacob Mordecai, Founder, and Proprietor from 1809 to 1818, of the Warrenton (N. C.) Female Seminary," A. J. H. S., *Publications*, VI (1897), 39-48; Alexander W. Weddell, "Samuel Mordecai: Chronicler of Richmond, 1786-1865," *Virginia Magazine of History and Biography*, LIII (1945), 271 ff.
24. These excerpts are from "Life of Alfred Mordecai in Mexico," etc., *op. cit.*

See also

Allen, Lewis F. "Founding of the City of Ararat on Grand Island by Mordecai M. Noah," Buffalo Historical Society, *Publications*, I (1879), 305-328.

Berkowitz, Henry. "Notes on the History of the Earliest German Jewish Congregation in America," American Jewish Historical Society, *Publications*, IX (1901), 123.

Elzas, Barnett A. *A Century of Judaism in South Carolina 1800-1900*. Charleston, 1904. (Reprinted from the Centennial Edition of the *News and Courier*, May, 1904.)

Ezekiel, Herbert T., and Lichtenstein, Gaston. *The History of the Jews in Richmond from 1769 to 1917*. Richmond: H. T. Ezekiel, 1917.

Falk, Sampson. "A History of the Israelites in Buffalo," Buffalo Historical Society, *Publications*, I (1879), 289-304.

Friedenberg, Albert M. "Calendar of American Jewish Cases," A. J. H. S., *Publications*, XII (1904), 87-88. "The Correspondence of Jews with President Martin Van Buren," A. J. H. S., *Publications*, XXII (1914), 71-72.

Goldberg, Isaac. *Major Noah: American-Jewish Pioneer*. Philadelphia: Jewish Publication Society of America, 1936.

Hersch, Virginia. *Storm Beach*. Boston: Houghton Mifflin Co., 1933. *Woman under Glass. Saint Teresa of Avila*. New York: Harper & Brothers, 1930. In these two books, the first about her beloved Charleston, the second about St. Teresa of Avila, the grandniece of Penina Moïse preserves the literary tradition of the Moïse family. The latter book is dedicated to Miss Hersch's mother, Georgie Moïse Davis.

Jacobs, Joseph. "The Original of Scott's Rebecca," A. J. H. S., *Publications*, XXII (1914), 53-60.

Kohler, Max J. "Isaac Harby, Jewish Religious Leader," A. J. H. S., *Publications*, XXXII (1931), 39. "Judah Touro, Merchant and Philanthropist," A. J. H. S., *Publications*, XIII (1905), 93-111.

Kohut, George A. "A Literary Autobiography of Mordecai Manuel Noah. With an Introduction," A. J. H. S., *Publications*, VI (1897), 113-21.

London, Hannah. In Daughters of the American Revolution, *Magazine* (February, April, December, 1926).

Moïse, Lucius C. *Biography of Isaac Harby*. Columbia: R. L. Bryan Co., 1931. See especially "The Reformed Society of Israelites of Charleston, S. C., 1824-1833," p. 7.

Morais, Henry S. *Eminent Israelites of the Nineteenth Century*. Philadelphia, 1880. Pp. 335 ff.

Mordecai, Alfred. "Life of Alfred Mordecai as Related by Himself." Edited by James A. Padgett, *North Carolina Historical Review*, XXII (1945), 58-108. "Life of Alfred Mordecai in Mexico, in 1865-1866, as Told in His Letters to His Family." Edited by James A. Padgett, *North Carolina Historical Review*, XXII (1945), 198-227.

Mordecai, Gratz. "Notice of Jacob Mordecai, Founder and Proprietor from 1809-1818, of the Warrenton (N. C.) Female Seminary," A. J. H. S., *Publications*, VI (1897), 39-48.

Noah, Mordecai. "Address by Mordecai M. Noah," A. J. H. S., *Publications*, XXI (1913), 230-52.

Osterweis, Rollin G. *Rebecca Gratz*. New York: G. P. Putnam's Sons, 1935.

Philipson, David. *Letters of Rebecca Gratz*. Philadelphia: Jewish Publication Society of America, 1929. "Some Unpublished Letters of Rebecca Gratz," A. J. H. S., *Publications*, XXIX (1924), 53-60.

Pool, David de Sola. "Gershom Mendes Seixas' Letters, 1813-1815, to His Daughter Sarah (Seixas) Kursheedt and Son-in-Law, Israel Baer Kursheedt," A. J. H. S., *Publications*, XXXV (1939), 204.

Richman, Julia. "The Jewish Sunday School Movement in the United States." *The Jewish Quarterly Review*, XII (1900), 563-601.

Wedell, Alexander W. "Samuel Mordecai: Chronicler of Richmond, 1786-1865," *Virginia Magazine of History and Biography*, LIII (1945), 265-87.

CHAPTER X

1. Albert M. Friedenberg, "A German Jewish Poet on America," American Jewish Historical Society, *Publications*, XIII (1905), 91-92.

2. Marquis, James, *Andrew Jackson* (Indianapolis: Bobbs-Merrill Co., 1937), pp. 393, 495-96.

3. Quoted by David S. Muzzey, *An American History* (New York: Ginn & Co., 1925), p. 230.

4. Saul M. Ginsburg, "Max Lilienthal's Activities in Russia; New Documents," A. J. H. S., *Publications*, XXXV (1939), 49 ff.

5. Albert M. Hyamson, "British Projects for the Restoration of Jews to Palestine," A. J. H. S., *Publications*, XXVI (1918), 134.

6. Max J. Kohler, "Jews and the Anti-Slavery Movement, II," A. J. H. S., *Publications*, IX (1901), 53 ff.

7. Augusta Levy, "Recollections of a Pioneer Woman of La Crosse," edited by Albert H. Sanford, State Historical Society of Wisconsin, *Proceedings for 1911* (Madison: The Society, 1912), pp. 201-215.

8. H. Eliassof, "The Jews of Chicago," A. J. H. S., *Publications*, XI (1903), 118-119.

9. Guido Kisch, ed., "A Voyage to America Ninety Years Ago. The Diary of a Bohemian Jew on His Voyage from Hamburg to New York, 1847," A. J. H. S., *Publications*, XXXV (1939), 65-113; Josephine Goldmark, *Pilgrims of '48* (New Haven: Yale University Press, 1930), *passim*.

10. J. A. Wax, "Isidor Bush," *Historia Judaica*, V (October, 1943), 183-203.

11. Sampson Falk, "A History of the Israelites in Buffalo," Buffalo Historical Society, *Publications*, I (1879), 292-303.

12. J. D. Eisenstein, "The History of the First Russian-American Jewish Congregation," A. J. H. S., *Publications*, IX (1901), 69.

13. Henry Cohen, "Henry Castro, Pioneer and Colonist," A. J. H. S., *Publications*, V (1897), 39.

14. Charles A. and Mary R. Beard, *The Rise of American Civilization*, 2 vols. (New York: Macmillan Co., 1929), vol. I, 611.

15. David Philipson, *Letters of Rebecca Gratz* (Philadelphia: The Jewish Publication Society of America, 1929), pp. 357, 393.

16. Henry Cohen, "Settlement of the Jews in Texas," A. J. H. S., *Publications*, II (1893), 139-40.

17. Albert M. Friedenberg, "Solomon Heydenfeldt: A Jewish Jurist of Alabama and California," A. J. H. S., *Publications*, X (1902), 138.

18. L. L. Waters, "Intrepid Artist Explorer," *Liberal Judaism* (June, 1946), pp. 43-50.

19. S. N. Carvalho, *Incidents of Travel* (New York, 1857), *passim*.

See also

The American Jewish Year Book. 5665 (1902-1903). *See* "Jewish Statistics," p. 143.

Blunt, John E. "An Enquiry into the Civil Disabilities of the Jews in England," in his *History of the . . . Jews in England*. London, 1830.

Cohen, Henry. "Henry Castro, Pioneer and Colonist," A. J. H. S., *Publications*, V (1897), 39. "Settlement of the Jews in Texas," A. J. H. S., *Publications*, II (1893), 139-40, 146-47.

Deutsch, Gotthard. "Dr. Abraham Bettman, a Pioneer Physician of

Cincinnati (1806-1901)," A. J. H. S., *Publications*, XXIII (1934), 105-116.

Dickens, Charles. Letter from Charles Dickens, Esq., Naples, June 1, 1845, in the *St. Louis Weekly Reveille*, July 14, 1845.

Dunbar, Seymour. *History of Travel in America*. New York: Tudor Publishing Co., 1937. Pp. 530-31.

Dushkin, Alexander M. *Jewish Education in New York City*. New York: The Bureau of Jewish Education, 1918.

Eisenstein, J. D. "The History of the First Russian-American Jewish Congregation. The Beth Hamedrosh Hagodol," A. J. H. S., *Publications*, IX (1901), 64.

Eliassof, H. "The Jews of Chicago," A. J. H. S., *Publications*, XI (1904), 119.

Falk, Sampson. "A History of the Israelites in Buffalo," Buffalo Historical Society, *Publications*, I (1879), 292.

Felsenthal, Bernhard. "On the History of the Jews in Chicago," A. J. H. S., *Publications*, II (1893), 24.

Friedenberg, Albert M. "A German Jewish Poet on America," A. J. H. S., *Publications*, XIII (1905), 91-92. "Letters of a California Pioneer," A. J. H. S., *Publications*, XXXI (1928), 135-71. "Solomon Heydenfeldt: A Jewish Jurist of Alabama and California," A. J. H. S., *Publications*, X (1902), 129-40.

Ginsburg, Saul M. "Max Lilienthal's Activities in Russia; New Documents," A. J. H. S., *Publications*, XXXV (1939), 50.

Goldmark, Josephine. "The Forty-eighters in the United States," in her *Pilgrims of '48*. New Haven: Yale University Press, 1930. P. 248.

Grinstein, Hyman B. *The Rise of the Jewish Community of New York, 1654-1860*. Philadelphia: Jewish Publication Society of America, 1945. *Passim*.

Hyamson, Albert M. "Restoration of Jews to Palestine," A. J. H. S., *Publications*, XXVI (1918), 134.

The Jewish People, Past and Present. 2 vols. New York: Jewish Encyclopedic Handbooks, Central Yiddish Culture Organization, 1946-48. Pp. 219-20.

Kisch, Guido. "Two American Jewish Pioneers of New Haven," *Historia Judaica*, IV (1942). "A Voyage to America Ninety Years Ago." Edited by Guido Kisch, A. J. H. S., *Publications*, XXXV (1939), 65-113.

Kohler, Max J. "Educational Reforms in Europe in Their Relation to Jewish Emancipation, 1778-1919," A. J. H. S., *Publications*, XXVIII (1921), 83-132. "Jews and the Anti-Slavery Movement, II," A. J. H. S., *Publications*, IX (1901), 53-56. "The German-Jewish Migration to America, 1848," A. J. H. S., *Publications*, IX (1901), 87-105.

Kurath, H. "Dialect Areas, Settlement Areas and Culture Areas in the United States," in C. Ware, ed., *Cultural Approach to History*. New York: Columbia University Press, 1940. P. 339.

Lebowich, Joseph. "The Jews in Boston till 1875," A. J. H. S., *Publications*, XII (1904), 110.

Lestschinsky, Jacob. "The Economic and Social Development of the Jewish People," in *The Jewish People*, I (1946), 361-406.

Levy, Augusta. "Recollections of a Pioneer Woman of La Crosse." Edited by Albert H. Sanford, State Historical Society of Wisconsin, *Proceedings for 1911*. Madison, The Society, 1912. Pp. 201-215.

Lindo, Alicia. "A Sketch of the Life of David Lindo," A. J. H. S., *Publications*, XXIII (1915), 37-41.

Macaulay, T. B. "Civil Disabilities of the Jews," *Occident*, II (1844), 127 ff.

Margolis, Max L., and Marx, Alexander. *A History of the Jewish People*. Philadelphia: Jewish Publication Society of America, 1938. P. 645.

Mordecai, Alfred. "Life of Alfred Mordecai as Related by Himself." Edited by James A. Padgett, *North Carolina Historical Review*, XXII (1945), 90-91.

Moses, Alfred G. "The History of the Jews of Montgomery," A. J. H. S., *Publications*, XIII (1905), 85.

Nevins, Allan, and Commager, Henry S. *The Pocket History of the United States*. New York: Pocket Books Inc., 1943. P. 196.

Rivkind, Isaac. "A Pocket Edition Prayer Book for German Jewish Emigrants to America, 1842," A. J. H. S., *Publications*, XXXV (1939), 207-212.

Sulzberger, David. "Growth of Jewish Population in the United States," A. J. H. S., *Publications*, VI (1897), 143.

Trachtenberg, Joshua. *Consider the Years*. Easton, Penn.: Centennial Committee of Temple Brith Sholom, 1944. P. 234.

Wax, James A. "Isidor Bush, American Patriot and Abolitionist," *Historia Judaica*, V (October 1943), 183-203.

Wright, Richardson L. *Hawkers & Walkers in Early America*. Philadelphia: J. B. Lippincott Co., 1927. P. 92.

CHAPTER XI

1. David Philipson, *Letters of Rebecca Gratz* (Philadelphia: Jewish Publication Society of America, 1929), pp. 341-45.
2. Max J. Kohler, "The Jews and the American Anti-Slavery Movement," American Jewish Historical Society, *Publications*, V (1897), 141-43.
3. Max J. Kohler, "Jews and the American Anti-Slavery Movement. II," A. J. H. S., *Publications*, IX (1901), 46.
4. Kohler, "The Jews and the American Anti-Slavery Movement," A. J. H. S., *Publications*, V (1897), 144.
5. Kohler, "Jews and the American Anti-Slavery Movement. II," A. J. H. S., *Publications*, IX (1901), 53-55.

6. Philip S. Foner, *Jews in American History, 1654-1865* (New York: International Publishers, 1946), pp. 54 ff.; Rheta C. Dorr, *Susan B. Anthony* (New York: Frederick A. Stokes Co., 1928), p. 70.

7. Kohler, "The Jews and the American Anti-Slavery Movement," A. J. H. S., *Publications*, V (1897), 152-53.

8. *Ibid.*, p. 154.

9. Cyrus Adler, and Albert M. Friedenberg, "Reference to Jews in the Correspondence of John J. Crittenden," A. J. H. S., *Publications*, XXIII (1915), 123-26.

10. Leon Hühner, "Some Jewish Associates of John Brown," A. J. H. S., *Publications*, XXIII (1915), 63-64.

11. Kohler, "The Jews and the American Anti-Slavery Movement," A. J. H. S., *Publications*, V (1897), 147, 150-51.

12. Henry S. Morais, *Eminent Israelites of the Nineteenth Century* (Philadelphia, 1880), pp. 287-91; Foner, *op. cit.*, pp. 61-62.

13. *Occident*, XIX (November, 1861), 356-66.

14. *Occident*, XIX (April, 1861), 1-7.

15. *Occident*, XIX (August, 1861), 194-201.

16. Philipson, *op. cit.*, 426-27.

17. Alfred Mordecai, "The Life of Alfred Mordecai as Related by Himself," edited by James A. Padgett, *North Carolina Historical Review*, XXII (1945), 105.

18. Alfred Mordecai, "Life of Alfred Mordecai in Mexico, in 1865-1866, as Told in His Letters to His Family," edited by James A. Padgett, *North Carolina Historical Review*, XXII (1945), 211.

19. Allan Nevins and Henry S. Commager, *The Pocket History of the United States* (New York: Pocket Books, 1943), p. 240.

20. Isaac Markens, "Lincoln and the Jews," A. J. H. S., *Publications*, XVII (1909), 109.

21. Oppenheim MSS. (Package IV), "Portfolio, Israel Moses. Civil War." 114 pp.

22. Max J. Kohler, "Judah P. Benjamin: Statesman and Jurist," A. J. H. S., *Publications*, XII (1904), 75.

23. The *Occident* was thoroughly combed for all pertinent data on this period. It is not necessary to itemize separate quotations as to page and volume. The student will find these volumes extremely useful. The preceding paragraph, for example, used volumes XIX and XX, from April, 1861, through February, 1863.

24. L. H. Roddis, "Phineas J. Horwitz—the Fourth Chief of the Bureau of Medicine, 1865-1869," United States Navy, *Bulletin* (Washington, 1935).

25. Morais, *op. cit.*, 149-53.

26. Kohler, "Judah P. Benjamin: Statesman and Jurist," A. J. H. S., *Publications*, XII (1904), 63.

27. *Ibid.*

28. Simon Wolf, *American Jew, as Patriot, Soldier, and Citizen* (Philadelphia, 1895), pp. 101-102, 109-111.
29. *Ibid.*, p. 374; *Universal Jewish Encyclopedia*, 10 vols. (New York: The Universal Jewish Encyclopedia, Inc., 1939-43), vol. III, 251; see also *Florida Historical Quarterly*, II (April and July, 1909).
30. Henry Cohen, "A Modern Maccabean," A. J. H. S., *Publications*, VI (1897), 36-37.
31. *Universal Jewish Encyclopedia*, IX (1939-43), 624.
32. Foner, *op. cit.*, pp. 63 ff.; Hyman B. Grinstein, *The Rise of the Jewish Community of New York, 1654-1860* (Philadelphia: Jewish Publication Society of America, (1945), p. 544; Morais, *op cit.*, p. 156.
33. Markens, *op. cit.*, p. 127.
34. *Abraham Lincoln: His Speeches and Writings*, edited by Roy P. Basler (Cleveland: World Publishing Co., 1946).
35. Markens, *op. cit.*, p. 127.
36. Since this chapter was written, an excellent, detailed study of "Jewish Chaplains during the Civil War" has been published by Rabbi Bertram W. Korn in *American Jewish Archives*, I (June, 1948), 6-22.
37. Myer S. Isaacs, "A Jewish Army Chaplain," A. J. H. S., *Publications*, XII (1904), 127-133.
38. *Ibid.*
39. Charles A. and Mary R. Beard, *The Rise of American Civilization*, 2 vols. (New York: Macmillan Co., 1929), vol. II, 91-92.
40. Joseph Lebowich, "General Ulysses S. Grant," A. J. H. S., *Publications*, XVII (1909), 71-72.
41. "Appendix III. A Birdseye View of Jewish Civic Activity and Patriotism All Over the World during Our Civil War," A. J. H. S., *Publications*, XXIX (1924), 125.
42. Markens, *op. cit.*, p. 120.
43. *Ibid.*, p. 117.
44. Lebowich, *op. cit.*, p. 73.
45. "Appendix III," *op. cit.*, pp. 119-120.
46. Quoted by Carl Sandburg, *Abraham Lincoln, the War Years*, 2 vols. (New York: Harcourt Brace & Co., 1939), vol. II, 176.
47. *Jewish National Monthly*, LX (March, 1946), 232.
48. Lebowich, *op. cit.*, pp. 74-75.
49. *Ibid.*, p. 79.
50. Markens, *op. cit.*, p. 143.

See also

Adler, Cyrus, and Friedenberg, Albert M. "References to Jews in the Correspondence of John J. Crittenden," American Jewish Historical Society, *Publications*, XXIII (1915), 126.
"Appendix II" (The Board of Delegates of American Israelites), A. J. H. S., *Publications*, XXIX (1924), 84.

"Appendix III. A Birdseye View of Jewish Civic Activity and Patriotism All Over the World during Our Civil War," A. J. H. S., *Publications*, XXIX (1924), 119-120.

Cohen, Henry. "A Modern Maccabean," A. J. H. S., *Publications*, VI (1897), 36-37.

Felsenthal, Bernhard. "Adolphe Cremieux," in Emma Felsenthal, *Bernhard Felsenthal, Teacher in Israel; Selections from His Writings*. New York: Oxford University Press, 1924. Pp. 248-249.

Felsenthal, Emma. *Bernhard Felsenthal, Teacher in Israel; Selections from His Writings, with Biographical Sketch and Bibliography by His Daughter*. New York: Oxford University Press, 1924. P. 288.

Hühner, Leon. "Some Jewish Associates of John Brown," A. J. H. S., *Publications*, XXIII (1915), 63-64.

Isaacs, Myer S. "A Jewish Army Chaplain," A. J. H. S., *Publications*, XII (1904), 127.

Kohler, Max J. "The Board of Delegates of American Israelites, 1859-1878. Including the Correspondence of Myer S. Isaacs with General F. Butler as to the Status of the Jews at the Time of Our Civil War," A. J. H. S., *Publications*, XXIX (1924), 77-78. "The Jews and the American Anti-Slavery Movement," A. J. H. S., *Publications*, V (1897), 141. "Jews and the American Anti-Slavery Movement. II," A. J. H. S., *Publications*, IX (1901), 46. "Judah P. Benjamin: Statesman and Jurist," A. J. H. S., *Publications*, XII (1904), 75.

Abraham Lincoln: His Speeches and Writings. Edited by Roy P. Basler. Cleveland: World Publishing Co., 1946.

Lebowich, Joseph. "General Ulysses S. Grant and the Jews," A. J. H. S., *Publications*, XVII (1909), 71.

Markens, Isaac. "Lincoln and the Jews," A. J. H. S., *Publications*, XVII (1909), 109, 125-26.

Mordecai, Alfred. "Life of Alfred Mordecai in Mexico, in 1865-1866, as Told in His Letters to His Family," edited by James A. Padgett, *North Carolina Historical Review*, XXII (1945), 211.

Morais, Henry S. *Eminent Israelites of the Nineteenth Century*. Philadelphia, 1880. Pp. 153-57, 195-201.

"Popular Movements," *The Nation*, VI (May 28, 1868), 427-28.

Roddis, L. H. "Phineas J. Horwitz, the Fourth Chief of the Bureau of Medicine, 1865-1869," United States Navy, *Bulletin*, (1935).

Sandburg, Carl. *Abraham Lincoln, the War Years*. 2 vols. New York: Harcourt, Brace and Co., 1939. *Passim.*

Sulzberger, David. "Growth of the Jewish Population in the United States," A. J. H. S., *Publications*, VI (1897), 143.

    "In the *History of the Jews up to the Present Time*, 2nd edition, Boston, 1848, compiled and published by M. A. Berk, he says: 'From the best information it would appear that there are about 50,000 Jews in the United States. From 12,000 to 13,000 of this number are supposed to reside in the city of New York, 4000 in Philadelphia, and Baltimore 1000 . . .' "

Sumner, William G. *Folkways: a Study of the Sociological Importance of Usages, Manners, Customs, Mores, and Morals.* Boston, c. 1906. Pp. 110-111.

Wax, James A. "Isidor Bush, American Patriot and Abolitionist," *Historia Judaica*, V (October, 1943), 200.

Wolf, Simon. *The American Jew as Patriot, Soldier and Citizen.* Philadelphia, 1895. Pp. 109-111.

CHAPTER XII

1. *Asmonean* (October 24, 1851).
2. Semen M. Dubnow, *Jewish History* (London, Published for the Jewish Historical Society of England by Macmillan, 1903), p. 22.
3. Albert M. Friedenberg, "American Jewish Journalism to the Close of the Civil War," American Jewish Historical Society, *Publications*, XXVI (1918), 270-71, 272.
4. *Allgemeine Zeitung des Judenthums* was used to correlate events of importance in Europe and America. Only occasional copies were consulted during specific times of stress or historic importance. The *Asmonean* and the *Occident* were used chronologically.
5. Henry S. Morais, *Eminent Israelites of the Nineteenth Century* (Philadelphia, 1880), p. 222.
6. *Asmonean*, vols. I-XVII, *passim*.
7. Morais, *op. cit.*, pp. 195 ff.
8. David Philipson, *Letters of Rebecca Gratz* (Philadelphia: Jewish Publication Society of America, 1929), p. 108.
9. *Ibid.*, p. 193.
10. *Occident* (April, 1843), pp. 28-32. No attempt will be made to identify quotations from the *Occident* except for the quotations that are of particular significance to the scholar or student. This chapter originally had 436 footnotes.
11. *Occident* (September, 1843), pp. 301-307.
12. *Occident* (April, 1845), pp. 496-510.
13. *Occident* (February, 1845), pp. 538-43. Italics mine.
14. *Occident* (January, 1845), p. 512.
15. *Occident* (May, 1847), pp. 87-90.
16. *Occident* (January, 1848), pp. 510-11.
17. *Occident* (December, 1848), pp. 431-35.
18. *Occident* (January, 1849), pp. 137-49.
19. *Occident* (January, 1862), pp. 476-80.
20. Sampson Falk, "A History of the Israelites in Buffalo," Buffalo Historical Society, *Publications*, I (1879), 301.
21. *Occident* (December, 1866), pp. 419-24.

22. *Occident* (March, 1868), pp. 593-601.
23. Michael A. Mikkelson, *The Bishop Hill Colony* (Baltimore: Johns Hopkins University Press, 1892). This scroll is now on exhibit at the library of the Jewish Theological Seminary of America.

See also

Allgemeine Zeitung des Judenthums. Its files may be consulted at the Jewish Theological Seminary. Some volumes are also in the Newberry Library.

Friedenberg, Albert M. "The Jews and the American Sunday Laws," American Jewish Historical Society, *Publications*, XI (1903), 101.

Jacobs, William. *The Jews' Reasons for Believing in One God Only.* New York: G. Vale, 1849.

Kisch, Guido. "Israels Herold," *Historia Judaica*, II (1940), 3-22.

Lebeson, Anita L. *Jewish Pioneers in America, 1492-1848.* New York: Brentano, 1931. Pp. 309-310.

Leeser, Isaac. *The Twenty-four Books of the Holy Scriptures: Carefully Translated According to the Massoretic Text, after the Best Jewish Authorities.* London, 5626. 1865. (Prince Louis Lucien Bonaparte Collection in Newberry Library.)

Memoir of Maria . . . the Converted Jewess. New York, 1847.
　　From the fourth London edition. (Published for the Sunday-School Union of the Methodist Episcopal Church, 20 Mulberry Street.)

M'Neile, Rev. Hugh. "The Jews and Judaism," *Exeter Hall Lectures*, IX (February 14, 1854), 424.

Montefiore, Sir Moses. "Sir Moses Montefiore's Report to the Board of Deputies of British Jews," *Occident*, XXIV (December 1866), 419-24.

Occident and American Jewish Advocate. Edited by Isaac Leeser. 26 vols. Philadelphia, 1843-69. (Suspended 1852-53.)

Philipson, David. "The Progress of the Jewish Reform Movement in the United States," *Jewish Quarterly Review*, X (1897-98), 64.

Richman, Julia. "The Jewish Sunday School Movement in the United States," *Jewish Quarterly Review*, XII (1900), 572.

CHAPTER XIII

1. Emma Lazarus, *Songs of a Semite* (New York, 1882), p. 53. Since this chapter was written, the writer has read with interest a monograph edited by Morris U. Schappes, *Emma Lazarus, Selections from Her Poetry and Prose* (New York: Cooperative Book League, Jewish-American Section, International Workers Order, 1944).

2. Ruth L. Benjamin, "Marcus Otterbourg, United States Minister to Mexico in 1867," American Jewish Historical Society, *Publications*, XXXII (1931), 95.

3. "Reform Movement Among the Jews," *The Nation*, VI (June 18, 1868), 488-89.

4. Lucius C. Moïse, *Biography of Isaac Harby* (Columbia: R. L. Bryan Co., 1931), especially section titled "Reformed Society of Israelites."

5. David Philipson, "The Progress of the Jewish Reform Movement in the United States," *Jewish Quarterly Review*, X (1897), 62.

6. *Occident* (October, 1843), pp. 336-42, 352-53; (November, 1843), pp. 384-90; (December, 1843), pp. 436-37.

7. *Occident* (October, 1848), pp. 330-38, 357-60.

8. Isaac M. Wise, *Reminiscences*, translated by David Philipson (Cincinnati: L. Wise & Co., 1901), pp. 51 ff. The quotation is on pp. 55-57.

9. David Philipson, *The Reform Movement in Judaism* (New York: Macmillan Co., 1931), pp. 334 ff.

10. *Ibid., passim.*

11. *Ibid.*, p. 336.

12. Wise, *op. cit.*, p. 18.

13. *Ibid.*, p. 78.

14. *Ibid.*, p. 79.

15. *Ibid.*, p. 86.

16. Julia Richman, "The Jewish Sunday School Movement in the United States," *Jewish Quarterly Review*, XII (1900), 564-65.

17. Emile Durkheim, *The Elementary Forms of Religious Life* (New York: Macmillan Co., 1915), p. 427; Hyman G. Enelow, *What Do Jews Believe?* (Cincinnati: Press of C. J. Krehbiel & Co., 1908).

18. *Jewish Layman* (December, 1944).

19. In the preparation of this summary the following books were utilized: David de Sola Pool, "Judaism and the Synagogue," in Oscar Janowsky, ed., *The American Jew* (New York: Harper & Brothers, 1942); Moshe Davis, "Jewish Religious Life and Institutions in America," in Louis Finkelstein, ed., *The Jews*, 2 vols. (New York: Harper & Brothers, 1950); *American Jewish Year Book*, XLIX (5708) (1947-48).

20. David de Sola Pool, *op. cit.*, p. 41.

21. Robert Gordis, *Conservative Judaism, an American Philosophy* (New York: Published for the National Academy of Adult Jewish Studies of the Jewish Theological Seminary of America, Behrman House, 1945), p. 79. S. Schechter, *Studies in Judaism* (Philadelphia: Jewish Publication Society of America, 1908).

22. Louis Finkelstein, "Modern Theology," *Jewish Quarterly Review*, new series XIII (1922-23), 239-43.

23. Mordecai M. Kaplan, *Judaism as a Civilization* (New York: Macmillan Co., 1934), p. 91.

24. Mordecai M. Kaplan, ed., *The Jewish Reconstructionist Papers* (New York, 1936), *passim.*
25. *Occident* (December, 1848), pp. 431-35.
26. *Occident* (December, 1851).
27. Simon Wolf, *The American Jew as Patriot, Soldier and Citizen* (Philadelphia, 1895), p. 542; Joseph Lebowich, "General Ulysses S. Grant and the Jews," A. J. H. S., *Publications*, XVII (1909), 71-79.
28. Cyrus Adler, "Jews in American Diplomatic Correspondence," A. J. H. S., *Publications*, XV (1906), p. 49.
29. Herbert T. Ezekiel and Gaston Lichtenstein, *The History of the Jews of Richmond from 1769 to 1917* (Richmond H. T. Ezekiel, 1917).
30. *Harper's Weekly*, XXIX (1885), 237.
31. William A. Christian, *Richmond, Her Past and Present* (Richmond: L. H. Jenkins, 1912), p. 325.
32. Cyrus Adler and Aaron M. Margalith, "American Intercession on Behalf of Jews in the Diplomatic Correspondence of the United States, 1840-1938," A. J. H. S., *Publications*, XXXVI (1943), 323; "Proceedings of the Virginia Historical Society," *Virginia Magazine of History and Biography*, XXV (1917), xl.
33. Adler and Margalith, *op. cit.*, p. 324.
34. Christian, *op. cit.*, p. 395.
35. Adler and Margalith, *op. cit.*, pp. 325-27.
36. *Ibid.*, p. 339.
37. *Ibid.*, p. 340.
38. *Ibid.*, p. 341.
39. *Ibid.*
40. *Allgemeine Zeitung des Judenthums* (Leipsig, 1886). Keiley references on pp. 28, 35, 53, 315.
41. *National Cyclopedia of American Biography* (New York: J. T. White & Co., 1893-), vol. XIII, 433.
42. Adler and Margalith, *op. cit.*, p. 346.
43. Alexander Marx, *Studies in Jewish History and Booklore* (New York: The Jewish Theological Seminary of America, 1944), p. 364.
44. Allen F. Lesser, "Adah Isaacs Menken: A Daughter of Israel," A. J. H. S., *Publications*, XXXIV (1937), 145.
45. R. L. Rusk, *Letters to Emma Lazarus* (New York: Columbia University Press, 1939), p. 31.
46. Emma Lazarus, "The Jewish Problem," *The Century Illustrated Monthly Magazine*, XXV, new series III (1882-1883), 611.
47. *Ibid.*, p. 610.
48. Lazarus, *Songs of a Semite* (New York, 1882), *passim*; *Admetus and other poems* (New York: Hurde and Houghton, 1871), *passim.*
49. Rusk, *op. cit.*, pp. 8, 35.
50. Lazarus, "The Jewish Problem," *The Century Illustrated Monthly Magazine*, XXV, new series, III (1882-1883), 608.

51. *Universal Jewish Encyclopedia*, 10 vols. (New York: Universal Jewish Encyclopedia, Inc., 1939-43), vol. V, 618.
52. Montagu F. Modder, *The Jew in the Literature of England* (Philadelphia: The Jewish Publication Society of America, 1944), pp. 245-46. Italics mine.
53. Benjamin H. Hartogensis, "The Russian Night School of Baltimore," A. J. H. S., *Publications*, XXXI (1928), 226.
54. Fannie M. Brody, "The Hebrew Periodical Press in America, 1871-1931: a Bibliographical Survey," A. J. H. S., *Publications*, XXXIII (1934), 130. The quotation appears on p. 127.

See also

Abrahams, I. "Marriages Are Made in Heaven," *Jewish Quarterly Review*, II (1890), 177.

Adler, Cyrus. *I Have Considered the Days.* Philadelphia: Jewish Publication Society of America, 1945. "Jews in American Diplomatic Correspondence," American Jewish Historical Society, *Publications*, XV (1906), 19, 30.

Allgemeine Zeitung des Judenthums, October 30, 1896, January 24, 1896. P. 1.

Bamberger, Bernard J. "Challenge of Liberal Judaism," *Liberal Judaism* (July, 1946), pp. 20-23.

Durkheim, Emile. *The Elementary Forms of Religious Life.* New York: Macmillan Co., 1915. P. 427.

Eisendrath, M. N. "The March of Reform in America," *Liberal Judaism* (March, 1946), p. 14.

Enelow, Hyman G. *What Do Jews Believe?* Cincinnati: Press of C. J. Krehbiel and Co., 1908.

Feldman, Abraham J. "Building a Modern Synagogue," *The Jewish Layman* (December, 1944).

Finkelstein, Louis. "Is There a God?" *Jewish Quarterly Review*, new series, XIII (1922-23), 243. "Modern Theology," *Jewish Quarterly Review*, new series XIII (1922-23), 239-243.

Fox, G. G. "American Reform Judaism," *Christian Century* (October 28, 1942).

Gordis, Robert. *Conservative Judaism, an American Philosophy.* New York: Published for the National Academy of Adult Jewish Studies of the Jewish Theological Seminary of America, Behrman House, 1945. Pp. 79, 83.

Harris, Maurice H. "Are the Jews a Nation Today," *Jewish Quarterly Review*, II (1890), 166-71.

Hirsch, S. A. "Early English Hebraists," *Jewish Quarterly Review*, XII (1900), 34-88.

James, Henry. *The American Scene.* New York: Harper & Brothers, 1907. Pp. 127 ff.

James, William. *Essays on Faith and Morals.* New York: Longmans, Green & Co., 1943. P. 22.

Kaplan, Mordecai M. *Judaism as a Civilization.* New York: Macmillan Co., 1935. P. 91. *The Jewish Reconstructionist Papers.* New York, 1936. P. 95. *The Reconstructionist Viewpoint* (Pamphlet). New York, 1945. P. 5.

Lecky, William E. "The Art of Writing History," *The Forum,* XIV (1893), 715-24.

Liberal Judaism (June-July, 1947), p. 7.

Liebman, J. L. *Peace of Mind.* New York, 1946. *Passim.*

Marx, Alexander. *Studies in Jewish History and Booklore.* New York: Jewish Theological Seminary of America, 5704, 1944. Pp. 392 ff.

Moïse, Lucius C. "Reformed Society of Israelites," in his *Biography of Isaac Harby.* Columbia: R. L. Bryan Co., 1931. P. 39.

Montagu, Lily H. "Spiritual Possibilities of Judaism Today," *Jewish Quarterly Review,* XI (1898-99), 216-31.

Morais, Henry S. *Eminent Israelites of the Nineteenth Century,* Philadelphia, 1880. P. 223.

Newman, Louis I. *Jewish Influence on Christian Reform Movements.* New York: Columbia University Press, 1925.

Occident (December, 1848), 431-35; (December, 1851).

Parsons, Talcott. "The Theoretical Development of the Sociology of Religion," *Journal of the History of Ideas,* V (1944), 176-90.

Philipson, David. *The Reform Movement in Judaism.* New York: Macmillan Co., 1931. Pp. 63, 77-78.

> "The first congregation organized as a reformed congregation was the Har Sinai of Baltimore. In April, 1842, a number of young men, influenced by the Hamburg Temple movement, formed themselves into a society known as the Har Sinai Verein; they adopted the Hamburg Temple prayerbook for their services, which were conducted by several of their own number. Three years later, in 1845, the Emmanuel congregation of New York, at present the largest congregation in the land, was organized by a number of young men . . ."

Polish, David, "Peretz Smolenskin's Contribution to Jewish Thought," *Reconstructionist,* June 11, 1943.

Pool, David de Sola. *Jehuda Halevi's Defense of His Faith.* New York: The Union of Orthodox Jewish Congregations of America, c. 1925. P. 89. "Judaism and the Synagogue," in Oscar Janowsky, ed. *The American Jew, a Composite Portrait.* New York: Harper & Brothers, 1942. Pp. 28 ff., 53. *The Seventieth Street Synagogue of the Congregation Shearith Israel (Founded in the City of New York in 1655.) The Story of a Building on the Occasion of Its Jubilee.* New York, 1947.

"Reform Movement Among Jews," *The Nation,* VI (1868), 488.

Richman, Julia. "The Jewish Sunday School Movement in the United States," *Jewish Quarterly Review,* XII (1900), 564-65.

Schechter, S. *Studies in Judaism*. Philadelphia: Jewish Publication Society of America, 1908.

Simon, C. J. "The Position of Faith in the Jewish Religion," *Jewish Quarterly Review*, II (1890), 55-61.

Sulzberger, David. "The Beginnings of Russo-Jewish Immigration to Philadelphia," A. J. H. S., *Publications*, XIX (1910), 126-29.

Tractenberg, Joshua. *Consider the Years: the Story of the Jewish Community of Easton, 1752-1942*. Easton, Penn.: Centennial Committee of Temple Brith Sholom, 1944. P. 13.

Wallach, L. "The Beginnings of the Science of Judaism in the Nineteenth Century," *Historia Judaica*, VIII (April, 1946), 33-60.

Wenley, R. M. "Judaism and Philosophy of Religion," *Jewish Quarterly Review*, X (1897-98), 25.

Wise, Isaac. *Reminiscences*. Translated by David Philipson. Cincinnati: L. Wise and Co. 1901. P. 17.

CHAPTER XIV

1. Jacques de Beauval Basnage, *Histoire des Juifs*, 9 vols. in 15 vols. (The Hague, 1716).

2. H. L. Mencken, *Prejudices. Fourth Series* (New York: Alfred A. Knopf, 1924), pp. 72-73.

3. Marcus Lee Hansen, *The Atlantic Migration, 1607-1860*. Edited by A. M. Schlesinger (Cambridge: Harvard University Press, 1940), p. 26.

4. Gordon W. Allport and Bernard M. Kramer, *Some Roots of Prejudice* (New York: Committee on Community Interrelations of the American Jewish Congress, 1946).

5. Hilaire Belloc, *The Jews* (London: Constable Co., 1922), pp. 147-48.

6. *The Dearborn Independent* has been consulted. Only extensive quotations need be identified.

7. Werner Sombart, *The Jews and Modern Capitalism* (London: T. F. Unwin, 1913), pp. 248 ff.

8. Frances M. Trollope, *Domestic Manners of the Americans* (London, 1832), pp. 259 and *passim*.

9. *Ibid.*, p. 362.

10. *Ibid.*, p. 327.

11. Charles Dickens, *Life and Adventures of Martin Chuzzlewit*, 2 vols. (London: Chapman and Hall), vol. II, 145-46.

12. Charles Dickens, *American Notes* (London, 1842), vol. II, 290-91.

13. Alexis C. de Tocqueville, *Democracy in America*, 2 vols. (New York, 1898), chapter XIV, "Some Reflections on American Manners."

14. James B. Bryce, *The American Commonwealth*, 2 vols. (New York: Macmillan Co., 1910), vol. II, 304-306.
15. Dennis W. Brogan, *The American Character* (New York: Alfred A. Knopf, 1944), p. 99.
16. Robert Louis Stevenson, *Letters* (London, 1899), p. 230.
17. Nina Morais, "Jewish Ostracism in America," *North American Review*, CXXXIII (1881), 266 ff.
18. Boston, 1886.
19. William Rosenau, "Cardinal Gibbons and His Attitude Toward Jewish Problems," American Jewish Historical Society, *Publications*, XXXI (1928), 220.
20. *Forum*, XIV (1893), 607 ff.
21. *Forum*, XV (1893), 172-82.
22. Anatole Leroy-Beaulieu, *Israel among the Nations* (London, 1896), p. 230.
23. North Shore Congregation Israel, *Bulletin* (April 5, 1946).
24. *Jews in America*. By the Editors of *Fortune* Magazine (New York, 1936).
25. Ben Hecht, *A Guide for the Bedeviled* (New York: Charles Scribner's Sons, 1944).
26. K. Dunlap, "The Great Aryan Myth," *Scientific Monthly*, LIX (October, 1944), 296-300.
27. Wallace Stegner, "Who Persecutes Boston?" *The Atlantic Monthly*, CLXXIV (July, 1944), p. 50.
28. *Ibid.*, p. 47.
29. *Congress Weekly* (December 22, 1944).
30. *Time* (April 14, 1947).

See also

Dawes, Anna L. *The Modern Jew; His Present and Future*. New York: Office of the American Jew, 1884. Pp. 41-42.
Fleg, Edmond. *The Jewish Anthology*. Translated by Maurice Samuel. New York: Harcourt, Brace and Co., 1925. P. 222.
Forum, XIV (1893), 608 ff.

CHAPTER XV

1. M. Rosenfeld, "On the Ocean." Translated from the Yiddish by Alice Lucas. *Jewish Quarterly Review*, XII (1900), 91.
2. Edmund J. James, et al., *The Immigrant Jew in America* (New York, 1906).
3. Samuel Gompers, *Seventy Years of Life and Labor*, 2 vols. (New York: E. P. Dutton & Co., 1925), *passim*.
4. L. Levine, *Women's Garment Workers* (New York, 1924), pp. 18 ff.
5. *Jewish Review*, III (July, 1945).

6. Maurice R. Davie, *World Immigration* (New York: Macmillan Co., 1936), p. 166; S. Joseph, *Jewish Immigration to the United States from 1881 to 1910.* Ph.D. thesis, Columbia University (New York, 1914).
7. "Yiddish Press—75 Years Old," *Congress Weekly* (March 2, 1945).
8. S. Joseph, *History of the Baron de Hirsch Fund* (New York: Jewish Publication Society of America, 1935).
9. *Hispanic American Historical Review*, XIX (1939), 185-203.
10. Gabriel Davidson, *Our Jewish Farmers and the Story of the Jewish Agricultural Society* (New York: L. B. Fischer, 1943), p. 35.
11. Elkan N. Adler, *About Hebrew Manuscripts* (London: H. Frowde, 1905), p. 87.
12. G. Herbert Cone, "New Matter Relating to Mordecai M. Noah," *A. J. H. S., Publications*, XI (1903), 136.
13. Lucien Wolf, "The Zionist Peril," *Jewish Quarterly Review*, XVII (1905), 1-25.
14. Hilaire Belloc, *The Jews* (London: Constable & Co., 1922), pp. 301-302.
15. *New Palestine* (July 27, 1945).
16. *Chicago Times* (August 15, 1946).
17. A. T. Mason, *Brandeis. A Free Man's Life* (New York: The Viking Press, 1946).

See also

Davidson, Gabriel. *Our Jewish Farmers and the Story of the Jewish Agricultural Society.* New York: L. B. Fischer, 1943. "The Palestine Colony in Michigan. An Adventure in Colonization," American Jewish Historical Society, *Publications*, XXIX (1924), 61-62.
Harper's Weekly, LXI (1907), 511-12.
Marx, Alexander. *Studies in Jewish History and Booklore.* New York: Jewish Theological Seminary of America, 5704, 1944. P. 392.
Modder, Montagu F. *The Jew in the Literature of England.* Philadelphia: Jewish Publication Society of America, 1944. P. 246.

CHAPTER XVI

1. *American Jewish Year Book* (1946-47), p. 127.
2. Mordecai M. Kaplan, *The Future of American Jews* (New York: Macmillan Co., 1948), p. 33.
3. Louis D. Brandeis, *Brandeis on Zionism. A Collection of Addresses and Statements* (Washington, D. C., 1942).
4. Kaplan, *op. cit.*, pp. 524 ff.
5. Sophia M. Robison, ed., *Jewish Population Studies* (New York: Conference on Jewish Relations, 1943), *passim*.
6. F. L. Mott, *American Journalism* (New York: Macmillan Co., 1941), pp. 549-51.

7. *Reconstructionist*, June 9, 1944, pp. 24-27.
8. "Roosevelt's Own List of 23 Leading Americans," *This Week Magazine*, June 20, 1948.
9. John Hersey wrote this biographical sketch of Baruch published in the *New Yorker*, in 1948. The quotations are in the issue of January 3, 1948.
10. *Universal Jewish Encyclopedia*, 10 vols. (New York: Universal Jewish Encyclopedia, Inc., 1939-43), vol. IV, 407; Matthew Josephson, "Jurist," *New Yorker* (November 30, December 7, December 14, 1940).
11. George S. Hellman, *Benjamin N. Cardozo, American Judge* (New York: Whittlesey House, 1940).
12. *New York Times*, October 24, 1937.
13. Hellman, *op. cit.*, p. 79.
14. *Ibid.*, p. 207; see also Benjamin Nathan Cardozo, *Selected Writings*, edited by Margaret E. Hall (New York: Fallon Publications, 1947), *passim*.
15. *The Menorah Journal* (New York: The Intercollegiate Menorah Association, Spring, 1948).
16. *National Jewish Monthly* (December, 1947).
17. *Harper's Weekly* (November 13, 1915), pp. 460-62.
18. The *Universal Jewish Encyclopedia* has an excellent section on the Jewish soldier. See also Frank Gervasi, "The Jew as a Soldier," *Collier's* (April 22, 1944); Joshua Bloch, "Where Is the Record?" *Congress Weekly*, (March 26, 1943); Samuel C. Kohs, "Jews in the United States Armed Forces," *Yivo* (1945); Joseph G. Fredman and L. A. Falk, *Jews in American Wars* (New York: Jewish War Veterans of the United States, 1942); *American Jews in World War II. The Story of 550,000 Fighters for Freedom*, compiled by the Bureau of War Records of the National Jewish Welfare Board, 2 vols. (New York, 1947); *Move Out. Verify. Combat Story of the 743rd Tank Battalion;* See also *Saturday Evening Post* (October 19, 1946).
19. *Liberal Judaism* (May, 1946).
20. Israel S. Wechsler, *The Neurologist's Point of View* (New York: L. B. Fischer, 1945), p. 195.
21. *New Yorker* (June 12, 1948), 30-41.
22. Emma Lazarus, "The Jewish Problem," *The Century Illustrated Monthly Magazine*, XXV, new series III (1882-83), 611.
23. *New York Herald Tribune* (January 21, 1948).
24. *New York Herald Tribune*, (April 5, 1948).
25. Nathan Goldberg, "Population Trends in U. S.," *Jewish Affairs*, II (April 15, 1948); *American Jewish Year Book*, XXXXVIII, 599-600; Nathan Goldberg, *Economic Trends among American Jews* (New York: Office of Jewish Information, 1946).

26. Leo L. Honor, "Jewish Education in the United States," *The Jewish People, Past and Present,* 2 vols. (New York: Jewish Encyclopedic Handbooks, Central Yiddish Culture Organization, 1946-48), vol. II, 151-71.
27. Quoted by permission from a letter dated January 8, 1943, by Judge Ulysses S. Schwartz.

See also

American Jewish Year Book, XXXXVII, 641 ff., XXXXVIII, 599-600.
Goldberg, N. "Population Trends in U. S.," in *Jewish Affairs,* II, no. 5 (April 15, 1948).
U. S. Department of Commerce. Bureau of the Census. *Religious Bodies:* 1936. Vol. II, part I. Washington, 1941.
Weizmann, Chaim. *Trial and Error.* New York: Harper & Brothers, 1949.
Zielonka, Martin. "The Fighting Jew," A. J. H. S., *Publications,* XXXI (1928), 215-216.

CHAPTER XVII

The author would like to acknowledge and thank the following for help in assembling data for this chapter:
Mrs. Robert Aronson; Rabbi Philip S. Bernstein; Isadore H. Braun; Sarah Elkin Braun; Marianne L. Goldstein; Jacob J. Gordon; Rabbi A. J. Heschel; Mrs. Marvin Jacobson; Dr. Lawrence Marwick; Dr. Isidore S. Meyer; Mrs. Leah Mishkin; Professor Jack Silber.

1. Rabbi Morris Silverman, ed., *High Holiday Prayer Book* (Hartford: Prayer Book Press, 1951).
2. Edwin Markham, "The Pilgrim," in *Masterpieces of Religious Verse,* New York: Harper, 1948.
3. Drew Middleton, "Who Lost the Yom Kippur War?" in *The Atlantic* (March, 1974), pp. 45-55.
4. Paul Tillich, *Dynamics of Faith* (New York: Harper, 1957), pp. 12, 67, 78.
5. Alfred Kazin, "The Jew as Modern American Writer," *The Commentary Reader,* (New York: Atheneum, 1966), p. XIX.
6. *Saturday Review* (January 31, 1970).
7. Abba Eban, *The Meaning of Jewish History* (Society of Jewish Bibliophiles, 1964), p. 17.
8. Simon N. Herman, *Israelis and Jews: The Continuity of an Identity* (Under the editorship of Dr. Moshe Davis) (New York: XX, 1970), pp. 199, 202, 204-205.
9. Joachim Prinz, *The Dilemma of the Modern Jew* (New York: 1962), pp. 184 ff. Prinz discusses the dilemma of the American Jew: to be or not to be. On p. 216 he pleads against "the watering down of the Jewish heritage."

10. *Two Generations in Perspective.* "The American Jewish Congress," p. 265.
11. Ibid., pp. 270-271.
12. *The American Jew: A Reappraisal,* pp. 118-119.
13. Ibid., pp. 340-341.
14. *American Jewish Year Book* (1970), pp. 90-91 ff.
15. Ibid., p. 148.
16. New York *Times,* (October 24, 1971).
17. Edward H. Flannery, *The Anguish of the Jews; Twenty-three Centuries of Anti-Semitism,* Preface, (New York: Macmillan).
18. Ibid., p. 205.
19. Ibid., pp. 221 ff.
20. Ibid., pp. 255 ff.
21. *American Jewish Year Book* (1970), p. 148.
22. *The American Jew: A Reappraisal,* pp. 382-386.
23. *Congress Weekly* (April 2, 1951).
24. *Congress Weekly* (November 26, 1951).
25. *Congress Weekly* (December, 1953).
26. *Congress Weekly* (May 23, 1955).
27. *Congress Weekly* (April 1, 1957).
28. *Congress Weekly* (January 3, 1958), pp. 10-12.
29. *Congress Weekly* (September, 1958).
30. *Congress Weekly* (February 8, 1960).
31. Rabbi Eugene B. Borowitz, "Aspects of Jewish Theology" in *Image of the Jews,* pp. 27-29.
32. Milton Steinberg, *Anatomy of Faith.* Edited with an Introduction by Arthur A. Cohen. (New York: 1960), pp. 73-74.
33. A. Leland Jamison, Introduction to Emil L. Fackenheim's "The Human Condition after Auschwitz: A Jewish Testimony a Generation Later," E. G. Rudolph Lectures in Judaic Studies, Syracuse University Imprints, April 1971, p. i.
34. Martin Buber, *Believing Humanism* (New York: Simon & Schuster, 1967), p. 231.
35. Maurice Friedman, Introduction to *Believing Humanism* p. 23.
36. *Two Generations in Perspective,* p. 457.
37. Ibid., pp. 370 ff.
38. Ibid., pp. 290-299.
39. *America* (March 10, 1973), editorial.
40. Arthur A. Cohen, *The Natural and Supernatural Jew* (New York: 1962), pp. 234-239, 259, 313.
41. Abraham J. Heschel, *The Prophets* (New York: 1962), pp. X and 5.
42. Abraham J. Heschel, "The Meaning of Jewish Existence," in *Mid-Century* (New York: 1955), pp. 86 ff.
43. Ibid., pp. 25, 31, 43, 78.
44. Ibid., pp. 86-87, 94-95.

45. *The Eternal Light*. A Conversation with Doctor Abraham Joshua Heschel, NBC-TV network (February 4, 1973, date of publication).

46. W. D. Davies, "Conscience, Scholar, Witness," in *America*, devoted to Abraham Joshua Heschel (March 10, 1973).

47. *Upstate New York* (December 3, 1972).

48. Philip S. Bernstein, *Rabbis at War* (American Jewish Historical Society: 1971). *What Jews Believe* (New York: 1953). And especially his "Testament of Faith," a sermon he preached in honor of the Seventy-fifth anniversary of Jewish War Veterans (1896–1971).

49. Philip S. Bernstein, *The Fighting Jew . . . A Moral Dilemma*, passim (New York: Park Avenue Synagogue, March 12, 1971).

50. Philip S. Bernstein, Preface to *Rabbis at War*, passim.

51. Yehuda Bauer, *Flight and Rescue*, p. 255.

52. *Near East Report*, XVIII, No. 1 (January 2, 1974), p. 3.

53. Oscar I. Janowsky, ed., *The American Jew: A Reappraisal* (Philadelphia: 1965), pp. 153 ff.

54. Ibid., p. 381.

55. Annual of the Thirty-eighth Issue of the *Yearbook of American Churches*, pp. 48-49.

56. *American Jewish Year Book*, Vol. 73 (New York: 1972), p. 384.

57. *Newsweek* (March 1, 1971).

58. *Mid-Century: Religious Trends in American Jewry*. p. 251.

59. Emil L. Fackenheim, "The Dilemma of Liberal Judaism" in *Commentary Reader* (October, 1960), p. 439.

60. Ibid., pp. 448-449.

61. Leo Baeck, *Judaism and Christianity*, p. 180.

BIBLIOGRAPHY

Abrabanel, Solomon. *The Complaint of the Children of Israel.* London, 1736.

Abraham, Lewis. "Correspondence between Washington and Jewish Citizens," American Jewish Historical Society, *Publications,* III (1894), 87-96.

Abraham ben Meir Aben Ezra. *The Beginnings of Wisdom: An Astrological Treatise by Abraham ibn Ezra.* Edited by Raphael Levy and Francisco Cantera Burgos. Baltimore: Johns Hopkins Press, 1939.

Abraham ben Mordecai Farissol. *Itinera Mundi, Sic Dicta Nampe Cosmographia Autore Abrahams Peritsol.* Oxonii, 1691.

Abrahams, Edmund H. "Some Notes on the Early History of the Sheftells of Georgia," A.J.H.S., *Publications,* XVII (1909), 167-86.

Abrahams, Israel. *Chapters on Jewish Literature.* Philadelphia: Jewish Publication Society of America, 1899.

——. "Isaac Abendana's Cambridge Mishnah and Oxford Calendars," Jewish Historical Society of England, *Transactions,* VIII (1819), 99-121.

——. *Jewish Life in the Middle Ages.* New York: Macmillan Co., 1896.

——. "Joachim Gaunse: A Mining Incident in the Reign of Queen Elizabeth," J.H.S.E., *Transactions,* IV (1903), 83-101.

——. "Marriages Are Made in Heaven," *Jewish Quarterly Review,* II (1890), 172-77.

——, and Sayle, C. E. "The Purchase of Hebrew Books by the English Parliament in 1647," J.H.S.E., *Transactions,* VIII (1918), 63-77.

Abrahams, Lionel B. "The Condition of the Jews of England at the Time of Their Expulsion in 1290," J.H.S.E., *Transactions,* II (1894-95), 76-105.

——. "The Economic and Financial Position of the Jews in Mediaeval England," J.H.S.E., *Transactions,* VIII (1918), 171-88.

——. "Sir I. L. Goldsmid and the Admission of the Jews of England to Parliament," J.H.S.E., *Transactions,* IV (1903), 116-76.

Academia das Sciencias de Lisboa Commissão Portuguesa de Exposição de Madrid. *Centenario do Descobrimento da America.* Lisbon, 1892.

Academia Española. *Diccionario de la Lengua Castellana.* 4 vols. Madrid, 1726.

Adair, James. *The History of the American Indians.* London, 1775.

Adams, Hannah. *An Abridgement of the History of New-England.* Boston, 1805.

———. *The History of the Jews from the Destruction of Jerusalem to the Nineteenth Century.* 2 vols. Boston, 1812.

———. *A Summary History of New-England.* Dedham, 1799.

Adams, Herbert B., and Hollander, J. H. "A Sketch of Haym Salomon. From an Unpublished MS. in the Papers of Jared Sparks," A.J.H.S., *Publications,* II (1894), 5-19.

———, and Wood, Henry. *Columbus and His Discovery of America.* Baltimore: Johns Hopkins Press, 1892.

Adler, Cyrus. "Adolphus S. Solomons and the Red Cross," A.J.H.S., *Publications,* XXXIII (1934), 211-30.

———. "A Contemporary Memorial Relating to Damages to Spanish Interests in America Done by Jews of Holland (1634)," A.J.H.S., *Publications,* XVII (1909), 45-51.

———. *I Have Considered the Days.* Philadelphia: Jewish Publication Society of America, 1945.

———. "Jews in American Diplomatic Correspondence," A.J.H.S., *Publications,* XV (1906), 1-117.

———. "Jews in the American Plantations Between 1600-1700," A.J.H.S., *Publications,* I (1892), 105-108.

———. "Original Unpublished Documents Relating to Thomas Tremino de Sobremonte (1683)," A.J.H.S., *Publications,* XVII (1909), 27-31.

———. "A Political Document of the Year 1800," A.J.H.S., *Publications,* I (1892), 111-15.

———. "Trial of Jorge de Almeida by the Inquisition in Mexico," A.J.H.S., *Publications,* IV (1896), 29-79.

———, and Friedenberg, Albert M. "References to Jews in the Correspondence of John J. Crittenden," A.J.H.S., *Publications,* XXIII (1915), 117-27.

———, and Margalith, Aaron M. "American Intercession on Behalf of Jews in the Diplomatic Correspondence of the United States. 1840-1938," A.J.H.S., *Publications,* XXXVI (1943), 3-419.

Adler, Elkan N. *About Hebrew Manuscripts.* London: H. Frowde, 1905.

———. *Auto de Fé and Jew.* London: H. Frowde, 1908.

———. "The Inquisition in Peru," A.J.H.S., *Publications,* XII (1904), 5-37.

———, ed. *Jewish Travellers.* London: G. Routledge and Sons, 1930. (*The Broadway Travellers,* vol. XX. Series edited by Sir E. Denison Ross and Eileen Power.)

———. "A Letter of Menasseh ben Israel," J.H.S.E., *Transactions,* V (1908), 174-83.

Adler, Marcus N. "The Itinerary of Benjamin of Tudela," *Jewish Quarterly Review,* XVII (1905).

Adler, Michael. "History of the 'Domus Conversorum' from 1290 to 1891," J.H.S.E., *Transactions,* IV (1903), 16-75.

Alguns Documentos do Archivo Nacional da Torre do Tombo, acerca das navegações e conquistas portuguezas. Lisbon: Academia das Sciencias de Lisboa, 1892.

Allen, Lewis F. "Founding of the City of Ararat on Grand Island by Mordecai M. Noah," Buffalo Historical Society, *Publications*, I (1879), 305-328.

Allgemeine Zeitung des Judenthums. Leipzig.

Allport, Gordon W., and Kramer, Bernard M. *Some Roots of Prejudice.* New York: Committee on Community Interrelations of the American Jewish Congress, 1946.

Almeida Prado, Jorge de. "Inquisition in New World, Denunciation Against," A.J.H.S., *Publications*, IV (1896), 68.

———. *Pernambuco e as Capitanias do Norte do Brasil (1530-1630).* 4 vols. São Paulo: Companhia Editora Nacional, 1939-42.

Alvarez Pedroso, Armando, *Cristobal Colon.* Havana: Cultural, s. a., 1944.

Alvord, Clarence W. *The Mississippi Valley in British Politics.* 2 vols. Cleveland: Arthur H. Clark Company, 1917.

Amador de los Rios, José. *História Social, Política y Religiosa de los Judíos de España y Portugal.* 3 vols. Madrid, 1875.

Amaral Gurgel, L. *Ensaios Quinhentistas.* São Paulo: J. Fagundes, 1936.

"The American Celebration," J.H.S.E., *Transactions*, V (1908), 299-305.

American Jewish Year Book, 1889-1948. Philadelphia: Jewish Publication Society of America.

André, Marius. "La Véridique Aventure de Christophe Colomb," *Revue de l'Amérique Latine*, XIII (1927), 1-22.

Andrews, Charles M. *Colonial Folkways: A Chronicle of American Life in the Reign of the Georges.* New Haven: Yale University Press, 1919.

Anthiaume, Albert. *L'Astrolabe-Quadrant du Musée des Antiquités de Rouen.* Paris: G. Thomas, 1910.

"Appendix II." (The Board of Delegates of American Israelites.) A.J.H.S., *Publications*, XXIX (1924), 83-116.

"Appendix III." (A Birdseye View of Jewish Civic Activity and Patriotism All Over the World During Our Civil War.) A.J.H.S., *Publications*, XXIX (1924), 117-28.

Archivo Storico Italiano, Appendice, No. 10-12, tomo II, Firenze, 1845.

The Asmonean. A Family Journal of Commerce, Politics, Religion, and Literature, Devoted to the Interests of the American Israelites. 18 vols. New York, 1849-58.

Atherton, Gertrude. *Adventures of a Novelist.* New York: Liveright, 1932.

Atkinson, Henry A. "Anti-Semitism Assails America," *Opinion*, XIV (December, 1943), 6-7.

Azevedo, João Lucio d'. *Historia dos Christãos Novos Portugueses.* Lisbon: Livraria Clássica Editora de A.M. Teixeira, 1922.

————. "Noticias de Portugal de 1578-1580," *Lusitania*, (1924), pp. 33-39.

Bacon, Francis. *New Atlantis*. Edited with introduction and notes by Alfred B. Gough. Oxford: Clarendon Press, 1915.

Baldwin, Leland D. *The Story of the Americas. The Discovery, Settlement and Development of the New World*. New York: Simon and Schuster, 1943.

Ballesteros y Beretta, Antonio. *Cristóbal Colón y el Descubrimiento de América*. 2 vols. Barcelona: Salvat Editores, 1945.

Bamberger, Bernard J. "Challenge of Liberal Judaism," *Liberal Judaism* (July, 1946).

Baron, Salo W. *The Jewish Community. Its History and Structure to the American Revolution*. 3 vols. Philadelphia: Jewish Publication Society of America, 1942.

————. *A Social and Religious History of the Jews*. 3 vols. New York: Columbia University Press, 1937.

Baroway, Aaron. "The Cohens of Maryland," *Maryland Historical Magazine*, XVIII (1923), 357-76.

Barros, João de. *Da Asia*. 13 parts in 24 vols. Lisbon, 1777-88.

————. *L'Asia*. Venice, 1562.

Basnage de Beauval, Jacques. *Histoire des Juifs*. 9 vols. in 15 vols. The Hague, 1716.

Batalha Reis, Hayme. *Estudos Geográficos e Históricos*. Lisbon: Agência Geral das Colónias, 1941.

Beals, Carleton. *America South*. Philadelphia: J. B. Lippincott Co., 1937.

Beard, Charles A. "Written History as an Act of Faith," *American Historical Review*, XXXIX (1933-34), 219-31.

————, and Beard, Mary R. *The American Spirit*. New York: Macmillan Co., 1942.

————. *The Rise of American Civilization*. 2 vols. New York: Macmillan Co., 1929.

Beazley, Charles R. "Prince Henry of Portugal and His Political, Commercial, and Colonizing Work," *American Historical Review*, XVII (1911-12), 252-67.

————. *Prince Henry the Navigator*. New York, 1895.

Becker, Carl L. *Everyman His Own Historian*. New York: F. S. Crofts and Co., 1935.

Bell, Aubrey F. G. *Gaspar Corrêa*. London: Oxford University Press, 1924.

Belloc, Hilaire. *The Jews*. London: Constable and Co., 1922.

Benjamin, Ruth L. "Marcus Otterbourg, United States Minister to Mexico in 1867," A.J.H.S., *Publications*, XXXII (1931), 65-98.

Bensaude, Joaquim. *L'astronomie nautique au Portugal à l'époque des grandes découvertes*. Bern: M. Drechsel, 1912.

————. *Histoire de la science nautique portugaise à l'époque des grandes découvertes.* Genève: Société Sadag, 1914.

————. *Lacunes et surprises de l'historie des découvertes maritimes.* Coimbra: Imprensa da Universidade, 1930.

————. *Les légendes allemandes sur l'histoire des découvertes maritimes portugaises.* Genève: A. Kundig, 1917-20.

————, ed. *Regimento do Estrolabio e do Quadrante.* Introduction by Joaquim Bensaude. Munich: C. Kuhn, 1914.

Berdiaev, Nikolai A. *Solitude and Society.* New York: Charles Scribner's Sons, 1939.

Berkowitz, Henry. "Notes on the History of the Earliest German Jewish Congregation in America," A.J.H.S., *Publications,* IX (1901), 123-27.

Bethencourt, Cardozo de. "Notes on the Spanish and Portuguese Jews in the United States, Guiana, and the Dutch and British West Indies during the Seventeenth and Eighteenth Centuries," A.J.H.S., *Publications,* XXIX (1925), 7-38.

Biet, Antoine. *Voyage de la France equinoxiale en l'isle de Cayenne, entrepris par les François en l'année MDCLII.* Paris, 1664.

Bloch, Joshua. "Early Hebrew Printing in Spain and Portugal," New York Public Library, *Bulletin,* XLII (1938), 371-420.

————. "Venetian Printers of Hebrew Books," New York Public Library, *Bulletin,* XXXVI (1932), 71-92.

————. "Where is the Record?" *Congress Weekly,* March 26, 1943.

Bloom, Herbert I. "The Dutch Archives, with Special Reference to American Jewish History," A.J.H.S., *Publications,* XXXII (1931), 7-21.

————. *The Economic Activities of the Jews of Amsterdam in the Seventeenth and Eighteenth Centuries.* Williamsport, Penn.: Bayard Press, 1937.

————. "A Study of Brazilian Jewish History 1623-1654, Based Chiefly upon the Findings of the Late Samuel Oppenheim," A.J.H.S., *Publications,* XXXIII (1934), 43-125.

Blunt, John E. *A History of the Establishment and Residence of the Jews in England; with an Enquiry into Their Civil Disabilities.* London, 1830.

Boas, Ralph P. "The Problem of American Judaism," *Atlantic Monthly,* CXIX (1917), 145-52.

Bogen, Boris D. *Born a Jew.* New York: Macmillan Co., 1930.

Boissonnade, Prosper M. *Life and Work in Medieval Europe,* (fifth to fifteenth centuries). Translated by Eileen Power. London: Alfred A. Knopf, 1927.

Bradley, Edward Sculley. *Henry Charles Lea, a Biography.* Philadelphia: University of Pennsylvania Press, 1931.

Brandeis, Louis D. *Brandeis on Zionism. A Collection of Addresses and Statements.* Washington, 1942

Brav, Aaron. "Müng's 'Jewish Physicians in the Middle Ages,'" *Jewish Quarterly Review*, XIV (1923-24), 375-77.

Bregstone, Philip P. *Chicago and Its Jews, a Cultural History*. Chicago: Privately published, 1933.

Brody, Fannie M. "The Hebrew Periodical Press in America, 1871-1931: A Bibliographical Survey," A.J.H.S., *Publications*, XXXIII (1934), 127-70.

Brogan, Dennis W. *American Character*. New York: Alfred A. Knopf, 1944.

Brooks, John G. "Who Is the American?" *The Chautauquan*, XLVIII (1907), 174-88.

Bryce, James B. *The American Commonwealth*. 2 vols. New York: Macmillan Co., 1910.

Byars, William Vincent. *B. & M. Gratz, Merchants in Philadelphia, 1754-1798*. Jefferson City, Mo.: Hugh Stephens Printing Co., 1916.

———. "The Gratz Papers," A.J.H.S., *Publications*, XXIII (1915), 1-23.

Calisch, Edward N. *The Jew in English Literature*. Richmond, The Bell Book and Stationery Co., 1909.

Calmon, Pedro. "O Brasil e Portugal de 1500," *Jornal de Commercio* (1939), 555-65.

———. *Historia da Civilização Brasileira*. São Paulo: Companhia Editora Nacional, 1935.

———. *Historia do Brasil*. São Paulo: Companhia Editora Nacional, 1939.

The Cambridge Medieval History. Edited by H. M. Gwatkin, J. P. Whitney. 8 vols. in 16 vols. New York: Macmillan Co., 1911-36.

Caminha, Pedro Vaz de. *A Carta de Pero Vaz de Caminha, com um Estudo do Jaime Cortesão*. Rio de Janeiro: Livros de Portugal, 1943.

Camões, Luiz de. *The Lusiad*. Translated by Richard Fanshawe. Cambridge: Harvard University Press, 1940.

Campos, Agostinho de. "Sobre a 'Decadencia' e a 'Ignorancia' da Espanha," *Lusitania* (1926-27), 399-408.

Canabrava, Alice P. *O Comércio Português no Rio da Prata (1580-1640)*. São Paulo: Universidade de São Paulo, 1944. (Boletim XXXV História da Civilização Americana, n. 2.)

Canoutas, Seraphim G. *Christopher Columbus, a Greek Nobleman; a Disquisition Concerning the Origin and Early Life of the Great Discoverer and a Refutation of the Charges Against Him which Have Appeared in Certain Recent Publications*. New York: St. Marks Printing Corp., 1943.

Cantera Burgos, Francisco. *Abraham Zacut, Siglo XV*. Madrid: M. Aguilar, 1935.

———. "Notas para la Historia de la Astronomia en la España Medieval; el Judio Salmantino Abraham Zacut," *Revista de la Academia de Ciencias Exactas, Físico-Químicas y Naturales de Madrid*, XXVII (1931), 63-398.

Carbia, Romulo D. *La Carta de Navegar Atribuída a Toscanelli (1474).* Buenos Aires, Imprenta de la Universidade, 1932.

———. *Origen y Patria de Cristóbal Colón.* Buenos Aires: Talleres Gráficos, 1918.

———. *La Investigación Científica y el Descubrimiento de América.* Buenos Aires: Talleres Gráficos San Pablo, 1937.

Cardozo, Benjamin N. *Selected Writings of Benjamin Nathan Cardozo.* Edited by Margaret E. Hall. New York: Fallon Publications, 1947.

The Cartwright Petition of 1649. Facsimile. Published by Sutro Library Associates. San Francisco, 1941.

Carvalho, S. N. *Incidents of Travel.* New York: Derby and Jackson, 1857.

Casas, Bartolome de las. *An Account of the First Voyages and Discoveries Made by the Spaniards in America.* London, 1699.

Catálogo da Livraria Portugalia. Lisbon, 1947.

Cha Masser, Lunardo da. "Relazione de Lunardo da Cha Masser," *Centenario do Descobrimento da America. Memorias da Commissão Portugueza.* Lisbon, 1892.

———. Relizione di Leonardo da Ca' Masser," *Archivo Storico Italiano,* Appendice, No. 10-12, tomo II. Firenze, 1845.

Christian, William A. *Richmond, Her Past and Present.* Richmond: L. H. Jenkins, 1912.

Church, George E. *Aborigines of South America.* Edited by Clement R. Markham. London: Chapman and Hall, 1912.

Cirot, Georges. "Notes sur les 'Juifs Portugais' de Bordeaux," *Revista da Universidade de Coimbra,* XI (1933), 158-72.

Clemens, Samuel^L. "Concerning the Jews," *Harper's New Monthly Magazine,* XCIX (1899), 527-35.

Cochut, P. A. *Law, son système et son époque.* Paris, 1853.

Cohen, Henry. "A Brave Frontiersman," A.J.H.S., *Publications,* VIII (1900), 59-74.

———. "Henry Castro, Pioneer and Colonist," A.J.H.S., *Publications,* V (1897), 39-43.

———. "A Modern Maccabean," A.J.H.S., *Publications,* VI (1897), 31-37.

———. "Settlement of the Jews in Texas," A.J.H.S., *Publications,* II (1893), 139-56.

Cohen, Herman. "The Modern Jew and the New Judaism," *Fortnightly Review,* new series LIX (1896), 457-62, 624-34.

Cohen, Israel. *Vilna.* Philadelphia: Jewish Publication Society of America, 1943.

Cohn, David L. *The Good Old Days.* New York: Simon and Schuster, 1940.

Coleman, Edward D. "The Jew in English Drama," *New York Public Library, Bulletin,* XLII (1938), 827.

————. "Jewish Prototypes in American and English *Romans* and *Drames À Clef*," A.J.H.S.; *Publications*, XXV (1939), 227-80.

————. "Plays of Jewish Interest on the American Stage, 1752-1821," A.J.H.S., *Publications*, XXXIII (1934), 171-98.

Collecção de Livros Ineditos de Historia Portugueza. 3 vols. Lisbon, 1790. (Academia das Sciencias de Lisboa.)

Collins, Victor. *Attempt at a Catalogue of the Library of the Late Prince Louis-Lucien Bonaparte*. London, 1894.

Colombo, Cristoforo. *Carta a Luis de Santangel de las Islas Halladas en las Indias*. 1493.

————. *Codice Diplomatico Colombo-Americano*. Geneva, 1823.

————. *The Journal of Christopher Columbus (during His First Voyage, 1492-93)*. Edited by Clements R. Markham. London, 1893. (Works issued by the Hakluyt Society, vol. 86).

————. *The Letter in Spanish of Christopher Columbus*, written on his return from his first voyage, and addressed to Luis de Sant Angel, 15 February—14 March 1493. Facsimile edition. London, 1889.

Colon, Diego. *The First Extant Letter from America of Diego Columbus*. Dated January 12, 1512. London, 1929. (Description of the letter, published by Maggs Brothers.)

————. *Memorial de Don Diego Colon*. London, 1854.

Colon, Fernando. "The History of the Life and Actions of Admiral Christopher Colon, and of His Discovery of the West Indies, called the New World, Now in Possession of His Catholic Majesty. Written by His Own Son, Don Ferdinand Colon," in *A General Collection of the Best and Most Interesting Voyages and Travels in All Parts of the World*. Edited by John Pinkerton. 17 vols. London, 1808-14. Vol. XII, 1-155.

The Columbia Encyclopedia. Compiled by Clarke F. Ansley. New York: Columbia University Press, 1935.

Cone, G. Herbert. "New Matter Relating to Mordecai M. Noah," A.J.H.S., *Publications*, XI (1903), 131-37.

Congress Weekly, December 22, 1944; March 2, 1945.

Connecticut (Colony). *The Public Records of the Colony of Connecticut, (1636-1776)*. 15 vols. Hartford, 1850-90.

Conway, George R. G. "Hernando Alonzo, a Jewish Conquistador with Cortes in Mexico," A.J.H.S., *Publications*, XXXI (1928), 9-31.

Cooley, Charles H. *Sociological Theory and Social Research*. New York: Henry Holt and Co., 1930.

"Corn, Its Products and Uses," in U. S. Dept. of Agriculture *Bulletin*, Agricultural Research Administration, Bureau Agricultural Industrial Chemistry. February, 1947.

Corrêa, Gaspar. *Lendas da India*. 4 vols. Lisbon, 1858.

————. "The Three Voyages of Vasco da Gama and His Viceroyalty." From the *Lendas da India* of Gaspar Corrêa, translated by Henry E.

J. Stanley. London, 1869. (Works issued by the Hakluyt Society, vol. XLII).

Cortesão, Armando. *Cartógrafia e Cartografos Portugueses dos Séculos XV e XVI.* 2 vols. Lisbon: Edição da "Seara Nova," 1935.

Cortesão, Jaime. "Do Siglio Nacional sôbre os Descobrimentos," *Lusitania* (1924), pp. 45-81.

————. L'expansion des Portugais dans l'histoire de la civilization. Bruxelles, Belgique: A. Puvrez, 1930.

————. "Le secret portugais des découvertes," *Lusitania,* (1924), 160-63.

Costa, Candido. *As Duas Americas.* Lisbon, J. Bastos, 1900.

Coudenhove-Kalergi, Heinrich H. *Anti-Semitism Throughout the Ages.* London: Hutchinson and Co., 1935.

Couto, Gustavo do Monsenhor, "O Cosmografo Fernam Vaz Dourado, Fronteiro da India e a Sua Obra," *Boletim da Sociedade de Geografia de Lisboa,* Serie 46ª, no. 7-8 (Julho-agosto, 1928), 175.

Cox, Isaac Joslin. "Alien Strands in the Racial Fabric of Chile." Unpublished MS.

Cronbach, Abraham. *Religion and Its Social Setting.* Cincinnati: The Social Press, 1933.

Crone, Gerald R., ed. *The Voyages of Cadamosto.* London, 1937. (Works issued by the Hakluyt Society, series 2, vol. LXXX.)

Cumberland, Richard. *The Jew.* Act III. Scene ii.

Cumston, Charles G. *An Introduction to the History of Medicine, from the Time of the Paraohs to the End of the XVIIIth Century.* New York: Alfred A. Knopf, 1926.

Cundall, Frank, Davis, N. Darnell, and Friedenberg, Albert M. "Documents Relating to the History of the Jews in Jamaica and Barbados in the Time of William III," *A.J.H.S., Publications,* XXIII (1915), 25-29.

Daly, Charles P. *The Settlement of the Jews in North America.* Edited with notes and appendices by Max J. Kohler. New York, 1893.

David, Maurice. *Who was "Columbus?"* New York: The Research Publishing Co., 1933.

Davidson, Gabriel. *Our Jewish Farmers and the Story of the Jewish Agricultural Society.* New York: L. B. Fischer, 1943.

————. "The Palestine Colony in Michigan. An Adventure in Colonization," *A.J.H.S., Publications,* XXIX (1924), 61-74.

Davie, Maurice Rea. *World Immigration; with Special Reference to the United States.* New York: Macmillan Co., 1936.

Davis, Helen I. "Bret Harte and His Jewish Ancestor, Bernard Hart," *A.J.H.S., Publications,* XXXII (1931), 99-111.

Davis, N. Darnell. "Notes on the History of the Jews in Barbados," *A.J.H.S., Publications,* XVIII (1909), 129-48.

————. *Songs of Exile.* Philadelphia, 1901.

Dawes, Anna L. *The Modern Jew; His Present and Future.* New York: Office of the American Hebrew, 1884.

Dearborn Independent. Dearborn, Michigan, January, 1920—December 31, 1927.

Deiler, John Hanno. *The Settlement of the German Coast of Louisiana and the Creoles of German Descent.* Philadelphia: Americana Germanica Press, 1909.

Deutsch, Gotthard. "Dr. Abraham Bettman, a Pioneer Physician of Cincinnati (1806-1901)," A.J.H.S., *Publications*, XXIII, 105-116.

Dickens, Charles. *American Notes.* London, 1842.

———. "Letter. Naples, June 1, 1845," in *St. Louis Weekly Reveille*, Monday, July 14, 1845.

———. *Life and Adventures of Martin Chuzzlewit.* London: Chapman and Hall, no date.

Diffie, Bailey W. *Latin-American Civilization: Colonial Period.* Harrisburg, Penn.: Stackpole Sons, 1945.

Dorr, Rheta C. *Susan B. Anthony.* New York: Frederick A. Stokes Co., 1928.

Drayton, John. *Memoirs of the American Revolution.* 2 vols. Charleston, 1821.

Dublin, Frances. "Jewish Colonial Enterprise in the Light of the Amherst Papers (1758-1763)," A.J.H.S., *Publications*, XXXV (1939), 1-25.

Dubnow, Semen M. *Evrei v Rossii i zapadnoĭ Evrope.* Moscow, 1923.

———. *History of the Jews in Russia and Poland, from the Earliest Times until the Present Day.* 3 vols. Philadelphia: Jewish Publication Society of America, 1916-20.

———. *Jewish History.* London: Published for the Jewish Historical Society of England by Macmillan, 1903.

Duff, Charles. *The Truth About Columbus.* London: Grayson and Grayson, 1936.

Duhem, Pierre M. M. *Le système du monde; histoire des doctrines cosmologiques de Platon à Copernic.* 5 vols. Paris: A. Hermann et fils, 1913-17.

Dunlap, K. "The Great Aryan Myth," *Scientific Monthly*, LIX (October 1944), 296-300.

Dunbar, Seymour. *A History of Travel in America.* New York: Tudor Publishing Co., 1937.

Durkheim, Emile. *The Elementary Forms of Religious Life.* New York: Macmillan Co., 1915.

Dushkin, Alexander M. *Jewish Education in New York City.* New York: Bureau of Jewish Education, 1918.

Dutertre, Jean Baptiste. *Histoire générale des Antilles habitées par les François.* 4 vols. Paris, 1667-71.

Dyer, Albion M. "Points in the First Chapter of New York Jewish History," A.J.H.S., *Publications*, III (1894), 41-60.

——. "Site of the First Synagogue of the Congregation Shearith Israel of New York," A.J.H.S., *Publications*, VIII (1900), 25-41.

Eannes de Azurara, Gomes. *The Chronicle of the Discovery and Conquest of Guinea.* 2 vols. London, 1896-99. (Works issued by the Hakluyt Society, vols. 95, 100.)

"The Earliest Extant Minute Books of the Spanish and Portuguese Congregation Shearith Israel in New York, 1728-1786," A.J.H.S., *Publications*, XXI (1913), 1-171.

Eckstein, Walter. "Rousseau and Spinoza," *Journal of the History of Ideas*, V (1944), 259-91.

Eisendrath, M. N. "The March of Reform in America," *Liberal Judaism*, March, 1946.

Eisenstein, J. D. "The History of the First Russian-American Jewish Congregation. The Beth Hamedrosh Hagodol," A.J.H.S., *Publications*, IX (1901), 63-74.

Elbogen, Ismar. *A Century of Jewish Life.* Philadelphia: Jewish Publication Society of America, 1944.

Eliassof, H. "The Jews of Chicago," A.J.H.S., *Publications*, XI (1903), 117-30.

Ellis Junior, Alfredo. "Alguns Paulistas dos Seculos XVI e XVII Subsidio para a Historia de S. Paulo," *Revista do Instituto Historico e Geographico Brasileiro*, Tomo especial, III (1927), 409-437.

Elzas, Barnett A. *A Century of Judaism in South Carolina 1800-1900.* Charleston, 1904. (Reprinted from the Centennial edition of the *News and Courier*, May, 1904.)

——. *The Jews of South Carolina.* Charleston: The Daggett Printing Co., 1903.

Emden, Paul H. "The Brothers Goldsmid and the Financing of the Napoleonic Wars," J.H.S.E., *Transactions*, XIV (1940), 225-46.

Encyclopedia Britannica (11th edition), "Pinto Fernão Mendes," XXI, 629.

Enelow, Hyman G. *What Do Jews Believe?* Cincinnati: Press of C. J. Krehbiel and Co., 1908.

Entwistle, William J. "The 'Lusiads,' Da Gama and Modern Criticism," *Lusitania* (1927), pp. 69-88.

Epstein, Isidore. "Judah Halevi as Philosopher," *Jewish Quarterly Review*, XXV (1934-35), 201-225.

Essays on Maimonides, an Octocentennial volume. Edited by Salo Wittmayer Baron. New York: Columbia University Press, 1941.

Exeter Hall Lectures. IX, February 14, 1854.

Eyre, Edward. *European Civilization, Its Origin and Development.* By various contributors under the direction of Edward Eyre. 7 vols. New York: Oxford University Press, 1934-39.

Ezekiel, Herbert T., and Lichtenstein, Gaston. *The History of the Jews of Richmond from 1769 to 1917.* Richmond: H. T. Ezekiel, 1917.

Falk, Sampson. "A History of the Israelites in Buffalo," Buffalo Historical Society, *Publications* I (1879), 289-304.

Faulkner, Harold U. *American Political and Social History.* New York: F. S. Crofts and Co., 1939.

Fawtier, Robert. "The Jews in the 'Use of York,' " *Bulletin of the John Rylands Library,* V (Manchester, 1918-20), 381-85.

Feldman, Abraham J. "Building a Modern Synagogue," *The Jewish Layman,* December, 1944.

Felsenthal, Bernhard. *The Beginnings of the Chicago Sinai Congregation. A Contribution to the Inner History of American Judaism.* Chicago, 1898.

————. "The Jewish Congregation in Surinam," A.J.H.S., *Publications,* II (1894), 29-30.

————. *Kol Kore Bamidbar "Ueber Jüdische Reform."* Chicago, 1859.

————. "On the History of the Jews in Chicago," *A.J.H.S., Publications,* II (1894), 24.

————. *The Wandering Jew.* Chicago, 1872.

————, and Eliassof, Herman. *History of KAM (Congregation of the Men of the West).* Chicago, 1897.

Felsenthal, Emma. *Bernhard Felsenthal, Teacher in Israel; Selections from His Writings, with Biographical Sketch and Bibliography by His Daughter.* New York: Oxford University Press, 1924.

Fernandes, Valetim. *Reportorio dos Tempos . . . Reproduction Facsimile . . . Edition 1563.* Genève: Société Sadag, 1917.

Fernandez y Gonzalez, Francisco. *Instituciones Jurídicas del Pueblo de Israel en los Diferentes Estados de la Península Ibérica.* Madrid, 1881.

Feuchwanger, Ludwig. "Reflections on Anglo-Jewish History," *Historia Judaica,* IX (October, 1947).

Ficalho, Francisco M. *Garcia da Orta e o Seu Tempo.* Lisbon, 1886.

————. *Viagens de Pedro da Covilham.* Lisbon, 1898.

"Find Quaint Sect of Jews in Mexico," *Chicago Sunday Times,* November 4, 1945. P. 16.

Finkel, Joshua. "An Eleventh Century Source for the History of Jewish Scientists in Mohammedan Land (Ibn Said)," *Jewish Quarterly Review,* new series XVIII (1927-28), 45-54.

Finkelstein, Louis. "Is There a God?" *Jewish Quarterly Review,* new series XIII (1922-23), 243.

————, ed. *The Jews, Their History, Culture, and Religion.* 2 vols. New York: Harper and Brothers, 1950.

————. "Modern Theology," *Jewish Quarterly Review,* new series XIII (1922-23), 239-43.

Fisher, Sydney G. "Alien Degradation of American Character," *The Forum,* XIV (1892-93), 608-615.

Fleg, Edmond. *The Jewish Anthology.* Translated by Maurice Samuel. New York: Harcourt, Brace and Co., 1925.

————. *Why I am a Jew*. New York: Bloch Publishing Co., 1929.

Florida Historical Quarterly, II (April, July, 1909).

Flügel, John C. *The Psychology of Clothes*. London: L. and V. Woolf at the Hogarth Press, and the Institute of Psychoanalysis, 1930.

Foner, Philip S. *The Jews in American History, 1654-1865*. New York: International Publishers, 1946.

Fontoura da Costa, Abel. "L'Almanach Perpetuum de Abraham Zacut," *III° Congrès International d'Histoire des Sciences, Actes, Conférences et Communications*, Lisbon, 1936, pp. 137-46.

————. *A Marinharia dos Descobrimentos*. Lisbon, 1933.

For the Honor of the Nation: Patriotism of the American Jew Hailed by Christian Historians. By S. E. McCall, C. M. Eliot, W. T. Manning, and others. New York: 1939.

Forjaz de Sampaio, Albino. *Historia da Literatura Portuguesa*. 3 vols. Paris, 1929-32.

Forum, XIV (1893), 607, 608 ff.; XV (1893), 172-82.

Fox, G. G. "American Reform Judaism," *Christian Century*, October 28, 1942.

Frank, Murray. "Emma Lazarus—Symbol of Liberty," *Chicago Jewish Forum*, Summer, 1948.

Frank, Waldo. "The Jews *Are* Different," *Saturday Evening Post*, CCXIV (March 21, 1942), 27, 53 ff.

————. *The Re-Discovery of America*. New York: 1929.

Fredman, Joseph G., and Falk, L. A. *Jews in American Wars*. New York: Jewish War Veterans of the United States, 1942.

Freitas, Jordão de. "O Descobrimento Pre-Colombino da America Austral Pelos Portugueses," *Lusitania*, (1926), pp. 315-27.

Freudenthal, J. "On the History of Spinozism," *Jewish Quarterly Review*, VIII (1896), 17-70.

Freund, Miriam K. *Jewish Merchants in Colonial America; Their Achievements and Their Contributions to the Development of America*. New York: Behrman's Jewish Book House, 1939.

Freyre, Gilberto. *Brazil, an Interpretation*. New York: Alfred A. Knopf, 1945.

————. *Casa Grande & Senzala: Formação da Familia Brasileira sob o Regimen de Economia Patriarchal*. Rio de Janeiro: Maia and Schmidt, 1933.

————. *The Masters and the Slaves [Casa-grande & Senzala]. A Study in the Development of Brazilian Civilization*. New York: Alfred A. Knopf, 1946.

————. *Mucambas do Nordeste, Algunas Notas sobre o Typo de Casa Popular mais Primitivo do Nordeste do Brasil*. Rio de Janeiro: Ministerio da Educação e Saude, [1937].

————. "Os Comecos da Literatura Israelita na America," in *Os Judeus na História do Brasil*. Rio de Janeiro: U. Zwerling, 1936, pp. 97-98.

————. *Sobrados e Mucambos: Decadencia do Patriarchado Rural no Brasil.* São Paulo: Companhia Editora Nacional, 1936.

————. "Some Aspects of the Social Development of Portuguese America," in *Concerning Latin American Culture.* Edited by Charles C. Griffin. New York: Columbia University Press, 1940.

Friedenberg, Albert M. "American Jewish Journalism to the Close of the Civil War," A.J.H.S., *Publications,* XXVI (1918), 270-73.

————. "Calendar of American Jewish Cases," A.J.H.S., *Publications,* XII (1904), 87-99.

————. "The Correspondence of Jews with President Martin van Buren," A.J.H.S., *Publications,* XXII (1914), 71-100.

————. "A German Jewish Poet on America," A.J.H.S., *Publications,* XIII (1905), 89-92.

————. "The Jews and the American Sunday Laws," A.J.H.S., *Publications,* XI (1903), 101-115.

————. "Letters of a California Pioneer," A.J.H.S., *Publications,* XXXI (1928), 135-71.

————. "Solomon Heydenfeldt: a Jewish Jurist of Alabama and California," A.J.H.S., *Publications,* X (1902), 129-40.

————. "Wätjen's 'Colonial Empire in Brazil,'" *Jewish Quarterly Review,* new series XIV. (1923-24), 379-83.

Friedenwald, Harry. "Jewish Physicians in Italy: Their Relation to the Papal and Italian States," A.J.H.S., *Publications,* XXVIII (1922), 133-211.

————. *The Jews and Medicine.* 2 vols. Baltimore: Johns Hopkins Press, 1944.

Friedenwald, Herbert. "Jacob Isaac and His Method of Converting Salt Water into Fresh Water," A.J.H.S., *Publications,* II (1893), 111-17.

————. "Jews Mentioned in the Journal of the Continental Congress," A.J.H.S., *Publications,* I (1892), 65-89.

————. "A Letter of Jonas Phillips to the Federal Convention," A.J.H.S., *Publications,* II (1893), 107-110.

————. "Material for the History of the Jews in the West Indies," A.J.H.S., *Publications,* V (1897), 45-101.

————. "Memorials Presented to the Continental Congress," A.J.H.S., *Publications,* II (1893), 119-27.

————. "Some Newspaper Advertisements of the Eighteenth Century," A.J.H.S., *Publications,* VI (1897), 49-59.

Friedman, Lee M. "Aaron Lopez's Family Affairs from 'The Commerce of Rhode Island,'" A.J.H.S., *Publications,* XXXV (1939), 295-304.

————. "Cotton Mather and the Jews," A.J.H.S., *Publications,* XXVI (1918), 201-210.

————. *Early American Jews.* Cambridge: Harvard University Press, 1934.

————. "Gabriel Milan, the Jewish Governor of St. Thomas," A.J.H.S., *Publications*, XXVIII (1922), 213-21.

————. *Jewish Pioneers and Patriots*. Philadelphia: Jewish Publication Society of America, 1942.

————. "Moses Michael Hays," A.J.H.S., *Publications*, XXXV (1939), 288-95.

————. *Rabbi Haim Isaac Carigal: His Newport Sermon and His Yale Portrait*. Boston: Privately printed [D. B. Updike, The Merrymount Press], 1940.

————. "Rowland Gideon, an Early Boston Jew, and His Family," A.J.H.S., *Publications*, XXV (1939), 27-37.

Fromm, Erich. *Escape from Freedom*. New York: Farrar and Rinehart, 1941.

Gama, Vasco da. *Diário da viagem de Vasco da Gama*. 2 vols. Porto; Livraria Civilização, 1945. (Alvardo Velho, supposed author.)

Gandía, Enrique de. *Historia de Cristóbal Colón*. Buenos Aires: Editorial Claridad, 1942.

Garcia, Rodolpho. "Os Judeus no Brasil Colonial," in *Os Judeus na História do Brasil*. Rio de Janeiro: U. Zwerling, 1936, pp. 9-46.

Garcia de la Riega, Celso. "Cristóbal Colón ¿Espanol?" *Boletin de la Sociedad Geográfica de Madrid*, XL, suppl. (1898), 1-43.

Gaster, Moses. "Yiddish Literature in the Middle Ages," Royal Society of Literature, *Transactions*, new series VII (1927), 105-131.

Gayarré, Charles. *History of Louisiana*. 4 vols. New York, 1854-66.

Gervasi, Frank. "The Jew as a Soldier," *Collier's*, April 22, 1944.

Gibbon, Edward. *History of the Decline and Fall of the Roman Empire*. 6 vols. New York, 1880.

Giddings, Franklin H. *Studies in the Theory of Human Society*. New York: Macmillan Co., 1922.

Ginsburg, Saul M. "Max Lilienthal's Activities in Russia; New Documents," A.J.H.S., *Publications*, XXXV (1939), 39-51.

Godbey, Allen H. *The Lost Tribes a Myth; Suggestions Toward Rewriting Hebrew History*. Durham, N. C.: Duke University Press, 1930.

Goff, Frederick R. "The Letter of Christopher Columbus Concerning the Islands of India," *The Library of Congress Quarterly Journal*, III, No. 3 (1946), 3-7.

Goldberg, Isaac. *Major Noah: American-Jewish Pioneer*. Philadelphia: Jewish Publication Society of America, 1936.

Goldberg, Nathan. *Economic Trends among American Jews*. New York: Office of Jewish Information, 194–.

————. "Occupational Patterns of American Jews," *The Jewish Review*, III (July 1945). Reprint.

————. "Population Trends in U.S.," *Jewish Affairs*, II, no. 5 (April 15, 1948).

Goldman, Solomon, *The Jew and the Universe*. New York: Harper & Brothers, 1936.

Goldmark, Josephine C. *Pilgrims of '48*. New Haven: Yale University Press, 1930.

Gompers, Samuel. *Seventy Years of Life and Labor*. 2 vols. New York: E. P. Dutton and Company, 1925.

González Obregón, Luis. *The Streets of Mexico*. San Francisco: G. Fields, 1937.

Gordis, Robert. *Conservative Judaism. An American Philosophy*. New York: Published for the National Academy of Adult Jewish Studies of the Jewish Theological Seminary of America, Behrman House, 1945.

———. *The Wisdom of Ecclesiastes*. New York: Behrman House, 1945.

Gordon, Albert I. *Jews in Transition*. Minneapolis: University of Minnesota Press, 1949.

Gottheil, Richard J. H. "Columbus in Jewish Literature," A. J. H. S., *Publications*, II (1894), 129-37.

———. "Contributions to the History of the Jews in Surinam," A. J. H. S., *Publications*, IX (1901), 129-42.

Graetz, Heinrich H. *History of the Jews, from the Earliest Times to the Present Day*. 5 vols. London: D. Nutt, 1891-1901.

Grande Enciclopédia Portuguesa e Brasileira. 20 vols. Lisbon: Editorial Enciclopédia, 1935.

Gravier, Gabriel. *La Lettre et la Carte de Toscanelli à Fernam Martins, et à Christophe Colomb d'après Henry Vignaud*. Rouen: E. Cagniard, 1902.

Greenlee, William B. "The Background of Brazilian History," *The Americas*, II (1945), 151-64.

———. "The Captaincy of the Second Portuguese Voyage to Brazil, 1501-1502," *The Americas*, II (1945), 3-12.

———. "A Descriptive Bibliography of the History of Portugal," *Hispanic American Historical Review*, XX (1940), 491-516.

———. "The First Half Century of Brazilian History," *Mid-America*, new series XIV (1943), 91-120. (Revised reprint.)

———. *The Voyage of Pedro Álvarez Cabral to Brazil and India*. London, 1938. (Works issued by the Hakluyt Society, series II, no. 81.)

Greenough, George B. *Address to the Royal Geographical Society of London*. London, 1840.

Griffin, Charles C., ed. *Concerning Latin American Culture*. Papers read at Byrdcliffe, Woodstock, New York; August, 1939, and edited by Charles C. Griffin. New York: Published by Columbia University Press for the National Committee of the United States of America on International Intellectual Cooperation, 1940.

Grinstein, Hyman B. "A Haym Salomon Letter to Rabbi David Tevele Schiff, London, 1784," A. J. H. S., *Publications*, XXXIV (1937), 107-16.

———. "The Memoirs and Scrapbooks of the Late Dr. Joseph Isaac Bluestone of New York City," A. J. H. S., *Publications*, XXXV (1939), 53-64.

———. *The Rise of the Jewish Community of New York: 1654-1860.* Philadelphia: Jewish Publication Society of America, 1945.

Gùimarães, Argeu. "Os Judeus Portuguezes e Brasileiros na America Hespanhola," *Journal de la Société des Américanistes de Paris*, new series, XVIII (1926), 297-312.

Gunther, Robert W. *The Astrolabes of the World.* 2 vols. Oxford: The University Press, 1932.

Gutstein, Morris A. *Aaron Lopez and Judah Touro: a Refugee and a Son of a Refugee.* New York: Behrman's Jewish Book House, 1939.

———. *The Story of the Jews of Newport; Two and a Half Centuries of Judaism, 1658-1908.* New York: Bloch Publishing Co., 1936.

Hackenburg, William B. "Outline of a Plan to Gather Statistics Concerning the Jews of the United States," A. J. H. S., *Publications*, XII (1904), 157-61.

Halevi, Jehudah. "Israel's Duration," translated by Nina Davis, *Jewish Quarterly Review*, X (1897-98), 627.

———. "A Love Song," translated by Nina Davis, *Jewish Quarterly Review*, X (1897-98), 628.

———. "Song of the Oppressed," translated by Nina Davis, *Jewish Quarterly Review*, X (1897-98), 627.

———. "Where Shall I Find Thee?" translated by Nina Davis, *Jewish Quarterly Review*, X (1897-98), 117-18.

Hamy, Jules T. E. "Cresques lo Juheu," *Annales de Géographie*, I (1891-92). Bibliographie, p. 433.

———. *Cresques, lo Juheu: Note Sur un Géographe Juif Catalan de la Fin du XIV Siècle.* Angers: A Burdin, 189–.

———. "Jaffuda Cresques (Jaime Ribes). Commentaires sur quelques documents . . . publiés par D. Miguel Bonet sur ce géographe juif catalan," *Bulletin de Geographie Historique et Descriptive*, France, Comité des Travaux historiques et scientifiques, Année 1897, no. 3 (1898), 381-88.

———. *Mecia de Viladestes, Cartographe Juif Majorcain du Commencement du XV siècle.* Macon: Protat frères, 1902.

———. "Note sur le Mappemonde de Diego Ribero (1529)." Paris, 1887. (*Bulletin de Géographie Historique et Descriptive*, 1887, no. 1).

———. "Notice sur une carte Marine inédite du Cosmographe Majorcain Gabriel de Vallsecha," 1896.

———. *Portolan Charts of the XVth, XVIth, and XVIIth Centuries.* New York, 1912.

Hanotaux, Gabriel. *Histoire des colonies françaises et de l'expansion de la France dans le monde.* 6 vols. Paris: Société de l'histoire nationale, 1929-33.

Hansen, Marcus L. *The Atlantic Migration 1607-1860; A History of the Continuing Settlement in the United States.* Edited by A. M. Schlesinger. Cambridge: Harvard University Press, 1940.

Hapgood, Norman. Series of articles on Jewish problems in *Harper's Weekly*, LXI (August-November 1915).

Harris, Maurice H. "Are the Jews a Nation Today?" *Jewish Quarterly Review*, II (1890), 166-71.

Harrisse, Henry. *Christophe Colomb: son origine, sa vie, ses voyages, sa famille et ses descendants.* 2 vols. Paris, 1884-85.

———. *Notes on Columbus.* New York: 1866.

Hart, Gustavus N. "A Biographical Account of Ephraim Hart and His Son, Dr. Joel Hart of New York," A. J. H. S., *Publications*, IV (1894), 215-18.

Hartogensis, Benjamin H. "The Russian Night School of Baltimore," A. J. H. S., *Publications*, XXXI (1928), 225-28.

Hartstein, Jacob I. "The Polonies Talmud Torah of New York," A. J. H. S., *Publications*, XXXIV (1937), 123-41.

Harvey, Gabriel. *The Prototype of Shylock, Lopez the Jew, Executed 1594.* Harrow Weald, Middlesex, 1927.

Hecht, Ben. *A Guide for the Bedevilled.* New York: C. Scribner's Sons, 1944.

Heineman, David E. "The Startling Experience of a Jewish Trader during Pontiac's Siege of Detroit in 1763," A. J. H. S., *Publications*, XXIII (1915), 31-35.

Hellman, George S. *Benjamin N. Cardozo, American Judge.* New York: Whittlesey House, 1940.

Henriques, Henry S. Q. "Jews and English Law," *Jewish Quarterly Review*, XII (1900), 662-73. Also London, 1908 edition.

———. "Reflections on the History of the Anglo-Jewish Community," J. H. S. E., *Transactions*, IX (1918-20), 131-42.

Herculano de Carvalho e Araujo, Alexandre. *Historia da Origem e Estabelecimento da Inquisação em Portugal.* 3 vols. Lisbon, 1885.

———. *History of the Origin and Establishment of the Inquisition in Portugal.* Translated by J. C. Branner. Stanford University, California: The University, 1926.

Hersch, Virginia. *Storm Beach.* Boston and New York: Houghton Mifflin Co., 1933.

———. *Woman Under Glass, Saint Teresa of Avila.* New York: Harper & Brothers, 1930.

Hersey, John. "The Old Man" [Bernard Mannes Baruch], *New Yorker* (January 3, 1948), 28-37.

Hevesy, André de. *The Discoverer: a New Narrative of the Life and Hazardous Adventures of the Genoese, Christopher Columbus.* London: Thornton Butterworth, 1929.

Higby, Chester P. *History of Europe (1492-1815)*. Boston: Houghton Mifflin Co., 1927.

Hilfman, P. A. "Notes on the History of the Jews in Surinam," A. J. H. S., *Publications*, XVIII (1909), 179-207.

———. "Some Further Notes on the History of the Jews in Surinam," A. J. H. S., *Publications*, XVI (1907), 7-22.

Hirsch, S. A. "Early English Hebraists. Roger Bacon and His Predecessors," *Jewish Quarterly Review*, XII (1899-1900), 34-88.

Hirschfeld, Hartwig. "An English Voice on the Emancipation of the Jews," J. H. S. E., *Transactions*, VI (1912), 128-37.

Hirsh, Iyda R. "The Mears Family and Their Connections, 1696-1824," A. J. H. S., *Publications*, XXXIII (1934), 199-210.

Hispanic Society of America. *Facsimiles of Portolan Charts Belonging to the Hispanic Society of America*. With an introduction by Edward Luther Stevenson. New York, 1916.

História da Colonização Portuguesa do Brasil. Edição Monumental Comemorativa do Primeiro Centenario da Indipendencia do Brasil. 3 vols. Pôrto: Litografia nacional, 1921-24.

Hollander, J. H. "Documents Relating to the Attempted Departure of the Jews from Surinam in 1675," A. J. H. S., *Publications*, VI (1897), 9-29.

———. "Some Unpublished Material Relating to Dr. Jacob Lumbrozo, of Maryland," A. J. H. S., *Publications*, I (1892), 25-39.

Holmes, Abiel. *The Annals of America*. 2 vols. Cambridge, 1829.

Holmes, John H. *Palestine Today and Tomorrow: a Gentile's Survey of Zionism*. New York: Macmillan Co., 1929.

Honor, Leo L. "Jewish Education in the United States," *Jewish People*, II (1946), 151-71.

Houben, Heinrich H. *Christopher Columbus: the Tragedy of a Discoverer*. London: G. Routledge and Sons, 1935.

Hühner, Leon. "Asser Levy. A Noted Jewish Burgher of New Amsterdam," A. J. H. S., *Publications*, VIII (1900), 9-23.

———. "The First Jew to Hold the Office of Governor of One of the United States," A. J. H. S., *Publications*, XVII (1909), 187-95.

———. "Francis Salvador. A Prominent Patriot of the Revolutionary War," A. J. H. S., *Publications*, IX (1901), 107-122.

———. "Isaac de Pinto, a Noted European Publicist and Defender of Great Britain's Policy during the American Revolution," A. J. H. S., *Publications*, XIII (1905), 113-26.

———. "Jews in Connection with the Colleges of the Thirteen Original States Prior to 1800," A. J. H. S., *Publications*, XIX (1910), 101-124.

———. "The Jews of Georgia from the Outbreak of the American Revolution to the Close of the 18th Century," A. J. H. S., *Publications*, XVII (1909), 89-108.

———. "The Jews of South Carolina from the Earliest Settlement to the End of the American Revolution," A. J. H. S., *Publications*, XII (1904), 39-61.

———. "The Jews of Virginia from the Earliest Times to the Close of the Eighteenth Century," A. J. H. S., *Publications*, XX (1911), 85-105.

———. *The Life of Judah Touro, 1775-1854*. Philadelphia: Jewish Publication Society of America, 1946.

———. "Some Additional Notes on the History of the Jews of South Carolina," A. J. H. S., *Publications*, XIX (1910), 151-56.

———. "Some Jewish Associates of John Brown," A. J. H. S., *Publications*, XXIII (1915), 55-78.

———. "Some Notes on the Career of Colonel David S. Franks," A. J. H. S., *Publications*, X (1902), 166-68.

Humboldt, Alexander. *Cosmos: essai d'une description physique du monde*. 3 vols. Milan, 1846-51.

Hyamson, Albert M. "British Projects for the Restoration of Jews to Palestine," A. J. H. S., *Publications*, XXVI (1918), 127-64.

———. *History of the Jews in England*. London: Methuen and Co., 1928. (Also London, 1908 edition.)

———. "Restoration of Jews to Palestine," A. J. H. S., *Publications*, XXVI (1918), 134.

Inman, Samuel G. *Latin America, Its Place in World Life*. Chicago: Willet, Clark and Co., 1937.

Irving, Washington. *The Life and Voyages of Christopher Columbus*. 3 vols. New York, 1850.

Isaac, Myer S. "A Jewish Army Chaplain," A. J. H. S., *Publications*, XII (1904), 127-33.

Jackson, Ada. *Behold the Jew*. New York: Macmillan Co., 1944.

Jacobs, Joseph. "Aaron of Lincoln," *Jewish Quarterly Review*, X (1898), 629-48.

———. *George Eliot, Matthew Arnold, Browning, Newman*. London, 1891.

———. *Jewish Contributions to Civilization*. Philadelphia: Jewish Publication Society of America, 1944.

———. *The Jews of Angevin England*. London, 1893.

———. "The Original of Scott's Rebecca," A. J. H. S., *Publications*, XXII (1914), 53-60.

———. "Report of the Committee on Indexing American Jewish Periodicals of the American Jewish Historical Society," A. J. H. S., *Publications*, XIII (1905), xix-xxiii.

———. *The Story of Geographical Discovery*. London, 1899.

———. *Studies in Jewish Statistics*. London, 1891.

———. "The Typical Character of Anglo-Jewish History," *Jewish Quarterly Review*, X (1898), 217-37.

Jacobs, William. *The Jews' Reasons for Believing in One God Only*. New York; G. Vale, 1848.

James, Edmund J. and others. *The Immigrant Jew in America.* New York, 1906.

James, Henry. *The American Scene.* New York: Harper & Brothers, 1907.

James, Marquis. *Andrew Jackson.* Indianapolis: Bobbs-Merrill Co., 1937.

James, Preston E. *Latin America.* New York: Odyssey Press, 1942.

James, William. *Essays on Faith and Morals.* New York: Longmans, Green and Co., 1943.

Jameson, John F., ed. *Narratives of New Netherland, 1609-1664.* New York: Charles Scribner's Sons, 1909.

Jane, Cecil. "The Letter of Columbus Announcing the Success of His First Voyage," *Hispanic American Historical Review,* X (1930), 33-50.

————. "The Question of the Literacy of Columbus in 1492," *Hispanic American Historical Review,* X (1930), 500-16.

————, ed. *Select Documents Illustrating the Four Voyages of Columbus.* London, 1930. (Works issued by *the Hakluyt Society,* series II, vol. XV.)

Janowsky, Oscar, ed. *The American Jew, a Composite Portrait.* New York: Harper & Brothers, 1942.

Jastrow, Morris, Jr. "Documents Relating to the Career of Isaac Franks," A. J. H. S., *Publications,* V (1897), 7-34.

Jayne, Kingsley G. *Vasco da Gama and His Successors, 1450-1580.* London: Methuen and Co., 1910.

Jervis, Walter W. *The World in Maps.* London: G. Philip and Son, 1936.

The Jewish Encyclopedia. 12 vols. New York: Funk and Wagnalls Co., 1901-1906.

The Jewish Library. Edited by Leo Jung. New York: Macmillan Co., 1928.

Jewish National Monthly, LX, no. 7 (March, 1946), 232.

The Jewish People, Past and Present. 2 vols. New York: Jewish Encyclopedic Handbooks, Central Yiddish Culture Organization, 1946-48.

Jewish Quarterly Review. 20 vols. London, 1888-1908. Superseded by the *Jewish Quarterly Review,* new series. Philadelphia, 1910.

The Jewish Question and the Mission of the Jews. New York, 1894.

Jewish Review, III, no. 2 (July, 1945).

Jews in America. By the Editors of *Fortune* Magazine. New York, 1936.

Jones, C. K. Review of "Los León Pinelo; la ilustre familia marrana del siglo XVII," by Bolesleo Lewin. *Hispanic American Historical Review,* XXIII (1943), 531-32.

Jones, Charles C., Jr. "The Settlement of the Jews in Georgia," A. J. H. S., *Publications,* I (1892), 5-12.

Joseph, S. *History of the Baron de Hirsch Fund.* New York: Jewish Publication Society of America, 1935.

————. *Jewish Immigration to the United States from 1881-1910.* Ph D. thesis, Columbia University. New York, 1914.

Josephson, Matthew. "Jurist" [Felix Frankfurter], *New Yorker*, November 30, December 7, December 14, 1940.

The Journal of Christopher Columbus (during His First Voyage, 1492-93). London, 1893.

A Journal of the First Voyage of Vasco da Gama, 1497-1499. Translated by E. C. Ravenstein. London, 1898. (Works issued by the Hakluyt Society, no. 99.)

Os Judeus na História do Brasil. Edited by Uri Zwerling. Rio de Janeiro, U. Zwerling, 1936.

Kahn, E. J., Jr. "The Years Alone" [Mrs. Franklin Delano Roosevelt], *New Yorker* (June 12, 1948), 30-41.

Kagan, Soloman R. *Jewish Contributions to Medicine in America, from Colonial Times to the Present.* Boston: The Boston Medical Publishing Co., 1939.

Kampen, Nicholaas G. van. *Geschichte der Niederlande.* Hamburg, 1831-33.

Kaplan, Mordecai M. *The Future of American Jew.* New York: Macmillan Co., 1948.

Kaplan, M. M., ed. *The Jewish Reconstructionist Papers.* New York, 1936.

————. *Judaism as a Civilization: Toward a Reconstruction of American-Jewish Life.* New York: Macmillan Co., 1934.

————. *The Reconstructionist Viewpoint* (Pamphlet). New York: 1945.

Katz, Solomon. *The Jews in the Visigothic and Frankish Kingdoms of Spain and Gaul.* Cambridge, Mass.: The Mediaeval Academy of America, 1937.

Katzenstein, Julius. *History and Destiny of the Jews.* Garden City, New York: Garden City Publishing Co., 1936.

Kayserling, Meyer. *Biblioteca Española—Portugueza—Judaica, Dictionnaire bibliographique des auteurs juifs.* Strasbourg, 1890.

————. *Christopher Columbus and the Participation of the Jews in the Spanish and Portuguese Discoveries.* New York, 1894.

————. "The Earliest Rabbis and Jewish Writers of America," A. J. H. S., *Publications,* III (1895), 13-20.

————. *Geschichte der Juden in Portugal.* Leipzig, 1867.

————. "Isaac Aboah, the First Jewish Author in America," A. J. H. S., *Publications,* V (1897), 125-36.

————. *Die Juden in Navarra, den Baskenlaendern und auf den Balearen.* Berlin, 1861.

————. *Sephardim. Romanische poesien der Juden in Spanien.* Leipzig, 1859.

Kimble, George H. T. *Geography in the Middle Ages.* London: Methuen and Co., 1938.

Kisch, Guido. "Czechoslovak Jews and America," *Historia Judaica,* VI (1944), 123-38.

———. "German Jews in White Labor Servitude in America," A. J. H. S., *Publications*, XXXIV (1937), 11-49.

———. *In Search of Freedom. A History of American Jews from Czechoslovakia.* London: E. Goldston, 1949.

———. "Israels Herold, the First Jewish Weekly in New York," *Historia Judaica*, II (1940). Reprint.

———. "Two American Jewish Pioneers of New Haven: Sigmund and Leopold Waterman," *Historia Judaica*, IV (1942).

———, ed. "A Voyage to America Ninety Years Ago. The Diary of a Bohemian Jew on His Voyage from Hamburg to New York, 1847," A. J. H. S., *Publications* XXXV (1939), 65-113. (Diary of S. E. Rosenbaum.)

Kohler, Max J. "The Board of Delegates of American Israelites, 1859-1878. Including the Correspondence of Myer S. Isaacs with General Benjamin F. Butler as to the Status of the Jews at the Time of Our Civil War," A. J. H. S., *Publications*, XXIX (1925), 75-80.

———. "Civil Status of the Jews in Colonial New York," A. J. H. S., *Publications*, VI (1897), 81-106.

———. "Dr. Rodrigo Lopez, Queen Elizabeth's Jewish Physician, and His Relations to America," A. J. H. S., *Publications*, XVII (1909), 9-25.

———. "Educational Reforms in Europe in Their Relation to Jewish Emancipation—1778-1919," A. J. H. S., *Publications*, XXVIII (1921), 83-132.

———. *Haym Salomon, the Patriot Broker of the Revolution.* 1931.

———. "Incidents Illustrative of American Jewish Patriotism," A. J. H. S., *Publications*, IV (1894), 81-99.

———. "Isaac Harby, Jewish Religious Leader and Man of Letters," A. J. H. S., *Publications*, XXXII (1931), 35-53.

———. "Isaac Markens," A. J. H. S., *Publications*, XXXII (1931), 129-32.

———. "Jewish Activity in American Colonial Commerce," A. J. H. S., *Publications*, X (1902), 47-64.

———. "Jewish Rights at the Congresses of Vienna (1814-1815), and Aix-la-Chapelle (1818)," A. J. H. S., *Publications*, XXVI (1918) 33-125.

———. "The Jews and the American Anti-Slavery Movement," A. J. H. S. *Publications*, V (1897), 137-55.

———. "Jews and the American Anti-Slavery Movement. II," A. J. H. S., *Publications*, IX (1901), 45-56.

———. "The Jews in Newport," A. J. H. S., *Publications*, VI (1897), 61-80.

———. "Judah P. Benjamin; Statesman and Jurist," A. J. H. S., *Publications*, XII (1904), 63-85.

————. "Judah Touro, Merchant and Philanthropist," A. J. H. S., *Publications*, XIII (1905), 93-111.

————. "Notes," A. J. H. S., *Publications*, IV (1894), 219-25.

————. "Phases in the History of Religious Liberty in America, with Special Reference to the Jews," A. J. H. S., *Publications*, XI (1903), 53-73.

————. "Phases in the History of Religious Liberty in America with Particular Reference to the Jews. II," A. J. H. S., *Publications*, XIII 1905, 7-36.

————. "Phases of Jewish Life in New York Before 1800," A. J. H. S., *Publications*, III (1894), 73-86.

————. "The United States and German Jewish Persecutions," *Jewish Academy of Arts and Sciences*, no. 1 (1933).

————. "Unpublished Correspondence Between Thomas Jefferson and Some American Jews," A. J. H. S., *Publications*, XX (1911), 11-30.

Kohn, Hans. *A History of Nationalism in the East*. New York: Harcourt, Brace and Co., 1929.

Kohs, Samuel C. "Jews in the United States Armed Forces," *Yivo* (1945).

Kohut, George A. "The Contributions of Cyrus Adler to American Jewish History," A. J. H. S., *Publications*, XXXIII (1934), 17-42.

————. "Early Jewish Literature in America," A. J. H. S., *Publications*, III (1894), 103-47.

————. "Jellinek and America," A. J. H. S., *Publications*, XXXIII (1934), 237-49.

————. "Jewish Heretics in the Philippines in the Sixteenth and Seventeenth Century," A. J. H. S., *Publications*, XII (1904), 149-56.

————. "Jewish Martyrs of the Inquisition in South America," A. J. H. S., *Publications*, IV (1896), 101-87.

————. "A Literary Autobiography of Mordecai Manuel Noah. With an Introduction," A. J. H. S., *Publications*, VI (1897), 113-21.

————. "The Trial of Francisco Maldonado de Silva," A. J. H. S., *Publications*, XI (1903), 163-79.

————. "Who Was the First Rabbi of Surinam?" A. J. H. S., *Publications*, V (1897), 119-24.

Komroff, Manuel, ed. *Contemporaries of Marco Polo*. London: Boni and Liveright, 1928. (Includes "The Oriental Travels of Benjamin of Tudela, 1160-1173.")

Korn, Bertram W. "Jewish Chaplains during the Civil War," *American Jewish Archives*, I, no. 1 (1948), 6-22.

Korn, Harold. "Documents Relative to the Estate of Aaron Lopez," A. J. H. S., *Publications*, XXXV (1939), 139-43.

————. "Receipt Book of Judah Hays, June 20, 1759 to December 23, 1752," A. J. H. S., *Publications*, XXXIV (1937), 117-22.

Kraus, Michael. *A History of American History.* New York: Farrar and Rinehart, 1937.

Kuhn, Arthur K. "Hugo Grotius and the Emancipation of the Jews in Holland," A. J. H. S., *Publications,* XXXI (1928), 173-80.

Laet, Joannes de. *Iaerlyck Verhael van de Verrichtinghen der Geoctroyeer de West Indische Compagnie (1624-1626).* 'S-Gravenhage: M. Nijhoff, 1931-37.

Lafitau, Joseph F. *Histoire des découvertes et conquestes des Portugais dans le Nouveau Monde.* 4 vols. Paris, 1736.

La Harpe, Bernard de. *Journal historique de l'establissement des Français à la Louisiane.* New Orleans, 1831.

La Roncière, Charles G. M. B. de. *La carte de Christophe Colomb.* Paris: Les Éditions Historiques, 1924.

————. *La découverte de l'Afrique au moyen age, cartographes et explorateurs.* 3 vols. Cairo: Société Royale de Geographie de Égypte, 1924-27.

————. *Histoire de la découverte de la terre.* Paris: Librairie Larousse, [c1938].

Lasker, Bruno, ed. *Jewish Experiences in America; Suggestions for the Study of Jewish Relations with non-Jews.* New York: The Inquiry, 1930.

Lasswell, Harold D. *Democracy Through Public Opinion.* Menasha, Wisconsin: George Banta Publishing Co., c. 1941.

————. *Propaganda and Promotional Activities, an Annotated Bibliography.* Minneapolis: The University of Minnesota Press, 1935.

Lazarus, Emma. *Admetus and Other Poems.* New York: Hurde and Houghton, 1871.

————. *Emma Lazarus; Selections from Her Poetry and Prose.* Edited by Morris U. Schappes. New York: Cooperative Book League, Jewish-American Section, International Workers Order [1944].

————. "The Jewish Problem," *The Century Illustrated Monthly Magazine,* XXV, new series III (1882-83), 602-611.

————. *The Letters of Emma Lazarus, (1868-1885).* Edited by Morris U. Schappes. New York: New York Public Library, 1949.

————. *Songs of a Semite: The Dance to Death, and Other Poems.* New York, 1882.

Lea, Henry C. *The Inquisition in the Spanish Dependencies,* New York: Macmillan Co., 1908.

Lebeson, Anita L. "The American Jewish Chronicle," in *The Jews,* edited by Louis Finkelstein. 2 vols. New York: Harper & Brothers, 1950. Vol. I, 313-53.

————. "American Jewish History, the Task and the Challenge," *Historia Judaica,* IX (1947), 1-34.

————. "Hannah Adams and the Jews," *Historia Judaica,* VIII, no. 2 (October, 1946).

————. "Jewish Cartographers: a Forgotten Chapter of Jewish History," *Historia Judaica,* XI (1949), 155-74.

————. *Jewish Pioneers in America, 1492-1848.* New York: Brentano, 1931.

————. "On the Writing of American Jewish History," A. J. H. S., *Publications,* XXXIX (1950), 303-312.

————. "The Tale of Gabriel," *Young Judean,* February, 1945.

Lebowich, Joseph. "General Ulysses S. Grant and the Jews," A. J. H. S., *Publications,* XVII (1909), 71-79.

————. "The Jews in Boston till 1875," A. J. H. S., *Publications,* XII (1904), 101-112.

Lecky, William E. "The Art of Writing History," *The Forum,* XIV (1892-93), 715-24.

————. *History of the Rise and Influence of the Spirit of Rationalism in Europe.* 2 vols. New York, 1886.

Le Conte, René. "Les Allemands à la Louisiane au XVIII° siècle," *Journal de la Société des Américanistes de Paris,* new series, XVI (1924).

Lee, Sidney L. "Elizabethan England and the Jews," New Shakespere Society, *Transactions,* series I (1887-92).

————. "The Original of Shylock," *The Gentleman's Magazine,* CCXLVI (1880), 185-200.

Leeser, Isaac, tr. *The Twenty-four Books of the Holy Scriptures Carefully Translated According to the Massoretic Text, after the Best Jewish Authorities.* London, 5625 (1865). (Prince Louis Lucien Bonaparte Collection in Newberry Library.)

Leite, Serafim. *História da Companhia de Jesus no Brasil.* 6 vols. Lisbon: Livraria Portugália, 1938.

Leite, Solidonio. *Da Influencia do Elemento Judaico no Descobrimento e Commercio do Brasil (Seculos XVI e XVII).* Rio de Janeiro: Congresso de Historia Nacional, Instituto Historico Brasileiro, 1938.

Leroy-Beaulieu, Anatole. *Israel Among the Nations: a Study of the Jews and Antisemitism.* New York, 1896.

Lesser, Allen F. "Adah Isaacs Menken: a Daughter of Israel," A. J. H. S., *Publications,* XXXIV (1937), 143-47.

Lester, Charles E. *The Life and Voyages of Americus Vespucius.* New York, 1846.

L'Estrange, Hamon. *Americans No Iewes, or Improbabilities That the Americans Are of That Race.* London, 1652.

Lestschinsky, Jacob. "The Economic and Social Development of the Jewish People," *The Jewish People,* I (1946), 361-406.

Levi, David. *Letters to Dr. Priestley, in Answer to Those He Addressed to the Jews.* New York, 1794.

Levin, Schmarya. *Youth in Revolt.* Translated by Maurice Samuel. New York: Harcourt, Brace and Co., c. 1930.

Levine, L. *Women's Garment Workers.* New York, 1924.

Levinger, Lee J. *Anti-Semitism in the United States: Its History and Causes.* New York: Bloch Publishing Co., 1925.

Levy, Augusta. "Recollections of a Pioneer Woman of La Crosse." Edited by Albert H. Sanford. State Historical Society of Wisconsin, *Proceedings for 1911.* Madison: The Society, 1912, pp. 201-215.

Levy, Raphael. *The Astrological Works of Abraham ibn Ezra.* Baltimore: Johns Hopkins Press, 1927.

Levy S. "John Dury and the English Jewry," J. H. S. E., *Transactions,* IV (1903), 76-82.

Lewin, Boleslao. *El Judío en la Época Colonial.* Buenos Aires: Colegio Libre de Estudios Superiores, 1939.

———. "Los Leon Pinelo; la Ilustre Familia Marrana de Siglo XVII," *Hispanic American Historical Review,* XXIII (1943), 531-32. (Review by C. K. Jones).

Liebmann, Walter H. "The Correspondence Between Solomon Etting and Henry Clay," A. J. H. S., *Publications,* XVII (1909).

Lincoln, Abraham. *Abraham Lincoln: His Speeches and Writings.* Edited by Roy P. Basler. Cleveland: World Publishing Co., 1946.

Lindo, Alicia. "A Sketch of the Life of David Lindo," A. J. H. S., *Publications,* XXIII (1915), 37-41.

Lindo, Elias H. *The History of the Jews of Spain and Portugal.* London, 1848.

Linton, Ralph, ed. *The Science of Man in the World Crisis.* New York: Columbia University Press, 1945.

Lobo d' Ávila, Arthur. *Cristóbal Colón.* Lisbon: Tip. da Emprêsa Nacional de Publicidade, 1939.

Locke, John. "Letters Concerning Toleration," in his *Works.* 3 vols. London, 1740. Vol. II, 249-76.

———. "Two Treatises of Government," *Ibid.,* 110 ff.

Lollis, Cesare de. *Cristoforo Colombo.* Rome: Fratelli Treves, c. 1923.

London, Hannah R. "Portraits of Jews by Thomas Sully," *Daughters of the American Revolution Magazine,* LX (1926), 85-89.

———. "Portraits of Jews Painted by Gilbert Stuart," *Daughters of the American Revolution Magazine,* LX (1926), 213-216.

———. "Some Pre-Revolutionary Portraits," *Daughters of the American Revolution Magazine,* LX (1926), 725-30.

Lopes de Mendonça, Henrique. *Estudos sobre Navios Portuguezes nos Seculos XV e XVI.* Lisbon, 1892.

Lotz, Philip H. *Distinguished American Jews.* New York: Association Press, 1945.

"The Lyons Collection," A.J.H.S., *Publications,* XXI (1913); XXVII (1919). Two entire volumes.

Macaulay, Thomas B. "Civil Disabilities of the Jews," *Occident and American Jewish Advocate,* II (1844), 127 ff.

———. *Essay and Speech on Jewish Disabilities*. Edinburgh: Ballantyne, Hanson and Co., 1909.

McKenney, Thomas L., and Hall, James. *History of the Indian Tribes of North America*. 3 vols. Philadelphia, 1848-50.

Madariaga, Salvador de. *Christopher Columbus*. New York: Macmillan Co., 1940.

Magnus, Katie. *Outlines of Jewish History from B. C. E. 586 to C. E. 1929*. Philadelphia: Jewish Publication Society of America, 1929.

Mallery, Garrick. *Israelite and Indian. A Parallel in Planes of Culture*. Salem, Mass., 1889.

Manasseh ben Joseph ben Israel. *The Hope of Israel*. London, 1651.

———. *Menasseh ben Israel's Mission to Oliver Cromwell*: being a reprint of the pamphlets published by Menasseh ben Israel to promote the re-admission of the Jews to England, 1649-1656. Edited by Lucien Wolf. London: Published for the Jewish Historical Society of England by Macmillan and Co., 1901.

Manuel. *Carta de El-Rei D. Manuel ao Rei Catholico Narrando—Lhe As Viagens Portuguezas á India desde 1500 até 1505*. Reimprcssa sobreo prototype romano de 1505, vertida em linguagem e annotada por prospero peragalio. In *Centenario do Descobrimento da America. Memorias da Commissão Portugueza*. Lisbon, 1892.

Manuel II, King of Portugal. *Livros Antigos Portuguezas 1489-1600 da Bibliotheca de Sua Majestade Fidelissima*. 3 vols. London: Maggs Brothers, 1929-35. Vol. I.

Marcel, Gabriel A. *Reproductions de cartes & de globes relatifs à la découverte de l'Amérique du XV* au XVIII* siècle*. Paris, 1893.

Marchant, Alexander. "The Discovery of Brazil: A Note on Interpretations," *The Geographical Review*, XXXV (1945), 296-300.

Marcondes de Souza, Thomas O. *O. Descobrimento da América e a Suposta Prioridade dos Portugueses*. São Paulo: Editorial Brasiliense, 1944.

Marcondes Homen de Mello, Francisco I. *Atlas do Brazil*. Rio de Janeiro: F. Briguiet and Cia., 1909.

Marcus, Jacob R. *The Jew in the Medieval World*. Cincinnati: The Union of American Hebrew Congregations, 1938.

Margolis, Max L., and Marx, Alexander. *A History of The Jewish People*. Philadelphia: Jewish Publication Society of America, 1938.

Margry, Pierre, ed. *Découvertes et établissements des français dans l'ouest et dans le sud de l'Amérique septentrional (1614-1754)*. 6 vols. Paris, 1876-86.

Markens, Isaac. "Lincoln and the Jews," A.J.H.S., *Publications*, XVII (1909), 109-165.

Marx, Alexander. "Aims and Tasks of Jewish Historiography," A.J.H.S., *Publications*, XXVI (1918), 11-32.

———. "Societies for the Promotion of the Studies of Jewish History," A.J.H.S., *Publications*, (1911), 1-9.

————. *Studies in Jewish History and Booklore*. New York: The Jewish Theological Seminary of America, 1944.

Mason, Alpheus T. *Brandeis, a Free Man's Life*. New York: Viking Press, 1946.

Massachusetts (Colony) Laws, Statutes, etc. *The Colonial Laws of Massachusetts*. Reprinted from the edition of 1672 with the supplements through 1686. Published by order of the City Council of Boston, under the supervision of William H. Whitmore. Boston, 1887.

Masserman, Paul, and Baker, Max. *The Jews Come to America*. New York: Bloch Publishing Co., 1932.

Means, Philip A. *Newport Tower*. New York: Henry Holt and Co., 1942.

Meisels, Isaac S. "Don Isaac Abarbanel," *Jewish Quarterly Review*, II (1890), 37-52.

Mello, Francisco M. de. *Espanáforas de Vária História Portuguesa*. Coimbra: Impr. da Universidade, 1931.

Mencken, H. L. *Prejudices. Fourth Series*. New York: Alfred A. Knopf, 1924.

Mendes dos Remedios, Joaquim. *Os Judeus em Portugal*. Coimbra, 1895.

Mendes Pinto, Fernão. *Peregrinação*. 4 vols. Lisbon: Livraria Ferreira, 1908-1910.

————. *The Voyages and. Adventures of Ferdinand Mendez Pinto, the Portuguese (Done into English by Henry Cogan)*. London, 1891.

The Menorah Journal. New York, The Intercollegiate Menorah Association, 1948 (Spring number).

Mersand, Joseph. *Traditions in American Literature: A Study of Jewish Characters and Authors*. New York: The Modern Chapbooks, 1939.

Meyer, Isidore S. "Hebrew at Harvard, (1636-1760). A Résumé of the Information in Recent Publications," *A.J.H.S., Publications*, XXXV (1939), 145-70.

Michaëlis de Vasconcellos, Carolina. "Uriel da Costa, Notes Suplementares relativas a Sua Vida e Sua Obra," *Lusitania*, (1924), pp. 5-22.

Mikkelson, Michael A. *The Bishop Hill Colony, a Religious Communistic Settlement in Henry County, Illinois*. Baltimore: Johns Hopkins Press, 1892.

Miller, George J. "James Alexander and the Jews, Especially Isaac Emanuel," *A.J.H.S., Publications*, XXXV (1939), 171-88.

"The Minis Family." By the Genealogical Editor. *The Georgia Historical Quarterly*, I (1917), 45-49.

Minkin, Jacob S. *Abarbanel and the Expulsion of the Jews from Spain*. New York: Behrman's Jewish Book House, 1938.

Miscelânea de Estudos em Honra de D. Carolina Michaëlis de Vasconcellos. Coimbra: Imprensa da Universidade, 1933.

Modder, Montagu F. *The Jew in the Literature of England*. Philadelphia: Jewish Publication Society of America, 1944.

Moïse, Lucius C. *Biography of Isaac Harby*. Columbia: R. L. Bryan Co., 1931.

Monin, José. *Los Judíos en la America Española. 1492-1810.* Buenos Aires: Biblioteca Yavne, 1939.

Monis, Judah. *A Grammar of the Hebrew Tongue.* Boston, 1735.

Montagu, Lily H. "Spiritual Possibilities of Judaism Today," *Jewish Quarterly Review,* XI (1898-99), 216-31.

Montefiore, Sir Moses. "Sir Moses Montefiore's report to the Board of Deputies of British Jews," *Occident,* XXIV (December, 1866), 419-24.

Moore, Nathaniel F. *Diary. A Trip from New York to the Falls of St. Anthony in 1845.* Edited by Stanley Pargellis and Ruth Lapham Butler. Chicago: Published for the Newberry Library by the University of Chicago Press, 1946.

Morais, Henry S. *Eminent Israelites of the Nineteenth Century.* Philadelphia, 1880.

Morais, Nina. "Jewish Ostracism in America," *North American Review,* CXXXIII (1881), 265-75.

Morais, Sabato, "Mickvé Israel Congregation of Philadelphia," A.J.H.S., *Publications,* I (1892), 13-24.

Mordecai, Alfred. "The Life of Alfred Mordecai as Related by Himself," edited by James A. Padgett, *North Carolina Historical Review,* XXII, no. 1 (1945), 58-108.

————. "Life of Alfred Mordecai in Mexico, in 1865-1866, as Told in His Letters to His Family," edited by James A. Padgett, *North Carolina Historical Review,* XXII, no. 2 (1945), 198-227.

Mordecai, Gratz. "Notice of Jacob Mordecai, Founder, and Proprietor from 1809 to 1818, of the Warrenton (N. C.) Female Seminary," A.J.H.S., *Publications,* VI (1897), 39-48.

Morison, Samuel E. *Admiral of the Ocean Sea: A Life of Christopher Columbus.* 2 vols. Boston: Little, Brown and Co., 1942.

————. "Columbus and Polaris," *American Neptune,* I (1941), 6-25, 123-37.

————. *Portuguese Voyages to America in the Fifteenth Century.* Cambridge: Harvard University Press, 1940.

————. "The Route of Columbus Along the North Coast of Haiti, and the Site of Navidad," American Philosophical Society, *Transactions,* new series XXXI (1940), 239-85.

Moses, Alfred G. "The History of the Jews of Montgomery," A.J.H.S., *Publications,* XIII (1905), 83-88.

Moses ben Maimon. *The Guide to the Perplexed of Maimonides.* 3 vols. London, 1881-85.

Mott, Frank Luther. *American Journalism; a History of Newspapers in the United States Through 250 Years, 1690 to 1940.* New York: Macmillan Co., 1941.

Move Out Verify. The Combat Story of the 743rd Tank Battalion.

Myers, Gustavus. *The History of American Idealism.* New York: Boni and Liveright, 1925.

Nachod, Oskar. "Die Älteste Abend-ländische Manuskript-Spezialkarte von Japan von Fernão Vaz Domado 1568," *Atti del X Congresso Internazionale di Geografia, Roma MCMXIII*. Rome, 1915.

Namier, Lewis B. *The Jews in the Modern World*. London, 1934.

National Cyclopedia of American Biography. New York: J. T. White and Co., 1893.

National Jewish Welfare Board. *American Jews in World War II. The Story of 550,000 Fighters for Freedom*. Compiled by the Bureau of War Records of the National Jewish Welfare Board. 2 vols. New York, 1947.

Navarrete, Martín Fernández de. *Colección de los Viages y Descubrimientes que Hicieron por Mar los Españoles desde Fines del Siglo XV*. 5 vols. Madrid, 1825-37.

Necarsulmer, Henry. "The Early Jewish Settlement at Lancaster, Pennsylvania," A.J.H.S., *Publications*, IX (1901), 29-44.

Netscher, Pieter Marinas. *Les Hollandais au Brésil, notice historique sur les Pays-Bas et le Brésil au XVIIe siècle*. La Haye: Belinfante frères, 1853.

Neuman, Abraham A. *The Jews in Spain, Their Social, Political and Cultural Life During the Middle Ages*. 2 vols. Philadelphia: Jewish Publication Society of America, 1942.

————. "Some Phases of the Conditions of the Jews in Spain in the Thirteenth and Fourteenth Centuries," A.J.H.S., *Publications*, XXII (1914), 61-70.

Neumann, Joshua N. "Some Eighteenth Century American Jewish Letters," A.J.H.S., *Publications*, XXXIV (1937), 75-106.

Nevins, Allan, and Commager, Henry S. *The Pocket History of the United States*. New York: Pocket Books, Inc., 1943.

Newberry Library. *Bulletin*. No. 5. Chicago, September, 1946.

Newman, Ernest. *The Life of Richard Wagner*. 4 vols. London: Cassell, 1933-47.

Newman, Louis I. *Jewish Influence on Christian Reform Movements*. New York: Columbia University Press, 1925.

————. *The Talmudic Anthology*. New York, 1945.

Newport Historical Society. *Early Religious Leaders of Newport*. Newport, R. I.: Newport Historical Society, 1918.

Newton, Arthur P., ed. *The Great Age of Discovery*. London: University of London Press, 1932.

New York Evening Post, December 17, 1744.

Nieuhof, Johan. *Voyages and Travels into Brazil*. In *A General Collection of the Best and Most Interesting Voyages and Travels in All Parts of the World*. Edited by John Pinkerton. 17 vols. London, 1808-14. Vol. XIV.

————. "Voyages and Travels into Brazil and the East Indies." In

Awnskam Churchill, comp., *A Collection of Voyages and Travels.* London, 1704.

Noah, Mordecai M. [Address delivered at Grand Island, New York, in September, 1825], A.J.H.S., *Publications,* XXI (1913), 229-52.

Nordau, Max S. *The Interpretation of History.* London: Rebman, 1910.

Nordenskiöld, Niles A. E. *Facsimile-Atlas to the Early History of Cartography.* Stockholm, 1889.

———. *Periplus, an Essay on the Early History of Charts and Sailing-Directions.* Stockholm, 1897.

North Shore Congregation Israel. *Bulletin,* April 5, 1946.

Nowell, Charles E. "The Columbus Question," *American Historical Review,* XLIV (1939), 802-822.

———. "The Discovery of Brazil—Accidental or Intentional?" *Hispanic American Historical Review,* XVI (1936), 311-38.

Nunn, George E. *The Geographical Conceptions of Columbus; a Critical Consideration of Four Problems.* New York: American Geographical Society, 1924.

O'Brien, George A. T. *An Essay on Mediaeval Economic Teaching.* London: Longmans, Green and Co., 1920.

Occident and American Jewish Advocate. Edited by Isaac Lesser. 26 vols. Philadelphia, 1843-69. (Suspended December, 1852—March, 1853.)

Oliveira, Miguel de. *História Eclesiástica de Portugal.* Lisbon: União Gráfica, 1940.

Oppenheim, Samuel. "The Early History of the Jews in New York, 1654-1664. Some New Matter on the Subject," A.J.H.S., *Publications,* XVIII (1909), 1-91.

———. "An Early Jewish Colony in Western Guiana, 1658-1666, and Its Relation to the Jews in Surinam, Cayenne and Tobago," A.J.H.S., *Publications,* XVI (1907), 95-186.

———. "An Early Jewish Colony in Western Guiana: Supplemental Data," A.J.H.S., *Publications,* XVII (1909), 53-70.

———. "The First Settlement of the Jews in Newport; Some New Matter on the Subject," A.J.H.S., *Publications,* XXXIV (1937), 1-10.

———. "Jewish Owners of Ships Registered at the Port of Philadelphia, 1730-1775," A.J.H.S., *Publications,* XXVI (1918), 235-36.

———. "The Jews and Masonry in the United States Before 1810," A.J.H.S., *Publications,* XIX (1910), 1-94.

———. "Letter of Jonas Phillips, July 28, 1776, Mentioning the American Revolution and the Declaration of Independence," A.J.H.S., *Publications,* XXV (1917), 128-31.

———. "A List of Jews Made Denizens in the Reigns of Charles II and James II, 1661-1687," A.J.H.S., *Publications,* XX (1911), 109-13.

———. "More About Jacob Barsimson, the First Jewish Settler in New York," A.J.H.S., *Publications,* XXIX (1925), 39-52.

————. "The Question of the Kosher Meat Supply in New York in 1813: with a Sketch of Earlier Conditions," A.J.H.S., *Publications*, XXV (1917), 31-62.

————. "Two Letters of Solomon Bush, a Revolutionary Soldier," A.J.H.S., *Publications*, XXIII (1915), 177-178.

Orta, Garcia da. *Colloquies on the Simples & Drugs of India*. Translated by Sir Clements Markham. London: H. Sotheran and Co., 1913.

Osterweis, Rollin G. *Rebecca Gratz*. New York: G. P. Putnam's Sons, 1935.

Otero Sanchez, Prudencio. *España, Patria de Colón*. Madrid: Biblioteca Nueva, 1922.

Paine, Thomas. "Age of Reason." In *Basic Writing of Thomas Paine*. New York: Willey Book Co., 1942.

Parker, George F. "What Immigrants Contribute to Industry?" *The Forum*, XIV (1892-93), 600-607.

Parkes, James W. *The Jew in the Medieval Community, a Study of His Political and Economic Situation*. London: The Soncino Press, 1938.

Parsons, Talcott. "The Theoretical Development of the Sociology of Religion," *Journal of the History of Ideas*, V (1944), 176-90.

Patai, Raphael. "Problems and Tasks of Jewish Folklore and Ethnology," *Journal of American Folklore*, LIX (1946), 25-39.

Peddie, Robert A. *An Outline of the History of Printing*. London: Grafton and Co., 1917.

————, ed. *Printing, a Short History of the Art*. London: Grafton and Co., 1927.

Peixoto, Afranio. "Israel Continuará." In *Os Judeus na História do Brazil*. Rio de Janeiro: U. Zwerling, 1936.

Pereira da Silva, Luciano. "A Arte de Navegar dos Portugueses desde o Infante a D. João de Castro," *História da Colonização Portuguesa do Brasil*, I (1921), 29-104.

————. *Astrolábios Existentes em Portugal*. Lisbon: Tip. dos Camos. de Ferro do Estado, 1917.

————. "A Concepção Cosmológica nos 'Lusíadas,'" *Lusitania*, (1925), 263-89.

————. "Kamal, Tábuas do India e Tavoletas Náuticas," *Lusitania*, (1924), 363-71.

————. "A Propósito das Leituras do Infante," *Lusitania*, (1924), 23-27.

Peters, Madison C. *Justice to the Jew: the Story of What He has Done for the World*. New York: McClure Co., 1908.

Philipson, David. "The Cincinnati Community in 1825," A.J.H.S., *Publications*, X (1902), 97-99.

————. "The Jewish Pioneers of the Ohio Valley," A.J.H.S., *Publications*, VIII (1900), 43-57.

———. *Letters of Rebecca Gratz.* Philadelphia: Jewish Publication Society of America, 1929.

———. "The Progress of the Jewish Reform Movement in the United States," *Jewish Quarterly Review,* X (1897-98), 52-99.

———. *The Reform Movement in Judiasm.* New York: Macmillan Co., 1931.

———. "Some Unpublished Letters of Rebecca Gratz," A.J.H.S., *Publications,* XXIX (1924), 53-60.

Phillips, N. Taylor. "Family History of the Reverend David Mendez Macado," A.J.H.S., *Publications,* II (1893), 45-61.

———. "Items Relating to the History of the Jews of New York," A.J.H.S., *Publications,* XI (1903), 149-61.

———. "A Landmark," A.J.H.S., *Publications,* I (1892), 91-92.

———. "The Levy and Seixas Families of Newport and New York," A.J.H.S., *Publications,* IV (1894), 189-214.

———. "Rev. Gershom Mendez Seixas," *American Jewish Year Book,* 1904-1905.

Phillips, Rosalie S. "A Burial Place for the Jewish Nation Forever," A.J.H.S., *Publications,* XVIII (1909), 93-122.

Pierson, Donald. "The Brazilian Racial Situation," *The Scientific Monthly,* LVIII (1944), 227-32.

———. *Negroes in Brazil, a Study of Race Contact at Bahia.* Chicago: University of Chicago Press, 1942.

Pinheiro Chagas, Manuel. *Diccionario Popular, Historico, Geographico, Mythologico, Biographico.* Lisbon, 1876-90.

Pinkerton, John, ed. *A General Collection of the Best and Most Interesting Voyages and Travels in All Parts of the World.* 17 vols. London, 1808-14. (Includes Rabbi Benjamin of Tudela, vol. VII.)

Pirenne, Henri. *A History of Europe, from the Invasions to the XVI Century.* London: G. Allen and Unwin, 1939.

Pires de Lima, J. A. *Mouros, Judeus e Negros na História da Portugal.* Pôrto: Livraria Civilização, 1940.

Pohl, Frederick J. *Amerigo Vespucci, Pilot Major.* New York: Columbia University Press, 1944.

Polish, David. "Peretz Smolenskin's Contribution to Jewish Thought," *Reconstructionist,* June 11, 1943.

Pool, David de Sola. "Gershom Mendes Seixas' Letters, 1813-1815, to His Daughter Sarah (Seixas) Kursheedt and Son-in-Law Israel Baer Kursheedt," A.J.H.S., *Publications,* XXXV (1939), 189-205.

———. "Hebrew Learning Among the Puritans Prior to 1700," A.J.H.S., *Publications,* XX (1911), 31-83.

———. "Henry Pereira Menoes," A.J.H.S., *Publications,* XXXV (1939), 316-19.

———. *Jehuda Halevi's Defense of His Faith.* New York: The Union of Orthodox Jewish Congregations of America, c. 1925.

————. "Judaism and the Synagogue," in Oscar Janowsky, ed., *The American Jew*. New York: Harper & Brothers, 1942.

————. *The Seventieth Street Synagogue of the Congregation Shearith Israel (Founded in the City of New York in 1655). The Story of a Building on the Occasion of Its Jubilee*. New York, 1947.

"Popular Movements," *The Nation*, VI (May 28, 1868), 427-28.

Portugal. Agência Geral das Colónias. *Os Sete Únicos Documentos de 1500, Conservados em Lisboa, Referentes a Viagem de Pedro Alvares Cabral*. Lisbon: Agência Geral das Colónias, 1940.

Prestage, Edgar. *The Portuguese Pioneers*. London: A. and C. Black, 1933.

Priestley, Herbert I. *The Coming of the White Man, 1492-1848*. New York: Macmillan Co., 1929.

Priestley, Joseph. *A Comparison of the Institutions of Moses with Those of the Hindoos and Other Ancient Nations*. Northumberland, 1799.

————. *Letters to the Jews: Inviting Them to an Amicable Discussion of the Evidences of Christianity*. Birmingham, 1787.

Ptolemaeus, Claudius. *Geographiae opus*. Argentine, 1513.

"Publications Received. *Publications of the American Jewish Historical Society*. Number 9, 1901," *The South Carolina Historical and Genealogical Magazine*, III (1902), 59-64.

Purchas, Samuel. *Hakluytus Posthumus, or Purchas His Pilgrimes*. 20 vols. Glasgow: J. MacLehose and Sons, 1905-1907.

Rabinowitz, L. "Literary Connections between Abrabanel and England," J.H.S.E., *Transactions*, XIV (1940), 131-39.

Rae, George M. *The Syrian Church in India*. London, 1892.

Raffalovitch, I. "The Condition of Jewry and Judaism in South America," Central Conference of American Rabbis, *Yearbook*, 1930.

Raskin, A. H. "Sidney Hillman, 1887-1946," *American Jewish Year Book*, XLIX (1947-48).

Ravenstein, Ernest G. *Martin Behaim, His Life and His Globe*. London: G. Philip and Son, 1908.

Recent Social Trends in the United States: Report of the President's Research Committee on Social Trends. 2 vols. New York: McGraw Hill Book Co., 1933.

"The Reform Movement Among the Jews," *The Nation*, VI (June 18, 1868), 488-89.

Regimento do Estrolabio e do Quadrante. Introduction by Joaquim Bensaude. Munich: C. Kuhn, 1914.

Renard, Georges F., and Weulerssee, G. *Life and Work in Modern Europe (Fifteenth to Eighteenth Centuries)*. London: Alfred A. Knopf, 1926.

Revista de Estudos Hebraicos. Vol. I Lisbon: Publicado Pelo Instituto de Estudos Hebraicos de Portugal, 1928. (This was the only volume published.)

Rhode Island (Colony). *Records of the Colony of Rhode Island and Providence Plantations in New England.* 10 vols. Providence, 1856-65.

Ribeiro, Patrocinio. *A Nacionalidade Portuguesa de Cristovam Colombo. The Portuguese Nationality of Christopher Columbus.* Lisbon: Livraria Renascença, J. Cardoso, 1927.

Richman, Julia. "The Jewish Sunday School Movement in the United States," *The Jewish Quarterly Review,* XII (1900), 563-601.

Riis, Jacob A. *The Children of the Poor.* New York: Charles Scribner's Sons, 1923.

————. "Special Needs of the Poor in New York," *The Forum,* XIV (1892-93), 492-502.

Ringel, Mosheh R. "Further Information Concerning the Colony 'Sholam' on Yageville Hill, Ulster County, New York," A.J.H.S., *Publications,* XXXV (1939), 306-309.

Rios, Fernando de los. "The Action of Spain in America," In *Concerning Latin American Culture.* Edited by Charles C. Griffin. New York: Columbia University Press, 1940. pp. 49-78.

————. "Spain in the Epoch of American Colonization," In *Concerning Latin American Culture, op. cit.,* pp. 25-48.

Rivkind, Isaac. "Early American Hebrew Documents," A. J. H. S., *Publications,* XXXIV (1937), 51-74.

————. "A Pocket Edition Prayer Book for German Jewish Emigrants to America, 1842," A.J.H.S., *Publications,* XXXV (1939), 207-12.

Robertson, William. *The History of America.* 2 vols. London, 1778.

Robinson, James H. *The Ordeal of Civilization, a Sketch of the Development and World-Wide Diffusion of Our Present-Day Institutions and Ideas.* New York: Harper & Brothers, 1926.

————, and Breasted, James H. *A General History of Europe, from the Origins of Civilization to the Present Time.* Boston: Ginn and Co., 1921.

Robison, Sophia M., ed. *Jewish Population Studies.* New York: Conference on Jewish Relations, 1943.

Roddis, Louis H. "Phineas J. Horwitz—the Fourth Chief of the Bureau of Medicine, 1865-1869," United States Navy, *Bulletin,* (1935).

Rodrigues, José Honorio, and Ribeiro, Joaquim. *Civilização Holandesa no Brasil.* São Paulo: Companhia Editora Nacional, 1940.

Rogachevskiĭ, Vasiliĭ L'vovich. *Russko-Evreĭskaĭa Literatura.* Moscow, 1922.

Roos, J. S. "Additional Notes on the History of the Jews of Surinam," A.J.H.S., *Publications,* XIII (1905), 127-36.

"Roosevelt's Own List of 23 Leading Americans," *This Week Magazine,* June 20, 1948.

Roper, R. C. "Thomas Paine: Scientist—Religionist," *Scientific Monthly,* LVIII (February, 1944), 101-11.

Rosenau, William. "Cardinal Gibbons and His Attitude Toward Jewish Problems," A.J.H.S., *Publications,* XXXI (1928), 219-24.

Rosenbach, Abraham S. W. "An American Jewish Bibliography being a List of Books and Pamphlets by Jews or Relating to Them, Printed in the United States, from the Establishment of the Press in the Colonies until 1850," A.J.H.S., *Publications*, XXX (1926), 1-467.

———. "Notes on the First Settlement of Jews in Pennsylvania, 1655-1703," A.J.H.S., *Publications*, V (1897), 191-98.

Rosendale, Simon W. "A Document Concerning the Franks Family," A.J.H.S., *Publications*, I (1892), 103-104.

Rosenfeld, M. "On the Ocean," translated from the "Yiddish" by Alice Lucas, *Jewish Quarterly Review*, XII (1900), 89-91.

Roth, Cecil. "The Anglo-Jewish Tradition," *The National Jewish Monthly*, LX (1946), 194.

———. *A Bird's-Eye View of Jewish History*. Cincinnati: Department of Synagogue and School Extension of the Union of American Hebrew Congregations, 1935.

———. "The Challenge to Jewish History," J.H.S.E., *Transactions*, XIV (1940), 1-38.

———. *A History of the Jews in England*. Oxford: Clarendon Press, 1941.

———. *A History of the Marranos.* Philadelphia: Jewish Publication Society of America, 1932.

———. *The House of Nasi. Doña Gracia.* Philadelphia: Jewish Publication Society of America, 1948.

———. "A Jewish Voice for Peace in the War of American Independence. The life and Writings of Abraham Wagg, 1719-1803," A.J.H.S., *Publications*, XXXI (1928), 33-75.

———. *A Life of Menasseh ben Israel, Rabbi, Printer, and Diplomat.* Philadelphia: Jewish Publication Society of America, 1934.

———. "New Light on the Resettlement," J.H.S.E., *Transactions*, XI (1928), 112-42.

———. *A Short History of the Jewish People, 1600 B.C.—A.D. 1935.* London: Macmillan and Co., 1936.

Rubens, Alfred. *Anglo-Jewish Portraits: a Biographical Catalogue*. London: The Jewish Museum, 1935.

———. "Early Anglo-Jewish Artists," J.H.S.E., *Transactions*, XIV (1940), 9-129.

Ruge, Sophus. *Historia da Época dos Descobrimentos*. Paris: Aillaud e Bertrand, 190-.

Rumney, J. "Anglo-Jewry as Seen Through Foreign Eyes," J.H.S.E., *Transactions*, XIII (1936), 323-40.

Ruppin, Arthur. *The Jews in the Modern World*. London: MacMillan, 1934.

Rusk, Ralph L. *Letters to Emma Lazarus*. New York: Columbia University Press, 1939.

Russell, Bertrand. *A History of Western Philosophy and Its Connection with Political and Social Circumstances from the Earliest Times to the Present Day*. New York: Simon and Schuster, 1945.

Russell, Charles E. *Haym Salomon and the Revolution*. New York: Cosmopolitan Book Corporation, 1930.

Sacchi, Federico. *I Tipografi Ebrei di Soncino*. Cremona, 1877.

Sachse, Julius F. "Jacob Philadelphia, Mystic and Physicist," A.J.H.S., *Publications*, XVI (1908), 73-83.

Samuel, Wilfred S. "A Review of the Jewish Colonists in Barbados in the Year 1680," J.H.S.E., *Transactions*, XIII (1936), 1-111.

Sandburg, Carl. *Abraham Lincoln, the War Years*. 2 vols. New York: Harcourt, Brace and Co., 1939.

Schapiro, Israel. "Ephraim Deinard," A.J.H.S., *Publications*, XXXIV (1937), 149-63.

Schappes, Morris U. "August Bondi, Anti-Slavery Fighter," *Jewish Life*, November 1949.

———. "Ernestine L. Rose," *Journal of Negro History*, XXXIV (July, 1949), 344-55.

———. "Toward the Biography of Judah Touro," *Jewish Life*, April, 1947.

Schechter, S. *Studies in Judaism*. Philadelphia: Jewish Publication Society of America, 1908.

Schleiden, Matthias J. *The Importance of the Jews for the Preservation and Revival of Learning during the Middle Ages*. London, Siegle, Hill and Co., 1911.

Scholem, Gershom G. *Major Trends in Jewish Mysticism*. New York: Schocken Books, c. 1946.

Schonfield, Hugh J. *The History of Jewish Christianity from the First to the Twentieth Century*. London: Duckworth, [1935].

Schwartz, Ernst, and Te Velde, Johan C. "Jewish Agricultural Settlement in Argentina: the ICA Experiment," *Hispanic American Historical Review*, XIX (1939), 185-203.

Schwarz, Leo W., ed. *A Golden Treasury of Jewish Literature*. New York: Farrar and Rinehart, c. 1937.

Seignobos, Charles. *The Rise of European Civilization*. London: J. Cape, [1939].

Sergio, Antonio. Review of "Episodios Dramaticos da Inquisição Portuguesa," by Antonio Baião, *Lusitania* (1924), 446-48.

Sewall, Samuel. "Diary," Massachusetts Historical Society, *Collections*, Fifth Series, V (1878).

Seybolt, Robert F. "Hebrew in the Schools of Colonial America," A.J.H.S., *Publications*, XXXII (1931), 113-14.

Shpall, Leo. "The First Synagogue in Louisiana," *The Louisiana Historical Quarterly*, XXI (1938), 518-31.

———. "The Sheftalls of Georgia," *The Georgia Historical Quarterly*, XVII (1943), 339-49.

Sherman, Charles B. *Yidden Un Andere Etnische Grupez.* New York, 1948.

Silber, Mendel. "America in Hebrew Literature," A.J.H.S., *Publications*, XXII (1914), 101-137.

Simon, Mrs. Barbara A. *The Ten Tribes of Israel Historically Identified with the Aborigines of the Western Hemishere.* London, 1836.

Simon, O. J. "The Position of Faith in the Jewish Religion," *Jewish Quarterly Review*, II (1890), 53-61.

Sisson, C. J. "A Colony of Jews in Shakespeare's London," in *Essays and Studies by Members of the English Association*, XXIII (Oxford, 1938), 38-51.

Sivarama Menon, Cherubala P. *Early Astronomy and Cosmology.* London: G. Allen and Unwin, 1932.

Solis, Elvira N. "Some References to Early Jewish Cemeteries in New York City," A.J.H.S., *Publications*, VIII (1900), 135-40.

Solis-Cohen, Solomon. "Note Concerning David Hays and Esther Etting His Wife, and Michael Hays and Reuben Etting, Their Brothers, Patriots of the Revolution," A. J. H. S., *Publications*, II (1893), 63-72.

Solomons, Israel. "David Nieto and Some of His Contemporaries," J.H.S.E., *Transactions*, XII (1931), 1-101.

———. "Satirical and Political Prints on the Jews' Naturalization Bill, 1753," J.H.S.E., *Transactions*, VI (1912), 205-33.

Sombart, Werner. *The Jews and Modern Capitalism.* London: T. F. Unwin, 1913.

Sorokin, Pitirim A. *The Crisis of Our Age.* New York: E. P. Dutton and Co., 1943.

———. *Man and Society in Calamity, the Effects of War, Revolution, Famine, Pestilence upon Human Mind, Behavior, Social Organization and Cultural Life.* New York: E. P. Dutton and Co., 1942.

———. *Social and Cultural Dynamics.* 4 vols. New York: American Book Co., 1937-41.

———. *Social Mobility.* New York: Harper & Brothers, 1927.

———. "Socio-Cultural Trends in Euro-American Culture during the Last Hundred Years," in *A Century of Social Thought: A Series of Lectures Delivered at Duke University during the Academic Year 1938-39.* Durham: Duke University Press, 1939.

Sousa Holstein, Francisco de Borja P. M. A. *A Escola de Sagres e as Tradições do Infante D. Henrique.* Lisbon, 1877.

Sousa Viterbo, Francisco M. de. *Trabalhos Nauticos dos Portuguezes nos Seculos XVI e XVII.* 2 vols. Lisbon: Academia Real das Sciencias, 1898-1900.

The South American Handbook. London: South American Publications, 1942.

Southey, Robert. *History of Brazil.* 3 vols. London, 1810-1819.

Souto Maior, Pedro. *Fastos Pernambucanos.* Rio de Janeiro: Imprensa Nacional, 1913.

Spargo, John. *The Jew and American Ideals.* New York: Harper & Brothers, [c. 1921].

Spiegel, Hans W. "An Early English Intervention on Behalf of Foreign Jewry," A.J.H.S., *Publications*, XXXV (1939), 213-17.

Spinoza, Benedictus de. *Philosophy of Benedict de Spinoza.* Translated from the Latin by R. H. M. Elwes. New York: Tudor Publishing Co., 1933.

Stegner, Wallace. "Who Persecutes Boston?" *The Atlantic Monthly,* CLXXIV (July, 1944), 45-52.

Steinschneider, Moritz. *Die Hebraeischen uebersetzungen des Mittelalters und die Juden als Dolmetscher.* 2 vols. Berlin, 1893.

――――. *Eine unbekannte Incunabel mit Holzchnitten. [1490]; Der Buchdruck des 15 Jahrhunderts.* Berlin, 1929.

Stephens, Henry M. *Portugal.* New York, 1898.

Stevens, G. W. "France as Affected by the Dreyfus Case," *Harper's New Monthly Magazine,* XCIX (1899), 792-98.

Stevenson, Edward L. *Christopher Columbus and His Enterprise.* New York(?) 1914(?)

――――. *Early Spanish Cartography of the New World, with Special Reference to the Wolfenbüttel-Spanish Map and the Work of Diego Ribero.* Worcester, Mass.: The Davis Press, 1909.

――――. *Portolan Charts; Their Origin and Characteristics.* New York: Knickerbocker Press, 1911.

Stevenson, Robert Louis. *Letters.* London, 1899.

Stiles, Ezra. *Extracts from the Itineraries and Other Miscellanies . . . with a Selection from His Correspondence.* Edited by Franklin B. Dexter. New Haven: Yale University Press, 1916.

――――. *The Literary Diary of Ezra Stiles.* Edited by Franklin B. Dexter. 3 vols. New York: Charles Scribner's Sons, 1901.

Stokes, H. P. "The Relationship Between the Jews and the Royal Family of England in the Thirteenth Century," J.H.S.E., *Transactions*, VIII (1918), 153-70.

Stonehill, Charles A. *The Jewish Contribution to Civilization.* London: C. A. Stonehill, 1940.

Straus, Donald B. *Hickey-Freeman Company and Amalgamated Clothing Workers of America.* Washington, D. C., 1949.

Straus, Oscar S. "New Light on the Career of Colonel David S. Franks," A.J.H.S., *Publications*, X (1902), 101-108.

――――. *Under Four Administrations, from Cleveland to Taft.* Boston: Houghton Mifflin Co., 1922.

Sulzberger, David. "The Beginnings of Russo-Jewish Immigration to Philadelphia," A.J.H.S., *Publications*, XIX (1910), 125-50.

――――. "Growth of Jewish Population in the United States," A.J.H.S., *Publications*, VI (1897), 141-49.

Sumner, William G. *Folkways: a Study of the Sociological Importance of Usages, Manners, Customs, Mores, and Morals.* Boston, c. 1906.

Sweet, William W. *A History of Latin America.* New York: Abingdon Press, 1929.

Swiren, Max. "Defendants Brief. Appellate Court of Illinois." No. 44,500. October, 1948.

Teixeira, Pedro. *The Travels of Pedro Teixeira.* Translated and annotated by William F. Sinclair and Donald Ferguson. London, 1902. (Works issued by the Hakluyt Society. Series II, vol. IX).

Thacher, John B. *Christopher Columbus.* 3 vols. New York: G. P. Putnam's Sons, 1903-1904.

Thiers, Adolphe. *The Mississippi Bubble.* New York, 1859.

Thompson, James W. *The Middle Ages, 300-1500.* 2 vols. New York: Alfred A. Knopf, 1931.

Thorowgood, Thomas. *Iewes in America, or Probabilities that Those Indians Are Judaical, Made More Probable by Some Additionals to the Former Conjectures.* London, 1660.

Tocqueville, Alexis C. *Democracy in America.* 2 vols. New York, 1898.

Toro, Alfonso. *La Familia Carvajal.* 2 vols. Mexico: Editorial Patria, 1944.

————, ed. *Los Judíos en la Nueva España: Selección de Documentos del Siglo XVI. Correspondientes al Ramo de Inquisición.* Mexico: Talleres Gráficos de la Nación, 1932.

Tout, T. F. "Mediaeval Forgers and Forgeries," *Bulletin of the John Rylands Library,* V (Manchester, 1918-20), 208-234.

Tovey, De Blossiers. *Anglia Judaica: or, the History and Antiquities of the Jews in England.* Oxford, 1738.

Trachtenberg, Joshua. *Consider the Years: the Story of the Jewish Community of Easton. 1752-1942.* Easton, Penn.: Centennial Committee of Temple Brith Sholam, 1944.

————. *The Devil and the Jews. The Medieval Conception of the Jew, and Its Relation to Modern Antisemitism.* New Haven: Yale University Press, 1943.

————. "Religion," in *American Jewish Year Book,* XLIX (1947-48).

"Trial of Gabriel de Granada by the Inquisition in Mexico, 1642-1645," translated from the original by David Fergusson. Edited with notes by Cyrus Adler, A.J.H.S., *Publications,* VII (1899), 1-127.

Trollope, Mrs. Frances M. *Domestic Manners of the Americans.* London, 1832.

The Two Hundred and Fiftieth Anniversary of the Settlement of the Jews in the United States, 1655-1905. New York: American Jewish Historical Society, 1906.

Ulloa, Luis. *El Pre-descubrimiento Hispano-Catalán de América en 1477. Xristo-Ferens Colom, Fernando el Católico y la Cataluña Española.* Paris, Librairie Orientale et Américaine, Maisonneuve Fréres, 1928.

Universal Jewish Encyclopedia. 10 vols. New York: Universal Jewish Encyclopedia, Inc., 1939-43.

U. S. Department of Commerce, Bureau of the Census. *Religious Bodies: 1936.* Vol. II, part I, Washington, 1941.

U. S. Hydro-graphic Office. *Sailing Directions for South America.* Washington, 1935.

Usque, Samuel. *Consolaçam as Tribulacõens de Israel.* Ferrara, 1553.

Van Etten, Ida M. "Russian Jews as Desirable Immigrants," *The Forum,* XV (1893), 172-82.

Varnhagen, Francisco Adolpho de. *Examen de quelques points de l'histoire géographique du Bresil.* Paris, 1858.

———. *Historia das Lutas com os Hollandezes no Brazil desde 1624 a 1654.* Lisbon, 1872.

Veen, Harm R. S. van der. *Jewish Characters in Eighteenth Century English Fiction and Drama.* Groningen, Batavia: J. B. Wolters' uitgevers-maatschappij n. v., 1935.

Velho, Alvaro. *Roteiro da Primeira Viagem de Vasco da Gama.* Lisbon: Agência Geral das Colónias, 1940.

Vignaud, Henry. "Columbus a Spaniard and a Jew," *American Historical Review,* XVIII (1913), 505-512.

———. *Toscanelli and Columbus. The Letter and Chart of Toscanelli.* New York: E. P. Dutton and Co., 1902.

Villiers du Terrage, Baron Marc de. *Histoire de la fondation de la Nouvelle-Orléans, 1717-1722.* Paris: Imprimerie Nationale, 1917.

Vining, Edward P. *An Inglorious Columbus.* New York, 1885.

Virginia Historical Society. "Proceedings," *The Virginia Magazine of History and Biography,* XXV (1917), i-lii. (Reference to Anthony M. Keiley on p. xl.)

Waddell, Helen J. *Mediaeval Latin Lyrics.* London: Constable and Co., 1929.

———. *The Wandering Scholars.* London: Constable and Co., 1927.

Wagenknecht, Edward C. *Mark Twain, the Man and His Work.* New Haven: Yale University Press, 1935.

Waldseemüller, Martin. *Cosmographiae Introductio.* Deodate, 1507.

———. *The Cosmographiae Introductio . . . Followed by the Four Voyages of Amerigo Vespucci.* New York: United States Catholic Historical Society, 1907.

Wallech, L. "The Beginnings of the Science of Judaism in the Nineteenth Century," *Historia Judaica,* VIII (April, 1946), 33-60.

Ware, Caroline F., ed. *The Cultural Approach to History.* New York: Columbia University Press, 1940. (Papers edited for the American Historical Association.)

Waters, L. L. "Intrepid Artist Explorer," *Liberal Judaism* (June, 1946), 43-50.

Wax J. A. "Isidor Bush, American Patriot and Abolitionist," *Historia Judaica*, V (October, 1943), 183-203.

Waxman, Meyer. *A History of Jewish Literature*. 4 vols. New York: Bloch Publishing Co., 1930.

Wechsler, Israel S. *The Neurologist's Point of View, Essays on Psychiatric and Other Subjects*. New York: L. B. Fischer, 1945.

Weddell, Alexander W. "Samuel Mordecai: Chronicler of Richmond, 1786-1865," *Virginia Magazine of History and Biography*, LIII (1945), 265-87.

Wedel, Theodore O. *The Mediaeval Attitude toward Astrology, Particularly in England*. New Haven: Yale University Press, 1920.

Weiss-Rosmarin, Trude. "Gersonides—Philosopher, Exegete and Inventor," *Opinion*, XV (1945), 6-7.

Weizmann, Chaim. *Trial and Error. The Autobiography of Chaim Weizmann*. New York: Harper & Brothers, 1949.

Wenley, R. M. "Judaism and Philosophy of Religion," *Jewish Quarterly Review*, X (1897-98), 18-40.

Wertenbaker, Thomas J. *American People: a History*. New York: Charles Scribner's Sons, 1926.

White, Lynn, Jr. "Technology and Invention in the Middle Ages," *Speculum*, XV (1940), 141-59.

Wiernik, Peter. *History of the Jews in America, from the Period of the Discovery of the New World to the Present Time*. New York: The Jewish Press Publishing Co., 1912.

Willner, Rev. W. "Ezra Stiles and the Jews (1727-1795)," A.J.H.S., *Publications*, VIII (1900), 119-26.

Wilson, William J. "The Spanish Discovery of the South American Mainland," *Geographical Review*, XXXI (1941), 283-99.

Winsor, Justin, ed. *Narrative and Critical History of America*. 8 vols. Boston, 1884-89.

Wirth, Louis. *The Ghetto*. Chicago: University of Chicago Press, 1928.

Wise, Isaac M. *Reminiscences*. Translated by David Philipson. Cincinnati: L. Wise and Co., 1901.

Wolf, Lucien. "American Elements in the Re-Settlement," J.H.S.E., *Transactions*, III (1899), 76-100.

———. "Crypto-Jews Under the Commonwealth," J.H.S.E., *Transactions*, I (1893-94), 55-88.

———. "The Disraeli Family," J.H.S.E., *Transactions*, V (1908), 202-218.

———. "The Jewry of the Restoration, 1660-1664," J.H.S.E., *Transactions*, V (1908), 5-33.

———. "Jews in Elizabethan England," J.H.S.E., *Transactions*, XI (1928), 1-91.

———. "Status of the Jews in England after the Re-Settlement," J.H.S.E., *Transactions*, IV (1903), 177-93.

————. "The Zionist Peril," *Jewish Quarterly Review*, XVII (1905), 1-25.

Wolf, Simon. *The American Jew as Patriot, Soldier, and Citizen*. Philadelphia, 1895.

Wood, Margaret M. *The Stranger: a Study in Social Relationships*. New York: Columbia University Press, 1934.

Woofter, Thomas J. *Races and Ethnic Groups in American Life*. New York: MacGraw-Hill Book Co., 1933.

Wright, Richardson L. *Hawkers & Walkers in Early America*. Philadelphia, J. B. Lippincott Co., 1927.

Wroth, Lawrence C. *The Way of a Ship*. Portland, Me.: The Southworth-Anthoensen Press, 1937.

Yule, Sir Henry, ed. and tr. *Cathay and the Way Thither; Being a Collection of Medieval Notices of China*. London, 1913-16. (Works issued by the Hakluyt Society, series II, vols. XXXIII, XXXVII, XXXVIII, XLI.)

Zacuto, Abraham ben S. *Almanach Perpetuum Celestium Motuum* (*Radix 1473*). Translated by Joseph Vizinho. Genève: Société Sadag, 1917.

Ziegler, Jacob. *Terrae Sanctae*. Argentorati, 1536.

Zielonka, Martin. "The Fighting Jew," A.J.H.S., *Publications*, XXXI (1928), 211-17.

————. "Francisco Rivas," A.J.H.S., *Publications*, XXXV (1939), 219-25.

INDEX

637